Doctors Academy Preparation Guide

BMAT

for 2021 and 2022 Tests

1000+ Questions and Answers with Comprehensive Explanations

- Includes Complete Mock Tests (Sections 1, 2 and 3)
- Follows the Official BMAT Specification
- Reflects Changes to the Test Introduced in 2020

A Lakshmi

T R Enoch

S Z Y Ooi

Content Edited and Approved by the Higher Educational Divisions of the Doctors Academy Group (Intl), College of Physicians and Surgeons of Cardiff and the Academy for Advanced Scientific Communication in English.

DOCTORS ACADEMY
BETTER EDUCATION. BETTER HEALTH.

AASCE
The Academy for Advanced Scientific Communication in English

College of Physicians and Surgeons of Cardiff
Eruditio. Novatio. Excellentia. Misericordia.

Doctors Academy Publications, November 2020 (Reprint March 2021)

Doctors Academy Preparation Guide

BMAT

for 2021 and 2022 Tests

Miss Aiswarya Lakshmi
Medical Student
Downing College
University of Cambridge, UK

Miss Tanya Rebekah Enoch
Medical Student, Cardiff University
Coordinator, Medical Admissions Test
Doctors Academy Group (Intl), Cardiff, UK

Mr Setthasorn Zhi Yang Ooi
Medical Student, Cardiff University
Director, Medical School Interview Preparation Courses
Doctors Academy Group (Intl), Cardiff, UK

Content Edited and Approved by the Higher Educational Divisions of the Doctors Academy Group (Intl), College of Physicians and Surgeons of Cardiff and the Academy for Advanced Scientific Communication in English.

DOCTORS ACADEMY
BETTER EDUCATION. BETTER HEALTH.

AASCE
The Academy for Advanced Scientific Communication in English

College of Physicians and Surgeons of Cardiff
Eruditio. Novatio. Excellentia. Misericordia.

Doctors Academy Publications, November 2020 (Reprint March 2021)

1st Edition, November 2020, Doctors Academy Publications (Reprint March 2021)

Electronic version published at	:	Doctors Academy, 189, Whitchurch Road, Cardiff, CF14 3JR, United Kingdom
Print version printed and published at	:	Abbey Bookbinding and Print Co., Unit 3, Gabalfa Workshops, Clos Menter, Cardiff CF14 3AY
ISBN	*:*	*978-93-80573-74-8*
Cover page design	:	Sreekanth S.S
Typesetting	:	Lakshmi Sreekanth
Contact	:	publishing@doctorsacademy.org.uk

Preface

The BMAT (BioMedical Admissions Test) is an admissions test used by a number of medical and dental schools (and some biomedical programmes) in the United Kingdom, Croatia, Hungary, Kazakhstan, Malaysia, Poland, Russia, Singapore, Spain and Thailand to assess a range of analytical skills and thinking abilities in a prospective candidate. The skills appraised include the candidate's ability to interpret data from tables and graphs, his/her aptitude to critically evaluate and distil information from scientific and literary passages, and his/her proficiency to apply academic knowledge in a range of complex scenarios. The challenge of the BMAT is not simply due to the breadth of the knowledge needed to answer the questions but, rather, the need for the candidates to answer accurately and judiciously within a very short time. The time constraints place the candidate under immense pressure during the two-hour written test.

The test consists of three sections: a one-hour Thinking Skills paper (Section 1); a 30-minute Scientific Knowledge and Applications paper (Section 2); and a 30-minute Writing Task (Section 3). In order to mirror the test, this book is divided into three sections. Section 1 comprises of 185 Problem Solving, 189 Data Analysis and 52 Critical Thinking questions. Section 2 encompasses 100 questions in each of the following four subjects: Biology; Chemistry; Physics; and Mathematics. A copy of the official specification has been included before each topic in Section 2. In addition, a checklist is provided so that the candidate can monitor his/her level of preparedness and progress. Answers and detailed explanations are provided for Sections 1 and 2. Section 3 consists of five essays which have been marked with examiners' comments. Model essay answers are also included. These will allow the candidate to recognise the standard and vocabulary required, appreciate the importance of articulating an argument and a counterargument, and comprehend the significance of a robust discussion and formulating an effective conclusion. The book also contains three mock tests which follow the changes introduced to the test in 2020 and include sample answer sheets with detailed explanations. It is recommended that these tests should be practised under timed conditions in order to replicate a realistic test environment.

With over 1000 questions, this book is an essential "must-have" in a candidate's preparation for the BMAT. It is envisaged that this book, with a wide range of exercises and varying levels of difficulty, will allow the candidate to appreciate the type and style of questions that can be expected in the BMAT. It will also provide him/her with the opportunity to refine and optimise his/her technique in answering questions in an efficacious manner. The book is thus a consummate preparation tool for a candidate who aspires to achieve a high score in the BMAT and maximise his/her chances of getting into the medical or dental school of his/her choice.

We, as authors, have sat the BMAT recently and were fortunate to achieve a very credible score which undoubtedly enhanced our chances of securing interviews and places in the medical schools of our choice. We firmly believe that, with early preparation and ample practice, one will learn to recognise patterns, become aware of the nuances of various answer options, and avoid potential distractors that are present in all questions.

We sincerely hope that this book proves valuable in a candidate's preparation for the BMAT.

We wish you all the very best.

A Lakshmi, T R Enoch, S Z Y Ooi

OVERVIEW OF BMAT

I. Universities Requiring BMAT

Name of Institution	Type of Course
Brighton and Sussex Medical School (B74), UK	A100 Medicine
Imperial College London (I50), UK	A100 Medicine
Lancaster University (L14), UK	A100 Medicine & Surgery A104 Medicine & Surgery with a Gateway Year
University College London (U80), UK	A100 Medicine
University of Cambridge (C05), UK	A100 Medicine
University of Leeds (L23), UK	A100 Medicine A101 Gateway Year to Medicine; A200 Dentistry
University of Manchester Medical School, UK (for some groups of international applicants only; check the University's website)	A106 MBChB Medicine A104 MBChB Medicine (with foundation year)
University of Oxford (O33), UK	A100 Medicine A101 Graduate Medicine BC98 Biomedical Sciences
Keele University (K12), UK (for 'overseas for fees' students only; check the University's website).	A100 Medicine
Universidad de Navarra, Spain	Medicine
University of Pécs, Hungary	Medicine, Dentistry
Chiang Mai University, Thailand	Doctor of Medicine
Chulalongkorn University, Thailand	Doctor of Medicine
Khon Kaen University, Thailand	MD02 Medicine (Northeast Thailand applicants); MDX Medicine (other applicants)
King Mongkut's Institute of Technology Ladkrabang Faculty of Medicine, Thailand	Medicine
Lee Kong Chian School of Medicine (LKCMedicine), Singapore	Medicine: MBBS degree jointly awarded by Imperial College London and Nanyang Technological University, Singapore
Mahidol University, Faculty of Medicine Ramathibodi Hospital; Mahidol International Dental School, Thailand	Medicine; Dentistry
Navamindradhiraj University, Faculty of Medicine Vajira Hospital, Thailand	MD Doctor of Medicine
Srinakharinwirot University, Thailand	A10S Doctor of Medicine (joint programme with the University of Nottingham)
Suranaree University of Technology, Thailand	MD Doctor of Medicine

Thammasat University: CICM and Dentistry, Thailand	642901 Doctor of Medicine 642902 Doctor of Dental Surgery (bilingual English/Thai)
University of Malaya, Malaysia	Medicine
University of Rijeka, Faculty of Medicine, Croatia	MD Medicine
University of Zagreb, Croatia	Doctor of Medicine (in English)
Medical University of Warsaw, Poland	DM Doctor of Medicine DMD Doctor of Dental Medicine
Pirogov Russian National Research University, Russia	General Medicine Biology
Nazarbayev University School of Medicine, Kazakhstan	MD (Postgraduate Medicine)

II. Format of BMAT

Test Section	Time Allocated	Number of questions	Skills required
1. Thinking Skills	1 hour	32 multiple-choice questions	• Solve problems • Think critically
2. Scientific Knowledge and Applications	30 minutes	27 multiple-choice questions	• Apply scientific knowledge typically learned in school in Science and Mathematics by the age of 16 (for example, GCSE in the UK and IGCSE internationally).
3. Writing Task	30 minutes	One writing task from a choice of three	• Select, develop and organise ideas • Communicate effectively in writing and present ideas clearly and concisely

III. Section 1 - Thinking Skills (1 hour)

- <u>16 Problem Solving questions</u>

  Problem solving requires the capacity to:
  - select relevant information
  - identify similarity
  - determine and apply appropriate procedures.

- <u>16 Critical Thinking questions</u>

  Presents a series of logical arguments and requires you to:
  - summarise conclusions
  - draw conclusions
  - identify assumptions
  - assess the impact of additional evidence
  - detect reasoning errors

- match arguments
- apply principles.

Both Problem Solving and Critical Thinking are assessed by multiple-choice questions. In each case, a stimulus is presented, followed by the stem (question) and five options. One of the options is the correct answer (key) and the remaining four options (distractors) are wrong. In Critical Thinking, the stimulus is a passage of text. In Problem Solving, the stimulus may include a diagram, a table of information (a railway timetable for example), or a graph. The options may also be graphs or diagrams.

Please note that, from the 2020 test, the section on Data Analysis has been integrated into the Problem Solving component. This means, there will be no data sets (approximately a page of text or data followed by four or five questions). However, this book includes questions on Data Analysis since the skills required to solve them are transferrable for answering the Problem Solving and Critical Thinking components. In addition, if single stem questions based on data should appear in the test, a thorough revision of Data Analysis style questions will prove to be immensely beneficial.

IV. Section 2 - Scientific Knowledge and Applications (30 minutes)

Subject	Number of questions
Biology	7
Chemistry	7
Physics	7
Mathematics	6
TOTAL	**27**

The questions in Section 2 are based on the specification published on the official BMAT website (www.admissionstesting.org). For ease, a copy of this specification is included before the start of each topic in Section 2. In addition, a checklist is provided so that you can monitor the progress of your revision. It is imperative that you revise the topics in the specification carefully and understand the concepts since this will help in answering the questions correctly. Certain formulae and definitions need to be memorised for the test; these are stated in the specification.

General Advice for Sections 1 and 2:

- It needs to be appreciated that there is an element of time pressure in the BMAT test; however, try to answer all the questions.
- If you are unsure of a question, move on to another question and come back to it later.
- Ensure that all of the answers are transferred onto the answer sheet within the time set for each section.
- If you are unsure of an answer and are running out of time, choose whichever option you think is most likely, since there is no negative marking in the test.
- <u>**Calculators are not allowed in the test.**</u>

V. Section 3: Writing Task (30 minutes)

- A selection of three tasks will be available, from which one must be chosen.
- The main essay title will be based on a topic of general (e.g., a literary quote), scientific or medical interest.
- Questions will provide a short proposition (three prompt questions) and it requires you to consider one of the following tasks.
  - ***Explanation of the proposition:*** you will be asked to explain the proposition or part of it, or its implications.
  - ***Generation of a counter-argument:*** you will be asked to look at the other side of the argument by proposing or commenting on a counter-argument or counter-proposition.
  - ***Reconciliation of the two sides:*** you will be asked to offer some sort of resolution or reconciliation for two opposing positions (or elements of those positions) explored in the answer.

General Advice for Section 3:

- Planning a structure to your answer is essential. You should spend approximately 8-10 minutes on planning.
- Proper planning will help you prevent digressing from the topic.
- Plan the answer on the question paper.
- Make sure that the answer has a clear structure in which the question is explained, a discussion is presented, and a conclusion is made.
- If facts are included, ensure that they are correct and support the argument. If examples or quotes are used, keep them short.
- Answer every aspect of the question. If all parts of the question are not addressed, the essay will not be able to score a 3 or higher for content.

Towards the end of the test, take a minute or two to look over your answer and ask:

- Have you addressed all parts of the question in a relevant way?
- Have you organised your thoughts clearly?
- Have you used your general knowledge and opinions appropriately?
- Have you considered other viewpoints and counter-arguments, and justified your opinions?

VI. Scoring and Reporting

- For both Thinking Skills (Section 1) and Scientific Knowledge and Applications (Section 2), answer sheets are scanned and verified, followed by automated marking, psychometric analysis, test calibration and the issuing of results.
- For Sections 1 and 2, scores will be reported (to one decimal place) on a 9-point BMAT scale. Questions in Sections 1 and 2 are worth 1 mark each. Total raw marks for each section are converted to BMAT's scale, which runs from 1 (low) to 9 (high). In recent years, the majority of good students have scored between 4.5 and 6.0 in Sections 1 and 2, with very good students scoring between 6.0 and 7.0 and excellent students scoring above 7.0.
- The Writing Task (Section 3) is marked by Cambridge Assessment Admissions Testing examiners (two examiners). Each examiner gives two scores – one for quality of content (on a scale of 0–5), and one for quality of written English (on the scale A, C, E).

- If the two marks for content are the same or no more than one mark apart, you will get the average of the two marks.
- An image of the response will be supplied to each institution to which you have applied. In addition to the scores, the task provides the institution with a basis for qualitative assessment of writing skills.

Section 3 Marking Criteria – Content:

Scores are awarded on a scale from 1 to 5.

Score 1

An answer that has some bearing on the question, but which does not address the question in the way demanded, is incoherent or unfocussed.

Score 2

An answer that addresses most of the components of the question and is arranged in a reasonably logical way. There may be significant elements of confusion in the argument. The candidate may misconstrue certain important aspects of the main proposition or its implication or may provide an unconvincing or weak counter proposition.

Score 3

A reasonably well-argued answer that addresses ALL aspects of the question, making reasonable use of the material provided and generating a reasonable counter- proposition or argument. The argument is relatively rational. There may be some weakness in the force of the argument or the coherence of the ideas, or some aspect of the argument may have been overlooked.

Score 4

A good answer with few weaknesses. ALL aspects of the question are addressed, making good use of the material and generating a good counter proposition or argument. The argument is rational. Ideas are expressed and arranged in a coherent way, with a balanced consideration of the proposition and counter proposition.

Score 5

An excellent answer with no significant weaknesses. ALL aspects of the question are addressed, making excellent use of the material and generating an excellent counter proposition or argument. The argument is cogent. Ideas are expressed in a clear and logical way, considering a breadth of relevant points and leading to a compelling synthesis or conclusion.

An answer judged to be irrelevant, trivial, unintelligible or missing will be given a score of 0.

Section 3 Marking Criteria - Quality of English:

Scores are awarded on a scale from A to E.

Band A - Good use of English.

- fluent
- good sentence structure
- good use of vocabulary
- sound use of grammar
- good spelling and punctuation

- few slips or errors

Band C - Reasonably clear use of English.

There may be some weakness in the effectiveness of the English:

- reasonably fluent/not difficult to read
- simple/unambiguous sentence structure
- fair range and appropriate use of vocabulary
- acceptable grammar
- reasonable spelling and punctuation
- some slips/errors

Band E - Rather weak use of English.

- hesitant fluency/not easy to follow at times
- some flawed sentence structure/paragraphing
- limited range of vocabulary
- faulty grammar
- regular spelling/punctuation errors
- regular and frequent slips or errors

If you have crossed out sections or added information, the essay will be judged based on the quality of the resulting use of English (i.e., the crossed-out text will be ignored, and inserted text will be read as if it were originally in place). An essay that is judged to be below the level of an E will receive an X.

VII. Attainment of Previous Years (2017-2019)

2019:

Mode for Section 1: 4.0

Mode for Section 2: 3.5

Mode for Section 3: 3A

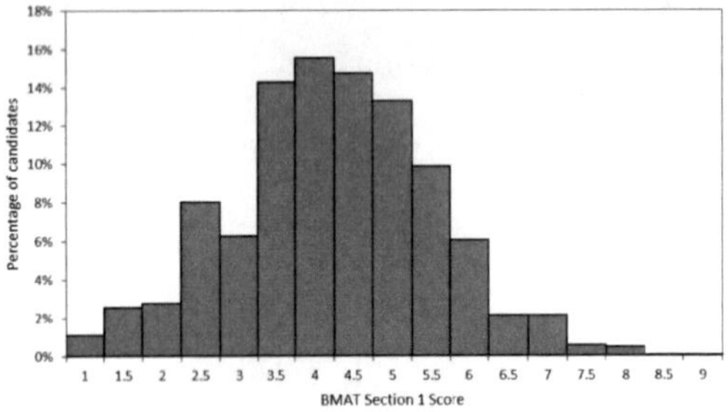

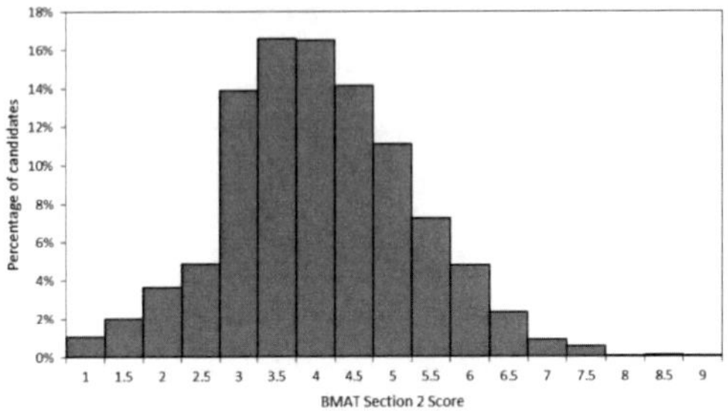

2018:

Mode for Section 1: 4.0

Mode for Section 2: 4.0

Mode for Section 3: 3A

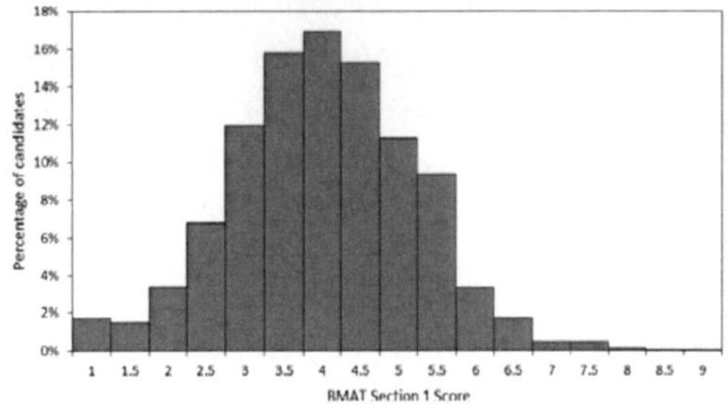

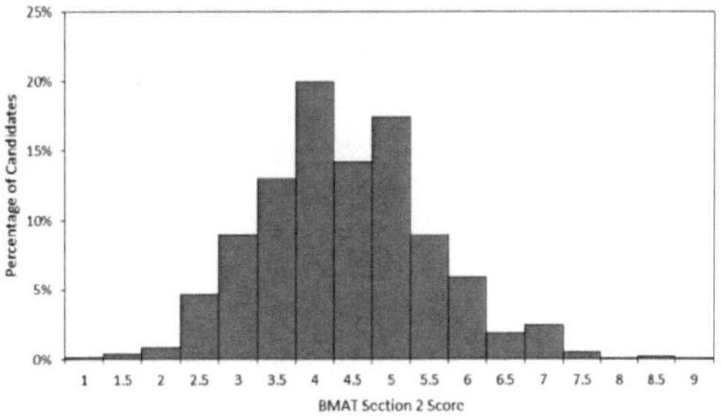

2017:

Mode for Section 1: 4.5

Mode for Section 2: 4.5

Mode for Section 3: 3A

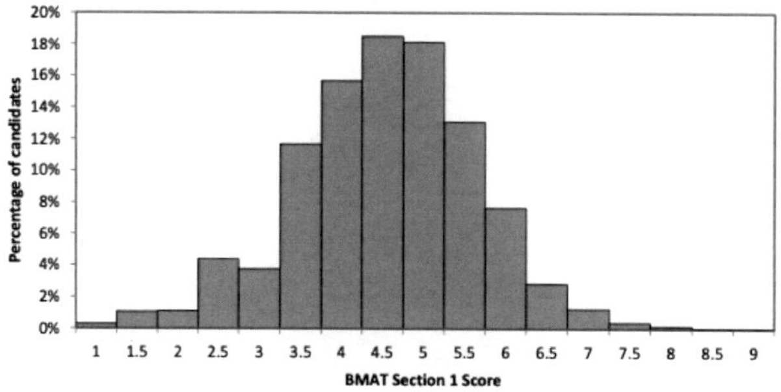

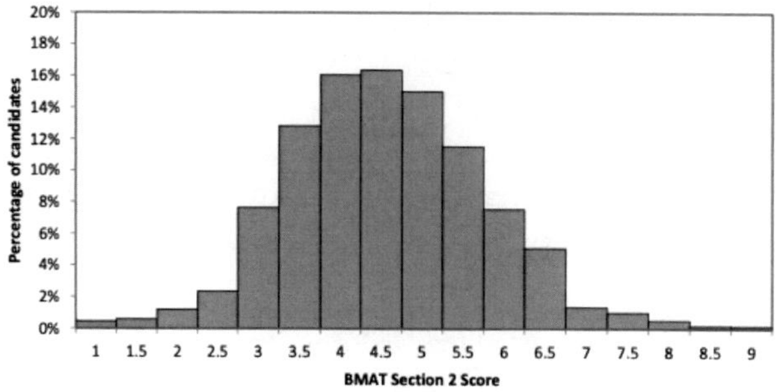

VIII. On Test Day

- Take a black ink pen, a pencil and an eraser.
- You are not allowed to use a calculator, dictionary or correction fluid.
- You are not allowed rough paper, but you can write on the question papers to mark key information, work out problems, make notes and draw diagrams. For Section 3, plan your response on the question paper.
- Each section has a time limit. You cannot use any time from one section to work on other sections.

CONTENTS

SECTION 1

CT	CRITICAL THINKING	Questions

Question 1

People with two copies of a version of the APOE gene called APOE4 are 14 times more likely to develop Alzheimer's disease compared to people with two copies of the APOE3 version of the gene. Those people were also more than twice as likely to test positive for the coronavirus than people with two copies of the APOE3 version. The results come from a study of more than 600 people in England diagnosed with coronavirus from March 16th to April 26th, 2020. Of 622 people who tested positive for the coronavirus, 37 had two copies of APOE4. On a population scale, this means that approximately 410 of every 100,000 people with two copies of APOE4 would test positive. That compares with 179 of every 100,000 people with two copies of APOE3 testing positive. As a result, individuals with two copies of APOE4, a gene that raises one's risk of developing Alzheimer's disease, are also more susceptible to coronavirus.

Which one of the following, if true, most weakens the argument above?

A. Individuals with Alzheimer's disease are more likely to be infected with coronavirus compared to a healthy individual.
B. When a further 40000 people tested positive for coronavirus, more than 35000 of these people had two copies of APOE3.
C. The APOE4 gene results in the development of coronavirus.
D. If an individual has two copies of the APOE3 gene, he or she will not develop Alzheimer's disease.
E. An individual who is infected with coronavirus is more likely to develop Alzheimer's disease due to the presence of the APOE4 gene.

Question 2

Much of the push toward self-driving cars has been underwritten by the hope that they will save lives, by preventing more injuries and deaths compared to human-driven cars. These self-driving cars have a variety of other safety technologies that use hardware (sensors, cameras and radar) and software to help vehicles identify certain safety risks so they can warn the driver of the appropriate actions to avoid a crash. Statistics suggest that more than 90% of car crashes in the UK are thought to involve some form of driver error. It is clear that self-driving cars should not have a speed limit on roads, due to their safety features, and the speed limit for these cars can be removed without causing more road fatalities.

Which one of the following is an assumption made in this passage?

A. The Government should not impose a speed limit on roads.
B. The safety features of self-driving cars reduce the chances of fatal road accidents for self-driving cars travelling at higher speeds.
C. If there was no speed limit, self-driven cars would drive at lower speeds, therefore reducing their risk of a fatality.
D. The public do not want a speed limit on the roads.
E. The roads have not become busier since self-driving cars were introduced.

Question 3

In order for a child to go to school, he or she must have had a range of vaccinations. Before a vaccination, doctors will not administer a vaccine if a child has a very high temperature, vomiting or diarrhoea on the day of the appointment. The inactivated polio vaccine must be used to prevent polio in toddlers. Susan is a three-year-old toddler who develops a high temperature after being administered the inactivated polio vaccine. Since she did not have this temperature before the vaccine, it must be due to the inactivated polio vaccine.

Which one of the following best illustrates a flaw in the reasoning?

A. It assumes that the inactivated polio vaccine is necessary to prevent polio.
B. It ignores the other potential issues caused by the inactivated polio vaccine.
C. It assumes that high temperature is the only side-effect of the inactivated polio vaccine.
D. It assumes that the high temperature definitely occurred due to the inactivated polio vaccine.
E. It ignores the action of the immune system, which may be sufficient to prevent polio compared to the inactivated polio vaccine.

Question 4

Many studies have established a correlation between red meat and colorectal cancer. The analysis of eight cohort studies showed a 17 per cent increased risk per 100 grams red meat consumed per day. As a result, there is strong evidence that eating red meat increases the risk of developing colorectal cancer. The current advice, issued by the Government, says that adults who eat more than 90 grams of red and processed meat a day should reduce their intake to 70 grams a day, which is the average daily consumption in the UK. However, despite the clear evidence and advice, many individuals who consume red meat continue to consume large amounts and seek to minimise their risk of colorectal cancer by focusing on less important risk factors, such as exercise. This approach is obviously flawed, and the fact that some individuals feel this is a good way to reduce their risk of colorectal cancer proves that they are delusional.

Which of the following best illustrates the main conclusion of the passage?

A. Many individuals who consume large amounts of red meat ignore the largest risk factor, instead focusing on exercise.
B. The Government should ban the consumption of more than 90 grams of red meat a day in order to reduce the incidence of colorectal cancer.
C. An overwhelming number of studies have proven the link between red meat and colorectal cancer.
D. The biggest risk factor of colorectal cancer is red meat.
E. Some individuals who consume large amounts of red meat are delusional.

Question 5

A drinks company conducted a survey on its staff to assess if there was a correlation between the musical instruments that employees played and their favourite drink. The findings were as follows:

Some violinists liked coffee and some of them liked Fanta.
All employees liked tea.
None of the flutists liked Fanta, but all of them, as well as some drummers, liked hot chocolate.
All drummers liked chocolate milkshakes.

Based on the findings, which one of the below must be true?

A. Some violinists liked coffee and Fanta.
B. Some drummers liked Fanta.
C. Some drummers liked three drinks.
D. Some of the flutists liked more than three drinks.
E. Some of the violinists liked tea but did not like coffee or Fanta.

Question 6

Hydroxychloroquine is a drug that prevents malaria in developing countries. As a result, there is an interest in hydroxychloroquine for the prevention of coronavirus. This has stemmed from studies in the laboratory that have suggested that the antimalarial drug could block viral entry into cells and slow viral replication. In a study of 821 people who had been exposed to someone with a confirmed case of coronavirus, 11.8 percent of people taking hydroxychloroquine and 14.3 percent of people taking a placebo developed symptoms. Therefore, hydroxychloroquine has been proposed to prevent the spread of coronavirus amongst key workers.

Which one of the following is an assumption made in this passage?

A. There is a significant difference in the number of cases of coronavirus when individuals take hydroxychloroquine compared to the placebo.
B. Hydroxychloroquine can be used to prevent the spread of coronavirus because it interferes with the communication of cells in the immune system as happens in the prevention of malaria.
C. Both coronavirus and malaria use similar mechanisms to infect individuals.
D. Hydroxychloroquine is the most effective preventative measure against malaria.
E. Coronavirus is a more complex infection compared to malaria.

Question 7

In 2001, Portugal became the first country to decriminalise the possession and consumption of all illicit substances. Rather than being arrested, those caught with a personal supply might be given a warning, a small fine, or told to appear before a local commission - a doctor, a lawyer and a social worker - about treatment, harm reduction, and the support services that were available to them. The opioid crisis soon stabilised, and the ensuing years saw dramatic drops in problematic drug use, HIV and hepatitis infection rates, overdose deaths, drug-related crime and incarceration rates. HIV infection plummeted from an all-time high in 2000 of 104.2 new cases per million to 4.2 cases per million in 2015. The data behind these changes has been studied and cited as evidence by harm-reduction movements around the globe. Therefore, the reduction of drug use in Portugal is due to the decriminalisation of possession and consumption of all illicit substances.

Which one of the following, if true, most weakens the argument above?

A. Portugal's remarkable recovery could not have happened without the enormous cultural shift, and a change in how the country viewed drugs and addiction.
B. The decriminalisation of possession and consumption of all illicit substances caused a reduction in drug use.
C. No other factors influenced the reduction of drug use between 2001-2015.
D. In 2020, there are now 1.2 new cases per million of HIV infection.
E. Portugal decriminalised drug possession due to the large amounts of drugs present in the country prior to 2001.

Question 8

Twenty years ago, Norway moved its focus from punishment to rehabilitation of offenders (including for those who were imprisoned). This was followed by large reductions in reoffending rates. Compared to a reoffending rate of around 50% within a year in the UK, whose prison system focuses more on punishment, Norway's is around 25% in five years. A lot of people processed within the criminal justice system have vulnerabilities that can make them more prone to offending, which might suggest why rehabilitation can be so successful. Recent evidence suggests that the UK prison population has serious levels of self-harm. In addition, a recent report finds that 90% of the UK's prison population suffer from mental health problems. Releasing such people without investing in their treatment is bound to result in reoffending. As a result, rehabilitation is mor e successful than punishment for offending individuals.

Which one of the following is an assumption made in this passage?

A. Norway has decriminalised the use of certain drugs, which has led to less people being convicted.

B. Individuals who suffer from mental health problems are more likely to reoffend.

C. The reoffending rates in Norway have only decreased due to the change in focus from punishment to rehabilitation.

D. Other countries which have focused on rehabilitation have also witnessed a reduction in their reoffending rates.

E. The success of a prison system is determined by the reoffending rates.

Question 9

A team of researchers from Surrey detailed the development of a technique that is able to detect key explosives. The new detection method is able to analyse nitrotoluenes, trinitrotriazine and nitroglycerine faster than current thermal based detection systems used in today's airports, while also reducing false positive reports. The new method, which uses swabs to collect samples of these explosives, is able to detect the aforementioned chemicals in 30 seconds. Surrey's swab spray technique is able to achieve higher sensitivity results than previously published works and was also tested on dirty surfaces such as new and used keyboards. As a result, the quicker detection of these explosives could help prevent high-profile terrorist attacks.

Which one of the following is the main assumption made in this passage?

A. High profile terrorist attacks are only due to explosives.

B. Explosives used in high profile terrorist attacks include nitrotoluenes, trinitrotriazine and nitroglycerine.

C. Thermal based detection systems are not able to detect explosives as quickly as this new technique.

D. All high-profile terrorist attacks can be prevented by this new technique.

E. Used keyboards have a lower sensitivity to the swab technique compared to new keyboards.

Question 10

A psychological phenomenon nicknamed the 'Return Trip Effect', is described as when the journey home feels shorter than the outward trip. Many psychologists believe that the 'Return Trip Effect' has to do with the subjective experience of time. At the biological level, humans possess a number of internal clocks that are relatively precise. The heart beats to a steady rhythm, and human bodies go through daily cycles. However, at the psychological level, the perception of time is imprecise and greatly influenced by one's mood. One explanation for the 'Return Trip Effect' involves familiarity. The idea is that the subjective perception of time slows down during unfamiliar experiences (resulting in the outbound journey feeling longer than the return trip). Needless to say, the exact mechanisms behind the 'Return Trip Effect' are still unknown and psychologists are still researching into the exact causes behind this phenomenon.

Which one of the following can be reliably concluded from the passage above?

A. Psychologists cannot definitely state the reasons behind the 'Return Trip Effect'.

B. The 'Return Trip Effect' always results in the journey home feeling shorter than the outward trip.

C. More recent research has concluded that the 'Return Trip Effect' was more apparent in individuals who had higher levels of anticipation.

D. The 'Return Trip Effect' is due to the subjective experience of time.

E. All individuals who have been on an outward trip and the journey home have experienced a type of 'Return Trip Effect'.

Question 11

The bizarre life of the sea's middle depths has long been a challenge to see, study and fathom. The creatures of that realm live under crushing pressures at icy temperatures in pitch darkness. Consequently, it is estimated that up to half the creatures of the sea remain undiscovered — mainly the otherworldly ones of the middle depths. A recently discovered organism is the siphonophore, with an estimated length of 150 feet, which is considered to be one of the longest oceanic creatures.

Which of the following best expresses the main conclusion of the passage above?

A. The siphonophore is considered to be one of the longest oceanic creatures.

B. Up to half of sea creatures may be undiscovered.

C. Creatures in the middle depths of the sea live under crushing pressures at icy temperatures in pitch darkness.

D. Studying the sea's middle depths has always been one of the greatest challenges that humans have encountered.

E. Most of the creatures in the darkest depths have yet to be discovered.

Question 12

This new technological product will enable elite football teams to monitor players. It combines techniques from artificial intelligence and machine learning to facilitate the rapid pattern matching needed to contextualise tactical activities. As a result, top teams will be able to use it to root out the weak links in their teams as well as from the opposition quickly and accurately. Currently, many football clubs use automated camera tracking technology to collect data on players. However, this new product can collect individual's data at 65% more accuracy. The study analysed English Premier League players by synchronising high-intensity distance data with the video footage of each game. This analysis clearly unveiled the unique physical profile that exists for each distinct tactical role.

Which one of the following would most weaken this argument?

A. This new technological product could be modified to help schools monitor their pupils.

B. If top teams root out their weak links, they are 74% more likely to win the match.

C. This new technological product took 25% more time to process all of the individual player data compared to automated camera tracking technology.

D. This new technological product can collect the most accurate player data.

E. A football team is more likely to win if it can identify out weak players in the opposing team.

Question 13

Lots of evidence have concluded that interacting with pets reduces people's stress. Good interactions have a profound effect on health because it causes changes in the levels of oxytocin and beta endorphins. The downside is that pets can also cause stress and be expensive to families. As a result, many reports — particularly those that come from medical professionals, who are inexperienced in this field — find negative effects to owning a pet. The reporting bias is in favour of the positive studies; the study that showed that cat owners were usually more depressed than people who don't have any pets was not popular. Therefore, pet-keeping does not have any major effect on health in either direction.

Which one of the following best states an assumption made in this argument?

A. It assumes that changes in the levels of oxytocin and beta endorphins are due to reduced stress.
B. It assumes that all cat owners are more depressed than people who do not have any pets.
C. It assumes that medical professionals do not have any expertise on the effect of pets on human health.
D. It assumes that the positive benefits of having a pet is equivalent to the downsides.
E. It assumes that all pets cause stress and are expensive to families.

Question 14

School administrators say uniforms are as much about safety and convenience as they are about inclusion. Students feel like they're part of a team, parents save money, and teachers don't have to worry about losing sight of them at the playground or on a field trip. However, requiring toddlers to wear khakis and collared shirts is part of a broader fast-forwarding of childhood. It reflects the culture's obsession on turning school, even nursery, into work. In addition, it indicates to student to follow the rules and not to colour outside the lines. Furthermore, uniforms represent a growing source of revenue. The lead-up to the school year is a crucial time for the country's largest chains. It is the second-largest shopping event of the year, behind the holiday season. As a result, many people believe uniforms should be banned in schools; it stifles creativity and individualism.

Which of the following best illustrates a flaw in this reasoning?

A. It ignores the fact that majority of students prefer wearing school uniform compared to own clothes.
B. It assumes that creativity and individualism can only be expressed in the clothes worn by pupils at school.
C.
D. It assumes that many of school administrators are not in favour of school uniforms.
E. It ignores the fact that schoolgirls do less exercise in their school uniform skirts compared to boys over a two-week period.

Question 15

Based on lab studies, researchers were able to demonstrate that the bumblebees' propensity to damaging leaves had a strong correlation with the amount of pollen they can obtain: Bumblebees damage leaves much more frequently when there is little or no pollen available to them. They also found that damage inflicted on plant leaves had dramatic effects on flowering time in different plant species. Tomato plants subjected to bumblebee biting flowered up to 30 days earlier than those that hadn't been targeted, while mustard plants flowered about 14 days earlier when damaged by the bumblebees. As a result, bumblebees can influence flowering time of all plant species, depending on the amount of pollen available on the plant.

Which of the following best illustrates a flaw in this reasoning?

A. Assumes that pollen always affects the bumblebees' propensity to damaging leaves.
B. Ignores the fact that lab studies conducted on the bumblebees may be inaccurate.
C. Assumes that all plant species that are capable of flowering are affected by bumblebees.
D. Ignores the fact that only two plant species are mentioned in the passage.
E. Assumes that only pollen affects flowering time in plant species.

Question 16

To study the association between metabolism and sleep, researchers genetically modified C. elegans to "turn off" a neuron that controls sleep. These worms could still eat, breathe, and reproduce, but they lost their ability to sleep. With this neuron turned off, the researchers saw a severe drop in Adenosine Triphosphate (ATP) levels, which is the body's energy currency. "This suggests that sleep is an attempt to conserve energy; it's not actually causing the loss of energy," Raizen explained. In previous research, the van der Linden lab studied a gene in C. elegans called KIN-29. This gene is homologous to the Salt-Inducible Kinase (SIK-3) gene in humans, which was already known to signal sleep pressure. Surprisingly, when the researchers knocked out the KIN-29 gene to create sleepless worms, the mutant C. elegans accumulated excess fat - resembling the human obesity condition - even though their ATP levels lowered. The researchers hypothesized that the release of fat stores is a mechanism by which sleep is promoted, and that the reason KIN-29 mutants did not sleep is because they were unable to liberate their fat. To test this hypothesis, the researchers again manipulated the KIN-29 mutant worms; this time they expressed an enzyme that "freed" their fat. With that manipulation, the worms were again able to sleep. Raizen said this could explain one reason why people with obesity may experience sleep problems. "There could be a signalling problem between the fat stores and the brain cells that control sleep," he said.

Which of the following can be deduced from the passage?

A. If fat stores are not freed, then sleep is promoted.
B. KIN-29 is likely to be involved in the pathway that reduces the accumulation of fat by liberating it.
C. Fat stores cause lack of sleep in humans.
D. SIK-3 mutations in humans cause sleeplessness.
E. Sleep increases ATP levels.

Question 17

For those who can't or don't want to speak to a real person, apps that provide meditation training and breathing exercises are more popular, but little is known about whether they actually work. A study published in 2019 looked at those who had downloaded 93 of the most popular mental health apps in Google's app store. The researchers found that 94 per cent of people stopped opening these apps just 15 days after downloading them.

"There's good evidence that people who use these apps often get good results," says Torous.

"One of the issues with these apps is the perceived absence of a strong motivating therapeutic relationship with a therapist," says Grist. "How people use apps on their phone is very different to how we would sit with a therapist for 60 minutes."

Which one of the following statements is best supported by the above passage?

A. Video calls with therapists have been proven to be effective.
B. Those who do not want to speak to real people have found these apps extremely helpful.
C. Using the app does not act as a substitute for a therapist.

D. People tend to delete the app before there is time for any changes to be seen.
E. Help from therapists is more effective than the apps.

Question 18

Despite improvements in infant formula over its 150-year history, it is still associated with health risks for mother and infant compared with breastfeeding. Manufacturers try to limit these risks through changes to formula composition, which are often accompanied by health or nutrition claims that aid product differentiation or increase market value. Academics and regulators have raised concerns, however, that these claims are often unfounded and may undermine efforts to support breastfeeding. The current regulatory environment allows claims to be made for food products with low levels of evidence, but the potential harms associated with claims are higher for infant formula than for other foods. Infant formula is consumed by a substantial proportion of the world's infants, often in large volumes in relation to their body weight - typically 150-200 mL/kg/day for a young infant fed solely on formula milk, the equivalent of 11-14 L/day for a 70 kg adult. The developmental status of infants means that any potential harm associated with infant formula claims may have a high cumulative impact over their life. Mothers are also vulnerable during the period when they make infant feeding choices, with up to 20% experiencing a mental illness during pregnancy or the first year of their infant's life. Aggressive promotion of infant formula can influence decisions to use formula milk in place of breast milk, and health and nutrition claims are likely to contribute to this process by narrowing the perceived benefits of breast milk.

Which one of the following statements is best supported by the above passage?

A. Breastfeeding is associated with fewer health risks to the infant than formula milk.
B. Mothers are unable to make the right decisions about infant feeding choices due to mental illnesses associated with pregnancy.
C. The media has persuaded many mothers to replace breastmilk with formula milk.
D. Infant formula milk has improved substantially over the last few years.
E. Claims about the improved formula composition are supported by good evidence.

Question 19

They call it the "unreasonable effectiveness of mathematics". Physicist Eugene Wigner coined the phrase in the 1960s to encapsulate the curious fact that merely by manipulating numbers, one can describe and predict all manner of natural phenomena with astonishing clarity. This can be used from the movements of planets and the strange behaviour of fundamental particles to the consequences of a collision between two black holes billions of light years away. Now, some are wondering if maths can succeed where all else has failed, unravelling the laws of nature in the first place. It is a big ask. The question of how matter gives rise to a felt experience is one of the most vexing problems. Unsurprisingly, the first fleshed-out mathematical model of consciousness has generated huge debate about whether it can tell us anything sensible. However, as mathematicians work to hone and extend their tools for peering deep inside, they are confronting some eye-popping conclusions. Not least, what they are uncovering seems to suggest that if we are to achieve a precise description of consciousness, we may have to ditch our intuitions and accept that all kinds of inanimate matter could be conscious – maybe even the universe as a whole.

Which one of the following can reliably be concluded from the information in the above passage?

A. Mathematicians and physicians are trying to model consciousness.
B. The universe has consciousness.

C. Consciousness can accurately be modelled with equations which can be used to predict events in the universe.
D. The mathematical model describing consciousness assumes inanimate matter is conscious.
E. The question of how matter gives rise to a felt experience is answered if one assumes the universe is conscious.

Question 20

Asking how one would prefer to be addressed is a simple thing, and one that could have an important impact on improving communications in paediatric care. The recent #hellomynameis campaign encouraged health professionals to introduce themselves by name. Although this has helped break down barriers in one direction, it's time to take it to the next level. Simply asking a child's carer how they would like to be addressed immediately personalises the context of the conversation. It might be that calling parents 'Mum' and 'Dad' is not a problem, but always ask first; don't assume. This ask may be small, but it is an important step in respecting the role that parents have in healthcare teams. It helps them to feel appreciated for the knowledge and expertise they bring to the table.

What conclusion can be drawn from this extract?

A. Health care workers must always ask the parents or careers of the patient how they would like to be addressed.
B. Parents have an important role in the healthcare team.
C. Some parents feel disempowered when referred to as mum or dad by the healthcare workers.
D. A healthcare worker introducing themselves to the patient is an important part of communication.
E. The recent #hellomynameis campaign improved the communication between patients and healthcare workers.

Question 21

According to a study published in mid-2020, keeping schools closed to tackle the coronavirus pandemic is almost certain to increase educational inequalities between children from the richest and poorest families, as debate intensifies over the Government's push to reopen schools in England. Survey data from more than 4,000 families in England analysed by the Institute for Fiscal Studies found that by the end of this month, children in better-off families will have received a week and half more home learning than children in the poorest households during the closures.

Which of the following is the best statement of the flaw in the argument above?

A. Receiving more learning does not necessarily reflect the quality of learning and the inequalities.
B. If schools remained open, the educational inequalities would not have increased.
C. Richest families educate their children more.
D. If all children were given standard education during lockdown by all schools, then inequalities would reduce.
E. Reopening of schools earlier may not necessarily change the inequalities.

Question 22

Kabir's piano teachers says he must practise at home more often since otherwise he cannot pass his exam. She says he should play at least two pieces a day since doing this will mean that he will definitely do well in the exam.

What is a flaw in her argument?

A. Kabir can play one piece a day and still pass.
B. She assumes that Kabir will follow her advice.
C. If he does not pass, then it means that he didn't play more than two pieces a day.
D. Taking more lessons would be more beneficial to Kabir than doing more practise at home.
E. Even if Kabir plays more than two pieces a day, it does not mean he will definitely pass.

Question 23

A school play was scheduled to start at 6:00 pm. There is a 15-minute interval after the first three scenes. After the interval, there are five more scenes. The total time for all the scenes is 80 minutes. Therefore, the play will finish at 7:35 pm.

Which of the following is an assumption made in the passage?

A. None of the students forgot their lines.
B. Each scene lasted 10 minutes.
C. The play started exactly at 6:00 pm.
D. Eight scenes were performed.
E. The interval did not increase the time it takes to finish the whole play.

Question 24

Aditya and Huan decide to go for a run. They both begin their run at 4:40 pm from Huan's house. Aditya decides to run through the whole forest; she covers 8 km in total. Huan only runs a short distance into the forest and then comes back home. He covers 4 times less distance than Aditya. Huan reaches back at 5:00 pm. This means that Aditya will be back at 6:00 pm.

What assumption is made in the passage?

A. They both started at the same place.
B. The both ran the same route before Aditya carried on.
C. They both started at the same time.
D. They both ran at the same speed.
E. Huan ran 2 km in total.

Question 25

Afua wants to rely on renewable sources of energy for the electricity in her home. She is deciding whether to invest in solar panels or wind turbines. Wind turbines generate about 170 kWh of electricity per week. Solar panels generate 70 kWh of electricity per week. If she decides to buy the wind turbine, she will generate 100 kWh more electricity than if she bought the solar panels each week.

Which of the following is not an assumption that Afua has made?

A. The energy consumption in her household remains the same.
B. Solar panels always generate the same amount of electricity each week.
C. Wind turbines cannot produce more than 170 kWh of electricity per week even if it is a very windy day.

D. The weather will not affect the amount of electricity produced by the two renewable resources.
E. All of the above are valid assumptions.

Question 26

Every year, many people are diagnosed with skin cancer as a result of excessive UV light from sun exposure. Despite this, many people still do not use sun cream when they go out in the sun. If more people started wearing sun cream, especially in the summer, skin cancer can be prevented.

What is a flaw in this argument?

A. Not all skin types are susceptible to skin cancer.
B. It implies that wearing sun cream is sufficient to prevent skin cancer.
C. It ignores the fact that not everyone can afford to wear sun cream every time they are exposed to the sun.
D. Not everyone is aware of the damage done by UV radiation.
E. People need to be encouraged to wear sun cream as they are not aware of the benefits of this.

Question 27

The overall GCSE grades that pupils in a particular school are receiving is getting progressively worse, with an increasing number of pupils failing their exams. The quality of teaching has decreased in the last few years due to changes in regulation that made the class sizes much larger. Teachers have been struggling to manage large number of students in each class. Despite this, the school is refusing to recruit more teachers. If more teachers were employed and the class sizes were reduced, all the pupils will pass their GCSEs.

What is a flaw in this argument?

A. It ignores the fact that the school cannot afford to recruit more teachers.
B. It does not consider that the GCSE exams have become more difficult.
C. Teachers are demanding higher salaries, hence less are being recruited.
D. It ignores the fact there is a shortage of teachers in the country, therefore, more cannot be recruited.
E. It ignores to consider the fact that the new teachers will need to be trained, which will take time.

Question 28

High levels of bilirubin cause yellow discolouration of the skin and a yellow stain in the sclera of the eye. This condition is called jaundice. Some patients with jaundice present with vomiting and abdominal pain.

Which one of the following statements is supported by the passage?

A. A patient presents with vomiting and abdominal pain; he/she has jaundice.
B. A patient has high levels of bilirubin; therefore, he/she would have abdominal pain and vomiting.
C. Jaundice can be caused by a tumour in the head of the pancreas.
D. Some people with abdominal pain and vomiting do not have jaundice.
E. None of the above.

Question 29

Many flights are available from Heathrow, London to Delhi, India throughout the year. There is a much higher demand for the flights in the summer after schools have closed. Therefore, flights tickets would cost more after the schools close in the summer than any other time.

What assumption has been made?

A. There will be more flights to Delhi in the summer.
B. The flight charges will be higher if demand for them is greater.
C. Less people will want to fly to India in the summer when the flight charges are higher.
D. There are the same number of flights throughout the whole year.
E. There aren't enough flights to meet the demand in the summer.

Question 30

Many videos games today have a lot of gory and violent content. This could mean that children may become more aggressive and the crime rates can increase because people try to mimic what they see in these games. Parents must restrict, or even stop their children, from playing such games.

Which of the following best describes a flaw in this argument?

A. Playing violent video games does not necessarily mean children will mimic what they see in real life.
B. There are age restrictions in video games that limit younger children from playing them.
C. People are also exposed to violence by watching TV.
D. Not all video games have violence.
E. There has been a decrease in the number of violent video games being made.

Question 31

Smoking is harmful to our health. Many smokers are more likely to develop diseases such as lung cancer, chronic bronchitis and heart disease. Quitting smoking has many health benefits and will increase a person's life expectancy. It is never too late to quit, but many people do not wish to stop smoking, despite the risks it poses. If more people tried to quit smoking, then severe health problems can be avoided, and life expectancy would increase.

What conclusion can be drawn from this passage?

A. Smoking is harmful to the lungs.
B. Smoking is injurious to health and should be banned.
C. Many people are addicted to smoking; therefore, they cannot quit.
D. Not everyone is concerned about the health risks that are associated with the choices that they make.
E. Other factors may contribute to lung cancer, chronic bronchitis and heart disease.

Question 32

Workplaces that give their employees a higher salary tend to have more productive workers than the places that give their workers a lower salary for doing a similar job. Thus, if an employer wants to make workers more productive, then he or she must pay the employees a higher salary.

Which one of the following best demonstrates a flaw in the argument?

A. Some companies cannot afford to pay higher salaries for their workers.
B. Not all workplaces do the same type of work.
C. The productivity of the workers varies over the year.

D. Higher productivity is what leads to the workers being paid higher salaries.
E. Pressurising workers with deadlines would improve productivity.

Question 33

Many people in developed countries are becoming increasingly obese due to the sedentary lifestyles that they lead. This is often due to busy schedules, where individuals do not have enough time to exercise and prepare healthy food. If people had more free time, the health of the population will improve.

What assumption is made in this passage?

A. A sedentary lifestyle leads to obesity.
B. People in less developed countries are not becoming obese.
C. People will spend their spare time trying to improve their health and lifestyle.
D. It is not time-consuming to make healthy food.
E. Individuals will be less stressed if they had more spare time, which will ultimately improve their mental health.

Question 34

Many factories lack sufficient first-aid kits and often run out of them during the week. This means that workers who get injured in the workplace do not always get sufficient treatment or care for their injuries. If factories were well-equipped with these supplies and had plenty of stock, many of these accidents could be avoided.

Which of the following describes a flaw in this argument?

A. During some weeks, the supplies run out unexpectedly, despite having plenty in other weeks.
B. Some factories cannot afford to keep a huge stock of spare first-aid kits.
C. It implies that having sufficient first-aid kits will result in fewer accidents occurring.
D. It ignores the fact that not everyone has sufficient knowledge of how to use the first-aid kits.
E. Many of the injuries that workers may have cannot be treated, even if there are plenty of first-aid kits.

Question 35

Taking part in more extracurricular activities has improved Robert's grades at school. He claims that being busy kept him more motivated and productive while he studied; this has increased his educational attainment. Therefore, he believes that students struggling with schoolwork should take part in more extracurricular activities because this will improve their grades.

What is a flaw in this argument?

A. Doing more extracurricular activity means that some pupils may struggle to manage time and, as a result, their grades may actually drop.
B. Not all extracurricular activities help to improve grades.
C. Being more productive will help pupils manage time in the future.
D. Pupils should seek academic help if they are struggling with schoolwork, instead of participating in more extracurricular activities.
E. Participating in too many activities may cause students to burnout.

Question 36
Sophie claims that parents are buying mobile phones and tablets for very young children, in order to keep them entertained. Some children are spending many hours on these devices. She states that more children are struggling to communicate and interact with others. In addition, many individuals are also showing signs of obesity. Parents must not allow children to start using such devices from a young age; instead, they should find other ways to entertain their children. This will make sure that any behavioural and physical problems to their health in the future is minimised.

Which one of the following statements identify a flaw in the argument?

A. It ignores the fact that parents are too busy.
B. It only focuses on young children, and not older ones who are also using these devices.
C. Parents may not be aware of the risks that these devices have on their children.
D. It assumes that using these devices causes obesity and communication problems for children.
E. It does not state the disadvantages of children watching too much television.

Question 37
There's no reliable predictor of how fast dehydration would kill a person. Many survival blogs suggest that an average person can survive for somewhere from two days to a week without liquids. A person's health, the weather and the individual's physical activity levels will all contribute to determining the period of time that a person will survive without water. According to the Mayo Clinic, older people, children, individuals with chronic diseases, and people who work or exercise outside are at particular risk of dehydration. In a very hot environment, an adult can lose between 1 and 1.5 litres of sweat an hour. Generally, it appears as though humans can survive without any food for 30-40 days, as long as they are properly hydrated. Therefore, an individual is more likely to die from dehydration compared to starvation.

Which one of the following would most weaken this argument?

A. When 60 individuals were stranded in a desert for two months, majority of those who died were solely due to starvation.
B. More individuals died from dehydration compared to starvation in 2019.
C. The warmer the climate, the more likely that an individual will be dehydrated.
D. Children are 34% more likely to suffer from dehydration compared to adults.
E. A human cannot survive more than a week without water.

Question 38
Ancient footprints, first thought to belong to a pterosaur, may actually have been made by a large bipedal ancestor of crocodiles, that lived about 110 to 120 million years ago.
Martin Lockley and his colleagues found a set of fossilised footprints near Sacheon City, South Korea. The tracks were more detailed and well-preserved than similar ones discovered in 2012 about 50 kilometres away, which were thought to have been made by a giant flying reptile called a pterosaur. The newly discovered tracks are 18 to 24 centimetres long and include detailed skin impressions left by the animal's heels and toes. Lockley and his team say the size and skin patterns are consistent with those belonging to a large ancestor of modern crocodiles, called a crocodylomorph, that walked on two legs. The new findings suggest previously discovered footprints may also have been formed by a crocodylomorph, rather than a pterosaur, says Lockley. This was a surprise, he says. "No one knew that large bipedal crocs existed in the

early Cretaceous." Pedro Godoy, at Stony Brook University in New York, says he agrees that the tracks weren't made by a pterosaur, but thinks more evidence is needed before the footprints can be definitively assigned to an ancient crocodile. This is because the footprints are particularly large for a crocodylomorph from the Cretaceous period.

Which of the following best expresses the main conclusion of the above argument?

A. The footprints are from a pterosaur.
B. The footprints belong to a crocodylomorph.
C. Bipedal crocodiles existed in the early Cretaceous period.
D. It is not certain which species the footprints belong to because there is not sufficient evidence.
E. Crocodylomorphs are ancestors of modern crocodiles that walked on two legs.

Question 39

Zoom, the video-conferencing app that has seen a huge rise in downloads since quarantines were imposed around the world, is now being used by millions for work and social gatherings. In May 2020, Prime Minister Boris Johnson tweeted a picture of himself chairing a Cabinet meeting via the app. This led to questions about how secure it was for Government meetings. Zoom has angrily defended its security record, saying it would answer any questions the Government had. Prof Alan Woodward, a computer scientist at Surrey University thinks the Government needs to be careful: "In some ways, for a public broadcast, it doesn't matter if anyone can listen in - as was the case for the Number 10 briefing." "However, when the briefing is for the participants' ears only, we have used Microsoft Teams." "There is no evidence that Zoom has any problems in its latest versions but in these unprecedented times, it seems sensible only to use systems that are tried and tested. It does reinforce the message that whatever one uses, he or she should use the latest version," he added.

Which of the following best expresses the main conclusion of the above argument?

A. Skype is more secure than Zoom.
B. The latest version of Zoom is safe to use by the Government for secure meetings.
C. Although latest version of Zoom does not show any evidence of having any security issues, it is safer to use systems that have been tested and trusted.
D. Zoom is a very popular video-conferencing app.
E. Zoom will be used by the Government for future secure meetings.

Question 40

A sample consisted of 382 subjects (2-14 years of age) sustaining a fracture after low or moderate trauma. Males were at a higher risk of fractures than females; greater than two-thirds of injuries occurred after low-energy trauma and the upper limb was more frequently involved. With increasing age, the male/female ratio and time spent in sports participation increased ($p < 0.001$), while calcium intake and time spent in sedentary behaviours decreased ($p < 0.001$ and < 0.003, respectively). Gender discordance existed in pre-school children with respect to the anatomic location, and in school, children and adolescents with respect to the dynamics.

Which of the following best expresses the main conclusion of the above argument?

A. The injuries varied with gender.
B. The upper limb is more frequently fractured.
C. Men spent more time doing sports than women.
D. The fracture site varied between the genders.
E. Recurrent fractures have a similar trend in both genders.

Question 41

Acting against racism is everyone's responsibility. We now realise we cannot tackle COVID-19 unless we tackle racism. This realisation may be less obvious to some, who see the global outpouring of grief and anger at the killing of George Floyd in Minneapolis as either a distraction from or in conflict with efforts to contain the virus. Commentators in the BMJ make it clear that these two things are deeply interconnected and must be dealt together. Racism is a public health issue because it kills people. It is the underlying driver that puts people from ethnic minority groups at the centre of the pandemic. It is a co-factor for COVID-19 and a key social determinant of health.

Which of the following best expresses the main conclusion of the above argument?

A. Racism is a key issue during the COVID-19 pandemic the two aspects are interconnected since it puts people from the ethnic minority at the centre of the pandemic.
B. Racism kills people.
C. Some people think that the issues related to racism are just a distraction from the global pandemic or that it conflicts with the actions taken to try to contain the virus.
D. Racism is a co-factor for COVID-19.
E. COVID-19 cannot be eliminated unless racism is eliminated.

Question 42

The opening times of many supermarkets and shops are not suitable for those who are working during the week. This has meant that there is a large number of people who are heavily reliant on online shopping. Shops should remain open until the late evening; this would increase their sales as more people will be able to visit the stores.

What is the main assumption made in this passage?

A. If more people visit the stores, they will spend more in store than they would if they shopped online.
B. Online shopping will decrease.
C. People will visit the stores after work if they are open.
D. Shopping in store is cheaper.
E. Many supermarkets already stay open until the late evening.

Question 43

According to the US Centres for Disease Control and Prevention, drowning kills more children ages 1 to 4 than any other cause, with the exception of birth defects. In addition, 6,700 children attend hospital emergency rooms each year for injuries related to drownings; an equivalent of 18 children per day. An average of 379 children under age 15 die in reported drownings linked to pools or spas each year - this number increased to 395 deaths in 2017. In the age group 16-18, drowning is ranked as the third leading cause of death. Consequently, children under the age of 18 should not be allowed to enter large bodies of water, such as pools and spas, even when adult supervision is present.

Which one of the following statements, if true, would most strengthen the above argument?

A. Children under the age of 4 should not be allowed to enter any large body of water.
B. Children should be taught swimming at a much younger age, in order to prevent the chance of drowning.
C. More children under 15 died from drowning in 2017 due to the hot summer climate.
D. More than 60% of child drownings occur even when adult supervision is present.
E. Children are 80% more likely to drown at four years old compared to eight years old.

Question 44

One in three women in Europe inherited a gene variant from Neandertals, which results in increased fertility, fewer bleedings during early pregnancy and fewer miscarriages. The gene increases the production of progesterone, which is a hormone that plays an important role in the menstrual cycle and in pregnancy. Analyses of Biobank data from more than 450,000 participants - among them were 244,000 women - show that almost one in three women in Europe have inherited the progesterone receptor from Neandertals. Twenty-nine percent carry one copy of the Neandertal receptor and three percent have two copies.

Which one of the following, if true, most strengthens the argument above?

A. A woman with this gene variant will have a successful and healthy pregnancy.
B. The more copies of the gene variant, the more likely that a woman will have a healthy pregnancy.
C. European women are more likely to suffer from miscarriages compared to women of other ethnicities.
D. Molecular analyses revealed that women with this gene variant produce more progesterone receptors in their cells, which leads to an increased sensitivity to progesterone and protection against early miscarriages and bleeding.
E. Progesterone is the only hormone that is essential for a successful and healthy pregnancy.

Question 45

The positive effects from sports are achieved primarily through physical activity, but secondary effects bring health benefits such as psychosocial and personal development, and less alcohol consumption. Negative effects, such as the risk of failure, injuries, eating disorders, and burnout, are also apparent. Since physical activity is increasingly conducted in an organized manner, sport's role in society has become increasingly important over the years, not only for the individual but also for public health. The average energy intake is increasing, creating an energy surplus, and thus, we are seeing an increasing number of people who are overweight, which is a strong contributor to health problems. Physical activity and exercise have significant positive effects in preventing or alleviating mental illness, including depressive symptoms and anxiety- or stress-related disease. As a result, participating in sports is always beneficial, as long as personal capacities, social situations, and biological and psychological maturation are taken into account.

Which one of the following statements, if true, would most strengthen the above argument?

A. More pupils participate in sports during primary school compared to secondary school.
B. Participating in sports is always beneficial for all individuals.
C. In a recent survey, 38% of overweight individuals felt uncomfortable in participating in school sports.
D. Physical activity and exercise have significant positive effects in preventing or alleviating mental illness, including depressive symptoms and anxiety.
E. Participating in sports causes endorphins to be released, which triggers a positive feeling in the body.

Question 46

According to recent evidence, brain activity in different regions could directly result in phobias. In general, the origins of a phobia are tricky to unravel since they are often not related to simple experiences. Given the understanding of the amygdala's (present in the cerebral hemisphere of the brain) involvement in fear response, it is unsurprising that phobias are linked to heightened activity in this region. One study explored this phenomenon in people with arachnophobia. It found that if scientists told these individuals that they might encounter a spider, activity in their brains differed from control participants without a phobia. Activity in the lateral prefrontal cortex, praecuneus and visual cortex was comparatively lower. The authors say that these brain regions are key for the regulation of emotions; they help keep individuals level-headed. A reduction in their activity suggests a reduced ability to restrain fearful emotions.

Which one of the following statements, if true, would most strengthen the above argument?

A. When individuals were asked the reason behind their phobias, 67% said that they had personal experiences regarding that phobia.
B. Genes and the environment have a greater impact on phobias compared to brain activity.
C. Individuals over the age of 25 are more likely to have a phobia of spiders than heights.
D. One study also discovered that there was a disconnect between the amygdala and the prefrontal cortex region of the brain in individuals with a severe phobia, which normally helps an individual override or minimize the fear response.
E. Younger individuals, whose brains are not as developed, are more likely to have an irrational phobia compared to adults.

Question 47

Based on the substantial evidence that music offers numerous health benefits, many experts are asking for greater utilisation of music therapy within health care settings. Music therapists are poised and ready to assess, deliver and document music therapy treatment to support the patient as part of the interdisciplinary team. In addition, many researchers believe that music therapy could offer an alternative treatment option for some conditions – such as tension headaches. Based on the research to date, there is certainly evidence that humans have much more than just an emotional connection with music - it presents many additional health benefits as well.

Which one of the following statements, if true, would most strengthen the above argument?

A. More than 34% of individuals prefer music to reading.
B. Researchers found that patients who were played music after surgery experienced less pain and anxiety compared to those who were not.
C. Music therapy is less effective than other forms of therapy that patients can access.
D. Music therapy can be used to treat a range of mental illnesses, such as depression and anxiety.
E. According to a recent study, individuals are less than three times as likely to experience stress if they listen to music, compared to those who do not.

Question 48

According to recent figures, a homeless person dies on average every 19 hours in the UK. This has prompted calls for the Prime Minister to address the country's housing crisis. Data collated through coroners' enquiries, media coverage, family testimony and freedom of information requests reveals at least 235 people affected by homelessness have died over the last six months, ranging from the ages of 16 to 104 years old. The same figures from last year showed 449 deaths from homelessness were recorded in 12 months – on average one every 20 hours – this indicates that the frequency at which homeless people are dying has risen slightly, despite increased awareness of the issue. These horrific statistics can be reduced if the government allocates more money to prevent UK's housing crisis.

Which one of the following statements, if true, would most strengthen the above argument?

A. Homeless people are five times more likely to die compared to an individual who has a shelter.
B. When 20% more funding was invested into housing in 2019, 320 deaths due to homelessness occurred during a 12-month period.
C. A homeless person dies on average every 15 hours in the USA.
D. Not all individuals who are homeless want to be housed by the government.
E. When more charities were set up to aid the homeless in 2018, 140 people who were affected by homelessness died during a 12-month period.

Question 49

It has been reported that scientists have developed a blood test that can reliably predict whether a person will develop dementia within the next three years. If true, such a test would allow the detection of Alzheimer's, a type of dementia, at a point where treatments could be used to halt progression. A cohort of 525 healthy over-70s was recruited and followed over five years, regularly undergoing cognitive testing and providing blood samples in which thousands of molecules were measured. Using the blood samples provided, modern biomarkers were reported as correctly identifying nine out of ten of those who suffered cognitive decline and nine out of ten of those with normal cognitive function.

Which one of the following statements, if true, would most strengthen the above argument?

A. When the same study was repeated, the modern biomarkers correctly identified 80% of those who suffered cognitive decline.
B. Over 70s are the most likely individuals to develop Alzheimer's disease.
C. A blood test can reliably predict whether a person will develop dementia in the next three years.
D. Cognitive testing can always predict an individual's likelihood of developing dementia.
E. Modern biomarkers have identified 20 other cognitive diseases with 98% accuracy.

Question 50

Individuals tend to think of sleep as a time when the mind and body shut down. However, sleep is an active period in which a lot of important processing, restoration, and strengthening occurs. One of the vital roles of sleep is to help solidify and consolidate memories. Overnight, information is transferred from more tentative, short-term memory to stronger, long-term memory—a process called "consolidation." As a result, the best sleep habits are ones that are consistent and involve healthy routines, that allow anyone, regardless of their age, to meet sleep needs every night, and keep on top of life's challenges every day.

Which one of the following statements, if true, would most strengthen the above argument?

A. More processing, restoration and strengthening occurs while individuals are asleep compared to when they are awake.
B. Individuals with consistent sleep habits are twice as likely to remember events which occurred more than 5 years ago.
C. Sleep is the only time when individuals can solidify and consolidate memories.
D. A healthy sleep habit has a greater impact on health compared to diet and exercise.
E. The mind is twice as active when an individual is sleeping compared to when they are awake.

Question 51

While there are many alarming statistics, the good news is that quitting smoking reduces the risk of disease and death significantly. The risks drop further the longer a person refrains from smoking. In fact, some research says that quitting before the age of 40 reduces the risk of dying from smoking-related disease by about 90%. Within 2–5 years, the risk of a stroke reduces to half that of a non-smoker. The risks for mouth, throat, oesophagus and bladder cancer drop by half within 5 years of quitting, and 10 years for lung cancer. Soon after quitting, people experience many health benefits that can significantly improve their quality of life, such as an increased ease in breathing, a reduction in daily coughing and wheezing and an improvement in circulations through the hands and feet.

Which one of the following statements, if true, would most strengthen the above argument?

A. A smoker is three times more likely to develop oesophageal cancer compared to a non-smoker.
B. Quitting before the age of 40 reduces the risk of dying from smoking-related disease by about 90%.
C. Approximately 70% of individuals who strive to quit smoking will return within three months.
D. All individuals who quit smoking will have a better quality of life.
E. After one year of quitting, the risk of having a heart attack drops sharply.

Question 52

More than half the world's dwindling wild tiger population are threatened by roads built dangerously close to their habitats, and giant infrastructure projects planned across Asia could put tigers at even greater risk. Using a global dataset, Neil Carter at the University of Michigan, calculated that the tiger's current range, which mostly spans south and south-east Asia, contains 134,000 kilometres of roads. Based on average tiger density, he estimated that 57% of tigers live within five kilometres of these roads, which is considered dangerously close. According to the researcher's modelling, this proximity to roads could be decreasing the world's tiger population by more than 20%.

Which one of the following, if true, most strengthens the above argument?

A. Tigers that live near roads are more vulnerable because of their risk of being hit by vehicles and it also makes them more exposed to poachers.
B. More roads will be built in Nepal in the near future to connect all the villages.
C. Building roads close to the habitats of tigers endangers the life of the travellers that will use the roads.
D. Tigers are at more risk and vulnerable during the night when it is dark.
E. Building tiger friendly roads will prevent the lives of the tigers being endangered.

CT	CRITICAL THINKING	Answers

1. **B**

   Conclusion – Individuals with two copies of APOE4, a gene that raises one's risk of developing Alzheimer's disease, are also more susceptible to coronavirus.

   Evidence – Approximately 410 of every 100,000 people with two copies of APOE4 would test positive for coronavirus, compared to 179 of every 100,000 people with two copies of APOE3.

   A statement that weakens the argument would provide evidence to the contrary. **Option 'B'** states that when additional people who were tested positive for coronavirus, majority of them had copies of the APOE3 gene. This weakens the original conclusion; therefore, Option 'B' is correct. **Option 'A'** is not supported by the passage because the APOE4 gene increases the risk of developing coronavirus – not all individuals with Alzheimer's disease will have the APOE4 gene. **Options 'C' and 'D'** are incorrect because they are assertions which are not supported or explicitly stated in the passage. **Option 'E'** is also not mentioned, and the assumption is not based on any evidence in the passage.

2. **B**

   Conclusion – Speed limits for self-driving cars can be removed without causing more road fatalities.

   Evidence – Self- driving cars have many safety features and 90% of car crashes in the UK are caused by driver error.

   The assumption links the evidence to the conclusion. This passage describes improved safety features on self-driving cars that reduce the likelihood of road fatalities compared to human-driven cars. It concludes that this means there should be no speed limit, and that this would not affect the number of road fatalities. Therefore, **Option 'B'** correctly links the assumption that safety features will reduce the chances of self-driving cars, travelling at higher speeds, being involved in fatal road accidents. **Option 'C'** is not required to be true for the argument's conclusion to lead on from its reasoning. **Options 'A','D' and 'E'** are not relevant to the conclusion of the passage.

3. **D**

   Conclusion – Susan has developed a high temperature due to the inactivated polio vaccine.

   Evidence – Doctors will not administer a vaccine if a child has a very high temperature on the day of the appointment.

   Option 'D' correctly states that the development of a high temperature was not definitely caused by the polio vaccine – the conclusion and the evidence do not match. **Options 'A', 'B' and 'C'** are not assumptions because they are directly stated in the passage. **Option 'E'** is an irrelevant statement, and it also disagrees with a statement from the passage ('the inactivated polio vaccine must be used to prevent polio in toddlers').

4. **E**

   Conclusion – Some individuals who consume large amounts of red meat are delusional.

   Evidence - Many individuals who consume red meat continue to consume large amounts and seek to minimise their risk of colorectal cancer by focusing on less important risk factors, such as exercise.

The main conclusion is iterated in **Option 'E'**. If **Options 'A', 'C' and 'D'** are all accepted as true, they would all contribute towards supporting the statement given in **Option 'E'**, which is a valid conclusion from the passage. Therefore, Options 'A', 'C' and 'D' are all reasons given to support the main conclusion (Option 'E'). **Option 'B'** is not a valid conclusion because the passage does not suggest the banning of more than 90 grams of meat a day – it is merely advice from the government.

5. C

Since some violinists who like coffee are not necessarily the same ones who like coffee, **Options 'A' and 'E'** can be eliminated. Equally, there is insufficient evidence for **Option 'B'**; therefore, this is incorrect. All of the flutists liked hot chocolate and tea, but there is no evidence of them liking more than 3 drinks – **Option 'D'** is eliminated. All drummers like chocolate milkshakes and tea and some of them like hot chocolate. Therefore, there must be some drummers who like all three drinks – **Option 'C'** is correct.

6. B

Conclusion - Hydroxychloroquine has been proposed to prevent the spread of coronavirus amongst key workers.

Evidence – In a study of 821 people who had been exposed to someone with a confirmed case of coronavirus, 11.8 percent of people taking hydroxychloroquine and 14.3 percent of people taking a placebo developed symptoms.

The assumption would link the evidence to the conclusion. **Option 'B'** is correct because it makes the assumption that Hydroxychloroquine can be used to prevent the spread of coronavirus because it interferes with the communication of cells in the immune system as happens in the prevention of malaria.

Option 'A' is not an assumption because it would strengthen the argument that hydroxychloroquine can be used to treat coronavirus. **Option 'C'** contributes to the assumption, but it does not express the relationship between viruses and hydroxychloroquine. **Options 'D' and 'E'** are incorrect because they are opinions which are not based on the passage.

7. A

Conclusion - The reduction of drug use in Portugal is due to the decriminalisation of possession and consumption of all illicit substances.

Evidence - After the decriminalisation of possession and consumption of all illicit substances, Portugal saw dramatic drops in problematic drug use, HIV and hepatitis infection rates, overdose deaths, drug-related crime and incarceration rates.

Option 'B' is incorrect because it solely summarises the conclusion of the passage. **Option 'C'** is an assumption of the passage (only the decriminalisation of drugs contributed to a decline in drug use). As a result, Option 'C' is incorrect. **Option 'D'** is incorrect as it would strengthen the argument that decriminalisation has reduced drug use since it states a decline of HIV infections, which can be transmitted by sharing drug needles. **Option 'E'** is irrelevant to the passage since it has not stated the reason from the decriminalisation of drugs in 2001. Therefore, **Option 'A'** is correct because it provides an alternative explanation for the result in Portugal, thus weakening the argument that the decriminalisation was the sole reason for the reduction in drug use.

8. E

Conclusion - Rehabilitation is more successful than punishment for offending individuals.

Evidence - Compared to a reoffending rate of around 50% within a year in the UK, whose prison system focuses more on punishment, Norway's is around 25% in five years.
An assumption links the evidence to the conclusion. Therefore, Option 'E' is the correct answer. Option 'A' is incorrect because it is an assumption which is not based on the passage (the passage does not state that Norway has decriminalised the use of certain drugs). Option 'B' is incorrect since it is not related to the conclusion of rehabilitation being more successful compared to punishment. Option 'C' is a flaw in the argument as it assumes that only rehabilitation has contributed to a reduction in offending rates. Option 'D' strengthens the argument by stating that other countries that have adopted the rehabilitation approach have also witnessed a reduction in reoffending rates – however, this is not an assumption. Therefore, Option 'D' is incorrect.

9. B

Conclusion - The quicker detection of explosives could help prevent high-profile terrorist attacks.
Evidence - The new method is able to detect nitrotoluenes, trinitrotriazine and nitroglycerine in just 30 seconds.
The assumption must link the evidence to the conclusion; therefore, Option 'B' is the only assertion that mentions the three explosives and the relation to the prevention of high-profile terrorist attacks. Option 'B' is the correct answer. Option 'A' is incorrect because it is not mentioned in the passage (the assumption is too specific). Although Options 'C' and 'E' are factually based on the passage; they are not assumptions and can be eliminated. Option 'D' is incorrect because it generalises that all terrorist attacks can be prevented by the new technique.

10. A

Conclusion - The exact mechanisms behind the 'Return Trip Effect' are still unknown.
Evidence - Psychologists are still researching into the exact causes behind this phenomenon.
Therefore, the statement which best illustrates the conclusion is Option 'A'. Option 'B' is incorrect because it generalises that the 'Return Trip Effect' always results in the journey home feeling shorter than the outward trip - this is not supported by the passage. Option 'C' is not supported in the passage; as a result, it is incorrect. Option 'D' is incorrect because it gives a definitive reason behind this phenomenon; it is only suggested by the passage. Option 'E' generalises that all individuals have experienced the 'Return Trip Effect' - there is no evidence of this in the passage.

11. B

Conclusion - It is estimated that up to half the creatures of the sea remain undiscovered.
Evidence - The creatures of that realm live under crushing pressures at icy temperatures in pitch darkness.
Therefore, the statement which best illustrates the main conclusion is Option 'B'. Option 'A' is incorrect because it a statement from the passage, and not the main conclusion. Option 'C' gives a potential explanation for the conclusion; however, it is not the main conclusion. Option 'D' is incorrect because it is not stated or supported in the passage; it is an opinion. Option 'E' is incorrect since there is no statement regarding the discovery of creatures in the darkest depths of the ocean.

12. C

Conclusion - Top football teams will be able to use a new technological product to root out the weak links in their teams as well as from the opposition quickly and accurately.
Evidence - This new technological product can collect individual's data with 65% more accuracy compared to camera tracking technology.
A statement that weakens the evidence or provide a counterargument will weaken the aforementioned argument that this new technological product is better than the camera tracking technology. Therefore, **Option 'C'** is correct. **Option 'A'** is incorrect because it is not relevant to the passage. **Option 'B'** is incorrect since it strengthens the argument that top football teams would benefit from this new technology. **Option 'D'** generalises that this product collects the most accurate player data - this passage only mentions the new technological product and camera tracking technology (there may be other methods which are not stated in the passage). **Option 'E'** is an assumption based on the passage; it does not weaken the argument.

13. D

Conclusion - Pet-keeping does not have any major effect on health in either direction.
Evidence - There is evidence that interacting with pets reduces people's stress. Good interactions have a profound effect on health because it causes changes levels of oxytocin and beta endorphins. The downside is that pets can also cause stress and be expensive to families.
The assumption must link the evidence to the conclusion. Therefore, the conclusion that pet keeping does not impact human health must assume that all of the positive benefits of owning a pet are equivalent to all of the downsides - this is best illustrated in **Option 'D'**. **Option 'A'** is incorrect because it does not mention the conclusion that owning a pet has no impact on human health. **Option 'B'** is incorrect because it generalises that all cat owners are more depressed - this is not supported in the passage. **Option 'C'** is also a generalisation that all medical professions have no expertise in this particular field - this is not explicitly expressed in the passage. **Option 'E'** generalises that all pets cause stress - this is not stated in the passage.

14. B

Conclusion - Many people believe uniforms should be banned in schools.
Opinion - School uniforms stifle creativity and individualism.
Option 'B' is the main flaw because it best states that the opinion does not follow the conclusion. **Option 'A'** is incorrect because it is not stated or supported in the passage. **Option 'C'** is a generalisation that all toddlers wear uniform - this is not relevant to the conclusion. **Options 'D' and 'E'** are incorrect because they are not stated or implied in the passage.

15. C

Conclusion - Bumblebees can influence flowering time of all plant species, depending on the amount of pollen available on the plant.
Evidence - Tomato plants subjected to bumblebee biting flowered up to 30 days earlier than those that hadn't been targeted, while mustard plants flowered about 14 days earlier when damaged by the bumblebees.
The flaw will be illustrated in the statement which indicates that the conclusion does not follow the evidence. The evidence only mentions two plant species, but the conclusion generalises all plant species; therefore, **Option 'C'** is correct. **Option 'A'** is not stated in the

passage (bumblebees do not always damage leaves). **Option 'B'** is incorrect because it is irrelevant and not supported by the passage. **Option 'D'** contributes to the flaw; however, it does not mention the conclusion - therefore, it is incorrect. **Option 'E'** is not supported in the passage (the passage does not imply that only pollen affects flowering time in plant species).

16. B

Conclusion - There could be a signalling problem between the fat stores and the brain cells that control sleep in individuals with obesity.

Evidence - When researchers knocked out the KIN-29 gene to create sleepless worms, the mutant C. elegans accumulated excess fat - resembling the human obesity condition - even though their ATP levels are lowered.

The extract indicates that if fat stores are freed then sleep is promoted – **Option 'A'** is incorrect. When KIN-29 was knocked out in C. elegans, they were unable to liberate their fat. This suggests that KIN-29 is involved in the mechanism that reduces the accumulation of fat. As a result, **Option 'B'** is the correct answer. Fat stores not being liberated is shown to be related to sleep in this extract, but it cannot be concluded that there is a causal relation. **Option 'C'** is incorrect. It cannot be assumed that KIN-29 and SIK-3 produce the same effect on C. elegans and humans just because these two genes are homologous - there is no conclusive evidence for this in the passage. Therefore, **Option 'D'** is incorrect. **Option 'E'** is incorrect as the statement only says that sleep conserves energy and does not mention the increase in ATP levels.

17. C

Conclusion - "One of the issues with these apps is the perceived absence of a strong motivating therapeutic relationship with a therapist," says Grist. "How people use apps on their phone is very different to how we would sit with a therapist for 60 minutes."

Evidence - A study published in 2019 looked at those who had downloaded 93 of the most popular mental health apps in Google's app store. The researchers found that 94 per cent of people stopped opening these apps just 15 days after downloading them.

The statement that is best supported by the passage is that the app does not act as a substitute for a therapist. This is because the app is very different to a session with a real person. Therefore, **Option 'C'** is the correct answer. Nothing is mentioned about video calls - **Option 'A'** is incorrect. There is no information regarding the 6% of people who continued to use these apps for more than 15 days; as a result, **Option 'B'** is incorrect. There is no information that states that people delete the app before there is time to see effects. **Option 'D'** is incorrect. The extract states that there is an absence of a motivating therapeutic relationship when using apps, but this does not necessarily mean that the sessions with therapists are more effective. Consequently, **Option 'E'** is incorrect.

18. A

Conclusion - Aggressive promotion of infant formula can influence decisions to use formula milk in place of breast milk, and health and nutrition claims are likely to contribute to this process by narrowing the perceived benefits of breast milk.

Evidence - Despite improvements in infant formula over its 150-year history, it is still associated with health risks for mother and infant compared with breastfeeding.

The extract states that formula milk is associated with health risks for the mother and infant compared to breastfeeding. Therefore, **Option 'A'** is well supported since it states the conclusion. **Option 'B'** is not correct as the extract does not claim that mothers are unable to make the right decisions - it states that mothers are vulnerable during this period because 20% of them experience mental illness. The aggressive promotion of the formula milk influences the decision to use the formula milk in place of the breast milk; however, the extract does not state that it has persuaded any mothers to switch. As a result, **Option 'C'** is incorrect. Although the extract says infant formula milk has improved over the last 150 years, it is not certain if there have been any improvements in the last few years. There may not have been any improvements in the last few years – **Option 'D'** is not supported by the passage. The extract states that the claims regarding formula milk are often unfounded; therefore **Option 'E'** is false.

19. A

Conclusion - Humans may have to ditch intuitions and accept that all kinds of inanimate matter could be conscious – maybe even the universe as a whole.

Evidence - By manipulating numbers, one can describe and predict all manner of natural phenomena with astonishing clarity. This can be used from the movements of planets and the strange behaviour of fundamental particles to the consequences of a collision between two black holes billions of light years away. Now, some are wondering if maths can succeed where all else has failed, unravelling the laws of nature in the first place.

Option 'A' best describes the conclusion since mathematicians and physicists are trying to answer the question of felt experience. The passage never states that the universe has consciousness; it is suggesting that this could be possible. **Option 'B'** is incorrect. The extract says that the first model of consciousness was debated about whether it can tell an individual anything sensible, and therefore, it is not possible to conclude from the passage that the mathematical model of consciousness can predict the events that occur in the universe. As a result, **Option 'C'** is incorrect. **Option 'D'** is not true because the extract only asserts that humans may have to accept that inanimate matter could be conscious - it does not state that is an assumption that is made for the model. **Option 'E'** is not suggested in the passage; therefore, this cannot be the conclusion.

20. A

Conclusion - Asking how one would prefer to be addressed is a simple thing, and one that could have an important impact on improving communications in paediatric care.

Evidence - The recent #hellomynameis campaign encouraged health professionals to introduce themselves by name. Although this has helped break down barriers in one direction, it's time to take it to the next level. Simply asking a child's carer how they would like to be addressed immediately personalises the context of the conversation.

Option 'A' is best statement that demonstrates the conclusion. **Option 'B'** is not a conclusion that can be drawn from the extract - there is nothing said about the importance of their role. The section of the extract does not indicate that parents feel disempowered when referred to as 'Mum' or 'Dad'. Therefore, **Option 'C'** is incorrect. **Option 'D'** is true; however, it is not the conclusion. The #hellomynameis campaign is mentioned but its effectiveness is not discussed here; as a result, **Option 'E'** is not the correct answer.

21. A

Conclusion - According to a study published in mid-2020, keeping schools closed to tackle the coronavirus pandemic is almost certain to increase educational inequalities between children from the richest and poorest families, as debate intensifies over the Government's push to reopen schools in England.

Evidence - Survey data from more than 4,000 families in England analysed by the Institute for Fiscal Studies found that by the end of this month, children in better-off families would have received a week and half more home learning than children in the poorest households during the closures.

A flaw in an argument shows how the conclusion does not follow the reasoning. **Option 'A'** is the correct answer, as the conclusion that the educational inequalities between the richest and poorest families have increased is dependent on the reasoning that children in better-off families received a week and a half more home learning. A longer period of learning may not necessarily reflect a difference in the quality of teaching and so it is not sufficient to say the educational inequalities have increased. **Option 'B'** is just stating a possibility, it is not a flaw. **Option 'C'** is not a flaw as it just states something the argument would agree with. **Option 'D'** is providing a potential solution to the problem that the extract is stating. **Option 'E'** is not a flaw as the passage does not mention the idea of reopening schools earlier; it argues that the increase in the educational inequalities are encouraging the government to reopen schools.

22. E

Conclusion - Kabir's piano teacher says he should play at least two piano pieces a day.

Evidence - This will mean that he will definitely do well in the exam.

Option 'A' is not a flaw as his teacher only says that he will definitely pass if he played at least two pieces a day, and not that he will only pass if he does this. **Option 'B'** is not a flaw in her argument. **Option 'C'** does not find a flaw in the argument; it follows the argument. **Option 'D'** is not mentioned in the passage. **Option 'E'** is the correct answer as his teacher says that Kabir will definitely pass if he plays at least two pieces a day. However, doing this does not necessarily mean he will definitely perform well in the exam and pass.

23. C

If the play was delayed from starting at 6:00 pm, it would finish later than 7:35 pm. Therefore, **Option 'C' is the correct answer**. **Option 'A'** is not directly related to the time that the play ends. **Option 'B'** may not be true as all eight scenes lasted a total of 80 minutes and it doesn't say whether they were all the same length. The length of each individual scene does not impact the answer as we are given the total time taken for all the scenes. **Option 'D'** is not an assumption - the passage states there are three scenes before the interval and five after. **Option 'E'** is also not an assumption as the 15-minute interval was accounted for when calculating the time, the play should end that evening.

24. D

Conclusion - Aditya will be back at 6:00 pm.

Evidence - Aditya decides to run through the whole forest; she covers 8 km in total. Huan only runs a short distance into the forest and then comes back home. He covers 4 times less distance than Aditya. Huan reaches back at 5:00 pm.

Some of the statements are already mentioned in the passage, such as **Options 'A', 'C' and 'E'**. Therefore, these are not assumptions. **Option 'B'** does not affect the argument as the distance they both ran is already given. Therefore, the route they ran is irrelevant to draw the conclusion. As a result, **Option 'D' is the correct answer.**

25. A

Conclusion - If Afua decides to buy the wind turbine, she will generate 100 kWh more electricity than if she bought the solar panels each week.

Evidence - Wind turbines generate about 170 kWh of electricity per week. Solar panels generate 70 kWh of electricity per week.
The energy consumption in her household remaining the same is not an assumption since this does not affect the amount of electricity generated by the two renewable energy resources. As a result, **Option 'A' is the correct answer**. The rest are assumptions that have to be made for the conclusive statement because the value of electricity generated ought to change according to weather conditions. As a result, one would assume that she would always get 100kWh more energy by investing in the wind turbine. Afua is assuming that the same amount of electricity is produced by both resources each week despite the weather.

26. B

Conclusion - If more people started wearing sun cream, especially in the summer, skin cancer can be prevented.
Evidence - Every year, many people are diagnosed with skin cancer as a result of excessive UV light from sun exposure. Despite this, many people still do not use sun cream when they go out in the sun.
Option 'B' is the correct answer as the passage implies that wearing sun cream will prevent skin cancer. There may be other factors that contribute to skin cancer; therefore, sun cream may not be sufficient to prevent it. People may still get skin cancer despite using sun cream. **Options 'A' and 'C'** are irrelevant to the argument as it refers to the effectiveness of sun cream, and not to an individual's susceptibility to skin cancer or the cost of buying the sun cream. Similarly, **Options 'D' and 'E'** are referring to the fact that people are not aware of the facts related to this issue, and not the topic of sun cream preventing skin cancer.

27. B

Conclusion - If more teachers were employed and the class sizes were reduced, all the pupils will pass their GCSEs.
Evidence - The quality of teaching has decreased in the last few years due to changes in regulation that made the class sizes much larger. Teachers have been struggling to manage large number of students in each class.
Option 'B' is the correct answer. The passage assumes that the cause for the drop in GCSE grades are due to larger classes and fewer teachers in the school. The exams getting more difficult could be another factor that had resulted in more pupils failing. Therefore, the number of pupils who pass may not increase despite having more teachers. **Options 'A' and 'C'** are irrelevant to the argument as it is talking about the cost of recruiting teachers not improving the grades of the students. Similarly, **Options 'D' and 'E'** are only stating the difficulties of recruiting more teachers; it does not relate to the topic of the change in the GCSE grades of the school.

28. E

Conclusion - High levels of bilirubin cause yellow discolouration of the skin and a yellow stain in the sclera of the eye. This condition is called jaundice.
Evidence - Some patients with jaundice present with vomiting and abdominal pain.
None of the options are supported by the passage. **Option 'A' is not true** as this patient could have some other condition. **Option 'B' is incorrect** – not all patients with jaundice (high bilirubin levels) have abdominal pain and vomiting. Although a tumour in the head of the pancreas does cause jaundice, it is not mentioned or supported by the passage –

Option 'C' is incorrect. **Option 'D' is not true** as it cannot be assumed that people with these symptoms do not have jaundice.

29. B

Conclusion - Flights tickets would cost more after the schools close in the summer than any other time.

Evidence - There is a much higher demand for the flights in the summer after schools have closed.

For the conclusion to be valid, the argument assumes that flight charges will be higher if there is greater demand for them. This is not stated in the passage. Therefore, **Option 'B' is the correct answer**. The other statements are not relevant assumptions that need to be made to reach the conclusion.

30. A

Conclusion - Parents must restrict, or even stop their children, from playing such video games.

Evidence - Video games could mean that children become more aggressive and the crime rates can increase because people try to mimic what they see in these games.

Option 'A' is the correct answer as it contradicts the argument (thus, the flaw). Watching and playing violent games does not necessarily mean that children will imitate these; it could actually make children realise the negative side of violence and encourage them to not become aggressive. **Option 'B'** does not find a flaw in the argument; it just states that there are already some restrictions in place. **Option 'C'** is irrelevant - watching violence on TV does not make the contents in video games less gory. **Option 'D'** is also irrelevant as the passage refers to video games that have violence. **Option 'E'** does not find a flaw as the passage argues that children must be restricted from the violent video games that are already available to them.

31. D

Conclusion - It is never too late to quit, but many people do not wish to stop smoking, despite the risks it poses.

Evidence - If more people tried to quit smoking, then severe health problems can be avoided, and life expectancy would increase.

Option 'D' best illustrates the conclusion of the passage as many people are aware of the risks of smoking but despite this they continue to smoke. **Option 'A'** is a point that is made in the passage to support the conclusion. The passage does not imply that smoking should be banned, only that people should try to quit – **Option 'B' is incorrect**. **Option 'C'** is giving a reason why some people are unable to quit; however, this is not the conclusion. **Option 'E' is irrelevant** to the conclusion which focuses on quitting smoking.

32. D

Conclusion - Thus, if an employer wants to make workers more productive, then he or she must pay the employees a higher salary.

Evidence - Workplaces that give their employees a higher salary tend to have more productive workers than the places that give their workers a lower salary for doing a similar job.

Option 'D' is the correct answer as it reverses the cause and effect, in order to weaken the argument. The other options do not directly relate to the passage.

33. C

Conclusion - If people had more free time, the health of the population will improve.
Evidence - Sedentary lifestyles are often due to busy lifestyles, where individuals do not have enough time to exercise and prepare healthy food.
Option 'A' is not an assumption as it is mentioned in the passage. **Option 'B'** is not an assumption that needs to be drawn in order for the conclusion to be valid. **Option 'C'** is the assumption that has to be made in the passage. This is because having more free time does not necessarily mean people will spend it on exercise and making healthy food to improve their overall health. **Option 'D'** is a statement that does not support the passage; it is not an assumption. **Option 'E'** is not directly related to the topic discussed in the passage.

---

34. C

Conclusion - If factories were well equipped with these first aid supplies, and had plenty of stock, many accidents could be avoided.
Evidence - Many factories lack sufficient first-aid kits and often run out of them during the week. This means that workers who get injured in the workplace do not always get sufficient treatment or care for their injuries.
Option 'C' is the correct answer as it finds the flaw in the passage; first-aid kits could prevent the incidence of accidents. First-aid kits only help to treat the accidents that have already taken place - they will not prevent accidents from occurring. **Option 'A'** states a reason behind supplies running out. **Option 'B'** is irrelevant because the passage is stating what would occur if the first-aid kits were available; it does not mention anything about factories being able to afford them. **Options 'D' and 'E'** are irrelevant as the passage is arguing that the incidence of accidents can be reduced with first-aid kits.

---

35. A

Conclusion - Robert believes that students struggling with schoolwork should take part in more extracurricular activities because this will improve their grades.
Evidence - Taking part in more extracurricular activities has improved Robert's grades at school.
Option 'A' is the correct answer as it points out a flaw in Robert's argument that doing more activities will make one more motivated and productive. Some pupils may not be able to cope with too many activities if they cannot manage their time well. Therefore, their grades may drop in school. **Option 'B'** does not directly relate to Robert's argument. **Options 'C' and 'D'** are irrelevant to the passage. **Option 'E'** may seem like a flaw in the passage; however, it does not directly link academic achievement and grades with extracurricular activities.

---

36. D

Conclusion - Parents must not allow children to start using such devices from a young age; instead, they should find other ways to entertain their children.
Evidence - Some children are spending many hours on these devices. She states that more children are struggling to communicate and interact with others. In addition, many individuals are also showing signs of obesity.
Sophie assumes that if children spend too time on their phones and tablets, it will cause obesity and communication problems. However, there is no evidence in the passage to state that there is a casual relation between the two variables. Therefore, **Option 'D' is the correct answer.**

37. A

Conclusion - An individual is more likely to die from dehydration compared to starvation.

Evidence - An average person can survive for somewhere from two days to a week without liquids. However, it appears as though humans can survive without any food for 30-40 days, as long as they are properly hydrated.

To weaken the argument, the statement should provide evidence that an individual is more likely to die from starvation compared to dehydration. Therefore, **Option 'A'** is the correct answer. **Option 'B'** strengthens the argument that an individual is more likely to die from dehydration in 2019. **Option 'C'** is incorrect because it does not refer to the comparison between starvation and dehydration - it is not relevant to the conclusion. **Option 'D'** is incorrect since it compares children to adults rather than dehydration to starvation. **Option 'E'** is not relevant to the conclusion and is not supported by any evidence in the passage.

38. D

Conclusion - Ancient footprints, first thought to belong to a pterosaur, may actually have been made by a large bipedal ancestor of crocodiles, that lived about 110 to 120 million years ago.

Evidence - Lockley and his team say the size and skin patterns are consistent with those belonging to a large ancestor of modern crocodiles, called a crocodylomorph, that walked on two legs. The new findings suggest previously discovered footprints may also have been formed by a crocodylomorph, rather than a pterosaur, says Lockley.

Although the passage states that Lockley and his team believe that the footprints belong to a crocodylomorph and not a pterosaur, Godoy suggests that there isn't enough evidence to confirm that it belongs to a crocodylomorph as they are too large. Therefore, it is not known for certain which species the footprints belong to since there is not enough evidence to confirm this. As a result, **Option 'D' is the correct answer.** **Option 'E' is true**; however, it is not the conclusion of the passage.

39. C

Conclusion - There is no evidence that Zoom has any problems in its latest versions. However, in these unprecedented times, it seems sensible only to use systems that are tried and tested.

Evidence - Zoom has been questioned for its security regarding Government meetings.

The passage states that although the latest version of Zoom is said to be safe, it has not been tried and tested thoroughly enough to trust it. Therefore, it is safer to use systems that are trusted by the government for secure meetings. As a result, **Option 'C' is the correct answer**. **Option 'A'** is not stated in the passage. **Option 'D'** is true; however, it is not the conclusion of the passage. **Options 'B' and 'E'** are not stated in the article.

40. A

Conclusion - Males were at a higher risk of fractures than females; greater than two-thirds of injuries occurred after low-energy trauma and the upper limb was more frequently involved.

Evidence - With increasing age, the male/female ratio and time spent in sports participation increased ($p < 0.001$), while calcium intake and time spent in sedentary behaviours decreased ($p < 0.001$ and < 0.003, respectively). Gender discordance existed in pre-school children with respect to the anatomic location, and in school, children and adolescents with respect to the dynamics.

The main conclusion of the passage is that there were gender differences in the fractures. This is due to male subjects being more physically active compared to females. Therefore, **Option 'A' is the correct answer**. **Option 'E'** is not mentioned in this extract of the article. Although the other options are mentioned in the passage, they are supporting statements or facts; these options do not illustrate the main conclusion of the passage.

41. A

Conclusion - Commentators in the BMJ make it clear that racism and COVID-19 are deeply interconnected and must be dealt together.

Evidence - Racism is a public health issue because it kills people. It is the underlying driver that puts people from ethnic minority groups at the centre of the pandemic. It is a co-factor for COVID-19 and a key social determinant of health.

The passage states that racism is a very important issue in society, and it is everyone's responsibility to act against it. The global pandemic and the problems due to racism are deeply interconnected because those that are in the ethnic minority are the most affected. As a result, **Option 'A is the correct answer.** Although **Option 'B'** is true, it is not the conclusion of this passage. **Option 'C'** is mentioned in the passage; however, this is not the conclusion. **Options 'D' and 'E'** are also mentioned in the passage - however, these two statements support the main issues that the article is attempting to address.

42. A

Explanation:

Conclusion - Shops should remain open until the late evening; this would increase their sales as more people will be able to visit the stores.

Evidence - The opening times of many supermarkets and shops are not suitable for those who are working during the week. This has meant that there is a large number of people who are heavily reliant on online shopping.

Although having later closing times could mean that more people are able to visit the stores after work, it does not mean that the sales would increase. The passage assumes that people who visit the stores would spend more than they would have if they just shopped online; however, this is not necessarily the case. Therefore, **Option 'A' is the correct answer**. The customer could buy the same products as they would have bought online, meaning there is no change in their sales. **Option 'B'** is not an assumption that needs to be made to reach the conclusion. **Option 'C'** is not the main assumption to conclude the sales would increase. **Option 'D'** is not mentioned in the passage. **Option 'E'** is not directly related to the main message of the passage.

43. D

Explanation:

Conclusion - Children under the age of 18 should not be allowed to enter large bodies of water, such as pools and spas, even when adult supervision is present.

Evidence - An average of 379 children under age 15 die in reported drownings linked to pools or spas each year - this number increased to 395 deaths in 2017. In the age group 16-18, drowning is ranked as the third leading cause of death.

A statement that strengthens the argument will provide more evidence or data in order to support the conclusion. **Option 'D'** is correct because it provides the relevant statistics to prove that even when adult supervision is present, more than half of children drownings still occur. **Option 'A'** is incorrect because it is an opinion and does not strengthen the argument. **Option 'B'** may be supported by the passage, but it is not related to the conclusion that all children should be banned from large bodies of water. **Option 'C'** provides a potential reason for the increased number of deaths in 2017, however, it does not strengthen the argument. **Option 'E'** is implied in the passage, but it is not relevant to the argument.

44. D

Conclusion - One in three women in Europe inherited a gene variant from Neandertals, which results in increased fertility, fewer bleedings during early pregnancy and fewer miscarriages.

Evidence - The gene increases the production of progesterone, which is a hormone that plays an important role in the menstrual cycle and in pregnancy.

The statement which would strengthen the argument will provide more evidence that explains the reasoning behind the gene variant and the success of pregnancies. **Option 'D'** is correct since it is the only statement which provides a potential explanation for the reason behind the gene variant and the success of pregnancies. **Option 'A'** is incorrect because it is a generalisation that all women with this gene variant will have a healthy pregnancy. **Option 'B'** is not proven or explicitly stated in the passage – it is incorrect. The passage does not mention women of other ethnicities and their likelihood of suffering miscarriages; therefore, **Option 'C'** is incorrect. Option 'E' is also not stated in the passage, and as a result, cannot be reliable asserted. Consequently, **Option 'E'** is incorrect.

45. E

Conclusion - Participating in sports is always beneficial, as long as personal capacities, social situations, and biological and psychological maturation are taken into account.

Evidence - The positive effects from sports are achieved primarily through physical activity, but secondary effects bring health benefits such as psychosocial and personal development, and less alcohol consumption.

In order to strengthen the argument that sports is beneficial, the statement must provide additional evidence - **Option 'E'** is the correct answer. **Option 'A'** states the difference between sports in primary and secondary schools - it is not relevant to the conclusion. **Option 'B'** generalises that all individuals benefit from participating in sports - this is not supported by the passage. **Option 'C'** is incorrect because it does not provide additional evidence to the conclusion. **Option 'D'** does not strengthen the argument since it is directly stated in the passage.

46. D

Conclusion - According to recent evidence, brain activity in different regions could directly result in phobias.

Evidence - One study explored this phenomenon in people with arachnophobia. It found that if scientists told these individuals that they might encounter a spider, activity in their brains differed from control participants without a phobia. Activity in the lateral prefrontal cortex, praecuneus and visual cortex was comparatively lower. The authors say that these brain regions are key for the regulation of emotions; they help keep individuals level-headed.

The statement that would strengthen the argument that brain activity results in phobias is stated in **Option 'D'**; therefore, this is the correct answer. **Options 'A' and 'B'** weaken the argument because they provide alternative explanations behind the development of phobias. **Options 'C' and 'E'** are not relevant to the conclusion since neither mention the impact of brain in their arguments.

47. B

Conclusion - Many experts are asking for greater utilisation of music therapy within health care settings.

Evidence - This is based on the substantial evidence that music offers numerous health benefits to patients.

The correct statement should include more statistical evidence in order to strengthen the argument that music therapy poses many health benefits to patients. Therefore, **Option 'B'** is the correct answer. **Option 'A'** does not refer to the conclusion and the passage does not mention the benefits of reading. **Option 'C'** is incorrect because it suggests that music therapy is not effective - this weakens the argument. **Option 'D'** is an assumption that is not based on any evidence in the passage. **Option 'E'** does not mention the advantages of music in a healthcare setting; therefore, it is incorrect.

48. B

Conclusion - Deaths related to homelessness can be reduced if the government allocates more money to prevent this UK's housing crisis.

Evidence - Data collated through coroners' enquiries, media coverage, family testimony and freedom of information requests reveals at least 235 people affected by homelessness have died over the last six months, ranging from the ages of 16 to 104 years old. The same figures from last year showed 449 deaths from homelessness were recorded in 12 months – on average one every 20 hours – indicating that the frequency at which homeless people are dying has risen slightly, despite increased awareness of the issue.

To strengthen the argument that funding would reduce the number of deaths due to homelessness, the statement that provides more evidence to prove that funding does help would be correct. Therefore, the correct answer is **Option 'B'**. **Option 'A'** does not relate to the conclusion that funding specifically would aid in reducing homelessness. **Option 'C'** is not related to the passage - it does not state the impact of homelessness on other countries. **Option 'D'** is incorrect because it is an opinion which is not supported by the passage. **Option 'E'** is incorrect since it does not mention funding and, therefore, contribute to the conclusion.

49. E

Conclusion - Scientists may have developed a blood test that can reliably predict whether a person will develop dementia within the next three years.

Evidence - Using the blood samples provided, modern biomarkers were reported as correctly identifying nine out of ten of those who suffered cognitive decline and nine out of ten of those with normal cognitive function.

A statement that strengthens the argument will provide additional evidence or it will address the counterarguments. **Option 'E'** is correct because it provides more evidence into the reliability of modern biomarkers; thus, it strengthens the conclusion. **Option 'A'** is incorrect because it weakens the argument since only 80% of people were correctly identified as suffering from cognitive decline (in the first study, nine out of ten, or 90% of individuals were correctly identified). **Option 'B'** is incorrect because it is an assumption based on the passage and does not strengthen the argument. **Option 'C'** states that a blood test can reliably predict whether a person will develop dementia in the next three years; the passage states 'it has been reported'. Therefore, Option 'C' does not strengthen the argument. **Option 'D'** generalises that cognitive testing can always predict an individual's likelihood of developing dementia - this is not stated in the passage.

50. B

Conclusion - The best sleep habits are ones that are consistent and involve healthy routines.

Evidence - Overnight, information is transferred from more tentative, short-term memory to stronger, long-term memory—a process called "consolidation."

The statement that strengthens the argument that the best sleep habits should be consistent will provide more evidence behind this assertion. Therefore, the correct answer is **Option 'B'**. **Option 'A'** is an assumption that is not supported by the passage - it does not strengthen the argument. **Option 'C'** generalises that sleep is the only time when individuals can solidify and consolidate memories - there is no evidence of this in the passage. **Option 'D'** is irrelevant because the passage doesn't mention the impact of diet and exercise on health. **Option 'E'** does not strengthen the argument because it does not refer to the conclusion of consistent sleep habits in its reasoning.

51. E

Conclusion - Quitting smoking reduces the risk of disease and death significantly.

Evidence - Quitting before the age of 40 reduces the risk of dying from smoking-related disease by about 90%. Within 2–5 years, the risk of a stroke reduces to half that of a non-smoker. The risks for mouth, throat, oesophagus and bladder cancer drop by half within 5 years of quitting, and 10 years for lung cancer.

To strengthen the argument, the statement must refer to the advantages of quitting smoking - the correct answer is **Option 'E'**. **Option 'A'** is incorrect because it compares smokers to non-smokers, without mentioning those who have quit smoking. **Option 'B'** does not strengthen the argument since it is already stated in the passage. **Option 'C'** is not relevant to the argument that quitting smoking will improve an individual's quality of life. **Option 'D'** generalises that all individuals who quit smoking will have a better quality of life - this is not supported by evidence in the passage.

52. A

Conclusion - More than half the world's dwindling wild tiger population are threatened by roads built dangerously close to their habitats, and giant infrastructure projects planned across Asia could put tigers at even greater risk.

Evidence - Using a global dataset, Neil Carter at the University of Michigan, calculated that the tiger's current range, which mostly spans south and south-east Asia, contains 134,000 kilometres of roads. Based on average tiger density, he estimated that 57% of tigers live within 5 kilometres of these roads, which is considered dangerously close.

Option 'A' clarifies the reason behind the danger for tigers to be living near the roads. The extract only indicates that the tiger populations are threatened and decreasing as a result of roads being built. Therefore, Option 'A' strengthens this argument. **Option 'B'** is a fact which does not strengthen the argument of the tigers' lives being in danger. **Option 'C'** is not related to the issue of the tiger population being threatened. **Option 'D'** does not provide a connection between the tiger population and roads being built. **Option 'E'** suggests a solution for the problem, but does not strengthen the argument.

DA	DATA ANALYSIS	Questions

Questions 1-3 refer to the following information:

The National University of Singapore hosts an Inter-Hall Games (IHG) every year, where the student halls of the university compete to win trophies in each sport. The table below shows the final results of the table tennis IHG league at the end of the 2020 season. Each hall has played every other hall twice - once at a home game, and once away. Halls gain 3 points for a win, 1 point for a draw and 0 points for a loss. The teams in the table are ranked based on the number of points scored during the season. Some information in the table is missing.

Name of Hall	Win	Draw	Loss
Raffles	9	0	
Temasek	7	2	
Kent Ridge		1	3
Eusoff			4
Sheares	2		7
King Edward VII	0	1	

1. **How many points did Kent Ridge Hall score in this season?**
   A. 16
   B. 17
   C. 18
   D. 19
   E. More information needed

2. **How many games did Eusoff Hall draw?**
   A. 1 game
   B. 2 games
   C. 3 games
   D. 4 games
   E. 5 games

3. **How many more points did Eusoff Hall get compared to Sheares Hall?**
   A. 1
   B. 2
   C. 3
   D. 4
   E. 5

Questions 4-8 refer to the following information:

The table below shows the share prices in the month of May of different companies in the baking industry.

Name of Company	Number of shares (in 1,000s)	Share price in May (£)	Expected share price change in June
Khleb	20	0.20	-25%
BnB	29	0.25	+0%
Cakes	50	0.50	-50%
NY Bakes	20	0.40	+100%
Buttercup	17	0.50	+50%
Market value = Number of shares x Share price			

4. **Which of the companies is expected to have the greatest market value in June?**
   A. Khleb
   B. BnB
   C. Cakes
   D. NY Bakes
   E. Buttercup

5. **What is the ratio of the expected price of one share unit of Khleb to that of NY Bakes in June?**
   A. 16:3
   B. 5:3
   C. 3:16
   D. 3:5
   E. 1:16

6. **If BnB released an extra 21,000 shares at the expected share price in May, and Buttercup released an extra 43,000 shares at the expected share price in June, what would be the sum of the increase in market value for both companies to the nearest thousand?**
   A. £37,450
   B. £38,000
   C. £45,750
   D. £57,500
   E. £58,000

7. **Based on the data for May, how many percentage points would the price of Khleb need to change for the market value of Khleb to be equal to Cakes?**
   A. 425%
   B. 475%
   C. 525%
   D. 575%
   E. 625%

8. **Taking into consideration both the actual price in May and the predicted price in June, what was the average price of a share for all of the listed companies?**
   A. £0.35
   B. £0.36
   C. £0.41
   D. £0.44
   E. £0.45

Questions 9-12 refer to the following information:

The table below shows the exchange rate for £ to €.

(£1 = €?)	Day lowest	Day highest	End of the day
02.06.2015	1.15	1.25	1.20
26.06.2015	1.00	1.05	1.02
12.07.2015	1.25	1.30	1.25
04.08.2015	1.20	1.30	1.25
15.10.2015	1.10	1.20	1.15

9. On which of the following days was the difference between the day's lowest and highest values, as percentages of the end of the day value, the lowest? (It is not required to perform calculations for each of the days).

A. 02.06.2015
B. 26.06.2015
C. 12.07.2015
D. 04.08.2015
E. 15.10.2015

10. On 26.06.2015, Kevin exchanged £10,000 for euros and then decided to exchange an extra £40,000 on 12.07.2015. He then decided to exchange all the euros he bought for pounds on 15.10.2015. Kevin was unhappy with the outcome and claims that his timing was horrible. Which of the following is the worst outcome Kevin could have had from this exchange? The figures are rounded to the nearest thousand.

A. He made a profit of only £6,000.
B. He made a profit of only £10,000
C. He did not make a profit nor a loss.
D. He made a loss of £4,000.
E. He made a loss of £5,000.

11. A 10% exchange fee is applied to every transaction above £12,000. This fee is charged on the final currency received after conversion. Mario is planning to exchange his pounds for some euros for a year-end holiday trip. How many more euros would he get if he exchanged £35,000 on 04.08.2015 compared to 02.06.2015? Assume that the exchanges he makes use the end of the day values.

A. €1,250
B. €1,450
C. €1,575
D. €1,655
E. €1,800

12. The lowest value of 16.09.2015 is £1.05. What would be the expected highest value if the increase from its lowest to highest is the same as that of the increase in the average of the lowest value to the average of the highest value across the five dates?

A. £1.10
B. £1.13
C. £1.14
D. £1.15
E. £1.21

Questions 13-16 refer to the following information:

The table below shows the results of an IQ test taken by left-handed and right-handed participants. Assume that none of the participants of the survey are ambidextrous (i.e., both left-handed and right-handed). Some information in the table is missing.

IQ Score Range	Right-handed	Left-handed	Total
Below 70		2,895	
70-85	5,640	2,940	8,580
85-115	6,195		
Above 115	3,375	3,525	6,900
Total	19,335	17,145	36,480

13. How many right-handed participants scored below 70?

A. 3,850
B. 3,975
C. 4,125
D. 4,250
E. 4,400

14. How many participants who scored 85-115 were left-handed?

A. Between 5,500 and 6,500
B. Between 6,500 and 7,500
C. Between 7,500 and 8,500
D. Between 8,500 and 9,500
E. Between 9,500 and 10,500

15. What is the approximate ratio of the left-handed to right-handed participants in the score range with the second lowest ratio of right-handed to left-handed individuals?

A. 1:1
B. 1:1.3
C. 1:1.5
D. 1.3:1
E. 1.5:1

16. A group of left-handed participants took the survey and the new mean number of participants in both groups (right- and left-handed) are now 19,150. What is the expected number of new left-handed participants in each IQ score range?

A. 410
B. 455
C. 505
D. 550
E. 620

Questions 17-21 refer to the following information:

The diagram below shows the number of different symptoms presented by patients at GP clinics, which were recorded in a nationwide study across two years.

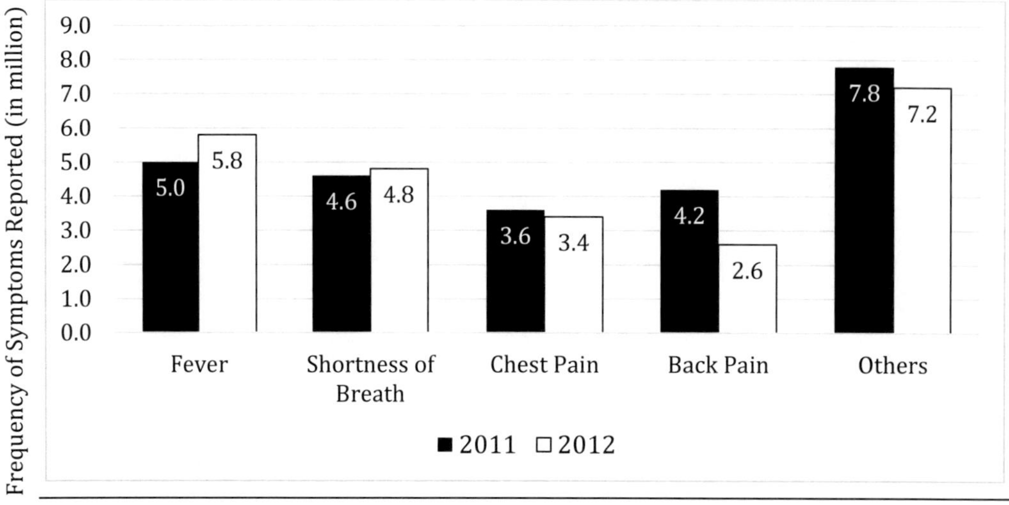

17. What is the total frequency of fevers recorded in 2012, chest pains in 2011, and back pains in 2012?

A. 11.2 million

B. 11.8 million

C. 12 million

D. 12.4 million

E. 13.6 million

18. What fraction of the total frequency of symptoms reported in 2012 is accounted for by chest pain?

A. $\frac{1}{4}$

B. $\frac{1}{5}$

C. $\frac{1}{6}$

D. $\frac{1}{7}$

E. $\frac{1}{9}$

19. What is the ratio of the total frequency of 'Others' symptoms in 2011 and 2012, to the average frequency of fevers in both years?

A. 3:1

B. 3:5

C. 5:3

D. 9:25

E. 25:9

20. What was the total frequency of symptoms of shortness of breath and back pain in 2011 and 2012?

A. 12.6 million
B. 14.6 million
C. 15.6 million
D. 16.2 million
E. 16.4 million

21. It was reported that all patients who presented at the GP clinics only complained of one symptom.
Approximately what percentage did the total number of patients decrease between 2011 and 2012?

A. 4.8%
B. 5.2%
C. 5.6%
D. 6.0%
E. 6.4%

Questions 22-25 refer to the following information:

The table below shows the cost of renting different types of boats at Boats of Britain. Some information in the table is missing.

Type of Boat	Deposit (£)	Rate per hour (£)
Rowboat	50	37.50
Bowrider Boat	90	72.50
Sailboat		95
Deck Boat	125	
Fishing Boat	165	200
Jet Boat		

- Every rent requires the payment of a non-refundable deposit fee.
- Customers renting the rowboat, bowrider boat, or sailboat have the option to hire a staff member to manoeuvre the boat. Hiring a member of staff costs £25 per hour.
- All rents for the deck boat, fishing boat, and jet boat are inclusive of a staff member who will manoeuvre the boat.
- All figures shown in the table, including the omitted ones, will effectively increase by 20% starting the 1st of April 2018. There will be no changes to the fee to hire a staff member.

22. Vegnesh and Praveena rented a rowboat for an hour on the 25th of March 2018. They returned a fortnight later for a 2-hour trip and decided to get a staff member on board to navigate the rowboat this time instead. How much more expensive was their second trip compared to the first trip?

A. £112.50
B. £121.00
C. £122.50
D. £125.00
E. £127.50

23. A pair of newlyweds celebrated the first day of the year 2018 by going on a sailboat ride for 5 hours. The average cost per person was £292.50.
If the couple did not opt for a staff member, how much was the deposit of the sailboat?

A. £90
B. £100
C. £110
D. £120
E. £130

24. Zavala went on a getaway alone during March in 2017 and decided to go on a 1-hour ride on the deck boat. As much as he enjoyed the staff on-board service, he felt that the trip ended too quickly. He returned during Christmas in the same year and decided to go for the cheapest boat option instead. Once again, he paid for the staff service. The second trip lasted for 4 hours but he still paid the same price as before. How much is the hourly rate for the deck boat?

A. £100
B. £115
C. £125
D. £145
E. £150

25. Nairobi and her family once rented the jet boat for 4 hours and had to pay £1,060, whilst Brooklyn and her family rented the same jet boat for 2 hours and had to pay £635. Both rents were in January 2018. How much more expensive is the hourly rate of the jet boat compared to its deposit?

A. £2.00
B. £2.50
C. £4.00
D. £5.00
E. £5.50

Questions 26-31 refer to the following information:
The table below shows the revenue report for Chelsea's Cafe for the years 2015 to 2019.

Year	Average number of customers per month (in 1,000s)	Average amount spent per customer (£)	Total cost of each customer (£)
2015	44	2.50	0.50
2016	52	2.20	0.60
2017	60	2.40	0.50
2018	58	2.10	0.40
2019	62	2.30	0.70
*Profit = Total revenue from sales - Cost			

26. **Which year had the lowest total revenue?**
    A. 2015
    B. 2016
    C. 2017
    D. 2018
    E. 2019

27. **What was the approximate difference between the total revenue in 2015 and 2016?**
    A. £45,600
    B. £48,500
    C. £52,800
    D. £54,000
    E. £55,500

28. **What was the increase in total profit between 2018 and 2019?**
    A. £2,400
    B. £3,600
    C. £4,800
    D. £6,000
    E. £7,200

29. **If the percentage increase in the average amount spent per customer from 2018 to 2019 continued from 2019 to 2020, what would be the closest estimate to the average amount spent by a customer in 2020?**
    A. £2.40
    B. £2.50
    C. £2.60
    D. £2.70
    E. £2.80

30. **What is the ratio between the average amount spent per customer in 2016 to the total cost of each customer in 2018?**
    A. 1:4
    B. 2:11
    C. 4:1
    D. 7:5
    E. 11:2

31. **If the total cost per unit stayed the same from the year 2015 onwards, but the average amount spent by the customer decreased by 30% each following year, in which year would Chelsea's Cafe start making a loss?**
    A. 2019
    B. 2020
    C. 2021
    D. 2022
    E. 2023

Questions 32-36 refer to the following information:

The diagram below shows the results of a survey looking at the number of units of different vehicles in different countries. The survey was taken in the year 2010. Assume that there are no other forms of vehicles in these countries.

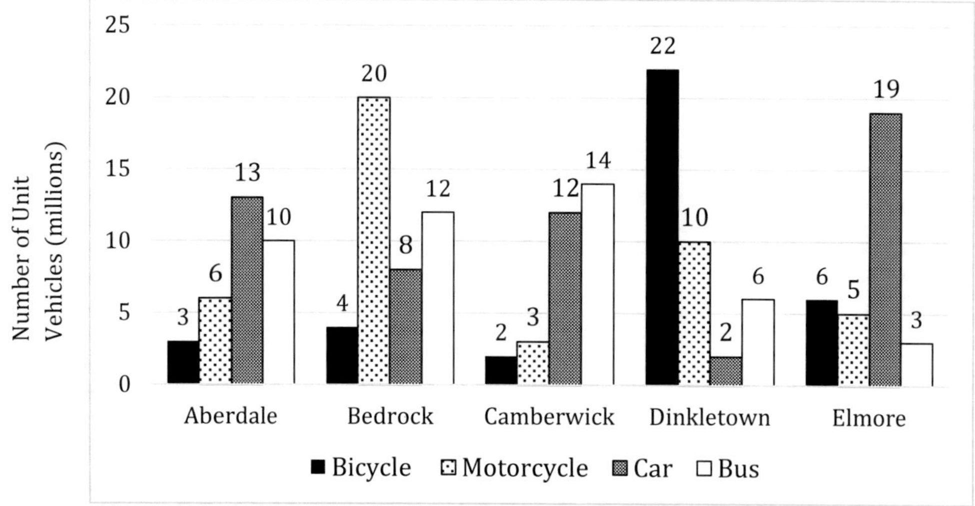

32. What percentage of all vehicles, in all 5 countries, are cars?

A. 25%
B. 30%
C. 35%
D. 40%
E. 50%

33. What is the ratio of all vehicles in Bedrock and Dinkletown to the total number of vehicles in Camberwick and Elmore?

A. 16:21
B. 32:41
C. 21:6
D. 21:16
E. 41:32

34. What is the percentage increase required in the number of vehicles in Aberdale to have the same number of vehicles in Dinkletown?

A. 10%
B. 15%
C. 20%
D. 22%
E. 25%

35. Assuming that all motorcycles and buses were manufactured in Ferrylake, what fraction of the vehicles in Aberdale and Dinkletown would they be responsible for?

A. $\frac{1}{9}$

B. $\frac{4}{7}$

C. $\frac{4}{9}$

D. $\frac{5}{7}$

E. $\frac{5}{9}$

36. The average cost of a bus is twice the average cost of a car in all markets. What is the ratio of the difference in total costs for both vehicles, to the sum of total costs for both vehicles?

A. 1:4

B. 7:17

C. 4:1

D. 17:7

E. 4:7

Questions 37-44 refer to the following information:

The hexagon represents students who wear glasses. The square represents those who play chess. The triangle represents those who are left-handed. The circle represents those who do well in school. Assume that no one is ambidextrous (i.e., both left-handed and right-handed). The diagram only consists of students.

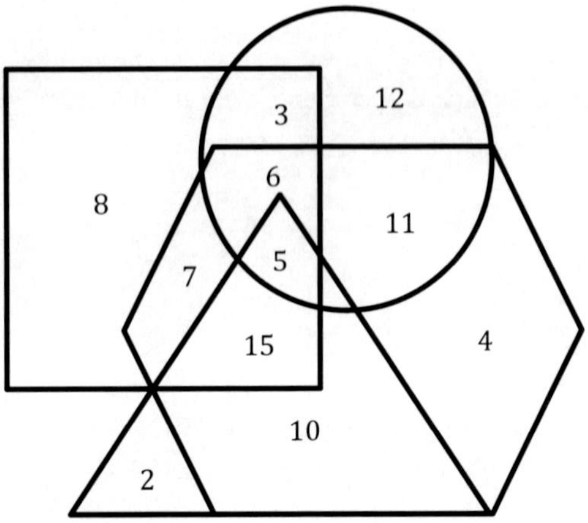

37. What is the number of students who wear glasses, are right-handed, and play chess but do not do well in school?

A. 4 students

B. 5 students

C. 6 students

D. 7 students

E. 11 students

38. What is the total number of students who wear glasses who are left-handed and play chess?

A. 5 students

B. 10 students

C. 11 students

D. 15 students

E. 20 students

39. What is the total number of students who wear glasses?

A. 47 students
B. 48 students
C. 52 students
D. 53 students
E. 58 students
F. 60 students

40. What is the number of students who do well in school and play chess?

A. 5 students
B. 9 students
C. 11 students
D. 14 students
E. 18 students
F. 30 students

41. What is the total number of students who do well in school or are right-handed but not both?

A. 19 students
B. 24 students
C. 32 students
D. 37 students
E. 59 students
F. 64 students

42. What is the total number of left-handed students who do not wear glasses and do well in school?

A. 0 students
B. 2 students
C. 4 students
D. 8 students
E. 10 students
F. 15 students

43. What is the total number of right-handed students who play chess but do not wear glasses?

A. 3 students
B. 8 students
C. 11 students
D. 23 students
E. 29 students
F. 36 students

44. Which of the following were not surveyed? Choose TWO options.

A. Right-handed students who play chess but do not wear glasses nor do well in school.
B. Left-handed students who wear glasses and do well in school but do not play chess.
C. Right-handed students who wear glasses but do not play chess nor do well in school.
D. Students who do not play chess nor do well in school nor wear glasses and are left-handed.
E. Students who do not do well in school nor play chess nor wear glasses and are right-handed.

Questions 45-49 refer to the following information:

Currency	1 Unit of Currency X
A	0.60
B	0.85
C	1.44
D	2.04
E	9.36
F	10.14
G	34.00
H	81.60
Commission charged at 10% of total currency	

45. What is the ratio of Currency H to Currency G?

A. 2.2:1
B. 1:2.5
C. 2.5:1
D. 5:12
E. 12:5

46. Excluding commission, how much Currency E would one receive if he/she converted 2,880 units of Currency C?

A. 443
B. 18,720
C. 20,592
D. 28,080
E. 36,040

47. Excluding commission, what is the difference between the value of 72 units of each Currency A and Currency C in units of Currency X?

A. 60
B. 64
C. 70
D. 82
E. 85

48. If one exchanges 612 units of Currency D, 2028 units of Currency F, and 9360 units of Currency E for the Currency of B, how many units of Currency B would one have, with commission excluded?

A. 425
B. 850
C. 1275
D. 1600
E. 2100

49. If one has 830 units of Currency X and he/she converts the right amount to get 10,200 units of Currency G, how much Currency A can he/she get with the remaining amount of Currency X? Commission is charged for each conversion.

A. 250
B. 270
C. 300
D. 450
E. 500

Questions 50-60 refer to the following information:

The graph below shows the h-index of five doctors during their postgraduate training: Foundation Years (FY) and Specialty Training (ST) years. The h-index is a metric that measures both the productivity and the citation impact of the publications of a researcher. Doctors become consultants after they complete their ST training.

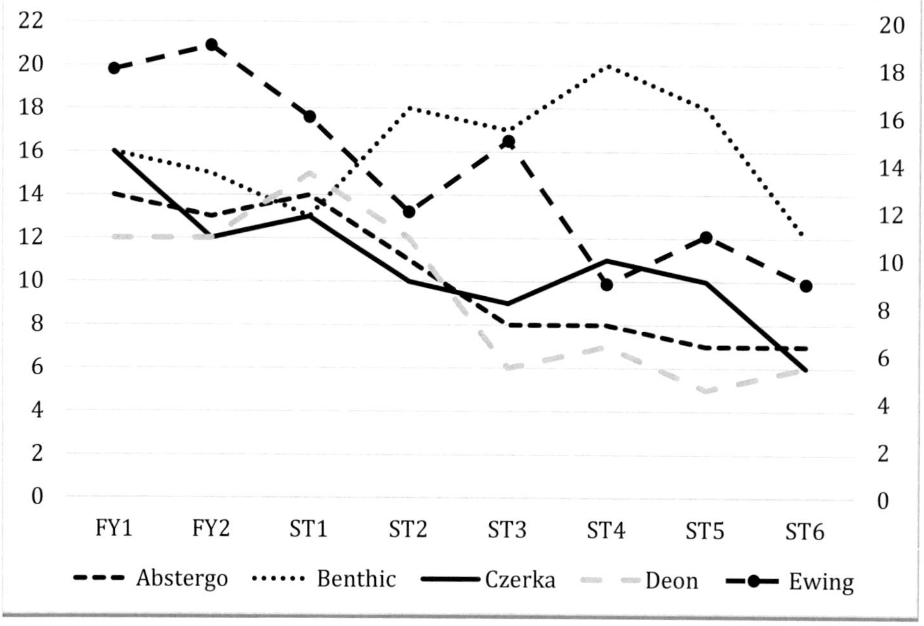

50. What was the difference in the combined h-index published by the five doctors between FY2 and ST1?

A. 5
B. 6
C. 7
D. 8
E. None of the above

51. What was the combined h-index, for all 5 doctors, mid-way between ST5 and ST6?

A. 40.5
B. 41
C. 42.5
D. 43
E. 45.5

52. Which doctor experiences the least number of decline in their h-index throughout their training from FY1 to ST6?

A. Abstergo
B. Benthic
C. Czerka
D. Deon
E. Ewing

53. Which year did the combined h-index for all five doctors have the same pattern with its preceding year as that between their FY2 and ST1 years?
    A. ST2
    B. ST3
    C. ST4
    D. ST5
    E. ST6

54. Using only information provided in the diagram, which doctor had the least decline in their h-index value at the end of their training compared to the start of his/her postgraduate training?
    A. Abstergo
    B. Benthic
    C. Czerka
    D. Deon
    E. Ewing

55. What is the magnitude of the greatest change in the h-index of the doctors within three consecutive training years?
    A. 7
    B. 8
    C. 9
    D. 10
    E. 11

56. What was the average h-index for each doctor in his/her training year FY1?
    A. 12.5
    B. 14.6
    C. 15.2
    D. 18.4
    E. 21.5

57. What is the difference between the average h-index of Abstergo and Ewing, across the entire course of their training years? Round the answer to one decimal place.
    A. 2.4
    B. 2.5
    C. 3.2
    D. 3.4
    E. 3.8

58. Which doctor has the median average h-index across the entire course of his/her training years?
    A. Abstergo
    B. Benthic
    C. Czerka
    D. Deon
    E. Ewing

59. Assume the mean h-indices of the doctors were rounded off to the nearest integer and these rounded values are expressed in a pie chart. What would be the greatest difference in the angle of the sector of any two individual doctors?
    A. 30°
    B. 36°

C. 42°
D. 45°
E. 60°

60. Assume that Benthic's h-index remains constant indefinitely after ST6. Deon's h-index increases steadily at one and a half of the rate of that in ST5 to ST6. After how many years of being a consultant would Deon's h-index match with Benthic's h-index?

A. 4 years
B. 5 years
C. 6 years
D. 7 years
E. 8 years

Questions 61-67 refer to the following information:

The acapella groups at the University of Music decided to raise funds for their local orphanages as the Christmas season is around the corner. The groups agreed that to divide the total funds between two homes - that is, Littlewood and New Beginnings - in the ratio of 2:1. New Beginnings received £51.60 from this initiative.

The table below summarises the total number of songs for each student group and how much money they managed to raise. Some information in the table is missing.

Group	Number of songs	Amount of funds raised (£)
Noteworthy		24.60
Clef Hangers		25.20
Treblemakers	8	28.00
Wrecking Belles	5	
Chord of the Rings	10	42.00

61. How much did Wrecking Belle manage to raise?

A. £32.50
B. £33.00
C. £35.00
D. £38.50
E. £42.40

62. Let the two groups with an unknown number of songs be Group X and Group Y, in no particular order. Chord of the Rings and Group X performed the same number of songs. If the mean amount of funds raised per song in this whole initiative is exactly £3.87, how many songs did Group Y perform?

A. 6
B. 7
C. 8
D. 9
E. 10

63. All acapella groups raised a certain amount of funds such that the mean funds raised per song are *perfect* numbers. This means that if the funds raised by a particular group were to be divided by its number of songs, one would get a maximum of 2 decimal places (i.e., £.pp). Using the information provided in Q62, which group is likely to be Group Y, and what is the mean number of funds raised per song by that group?
   A. Noteworthy; £3.50
   B. Clef Hangers; £3.50
   C. Noteworthy; £3.60
   D. Clef Hangers; £3.60
   E. More information needed

64. The amount of money raised per song of each group is expressed in a pie chart. Using the information from Q62 and Q63, the third biggest sector of the pie chart would correspond to:
   A. Noteworthy
   B. Clef Hangers
   C. Treblemakers
   D. Wrecking Belles
   E. Chord of the Rings

65. The amount of money raised by each group is expressed in a pie chart. Using the information from Q62 and Q63, the biggest sector has an angle that is at least 1.5 times greater in size to how many other sectors?
   A. 0
   B. 1
   C. 2
   D. 3
   E. 4

66. Littlewood generously gave some money to New Beginnings such that they both receive the same amount. What proportion of Littlewood's funds was donated to New Beginnings?
   A. 10%
   B. 20%
   C. 25%
   D. 40%
   E. 50%

67. Another student group, Local Vocals, joined in at the last minute and performed 5 songs. The average of the amount raised per group became £32.50. How much did Local Vocals raise per song, on average, from their performance?
   A. £4.08
   B. £8.40
   C. £8.04
   D. £20.40
   E. £40.20
   F. £42.00

Questions 68-77 refer to the following information:

The table below shows the results of a survey looking at the key qualities needed to be successful in sports. The ratio of male to female participants in the survey is 1:1.

	Essential	Desirable	Irrelevant
Talent	30	20	70
Resilience	40	50	30
Discipline	60	60	0
Risk-taking	45	55	20
External support	20	70	30

68. What percentage of the participants of the survey said that 'Talent' is essential?

A. 20%

B. 25%

C. 33%

D. 40%

E. 50%

69. What is the ratio of the number of survey participants who deem 'Risk-taking' as desirable to the number of survey participants who deem 'Resilience' as essential?

A. 1:1.375

B. 1:8

C. 1.375:1

D. 4:5

E. 8:11

70. What percentage of the total responses were considered 'Irrelevant'?

A. 20%

B. 22%

C. 25%

D. 40%

E. 60%

71. What is the difference in the percentage of the total responses across all qualities due to 'Essential' compared to 'Desirable'?

A. 5%

B. 8%

C. 10%

D. 15%

E. 20%

72. Assuming that all of the 'Desirable' responses were regarded as 'Essential' by all respondents, which one of the qualities would correspond to the second highest 'Essential' responses?

A. Talent

B. Resilience

C. Discipline

D. Risk-taking

E. External support

73. What is the minimum possible fraction of female respondents who regarded 'External support' as 'Desirable'?
   A. $\frac{1}{4}$
   B. $\frac{1}{6}$
   C. $\frac{1}{8}$
   D. $\frac{1}{10}$
   E. $\frac{1}{12}$

74. Of the total responses that were regarded as 'Essential', what is the maximum possible percentage of responses due to males?
   A. 80%
   B. 90%
   C. 95%
   D. 98%
   E. 100%

75. What is the minimum possible percentage of 'Desirable' or 'Irrelevant' responses for the quality of 'Risk-taking' that was due to males?
   A. 10%
   B. 12%
   C. 15%
   D. 20%
   E. 25%

76. What is the minimum possible fraction of males that deemed 'Talent' as 'Essential' or 'Irrelevant'?
   A. $\frac{1}{2}$
   B. $\frac{1}{3}$
   C. $\frac{1}{6}$
   D. $\frac{2}{3}$
   E. $\frac{5}{6}$

77. Which one amongst the following statements is true?
   A. Female respondents may have only regarded 'Talent' as 'Essential' or 'Desirable'.
   B. The respondents who deem 'Discipline' as 'Essential' must be females only.
   C. All respondents who deem 'Talent' as 'Essential' or 'Desirable' may have deemed 'Discipline' as 'Essential'.
   D. More than two thirds of females may have deemed 'Resilience' as 'Irrelevant'.
   E. 50% of males deem 'External support' as 'Essential'.

Questions 78-85 refer to the following information:
The table below shows the 5-year growth of a bubble milk tea shop, Thirst-tea.

Year	Yearly Turnover (£)	Yearly Cost (£)	No. of Branches
2011	244,000	120,000	200
2012	290,000	124,000	220
2013	325,000	150,000	240
2014	350,000	165,000	250
2015	360,000	180,000	260

78. What was the second least profitable year for Thirst-tea?
A. 2011
B. 2012
C. 2013
D. 2014
E. 2015

79. Which year generated the least profit as a percentage of turnover?
A. 2011
B. 2012
C. 2013
D. 2014
E. 2015

80. Which year accounted for the lowest ratio of yearly cost to yearly profit?
A. 2011
B. 2012
C. 2013
D. 2014
E. 2015

81. What was the average increase per year, in the number of Thirst-tea branches, across the 5 years?
A. 10
B. 12
C. 14
D. 15
E. 20

82. If the trend of increase for the yearly turnover and cost between 2014 and 2015 were to continue, how many years, after 2015, will Thirst-tea take to reach a break-even point in its business?
A. 35 years
B. 36 years
C. 37 years
D. 38 years
E. 39 years
F. 40 years

83. What is the ratio of profit made by one branch in 2014 to profit made by one branch in 2011? Assume that, in any given year, all Thirst-tea branches have the same costs and profits.
A. 11:13
B. 13:11

C. 23:51
D. 31:37
E. 51:23
F. 37:31

84. Which year had a profit that is equal to the average profit per year across the 5 years?
A. 2011
B. 2012
C. 2013
D. 2014
E. 2015

85. Which year had the lowest average cost per unit branch?
A. 2011
B. 2012
C. 2013
D. 2014
E. 2015

Questions 86-95 refer to the following information:
The table below shows the profit analysis of a Canary Lane Bakery, in the year 2018. Assume that all items that were unsold were damaged, unless mentioned otherwise.
Some information in the table is missing.

Items	Total numbers sold	Total numbers damaged	Total numbers produced	Production cost per number (£)	Retail price (£)	Profit per number (£)
Bread	1,500		1,550	1.20	8.00	
Cookies	2,000	200		0.80		1.70
Macaroons		300	1,500	0.60	4.00	
Scones	1,800		2,000		5.50	4.25
Cupcakes	1,250	350		1.50		4.50

86. What was the ratio of the number of macaroons sold to the number of cupcakes sold in 2018?
A. 1:2
B. 2:3
C. 3:4
D. 4:5
E. 5:6

87. What was the total cost due to damaged items in the given year?
A. £1,150
B. £1,175
C. £1,200
D. £1,250
E. £1,500

88. What was the total additional profit that the bakery could have made in 2018 had there not been any damaged items and all items that were produced were sold?
A. £4,000
B. £4,125

C. £4,375
D. £4,500
E. £5,000

89. What was the total profit that the bakery would have made from macaroons and bread if they had sold all the items produced and there had been no damaged items?

A. £14,560
B. £14,650
C. £15,460
D. £15,640
E. £16,450
F. £16,540

90. Krantz visits the bakery to purchase 12 random items. Assuming that Canary Lane Bakery only sells these five items, what is the total amount of money can Krantz expect to spend?

A. £48.60
B. £62.40
C. £78.60
D. £81.80
E. £96.00

91. What would have been the total profit from the sale of the cupcakes if all the items produced were sold?

A. £5,625
B. £6,500
C. £7,200
D. £8,800
E. £9,600

92. Considering the cost to the bakery due to damaged items, what was the actual profit made from the sale of scones?

A. £6,800
B. £7,000
C. £7,200
D. £7,400
E. £7,500

93. Demarco spends £1,000 at Canary Lane Bakery. He wants to distribute the items at an upcoming charity drive; therefore, he wanted to make sure that his purchase allowed him to get the maximum number of items. How much profit will the bakery make from Demarco's purchase? Assume that the bakery only sells these five items.

A. £680
B. £700
C. £720
D. £750
E. £760

94. The 'profitability' of a product is defined as the amount of profit generated by an item per unit cost. A more profitable item is a product that generates more profit per unit cost. Which of the items sold at the bakery is the second least profitable?

A. Bread
B. Cookies
C. Macaroons

D. Scones
E. Cupcakes

95. Return of investment (ROI) is a performance measure used by companies to study the efficiency of an investment. It is measured by the ratio of the net profit made from an investment to its cost. The finance advisor of Canary Lane Bakery studies the ROI of each of the items sold at the bakery in 2018. Which item has the highest ROI? Assume that all items produced were sold and no items were damaged.

A. Bread
B. Cookies
C. Macaroons
D. Scones
E. Cupcakes

Questions 96-105 refer to the following information:

The graph below shows the trend in the number of laptops sold by five different companies across 6 years.

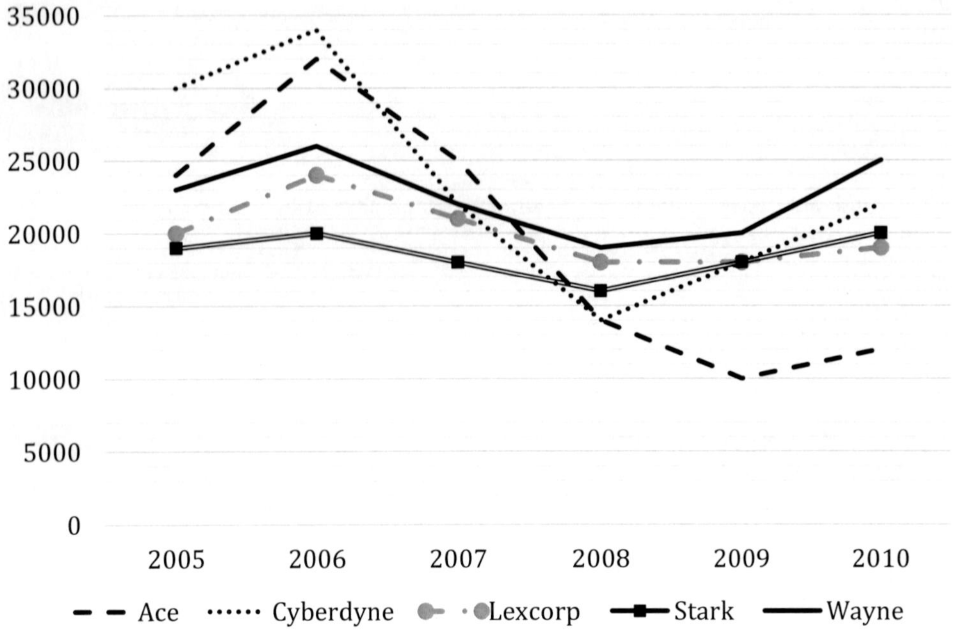

96. In 2007, what was the ratio of laptops sold by Stark compared to Lexcorp?

A. 2:3
B. 3:2
C. 5:6
D. 6:5
E. 6:7
F. 7:6

97. Which company sold the second greatest number of laptops across the 6 years?

A. Ace
B. Cyberdyne

C. Lexcorp
D. Stark
E. Wayne

98. What is the average number of laptops sold by Lexcorp per year, across the 6 years?
A. 16,000
B. 18,000
C. 20,000
D. 22,000
E. 24,000

99. What was the total number of laptops sold by all companies in the years 2005 to 2010 inclusive?
A. 620,000
B. 623,000
C. 626,000
D. 640,000
E. 650,000

100. In 2007, by how many percent was the number of laptops sold by Stark lower than that of Ace in the same year?
A. 20%
B. 24%
C. 28%
D. 30%
E. 35%

101. What is the difference in the average number of laptops sold by each company in the year 2005 compared to 2010?
A. 3,100
B. 3,200
C. 3,300
D. 3,400
E. 3,600

102. Expressed in a fraction, to what extent did the number of laptops drop in total, for all companies combined, between 2006 to 2009?
A. $\frac{13}{34}$
B. $\frac{14}{29}$
C. $\frac{15}{29}$
D. $\frac{21}{34}$
E. $\frac{31}{34}$

103. Between the years 2005 and 2010, by how much percent did the number of laptops sold by Ace drop from its highest number of sales to its lowest number of sales? Round the answer to the nearest integer.
A. 31%
B. 42%
C. 47%

D. 58%
E. 69%

104. If the trend for the increase in the number of laptops sold from 2009 to 2010 were to continue, how many years, after 2010, would it take for the number of laptops sold by Cyberdyne to be the same as that of Wayne?
A. 15 years
B. 20 years
C. 45 years
D. 52 years
E. None of the above

105. If the trend for the increase in the number of laptops sold from 2009 to 2010 were to continue, how many years, after 2010, would it take for the number of laptops sold by Ace to be the same as that of Lexcorp?
A. 6 years
B. 7 years
C. 8 years
D. 9 years
E. 10 years

Questions 106-115 refer to the following information:

The table below shows the number of various models of shoes available in different branches of a retail shoe company named Papoutsia. Papoutsia only sells five different models of shoes. These are the only five branches operating in Greece. All five models are also sold by other companies in Greece.

	Kallithea	Larissa	Athens	Patras	Heraklion
Model A	5	30	120	40	60
Model B	8	120	210	50	80
Model C	50	115	260	120	75
Model D	6	65	75	140	45
Model E	36	50	55	80	20

106. How many more pairs of shoes are stocked in Patras compared to Larissa?
A. 50 pairs
B. 55 pairs
C. 60 pairs
D. 65 pairs
E. 70 pairs

107. If the number of pairs of Model 'C' shoes at the store in Kallithea was increased by 90%, what percentage of shoes at the store would be Model 'E'?
A. 18%
B. 20%
C. 22%
D. 24%
E. 30%

108. If the number of pairs of Model 'B' shoes at Athens was reduced by 30%, what would be the ratio of the new number of Model 'B' shoes to the number of Model 'D' shoes in Athens?

A. 1.69:1
B. 1.75:1
C. 1.82:1
D. 1.96:1
E. 2.02:1

109. If the store in Patras increases its stock for Model 'A' shoes by 130%, by what percentage would they have to reduce their current count of Model 'E' shoes in order to keep the total number of shoes at the store the same?

A. 25%
B. 35%
C. 45%
D. 55%
E. 65%

110. What is the average number of pairs of shoes available per model in Heraklion?

A. 50
B. 52
C. 54
D. 55
E. 56

111. The total number of pairs of shoes available in each branch store is expressed in a pie chart. What is the angle of the sector that represents the branch store in Larissa? Use the values given in the table.

A. 60°
B. 65°
C. 70°
D. 72°
E. 75°

112. Model 'B' shoes are priced at £45 whereas Model 'D' shoes are priced at £65. Assuming all the Model 'D' shoes at Kallithea were to be sold out, how many Model 'B' shoes does the store need to sell to meet the same revenue generated from the sales of Model 'D'?

A. 5
B. 6
C. 7
D. 8
E. None of the above

113. Which one amongst the following statements is definitely true?

A. The store in Athens has the greatest number of shoes for four different models compared to the rest of the stores.
B. Model 'A' is the third most available shoe in three stores.
C. In Greece, there is more Model 'A' shoes available compared to Model 'E'.
D. Model 'C' is the second most available shoe in three stores.
E. The store in Kallithea has the least number of shoes for all models when compared to the rest of the stores.

114. Which one amongst the following statements is false?

A. The difference in the number of Model 'C' shoes available between the Patras branch and the Kallithea branch is greater than the difference in the number of Model 'D' shoes available between the Patras branch and the Athens branch.

B. In the Heraklion branch, there are more Model 'B' shoes than there are Model 'A' and Model 'E' shoes combined.

C. The percentage of Model 'E' shoes of all shoes available in the Larissa branch is greater than the percentage of Model 'A' shoes of all shoes available in the Athens branch.

D. None of the above.

115. Model 'C' is regarded as the best-selling model among all the shoes sold by Papoutsia. Which store branch has the greatest proportion of Model 'C' shoes of all the shoes available in the respective stores?

A. Kallithea

B. Larissa

C. Athens

D. Patras

E. Heraklion

Questions 116-120 refer to the following information:

A rain gauge is an instrument used to measure the amount of rain which falls in a particular area. The measurement is typically noted, in millimetres (mm), by the height of the water collected from the rain. The graph below shows the average rainfall in Penang and Sabah. Assume that the average monthly rainfall is the same every year.

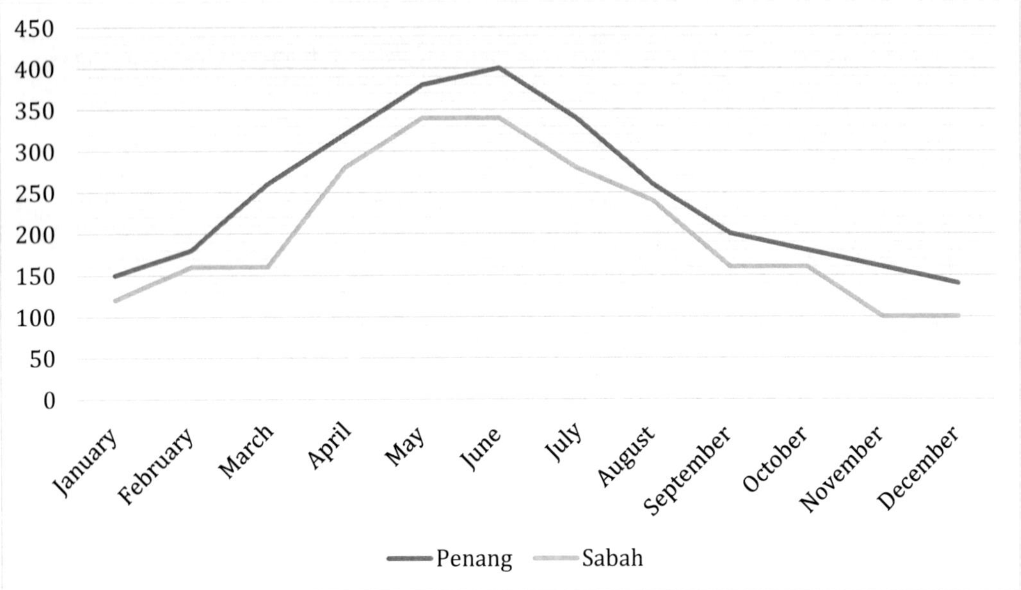

116. How many times, during the period July 2009 to April 2014 inclusive, is the average rainfall the same in two consecutive months in Sabah?

A. 18

B. 19

C. 20
D. 21
E. 22

117. From September 2013 to June 2020 inclusive, how many months is the average rainfall in Penang and Sabah higher than the previous month?

A. 18
B. 19
C. 21
D. 28
E. 29

118. How many times bigger is the greatest difference in the average rainfall between the two cities compared to the smallest difference in the average rainfall between the two cities?

A. 2.5
B. 3.33
C. 5
D. 8
E. 10

119. What is the ratio of the greatest change in the average rainfall between two consecutive months in Sabah to the smallest change in the average rainfall between two consecutive months in Penang?

A. 3:1
B. 3:2
C. 4:1
D. 6:1
E. 12:1

120. To the nearest 0.5 centimetres, what is the average rainfall difference between Penang and Sabah?

A. 3.5 cm
B. 4 cm
C. 4.5 cm
D. 5 cm
E. 5.5 cm

Questions 121-125 refer to the following information:
The diagram below shows the results of a survey taken on a group of individuals who presented to the GP. All of the individuals were tested for COVID-19. The symptoms that were noted were cough, shortness of breath, loss of taste, and fever.

Some information in the diagram is missing.

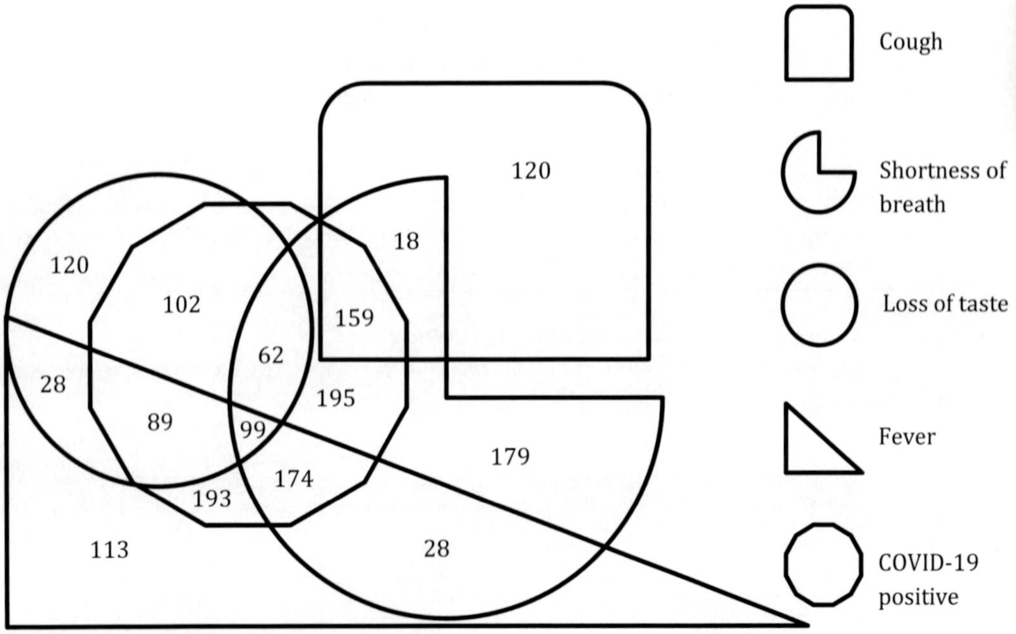

121. **How many patients, who were tested positive for COVID-19, complained of loss of taste and at least one other symptom?**
   A. 159 patients
   B. 195 patients
   C. 211 patients
   D. 250 patients
   E. 352 patients

122. **What is the total number of patients who presented with three symptoms?**
   A. 62 patients
   B. 89 patients
   C. 99 patients
   D. 159 patients
   E. 161 patients
   F. None of the above

123. **What is the total number of patients who presented with two symptoms?**
   A. 508 patients
   B. 558 patients
   C. 628 patients
   D. 658 patients
   E. 758 patients

124. Of all patients who presented with one symptom, what is the ratio of the number of patients who were tested positive for COVID-19 to those who weren't?

A. 3:4
B. 5:7
C. 5:14
D. 10:19
E. 35:38

125. Which one amongst the following statements is true?

A. No patients who were tested positive for COVID-19 were asymptomatic.
B. Some patients presented with shortness of breath and loss of taste but were tested negative for COVID-19.
C. Fever was the most common symptom among those who were COVID-19 positive.
D. Of those who presented with fever, the number of individuals who also had shortness of breath is the twice the number of individuals who had a loss of taste.
E. None of the above.

Questions 126 – 129 refer to the following information.

The table below shows the number of children who participate in six particular sports across schools in the UK.

	Boys	Girls
Hockey	60,000	35,000
Cricket	25,000	20,000
Swimming	12,000	34,000
Tennis	34,000	12,000
Netball	2,000	50,000
Football	85,000	82,000

126. Assuming that there are 800,000 girls and half a million boys across schools in the UK, and that all boys and all girls are equally likely to play any of the six sports, how many of the six sports are more likely to be played by girls compared to boys?

A. 1
B. 2
C. 3
D. 4
E. 5
F. 6

127. Assuming that there are half a million boys and one million girls across schools in the UK, what is the difference in percentage of boys playing these six sports compared to girls?

A. 20.3%
B. 21.2%
C. 23.3%
D. 24.5%
E. 36.8%
F. 41.2%
G. 43.6%

128. All children who play Hockey, Netball or Football have an individual afterschool session twice a week. All children who play Cricket, Swimming or Tennis have an individual afterschool session once every two weeks. Assume that 20% of the children who participate in the six sports are located in Wales, and children in Wales are not more or less likely to participate in any of the six sports. How many individual afterschool sessions are running in Wales with these six sports during a period of two weeks?

A. 139,300
B. 251,200
C. 278,600
D. 153,000
E. 557,200

129. Which of the following graphs correctly represents the proportion of girls who play tennis compared to the boys who play hockey?

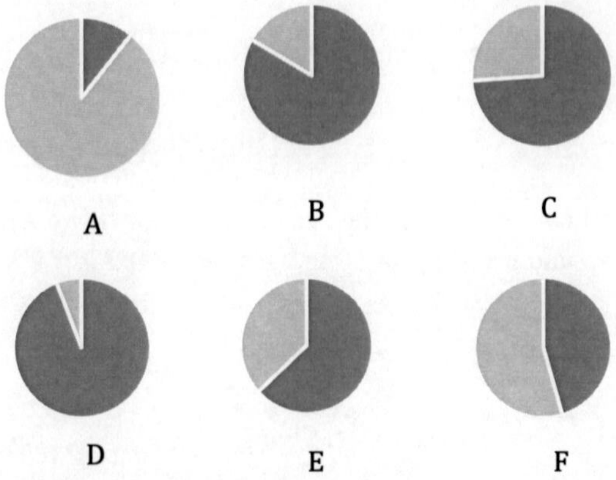

Questions 130 – 135 refer to the following information.

The following diagram displays different activities that children between the ages of 3 – 18 may participate in. The crescent represents children under the age of 10. The arrow represents those who attend formal education. The triangle represents those who spent more than 8 hours watching television. The heart represents those who participate in more than 3 sporting activities.

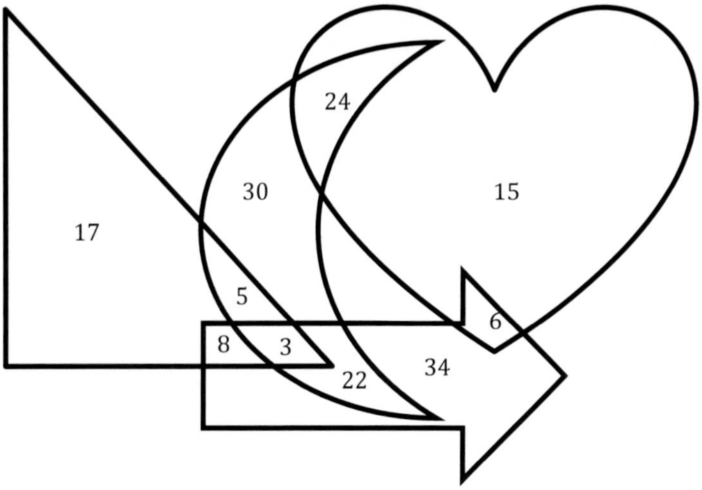

130. How many children over the age of 10 attend formal education and participates in 3 sporting activities?

A. 22
B. 25
C. 34
D. 40
E. 42
F. 48
G. 73

131. How many more children over the age of 10 do not attend formal education but watch more than 8 hours of television compared to children under the age of 10 who attend formal education and watch more than 8 hours of television?

A. 3 children
B. 7 children
C. 8 children
D. 11 children
E. 14 children
F. 25 children
G. 30 children

132. Assume that only 30% of all children under the age of 10 in Oxford were represented in the diagram. How many children under the age of 10 actually live in Oxford?

A. 30 children
B. 84 children
C. 100 children
D. 110 children
E. 180 children
F. 253 children
G. 280 children

133. Which row in the table below correctly identifies the percentages of the following scenario? Given that a child participates in more than 3 sporting activities, what is the probability that they are:

- under the age of 10
- in formal education?

	Under the Age of 10	In Formal Education
A	$\frac{8}{15}$	$\frac{2}{15}$
B	$\frac{8}{13}$	$\frac{2}{15}$
C	$\frac{8}{13}$	$\frac{2}{5}$
D	$\frac{8}{5}$	$\frac{2}{13}$
E	$\frac{8}{15}$	$\frac{2}{5}$

134. What is the total number of children under the age of 10 who are in formal education, or watch more than 8 hours of television, but not both?

A. 22 children
B. 25 children
C. 27 children
D. 30 children
E. 33 children
F. 38 children

135. How many more children under the age of 10 are represented in the diagram compared to children over the age of 10?

A. 2 children
B. 4 children
C. 6 children
D. 8 children
E. 10 children
F. 12 children
G. 14 children

136. A school wants to determine the relationship between GCSE and A-Level success amongst their students. They choose 10 pupils and record the proportion of A*s received at both GCSE and A-Level.

	Proportion of A*s at GCSE	Proportion of A*s at A-Level
Judy	0.10	0.68
Bella	0.87	0.98
Samuel	0.23	0.67
Maggie	0.92	0.45
Rebecca	0.45	0.67
Tim	0.50	0.25
Edward	0.98	1.00
Max	1.00	0.34
Emma	0.27	0.87
Lily	0.02	0.34

The school drew a bar chart but missed the names of the students. They also missed plotting one student in the graph below.

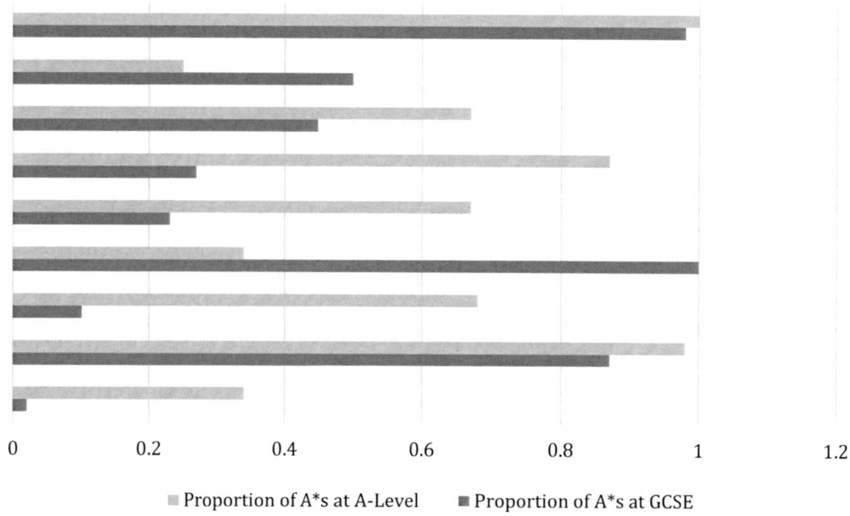

Which student did the school miss plotting on the graph?

A. Edward
B. Bella
C. Lily
D. Maggie
E. Max
F. None of the above

Questions 137 – 139 refer to the following information.

Jackie decides to sell cupcakes and soft drinks at her school in order to raise money for charity.

The prices for her cupcakes are as follows:

Cupcake flavour	Price
Chocolate	50 pence
Caramel	30 pence
Blueberry	20 pence
Cookie Dough	80 pence
Chocolate raspberry	90 pence

The prices for her soft drinks are as follows:

Soft Drink	Price
Fanta	£1.45
Pepsi	£1.65
Diet Coke	£1.30
Sprite	£1.20
7Up	£1.85

Students can buy two soft drinks and receive a Blueberry cupcake for free.

137. Today, Jackie decides that all cupcakes are 50% off. A student would like two Fantas, a Blueberry cupcake and a Cookie Dough cupcake. She pays with a £5 note. How much change should she get?

A. £1.10
B. £1.50
C. £1.70
D. £2.00
E. £2.20

138. Two weeks ago, Jackie's price for the Fanta was £2.50 and the price for the Sprite was £3.75. What is the difference in percentage decrease of the prices from two weeks ago compared to the prices in the table between Sprite and Fanta?

A. 14%
B. 26%
C. 40%
D. 42%
E. 68%

139. For a batch of 24 cupcakes, Jackie spends £3.60. Each soft drink comes in a pack of 12 for £13.20. Assuming she sells two cupcakes and one soft drink, what is the difference in the maximum and minimum profit that she can make?

A. £1.15
B. £1.20
C. £1.45
D. £1.85
E. £1.90
F. £2.05
G. £2.35

Questions 140 – 141 refer to the following graph.

The graph below shows the average monthly precipitation for two cities - Cardiff and London.

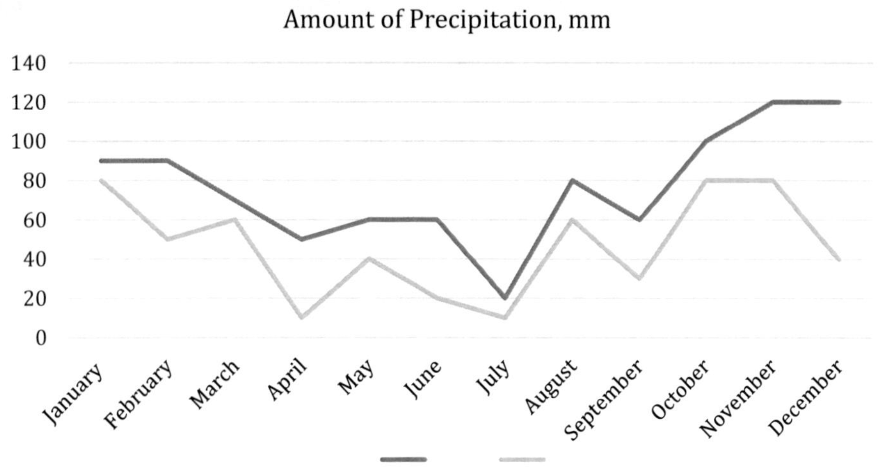

140. What is the average difference in monthly precipitation between Cardiff and London?

A. 30 mm
B. 40 mm
C. 50 mm
D. 60 mm
E. 70 mm
F. 80 mm
G. 90 mm

141. Assume that the average monthly precipitation is the same for every year. How many times during the period July 2016 to June 2020 inclusive is the average precipitation the same in 2 consecutive months in Cardiff?

A. 3
B. 4
C. 9
D. 10
E. 12
F. 15
G. 30

Questions 142 - 146 are based on the passage below.

Candy Land, a sweets company that specialises in personalised confectionary, recently realised that a large proportion of their customers had stopped purchasing their products. In order to address the problem, the company sent online questionnaires to all of their customers in order to assess the reason behind it. Candy Land has 6250 customers on its database. Only 80% of these customers have a device that can connect to the Internet. As a result, only 80% could be sent an online questionnaire. Out of the customers who received an online questionnaire, 4420 completed them.

The results were that, 2242 customers, almost exactly half (50.7%), had stopped buying sweets from Candy Land. A total of 880 (39%) of these customers complained about the price of the sweets. Of the customers who complained about the price of the sweets, 350 had complained once before and didn't witness any change to the price, and from those who did, 60% noticed a decrease in the quality of the sweets produced.

From those customers who did not complain about the price of the sweets, 681 gave the reason that they didn't think it was important. A total of 450 customers stated that the poor customer service was a greater contributing factor compared to the price of the sweets. In addition, 227 customers indicated that the variety of flavours and the taste of the sweets were more important than the price of the sweets. Assume that all of the customers who filled out the questionnaires did so honestly.

142. If a customer had stopped buying sweets from Candy Land, and had not complained about the price of sweets, what is the probability that the reasoning for this was that the variety of flavours and the taste of the sweets were more important than the price of the sweets?

A. $\frac{1}{3}$
B. $\frac{1}{6}$

C. $\frac{1}{12}$

D. $\frac{1}{24}$

E. $\frac{1}{48}$

143. Rounded to the nearest integer, what percentage of customers who were sent an online questionnaire did not respond?

A. 11%

B. 12%

C. 13%

D. 14%

E. 15%

144. How many customers noticed a decrease in the quality of the sweets after they had complained once regarding the price of the sweets?

A. 105 customers

B. 210 customers

C. 318 customers

D. 420 customers

E. 516 customers

145. What is the approximate difference in percentage of customers who had stopped buying the sweets from Candy Land because of the price compared to those who stated that the poor customer service was a greater contributing factor compared to the price of the sweets?

A. 4.5%

B. 9%

C. 11.5%

D. 19%

E. 25%

F. 31%

146. Candy Land's biggest competitor, Chocolate Bliss, has 20% more customers on its database compared to Candy Land. Chocolate Bliss sent the same online questionnaire to all of their customers (they could send the online questionnaire to only 60% of their customers on the database). Only 25% of the customers who were sent a questionnaire completed it. A total of 20% of the customers who were sent an online questionnaire by Chocolate Bliss had stopped buying their products. In addition, 20% of these customers said the price was unfair. How many customers at Chocolate Bliss stopped buying their products for reasons other than price?

A. 45 customers

B. 150 customers

C. 180 customers

D. 300 customers

E. 720 customers

147. Three shapes are shown below:

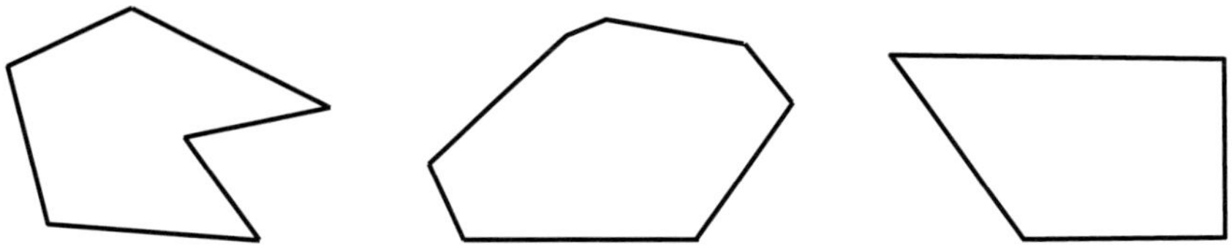

These shapes are joined together without overlapping in one of the figures below. Which of the Options below show the correct shape that the above three shapes form together?

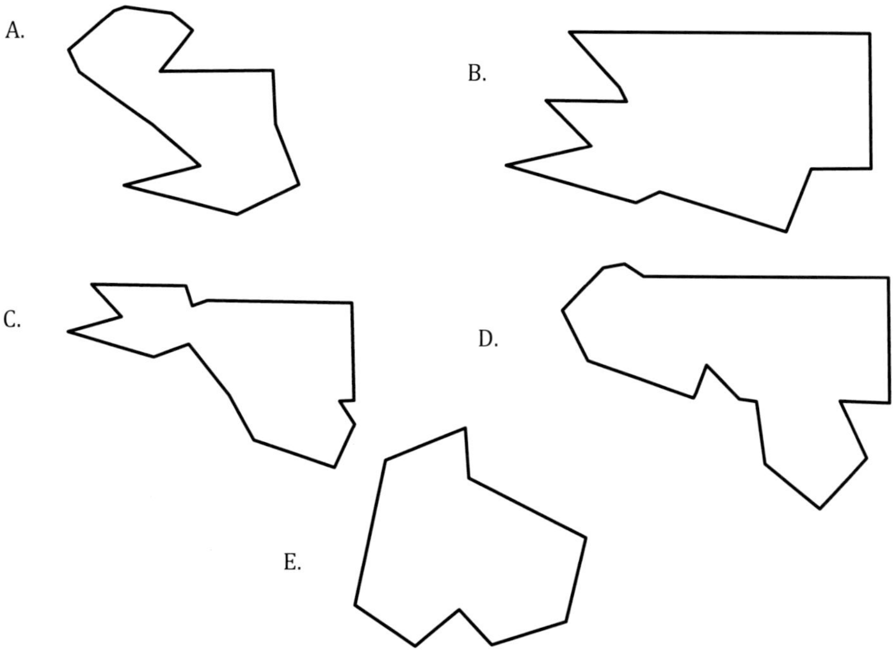

148. Tom is painting a wall that has an area 9 m². He is using different colours for the wall. The cost of each paint is given below. He paints the whole wall white initially as the first coat. Then he does alternate stripes of blue and red of equal width.

Paint Colour	Cost per m² of Area Painted
Blue	£0.40
White	£0.35
Red	£0.60

How much does it cost Tom to paint his wall?

A. £3.10
B. £4.50
C. £6.75
D. £7.65
E. £11.70

149. Dishwasher tablets are sold in packets of 3 different sizes.

Size	Number of tablets	Price
Small	20	£2.00
Medium	50	£3.50
Large	100	£6.50

A new offer is introduced by the company which means that all the medium sized packets contains 30% extra number of tablets and if a large packet is bought a small packet comes free with it.

A customer decides to buy 2 medium packets and one large packet.

Express the extra tablets that the customer gets under the offer as a percentage of the total number of tablets he/she has bought.

A. 10%
B. 20%
C. 25%
D. 30%
E. 35%

150. Illustrated below is a cube net:

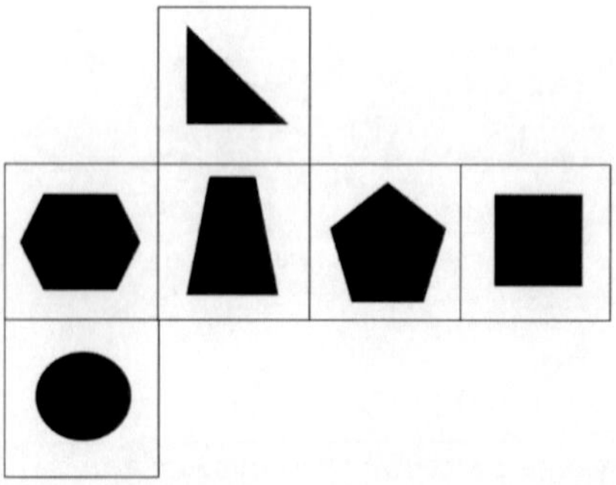

Which one of the following cubes can be made from the pattern displayed?

A.

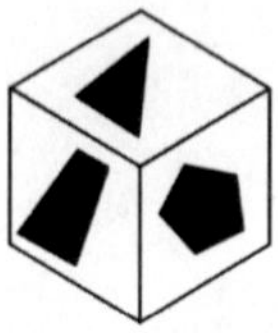

B.

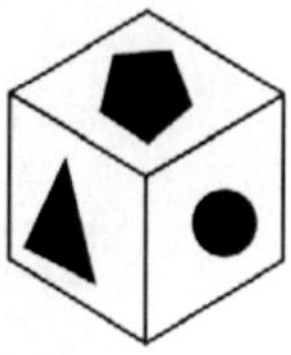

C.

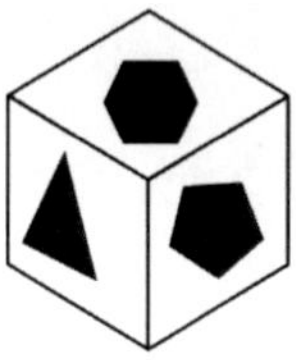

D.

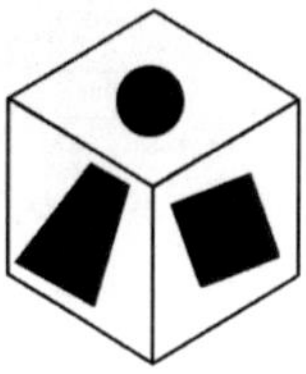

E.

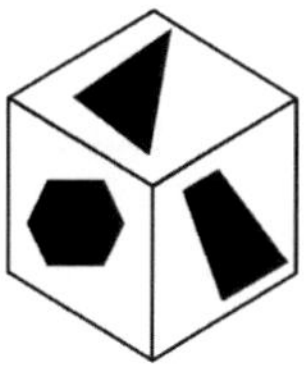

Data Analysis

151. A packet contains a mixture of nuts. The nuts are either plain or coated in chocolate. Some of the information in the table is missing.

Type of Nut	Plain	Chocolate Coated	Total
Peanut	16	16	32
Almond	15		40
Cashew nut			
Walnut		24	43
Total	117		180

There is a 2 in 7 chance that a chocolate coated nut is a cashew nut.
What is the probability that a cashew nut selected at random is plain?

A. $\frac{18}{65}$

B. $\frac{47}{65}$

C. $\frac{18}{63}$

D. $\frac{47}{117}$

E. $\frac{65}{180}$

152. The graph below shows the percentage of boys likely to do more than 30 minutes of exercise per day compared with the percentage of both girls and boys in a particular secondary school. The secondary school has pupils from Year 7 to Year 13.

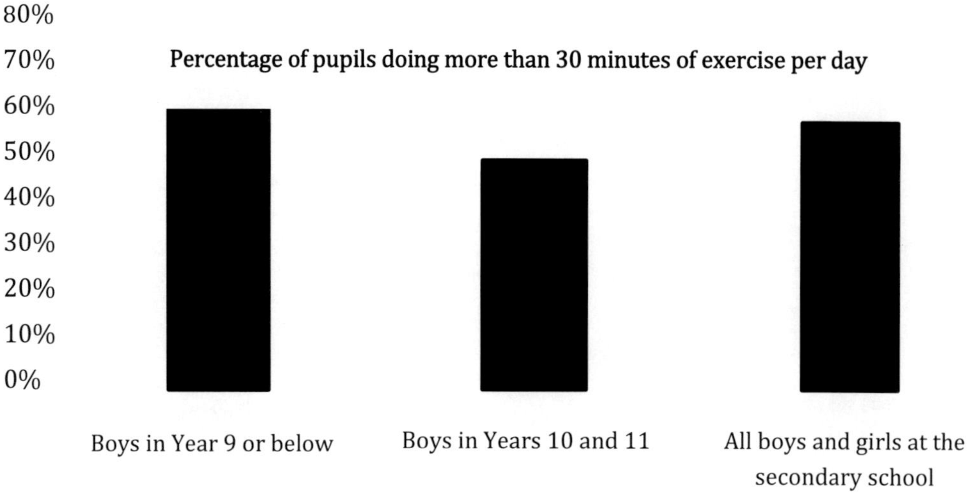

Which of the following statements can be deduced from the information provided?

1. A greater number of boys below Year 9 do more than 30 minutes of exercise than the boys in Years 10 or 11.
2. Boys are less likely to do more than 30 minutes of exercise each day as they get older.
3. Boys are more likely to do more exercise each day compared to girls at this school.
4. A greater proportion of boys do more than 30 minutes of exercise per day in Years 12 and 13 compared to Years 10 and 11.

A. 1 and 2 only
B. 1, 2 and 3 only
C. 2, 3 and 4 only
D. All of the above
E. None of the above

153. The table below shows the mid-year population estimates in 2014 in England:

2014 Mid-year population estimates

Category	Population
Rural, comprising:	9,260,892
Rural town and fringe	5,003,956
of which those in a sparse setting	192,085
Rural village and hamlet	4,256,936
of which those in a sparse setting	298,045
Urban, comprising:	45,055,726
Urban major conurbation	19,415,739
Urban minor conurbation	1,948,518
Urban city and town	23,691,469
of which those in a sparse setting	90,397
England	54,316,618

What percentage of the population live in settlements in sparse settings?

A. 0.4 %
B. 0.9%
C. 1.1%
D. 2.1%
E. 3.2%

154. The graph below shows the trends in single occasion risky drinking for students who drank in the past week by gender. They were between 12 and 17 years old, and the data was taken from 1984 to 2017:

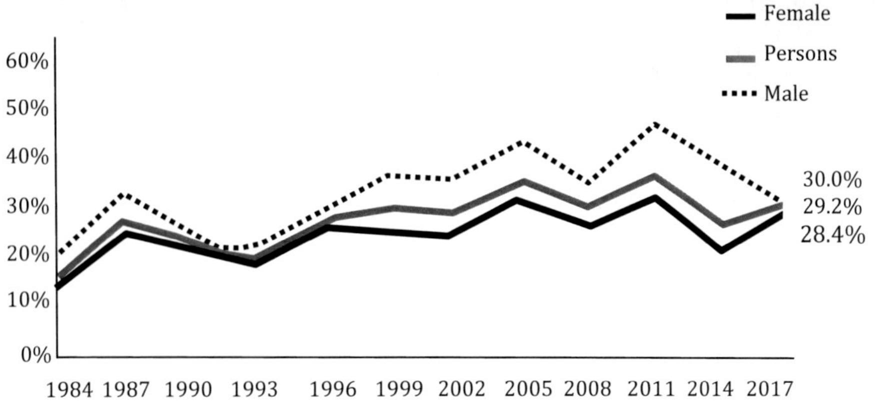

Which of the below statements can be reliably concluded from the data?

A. There has always been a significant difference between the risky drinking habits of male and female students.

B. There is a constant increase in the percentage of single occasion risky drinking.

C. Risky drinking for women has increased more than 3 times from 1984 to 2017.

D. The greatest rate in the decline of the percentage of female students involved in risky drinking was between 2011 and 2014.

E. There will always be a greater percentage of male students involved in single occasion risky drinking than the percentage of female students.

155. The data below demonstrates the consumer expenditure as a percentage of GDP in different countries:

Country	Consumer Spending as Percentage of GDP
China	37.0
United States	68.1
European Union	56.3
India	59.6
Russia	51.9
Indonesia	55.4
Brazil	63.4
Japan	58.6
Canada	57.5
Mexico	67.1

Which one amongst the following statements can be concluded from the data above?

A. The consumer spending in the United States is worth almost twice as much as that in China.

B. Prices of goods and services in China are much lower than the other countries.

C. Consumer spending in India is greater than that in Canada.

D. The China's GDP is almost twice that of the GDP in Mexico.

E. Consumer spending accounts for a greater proportion of the GDP in Brazil than it does in Indonesia.

156. Poppy and Lily had been given a book of questions to practice for their exam by their teacher. They were to submit the questions they did to the teacher every Friday night. The table shows the number of questions each person completed before the weekly deadline.

Date	Poppy	Lily	Number of correct questions that both girls achieved
1st May	56	24	21
8th May	57	25	34
15th May	49	29	33
22nd May	55	31	22
39th May	57	30	25
5th June	55	24	36
12th June	59	23	33
19th June	55	23	32

26th June	53	26	31
3rd July	53	29	37
10th July	52	34	23
17th July	58	21	26
24th July	50	24	29

Poppy was in the year below Lily. Therefore, she always managed to complete more questions than Lily since the book she got given contained easier questions.
How many questions did they both get correct when there was the biggest difference between the number of questions they had submitted?

A. 23 questions
B. 26 questions
C. 33 questions
D. 36 questions
E. 37 questions

157. **A school held two maths quizzes to select pupils to represent the school for a maths competition. The highest mark of the two quizzes were taken to select the pupils. The pupils who scored the top three highest marks were selected for the team.**
Any other pupil who scored a maximum of five marks less than the higher mark of the pupil who scored the lowest mark out of three pupils selected were kept as reserves.
The scores of the pupils are shown below:

Student	Quiz 1	Quiz 2
1	50	22
2	47	52
3	45	23
4	49	29
5	46	35
6	49	49
7	27	35
8	56	51
9	33	33
10	50	44
11	51	46
12	55	53

How many pupils were kept as a reserve?

A. 1 pupil
B. 2 pupils
C. 3 pupils
D. 4 pupils
E. 5 pupils

158. A survey was conducted to determine the number of minutes that workers from five different offices exercised per week:

Number of minutes of exercise:	Office A	Office B	Office C	Office D	Office E	Total
0	2	4	0	12	9	27
15	12	3	12	14	4	45
30	23	27	27	25	2	104
60	12	14	33	13	16	85
90	1	6	1	9	38	55
Total	50	54	73	70	69	316

One of the values in the table has been entered incorrectly, but the total of all the rows and columns were worked out prior to this error in typing; therefore, these are correct.
Which value was typed incorrectly?

A. 12
B. 13
C. 23
D. 25
E. 27

Questions 159 - 163 relate to the following information.

An online retail company measures the type of products sold annually using the following charts. Assume that the online retail company only sells these 6 categories of products in both 2019 and 2020. There were 25% more products sold in 2019 compared to 2020.

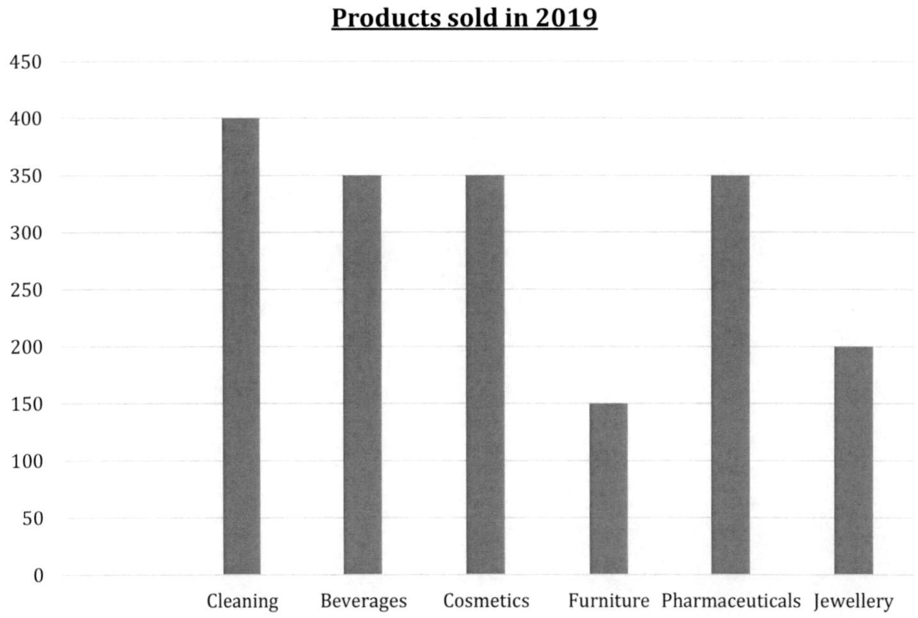

Products sold in 2020

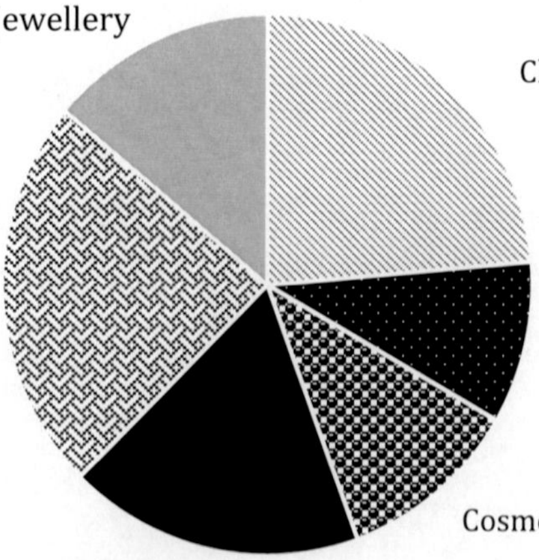

The angle of each category in 2020 is as follows:
Cleaning - 85°
Beverages - 35°
Cosmetics - 40°
Furniture - 65°
Pharmaceuticals - 85°
Jewellery - 50°

159. What was the difference in percentage decrease in the number of cleaning products compared to the number of beverages sold between 2019 and 2020?

A. 5%
B. 10%
C. 15%
D. 35%
E. 40%
F. 45%
G. 60%

160. How many more pharmaceutical products were sold compared to jewellery in 2020?

A. 140
B. 150
C. 180
D. 200
E. 240
F. 320
G. 340

161. What is the difference in probability that a randomly chosen product is a cosmetic in 2019 compared to 2020?

A. $\frac{1}{6}$
B. $\frac{1}{12}$

C. $\frac{1}{24}$
D. $\frac{2}{3}$
E. $\frac{3}{8}$
F. $\frac{1}{4}$

162. In 2019, one carat of gold sells for £10.50. Half of the jewellery sold in 2019 is 18 carat gold and the remainder are 12 carat gold. In 2020, one carat of gold sells for 50% less. All of the jewellery sold in 2020 are 6 carat gold.
What is the total amount of money made from jewellery in 2019 and 2020?

A. £39900
B. £44100
C. £37800
D. £44300
E. £44500

163. Which type of product saw the greatest decrease from 2019 to 2020?

A. Cleaning
B. Beverages
C. Cosmetics
D. Furniture
E. Pharmaceuticals
F. Jewellery

Questions 164 to 167 refer to the following information.

Sally's Boutique is a high-end store which sells a variety of clothes. Sally wanted to understand the most popular clothing types that her customers liked to purchase.

The following diagram represents all of the female customers who purchased items at Sally's boutique in 2020. The L-shape represents females under the age of 18. The hexagon represents those who purchased jumpsuits. The cross represents those purchased an item that was pink. The parallelogram represents those who purchased more than four different items in one purchase. The circle represents those who purchased summer dresses.

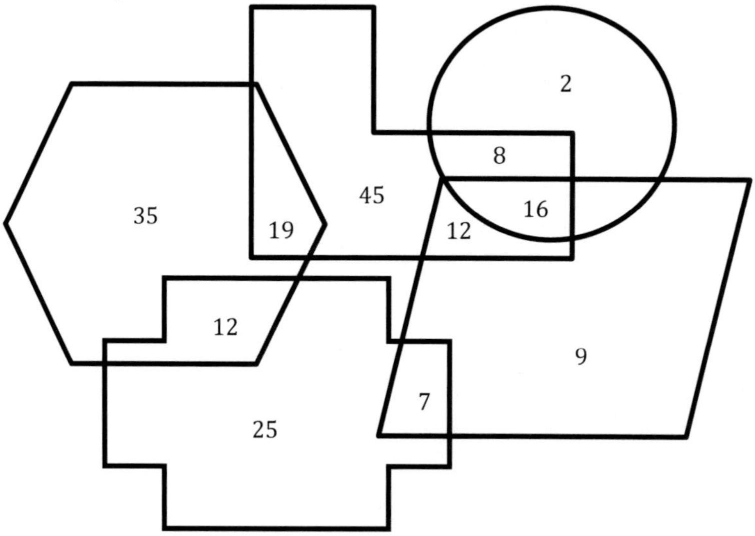

The following graph demonstrates the difference in the number of clothing items sold between 2013 and 2020.

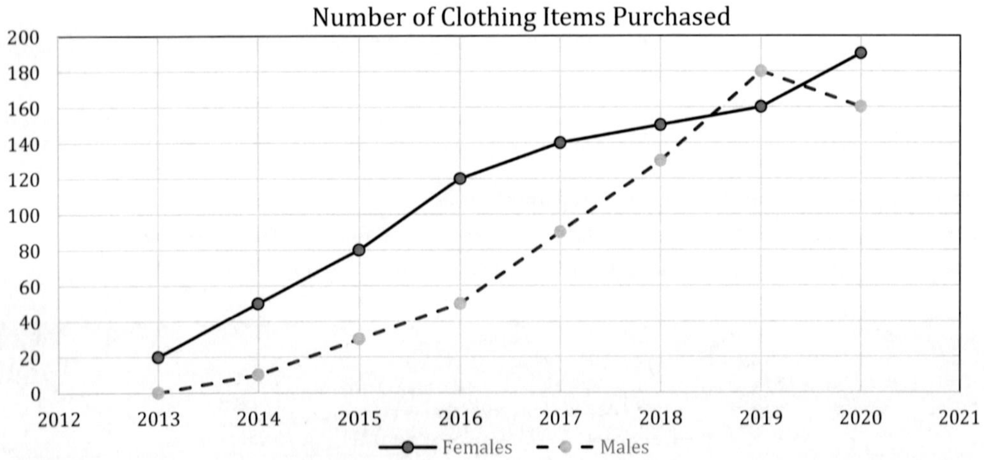

164. How many more females under the age of 18 purchased summer dresses and four different items in one purchase compared to females over the age of 18 who purchased only summer dresses?

A. 4 females
B. 6 females
C. 8 females
D. 12 females
E. 14 females
F. 26 females

165. What percentage, to the nearest percent, of females who purchased items at Sally's Boutique in 2020 were under 18?

A. 23%
B. 37%
C. 48%
D. 53%
E. 65%
F. 73%

166. Given that a female is over the age of 18, what is the probability of her purchasing a pink jumpsuit in 2020?

A. $\frac{2}{15}$

B. $\frac{7}{18}$

C. $\frac{3}{25}$

D. $\frac{7}{20}$

E. $\frac{7}{18}$

167. What was the difference in percentage increase in the number of items purchased by males and females between 2014 - 2017?

A. 24%
B. 38%
C. 135%
D. 480%
E. 620%
F. 740%

Questions 168 - 171 refer to the following information.

The following table refers to the profit made from exports and imports of several countries around the world in 2019. Some information in the table is missing.

Country	Total Profit (billions USD)	Total imports (billions USD)	Total exports (billions USD)	Vehicles (% of total exports)	Precious metals (% of total exports)	Pharmaceuticals (% of total exports)
Barbados		0.4	1.7	2.7	21.7	17.8
United Arab Emirates (UAE)	35	250		1.8	34.8	16.7
Spain	87	284		12.5	3.5	4.4
UK	65	630	695	8.8	9.0	5.8
India		312	478	10.8	12.5	1.2
Japan	21	685		49.6	13.2	4.5
China	5000		27000	20.9	12.8	6.2
Canada		446	485	2.7	5.1	0.8
Australia	58		272	16.5	3.4	1.3

168. Which country had the biggest total profit compared to the total value of the exports?

A. Barbados
B. China
C. India
D. UK
E. Spain
F. UAE

169. Assuming that 1 US Dollar equals 110 Japanese Yen, approximately how much more money, to the nearest trillion Japanese Yen, in exports did Japan make selling vehicles compared to precious metals and pharmaceuticals combined?

A. 16 trillion Japanese Yen
B. 19 trillion Japanese Yen
C. 23 trillion Japanese Yen
D. 32 trillion Japanese Yen
E. 36 trillion Japanese Yen
F. 43 trillion Japanese Yen

170. **Which country had the highest value of exports from pharmaceuticals?**
    A. Australia
    B. China
    C. Canada
    D. Barbados
    E. UAE
    F. India

171. **In 2020, India exported 10% more and imported 40% less. Assume that the percentages of the total exports were the same as 2019. How much money, to the nearest billion USD, was made from exporting vehicles from India in 2020?**
    A. 52 billion USD
    B. 55 billion USD
    C. 57 billion USD
    D. 61 billion USD
    E. 63 billion USD
    F. 68 billion USD

Questions 172 - 175 refer to the following information.
The price of a coffee latte at two rival coffee shops, Coffee House and The Roasted Bean, are plotted below:

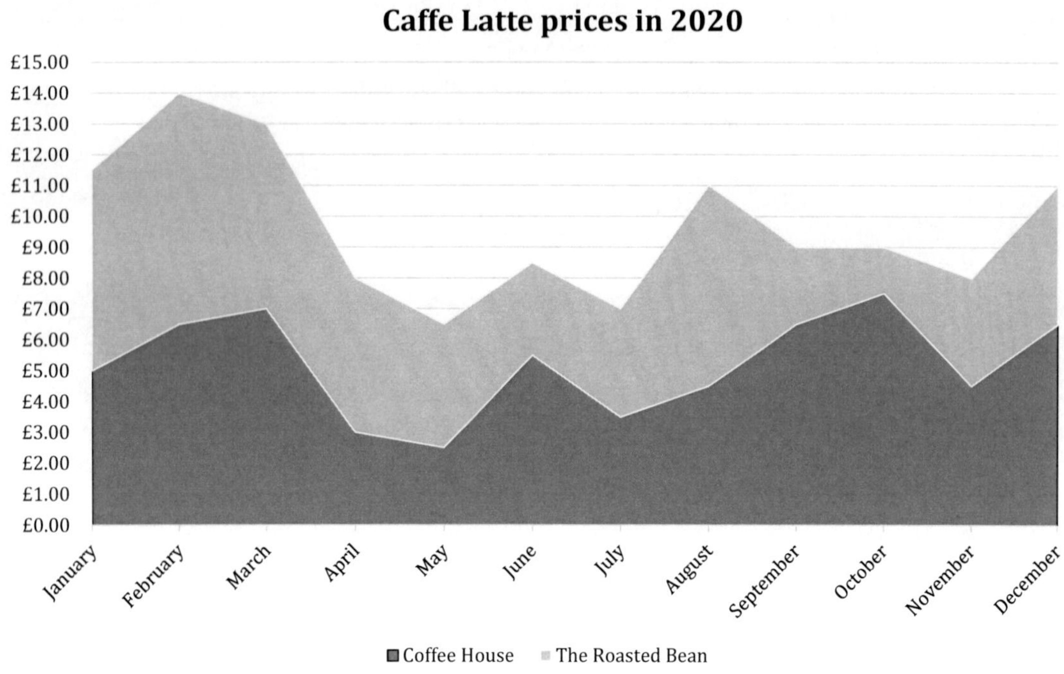

The total profit made from these two coffee shops in a typical week is illustrated in the graph below:

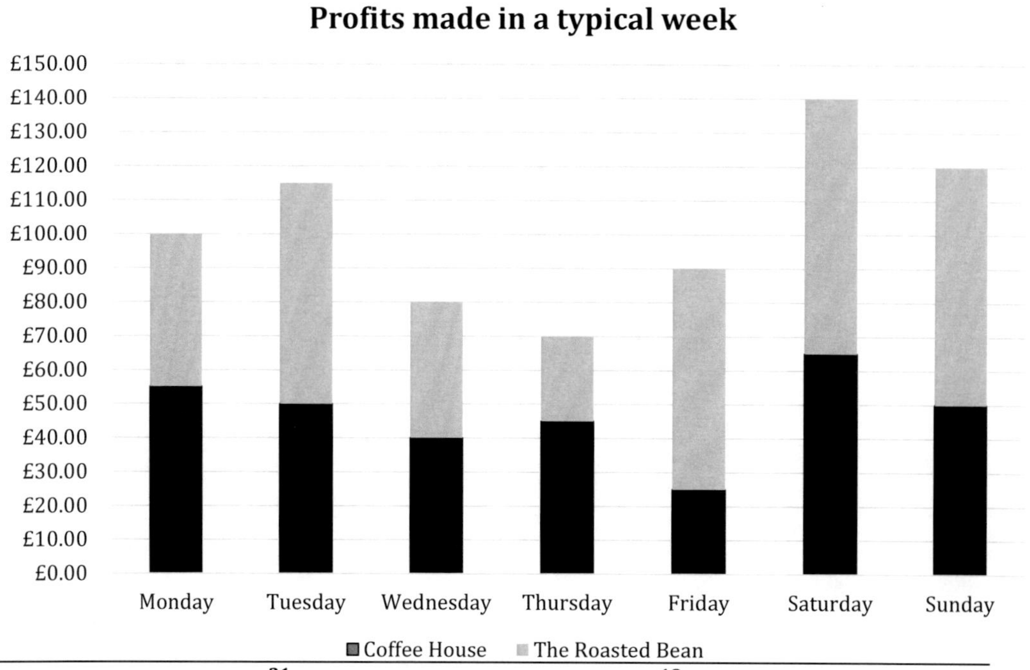

172. **On a typical Saturday, $\frac{21}{26}$ of the profits in Coffee House and $\frac{18}{25}$ of the profits in The Roasted Bean in October are generated by Caffe Lattes. What is the total number of Coffee Lattes purchased during this time period from these two coffee shops?**

A. 7
B. 17
C. 24
D. 36
E. 43
F. 50

173. **A Flat White Coffee is 20% cheaper than a Coffee Latte in Coffee House, but 30% more expensive in The Roasted Bean. In April, Julian purchases two Flat White Coffee, one from each coffee shop. Assume that £1 is equivalent to $1.30. He pays with a $5 note in Coffee House and a $10 note in The Roasted Bean. What is the total amount of change, in $, that he receives?**

A. $1.27
B. $3.43
C. $5.36
D. $5.45
E. $6.10
F. $7.24

174. **What is the difference in the weekly profits between Coffee House and The Roasted Bean?**

A. £55.00
B. £60.00
C. £65.00

D. £70.00
E. £75.00
F. £80.00

175. Considering that there are exactly four weeks in February, and 8 Coffee Lattes are sold every two weeks, what is the approximate percentage of The Roasted Bean's profit in February that is from Coffee Lattes?

A. 8%
B. 11%
C. 13%
D. 16%
E. 19%
F. 23%
G. 31%

Questions 176-180 refer to the following information.

A restaurant decides to summarise their most popular dishes in 2017 and 2020 in the table below:

Dish	2020 (% of total number of dishes ordered)	2017 (% of total number of dishes ordered)
Parmesan Chicken Cutlets	30	14
Chicken Dumplings	29	3
Chicken Fajitas	15	8
Mexican Chicken Pasta	5	14
Grilled Chicken Breast	2	45
Thai Peanut Skillet Chicken	7	1
Chicken Teriyaki Pineapple Bowls	12	15
Total	**100**	**100**

The total number of dishes ordered in 2017 was 1200. The number of total dishes ordered increased by 35% in 2020.

176. How many more Chicken Fajitas were ordered in 2020 compared to 2017?

A. 50
B. 84
C. 96
D. 147
E. 180
F. 263

177. What is the percentage increase of the number of Chicken Teriyaki Pineapple Bowls ordered between 2017 and 2020?

A. 3%
B. 6%
C. 8%
D. 10%
E. 13%

178. What is the percentage difference, to the nearest percent, of the number of Mexican Chicken Pasta dishes ordered in 2017 compared to 2020?

A. 46%
B. 52%
C. 62%
D. 65%
E. 143%
F. 278%

179. Chicken Dumplings are the most expensive in both years - each dish costs £16.50. Grilled Chicken Breasts cost 10% less than Chicken Dumplings and Thai Peanut Skilled Chicken costs 15% less than Grilled Chicken Breasts in 2017 but 35% more than Chicken Dumplings in 2020. What is the difference in price of Thai Peanut Skilled Chicken between 2020 and 2017?

A. £9.07
B. £10.27
C. £11.57
D. £12.27
E. £13.07
F. £14.87

180. In 2020, the restaurant forgot to include the Creamed Spinach Chicken dish, which accounted for 180 dishes on top of those shown. What percentage of the total number of dishes ordered did Parmesan Chicken Cutlets actually represent in 2020?

A. 14%
B. 18%
C. 22%
D. 27%
E. 30%
F. 46%

Questions 181-184 refer to the following information.

The following diagram shows different subjects taken at GCSE by Year 11 students in Cathedral School, Cardiff in 2020. Each black dot represents 2 students and each grey dot represents 5 students.

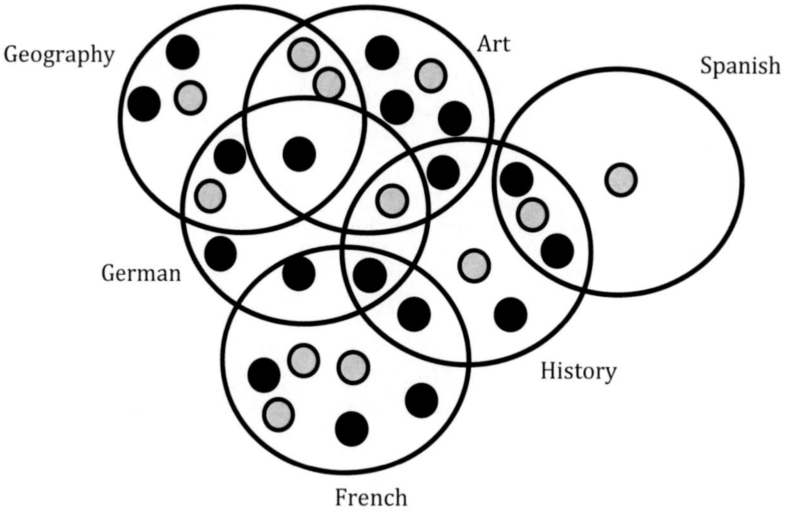

181. Only 80% of all of the students in Year 11 are represented in the diagram above. What percentage of students in the whole year study French?
   A. 20.5%
   B. 21%
   C. 21.5%
   D. 22%
   E. 22.5%
   F. 23%

182. Given that a student studies History, what is the probability that s/he studies Spanish or Art?
   A. $\frac{11}{27}$
   B. $\frac{16}{27}$
   C. $\frac{18}{27}$
   D. $\frac{21}{27}$
   E. $\frac{23}{27}$

183. The number of students who study Welsh is three times less than the number of students who study French. Exactly 20% less students study Psychology compared to Art. How many more students study Psychology compared to Welsh?
   A. 15 students
   B. 21 students
   C. 39 students
   D. 46 students
   E. 53 students

184. Assume that there were 80% more students who studied Geography and German in 2020 compared to 2019, and 75% less students who studied French and German in 2020 compared to 2019. In 2019, what was the difference in the number of students who studied Geography and German compared to History and Spanish?
   A. 5 students
   B. 7 students
   C. 10 students
   D. 11 students
   E. 13 students
   F. 15 students

Data Analysis

Questions 185-189 refer to the following information:
Two banks, Bank A and Bank B, offer different interest rates for amounts less than or more than £5000.

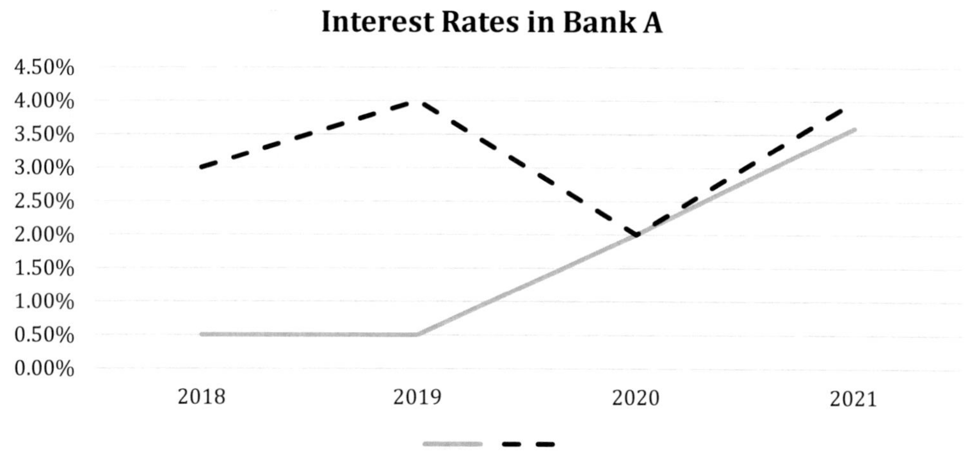

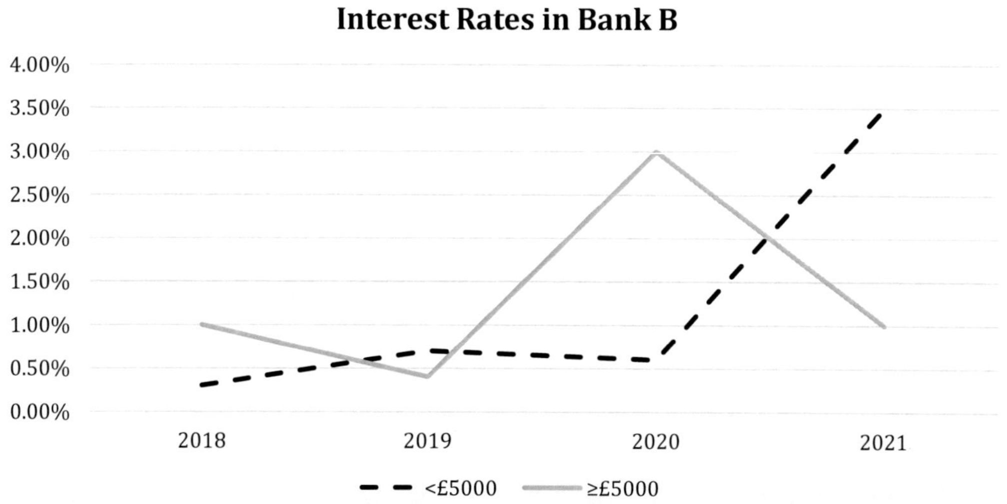

185. Gracie invests £6000 in Bank A and £5000 in Bank B at the start of 2018. At the end of 2019, how much more money is in Bank A compared to Bank B?

A. £1357
B. £1372
C. £1386
D. £1389
E. £1459
F. £1500

186. If Jacob invests £2000 in Bank A and £10000 in Bank B at the start of 2019, what is the total amount of money he would have in both Banks by the end of 2020?

A. £12291.30
B. £12381.40

C. £12391.40
D. £12481.30
E. £12484.60
F. £12492.30

187. Thomas invests £4000 in Bank B at the start of 2019. He invests an additional £3000 into the same bank account at the start of 2020. How much money is in Thomas' bank account at the end of 2020?

A. £4028.38
B. £7028.46
C. £7133.42
D. £7238.84
E. £7487.38
F. £8456.68

188. Jason invests £5000 into Bank A at the start of 2018. What is the percentage increase of money in his bank account between the end of 2018 and the end of 2020?

A. 1%
B. 2%
C. 3%
D. 4%
E. 5%
F. 6%

189. In 2022, the interest rate is predicted to increase to 5% for amounts greater than or equal to £5000 in both Bank A and Bank B. Rachel invests £6000 in both Banks at the start of 2020. Assume that the 2022 predictions are correct. What is the difference in the amount of money present in each of Rachel's bank accounts at the end of 2022?

A. £126.15
B. £129.15
C. £131.15
D. £132.15
E. £135.15
F. £137.15

DA	DATA ANALYSIS	Answers

1. D

Explanation:

There are six halls in total. Each hall plays with five other halls twice - hence, each hall plays 10 games in total. Thus, the number of games won by Kent Ridge is **10 - 1 (draw) - 3 (loss) = 6**. This accounts for 18 points. Kent Ridge Hall scored one point from the one tied game. In total, the **Kent Ridge Hall scored 19 points.**

2. E

Explanation:

Given that each hall plays 10 games, one should be able to work out the figures in bold shown below:

Hall	W	D	L
Raffles	9	0	**1**
Temasek	7	2	**1**
Kent Ridge	6	1	3
Eusoff			4
Sheares	2	**1**	7
King Edward VII	0	1	**9**

By logic, the total number of games won in the table is equal to the total lost. From the above table, the total number of games lost is 25. Given that the total won is equal to 25 too, the number of games won by Eusoff Hall must be one. **Hence, the number of games drawn by Eusoff Hall is five.**

3. A

Explanation:

One should have completed the table as below:

Hall	W	D	L
Eusoff	1	5	4
Sheares	2	1	7

The number of points scored by Eusoff Hall is:

(1 x 3) + (5 x 1) = 8

However, the number of points scored by Sheares Hall is:

(2 x 3) + (1 x 1) = 7

The difference is one.

4. **D**

Explanation:

This question can be solved by eliminating some of the options which will clearly not have the greatest market value. For example, comparing Khleb and BnB, it can be extrapolated that Khleb will have a share price that is lower than BnB's. Given that Khleb also has lesser shares, it will definitely not have the greatest market value. Comparing Cakes and BnB, they will both have the same share price in June; however, Cakes has more shares. Hence, BnB can be eliminated. Comparing NY Bakes and Buttercup, NY Bakes will have a greater share price in June and also more shares than Buttercup. Hence, Buttercup can be eliminated. At this point, only Cakes and NY Bakes will have to be compared. Cakes will have a share price of £0.25 whereas NY Bakes will have a share price of £0.80, which is more than three times of that than Cakes. However, given that Cakes only have 2.5 times more shares than NY Bakes, this means that **NY Bakes will have a greater market value**.

5. **C**

Explanation:

Share price of Khleb: 0.20 x 0.75 = **£0.15**

Share price of NY Bakes: 0.40 x 2 = **£0.80**

Ratio = 0.15 : 0.80 - **3:16**

6. **B**

Explanation:

Increase in market value for BnB: 21,000 x 0.25 = **£5,250**

Increase in market value for Buttercup: 43,000 x 0.50 x 1.5 = **£32,250**

Total increase in market value: 5,250 + 32,250 = **£37,500 (£38,000 rounded off to the nearest thousand)**

7. **C**

Explanation:

To make the calculations quicker, omit the '000' at the end of the figures.

Market value of Cakes: 50 x 0.50 = **25**

Price needed for the number of shares Khleb has: $\frac{25}{20}$ = **£1.25**

Percentage increase of Khleb share price: $\frac{1.25 - 0.20}{0.20}$ x 100 = **525%**

8. **C**

Explanation:

Total share price in May: 0.20 + 0.25 + 0.50 + 0.40 + 0.50 = **£1.85**

Total predicted share price in June:

(0.20 x 0.75) + 0.25 + (0.50 x 0.5) + (0.40 x 2) + (0.50 x 1.5) = **£2.25**

Total share prices in both months:

1.85 + 2.25 = **£4.10**

Average price of a share: 4.10 ÷ 10 = **£0.41**

9. **C**

Explanation:

This question can be solved by evaluating the numbers given based on the formula:

$$\text{Percentage} = \frac{\text{Day highest} - \text{Day lowest}}{\text{End of day}} \times 100$$

This means the percentage will increase proportionally with an increase in (Day highest - Day lowest) and it will decrease proportionally with an increase at the 'End of day' value.

The best way to start is to look at the two dates which have the greatest 'End of day' values. The dates 12.07.2015 and 04.08.2015 have the same 'End of day' value. However, the (Day highest - Day lowest) in 12.07.2015 is half of that of 04.08.2015. Thus, 12.07.2015 must have a lower percentage. The (Day highest - Day lowest) value for 12.07.2015 is €0.05. Given that all (Day highest - Day lowest) values for other days are either €0.05 or €0.10, **12.07.2015 has the smallest (Day highest - Day lowest) value possible. Hence, it must have the lowest percentage.**

10. C

Explanation:

For Kevin to have made a loss, he must have exchanged the pounds at the euros' lowest rate (1.00 and 1.25) and changed the euros back to pounds at its highest rate (1.20).

Amount of euros Kevin had before exchanging back:

(1.00 x 10,000) + (1.25 x 40,000) = **€60,000**

Amount of pounds received in return:

60,000 ÷ 1.20 = **£50,000**

£50,000 is the same amount of money Kevin initially invested in the exchange. Hence, **he did not make a profit nor a loss.**

11. C

Explanation:

The difference in the number of euros received per pound is €0.05.

Hence, the extra euros he would make is:

(1 - 0.1) x 35,000 x 0.05 = **€1,575**

12. B

Explanation:

Average of the lowest value: $\frac{1.15 + 1.00 + 1.25 + 1.20 + 1.10}{5}$ = **£1.14**

Average of the highest value: $\frac{1.25 + 1.05 + 1.30 + 1.30 + 1.20}{5}$ = **£1.22**

Increase in average values: 1.22 - 1.14 = **£0.08**

Highest value on 16.09.2015: 1.05 + 0.08 = **£1.13**

13. C

Explanation:

Total number of right-handed participants = **19,335**

Total number of right-handed participants who scored 70 and above:

5,640 + 6,195 + 3,375 = **15,210**

Total number of right-handed participants who scored below 70:

19,335 - 15,210 = **4,125**

14. C

Explanation:

One method of solving this question is by subtracting all the relevant numbers from the total.

Total right-handed participants who scored between 85 -115:

17,145 - 3,525 - 2,940 - 2,895 = **7,785**

Alternatively, one could make a smart guess by looking at the numbers given for left-handed participants. It can be extrapolated that the total number of people who scored below 85 approximately add up to slightly below 6,000. Adding this with the total of participants who scored above 115, one will be an approximate number that is slightly below 9,500. Subtracting this from 17,000, it can be estimated that the result is approximately 7,500. However, given that 17,000 is a figure rounded down and 9,500 is an overestimation, this infers that the final result will definitely be slightly greater than 7,500. Hence, **the number falls between 7,500 and 8,500.**

15. D

Explanation:

One should be able to fill in the table as below.

IQ Score	Right-handed	Left-handed
Below 70	4,125	2,895
70-85	5,640	2,940
85-115	6,195	7,785 or 7,500 - 8,500
Above 115	3,375	3,525

The question asks for the second lowest ratio of right-handed to left-handed individuals. From the numbers above, the group for 'Below 70' and '70-85' will have ratios greater than the other two groups as the number of right-handed individuals is greater than those who are left-handed. Comparing the '85-115' and 'Above 115' group, one can see that the 'Above 115' group has a ratio that approximates near to 1 : 1. The '85-115' group has a ratio of 1 : 1.3 (approximately 6,000 : 7,800). Therefore, it has a lower ratio than the 'Above 115' group.

Assuming that one did not work out the number 7,785 from the earlier question, one should be able to tell that the ratio is 1 : 1.3 and not 1 : 1.5 as 6,000 x 1.5 = 9,000, which is clearly out of the 7,500 to 8,500 range.

Given that the question wants the ratio to be expressed in terms of left-handed to right-handed participants, **the answer is 1.3 : 1.**

16. B

Explanation:

Given that the new mean is 19,150, this means that the new total number of participants is:

19,150 x 2 = **38,300**

The new group of participants has: 38,300 - 36,480 = **1,820 individuals**

Given that there are four ranges in the table, each range is expected to have:

1,820 ÷ 4 = **455 individuals**

17. C

Explanation:

Frequency of fevers in 2012: **5.8 million**

Frequency of chest pains in 2011: **3.6 million**

Frequency of back pains in 2012: **2.6 million**

Total: 5.8 + 3.6 + 2.6 = **12 million**

18. D

Explanation:

Frequency of chest pains in 2012: **3.4 million**

Total frequency of symptoms recorded in 2012:

5.8 + 4.8 + 3.4 + 2.6 + 7.2 = **23.8 million**

Fraction of chest pains: $\frac{3.4}{23.8} = \frac{1}{7}$

19. E

Explanation:

Total frequency of other symptoms in both years: 7.2 + 7.8 = <u>15</u>

Average frequency of fevers across both years: $\frac{5.0 + 5.8}{2} = \underline{5.4}$

Ratio - 15 : 5.4 = <u>25 : 9</u>

20. D

Explanation:

Total frequency of shortness of breath: 4.6 + 4.8 = <u>9.4 million</u>

Total frequency of back pains: 4.2 + 2.6 = <u>6.8 million</u>

Total frequency of both: 9.4 + 6.8 = <u>16.2 million</u>

21. C

Explanation:

Total number of patients in 2011: 5.0 + 4.6 + 3.6 + 4.2 + 7.8 = <u>25.2 million</u>

Total number of patients in 2012: 5.8 + 4.8 + 3.4 + 2.6 + 7.2 = <u>23.8 million</u>

Percentage decrease in the number of patients:

$\frac{25.2 - 23.8}{25.2} \times 100 = \underline{5.6\% \text{ (approximately)}}$

22. A

Explanation:

Given that Vegnesh and Praveena 'decided to get a staff member instead' on their second trip, one can infer that they did not hire a staff the first time around.

Cost of trip in March 2018: 50 + 37.50 = <u>£87.50</u>

Cost of trip in April 2018: (50 x 1.20) + 2 x (37.50 x 1.20) + (2 x 25) = <u>£200</u>

Increase in cost: £200 - £87.50 = <u>£112.50</u>

23. C

Explanation:

Total cost of rent: 292.50 x 2 = <u>£585</u>

Deposit + (5 x 95) = 585

Deposit = <u>£110</u>

24. E

Explanation:

Let the rate per hour for the Deck Boat be 'D'.

Cost of first trip: 125 + D + 25 (staff service) = <u>£ (150 + D)</u>

His second trip may have occurred later, but the year of his trips was in 2017.

Hence, the price of the rental is the same.

Therefore,

150 + D = 50 + [4 x (25 + 37.50)]

150 + D = 300

<u>D = £150</u>

<u>Therefore, the deck boat's hourly rate is £150.</u>

25. B

Explanation:

Let the deposit of the Jet Boat be 'D' and its hourly rate be 'R'.

Equation 1: D + 4R = 1,060

Equation 1 - Equation 2:
2R = 425
R = £212.50
Substitute R = 212.50 into Equation 2:
D + 2(212.5) = 635
D = £210
Difference between 'R' and 'D': 212.50 - 210 = **£2.50**

26. A

Explanation:

Before calculating the revenue for all the years, evaluate some of the data and eliminate some of the incorrect options. The years 2017 and 2019 will definitely not have the lowest revenue made as the average number of customers per month as well as the average amount spent per customer is higher than both 2016 and 2018.

When calculating the revenue generated for the remaining years, omit the 1,000 for the number of customers as it is constant for all years. In addition, ignore multiplying the figures with 12 months as this is a constant for all calculations as well.

2015: 44 x 2.50 = **£110**
2016: 52 x 2.20 = **£114.40**
2018: 58 x 2.10 = **£121.80**
2015 was the year with the lowest revenue generated.

27. C

Explanation:

Using the values from the question before, the quickest way to solve this is to first find the difference in the revenue per month.

Difference between monthly revenue in 2015 and 2016:
114.40 - 110 = **£4,400 (with 1,000 included)**
Revenue difference between the years: £4,400 x 12 = **£52,800**

28. E

Explanation:

Average profit made per month in 2018: (2.10 - 0.40) x 58,000 = **£98,600**
Average profit made per month in 2019: (2,30 - 0.70) x 62,000 = **£99,200**
Difference in average profit made per month: 99,200 - 98,600 = **£600**
Difference in profit made between both years: 600 x 12 = **£7,200**

29. B

Explanation:

The quickest way to solve this is by recognising that £2.30 has to be upscaled, similarly to the way £2.10 was upscaled to £2.30. On top of that, as working with decimals can get messy at times, omit the decimals in the calculations, and then add them back in at the end. As the numbers involved do not cancel each other out, it would be easier to find ways to make calculations as simple and as straightforward as possible.

$\frac{23 \times 23}{21}$ = **25.2 (this represents £2.51 which is closest to £2.50)**

30. E

Explanation:

Average amount spent per customer in 2016: **£2.20**
Total cost per customer in 2018: **£0.40**

Ratio - 2.20 : 0.40 = **11 : 2**

31. B

Explanation:

Chelsea's Cafe will start making a loss when the amount spent per customer is lesser than the total cost of each customer.

This question requires one to apply a **30% decrease to the average spend per customer in 2015 for a few times until a value below £0.50 is reached.** This can be done by multiplying 0.7 to £2.50. This process (i.e., multiplying each answer by 0.7) is repeated until an answer is found that is lower than £0.50.

One will find that after 0.7 is multiplied the 5th time, the value becomes £0.42. **Hence, it takes 5 years (i.e., 2020) for Chelsea's Cafe to make a loss.**

32. B

Explanation:

The number of vehicles in the survey is 180 million and the total number of cars is 54 million.

Hence, the percentage of vehicles that are cars is:

$\frac{54}{180}$ x 100 = **30%**

33. D

Explanation:

The total number of vehicles in Bedrock and Dinkletown combined is 84 million and the total number in Camberwick and Elmore is 64 million.

The ratio is **84:64 = 21:16**

34. E

Explanation:

The total number of vehicles in Aberdale is 32 million, and the total number of vehicles in Dinkletown is 40 million.

The percentage increase required would be:

$\frac{40 - 32}{32}$ x 100 = **25%**

35. C

Explanation:

The total number of vehicles in Aberdale and Dinkletown combined is 72 million. The total number of motorcycles and buses in these two countries is 32 million. *Hence, the fraction would be:*

$\frac{32}{72} = \mathbf{\frac{4}{9}}$

36. A

Explanation:

The total number of cars in the survey is 54 million and the total number of buses is 45 million. Given that the cost of a bus is twice the cost of a car, let the costs of a car and a bus to be 'x' and '$2x$'.

Total cost of all cars: **54x**

Total cost of all buses: 45 x $2x$ = **90x**

Sum of both costs: $54x + 90x$ = **144x**

Difference in both costs: $90x - 54x$ = **36x**

Ratio: $36x : 144x$ = **1 : 4**

37. D

Explanation:

In questions such as this, be careful with the diagram. Labelling the shapes would help in solving this question.

38. E

Explanation:

This scenario described involves the overlap of the hexagon, triangle, and square. That gives an area of 5 + 15 = 20.

39. E

Explanation:

Add up all the numbers in the hexagon:

6 + 7 + 5 + 11 + 15 + 4 + 10 = 58

40. D

Explanation:

This scenario described involves the overlap of the circle and the square. That gives an area of 3 + 6 + 5 = 14.

41. B

Explanation:

The scenario described counts for none of the numbers which are in the circle except for '5', and the rest of the numbers that are outside the triangle.

i) *none of the numbers which are in the circle except for '5'*: This is because all the numbers '3', '6', '12', and '11' account for students who are right-handed and do well in their exams.

ii) *the rest of the numbers that are outside the triangle*: the rest of the numbers outside the triangle, which are '4', '7' and '8' accounts for right-handed students.

Hence, the total is 8 + 7 + 5 + 4 = 24

42. A

Explanation:

Carefully analysing the diagram will give the **answer of 0.**

43. C

Explanation:

The question is looking for the area in the diagram that is not within the triangle nor the hexagon but is within the square. That gives 3 + 8 = 11.

44. B; E

Explanation:

Option 'B' accounts for the blank space bounded by the triangle, circle, and square. **Option 'E'** accounts for the space outside the diagram.

45. E

Explanation:

Ratio 'H' to 'G': 81.60 : 34.00 = 12 : 5

This requires careful simplification of the numbers. However, it would be easier to ignore the decimal places and focus on reducing **816 : 340.**

46. B

Explanation:

Exactly 2,880 units of Currency C is equivalent to:

$\frac{2880}{1.44}$ = **2,000 units** of Currency X

This is equal to:

2,000 x 9.36 = **18,720** units of Currency E

---

47. C

Explanation:

0.60 unit of Currency A = **1 unit of Currency X**

72 units of Currency A: 72 ÷ 0.60 = **120 units of Currency X**

1.44 unit of Currency C = **1 unit of Currency X**

72 units of Currency C: 72 ÷ 1.44 = **50 units of Currency X**

Difference in the units of Currency X: 120 - 50 = **70 units of Currency X**

---

48. C

Explanation:

2.04 unit of Currency D = **1 unit of Currency X**

612 units of Currency A: 612 ÷ 2.04 = **300 units of Currency X**

10.14 unit of Currency F = **1 unit of Currency X**

2,028 units of Currency F = 2,028 ÷ 10.14 = **200 units of Currency X**

9.36 unit of Currency E = **1 unit of Currency X**

9,360 units of Currency E: 9,360 ÷ 9.36 = **1,000 units of Currency X**

Total units of Currency X: 300 + 200 + 1,000 = **1,500 units of Currency X**

1,500 units of Currency X: 1,500 x 0.85 = **1,275 units of Currency B**

---

49. B

Explanation:

34 units of Currency G = **1 unit of Currency X**

10,200 units of Currency G: 10,200 ÷ 34 = **300 units of Currency X**

With 10% commission, this will cost **300 x 1.1 = 330 units of Currency X**.

The remaining amount of Currency X is **830 - 330 = 500 units**. During the conversion of Currency X to Currency A, 10% is lost due to commission.

Hence, **500 x 0.9 = 450 units** of Currency X is converted to **450 x 0.60 = 270** units of Currency A.

---

50. E

Explanation:

Total papers published for FY2: 13 + 15 + 12 + 12 + 19 = **71**

Total papers published for ST1: 14 + 13 + 13 + 15 + 16 = **71**

The **difference in the total number of papers published is 0.**

---

51. E

Explanation:

One way to do this is to find the midpoint of each pair of values between years ST5 and ST6, followed by adding up all the midpoints. However, there is a more time-efficient method for solving this. That is, by adding up all the h-index numbers in ST5 and ST6, followed by dividing the final result by 2. One will arrive at the same answer in a shorter time.

Total h-index in ST5 and ST6: 7 + 18 + 10 + 5 + 11 + 7 + 12 + 6 + 6 + 9 = **91**

Combined h-index mid-way between ST5 and ST6: 91 ÷ 2 = **45.5**

52. D

Explanation:

Abstergo and Ewing had a drop in their h-index 4 times whilst Benthic and Czerka had a drop 5 times. Only Deon experienced a drop 3 times.

53. C

Explanation:

Between their FY2 and ST1 years, the **combined h-index remained constant**, as calculated in Q50. Hence, the question is looking for another year of which the combined h-index is the same as that of its preceding year.

Combined h-index of the following years: **ST2: 63; ST3: 55; ST4: 55; ST5: 51; ST6: 40**

Hence, the answer is ST4.

54. B

Explanation:

The declines (i.e., h-index of ST6 minus h-index of FY1) of the doctors are as follows:

Abstergo: 7; Benthic: 4 - **smallest decline**; Czerka: 10; Deon: 6; Ewing: 9

55. C

Explanation:

This question requires a careful analysis of the graph for the greatest change of two points that are within 3 training years apart. Deon had an h-index of 15 in ST1 and an h-index of 6 in ST3. This is the greatest difference found in the graph given.

56. C

Explanation:

Total h-index in FY1: $14 + 16 + 16 + 12 + 18 = \underline{76}$

Average h-index per doctor in FY1: $76 \div 5 = \underline{15.2}$

57. D

Explanation:

Mean h-index of Abstergo: $\frac{14+13+14+11+8+8+7+7}{8} = \frac{82}{8} = \underline{10.25}$

Mean h-index of Ewing: $\frac{18+19+16+12+15+9+11+9}{8} = \frac{109}{8} = \underline{13.625}$

Difference in mean h-index:

13.625 - 10.25 = 3.375 (3.4 rounded off to one decimal place)

58. C

Explanation:

The mean h-index for Abstergo (10.25) and Ewing (13.625) have been calculated in the previous question. The mean h-indices of the other doctors are as below.

Benthic: $\frac{16+15+13+18+17+20+18+12}{8} = \frac{129}{8} = \underline{16.125}$

Czerka: $\frac{16+12+13+10+9+11+10+6}{8} = \frac{87}{8} = \underline{10.875}$

Deon: $\frac{12+12+15+12+6+7+5+6}{8} = \frac{75}{8} = \underline{9.375}$

Alternatively, compare their total h-indices. As calculating the mean would require dividing all sums by 8, this means that the division of 8 is a constant.

Arranging their h-indices in ascending order, one would get:

Deon, Abstergo, Czerka, Ewing, and Benthic

Hence, the median mean h-index corresponds to Czerka.

59. C

Explanation:

Upon rounding the mean h-indices, one will calculate:

Abstergo: 10.25 = **10**; *Benthic:* 16.125 = **16**; *Czerka:* 10.875 = **11**; *Deon:* 9.375 = **9**; *Ewing:* 13.625 = **14**

The total mean h-index is 60. The greatest difference in angle corresponds to the greatest difference between two sectors. The smallest and biggest sector will belong to Deon (9) and Benthic (16) respectively. The difference between the two is 7. This value expressed in angles would be: $\frac{7}{60}$ x 360 = **42°**

60. A

Explanation:

Benthic's h-index remains at 12. In the graph, Deon's h-index increases as the rate of 1 per training year. Post ST6, his rate becomes an increase of 1.5 per training year. At ST6, Deon had an h-index of 6. For him to increase his h-index by 6, that will take him $\frac{6}{1.5}$ = **4 years**

61. C

Explanation:

New Beginnings received one third of the total amount. If they had received £51.60, a total of £51.60 x 3 = **£154.80 would have been raised.**

Funds raised by Wrecking Belles: £154.80 - £24.60 - £25.20 - £28.00 - £42.00 = **£35.00**

62. B

Explanation:

The total funds raised is £154.80. If the total amount of funds raised per song is exactly £3.87, then 40 songs were performed.

Hence, the number of songs performed by Group Y is:

40 - 10 - 10 - 8 - 5 = **7**

63. D

Explanation:

From Q62, the number of songs raised by Group Y is 7. The question requires one to decide which of the 2 groups - Noteworthy or Clef Hangers - performed 7 songs. Given that the mean is a *perfect* number, it must be Clef Hangers (£25.20) and **£25.30 ÷ 7 = £3.60**. If it was Noteworthy, the mean would have been **24.60 ÷ 7 = £3.5143....**

64. B

Explanation:

At this point, complete the table as below:

Group	Number of songs	Amount of funds raised (£)	Amount of funds raised per song (£)
Noteworthy	10	24.60	2.46
Clef Hangers	7	25.20	3.60
Treblemakers	8	28.00	3.50
Wrecking Belles	5	35.00	7.00
Chord of the Rings	10	42.00	4.20

The group with the third highest funds raised per song is **Clef Hangers**.

65. D

Explanation:

It is not required to express the amount of funds raised in angles and one can work with the numbers directly from the table. The process of converting the numbers to angle sizes is constant; hence, the numbers in the table are directly proportional to their angle sizes. Hence, 42 ÷ 1.5 = £28. This means that the sector corresponding to Chord of the Rings is at least 1.5 times bigger than that of Treblemakers. As a result, Chord of the Rings has an angle size that is also at least 1.5 times greater than that of Noteworthy and Clef Hangers. Hence, **3 groups in total fit the criteria in question.**

66. C

Explanation:

The total funds raised was **£154.80**. If split evenly, each home would receive **£77.40**. Littlewood initially had received **51.60 x 2 = £103.20**. The amount donated would be 103.20 - 77.40 = **£25.80**. That amount is equivalent to a proportion of:

$$\frac{25.80}{103.20} \times 100 = \underline{25\%}$$

67. C

Explanation:

There are 6 groups in total now. If the new mean is £32.50, that means the total amount raised in the initiative is £32.50 x 6 = **£195**. The amount of funds raised by Local Vocals is £195.00 - £154.80 = **£40.20**. Given that they performed 5 songs, their mean funds raised per song is £40.20 ÷ 5 = **£8.04.**

68. B

Explanation:

The total number of participants is 120. The number of participants who said 'Talent' is essential is 30. Expressed in percentage, this is:

$$\frac{30}{120} \times 100 = \underline{25\%}$$

69. C

Explanation:

Number of participants who deem 'Risk-taking' as 'Desirable': 55

Number of participants who deem 'Resilience' as 'Essential': 40

Ratio: 55 : 40 - 11 : 8 = 1.375 : 1

70. C

Explanation:

There are 120 responses for each quality and there are 5 qualities surveyed. The total number of responses is 120 x 5 = 600. The total number of 'irrelevant' responses is 70 + 30 + 20 + 30 = 150. Expressed as a percentage, this is:

$$\frac{150}{600} \times 100 = \underline{25\%.}$$

71. C

Explanation:

The total number of 'Essential' and 'Desirable' responses are 195 and 255 respectively. The difference between the two is 60. Expressed as a percentage to the total number of responses, this is:

$$\frac{60}{600} \times 100 = \underline{10\%.}$$

72. D

Explanation:

The sum of the 'Essential' and 'Desirable' responses are as below:

Talent: <u>50</u>; *Resilience:* <u>90</u>; *Discipline:* <u>120</u>; *Risk-taking:* <u>100</u> (second highest); *External support:* <u>90</u>

73. B

Explanation:

The number of participants who deemed 'External support' as 'Desirable' is 70. There are 60 males and 60 females in this survey. Of the 70, the minimum number of females must be 10. This is based on the assumption that all 60 males have contributed to the total of 70. Hence, the minimum fraction of female respondents that regarded 'External support' as 'Desirable' is:

$$\frac{10}{60} = \frac{\mathbf{1}}{\mathbf{6}}$$

74. E

Explanation:

The total number of males in this study is 60. All the responses that regarded the qualities as essential are 60 or below. It is possible that only males contributed to all of these responses. Hence, **<u>the answer is 100%.</u>**

75. D

Explanation:

The total number of 'Desirable' or 'Irrelevant' responses for 'Risk-taking' is 75. The minimum number of males of these 75 must be 15. This is based on the assumption that all 60 females contributed to this 75 as well. Hence, the minimum possible percentage of 'Desirable' or 'Irrelevant' responses that were due to males must be:

$$\frac{15}{75} \text{ x } 100 = \underline{20\%.}$$

76. D

Explanation:

The total number of responses that deem 'Talent' 'Essential' or 'Irrelevant' is 100. Of these 100, the minimum number of males must be 40. This is based on the assumption that all 60 females contribute to this 100. Hence, the minimum possible fraction of males is:

$$\frac{40}{60} = \frac{\mathbf{2}}{\mathbf{3}}.$$

77. C

Explanation:

This question requires a careful analysis of each statement:

<u>Option 'A'</u> - This is false because there are 60 female respondents and the total of essential and desirable responses for 'Talent' is 50. Hence, some females would have also regarded 'Talent' as 'Irrelevant'.

<u>Option 'B'</u> - This is false. No information supports this. It is possible that the respondents who deem 'Discipline' as 'Essential' are a mix of males and females.

<u>Option 'C'</u> - The total number of responses that deem 'Talent' as 'Essential' or 'Desirable' is 50. It is possible that all these 50 respondents contributed to the 60 responses that deem 'Discipline' as 'Essential'.

<u>Option 'D'</u> - This is false. Two thirds of the number of female respondents is 40. There are only 30 responses that deemed 'Resilience' as 'Irrelevant'.

Option 'E' - This is false. A total of 50% of males is equivalent to 30 respondents. There are only 20 responses that deem 'External support' as 'Essential'.

78. B

Explanation:

Profit = Yearly Turnover - Yearly Cost

(When performing calculations, ignore the '000' as they are constants for all the given values. This will apply for all the following explanations).

Profit for each year:

2011: 244 - 120 = **£124**; *2012:* 290 - 124 = **£166** (second lowest); *2013:* 325 - 150 = **£175**
2014: 350 - 165 = **£185**; *2015:* 360 - 180 = **£180**

Alternatively, qualitatively compare the turnover and cost values to obtain the year with the second lowest profit. One should go by the rule that profit increases with greater turnover and lesser cost.

79. E

Explanation:

The question requires a qualitative analysis of the data given on the table. The numbers are too complicated to calculate the percentage values for each given year.

The percentage required in the question is calculated by the profit made each year divided by the turnover for that particular year.

From Q78, the profit for each year is as below:

2011: 244 - 120 = **£124**; *2012:* 290 - 124 = **£166**; *2013:* 325 - 150 = **£175**
2014: 350 - 165 = **£185**; *2015:* 360 - 180 = **£180**

From the above values, the profit per turnover for the year 2015 is $\mathbf{\frac{180}{360} \times 100 = 50\%}$.

Considering the profits of the other years, they are at least 50% more than the corresponding turnover for the year.

To check this, multiply each of the profits by two. If the resulting number is more than the corresponding turnover, then it can be inferred that the profit is more than 50% of the turnover. For example, in the year 2011, the profit was £124. If this was 50% of the turnover, the turnover would be 124 x 2 = £248. Given that the turnover is £244 (which is less than £248), one can be certain that the percentage of profit per turnover is **more than 50%.**

80. B

Explanation:

From Q78, the profit for each year is as below:

2011: 244 - 120 = **£124**; *2012:* 290 - 124 = **£166**; *2013:* 325 - 150 = **£175**
2014: 350 - 165 = **£185**; *2015:* 360 - 180 = **£180**

This question requires one to look at the cost to profit ratio. In 2015, the ratio is 1:1. One can also estimate the ratio for 2011 as 1:1. Knowing these are useful in eliminating some of the answer options; however, they aren't useful as a reference point. This is because 1:1 is the highest ratio possible. In this question, the lowest ratio is required.

The ratio for 2012 approximates to 120 : 160 = 3 : 4. This can be of good reference. Looking at the numbers for 2013 and 2014, check their values by dividing their cost values by 3 and multiplying it by 4. For example, in 2013; $\frac{150}{3} \times 4 =$ **£200**. In 2014; $\frac{165}{3} \times 4 =$ **£220**.

As the resulting numbers are greater than the profit values given, it can be extrapolated that their turnover to profit ratio is greater than 0.75 : 1 (or 3 : 4). Hence, **2012 is the year with the lowest ratio.**

81. D

Explanation:

The increase in the number of branches across the 5 years is **260 - 200 = 60**. The average increase per year is $\frac{60}{4} = 15$. The total is divided by 4 because there were only 4 'increases' in between the 5 years.

82. B

Explanation:

The increase in turnover is £10. The turnover value in 2015 is £360. Let the number of years after 2015 be 'n'. After 'n' years, the turnover value would be 360 + 10n.

The increase in cost is £15. The cost value in 2015 is £180. After 'n' years, the cost value would be 180 + 15n.

For Thirst-tea to break-even, the turnover value must be equal to the cost value:

$360 + 10n = 180 + 15n$

$5n = 180$

$n = 36$

Hence, for a continuous trend, **it will take 36 years after 2015 for the company to break-even.**

83. F

Explanation:

The profit made in 2011 and 2014 is £124 and £185 respectively. The number of branches in 2011 and 2014 is 200 and 250 respectively. The profit per branch in 2011 is **124 ÷ 200 = 0.62**, whereas the profit per branch in 2014 is **185 ÷ 250 = 0.74**. The ratio for 2014 to 2011 is 0.74 : 0.62 = **37 : 31**.

84. B

Explanation:

From Q78, the profit for each year is as below:

2011: 244 - 120 = **£124**; *2012:* 290 - 124 = **£166**; *2013:* 325 - 150 = **£175**

2014: 350 - 165 = **£185**; *2015:* 360 - 180 = **£180**

The average profit across the 5 years is:

$$\frac{124 + 166 + 175 + 185 + 180}{5} = £166.$$

This is the same as the profit in 2012.

85. B

Explanation:

In scenarios like these, it can often look as if the question requires work with complicated numbers. However, that is often not the case. There should always be some form of hint or clue that makes the question fairly feasible. In cases where there are comparatives or superlatives, work out the answer through evaluating the data with simple numbers rather than to work with never-ending numbers with decimals.

In 2011, the average cost per branch was 120 ÷ 200 = 0.6. Multiply the number of branches for the following years with 0.6 in order to see whether the actual yearly cost is higher or lower than the expected ratio from 2011.

For example, in 2012, the number of branches was 220. If the yearly cost were to be the same as that of 2011, it would be **220 x 0.6 = £132**. However, given that its actual yearly cost is £124, its average cost per branch must be lower than 2011's.
It can be extrapolated that, for all other years, the actual yearly cost is greater than the expected 0.6 figure from 2011. This means that the average cost per branch in all other years (except 2012) is greater than 0.6. Hence, the only year which the average cost per branch is lower than in 2011 is 2012. Therefore, **2012 has the lowest average cost per branch.**

86. C

Explanation:

The table may not be complete; however, fill in all the blanks before attempting any of the questions:

Products	Total numbers sold	Total numbers damaged	Total numbers produced	Production cost per number (£)	Retail price (£)	Profit per number (£)
Bread	1,500	50	1,550	1.20	8.00	6.80
Cookies	2,000	200	2,200	0.80	2.50	1.70
Macaroons	1,200	300	1,500	0.60	4.00	3.40
Scones	1,800	200	2,000	1.25	5.50	4.25
Cupcakes	1,250	350	1,600	1.50	6.00	4.50

Number of macaroon units sold: 1,500 - 300 = **1,200**
Number of cupcake units produced: 1,250 + 350 = **1,600**
Ratio: 1,200 : 1,600 = **3 : 4**

87. B

Explanation:

The individual cost due to damaged items for each item is as below:
Bread: 50 x 1.20 = **£60**; *Cookies:* 200 x 0.80 = **£160**; *Macaroons:* 300 x 0.60 = **£180**
Scones: 200 x 1.25 = **£250**; *Cupcakes:* 350 x 1.50 = **£525**
Total cost due to damaged items: 60 + 160 + 180 + 250 + 525 = **£1,175**

88. B

Explanation:

The additional profit that could have been made due to damaged items, for each item, is as below:
Bread: 50 x 6.80 = **£340**; *Cookies:* 200 x 1.70 = **£340**; *Macaroons:* 300 x 3.40 = **£1,020**
Scones: 200 x 4.25 = **£850**; *Cupcakes:* 350 x 4.50 = **£1,575**
Total cost due to damaged items: 340 + 340 + 1,020 + 850 + 1,575 = **£4,125**

89. D

Explanation:

Total profit made from bread: 1,550 x £6.80 = **£10,540**
Total profit made from macaroons: 1,500 x £3.40 = **£5,100**

Total profit made from both items: £10,540 + £5,100 = **£15,640**

90. B

Explanation:

'Expected' values are the mean (i.e., average) of all the involved values. The mean retail price of the items in the bakery is $\frac{8.00 + 2.50 + 4.00 + 5.50 + 6.00}{5}$ = **£5.20**.

Since Krantz is purchasing 12 items, the expected amount of money spent will be:
12 x £5.20 = **£62.40.**

91. C

Explanation:

Total number of cupcakes produced: **1,600**
Profit made if all cupcakes made were sold: 1,600 x £4.50 = **£7,200**

92. D

Explanation:

Total profit made from scones: 1,800 x £4.25 = **£7,650**
Total loss due to damaged scones: 200 x £1.25 = **£250**
Actual profit made from scones: £7,650 - £250 = **£7,400**

93. A

Explanation:

To get the maximum number of units, Demarco should spend all his money on the cheapest item. The item with the cheapest retail price per unit is the cookies, which is £2.50 per unit. With £1,000, he would be able to purchase **£1,000 ÷ £2.50 = 400 units of cookies**. This brings a profit of **400 x £1.70 = £680** to the bakery.

94. E

Explanation:

One can approach this question by calculating the profit per cost of each item or by qualitatively interpreting the data to arrive at an answer.

Profitability = Profit ÷ Cost

If one were to calculate the profit per cost of each item, one would get:

Bread: £6.80 ÷ £1.20 = **5.67...**; *Cookies:* £1.70 ÷ £0.80 = **2.125**; *Macaroons:* £3.40 ÷ £0.60 = **5.67...**; *Scones:* £4.25 ÷ £1.25 = **3.4**

Cupcakes: £4.50 ÷ £1.50 = **3 (second least profitable product)**

If one was to evaluate the numbers:

First, note that the profitability of the bread and the macaroons are equal. The cost of making a unit of bread and the profit of selling a unit of bread are both exactly double that of macaroons. Hence, both cannot be the answer. Looking at the numbers, it can be extrapolated that that the profitability figures for both bread and macaroons are at least 5.

Estimate that the profitability figure for cookies is approximately 2, since 1.70 can be approximated to 1.60; hence, **1.60 : 0.80 = 2.**

It is fairly straightforward that the profitability figure of cupcakes is **£4.50 ÷ £1.50 = 3**.

The profitability figure of scones has to be greater than 3. This is because, if its figure were to be 3, then the profit per unit of scones would be **3 x £1.25 = £3.75**. Given that it is £4.25, the figure must be greater than 3.

At this point, one should be able to deduce that **cupcakes are the second least profitable product.**

95. A

Explanation:

To answer this question, focus on the column 'total units produced' and use the figures worked out in the previous question (Q94).

Essentially, ROI is the 'profitability' of a product multiplied with the total units produced. Bear in mind that all units produced are assumed to be sold.

Bread: £6.80 ÷ £1.20 = **5.67...**; *Cookies:* £1.70 ÷ £0.80 = **2.125**,

Macaroons: £3.40 ÷ £0.60 = **5.67...**; *Scones:* £4.25 ÷ £1.25 = **3.4**

Cupcakes: £4.50 ÷ £1.50 = **3**

The profitability of bread and macaroons are the same. However, more bread was sold. Hence, bread has a higher ROI than macaroons. Bread has a similar number of items sold as that of cupcakes. However, bread is much more profitable than cupcakes. Thus, bread has a higher ROI than cupcakes. Even though fewer units of bread were sold compared to cookies, bread was at least twice more profitable than cookies. Hence, it has a higher ROI than cookies. The number of units of bread sold is approximately 75% of the total units of scones sold. However, the profitability figure of scones is less than 75% of that of bread. The decimal 3.4 only approximates to about 60% of 5.67.... As a result, this means that **bread also has a higher ROI than scones.**

96. E

Explanation:

The number of laptops sold by Stark and Lexcorp in 2007 are 18,000 and 21,000 respectively. The ratio would be 18,000 : 21,000 = **6 : 7.**

97. E

Explanation:

Considering the graph, Wayne consistently sold more laptops than Lexcorp and Stark across the 6 years. Hence, these two companies can be put aside for the time-being. Cyberdyne and Ace had better sales than Wayne in earlier years; however, Wayne did better than both companies in the later years. Despite this, it's best to do some calculations for these 3 companies to be sure of their order.

(When performing calculations, ignore the '000' as they are constants for all the values. This will apply to the following explanations as well).

Ace: 24 + 32 + 25+ 14 + 10 + 12 = **117**

Cyberdyne: 30 + 34 + 22 + 14 + 18 + 22 = **140**

Wayne: 23 + 26 + 22 + 19 + 20 + 25 = **135**

From this, it can be deduced that **Wayne must be the company with the second highest number of sales across the 6 years.**

98. C

Explanation:

Total number of laptops sold by Lexcorp: 20 + 24 + 21 + 18 + 18 + 19 = **120**

Average number of laptops sold in 6 years: $\frac{120}{6} = 20$ **(20,000)**

99. B

Explanation:

From the previous question, the total number of laptops sold by Ace, Cyberdyne, Lexcorp, and Wayne are 117, 140, 120, and 135 respectively.

Total number of laptops sold by Stark: 19 + 20 + 18 + 16 + 18 + 20 = **111**

Total number of laptops sold by all 5 companies:

117 + 140 + 120 + 135 + 111 = 623 <u>(623,000)</u>

100. C

Explanation:

The number of laptops sold by Stark and Ace in 2007 is 18 and 25 respectively. Stark sold <u>25 - 18 = 7 laptops lesser than Ace</u>.

Express this as a percentage of the number of laptops sold by Ace:

$\frac{7}{25} \times 100 = \underline{28\%}.$

101. E

Explanation:

Average number of laptops sold by all 5 companies in 2005:

$\frac{24 + 30 + 20 + 19 + 23}{5} = \underline{23.2}$

Average number of laptops sold by all 5 companies in 2010:

$\frac{12 + 22 + 19 + 20 + 25}{5} = \underline{19.6}$

Difference in averages calculated: 23.2 - 19.6 = 3.6 <u>(3,600)</u>

102. A

Explanation:

Total number of laptops sold by all 5 companies in 2006:

32 + 34 + 24 + 20 + 26 = <u>136</u>

Total number of laptops sold by all 5 companies in 2009:

10 + 18 + 18 + 18 + 20 = <u>84</u>

The reduction in the total number of laptops sold is <u>136 - 84 = 52</u>. Expressed as a fraction, this is $\frac{52}{136} = \mathbf{\frac{13}{34}}$

103. E

Explanation:

The highest sales of Ace is 32 and the lowest is 10. The percentage decrease is:

$\frac{32 - 10}{32} \times 100 = \underline{68.75\%}$ (69% after rounding off)

104. E

Explanation:

The increase between 2009 and 2010 for Wayne and Cyberdyne is 5,000 and 4,000 respectively. **<u>Wayne has a steeper increase and a higher starting point as well</u>**. If the trend continues, both lines will never meet.

105. B

Explanation:

The increase for Ace is 2,000. The number of laptops sold in 2010 is 12,000. Let the number of years after 2010 be 'n'. After 'n' years, the number of laptops sold would be 12 + 2n.

The increase for Lexcorp is 1,000. The number of laptops sold in 2010 is 19,000. After 'n' years, the number of laptops sold would be 19 + n.

Given that the number of laptops sold will be the same:

12 + 2n = 19 + n

<u>n = 7</u>

Hence, for a continuous trend, it will take **7 years after 2010** for the number of laptops sold by both companies to be the same.

106. A

Explanation:

Total number of pairs of shoes in Patras: 40 + 50 + 120 + 140 + 80 = **430**

Total number of pairs of shoes in Larissa: 30 + 120 + 115 + 65 + 50 = **380**

Difference in the number of shoes stocked: 430 - 380 = **50**

107. D

Explanation:

The new number of Model 'C' shoes is 50 x 1.9 = **95.** The new total number of shoes in Kallithea is 5 + 8 + 95 + 6 + 36 = **150**. The percentage of Model 'E' shoes would be $\frac{36}{150}$ x 100 = **24%.**

108. D

Explanation:

The new number of Model 'B' shoes is 210 x 0.7 = **147**. The number of Model 'D' shoes in Athens is **75**. The required ratio would be 147 : 75 = **1.96 : 1.**

109. E

Explanation:

The initial number of Model 'A' shoes is 40. An increase of 130% would mean the increase in the shoe count is **40 x 1.3 = 52**. To maintain the same number of shoes at the store, the number of Model 'E' shoes must reduce accordingly. Given that the original number of Model 'E' shoes is 80, the percentage decrease in this must be:

$\frac{52}{80}$ x 100 = **65%.**

110. E

Explanation:

The average number of shoes available per model in Heraklion is:

$$\frac{60 + 80 + 75 + 45 + 20}{5} = \underline{56}$$

111. D

Explanation:

From previous questions, the total number of pairs of shoes in Kallithea, Larissa, Patras and Heraklion are 105, 380, 430 and 280 respectively. The total number of shoes in Athens is **120 + 210 + 260 + 75 + 55 = 720**. Hence, the total number of shoes in all 5 stores is **105 + 380 + 430 + 280 + 720 = 1,900**.

Expressed in a pie chart, the angle of Larissa's sector would be:

$\frac{380}{1{,}900}$ x 360 = **72°**

112. E

Explanation:

Total revenue from sales of Model 'D': 65 x 6 = **£390**

If all 8 pairs of Model 'B' shoes were sold, this would generate a revenue of:

45 x 8 = **£360**

Hence, it is **impossible to meet the revenue generated from Model 'D'**.

113. D

Explanation:

Option 'A' - This is false because the store in Athens has the greatest number of shoes for only three different models compared to the rest of the stores.

Option 'B' - This is false because Model 'A' is the third most available shoe in only two stores.

Option 'C' - While this is true for Papoutsia stores, it is not certain that it is the case for the whole of Greece. This is because the question has mentioned that the shoes are also sold by other retail companies.

Option 'E' - This is false because the store in Kallithea has the least number of shoes for only four models when compared to the rest of the stores.

114. B

Explanation:

Option 'A' - This is true. The difference in the number of Model 'C' shoes available between Patras and Kallithea (70) is greater than the difference in the number of Model 'D' shoes available between Patras and Athens (65).

Option 'B' - This is false. In the Heraklion branch, the number of Model 'B' shoes (80) is equal to the total of Model 'A' and Model 'E' shoes combined ($60 + 20 = 80$).

Option 'C' - This is true. The percentage of Model 'E' shoes of all shoes available in the Larissa branch ($\frac{50}{210} = \frac{5}{21}$) is greater than the percentage of Model 'A' shoes of all shoes available in the Athens branch ($\frac{120}{720} = \frac{1}{6}$).

115. A

Explanation:

From previous questions, the total number of pairs of shoes in Kallithea, Larissa, Athens, Patras and Heraklion are 105, 380, 720, 430 and 280 respectively. Kallithea is the only branch of which the proportion of Model 'C' shoes approximates to half of the shoes available in the store ($\frac{50}{105}$). **The proportion of Model 'C' shoes for the rest of the stores is well below half of the total number of shoes available in each respective store.**

116. B

Explanation:

In each given year, the number of times a 'flat' line occurs between 2 consecutive months in Sabah is 4. Hence, from 2010 to 2013, the 4 occurrences repeat 4 times;
4 x 4 = 16. In 2009, it occurs twice after July. In 2014, it occurs once before April. In total, the 'flat' line occurs **$16 + 2 + 1 = 19$ times**.

117. D

Explanation:

In each year, there is a general increasing trend in the average rainfall from January to June. Hence, there are 5 months in which we see an increasing trend. However, in Sabah, the month of March and June have the same average rainfall as the previous month. Thus, there are only 3 months that meet the criterion. However, there is a trick to this question. Looking at average rainfall in December compared to that in January, the average rainfall increases for both cities. Therefore, technically, in each year, there are 4 months (January, February, April and May) which have an average rainfall greater than its previous month.
Between 2014 and 2019, this occurrence repeats 6 times:

6 x 4 = 24

In 2013, this does not occur at any time after September. In 2020, this occurs 4 times as well. Hence, in total, there are **24 + 4 = 28 instances** where a month meets the criterion of the question.

118. C

Explanation:

The greatest difference in the average rainfall between the two cities: **100 mm**

The smallest difference in the average rainfall between the two cities: **20 mm**

Thus, the greatest difference is **5 times bigger than the smallest difference.**

119. E

Explanation:

The greatest change between the two consecutive months in Sabah: 120 mm (between April and March)

The smallest change in the average rainfall between the two cities: 10 mm (between December and January)

Thus, the ratio would be 120 : 10 = **12 : 1.**

120. B

Explanation:

First, work out the difference in the average rainfall for each month. Next, sum them up together to get: 30 + 20 + 100 + 40 + 40 + 60 + 60 + 20 + 40 + 20 + 60 + 40 = 530 mm = **53 cm**.

The average per month would be $\frac{53}{12} = 4\frac{5}{12}$

Rounded off to the nearest 0.5 cm is **4.5 cm.**

121. D

Explanation:

This question requires one to find the total number of patients who fall under the overlap of the circle and the 12-sided polygon and at least one other shape.

This will be: 62 + 89 + 99 = **250**

122. C

Explanation:

This is relatively straightforward. However, do keep in mind that being COVID-19 positive is not a symptom. The only area bounded by 3 shapes (that is not the 12-sided polygon) has **99 patients.**

123. B

Explanation:

Find the relevant figures which represent the overlap of any two shapes that is not the 12-sided polygon.

The total would be 62 + 159 + 18 + 28 + 174 + 28 + 89 = **558.**

124. E

Explanation:

Total number of patients with one symptom and was tested positive:

102 + 195 + 193 = **490**

Total number of patients with one symptom and was tested negative:

120 + 179 + 113 + 120 = **532**

Thus, the ratio is 490 : 532 = **35 : 38.**

125. E

Explanation:

Option 'A' - One cannot be certain of the number of patients who were asymptomatic and tested positive as that information is not provided in the diagram.

Option 'B' - This is false. All patients who presented with shortness of breath and loss of taste tested positive for COVID-19.

Option 'C' - This is false as shortness of breath is the most common symptom among those who tested positive.

Option 'D' - This is false. Of those who presented with fever, the number of individuals who also had shortness of breath is the same as the number of individuals who experienced a loss of taste.

---

126. D

Explanation:

Calculate how times greater the number of girls is compared to the number of boys:

$\frac{800000}{500000}$ = 1.6 times more girls than boys

Therefore, the sport played by girls must be 1.6 times greater than the sport played by boys, in order for girls to be more likely to participate in the sport.

Consider Hockey:

Number of girls = 35,000; Number of boys = 60,000

35000 x 1.6 = **56,000**

Since 56,000 is less than 60,000, **boys are more likely to play Hockey**.

Consider Cricket:

Number of girls = 20,000; Number of boys = 25,000

20000 x 1.6 = **32,000**

Since 32000 is more than 25000, **girls are more likely to play Cricket**.

Consider Swimming:

Number of girls = 34,000; Number of boys = 12,000

34000 x 1.6 = **54,400**

Since 54400 is more than 12,000, **girls are more likely to Swim**.

Consider Tennis:

Number of girls = 12,000; Number of boys = 34,000

12000 x 1.6 = **19,200**

Since 19,200 is less than 34,000, **boys are more likely to play Tennis**.

Consider Netball:

Number of girls = 50,000; Number of boys = 2,000

50000 x 1.6 = **80,000**

Since 80000 is more than 2,000, **girls are more likely to play Netball**.

Consider Football:

Number of girls = 82,000; Number of boys = 85,000

82000 x 1.6 = **131,200**

Since 131,200 is more than 85,000, **girls are more likely to play Football**.

Therefore, girls are more likely to participate in **Cricket, Swimming, Netball and Football** in this scenario.

127. A

Explanation:

Calculate the total number of boys who play these 6 sports:

60000 + 25000 + 12000 + 34000 + 2000 + 85000 = **218,000**

Calculate the total number of girls who play these 6 sports:

35000 + 20000 + 34000 + 12000 + 50000 + 82000 = **233,000**

Percentage of boys who play these 6 sports (total number of boys is half a million):

$\frac{218000}{500000}$ x 100 = **43.6%**

Percentage of girls who play these 6 sports (total number of girls is a million):

$\frac{233000}{1000000}$ x 100 = **23.3%**

Therefore, the difference in the percentages:

43.6% - 23.3% = **20.3%**

---

128. C

Explanation:

Calculate the number of children who play Hockey, Netball or Football in the UK:

60000 + 35000 + 2000 + 50000 + 85000 + 82000 = **314,000**

0.2 x 314000 = **62,800** (number of children who play Hockey, Netball or Football in Wales)

In one week:

62800 x 2 = **125,600** (number of individual sessions because each child has 2 sessions)

Therefore, over 2 weeks:

125600 x 2 =**251,200**

Calculate the number of children who participate in Cricket, Swimming or Tennis in the UK:

12000 + 34000 + 34000 + 12000 + 25000 + 20000 = **137,000**

0.2 x 137000 = **27,400** (number of children who play Hockey, Netball or Football in Wales)

In two weeks:

27400 x 1 = **27,400** (number of individual sessions because each child has 1 session every two weeks)

Therefore, total number of individual sessions:

251200 + 27400 = **278,600**

---

129. B

Explanation:

Girls who play tennis = 12,000; Boys who play hockey = 60,000

Therefore,

$\frac{60000}{12000}$ = **5** (5 times more boys play hockey compared to girls who play tennis)

Therefore, the section for boys who play hockey must be **5 times greater** than the section for girls who play tennis.

The pie chart that **best approximates this is Graph 'B'**.

---

130. E

Explanation:

Children under the age of 10 is represented by the crescent. Therefore, children over the age of 10 are situated **outside the crescent**. Those who attend formal education are represented by the **arrow**. The heart represents those who participate in more than 3 sporting activities. As a result, those who participates in only 3 sporting activities will be located **outside the heart**.

Therefore, the overall calculation:

$34 + 8 =$ **42**

131. E

Explanation:

Consider the children over the age of 10 who do not attend formal education but watch more than 8 hours of television:

Children over the age of 10: **outside the crescent**

Do not attend formal education: **outside the arrow**

Watch more than 8 hours television: **inside the triangle**

Therefore, the region which is within the triangle but outside the crescent and the arrow has: **17 children**

Consider the children under the age of 10 who attend formal education and watch more than 8 hours of television:

Children under the age of 10: **inside the crescent**

Attend formal education: **inside the arrow**

Watch more than 8 hours television: **inside the triangle**

Therefore, the overlap will represent the children under the age of 10 who attend formal education and watch more than 8 hours of television:

3 children

As a result, the difference is:

$17 - 3 =$ **14 children**

132. G

Explanation:

Calculate the number of children under the age of 10:

$24 + 30 + 5 + 3 + 22 = 84$

Since 84 represents 30% of the children under 10 in Oxford:

$84 \div 0.3 =$ **280 children**

Therefore, there are **280 children under the age of 10 in Oxford**.

133. A

Explanation:

Calculate the number of children who participate in more than 3 sporting activities (in the heart shape):

$24 + 15 + 6 = 45$ (this will be the denominator)

Under the age of 10:

Overlap of crescent and heart = 24 children

Therefore, the probability:

$$\frac{24}{45} = \mathbf{\frac{8}{15}}$$

In formal education:

Overlap of arrow and heart = 6 children

Therefore, the probability:

$$\frac{6}{45} = \mathbf{\frac{2}{15}}$$

134. C

Explanation:

Find the number of children under 10 who are in formal education but do not watch more than 8 hours of television:

Data Analysis

Number that is where the crescent and arrow overlaps, but not triangle –
22 children
Find the number of children under 10 who watch 8 hours of television but do not attend formal education:
Number of children where the crescent and triangle overlaps, but not the arrow:
5 children
Therefore, total number of children:
22 + 5 = **27 children**

135. B

Explanation:
Consider the number of children under the age of 10 (inside the crescent):
24 +30 + 5 + 3 + 22 = **84 children**
Consider the number of children over the age of 10 (outside the crescent):
15 + 6 + 34 + 8 + 17 = **80 children**
Therefore, difference in number:
84 – 80 = **4 children**

136. D

Explanation:
Consider the top bar:
Its data is consistent with **Edward** (0.98 at GCSE and 1.00 at A-Level)
Consider the second bar:
Its data is consistent with **Tim** (0.50 at GCSE and 0.25 at A-Level)
Consider the third bar:
Its data is consistent with **Rebecca** (0.45 at GCSE and 0.67 at A-Level)
Consider the fourth bar:
Its data is consistent with **Emma** (0.27 at GCSE and 0.87 at A-Level)
Consider the fifth bar:
Its data is consistent with **Samuel** (0.23 at GCSE and 0.67 at A-Level)
Consider the sixth bar:
Its data is consistent with **Max** (1.00 at GCSE and 0.34 at A-Level)
Consider the seventh bar:
Its data is consistent with **Judy** (0.10 at GCSE and 0.68 at A-Level)
Consider the eighth bar:
Its data is consistent with **Bella** (0.87 at GCSE and 0.98 at A-Level)
Consider the ninth bar:
Its data is consistent with **Lily** (0.02 at GCSE and 0.34 at A-Level)
*Therefore, the child who isn't on the graph is **Maggie**.*

137. C

Explanation:
Consider the two Fantas:
When a student buys two drinks, they will receive a Blueberry cupcake for free. Therefore, since this student is buying two Fantas, **the Blueberry cupcake will be free.**
The cost of the two Fantas:
£1.45 x 2 = **£2.90**
Consider the price of the Cookie Dough Cupcake at 50% off:
0.5 x 80 = **40 pence**

The overall amount to pay:
£2.90 + £0.40 = **£3.30**
From a £5 note, the change received:
£5.00 - £3.30 = **£1.70**

138. B

Explanation:

Percentage decrease = $\frac{\text{decrease}}{\text{original}}$ x 100

Original for Fanta is £2.50 and the original for Sprite is £3.75

Consider Fanta:

Percentage decrease = $\frac{2.50-1.45}{2.50}$ x 100

Percentage decrease = **42%**

Consider Sprite:

Percentage decrease = $\frac{3.75-1.20}{3.75}$ x 100

Percentage decrease = **68%**

Therefore, the difference in percentage decrease:
68% - 42% = **26%**

139. F

Explanation:

Consider the minimum profit:
Find the amount spent to make 1 cupcake: £3.60 ÷ 24 = **15 p**
The amount spent to make two cupcakes: 15 p x 2 = **30 p**
The cheapest cupcake is Blueberry (20 p). Therefore, two Blueberry cupcakes: 20 p x 2 = **40 p**
Minimum profit from two cupcakes: 40 p – 30 p = **10 p**
Find the amount spent to buy one soft drink: £13.20 ÷ 12 = **£1.10**
The cheapest soft drink is Diet Coke (£1.20).
Minimum profit from one soft drink: £1.20 – £1.10 = **10 p**
Therefore, the minimum profit from two cupcakes and one soft drink: 10 p + 10 p = **20 p**
Consider the maximum profit:
The amount spent to make two cupcakes: 15 p x 2 = **30 p**
The most expensive cupcake is Chocolate Raspberry (90 p). Therefore, two Chocolate Raspberry cupcakes: 90 p x 2 = **£1.80**
Minimum profit from two cupcakes: £1.80 – 30 p = **£1.50**
The amount spent to buy one soft drink: £13.20 ÷ 12 = **£1.10**
The most expensive soft drink is 7Up (£1.85).
Minimum profit from one soft drink: £1.85 – £1.10 = **75 p**
Therefore, the maximum profit from two cupcakes and one soft drink: £1.50 + 75 p = **£2.25**
The difference in maximum and minimum profits:
£2.25 – 20 p = **£2.05**

140. A

Explanation:

Find the difference between the monthly precipitation in each month:
January: 90 – 80 = **10**; February: 90 – 50 = **40**; March: 70 – 60 = **10**

April: 50 – 10 = **40**; May: 60 – 40 = **20**; June: 60 – 20 = **40**
July: 20 – 10 = **10**; August: 80 – 60 = **20**; September: 60 – 30 = **30**
October: 100 – 80 = **20**; November: 120 – 80 = **40**; December: 120 – 40 = **80**
Total difference:
10 + 40 + 10 + 40 + 20 + 40 + 10 + 20+ 30 + 20 + 40 + 80 = **360**
Average precipitation per month (divide by 12):
360 ÷ 12 = **30 mm**

141. E

Explanation:
Consider the period July 2016 – December 2016:
There is **one instance** of a straight line (November – December), which indicates the monthly precipitation is the same.
Consider the period January 2017 – December 2019:
Per year, there are 3 instances of a straight line (January – February, May – June and November – December). Therefore, in three years, there will be:
3 x 3 = **9 instances of straight lines between two consecutive months**
Consider the period January 2020 – June 2020:
There are **two instances** of a straight line (January – February and May – June), which indicates the monthly precipitation is the same.
Therefore, the total number of instances:
1 + 9 + 2 = **12**
There are **12 instances** where monthly precipitation between two consecutive months are the same.

142. B

Explanation:
Calculate the number of customers who did not complain about the price of the sweets:
2242 - 880 = **1362 customers**
The number of individuals who indicated that the variety of flavours and the taste of the sweets were more important than the price of the sweets: **227 customers**
Therefore, the probability:
$$\frac{227}{1362} = \frac{\mathbf{1}}{\mathbf{6}}$$

143. B

Explanation:
Calculate the number of people who received an online questionnaire:
0.8 x 6250 = **5000**
Calculate the number of people who didn't complete the online questionnaire:
5000 - 4420 = **580**
Therefore, the percentage of customers who did not respond:
$\frac{580}{5000}$ x 100 = 11.6% (**rounds to 12% to the nearest integer**)

144. C

Explanation:
Calculate the number of individuals who noticed a change in the price after one complaint:
880 - 350 = **530**
Since 60% of these people noticed a decrease in the quality of the sweets:
0.6 x 530 = **318 customers**

145. D

Explanation:

Consider the percentage of people who stopped buying sweets from Candy Land due to price: <u>39%</u>

Calculate the percentage of people who stopped buying sweets from Candy Land due to poor customer service: $\frac{450}{2242}$ is approximately **<u>20%</u>**

Therefore, the difference in percentage:

39% - 20% = **<u>19%</u>**

---

146. C

Explanation:

Calculate the number of customers Chocolate Bliss have: 1.2 x 6250 = 7500

Since only 60% of these customers could be sent an online questionnaire: 0.6 x 7500 = 4500

Calculate the number of customers at Chocolate Bliss who completed the online questionnaire: 0.25 x 4500 = 1125

Calculate the number of customers at Chocolate Bliss who had stopped buying their products: 0.2 x 1125 = 225

Since 20% of these customers thought that the price was unfair:

<u>A total of 80% stopped buying products for reasons other than price.</u>

Therefore,

0.8 x 225 = **<u>180 customers</u>**

---

147. A

Explanation:

Try to draw the individual shapes within the larger shape to see if it fits. **<u>Option 'A' is the only answer</u>** where all three shapes fit together with no overlap:

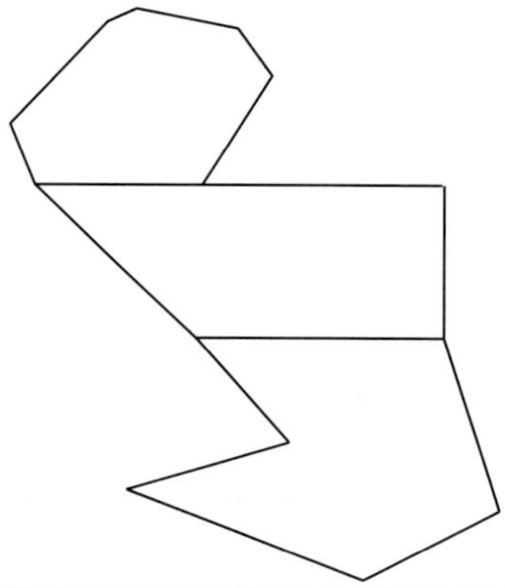

---

148. D

Explanation:

The base coat of white will cost him:

£0.35 x 9 = **<u>£3.15</u>**

As he did alternate stripes of blue and red as the second coat, each colour will occupy a total area of 4.5 m^2 as they are both painted with equal widths.

Therefore, the cost of the second coat will be:

(£0.40 x 4.5) + (£0.60 x 4.5) = **<u>£4.50</u>**

The total cost is:

£3.15 + £4.50 = **£7.65**

149. B

Explanation:

30% x 50 = **15 tablets**

Therefore, each medium packet contains 15 extra tablets. Buying 2 of these packets means that the customer gets an extra 30 tablets. Buying the large packet means that the small packet comes for free; hence, there are 20 extra tablets. In total, the customer receives:

30 + 20 = **50 extra tablets**

The total number of tablets are:

(50 x 2) + 100 + 50 = **250**

Express the extra tablets as a percentage of the total tablets the customer bought:

$\frac{50}{250} \times 100 = \underline{20\%}$

150. A

Explanation:

Try to visualise the net folding into a cube. Alternatively, one may take a clean cuboid rubber into the exam to draw the shapes on, in order to get the correct orientation. The base of the triangle is next to the trapezium in the net and when folded the pentagon will also come to lie adjacent to the triangle. **Option 'B' is incorrect** as the triangle and circle are on the wings of the net so when it is folded, these two shapes would lie opposite to each other. **Option 'C' is wrong** as shapes that are one square apart on the net will lie opposite to each other so the hexagon and pentagon cannot be next to each other. Similarly, to Option 'C', the trapezium and square are one space apart so they cannot be adjacent - **Option 'D' is wrong**. The positions of the shapes in **Option 'E' is incorrect** since the base of the triangle should be adjacent to the trapezium and not the hypotenuse.

151. B

Explanation:

The total number of chocolate coated nuts is:

180 – 117 = **63**

Exactly 2 in 7 of this is chocolate coated cashew nuts. *This is:*

63 ÷ 7 = 9

9 x 2 = **18**

The total number of cashew nuts are:

180– (32 + 40 + 43) = **65**

The total number of plain cashew nuts are:

65 – 18 = **47**

Therefore, the probability that a cashew nut is plain out of all the cashew nuts is:

$\frac{47}{65}$

152. E

Explanation:

Statement 1 may not be true as the absolute number of boys in each year is unknown. A greater proportion of boys below Year 9 who do more than 30 minutes of exercise does not equate to a greater number of boys than those in Years 10 or 11. **Statement 2 is not true** either as there is no information regarding Years 12 or 13 boys; hence, it cannot be assumed that the trend will continue. Without the information of pupils in Years 12 and

13, one cannot make valid comparisons between girls and boys. Therefore, **Statement 3 is incorrect**. Without any information about the proportion of boys doing more than 30 minutes of exercise in Years 12 and 13, **Statement 4 cannot be deduced** from the information provided.

153. C

Explanation:

For ease of calculation, one can round the numbers.

Therefore, the total number of people in sparse settings are:

$190,000 + 300,000 + 90,000 =$ **580,000**

This has to be expressed as a percentage of the total population (which is rounded to 54,000,000):

$$\frac{580,000}{54,000,000} \times 100 = \underline{1.1\ \%\ \text{approximately}}$$

154. D

Explanation:

Option 'A' is false as there is very little difference between male and female students between 1990 and 1993. **Option 'B' is false** as there is a slight overall increase; however, it isn't constant as there are some fluctuations in the trend. **Option 'C' is false** because the increase from 11% to 28.4% is less than 3 times from 1984 to 2017. **Option 'D' is correct** since the steepest negative gradient is in this period. **Option 'E' is not true** as the pattern of male students of having a greater percentage of single occasion risky drinking compared to female students may not continue into the future.

155. E

Explanation:

Option 'A' may not be true as the table only displays the consumer spending as a percentage of GDP; the actual amounts are not known. **Option 'B' cannot be concluded** from the information given. **Option 'C' may not be true** since the value of the GDP in each of the countries is not known. Even if the percentage of consumer spending in India accounts for a greater proportion of the GDP than in Canada, the actual amount is unknown. **Option 'D' also cannot be concluded** because there is no information regarding GDP. **Option 'E' is the correct answer** since it mentions the consumer spending as a proportion of GDP.

156. B

Explanation:

Since Poppy completes more questions than Lily, scan the table for a few values where Poppy completes a very high number of questions and Lily completes a low number of questions. These correspond to the days 17th July and 12th June. The difference in 17th July is 37 and the difference in 12th June is 36. Therefore, **17th July** shows the biggest difference in the number of questions. On this day they both got a **total of 26 questions correct**.

157. D

Explanation:

The highest marks on either quiz were by:

Student '8' – 56 (Quiz 1), Student '12' – 55 (Quiz 1) and the third one would be Student '12' – 53 (Quiz 2). However, since this student has already been chosen for the team, the third member is Student '2' – 52 (Quiz 2).

Anyone else who scores **52 – 5 = 47** or higher in either quiz will be kept as reserves.

These would include **Students '4', '6', '10' and '11'**. Therefore, there are **4 reserves.**

158. B

Explanation:

Calculate the sum of all the rows and columns. The sum of the column with workers from Office 'D' has a total of 73 instead of 70. Therefore, it must be a number from this column. This **eliminates Options 'C' and 'E'**. The sum of the column showing the number of workers doing 60 minutes of exercise totals to 88 instead of 85. Therefore, the **incorrect value was 13** in the column with workers from Office 'D' and the row showing those who do 60 minutes of exercise.

159. F

Explanation:

Calculate the number of products sold in 2019:

400 + 350 + 350 + 150 + 350 + 200 = **1800 products**

The number of cleaning products sold in 2019: **400**

The number of beverages sold in 2019: **350**

Since there were 25% more products sold in 2019 compared to 2020:

$x \times 1.25 = 1800$

$x = \frac{1800}{1.25}$

$x =$ **1440 products sold in 2020**

Calculate the number of cleaning products sold in 2020:

(There are 360° in a circle)

$\frac{85}{360} \times 1440 = \underline{340}$

Calculate the number of beverages sold in 2020:

$\frac{35}{360} \times 1440 = \underline{140}$

Percentage decrease:

$\frac{\textbf{decrease}}{\textbf{original}} \times \mathbf{100}$

Percentage decrease of cleaning products:

$\frac{400 - 340}{400} \times 100 = \underline{15\%}$

Percentage decrease of beverages:

$\frac{350 - 140}{350} \times 100 = \underline{60\%}$

Therefore, difference in percentage decrease:

60% - 15% = **45%**

160. A

Explanation:

Since there were 25% more products sold in 2019 compared to 2020:

$x \times 1.25 = 1800$

$x = \frac{1800}{1.25}$

$x =$ **1440 products sold in 2020**

Calculate the number of pharmaceutical products sold in 2020:

(There are 360° in a circle)

$\frac{85}{360} \times 1440 = \underline{340}$

Calculate the number of jewellery sold in 2020:

(There are 360° in a circle)

$\frac{50}{360}$ x 1440 = **200**

Therefore, the difference in pharmaceutical products compared to jewellery in 2020:

340 - 200 = **140**

---

161. B

Explanation:

Calculate the number of products sold in 2019:

400 + 350 + 350 + 150 + 350 + 200 = **1800 products**

The probability of a cosmetic product in 2019:

$\frac{350}{1800} = \frac{\mathbf{7}}{\mathbf{36}}$

Since there were 25% more products sold in 2019 compared to 2020:

x x 1.25 = 1800

$x = \frac{1800}{1.25}$

x = **1440 products sold in 2020**

Calculate the number of cosmetic products sold in 2020:

(There are 360° in a circle)

$\frac{40}{360}$ x 1440 = **160**

Therefore, probability of a cosmetic product in 2020:

$\frac{160}{1440} = \frac{\mathbf{1}}{\mathbf{9}}$

Therefore, difference in probability:

$\frac{7}{36} - \frac{1}{9} = \frac{\mathbf{1}}{\mathbf{12}}$

---

162. A

Explanation:

Number of jewellery sold in 2019:

200

Therefore, 100 are 18 carat gold:

100 x 18 x £10.50 = **£18,900**

100 are 12 carat gold:

100 x 12 x £10.50 = **£12,600**

Number of jewellery sold in 2020:

Since there were 25% more products sold in 2019 compared to 2020:

x x 1.25 = 1800

$x = \frac{1800}{1.25}$

x = **1440 products sold in 2020**

Calculate the number of jewellery sold in 2020:

(There are 360° in a circle)

$\frac{50}{360}$ x 1440 = **200**

One carat of gold in 2020 sells for 50% less:

£10.50 ÷ 1.5 = £7.00

200 jewellery are 6 carat gold:

6 x £7 x 200 = **£8400**

Therefore, total amount of money made on jewellery in 2019 and 2020:

£8400 + £12600 + £18900 = **£39,900**

---

163. B

Explanation:

Since there were 25% more products sold in 2019 compared to 2020:

x x 1.25 = 1800

$x = \frac{1800}{1.25}$

x = **1440 products sold in 2020**

Consider Cleaning products:

In 2019 - **400 products sold**

In 2020 - $\frac{85}{360}$ x 1440 = **340 products sold** (360° in a circle)

Difference: 400 - 340 = **40 more products in 2019 were sold**

Consider Beverages:

In 2019 - **350 products sold**

In 2020 - $\frac{35}{360}$ x 1440 = **140 products sold** (360° in a circle)

Difference: 350 - 140 = **210 more products in 2019 were sold**

Consider Cosmetics:

In 2019 - **350 products sold**

In 2020 - $\frac{40}{360}$ x 1440 = **160 products sold** (360° in a circle)

Difference: 350 - 160 = **190 more products in 2019 were sold**

Consider Furniture:

In 2019 - **150 products sold**

In 2020 - $\frac{65}{360}$ x 1440 = **260 products sold** (360° in a circle)

Difference: 260 - 150 = **110 more products in 2020 were sold**

Consider Pharmaceutical products:

In 2019 - **350 products sold**

In 2020 - $\frac{85}{360}$ x 1440 = **340 products sold** (360° in a circle)

Difference: 350 - 340 = **10 more products in 2019 were sold**

Consider Jewellery:

In 2019 - **200 products sold**

In 2020 - $\frac{50}{360}$ x 1440 = **200 products sold** (360° in a circle)

Difference: 200 - 200 = **0 more products in 2019 were sold**

Therefore, the greatest decrease from 2019 to 2020 was:

Beverages (210 more were sold in 2019)

---

164. B

Explanation:

Consider the number of females under the age of 18 who purchased summer dresses and four different items in one purchase:

- Under the age of 18 - inside the L-shape

- Summer dresses - inside the circle
- Four different items in one purchase - outside the parallelogram (because it is not more than four)

Looking at the diagram, there are **8 females** who are inside the L-shape and the circle, but outside the parallelogram.

Consider the number of females over the age of 18 who purchased summer dresses:

Since the diagram only represents females, individuals outside the L-shape are females over the age of 18. Therefore, there are **2 females** who are outside of the L-shape but inside the circle.

As a result, the difference in females: 8 - 2 = **6 females**

165. D

Explanation:

Calculate the number of females who are under 18:

19 + 45 + 12 + 16 + 8 = **100 females**

From the graph, the number of females who purchased clothing items in 2020: **190 females**

Therefore, the percentage: $\frac{100}{190}$ = **52.631...% (53% to the nearest percent)**

166. A

Explanation:

Calculate the number of females who are over 18:

Add the numbers **outside the L-shape:** 35 + 12 + 25 + 7 + 9 + 2 = **90 females**

Consider the number of females who are over 18 and who purchased a pink jumpsuit:

- Females over 18 - outside the L-shape
- Purchased a jumpsuit - inside the hexagon
- Purchased a pink item - inside the cross

Therefore, there were **12 females** who are outside the L-shape, but inside the hexagon and the cross.

The probability: $\frac{12}{90} = \mathbf{\frac{2}{15}}$

167. E

Explanation:

Percentage increase = $\frac{\text{increase}}{\text{original}}$ x 100%

Consider males:

- In 2014 - **10 items purchased**
- In 2017 - **90 items purchased**

Therefore, percentage increase: $\frac{90-10}{10}$ x 100% = 800%

Consider females:

- In 2014 - **50 items purchased**
- In 2017 - **140 items purchased**

Therefore, percentage increase: $\frac{140-50}{50}$ x 100% = **180%**

Therefore, difference in percentage increase: 800% - 180% = **620%**

168. A

Explanation:

Profit = Total exports - Total imports

Use approximations to quickly calculate an estimate.

Calculate the total profit of Barbados: 1.7 - 0.4 = 1.3

Therefore, the total profit compared to the total exports: $\frac{1.3}{1.7}$ = **0.76...**

Calculate the total exports by UAE: 35 + 250 = 285

Therefore, the total profit compared to the total exports: $\frac{35}{285}$ = **0.12....**

Calculate the total exports by Spain: 87 + 284 = 371

Therefore, the total profit compared to the total exports: $\frac{87}{371}$ = **0.23.....**

Calculate the total profit compared to the total exports of UK: $\frac{65}{695}$ = **0.09...**

Calculate the total profit of India: 478 - 312 = 166

Therefore, the total profit compared to the total exports: $\frac{166}{478}$ = **0.35.....**

Calculate the total exports by Japan: 21 + 685 = 706

Therefore, the total profit compared to the total exports: $\frac{21}{706}$ = **0.03.....**

Calculate the total profit compared to the total exports of China: $\frac{5000}{27000}$ = **0.18...**

Calculate the total profit of Canada: 485 - 446 = 39

Therefore, the total profit compared to the total exports: $\frac{39}{485}$ = **0.08...**

Calculate the total profit compared to the total exports of Australia: $\frac{58}{272}$ = **0.21...**

As a result, the country that had the biggest total profit compared to the total value of the exports was **Barbados**.

---

169. C

Explanation:

Calculate the percentage difference from exporting vehicles compared to precious metals and pharmaceuticals combined in Japan:

49.6 - (13.2 + 4.5) = **31.9%** (round to 30% for convenience)

Calculate the total exports by Japan: 21 + 685 = **706**

Therefore, 0.3 x 706 = 211.8

Therefore, **211.8 billion USD** more was made in Japan selling vehicles compared to precious metals and pharmaceuticals combined.

Since 1 US Dollar equals 110 Japanese Yen:

211.8 billion USD x 110 = 23298 billion Japanese Yen (approximately **23 trillion Japanese Yen**)

---

170. B

Explanation:

Use approximations to quickly calculate an estimate.

Looking at the table, China has the largest number of exports and the percentage of pharmaceuticals is the third highest (after Barbados and UAE). Therefore, there is only a need to consider Barbados, UAE and China.

Consider Barbados: 17.8% of 1.7 = **0.30... billion USD**

Consider UAE: 16.7% of total exports.

Calculate the total exports by UAE: 35 + 250 = 285

16.7% of 285 = **47.6...billion USD**

Consider China: 6.2% of 27000 = **1674... billion USD**

Therefore, **China** has the highest value of exports from pharmaceuticals.

171. C

Explanation:

*Since the question is asking the money made from exporting vehicles, **the information regarding imports can be disregarded.***

Calculate the value of exports by India in 2020: 110% of 478 = **525.8 billion USD**

10.8% of this was from vehicles: 10.8% of 525.8 = **56.7...billion USD** (rounded to 57 billion USD)

172. E

Explanation:

Consider the profits made in Coffee House on a Saturday from the graph:

£65

Since $\frac{21}{26}$ *are from Coffee Lattes:* $\frac{21}{26}$ x 65 = £52.50

From the first graph, a Coffee Latte from Coffee House in October costs **£7.50**

£52.50÷ £7.50 = **7 Coffee Lattes sold on Saturday**

Consider the profits made in The Roasted Bean on a Saturday from the graph:

140 - 65 = £75

Since $\frac{18}{25}$ *are from Coffee Lattes:* $\frac{18}{25}$ x 75 = £54

From the first graph, a Coffee Latte from The Roasted Bean in October costs **£1.50**

£54 ÷ £1.50 = **36 Coffee Lattes sold on Saturday**

Therefore, the total number of Coffee Lattes: 36 + 7 = **43 Coffee Lattes**

173. B

Explanation:

From the first graph, find the price of a Coffee Latte at Coffee House in April:

£3.00

A Flat White is 20% cheaper: £3.00 x 0.8 = **£2.40**

From the first graph, find the price of a Coffee Latte at The Roasted Bean in April:

£5.00

A Flat White is 30% more expensive: £5.00 x 1.3 = **£6.50**

Since £1 is equivalent to $1.30:

Convert £2.40 into $: 2.40 x 1.3 = **$3.12**

Convert £6.50 into $: 6.50 x 1.3 = **$8.45**

Therefore, the change received from a $5 note: $5.00 - $3.12 = **$1.88**

The change received from a $10 note: $10.00 - $8.45 = **$1.55**

Total change received: $1.88 + $1.55 = **$3.43**

174. A

Explanation:

Add the weekly profits of Coffee House using the second graph:

£55 + £50 + £40 + £45 + £25 + £65 + £50 = **£330**

Add the weekly profits of The Roasted Bean using the second graph:

£45 + £65 + £40 + £25 + £65 + £75 + £70 = **£385**

Therefore, the difference in weekly profits:

385 - 330 = **£55.00**

175. D

Explanation:

Calculate the total profits in The Roasted Bean each week:

£45 + £65 + £40 + £25 + £65 + £75 + £70 = **£385**

Therefore, in one month: 385 x 4 = **£1540**

Considering the first graph, in February, each Coffee Latte is: **£7.50**

In two weeks, 16 are sold: £7.50 x 16 = **£120**

Therefore, in a month: 120 x 2 = **£240**

Therefore, the percentage: $\frac{240}{1540} = \frac{12}{77}$

$\frac{12}{77}$ is approximately 16%

---

176. D

Explanation:

Calculate the total number of dishes ordered in 2020: 1.35 x 1200 = 1620

Calculate the number of Chicken Fajitas ordered in 2017: 8% of 1200 = 96

Calculate the number of Chicken Fajitas ordered in 2020: 15% of 1620 = 243

Therefore, the difference in Chicken Fajitas ordered between 2017 and 2020: 243 - 96 = 147

---

177. C

Explanation:

Calculate the total number of dishes ordered in 2020: 1.35 x 1200 = 1620

Calculate the number of Chicken Teriyaki Pineapple Bowls ordered in 2017:

0.15 x 1200 = 180

Calculate the number of Chicken Teriyaki Pineapple Bowls ordered in 2020:

0.12 x 1620 = 194.4

Therefore, the percentage increase: $\frac{194.4-180}{180}$ x 100 = 0.08 (8%)

---

178. B

Explanation:

Calculate the total number of dishes ordered in 2020: 1.35 x 1200 = 1620

Calculate the number of Mexican Chicken Pasta dishes ordered in 2017:

0.14 x 1200 = 168

Calculate the number of Mexican Chicken Pasta dishes ordered in 2020:

0.05 x 1620 = 81

Therefore, the percentage increase: $\frac{168-81}{168}$ x 100= 51.78... (52%)

---

179. A

Explanation:

Calculate the price of Grilled Chicken Breasts: 16.5 x 1.1 = **£18.15**

Since Thai Peanut Skillet Chicken costs 5% less than Grilled Chicken Breasts in 2017: 0.85 x 18.15 = 15.4275 (**£15.43** to the nearest pound)

Since Thai Peanut Skillet Chicken costs 35% more than Grilled Chicken Breasts in 2020: 18.15 x 1.35 = 24.5025 (**£24.50** to the nearest pound)

Therefore, the difference in prices: 24.50 - 15.43 = **£9.07**

180. D

Explanation:

Calculate the initial number of dishes ordered in 2020: 1.35 x 1200 = **1620**

Calculate the number of Parmesan Chicken Cutlets initially ordered in 2020:

0.3 x 1620 = **486**

Since 145 were unaccounted: 1620 + 180 = **1800 total dishes ordered**

Therefore, the percentage of these that are Parmesan Chicken Cutlets:

$\frac{486}{1800}$ x 100 = **27%**

181. E

Explanation:

Calculate the number of students represented in the diagram:

18 black dots and 11 grey dots: 18(2) + 12(5) = **96**

Let x be the number of students in the year:

x x 0.8 = 96; $x = 96 \div 0.8$; x = **120**

Therefore, there are 120 students in the whole year.

Calculate the number of students who study French:

6 black dots and 3 grey dots: 6(2) + 3(5) = **27**

The number of students who study French in the year: $\frac{27}{120}$ x 100 = **22.5%**

182. B

Explanation:

Calculate the number of students who study History:

6 black dots and 3 grey dots: 6(2) + 3(5) = **27**

Calculate the number of students who study Spanish and History:

2 black dots and 1 grey dot: 2(2) + 1(5) = **9**

Calculate the number of students who study Art and History:

1 black dot and 1 grey dot: 1(2) + 1(5) = **7**

Therefore, the overall probability: $\frac{7+9}{27} = \frac{\mathbf{16}}{\mathbf{27}}$

183. A

Explanation:

Calculate the number of students who study French:

6 black dots and 3 grey dots: 6(2) + 3(5) = **27**

Therefore, the number of students who study Welsh: 27 ÷ 3 = **9**

Calculate the number of students who study Art:

5 black dots and 4 grey dots: 5(2) + 4(5) = **30**

Therefore, the number of students who study Psychology: 30 x 0.8 = **24**

Therefore, the difference: 24 - 9 = **15 students**

184. D

Explanation:

Calculate the number of students who studied Geography and German in 2020:

2 black dots and 1 grey dot: 2(2) + 1(5) = 9

Let x be the number of students who studied Geography and German in 2019:

x x 1.8 = 9; $x = 9 \div 1.8$; x = **5**

Calculate the number of students who studied French and German in 2020:

2 black dots: 2(2) = 4

Let x be the number of students who studied History and Spanish in 2019:
$x \times 0.25 = 4$; $x = 4 \div 0.25$; $x = \underline{16}$
Therefore, the difference in the number of students: 16 - 5 = **11 students**

185. A

Explanation:
Consider Bank 'A':
From Graph 1, the interest rate in 2018 for more than £5000 is 3%.
At the end of 2018: £6000 x 1.03 = **£6180**
From Graph 1, the interest rate in 2019 for more than £5000 is 4%.
At the end of 2019: £6480 x 1.04 = **£6427.20**
Consider Bank 'B':
From Graph 2, the interest rate in 2018 for greater than or equal to £5000 is 1%.
At the end of 2018: £5000 x 1.01 = **£5050**
From Graph 2, the interest rate in 2019 for more than £5000 is 0.4%.
At the end of 2019: £5050 x 1.004 = **£5070.20**
Therefore, the difference: £6427.2 - £5070.2 = **£1357**

186. C

Explanation:
Consider Bank 'A';
From Graph 1, the interest rate in 2019 for less than £5000 is 0.5%.
At the end of 2019: £2000 x 1.005 = £2010
From Graph 1, the interest rate in 2020 for less than £5000 is 2%.
At the end of 2020: £2010 x 1.02 = **£2050.20**
Consider Bank 'B':
From Graph 2, the interest rate in 2019 for more than £5000 is 0.4%.
At the end of 2019: £10000 x 1.004 = £10040
From Graph 2, the interest rate in 2020 for more than £5000 is 3%.
At the end of 2020: £10040 x 1.03 = **£10341.20**
Therefore, the combined total: £10341.20 + £2050.20 = **£12391.40**

187. D

Explanation:
From Graph 2, the interest rate in 2019 for less than £5000 is 0.7%.
At the end of 2019: £4000 x 1.007 = **£4028**
Since £3000 is added to the same bank account: £4028 + £3000 = **£7028**
From Graph 2, the interest rate in 2020 for more than £5000 is 3%.
At the end of 2020: £7028 x 1.03 = **£7238.84**

188. B

Explanation:
From Graph 1, the interest rate in 2018 for greater than or equal to £5000 is 3%.
At the end of 2018: £5000 x 1.03 = **£5150**
From Graph 1, the interest rate in 2019 for more than £5000 is 4%.
At the end of 2019: £5150 x 1.04 = **£5356**
From Graph 1, the interest rate in 2020 for more than £5000 is 2%.
At the end of 2020: £5150 x 1.02 = **£5253**
Therefore, the percentage increase: $\frac{5253-5150}{5150} \times 100 = \underline{0.02\ (2\%)}$

189. B

Explanation:

Consider Bank 'A':

From Graph 1, the interest rate in 2020 for more than £5000 is 2%.

At the end of 2020: £6000 x 1.02 = **£6120**

From Graph 1, the interest rate in 2021 for more than £5000 is 4%.

At the end of 2021: £6120 x 1.04 = **£6364.80**

Since the interest rate increases to 5% in 2022: £6364.8 x 1.05 = **£6683.04**

Consider Bank 'B':

From Graph 2, the interest rate in 2020 for more than £5000 is 3%.

At the end of 2020: £6000 x 1.03 = **£6180**

From Graph 2, the interest rate in 2021 for more than £5000 is 1%.

At the end of 2021: £6180 x 1.01= **£6241.80**

Since the interest rate increases to 5% in 2022: 6241.8 x 1.05 = **£6553.89**

Therefore, the difference: £6683.04 - £6553.89 = **£129.15**

PS	PROBLEM SOLVING	Questions

1. **Hadley, Bartlett, Franco, Arturo, Zdenek, Maurice, Taillefer and Gaetana are all members of a committee, which consists of a President and a Vice President. The committee is temporarily divided into a few (i.e., more than one) departments when it comes to organising events. Each department has a Chair and a Vice-Chair while the rest are considered Volunteers. Each team has at least one Volunteer. To ensure the whole committee is monitored efficiently, the President and the Vice President will always work in different departments as Chairs or Vice-Chairs. Assume that the President and Vice President are of the same hierarchy. This applies to Chairs and Vice-Chairs as well.**
   For an upcoming event, the committee is divided such that no two departments have the same number of Volunteers working in them. Taillefer and Zdenek are of the same hierarchy and they work together. One of them also works alongside Gaetana, however, this is only temporary. Bartlett is best known for her designing skills and she enjoys taking the lead in the Publicity and Design Department when it comes to projects. She particularly likes to keep her department as small and focused. Zdenek, Gaetana and Hadley have no experience in designing, but Hadley and Gaetana are keen to learn the skill and Zdenek avoids it if given a choice.
   Who is Maurice?
   A. A Vice-Chair who is working alongside Zdenek.
   B. A Volunteer working under Gaetana's department.
   C. A Volunteer working alongside Arturo and no one else.
   D. The President of the committee.
   E. A Volunteer working under Taillefer's department.

2. **In a toy shop, all the alien toys are green as are all plushies. Dinosaurs are not aliens. Which of the following must be true?**
   A. All green toys are plushies or aliens.
   B. All dinosaurs are plushies.
   C. Dinosaur toys are not green.
   D. No alien toys are plushies.
   E. Some dinosaurs may be plushies.
   F. None of the above.

3. **Complete the following number sequence: 1, 4, 27, 256, 3,125, ...**
   A. 34284
   B. 37192
   C. 40008
   D. 46656
   E. 51125

4. **Two circular buttons of different sizes are in contact but they do not overlap one another. Button 1 has a radius that is five times bigger than that of Button 2's radius. Button 2 rolls around Button 1 in one full motion and returns to its original position.**
   How many times will Button 2 revolve till it reaches its initial position again?
   A. 4
   B. 4.5

C. 5
D. 5.5
E. 6

5. **Sheldon is 16 years older than Shenton. In 3 years, the sum of their ages will be 64. If the current year is 2020, at which year was Shenton born? (Assume that Shenton's birthday in 2020 has passed).**
   A. 1983
   B. 1990
   C. 1992
   D. 1999
   E. 2002

6. **During the new launch of the iShuffle touch-screen digital player, Kompani & Co. gave a 'buy one, free one' deal to the first 250 customers at their store. However, each customer is limited to only one purchase and both units must be in different colours. The common colours of the iShuffle were recorded as a percentage of the total of the first 250 customers. The records show that, of the iShuffles sold and given away for free, 58% were rose, 44% were alabaster, 32% were turquoise, 26% were shamrock and 18% were daffodil.**
   Which statement below must be true?
   A. No more than 55 customers purchased turquoise and shamrock iShuffles.
   B. A minimum of 6 customers purchased rose and alabaster iShuffles.
   C. The records above only included 445 customers.
   D. There was a minimum of 95 customers who did not purchase alabaster nor daffodil iShuffles.
   E. None of the above.

7. **This morning, Owen went running around a park that is situated nearby his place. After some time, he had completed one seventh of his intended distance. Upon completing another four rounds around the park, he had completed one fifth of the journey.**
   How many rounds did Owen set out to cover this morning?
   A. 60
   B. 70
   C. 95
   D. 120
   E. 140

8. **In a university, there are 300 students in the Year 2 cohort of the Law programme. All students are required to choose between EU Law and Tort Law as a compulsory module. No student is allowed to take up both modules. 65% of students take up Criminal Law, 72% of the students take up Company Law and 80% of the students take up Land Law. One other module offered by the university is Medical Law. All students are required to take four modules.**
   What is the percentage of students that took up Medical Law?
   A. 34%
   B. 44%
   C. 50%
   D. 75%
   E. 83%
   F. Can't tell

9. **Allaba is 3 km directly north of Messex. Toroto is situated 9 km directly south of Vincetown. Chance is 6 km directly west of Allaba and is 7 km directly east of Vincetown.**
   Which if the following cannot be reliably concluded from the information given above?
   A. Toroto is south of Messex.
   B. Allaba is north of Toroto.
   C. Vincetown is north of Messex.
   D. Toroto is west of Chance.
   E. Chance is east of Messex.

10. **Asia Rail is a train company that charges passengers at a rate of £1.40 per mile travelled, and an additional £3 for each international border it crosses during the journey. On the other hand, Tren & Co. charges passengers a flat rate of £40 regardless of the number of international borders crossed. It, however, charges a rate of 60 pence per mile travelled.**
    Rahul travels from Vietnam to Thailand for an outstation getaway trip. He knows that the journeys offered by both train services will pass through a country at some point of the journey. The price of the journey offered by both train services is the same.
    How many miles is Rahul travelling?
    A. 36.5 miles
    B. 38 miles
    C. 42.5 miles
    D. 46.25 miles
    E. 52 miles

11. **Tyron invests £4,000 in a bank account with an interest rate of 6% per annum. Assuming if he doesn't withdraw any money from the bank account, how much money will he have after 5 years? (Round off the answer to the nearest pound).**
    A. £4,897
    B. £5,353
    C. £8,280
    D. £12,523
    E. £41,943

12. **Pensel is a bookstore which sells different types of stationery. They give a 20% discount when a customer purchases 20 or more units of each item, and a 30% discount when a customer purchases 30 or more units. Parham visited the store one day to buy 22 pens and 10 rulers and paid £28.12. The next day, Jeremy pays £32.40 for 30 erasers and 25 pens while his friend, Shirley pays £24.50 for 50 rulers.**
    How much would Erick have to pay if he purchases 10 erasers, 20 rulers and 30 pens?
    A. £40.40
    B. £37.90
    C. £35.60
    D. £34.80
    E. £32.50

13. **There are five individuals in a family. The sum of the ages of each combination of the four individuals are 60, 62, 62, 64 and 80.**
    How old is the oldest individual in this family?
    A. 12 years old
    B. 14 years old
    C. 16 years old
    D. 18 years old

Problem Solving

E. 20 years old
F. 22 years old
G. 24 years old

14. Ollie normally buys a basket of watermelons from his local supermarket every weekend. This basket is said to weigh 10 kg but there is a 1% uncertainty to the scale. This means that the basket of watermelons could range from 1% above to 1% below the suggested weight.
Two weeks ago, the basket had four watermelons. Last week, there were six. This week's basket has two times the number of watermelons of the first week. The watermelons in the respective baskets turned out to have the same weight.
What is the maximum possible difference between the heaviest and lightest watermelon purchased by Ollie in the three weeks? (Assume that the weight of the basket is negligible).

A. 0.9805 kg
B. 1.0270 kg
C. 1.1315 kg
D. 1.2875 kg
E. 1.3565 kg

15. A group of engineering students are experimenting the model rockets they made. They fired two identical rockets towards each other at the same speed of 12.6 km/h. If it takes 0.2 seconds for the bodies of the rockets to fully cross each other, what was the length of the rockets?

A. 35 cm
B. 45 cm
C. 60 cm
D. 70 cm
E. 90 cm

16. Potato strips of varying length were placed in a hypertonic solution which caused them to decrease in length by 37%. They were then transferred to a hypotonic solution which causes them to increase in length by 22%.
What is the absolute percentage decrease in the original length of the strips?

A. 5%
B. 15%
C. 23.14%
D. 45.14%
E. 54.86%
F. None of the above

17. Meg's journey from her house to school involves walking to the bus station and catching a bus to school. The bus leaves the station at 25-minute intervals and the bus journey takes 45 minutes.
The school which Meg attends is a 10-minute walk from the bus stop where she gets off. If she arrives at the bus stop at 7:15 am, she gets to school at 8:25 am.
At what time wills she get to school if she arrives at the bus stop at 8:00 am?

A. 8:50 am
B. 9:05 am
C. 9:15 am
D. 9:25 am
E. 9:35 am
F. 9:45 am

18. Olly and Abigail are a couple who drive to and from work. Since their offices are in the same building, they normally carpool. One day, Olly has to stay back for 30 minutes as his company is rushing to complete an upcoming project. Given that they have to pick up their children from day-care, Abigail's friend offers her a lift to leave earlier so that she can fetch the children on time. The pick-up takes about 6 minutes. Abigail's friend drives a distance of 12 miles at the speed of 20 mph. Assuming that the day-care is along the route from work to home, at what speed does Olly have to drive to reach home at the same time as Abigail?
    A. 44 mph
    B. 50 mph
    C. 52 mph
    D. 60 mph
    E. 64 mph

19. Arendelle is a town that is located 10 miles northwest of another town called Corona. There are two other towns in the area, and they are named Monstropolis and Neverland. Every town is due North, South, East or West of at least two other towns.
    Which of one of the following statements below could be true?
    A. Neverland is 8 miles south of Arendelle and Monstropolis is 8 miles east of Arendelle.
    B. Monstropolis is 6 miles south of Arendelle and Neverland is 8 miles north of Corona.
    C. Neverland is 8 miles west of Corona and Monstropolis is 6 miles east of Arendelle.
    D. Monstropolis is 6 miles east of Arendelle and Neverland is 6 miles east of Corona.
    E. Neverland is 6 miles north of Corona and Monstropolis is 8 miles west of Corona.
    F. None of the above.

Problem Solving

20. Last year, 200,000 people in Country X were diagnosed with gonorrhoea. An average of 0.7 sexual partners was informed of the diagnosis. Of these, 3 in 5 have tests for gonorrhoea themselves. 25% of these tests come back positive.
    It was reported that each of the people diagnosed with gonorrhoea has an average of four sexual partners. Assume that none of them share sexual partners or have sex with each other. In addition to this, assume that the likelihood of having gonorrhoea is the same for those partners who are tested and those who are not.
    How many sexual partners who were not tested (whether informed or not) have gonorrhoea?
    A. 120,000
    B. 140,000
    C. 179,000
    D. 358,000
    E. 555,000
    F. 716,000

21. At a camp, the organiser has prepared four different meals for the participants - chicken rice, sandwich with crisps, stir-fried noodles and 'mini' pizzas. The participants in the camp are grouped and each group has four members. The students in the group queue up to collect their food. As the organiser distributes the food at random, he wants to make sure that no two consecutive students, in the same group, get the same meal. Assume that none of the participants have any dietary requirements nor preferences.
    Assuming that the organiser exhausted all possible orders of distributing the meals to the groups, what is the minimum total number of participants in the camp?
    A. 94
    B. 108
    C. 256

D. 432
E. 1024

22. **The average price of eight different types of chocolate bar in a given shop is £1.50, with the cheapest chocolate bar priced at 50 pence**
What is the maximum possible value for the most expensive chocolate bar?
A. £1.00
B. £2.50
C. £6.50
D. £7.00
E. £8.50
F. £9.50
G. £10.00

23. **Finn lives on a street with houses that are numbered oddly in a consecutive fashion. The total of all the house numbers along the street is 1,441.**
Which of the following information is required to determine the exact number of Finn's house?
1. At least four of the house numbers.
2. The relative position of Finn's house.
3. The greatest house number along the street.

A. 1 only
B. 2 only
C. 3 only
D. 2 and 3 only
E. 1 and 3 only

24. **Efa has a huge tank of 24 guppies, 9 of which are male. One day, she forgot to feed them, and two thirds of the guppies died, half of which were female. Over time, the females gave birth to some fries. Efa calculates that an average female guppy gives birth to 15 fries. However, only 40% of them survive after one week.**
Assuming if all female guppies give birth at the same time last week, how many live fish are there in the tank today?
A. 42 fish
B. 44 fish
C. 46 fish
D. 48 fish
E. 50 fish

25. **Four young men entered a cooking competition, where they are required to make a chicken dish. Meeko felt like he did not deliver his best, but he is grateful that he still managed to secure third place. Percy did better than the participant who made the roasted chicken and the participant who made the braised chicken did better than Roo. The participant who made the Hainanese chicken left the judges in awe and was awarded first place. Flit's *rendang* chicken did not come last, despite the meat being a bit overcooked.**
Which TWO of the following was not a result of the competition?
A. Flit came second.
B. Percy made braised chicken.
C. Roo came fourth.
D. Meeko made roasted chicken.

E. The braised chicken came in third place.
F. All of the above are true.

26. In a kindergarten, a group, which has b number of students, has a mean height of 96 cm. Another group, which has c number of students, has a mean height of 134 cm. When both groups are combined, the mean height of the group is 110 cm.
What is the value of c/b?

A. $\frac{5}{12}$
B. $\frac{7}{12}$
C. $\frac{19}{55}$
D. $\frac{36}{55}$
E. $\frac{48}{67}$
F. Can't tell

27. Harvey runs a business selling Mexican coffee buns at his local market. One day, he receives an order from a regular customer who requests 120 buns to be prepared for a school's Canteen Day, which begins at 8:00 am the following day. At any point, only 40 buns can go in the oven and the baking process will take 20 minutes. The buns would then need to be cooled down for 15 minutes before being packed. It takes Harvey an average of 10 seconds to pack each bun into a plastic bag. Harvey estimates that it will take him 35 minutes to deliver them. Assuming that Harvey prepares all the dough he needs the night before, what is the latest time Harvey has to start baking the buns the next morning?

A. 4:55 am
B. 5:30 am
C. 5:35 am
D. 6:03 am
E. 6:43 am

28. Lea arranges for herself a playlist of her 15 favourite songs, which she plays every day on her way to work. The playlist is such that each song will not be played again until all the other songs have been played. Lea normally selects the 'shuffle mode' so that the order of the songs are randomised. On her way to work this morning, the traffic was good so Lea arrived at work early and she only managed to listen to three songs during the journey.
How many other possible arrangements of songs could Lea have had during this morning's journey? (Assume that all the songs are of the same length).

A. 6
B. 36
C. 119
D. 978
E. 2,729

Questions 29-30 refer to the following information:

A salesman runs a 'spin-the-wheel' challenge to give out lucky draw prizes to customers who spend more than £20 on the company's products. The wheel consists of 6 different colours dedicated to a sector of the wheel. Each colour is dedicated to a number 1-6 and these colour-number matches are arranged in a consecutive clockwise manner. The wheel is placed vertically

upright and most of the wheel is covered in a black casing except for a small part where the pin points. This is where the colour spun can be seen.
Each customer is required to spin the wheel twice; the sum of the two numbers is subtracted from their product, e.g., If a customer spins "5" and "6", the resulting number will be (6 x 5) - (6 + 5) = 19. Prizes are given out to customers who manage to get numbers from 1 to 24.
A boy suspects that the salesman is not honest. He claims that the wheel is biased, and that area of the sectors are not equal. He adds that the probability of getting a negative, non-zero score is 0.64.

29. What is the probability of spinning a "1" on the wheel?

A. 0.4
B. 0.5
C. 0.6
D. 0.7
E. 0.8
F. Can't tell

30. How many times bigger is the area of Sector "1" compared to other sectors? Assume that all other sectors are of the same size.

A. $\frac{10}{3}$ times bigger
B. 5 times bigger
C. 7.5 times bigger
D. $\frac{35}{3}$ times bigger
E. 20 times bigger
F. Can't tell

31. Meredith is testing her arithmetic ability by playing with 6 six-faced die. She rolls all of them at once and she mentally calculates the product of the six figures obtained. For every round of die she rolls, what is the probability of her calculating a product that is even? (Assume that her calculations are all accurate).

A. $\frac{7}{8}$
B. $\frac{15}{16}$
C. $\frac{31}{32}$
D. $\frac{63}{64}$
E. $\frac{125}{126}$

32. Mariana is given a bottle and a cup. Their maximum capacities are half a litre and 300 ml respectively. None of these objects are graduated with marked lines. She is told to fetch exactly 0.4 litres of water from a nearby tap.
What is the minimum volume of water Mariana needs to ensure that she is able to fetch the right amount of water needed?

A. 300 ml
B. 400 ml
C. 500 ml
D. 900 ml
E. 1 litre
F. 1.2 litres

33. **A group of 16 friends hired a limousine for their school prom. The cost of the limousine was shared equally amongst them.**
If there had been 24 friends sharing the cost, the cost per passenger would have been £3 lower. Becca, one of the friends in the original group of 16, pays with a £20 note. How much change is she expected to receive?
A. £6.00
B. £9.00
C. £11.00
D. £13.00
E. £15.00
F. £17.00

34. **The word 'SURGEON' is coded as 'TTSHDNO', which itself is coded as 'UUTIEON'. What would be the second coding for the word 'PHYSICIAN'?**
A. RHAUIEIAN
B. OGXRJBJZM
C. QIZTHDHZO
D. PFWQIAIYN
E. RJAUGEGYP

35. **An average bullet train typically travels four times faster than a regular train. A regular train normally takes 12 minutes to travel from Touille to Kampong, which has a 7 kilometres distance.**
What is the speed of an average bullet train?
A. 120 km/h
B. 132 km/h
C. 140 km/h
D. 152 km/h
E. 160 km/h

Questions 36-37 refer to the following information:

A group of burglars divided themselves into three smaller groups to break into three different houses in a neighbourhood. This activated the alarm system in the three houses.

- The alarm of the first house makes a sound for 4 milliseconds, then goes off for 4 milliseconds and the process repeats.
- The alarm of the second house makes a sound for 5 milliseconds, then goes off for 5 milliseconds and the process repeats.
- The alarm of the third house makes a sound for 6 milliseconds, then goes off for 6 milliseconds and the process repeats.

All the alarms have just come on together a millisecond ago.

36. **When is the first time all three alarms will be quiet?**
A. 3 milliseconds later
B. 4 milliseconds later
C. 5 milliseconds later
D. 15 milliseconds later
E. 120 milliseconds later

37. **When is the next time all three alarms will come on together at the same time?**
A. 30 milliseconds later
B. 119 milliseconds later

Problem Solving

C. 0.12 seconds later
D. 959 milliseconds later
E. 0.96 seconds later

38. Two corpses were found in a forest. Radiocarbon dating is used to tell the age of the object from its date of death. The first corpse's age is the square of the second corpse. The age of the first corpse is an even number. Six years ago, the first corpse was 25 times the age of the second corpse.
What is the age difference between the two corpses?
A. 64
B. 72
C. 100
D. 120
E. 140

39. Nevaeh is the daughter of Quinn. Layla is Priscilla's mother. Maddox is Neveah's only brother. Quinn is the father of Rylee. Priscilla is Rylee's niece.
Which of the following statements is correct?
A. Priscilla and Neveah are cousins.
B. Quinn is Layla's daughter-in-law.
C. Maddox and Rylee are brothers.
D. Quinn is the grandmother of Priscilla.
E. Layla will be the aunt to Neveah's children.

40. Ms Wernicke plans to make apple juice for a New Year's dinner. She purchases 2 bottles of apple concentrate from her local supermarket. Each bottle has 1.25 litres of concentrate. She dilutes all the concentrate into a big bowl before serving it to her family members. During the party, both her two pairs of twins each drank 300ml of apple juice while her five nephews drank 250ml each. Ms Wernicke along with her four siblings and both their parents drank 350ml each. At the end of the night, there was 3,850ml of apple juice left in the bowl.
What ratio of the water to concentrate did Ms Wernicke use?
A. 3:1
B. 4:1
C. 4:3
D. 5:2
E. 7:2

41. Dalley's father owns an apple farm. Dalley plans to surprise his extended family with some apple crumble at their upcoming Christmas lunch party. Every morning, Dalley picks five apples from the farm. He knows that of his three siblings, who loves eating apples, eats an apple a day after their dinner. He estimates that he would need 15 apples in total. Once he has the number of apples needed, he will start baking the apple crumble.
What is the least number of days Dalley will take to save the number of apples needed to bake the crumble?
A. 5
B. 6
C. 7
D. 8
E. 9

42. My sister's phone passcode is twice my passcode, with 160 added to it. My brother's passcode is 160 more than double of my sister's passcode. My cousin's passcode is my brother's passcode multiplied by two, plus 160. All our passcodes are 4-digit numbers that do not begin with 0.
What is the biggest possible passcode that I can have?
A. 1109
B. 1219
C. 2359
D. 3449
E. 4879
F. Can't tell

43. Xyla and Yale want to know Zion's birthdate. Zion gives them 10 possible dates as below:

January	12	13		15		
February	12		14			
March				15	16	
April		13	14			17

Zion tells Xyla and Yale separately the month and the day of her birthday respectively. The conversation below follows.
Xyla: I don't know when Zion's birthday is, but I know that Yale doesn't know as well.
Yale: I initially didn't know when Zion's birthday was, but I know now.
Xyla: In that case, I know when Zion's birthday is too.
When is Zion's birthday?
A. 13th of January
B. 15th of January
C. 14th of February
D. 15th of March
E. 14th of April
F. None of the above

44. Adanna bought a shelf which was sold with a 40% discount off its original price *'s'*. She paid the cashier *'d'* dollars, and this included a 6% goods and services tax on the discounted price.
Which of the following represents *'s'* in terms of *'d'*?
A. $1.66d$
B. $\frac{d}{0.66}$
C. $0.66d$
D. $\frac{d}{(0.60)(1.06)}$
E. $(0.60)(1.06)d$
F. None of the above

45. An old lady tells her grandson, "All successful people are hardworking, but not all hardworking people are successful." Assume that the boy considers all famous people as successful and sad people as unsuccessful.
In the grandson's train of thought, which of the following is definitely false?
A. Some famous people are sad.
B. Some sad people are unsuccessful.
C. Some successful people are famous.
D. All famous people are hardworking.

46. Arthur sells durian packed in containers. There is a flat rate for the packaging fee and a rate per kilogram for the durian meat. It costs £16.40 for 4 kg of durian, and it costs £26.90 for 7 kg of durian.
    How much does 9 kg of durian cost?
    A. £33.90
    B. £25.10
    C. £41.40
    D. £35.10
    E. £39.80

47. A Biology teacher dilutes some concentrated glucose solution by 19:1 in preparation for her upcoming laboratory class. During the class, students use the prepared solution and dilute it further by 3:1 until their beaker is 90% full.
    If the full capacity of the beaker is 200 ml, how much concentrated glucose was used to prepare each beaker of diluted solution?
    A. 2.25 ml
    B. 2.5 ml
    C. 22.5 ml
    D. 25 ml
    E. 45 ml
    F. Can't tell

48. Rebekah enjoys using bath bombs whenever she uses the bathtub. A 'bath bomb' is a ball of hard-packed mixtures which effervesce when in contact with water. The ball has an initial volume of 140 cm^3. The packaging says that the ball reduces by 20% in size for the first 3 minutes then 30% for every subsequent minute.
    What size of the ball can Rebekah expect after 5 minutes, rounded off to the nearest cm^3?
    A. 25 cm^3
    B. 29 cm^3
    C. 32 cm^3
    D. 35 cm^3
    E. 41 cm^3

49. There were 21 students and a teacher in a Chemistry laboratory. Five students, who finished their work early, were about to leave for a break when one of them slipped and hit his head at the corner of the table. He fell to the floor and his head began to bleed. Everyone panicked while the teacher tried to control the situation. The lab assistant, who had arrived from the preparation room, was told by the teacher to call the ambulance. As the team of three paramedics arrived within the next 10 minutes, a third of the students, including the ones that were about to leave, had left the laboratory as they could not stand the sight of blood. Two of the school administrators had also arrived at the scene to speak with the teacher outside the laboratory. Thankfully, the paramedics were able to stabilise his neck and to mobilise him onto a stretcher.
    How many people were there in the laboratory before moving the boy out of the laboratory and into the ambulance?
    A. 17 people
    B. 18 people
    C. 19 people
    D. 20 people
    E. 21 people

50. The incomplete table below summarises the number of right leg dominant and left leg dominant football players by gender for the young adults at a local town. There are seven times as many females who are right leg dominant than females who are left leg dominant, and there are 12 times as many males who are right leg dominant than passed than males who are left leg dominant. None of the football players are both right and left leg dominant.

	Dominance	
Gender	Right Leg	Left Leg
Female		
Male		
Total		25

If there are 10 times as many young adults who are right leg dominant than young adults who are left leg dominant, what is the probability that a right leg dominant player selected at random is male?

A. 0.28
B. 0.4
C. 0.6
D. 0.72
E. 0.8
F. Can't tell

51. Reuben owns a business selling fresh banana milk. He is currently making the rota for the upcoming week for his employees Timothy, Noah and Zachary. Noah has informed Reuben beforehand that he will not be able to work on Thursday or Friday for the coming week. Timothy will work for five days and that will include Tuesday and Thursday. Zachary will have four days of work and his working days will be arranged in consecutively. Everyone will be required to work on Saturday, but they will be given a day off the following day. Each employee will either work for four or five days. During all weekdays, there must be two employees at the shop.
What days does Timothy work? (Assume that the first day of the week is Monday).

A. Tuesday, Wednesday, Thursday and Saturday
B. Monday, Wednesday, Thursday and Saturday
C. Monday, Tuesday, Friday and Saturday
D. Monday, Tuesday, Thursday, Friday and Saturday
E. Monday, Tuesday, Thursday and Saturday

52. Achara has two dogs, named Reggie and Miso. Their birthdays are two months apart and both birthdays coincidentally fall on the 15th of their respective months. On Achara's 18th birthday, her mother gets another dog, which happens to have a birthday that falls on the 15th of a particular month as well. Achara names this third dog Orsona as it was born five months after Miso's birthday. Achara is known to name her dogs such that the first letter is the same as the first letter of their birth month.
How many months after Orsona's birthday will Reggie have its birthday?

A. 3 months
B. 5 months
C. 6 months
D. 8 months
E. 9 months

Problem Solving

53. A music and drama school has 900 students where the male to female ratio is 1 to 1. Students in Year 2 must take up two compulsory language modules. In the first module, they get to choose between the French and Spanish language. In the second module, they have a choice between the Japanese and Korean language. A compulsory module is a module that is enrolled by students of all courses. All courses offered by the school are 3 years long. In 2019, one third of the Year 2 students decided to take up the French language. In the same year, a quarter of the Year 2 students took up the Japanese language. Assume that the intake of students every year is consistent. In addition, assume that the named language modules are not offered elsewhere in the programmes.
What is the difference between the minimum and the maximum number of boys that could have taken up both the Spanish and Korean language modules?
A. 25
B. 75
C. 100
D. 150
E. 200

Questions 54-57 refer to the following information:
Griffin takes the same modes of public transport to and from his factory where he works. Every morning, he takes the nearest ferry, that is a 5-minute walk from his place, to arrive at an underground station to catch the tube before walking 7 minutes to a central station to catch a bus. The bus stops at a station that is a 2-minute walk away from his factory. Griffin's boss is strict on having his employees arrive by 9:00 am each day.

Ferry	Underground Tube
7:43	7:47
7:49	8:00
7:59	8:15
8:05	8:21
8:14	8:30
8:26	8:37
8:44	8:42

- Underground costs £2.40 per journey. Each ride is 12 minutes long.
- Ferry costs £1.50 per journey. Each ride is 15 minutes long.
- Bus costs 60 p per journey.
- The fares are the same for weekdays and weekends.
- The bus starts operating from 6:09 am onwards and frequents every 10 minutes. Griffin's bus journey from the central station to her stop is usually 8 minutes long.

54. **What is the shortest travelling time possible for Griffin to arrive at his workplace?**
A. 52 minutes
B. 54 minutes
C. 55 minutes
D. 59 minutes
E. 60 minutes

55. One day, Griffin decided to take the taxi to the underground departure station instead of the ferry. He knows that it will take him 13 minutes to arrive at the underground station.
What is the latest time he should leave his place if he wants to arrive at the office 5 minutes early?
A. 7:33 am
B. 8:02 am
C. 8:15 am
D. 8:28 am
E. 8:42 am

56. Griffin goes to work 5 days per week for 40 weeks per year. Every other week, he has to go to work on a Saturday as well. Griffin is currently deciding if he should invest in an unlimited annual travel pass (valid for all modes of public transport). It is available for purchase at £1,250.
Between paying for the annual travel pass compared to paying for each journey individually, which is the cheaper option? How much will he save? Assume that he does not use public transport for any form of travel unrelated to work.
A. Purchase the annual pass; £370
B. Purchase the annual pass; £550
C. Purchase the annual pass; £730
D. Pay for individual journeys; £260
E. Pay for individual journeys; £400
F. Pay for individual journeys; £620

57. Griffin saves up enough money and now decides to drive to work, which is 27 km away. As he is new to driving, he often travels at an average speed of 20 m/s. However, he knows that the traffic normally increases his journey time by approximately 24 minutes. It takes him five minutes to park his car before arriving in person at the firm.
Approximately what is the latest time should Griffin leave his house for work?
A. 7:29 am
B. 7:43 am
C. 7:53 am
D. 8:08 am
E. 8:13 am

58. A series of numbers is given as 8, 5, 4, 9, 1, 7, 6, _, _, _. What are the three missing numbers?
A. 0, 2, 3
B. 2, 0, 3
C. 3, 0, 2
D. 0, 3, 2
E. 2, 3, 0
F. 3, 2, 0

59. A cheesemonger wants to prepare 12 equal sizes of cheese from a truckle of cheese (i.e., a cylindrical block of cheese). He intelligently does this with the least number of slices possible.
How many slices would he make to achieve this?
A. 3 slices
B. 4 slices
C. 5 slices
D. 6 slices
E. 7 slices

Problem Solving

60. Every year, a grandmother gives her grandchildren money at the end of the year based on their age (as of 1st of January) and their final exam results. Each child is given £10 plus £5 for every year that they are older than 10. Each child is also rewarded with £12 for every A+ achieved in their exam results. Callum is 17 and he achieved an A+ in his results this year. His sister, Suzie is four years younger than Callum, but she receives £7 more than the double amount that Callum gets. How many more A+ did Suzie get compared to Callum?
    A. 5
    B. 6
    C. 7
    D. 8
    E. 9

61. Benjamin, Christopher and Dominic are siblings who go to the same school and they cycle to and from school, which is placed 17 km from home. Benjamin cycles at a speed of 8 km/h, Christopher at a pace of 15 km/h and Dominic at 12 km/h. Benjamin finishes school an hour before Christopher who finishes school 20 minutes after Dominic. Assuming that they depart for home as soon as they finish, what order will the siblings arrive home?
    A. Benjamin, Christopher, Dominic
    B. Dominic, Christopher, Benjamin
    C. Christopher, Benjamin, Dominic
    D. Benjamin, Dominic, Christopher
    E. Dominic, Benjamin, Christopher
    F. Christopher, Dominic, Benjamin

62. A car travels from X to Y in 3.5 hours. The car has an average speed of 46 kilometres per hour for the first 2 hours and an average speed of 52 kilometres per hour for the whole journey. Assume that 1 kilometre per hour is 0.6 miles per hour.
    What was the car's average speed for the final one and a half hours of the journey?
    A. 36 mph
    B. 42 mph
    C. 56 mph
    D. 60 mph
    E. 72 mph
    F. 81 mph

63. A Mathematics teacher is teaching his class about the relationship between speed, distance and time. He tells them to imagine two swimmers who are swimming across the same given distance. The first swimmer, Joseph, does the breaststroke for half the time and the freestyle for the rest of it. The second swimmer, Daniel, does the freestyle for half the distance and the breaststroke for the rest of it. Both perform the freestyle stroke at the speed of 3 mph and the breaststroke at 1 mph. Joseph took 30 minutes to complete the distance.
    How long did Daniel take?
    A. 30 minutes
    B. 32 minutes
    C. 35 minutes
    D. 38 minutes
    E. 40 minutes

Questions 64-66 refer to the following information:

During a year-end clearance sale, the owner of a shoe shop decided to give a storewide discount offer to customers. The offer allows customers to enjoy a discount where the price of a pair of shoes is discounted by the square of the number of shoes purchased by the customer. For example, if a customer purchases two pairs of shoes which cost £100 each, he/she would have to pay £192 altogether.

64. Given the above information, how much would one have to pay if he/she purchases two pairs of shoes which cost £150 each and a third pair which costs £90?

A. £210
B. £244
C. £330
D. £363
E. £390

65. A group of 15 friends want to purchase the same model of shoe. Assuming that the cost price for all the shoes in the store is £20 and that the owner of the shop would ideally want to prevent making a loss, what is the minimum total amount of money that the group of friends is expected to pay in order for everyone to get the same model of shoe?

A. £2,775
B. £3,000
C. £3,375
D. £3,675
E. £3,900
F. Can't tell

66. A customer likes a particular model of shoe, which costs £192 per pair. This shoe is available in many different colours. She says that she is very fond of the previous pair that she has worn before. She wants to buy a few pairs of the same shoe this time around as the discount is very attractive.

What is the greatest number of shoes she can purchase in a single receipt?

A. 10
B. 11
C. 12
D. 13
E. 14
F. 15

67. The same customer in Question 65 purchases 'N' number of pairs of shoes and pays 'M' amount of money at checkout.

What is the value of 'N' if 'M' is at its maximum value?

A. 2
B. 5
C. 8
D. 11
E. 13

68. A chef runs a restaurant that is famous for making spicy noodles. The spicier the noodles, the better its taste - or at least, that's what customers enjoy most from his noodles. He also runs a side business of growing his own spices that are used in the recipe for his noodles as well. The cost of growing a kilogram of the spice is £96. The chef charges £2.40 for every 0.01 kg of spice added into a bowl of noodles. As an "incentive" for customers who enjoy increasing the

Problem Solving

level of spiciness in their noodles, he says that for every additional 5 grams of spice above the initial 10 grams, he reduces the extra cost by 20% lower than the linear increase of the given rate. What is the maximum amount of spice the chef can use whilst still making sure that its usage is cost-effective?

A. 20 grams
B. 25 grams
C. 30 grams
D. 35 grams
E. 40 grams

69. A school minibus can travel from Cardiff to Bristol in 36 minutes, provided it does not stop to pick up or drop off students. As the rear door takes a little more time to open compared to the front door, it normally takes about 100 seconds to drop off students and 80 seconds to pick up students. One day, the minibus picked up students from 8 stops and dropped students off at 6 stops.

What is the earliest estimated time of arrival at Bristol if the minibus departs from Cardiff at 8:00 am?

A. 8:49 am
B. 8:57 am
C. 9:01 am
D. 9:08 am
E. 9:13 am

70. Three different cakes may be purchased from a shop. The total price of Cake 1 and Cake 2 is £4.90. The total price of Cake 1 and Cake 3 is £6.10. The total price of Cake 2 and Cake 3 is £4.50.

How much more expensive is Cake 1 compared to Cake 3?

A. 20 pence
B. 40 pence
C. 60 pence
D. 80 pence
E. £1.00
F. £1.20
G. £1.40

71. Kaniel and his four friends are at a theme park for a day. They each spend some money on food during the trip. The mean and median amount of money spent by an individual is £16. The mode, however, is £25.

What must be the mean of the amount of money spent by three individuals in the group who spent the least?

A. £8
B. £10
C. £12
D. £14
E. Can't tell

72. The recipe Adrian uses to bake 16 lemon tarts requires 500 grams of crumbled cookies, 250 grams of butter, six lemons, two cans of condensed milk and four eggs. The cookies at his local supermarket are sold in packs of 100 grams and the butter is sold in blocks of 250 grams. The rest of the items can be purchased in single units. One day, he decides to bake for the neighbours along his street.

If each household in his neighbourhood is given an average of four tarts, what quantities of each ingredient must Adrian purchase?

A. 1,200 g of crumbled cookies, 500 g of butter, 16 lemons, 5 cans of condensed milk, 8 eggs

B. 1,375 g of crumbled cookies, 687.5 g of butter, 16.5 lemons, 5.5 cans of condensed milk, 11 eggs

C. 1,400 g of crumbled cookies, 687.5 g of butter, 17 lemons, 5.5 cans of condensed milk, 11 eggs

D. 1,400 g of crumbled cookies, 750 g of butter, 17 lemons, 5.5 cans of condensed milk, 11 eggs

E. 1,400 g of crumbled cookies, 750 g of butter, 17 lemons, 6 cans of condensed milk, 11 eggs

F. 2,000 g of crumbled cookies, 1,000 g of butter, 24 lemons, 8 cans of condensed milk, 16 eggs

---

73. Five friends are having a conversation.

Badrul: Only one of us is telling the truth.

Clyde: What Badrul says isn't true.

Klara: What Clyde says isn't true.

Naowarat: What Klara says isn't true.

Jihyo: What Naowarat says isn't true.

How many of them were not telling the truth?

A. 4

B. 3

C. 2

D. 1

E. 0

---

74. In a group of 50 adults who were 25 years old, a survey showed that 48% of them go to the cinemas at least once a month. Of these 48%, 5 in 6 of them go to the cinemas at least once a week. Exactly 35% of adults who go to the cinemas at least once a week do not subscribe to Netflix, while the rest do. Only 1 in 2 of the adults who go to the cinema less than once a month subscribe to Netflix.

What percentage of adults do not subscribe to Netflix?

A. 20%

B. 30%

C. 40%

D. 50%

E. 60%

---

75. Wanli, Carven, Sashi and Anthony are interim junior doctors on the Orthopaedic ward and their rota is flexible as long as they work in pairs. They must also obey the rule that the maximum number of consecutive days two doctors can work together is five, which Wanli and Carven now have. Sashi and Anthony have been working together for the last three days. If given a choice, Carven would normally try to avoid working with Anthony.

Who should work with Wanli the next day?

A. Carven

B. Sashi

C. Anthony

D. None of the above

76. In a BMAT Section 1 practice test, Andre scored higher than Karmen, who scored higher than Danyal. Firdaus scored higher than Danyal. Andre scored lower than Ciara.
Which of the following must be true?
A. Ciara scored lower than Danyal.
B. Firdaus and Andre attained the same scores.
C. Andre scored lower than Danyal.
D. Karmen and Firdaus attained the same scores.
E. Firdaus may have scored lower than Karmen.

77. Dates are often expressed in the format of dd/mm/yyyy. An example of such a date would be 01/01/1999. This date is made up of 3 different integers. What is the least number of days before 01/01/1999 that will give you a date that is made up of 4 different integers?
A. 3
B. 9
C. 10
D. 11
E. 15

78. The contents in table below show the product of the unknown integers in the first column and first row.
What does p + q + r + s equal to?
A. 195
B. 215
C. 250
D. 276
E. 280

	r	s
p	182	945
q	702	3,645

79. A school has four sports houses - Sapphire, Ruby, Emerald and Topaz. Each of them sends a representative for an upcoming triathlon and each student was assigned a number - I, II, III and IV. Every student also wore a shirt representing the colour of their house; sapphire - blue, ruby - red, emerald - green and topaz - yellow.
Barnabe wore Number III.
Cheung doesn't belong to the house Topaz nor did he wear a red shirt.
The student representing Sapphire wore IV. This student finished the race before the student who came third.
Only one student finished in the same position as the number of his shirt.
Demetrius finished the race before Barnabe.
Achille finished after Demetrius, but before the student who wore Number III.
Cheung finished first.
The student representing Ruby wore Number II.
Which of the following statements must be true?
A. Achille is from Topaz and was placed 3rd.
B. Cheung wore blue.
C. The student representing Emerald finished 4th.

D. The student who finished 3rd is from Ruby.
E. The student from Topaz wore I.

80. Every evening, Cindy buys a cup of bubble milk tea from Bobastry or Bubbleologist shops. To Cindy, both shops sell equally good bubble milk teas. However, given that they charge different prices, Cindy plans to work out which shop offers the best value for money for their drinks once the loyalty scheme has been taken into account. Bubbleologist and Bobastry sell each cup of bubble milk tea for £3.45 and £3.80 respectively. Bubbleologist uses a points system that offers 10 points for every full pound spent. Each point is worth 1p. Customers who collect sufficient points are entitled to a free cup of bubble milk tea. Bobastry offers a loyalty card which allows customers one stamp for every cup purchased. Upon collecting nine stamps, customers can trade the card for a free cup of bubble milk tea. In December, Cindy purchases her bubble milk tea from only one of these shops.
If Cindy had chosen the shop with the best value for money, which shop did she choose and how much did she save? Assume that Cindy had no stamps or points collected before December.
A. Bobastry, £2.80
B. Bubbleologist, £4.10
C. Bobastry, £3.90
D. Bubbleologist, £5.50
E. Bobastry, £5.25
F. Bubbleologist, £6.35

81. An anthropologist has a collection of 600 pieces of teeth each ranging from 1 to 600 years old (age from the date of death). No two pieces of teeth are of the same age. He keeps all these teeth in a display set. One day, he removes all the teeth which are multiples of 4. From the remaining set in the display, he then removes all the teeth which age is a multiple of 8. He then goes on to remove one third of the remaining set of teeth. Assume that each tooth has an average size of 3 mm x 4 mm x 5 mm and an average density of 2 g/cm^3.
What is the weight of the display set due to the remaining teeth?
A. 20 g
B. 32 g
C. 34 g
D. 36 g
E. 42 g

82. Hale looks at his analogue watch and reads the time as 11:26. What is the larger angle between the two hands on the clock?
A. 173°
B. 178°
C. 181°
D. 184°
E. 187°

Problem Solving

83. The table below shows the percentages of students from two different sports schools who represent their schools for different sports. Each student represents their school for only one sport. There are 1,500 students in School X. The number of students in School Y is 80% of that of School X. Table tennis, squash and badminton are considered as racquet sports.

	School X	School Y
Football	17.20	19.75
Table tennis	15.80	16.25
Baseball	20.60	13.25
Squash	9.40	17.50
Rugby	23.20	20.00
Badminton	13.80	13.25

How many more students in School X take up racquet sports compared to that in School Y?

A. 12 students
B. 21 students
C. 102 students
D. 120 students
E. 210 students

84. Harry and Harriet do not swim. Both Haroom and Harry ski. Both Hann and Haroom swim. Huzah does not ski or swim.

Which of the following is false?

A. Hann may only swim or ski and swim.
B. Harry only skis.
C. Huzah and Harry do the same sports.
D. Harriet may ski.
E. Huzah does not ski.

85. If you are overweight and below the age of 60, your risk of getting a Disease C is 1 in 3. For the same age group, if you are not overweight, you are half as likely to get the disease, but you are still twice as likely to get the disease as someone equal or above the age of 60. However, if you are overweight and equal or above the age of 60, you are twice as likely to get Disease C as someone in the younger age group. Research recently discovered a drug that gives off a side effect of increasing one's likelihood by 25% of getting Disease C.

If the guidelines state that patients who have a risk of developing a more than a 1 in 2 chance of getting Disease C should not be given the drug, to which patient groups can doctors safely prescribe the drug?

1. Overweight, below age of 60.
2. Overweight, equal or above age of 60.
3. Not overweight, below age of 60.
4. Not overweight, equal or above age of 60.

A. 2 only
B. 4 only
C. 3 and 4 only
D. 1, 2 and 3 only
E. 1, 3 and 4 only
F. All of the above

86. Ankara, Berlin, Cheyenne and Dakota are four friends who each enjoy a different genre of music: country, jazz, classical and dubstep. Ankara and Berlin enjoy accompanying their friend who is very keen to go for jazz nights. The fan of country music and Cheyenne often have dinner together at a restaurant where their friend plays classical music with a band. Berlin does not like country music but he will join his friend for concerts if the friend has a free ticket. Cheyenne never attends any of the jazz nights and she gives the excuse that she finds the place too crowded.
Who enjoys jazz music?
A. Ankara
B. Berlin
C. Cheyenne
D. Dakota
E. Can't tell

87. Capt. & Co. rents out fishing rods to visitors to fish at a nearby lake. They charge a standard flat rate as down payment and a half-hourly rate for the duration of the rental. Mahone rented one rod for six and a half hours and paid £73.50. Few days later, he returned with a few friends and rented three rods for half a day. They were charged £385.50.
How much would it cost one to rent two rods for 4 hours 30 minutes?
A. £53.50
B. £81.50
C. £107
D. £121
E. £163

88. There is a term derived from the Greek language that goes by *"paraskevidekatriaphobia"*, which translates to 'the fear of Friday the 13th'. This occurrence of Friday the 13th is often regarded as an unlucky day. Given that the 13th of March 2020 is a Friday, when was the previous time the 13th of a month happened to be a Friday?
A. September 2019
B. October 2019
C. November 2019
D. December 2019
E. January 2020
F. February 2020
G. None of the above

89. An optometrist shop is giving out free samples of contact lenses to 2,000 shoppers. The shop gives a dozen pairs of contact lenses to anyone who has purchased an item from them, and half a dozen pairs of contact lenses to anyone who did not make a purchase at their store.
If half of those who wear purchased items from their store and all of those who did not make a purchase at their store accept the free samples, how many pairs of contact lenses would the shop have given out in total?
A. 4,000
B. 6,000
C. 8,000
D. 10,000
E. 12,000
F. 14,000

Problem Solving

90. At a local food festival, the organisers give out some £15 food vouchers at the start of every hour, as part of a lucky draw. For every following hour, 1 in 5 of the vouchers on display are given out and another 25 are added. After 3 hours, there are 381 vouchers left on the display. How many vouchers were on display at the start of the festival?
A. 500
B. 625
C. 750
D. 875
E. 1,000

91. Five students competed in a race during their high school Sports Day. The results were said to be as follows: Sucre finished after Franklin, who finished after John. Theodore came before Sucre and David but still finished after Franklin. That would mean David finished:
A. Before Sucre and Franklin.
B. After Franklin, Sucre and John, but not necessarily Theodore.
C. After Franklin and Theodore, but before Sucre.
D. After John, Franklin, Theodore and Sucre.
E. After Franklin, John and Theodore, but not necessarily Sucre.

92. For a year-end assignment, a group of five students takes 3 weeks and 4 days to finish building a robot car. The students were only allowed to build the robot during school hours, which is 9:00 am to 5:00 pm on weekdays.
Assuming if the teacher had assigned one less student but gave them 10 hours a day instead, how much time will it take them to complete the project?
A. 2 weeks 3 days
B. 2 weeks 4 days
C. 3 weeks 1 day
D. 3 weeks 2 days
E. Same as the previous attempt
F. Can't tell

93. Ginnie buys 3,000 shares from a company which sells each share unit at 45 pence. Later in the month, she sells all the shares at the rate of 58 pence per share. She then buys 2,000 shares at 15 pence per share and sells half of them for 33 pence per share. There is a 10% charge for every transaction made. (i.e., If one buys shares for £10, they will have to pay £11. If one sells shares and was supposed to make £10, they will only receive £9.)
How much profit did Ginnie make?
A. £48
B. £156
C. £345
D. £590
E. £750

94. Justin works in a company which gives him a pay rise of $10r\%$ at the end of every full year since he joined them. He has worked in the company for 2 years and 4 months now. The letter 'r' represents the number of years of which he has worked in the company. If his current salary is £99,990, what was his salary when he first started at the company?
A. £25,250
B. £34,600
C. £50,500

D. £60,330
E. £75,750

95. An American man who has been framed for first-degree murder has eluded the Federal Bureau of Investigation (FBI) and is now believed to have crossed the federal border. He sends two letters, containing origami cranes, to his wife to let her know about his current whereabouts. He encodes his message just in case it falls into the wrong hands. On the paper cranes, he writes as below:
Letter 1: 724-466.
Letter 2: ....
You are a Central Intelligence Agency (CIA) agent who has got hold of these two letters and you suspect that the code will tell you his location. Your instincts tell you that Letter 1 has something to do with a *phone number*.
Assuming that your gut feeling is right, where do you think is the current whereabouts of the man?
A. Beirut
B. Dublin
C. Prague
D. Saigon
E. Riyadh
F. Zagreb

96. Two brothers, Mike and Sulley, both made automatic pet feeders for their school project. The feeders are made such that 0.4 kg of food is released once each day regardless of whether the food from the previous day has been finished. The feeders are connected to the boys' phones to send them a 'beep' notification when the food remaining is at 20% of its capacity. Mike's feeder has a capacity of 6 kg and Sulley's feeder has a capacity of 8 kg. The boys always fill the feeders at their maximum capacity. The brothers installed the feeders at 9:00 am on Day '0' and set the time of release of food at 12:00 pm daily.
Which two of the following are true?
A. Mike will receive a first 'beep' 4 days before Sulley.
B. Sulley will receive a first 'beep' 4 days before Mike.
C. The total food released by the time of the first 'beep' is 9.5 kg.
D. Within the first fortnight, Sulley and Mike will receive the 'beep' once.
E. Mike receives a 'beep' after 1.2 kg of food has been released.
F. Sulley receives a 'beep' when there is 1.6 kg of food left in the feeder.

97. Merida enjoys playing tennis with her father. This morning, they decided to focus their practice on the technique of serving. They brought 30 tennis balls with them to the court and seven plastic cones. The cones are used as targets and are placed at different parts of the service box. Each time she knocks a cone off, her father helps her to place it back at its original location. In the first round, she manages to hit all six targeted cones off twice. This, unfortunately, damaged one third of the cones. In the next round, she served 15 balls but this time, she had only focused on one cone as a target. During this round, as her father was putting the cone back at its place, he accidentally steps on one of the other cones and damages it. Realising that they lacked cones for practice, he rushed to the nearby shop to purchase six cones. When he returned, Merida told him that 50% of the initial batch of cones had been stolen by monkeys. In the final round of practice, Merida missed hitting any of the cones. She smashes half of the cones out of anger and was later reprimanded by her father for her temper.

How many cones were there left at the end of the three rounds?

A. 2 cones
B. 4 cones
C. 5 cones
D. 6 cones
E. 7 cones
F. 8 cones

98. Elias prepares two full 2-litre jugs of mixed syrup for a house party. Each of his friends are given cups of the same size. Whenever they pour themselves a cup of mixed syrup, they make sure to only fill seven eighths of the cup, which is equivalent to 175 ml.
What proportion of the final cup will be filled with mixed syrup?

A. 20%
B. 25%
C. 50%
D. 75%
E. 80%

99. I go to the gym whenever I feel like winding down from all of my university assignments. The minimum number of times I go to the gym in a week is once, that is, on Friday evenings. I am about to start a 6-year medical course at my university and each academic year is 9 months long. I learned that the Students' Union gym offers a membership deal of £20 per annum, which would allow me to pay only £2 for each time I enter the gym. Alternatively, I have a second option of paying £25 per month and with no extra charges. The gym is only open during the academic year.
Assuming I select the second option, what is the minimum number of times I would have to visit the gym each month, on average, to make sure that my decision is the cheaper option?

A. 10
B. 12
C. 14
D. 16
E. 18

100. You're about to get on a train to Aberdeen and you want to know if it's snowing. You call three random friends who are studying there and ask each if it's snowing. Each friend has a $\frac{1}{3}$ chance of telling you the truth and a $\frac{2}{3}$ chance of lying just to mess with you. All of them tell you "Yes" it is snowing.
What is the probability that it is actually snowing in Aberdeen?

A. $\frac{1}{27}$
B. $\frac{1}{9}$
C. $\frac{8}{27}$
D. $\frac{19}{27}$
E. $\frac{26}{27}$

101. A start-up tea company produces tea sets containing two teaspoons and 10 teacups. Ink is used to print its logo on the products too. The teaspoons are purchased from the supplier in boxes containing 180 units and the teacups come in boxes of 300 units each. The ink cartridge is sufficient to print 120 logos on either spoons or cups. A box of teaspoons costs £250 and a box of teacups is thrice the price of a box of teaspoons. The price of the ink cartridge is one fifth of that of a box of teaspoons.
How many tea sets can be produced from a budget of £26,000?
A. 640
B. 660
C. 680
D. 700
E. 720

102. A neighbourhood has two bakeries. The cakes from Bakery 'A' have two blueberries and three blackberries whereas the cakes from Bakery 'B' have a blackberry and four blueberries. In a local food festival, the display of cakes by the two bakeries had 282 blueberries and 163 blackberries.
How many of these cakes are from Bakery 'B'?
A. 37 cakes
B. 41 cakes
C. 44 cakes
D. 48 cakes
E. 52 cakes

103. A horde of hamsters has 2000 hamsters, where 42% of them are males. A total of 240 of the male hamsters have red eyes. The proportion of male and female hamsters who have red eyes are equal.
Approximately, how many hamsters with red eyes are females in the horde?
A. 300
B. 310
C. 320
D. 330
E. 340

104. Quinn has just given birth to a set of quintuplets - namely, Ashlyn, Blair, Courtney, Delia and Edeline. Each of these babies' weights are measured and recorded in their birth certificates. Edeline is lighter than Courtney. Blair is heavier than Ashlyn but lighter than Edeline. Delia is lighter than Ashlyn and Edeline.
If the babies are arranged, from left to right, in ascending order of their weights, who will be third from the right?
A. Ashlyn
B. Blair
C. Courtney
D. Delia
E. Edeline

105. A tennis academy coach asks his best players to play a few friendly matches against each other as practice for an upcoming tournament. Brian won a match against Dylan, whilst Zian won a match against Jack. Later, Dylan played a match against Zian and managed to win. The styles of tennis play of these players are either counterpunchers or aggressive baseliners. Jack plays as an aggressive baseliner whilst Brian plays a counterpunching game. To make sure

that each player is put out of their comfort zone, the coach organised the games such that players with the same game styles do not play with each other.
Given the information above, what is the next match that the coach should arrange and who is likely to win that match? (Assume that there are no upsets. An upset is when an underdog player wins the match against the player who had been expected to win).

A. Brian vs Jack; Jack wins
B. Dylan vs Jack; Dylan wins
C. Jack vs Brian; Brian wins
D. None of the above

106. It takes two builders six days to build a large kitchen in a house. If one more builder is hired to build the kitchen, how many days earlier does the work finish?

A. 1 day
B. 2 days
C. 3 days
D. 4 days
E. 5 days

107. Chloe and Natasha are a pair of twins who share a wardrobe. One of the accessories they share is headbands. They have 23 headbands altogether. There are four striped, six chequered, one plain white and seven floral headbands. The rest have a polka dot print.
How many headbands do they need to take from the wardrobe in order to get a matching pair?

A. 5
B. 6
C. 7
D. 8
E. 9

108. A total of 4750 individuals attended a K-Pop concert. Of all the tickets sold, only 95% showed up. Of these, 1 in 8 are males and the rest are females. Men are four times more likely to miss concerts as women.
How many females attended the concert?

A. 4200 females
B. 4250 females
C. 4325 females
D. 4375 females
E. 4450 females

Questions 109-111 refer to the following information:

A wrapping company provides services such as bubble wraps and sponge wraps for objects that are particularly fragile. The sponge wraps are 2 inches thick and a single layer of the wrap is used to completely surround the whole object. The bubble wraps are 0.5-inch thick but two layers of it are used to completely surround the whole object. Sponge wraps are priced by multiplying 25 pence with the largest dimension of the sponge wrap after it has wrapped around the object. Hence, a sponge wrap (around an object) which has dimensions of 10 x 20 x 8 inches would cost £5. Bubble wraps are priced by multiplying the £2 with the smallest dimension of the wrap after it has wrapped around the object. Hence, a bubble wrap (around an object) which has dimensions of 10 x 20 x 8 inches would cost £16. The company always packs objects with sponge wraps followed by wrapping it with bubble wraps, unless requested otherwise. For the questions below, assume that the sponge nor the bubbles are compressed when they are wrapped.

109. How much would it cost to wrap a glass box that has the dimensions 2 x 10 x 4 inches?

A. £13.00
B. £19.50
C. £21.50
D. £24.00
E. £33.50

110. How much more expensive would it cost to bubble wrap a box with dimensions of 16 x 17 x 11 inches compared to sponge wrap a box with dimensions of 4 x 20 x 18 inches?

F. 2.5 times
G. 3.25 times
H. 4 times
I. 5.5 times
J. 6.75 times

111. What is the largest cubic box that can be wrapped for £50?

A. 13 inches
B. 14 inches
C. 15 inches
D. 16 inches
E. 17 inches

112. Mr Hidayat provides one-to-one weekly badminton training sessions to the teenagers in his neighbourhood. On top of that, he also casually plays badminton with his best friend on both mornings over weekends and Wednesday evenings, every week. During the summer holidays, three of his students, Sakura and her two brothers went on a 3-month trip abroad. When Sakura and her siblings were away, Mr Hidayat restocks his shuttlecocks every 5 weeks. However, when Sakura and her siblings are around, Mr Hidayat restocks his shuttlecocks every 4 weeks. Assume that Mr Hidayat supplies the shuttlecocks for all the training sessions and games.
Including Sakura and siblings, how many students does Mr Hidayat have?

A. 9 students
B. 10 students
C. 11 students
D. 12 students
E. 13 students

113. In a music academy, all teenagers play the piano and all the children play the violin. None of the students who play the piano are children.
Which of the following must be true?

A. All students who play the violin are children.
B. Some teenagers play the violin.
C. Some children play the drums.
D. Some students who play the piano play the violin as well.
E. None of the above.

114. It is March 2021 and Santorino decides to prepare early for his application to medical school. He purchases a BMAT revision book from an online store. The expected time of arrival of the book, on the express service, is 2 weeks given the international delivery service as he resides overseas. However, given that Santorino opts for the regular service instead, the time of

Problem Solving

arrival of the book is likely to take 25% longer. On top of that, his country has just entered a further phase of 'lockdown' as the COVID-19 pandemic continues. He reads online that this will likely affect all posting services and that customers should expect the time of arrival of their mail to increase by 30%.

How many weeks will it take before Santorino receives his book?

A. 2.9 weeks
B. 3.25 weeks
C. 3.5 weeks
D. 4.4 weeks
E. 5.25 weeks

Questions 115-117 refer to the following information:

Global Food Village is a restaurant that serves a variety of cuisines. Customers are charged a certain amount for every 25 grams of any type of food taken, on top of their entry fee which is a fixed price. Assume that the weight of the plates and bowls used are negligible. Pushan, who is 22-years-old, was charged £20.20 for 0.9 kg of roasted lamb with potatoes. Khave, who is 35-years-old, paid £11.65 for 425 grams of fried rice. Children under the age of 12 pay half the price of the entry fee for adults and they are charged two thirds of the adult rate per 25 grams of food.

---

115. How much will it cost 60-year-old Flint for 375 grams of salmon sashimi?

A. £9.50
B. £10.75
C. £11.25
D. £13.00
E. £13.50

---

116. How much will it cost 11-year-old Melissa for 850 grams of mini chicken burgers?

A. £8.00
B. £9.50
C. £11.25
D. £12.20
E. £12.60

---

117. Henry visits the restaurant during his birthday month. He eats a meal which amounts to 1.175 kg of food.

He was given a special deal which requires him to solve as many Rubik's cubes as possible within 10 minutes. For every cube he solves, 50 grams of his meal will be considered free of charge at checkout.

If Henry only had to pay £17.95, what was the average time taken for Henry to solve a Rubik's cube?

A. 2 mins 30s
B. 2 mins 15s
C. 1 min 50s
D. 1 min 25s
E. 1 min 15s

Questions 118-122 refer to the following information:

Alexandra has five pet dogs, each of a different size. At each mealtime, Alexandra opens a pack of 5 kilograms of dog food and pours them into their respective bowls. As one can expect, dogs that are larger in size are provided with more food compared to smaller dogs. The pack of dog food is divided such that she will give the second smallest dog as much more than the smallest dog, as the third smallest gets than the second smallest, as the fourth smallest gets compared to the third smallest, etc. As a result, the portion of food received by the three largest dogs is eight times greater than that of the rest of the dogs combined.

W is the weight of dog food received by the smallest dog and D is the difference between the weight of dog food received by the smallest and second smallest dog.

118. What is the expression of the amount of food received by the second largest dog?

A. W
B. W + D
C. W + 2D
D. W + 3D
E. W + 4D
F. None of the above

119. Which of the following equations expresses the total food received by the dogs?

A. 5W = 5
B. 5D + 10W = 5
C. $W = \frac{D}{5}$
D. 5W + 10D = 5
E. $D = \frac{W}{5}$
F. None of the above

120. ***"The portion of food received by the three largest dogs is eight times greater than that of the rest of the dogs combined."***

Which of the following below represents the above statement?

A. 3W + 9D = 8(W + D)
B. 8(3W + 9D) = 2W + D
C. 8(2W + D) = 3W + D
D. 8(2W + D) = 3W + 9D
A. None of the above

121. Which of the equations below expresses W in terms of D?

A. 13D
B. $\frac{7D}{13}$
C. $\frac{8D}{5}$
D. $\frac{71D}{22}$
E. $\frac{D}{13}$
F. None of the above

122. Express 5 kg in terms of W.

A. 13D
B. $\frac{1}{27}$
C. $\frac{13}{27}$

Problem Solving

D. $\frac{13D}{27}$
E. $\frac{135D}{13}$

Questions 123-125 refer to the following information:
There are 36 nuts in a container. 1 in 3 of the nuts are pistachios. Of every 6 remaining nuts, 1 is a cashew. Exactly 10% of the nuts that are not pistachios nor cashews are almonds. The rest are hazelnuts.

123. If Nadia draws two nuts from the container without replacement, what is the most likely combination of nuts that she will draw?
A. Hazelnut and hazelnut.
B. Hazelnut and almond.
C. Cashew and hazelnut.
D. Pistachio and almond.
E. Hazelnut and pistachio.

124. If Nadia draws three nuts from the container without replacement, what is/ are the least likely combination(s) of nuts that she will draw?
1. Almond, almond and almond.
2. Cashew, almond and almond.
3. Cashew, cashew and almond.
4. Cashew, cashew and cashew.

A. 1 only
B. 2 only
C. 3 only
D. 2 and 3 only
E. 2 and 4 only

125. What is the minimum number of nuts Nadia will have to draw, without replacement, to guarantee that she will have at least one of at least three different types of nuts?
A. 5 nuts
B. 13 nuts
C. 19 nuts
D. 31 nuts
E. 35 nuts

126. Abbeytown is 30 miles directly north of Belville. Cork is 17 miles directly south of Davonmille. Epstone is situated 20 miles directly east of Belville, and 13 miles directly west of Cork.
Which of the following cannot be reliably concluded from this information?
A. Epstone is South of Abbeytown.
B. Belville is East of Davonmille.
C. Davonmille is North of Epstone.
D. Davonmille is North of Abbeytown.
E. Cork is East of Abbeytown.

127. Four children run a race. Alice, wearing a blue top, did not come last. The child who wore a red top had ran many races before, and, therefore, came first. Collin came third in the race.

Problem Solving

Bethany did better than the child in the green top, and the child who wore an orange top did better than Jacob.

The following statements are made:

1. Jacob wore a green top.
2. Alice came second.
3. Bethany wore an orange top.
4. The child wearing a green top came in 3rd place.
5. The child wearing an orange top was 3rd.

Which of the above statements are incorrect?

A. 1 and 2 only
B. 1 and 3 only
C. 2 and 4 only
D. 1 and 5 only
E. 2 and 5 only
F. 3 and 4 only
G. 3 and 5 only
H. 4 and 5 only

128. **A company devises a test to diagnose the presence of a certain disease amongst the elderly population. After many clinical trials, the test proves itself to be 95% accurate. In other words, on 5% of tests done on the elderly who do actually have the disease, the test will erroneously indicate that they do not have it. These 5% of tests are known as 'false negatives'. Similarly, on 5% of tests done on the elderly who do not actually have the disease, the test indicates incorrectly that they do have it. These 5% of tests are known as 'false positives'.**

The company tests 2000 elderly patients in a hospital for the presence of the disease. The table below provides the results as expected in terms of the test's 95% accuracy level.

	Disease actually present	Disease actually absent
Positive test results	1615 (true positive)	285 (false positive)
Negative test results	85 (false negative)	15 (true negative)
Total	1700	300

If an elderly patient has a positive test result, what is the difference in probability that s/he actually has the disease compared with the probability of she/he not having the disease?

A. $\frac{1330}{1900}$

B. $\frac{285}{1615}$

C. $\frac{1330}{1900}$

D. $\frac{1330}{2000}$

E. $\frac{100}{1900}$

F. $\frac{1300}{1900}$

129. A child chooses a marble from a large marble jar containing many marbles. There are three colours – Red, Blue and Orange. The child wants to choose six marbles in such a way that no two consecutive marbles have the same colour.
How many different ways can the child achieve this?
A. 32
B. 48
C. 72
D. 96
E. 108
F. 192
G. 729

130. Alfie says "Just one of us is telling the truth". Bert says "What Alfie says is true". Caitlin says "what Bert says is not true". Dave says "What Caitlin says is not true". Ellie says "What Dave says is true".
How many people are telling the truth?
A. 0
B. 1
C. 2
D. 3
E. 4
F. 5

131. A workers' union rewards its staff with free holidays when they fulfil certain criteria:

Holiday to Greece	Absences less than 3%
	Customer satisfaction rating of more than 3
	Complaints of less than 3% of the number of customers served*
Holiday to Spain	Absences less than or equal to 1%
	Customer satisfaction rating of 4 or more
	Complaints of less than or equal to 1% of the number of customers served*

***All staff served 2000 customers each**
The staff performed as follows:

	Johnson	Dwayne	Kristina	Carson	Molly
Attendance (%)	97	98	99	98	98
Customer Satisfaction rating	4	3	3	5	4
Number of complaints	49	60	39	20	59

Who is eligible for a free holiday?
A. Johnson only
B. Kristina only
C. Molly and Carson only
D. Molly and Dwayne only

E. Carson and Johnson only
F. Kristina and Johnson only

132. Three children are counting the number of sweets in a packet. Each child is accurate to within 3 sweets above or below the number of sweets they actually count. One child counts 7 sweets, one counts 9 sweets and one counts 11 sweets.
What is the minimum range in which the true number of sweets lies?

A. 2
B. 4
C. 6
D. 8
E. 10
F. 12

133. If an individual does not have Type II diabetes and does not smoke, the risk of developing Disease P is 1 in 8. If an individual has Type II diabetes, they are four times as likely to develop Disease P. If a person smokes, he/she is half as likely to develop Disease P as someone who does not smoke. A new injection is invented that halves anyone's total risk of developing Disease P for each dose administered. How many injection doses would an individual who has Type II diabetes have to take to reduce their risk to the same level as someone who smokes but did not have the injection?

A. 0 dose
B. 1 dose
C. 2 doses
D. 3 doses
E. 4 doses
F. 5 doses
G. 6 doses

134. The table below shows the results of a survey carried out on a small community to identifies different eye colours in the population. All individuals either had brown eyes or blue eyes. The bottom row of the table shows the percentage of each gender group that had brown eyes:

	3 to 16 years old		16 to 18 years old	
	Female	Male	Female	Male
Numbers tested	160	150	80	110
Percentage who had brown eyes	35%	30%	15%	60%

What percentage of all those surveyed had blue eyes (to the nearest whole number)?

A. 40%
B. 41%
C. 45%
D. 63%
E. 64%
F. 73%
G. 75%

135. Three are three cereal bar flavours - chocolate, caramel and honey - available in a shop. The chocolate cereals bars cost £0.70, caramel cereal bars cost 50 pence and honey cereal bars cost 25 pence. Judy spends exactly £3.50 on cereal bars.

2. She must have at least one chocolate cereal bar.
3. She must have more than two types of bar.
4. She must have more than 5 cereal bars altogether.

Which amongst the aforementioned statement(s) are correct?

A. 1 only
B. 2 only
C. 4 only
D. 1 and 2 only
E. 1 and 3 only
F. 1 and 4 only
G. 2 and 3 only
H. 2 and 4 only
I. 2 and 4 only
J. 1, 2 and 4 only

136. Three children - James, Sam and Jordan - walk around their local park. James takes 20 minutes to walk one lap, Sam takes 0.2 hours to walk one lap and Jordan takes 15 minutes to walk one lap. Assuming that all three children were in the same position 5 minutes ago, how long will it be until all three children meet again?

A. 25 minutes
B. 30 minutes
C. 55 minutes
D. 65 minutes
E. 115 minutes
F. 120 minutes

137. Five friends, Abby, Brooke, Callum, Dan and Elisabeth, are each sitting on one of the five chairs in a room. The chairs are in a straight line. One possible arrangement of the friends is, left to right, Abby, Brooke, Callum, Dan, Elisabeth. Another possible arrangement is Abby, Callum, Brooke, Dan, Elisabeth.
How many other arrangements are possible?

A. 100
B. 112
C. 116
D. 118
E. 120
F. 320

138. A company decides to fine employees when they are late. An employee who is late by more than 30 minutes is fined £20. Any employee who is late by more than 10 minutes but less than or equal to 30 minutes is fined £15.
The table below shows the scheduled time and the actual time that 8 employees arrived at the office.

Employee	Scheduled time	Actual time
1	12:35	13:05
2	10:25	11:00
3	14:55	14:25
4	09:15	09:20
5	08:16	08:50

6	15:47	15:49
7	12:39	12:29
8	14:56	15:07

All of the employees who were subjected to a fine paid the correct amount to the company. However, 20% of the money collected in fines were used to pay for an office upgrade.
How much money was used from the fines for the office upgrade?

A. £10
B. £11
C. £14
D. £17
E. £18
F. £21

139. On Wednesday, 36 students attended Drewstring Sixth Form for extra classes. Of the students who were supposed to attend the Sixth Form, only 90% of the students attended. Of the students who were supposed to attend, 1 in 4 are male, and the remainder are female students. Male students have a football match on this day, and, therefore, were three times more likely to miss Sixth Form compared to female students.
How many male students attended Drewstring Sixth Form on Wednesday?

A. 2
B. 3
C. 6
D. 7
E. 15
F. 17
G. 18
H. 20

140. A school surveys their pupils on subjects that they study. All of the students study English. Furthermore, 55% study Mathematics, 35% study Computer Science and 75% study French. The other subject that was surveyed was Geography. Assuming that every student studies 3 of the above subjects and that there are 120 students altogether, how many students study Geography?

A. 15
B. 20
C. 21
D. 40
E. 42
F. 47
G. 114

141. Sixty children go on a school trip. Two thirds of the girls on the trip ordered a ham sandwich, and two thirds of the class as a whole order a drink. Given that the school trip comprised of half boys and half girls, what is the difference between the minimum and maximum number of girls that could have ordered a ham sandwich and a drink?

A. 5
B. 10
C. 15
D. 20

Problem Solving

E. 25
F. 30
G. 35
H. 40

142. Matthew has forgotten his 5-digit pin code but remembers a few clues.
The second digit is the square of the first digit.
The sum of the first and the third digit is equivalent to 5 times the first digit.
The fourth digit is two more than the square of the first digit.
The sum of the fifth and third digit is equivalent to 10 minus two times the first digit.
The sum of all the digits is 57.
What is the first digit?

A. 3
B. 4
C. 5
D. 6
E. 7
F. 8

143. A group of adults hire out a cottage for the weekend. They split the cost of the villa between them, contributing £35 each. If there had been 10 more friends sharing the cost of the villa, each person would have had to contribute £21.
What was the overall cost of the cottage for the original group of adults?

A. £350
B. £525
C. £750
D. £755
E. £805
F. £930

144. Four different parents have one son each - Jacob, Jack, Josh and Joe. Jacob was born on the 27th May 2020, Jack was born on the 26th February 2020, Josh was born on the 21st November 2019 and Joe was born on the 10th March 2020.
Who amongst the four children were born on the same day?

A. Jacob and Jack only
B. Jacob and Josh only
C. Josh and Jack only
D. Jacob, Jack and Josh only
E. Jack, Josh and Joe only
F. Jacob, Jack and Joe only
G. Jacob, Jack, Josh and Joe only

145. The table below shows the annual number of members in different clubs available for primary school children.

	2020	2019	2018
Choir	23	24	30
Hockey	12	9	3
Chess	14	13	10
Coding	18	6	4
Orchestra	34	15	6

Orchestra	34	15	6
Journalism	16	19	27
Netball	10	2	0

What is the correct order in terms of highest to lowest increase between 2019 and 2020?

A. Orchestra, Coding, Netball, Hockey, Choir, Chess, Journalism
B. Orchestra, Coding, Netball, Hockey, Chess, Choir, Journalism
C. Journalism, Coding, Netball, Hockey, Chess, Choir, Orchestra
D. Orchestra, Hockey, Coding, Netball, Chess, Choir, Journalism
E. Coding, Netball, Chess, Hockey, Journalism, Choir, Chess
F. Journalism, Coding, Netball, Hockey, Chess, Choir, Orchestra
G. Orchestra, Choir, Chess, Netball, Hockey, Coding, Journalism

---

146. In a hospital, one large general ward is occupied by 16 patients. There are a total of 3 doctors, 4 nurses, 4 healthcare assistants and 24 visitors in this ward. Exactly 75% of visitors were about to leave when one of the sixteen patients has a cardiac arrest. In the two minutes before the 6 members of the crash team arrive, 50% of the visitors who were originally leaving plus all of the healthcare assistants leave the ward. Upon hearing the commotion, two senior doctors enter the ward and they hear the crash team pronounce the patient dead. How many 'living' people are left in the ward?

A. 29
B. 34
C. 33
D. 39
E. 45
F. 48
G. 52

---

147. Jamal, Lola and Graham have to run a distance of 18 km. Jamal runs at a pace of 15 kmph, Lola at a pace of 10 mph, and Graham 12.5 mph. Assume that 1 mile = 1.6 kilometres.
If Jamal sets off 5 minutes before Lola, and 17 minutes before Graham, what order will they arrive at the destination?

A. Jamal, Lola, Graham
B. Jamal, Graham, Lola
C. Graham, Lola, Jamal
D. Graham, Jamal, Lola
E. Lola, Jamal, Graham
F. Lola, Graham, Jamal

---

148. A team of 3 carpet fitters lay down a carpet in Hotel A. Each cm3 takes all three carpet fitters 15 minutes to lay down. This hotel has an area 288cm3 that must be carpeted. All carpet fitters work 6 hours every day. Assume that it takes 15 minutes for any number of carpet fitters to lay each cm3 of the carpet in Hotel A.
If six more carpet fitters were originally recruited, how many days would it have taken to finish carpeting for Hotel A?

A. 2 days
B. 4 days
C. 8 days
D. 9 days
E. 13 days

Problem Solving

149. Bank A pays 3% interest per annum. Bank B pays 4% interest per annum. Ally invests £8000 in Bank A and £7500 in Bank B. What is the difference in the value of the investment, to the nearest pound, in 2 years' time?

A. £323
B. £324
C. £347
D. £348
E. £375
F. £376
G. £438

150. A toy shop employee states that:

"All robots are sold with batteries and all toy cars are sold in packs of three. No items sold with batteries are toy cars".

Which of the following must be true?

A. Some toy car packs contain trucks.
B. All items sold in packs of three are toy cars.
C. Some robots are sold in packs of three.
D. Some items sold with batteries are also sold in packs of three.
E. None of the above.

Questions 151 - 153 refer to the following information.

There are 20 marbles in a bag:

$\frac{15}{30}$ are orange.

10% of those that are not orange are blue. The rest are lilac except one, which is maroon.

151. If Andy draws 2 marbles from the bag, without replacement, what is the most likely combination to draw?

A. Orange and Orange
B. Blue and Orange
C. Lilac and Orange
D. Lilac and Maroon
E. Blue and Blue
F. Blue and Maroon
G. Lilac and Blue
H. Maroon and Orange

152. If Andy draws 3 marbles from the bag, without replacement, what is the least likely (without being impossible) combination to draw?

A. Blue and Blue
B. Maroon and Maroon
C. Blue and Lilac
D. Lilac and Maroon
E. Maroon and Blue

153. How many marbles does Andy have to draw (without replacement) to guarantee getting at least one of at least three different colours?

A. 6 marbles
B. 8 marbles
C. 12 marbles

A Lakshmi, T R Enoch, S Z Y Ooi. Doctors Academy Publications, Cardiff, UK, 2020.

D. 13 marbles
E. 14 marbles
F. 17 marbles
G. 18 marbles
H. 19 marbles
I. 20 marbles

154. There are nine printers in an office. Together they take seven minutes to print a book with 560 pages. Three of the printers in the office stop working.
Assuming all the printers print at the same rate, how much longer does it take to print four books now?

A. 3.5 minutes
B. 4.7 minutes
C. 10.5 minutes
D. 14 minutes
E. 17 minutes

155. Clare and Sophie went shopping together. Clare bought three trousers and seven pairs of shoes spending £286. Sophie spent £227.75 by purchasing five trousers and two shoes.
Assuming that all the shoes had the same price and all the trousers cost the same, what is the price of one pair of shoes?

A. £25.75
B. £35.25
C. £51.50
D. £105.75
E. £180.75

156. A bag contains beads that weigh a total of 3 kg. To make a bracelet, 400 grams of beads are used by a company so that all the bracelets weigh the same. The company decided to increase the number of bracelets they make by using 40% less beads than before for each bracelet.
What is the weight of the beads that are left over after the maximum number of bracelets are made?

A. 60 grams
B. 120 grams
C. 240 grams
D. 320 grams
E. 380 grams

157. Cleaner 'A' charges £25 to clean a house with a maximum of six rooms in total. She charges an extra £1.00 for each additional room in the house. Cleaner 'B' charges £10 per session with an additional cost of £2 for each room in the house.
How many rooms will there be in a house where it costs the same to hire both the cleaners?

A. 8
B. 9
C. 12
D. 17
E. 28

158. A lock has a password that is created with five two-digit numbers:

54, 63, 74, 83, 91

Each two-digit number is used once in the password. No consecutive number shares more than one common factor.
Which one of the following options is the correct combination to open the lock?
A. 54 91 74 63 83
B. 63 91 74 54 83
C. 54 83 74 63 91

159. The prices to a rent a car are shown below:

Cars for rent
8 am – 5pm: £2 per hour
5pm – 10 pm: £3 per hour
10pm – 8am: £1 per hour
1 day (24 hours): £25
1 week: £170
Refundable deposit: £15

What is the cheapest price to rent a car for eight days from 8 am in the morning of the first day to 5 pm in the evening on the eighth day?
A. £174
B. £188
C. £193
D. £195
E. £200

160. Susan is raising money for charity by doing a run. Her mum said that she will pay her £5 for every kilometre she runs. Her grandparents said that they will pay her £10 if she runs between 5 to 6 km but they will pay her an extra £2 for every kilometre she runs above 6 km. Three of her friends have each sponsored £10 for her run. Her dad will match the total amount that she has raised after her run.
Susan ran 10 km.
How much money did she raise?
A. £96
B. £98
C. £156

D. £192
E. £196

161. In a multi-storey shopping mall, the clothes store is above the shop selling shoes and the cookie stall, but it is not above the cinema. The shop selling shoes is below the cinema, which is below the food court.
The cookie stall is:
A. Below all of the shops.
B. Below the clothes shop and above the shoe shop.
C. Below the food court and cinema but above the shoe shop.
D. Below the cinema but not necessarily the clothes shop.
E. Below the food court, cinema and clothes shop but not necessarily the shoe shop.

162. A tutor charges a base rate and a rate per minute for his lessons. A half an hour lesson costs £20. He charges £35 for an hour lesson. How much does a four-hour lesson cost?
A. £120
B. £125
C. £140
D. £145
E. £160

163. A girl wants to grow her hair to be 20 cm longer. It grows 4 cm per month, but at the end of each month she cuts it by 3 cm to keep her hair healthy. Once her hair is 20 cm longer, she will stop cutting it for a few months.
How long does it take for her hair to become 20 cm longer than it is now?
A. 16 months
B. 17 months
C. 18 months
D. 19 months
E. 20 months

164. A company that sells handwash increased the amount of soap in their bottles by 25% before Christmas. After New Year, they decided to decrease the amount of soap by reducing it by 15% of the current increased volume.
What change has there been to the volume of soap in the bottles after the reduction compared to the original volume?
A. Decreased by 6.25%.
B. Decreased by 15%.
C. Increased by 6.25%.
D. Increased by 10%.
E. Increased by 15%.

165. All the apples in a fruit basket are red, but not all the red fruits are apples. There are also some red grapes in the basket, but not all grapes are red. Not all the fruits in the basket are red.
Which statement below is definitely true?
A. All the grapes in the basket are red.
B. The basket contains fruits of more than one colour.
C. All apples are red.
D. There are more than 2 types of fruit in the basket.
E. The fruit basket contains some grapes that are not red.

Problem Solving

166. **Ria decided to buy a new phone and headphones with her birthday money. She spent 60% of the money she had for the phone, and the headphones cost 35% less than the phone she bought. What percent of her birthday money does she have left over?**
   A. 1%
   B. 5%
   C. 19%
   D. 95%
   E. 99%

167. **Passengers board a flight from Heathrow, London to fly to the John F. Kennedy International Airport in New York at 2 pm (BST – British Summer Time). The flight duration takes eight hours to the nearest hour.**
   Between what times can the passengers expect to land in New York (BST)?
   A. 9:29 pm – 10:29 pm
   B. 9:30 pm – 10:29 pm
   C. 9:29 pm – 10:30 pm
   D. 9:30 pm – 10:30 pm
   E. 9:29 pm – 10: 31 pm

168. **Somchai buys a bunch of bananas. The bunch has 11 hands each with 18 bananas. Each banana weighs 20 grams to the nearest 10 grams.**
   What is the smallest weight of the bunch of bananas (ignoring the weight of the stem)?
   A. 270 grams
   B. 432 grams
   C. 2970 grams
   D. 3960 grams
   E. 4752 grams

169. **There are people from four towns - Town A, Town B, Town C and Town D - who played sports at a common leisure centre. Everyone from Town A likes hockey and some like swimming. Of all the people from Town B, no one likes badminton, but everyone likes to swim. Some people in Town C like football and some like badminton. Everyone at the leisure centre likes running.**

   Which one amongst the following statements is true?
   A. Some people from Town C like football and badminton.
   B. There is no one who likes swimming who plays badminton.
   C. No-one from Towns A or B like badminton.
   D. Everyone who likes running likes hockey.
   E. Some people from Town A like three types of activities in the leisure centre.

170. **The ratio of boys to girls in a football club is 81:2. In the last two terms, the number of boys had decreased by 40% and the number of girls tripled.**
   What was the ratio of boys to girls two terms ago?
   A. 1215: 4
   B. 135: 6
   C. 405: 2
   D. 405: 6
   E. 162: 1

171. **A company made 20% profit on a washing machine. This profit was due to two factors - the manufacturing cost and because it was sold at an offer of 10% off on the original price that**

the company were selling it for. If the price of the washing machine is £450 after the offer, how much profit is made if it is sold at full price?

A. £50
B. £75
C. £100
D. £125
E. £150

172. Friedrich has a bag of 47 marbles of 6 different colours. He has 13 white marbles, 11 black ones, 9 gold ones, 6 green ones, 5 red ones and 3 blue ones. He picks one marble out each time and places it on a tray without looking.
How many times does he need to pick out marbles from the bag to ensure he has at least two marbles that are off the same colour?

A. 3
B. 6
C. 7
D. 12
E. 19

173. Valentina and Charlie decide to race around their housing estate. They would run a total of 9 km. Both of them run together at a constant speed of 2.5 km/h for 4 km until Valentina sees her friends and stops to talk to them for half an hour. Charlie carries on running at this pace. How fast must Valentina run to reach the end point of their race at the same time as Charlie?

A. 0.1 km/h
B. 2.0 km/h
C. 3.3 km/h
D. 3.5 km/h
E. 5.0 km/h

174. A shop has 2,500 shoes in stock. They sell shoes for both adults and children. Exactly 35% of the stock are children's shoes. Only 65 of the adults' shoes are made in Vietnam. The same proportion of children's shoes are also made in Vietnam.
How many shoes in the stock are from Vietnam?

A. 25
B. 35
C. 90
D. 100
E. 186

175. Brenda has to leave her dog in the kennel when she goes on a holiday. The cost to leave her dog there for the first night is £25. Consecutive nights cost her £17 per night. If she wanted her dog to be taken on long walks, it would cost her £8 per walk. However, if the dog is staying there for a week, the total cost of the walks for the whole week is £50. Brenda left her dog in the kennel for four nights and five days the first time and paid for him to be walked every day. Next month she is leaving him for seven nights and eight days. She will pay for him to be walked everyday again.
How much more will it cost her next month to leave her dog in the kennel?

A. £61
B. £69
C. £75
D. £86

E. £116

176. **Five pupils go and complain to a teacher. Lucy says only one person out of all five of them is not lying. Bill says that Lucy is lying. Jose claims Bill is lying. Bo states Jose is lying. When the teacher asks Amoli, she says Bo is not telling the truth.**
How many of pupils lied to the teacher?
A. 1
B. 2
C. 3
D. 4
E. 5

177. **In a dessert shop, all the cakes have chocolate in them, and all the tarts have fruits in them. None of the desserts with chocolate are tarts.**
Which of the following must be true?
A. Some of the cakes contain fruits.
B. Some of the desserts with chocolate have fruits in them.
C. All of the desserts with fruits are tarts.
D. There are at least 2 different types of fruit in each tart.
E. None of the above.

Problem Solving

178. **Iva is born in 2001 and she is older than Stella. Stella is older than Nuru, who are born in the 2002. Jamal is younger than Stella, but older than Peter.**
Who is Peter younger than?
A. Stella, Nuru and Iva.
B. Nuru, but not necessarily Iva or Stella.
C. Iva and Nuru, but not necessarily Stella.
D. Iva and Stella, but not necessarily Nuru.
E. Stella, but not necessarily Iva or Nuru.

179. **Children in a school were surveyed on the number of pets that they had. Between 40% and 50% of pupils owned a cat, and between 75% to 85% owned a dog. Less than 10% of the pupils had no pets at home.**
What percentage of children owned both a cat and a dog?
A. 15% - 35%
B. 15% - 45%
C. 25% - 35%
D. 25% - 45%
E. 35% - 45%

180. **Samantha is studying some insects. Species 'A' has one tail, 4 wings and 6 legs. Species 'B' has one tail, 2 wings and 2 legs. She picks a sample of bugs from a particular area of the field she is investigating. She counts a total of 68 tails from both species and 400 legs.**
What number of Species 'B' is present in the sample?
A. 2
B. 4
C. 32
D. 66
E. 67

181. **Anika has a purse with many coins. There are some 50 p coins, 20 p coins, 10 p coins and 2 p coins. She wants to pick 6 coins from her bag so that no two consecutive coins she picks out are the same.**

How many ways can she do this?

A. 729
B. 864
C. 972
D. 1024
E. 4096

182. Two cars are traveling on a straight road that is 20 km long. They are travelling in opposite directions but have the same speed. If they cross each other after 15 minutes from the start of the journey at either end of the road, what is their speed?

A. 1.30 kmh^{-1}
B. 15 kmh^{-1}
C. 40 kmh^{-1}
D. 60 kmh^{-1}
E. 80 kmh^{-1}

183. Ju makes and sells cupcakes. She gets an order for 50 cupcakes for a party at 6 pm. All the cupcakes that Ju makes are fresh and baked on the day of delivery. Her oven is small and can only bake 25 cupcakes at the same time which takes 30 minutes. She can prepare the mixture for all the cupcakes at the same time, a process which takes 15 minutes. Once the cupcakes are baked, they are left to cool for 10 minutes whilst the next batch are put in the oven to bake. After it has cooled, Ju starts decorating the cupcakes; this takes two minutes per cupcake. Afterwards, she must pack all the cupcakes securely for delivery; this takes 10 minutes. Her client lives 30 minutes away and Ju leaves an extra 10 minutes early to account for any traffic delays.

What is the latest time she can start making the cupcakes?

A. 1:55 pm
B. 2:55pm
C. 3:05 pm
D. 3:25pm
E. 3:35pm

184. There is a tin of biscuits in Carlos' home. His mother fills the tin with a packet of biscuits she bought. Each day, Carlos eats a $\frac{1}{4}$ of the biscuits in the tin for 3 days. On the fourth day, there were 27 biscuits left, which he shares with his sister.

How many biscuits did his mother fill the tin with?

A. 18
B. 27
C. 33
D. 64
E. 85

185. Amitola has 3 different colours of pens in her pencil case - black, blue and red. There is a 20% chance that she will pick a blue pen. There are twice the number of black pens than red pens. What is the minimum number of blue pens in her pencil case?

A. 2
B. 3
C. 4
D. 6
E. 8

PS	PROBLEM SOLVING	Answers

1. **B**

   Explanation:

   First, it is important to recognise that there are only eight individuals in the committee. Each department must have a Chair, a Vice-Chair and at least one Volunteer. This means that a department has a minimum of three individuals. Hence, the only possible number of departments that can be formed from the committee is two departments - one consisting of three members and the other having five - given that more than one department was formed and that no department has the same number of people.
   Taillefer and Zdenek must assume the role of the President and Vice President of the committee, given that they are of the same hierarchy and one of them temporarily works with Gaetana. Given that Zdenek avoids the Publicity and Design Department, this means that Bartlett and Taillefer are leading one department and Gaetana and Zdenek are leading the other. Hence, Hadley is the only Volunteer in Bartlett's department, given that Bartlett likes to keep her team small. This would mean that Maurice, Arturo and Franco are Volunteers in the other department led by Gaetana and Zdenek.

2. **E**

   Explanation:

   This question can be worked out by drawing a Venn diagram or by reasoning out the options with the statements given.
   Option 'A' - All alien toys are green but not all green toys are necessarily alien toys. For example, dinosaur toys could be green as well. Hence, this is incorrect.
   Option 'B' - It is possible that no dinosaurs are plushies.
   Option 'C' - There is a possibility that all dinosaurs may be green. Even though dinosaurs are not aliens and that all aliens are green, it is not certain that all green toys are aliens.
   Option 'D' - It cannot be certain that no alien toys are plushies.

3. **D**

   Explanation:

   The sequence goes such that the numbers 1, 2, 3, ... are given the power of the number itself.
   $1^1 = 1$; $2^2 = 4$; $3^3 = 27$; $4^4 = 256$; $5^5 = 3125$
   $6^6 = 46656$

4. **E**

   Explanation:

   This question is tricky and intuitively, many would think that the answer is 5. However, that is incorrect.
   To solve this question, first, identify the circumference of Button 2. Assume that Button 2 have radius 'r' and Button 1 have radius '5r'. This means that the circumference of Button 2 is $2\pi r$. The trick lies in the distance travelled by Button 2. It is erroneous to conclude that the distance travelled by Button 2 is equal to the circumference of Button 1. However, that is not the case. When Button 2 rolls itself around Button 1, the radius of

the circular distance travelled by the coin is measured from the centre of both coins. Hence, the radius of the circular motion is the sum of the radii of both circles:

<u>5r + r = 6r.</u>

Therefore,

Number of revolutions (n) x Circumference of Button 2

= Circumference of circular motion

n x 2πr = 2 x π x 6r

<u>n = 6</u>

5. **D**

Explanation:

Let Sheldon's current age be denoted as 'D' and Shenton's as 'T'.

Equation 1:

D - T = 16

<u>D = 16 + T</u>

Equation 2:

D + 3 + T + 3 = 64

<u>D = 58 - T</u>

Equation 1 + Equation 2:

2D = 74

<u>D = 37</u>

Substitute D = 37 into Equation 1:

37 = 16 + T

<u>T = 21</u>

Shenton's birth year: 2020 - 21 = <u>1999</u>

6. **D**

This question requires one to carefully work through each statement to verify if they are accurate.

<u>**Option 'A'**</u> - 32% and 26% of iShuffles purchased were turquoise and shamrock respectively. The maximum overlap of the two is 26%. This is equivalent to:

0.26 x 250 = 65 customers.

Therefore, Option 'A' is incorrect.

<u>**Option 'B'**</u> - 58% and 44% of iShuffles purchased were rose and alabaster respectively. The minimum overlap between the two is:

2% (i.e., 58 + 44 - 100 = 2%). This is equivalent to:

0.02 x 250 = 5 customers.

Hence, this is incorrect.

<u>**Option 'C'**</u> - This statement can be misleading if one adds up the percentages:

58 + 44 + 32 + 26 + 18 = 178%.

1.78 x 250 = 445 customers

However, it will be incorrect since the question has stated that each customer can make one purchase and each purchase includes two iShuffles.

<u>**Option 'D'**</u> - 44% and 18% of iShuffles purchased were alabaster and daffodil respectively. The minimum percentage of customers who did not purchase both is:

100 - 44 - 18 = 38%.

This is equivalent to:

0.38 x 250 = 95 customers.

As a result, <u>**Option 'D' is the correct answer.**</u>

Problem Solving

7. **B**

Explanation:

Extracting information from the question, *it can be deduced that 4 rounds are equivalent to :*

$\frac{1}{5} - \frac{1}{7} = \frac{2}{35}$ of the intended number of rounds.

Hence, the total number of rounds Owen set out to complete is:

$4 \div (\frac{2}{35}) = \underline{70}$

---

8. **E**

Explanation:

Given that there are 300 students, the total number of modules taken up by all of them is:

300 x 4 = 1200.

The number of students taking the following modules is:

Criminal Law: 0.65 x 300 = 195

Company Law: 0.72 x 300 = 216

Land Law: 0.80 x 300 = 240

EU Law + Tort Law = 300

Total number of modules taken (excluding Medical Law):

195 + 216 + 240 + 300 = 951

Number of students taking Medical Law:

1,200 - 951 = 249

Percentage of students taking Medical Law:

$\frac{249}{300}$ x 100 = 83%

---

9. **E**

Explanation:

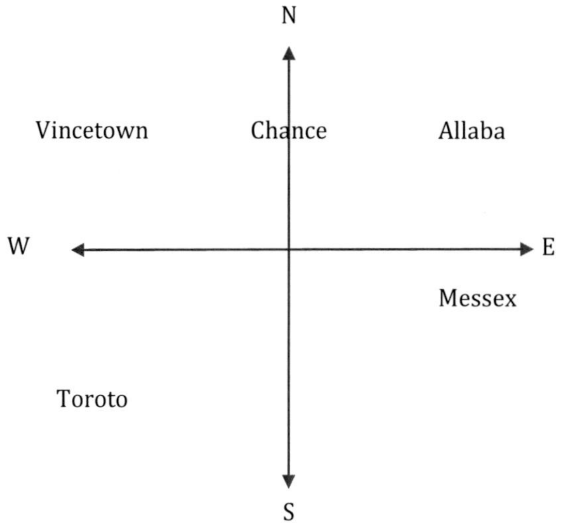

From the diagram above, it can be concluded that Chance is Northwest of Messex; hence, Option 'E' cannot be reliably concluded.

10. C

Explanation:

The question states that both train services will pass through a country in their journeys. This involves crossing an international border twice (i.e., to get into the country and to get out of it).

Let the total distance travelled by the trains be 'M'.

$1.4M + 2(3) = 40 + 0.6M$

$0.8M = 34$

<u>M = 42.5 miles</u>

11. B

Explanation:

After 1 year: 4,000 x 1.06 = **£4240.00**

After 2 years: 4,240 x 1.06 = **£4494.40**

After 3 years: 4,494.40 x 1.06 = **£4764.06**

After 4 years: 4,764.06 x 1.06 = **£5049.91**

After 5 years: 5,049.91 x 1.06 = **£5352.90**

12. A

Explanation:

Let the price of a pen, an eraser and a ruler be denoted as 'P', 'E' and 'R' respectively. This question tests your ability to solve mathematical problems using simultaneous equations.

Equation 1: (22P x 0.8) + 10R = <u>28.12</u>

Equation 2: (30E x 0.7) + (25P x 0.8) = <u>32.4</u>

Equation 3: (50R x 0.7) = <u>24.5</u>

From the given equations, it is easiest to find the value to R and that is, through working on Equation 3.

50R x 0.7 = 24.5

<u>R = £0.70</u>

Substitute R = 0.7 into Equation 1:

17.6P + 10(0.7) = 28.12; 17.6P = 28.12 - 7; 17.6P = 21.12

<u>P = £1.20</u>

Substitute P = 1.2 into Equation 2:

21E + 20(1.2) = 32.4; 21E = 32.4 - 24; 21E = 8.4

<u>E = £0.40</u>

Hence, to purchase 10 erasers, 20 rulers and 30 pens, it would cost a total of:

(10 x 0.4) + (20 x 0.7 x 0.8) + (30 x 1.2 x 0.7) = **£40.40**

13. F

Explanation:

Each child is included in four of the five totals. Therefore, adding these totals and dividing them by 4 will get the average of all four ages:

$$\frac{60+62+62+64+80}{4} = \underline{82}$$

The smallest total (60) is the sum of the ages of the four youngest individuals in the family.

Therefore, the age of the oldest individual:

82 - 60 = <u>22</u>

Problem Solving

14. D

Explanation:

The absolute uncertainty of the scale is:

10 x 0.01 = **0.1 kg**

This means that the weight of a basket of watermelons ranges from:

9.9 kg to 10.1 kg

Two weeks ago, 4 watermelons were purchased, hence, 8 watermelons were purchased in the third week. To get the maximum weight possible of a watermelon, take the maximum possible weight of the basket and divide it by the least number of watermelons (i.e., 4).

This would give:

10.1 ÷ 4 = **2.525 kg**

To get the minimum weight possible of a watermelon, take the minimum possible weight of the basket and divide it by the greatest number of watermelons (i.e., 8).

This would give:

9.9 ÷ 8 = **1.2375 kg.**

The difference in the weight of the heaviest and lightest watermelon is:

2.525 - 1.2375 = **1.2875 kg.**

15. D

Explanation:

Given that both rockets were travelling at the speed of 126 km/h, the relative speed of the two rockets must be:

12.6 x 2 = **25.2 km/h**

This is equivalent to:

25200 ÷ 3600 = **7 m/s.**

The total distance, in this case, is the sum of the lengths of both the rockets.

Let this be 2L:

Speed = Distance ÷ Time

7 = 2L ÷ 0.2

L :0.7m = 70 cm

16. C

Explanation:

Let the length of each potato strip be 'L':

The 37% decrease in length causes the final length of the strips to be:

L - 0.37L = **0.63 L**

After being transferred to the hypotonic solution, the strips increase in length by 22%.

This gives a final length of:

0.63L x 1.22 = **0.7686 L**

This means that the final length of the strips is 76.86% of their original length. *Hence, the magnitude of the percentage decrease is:*

100 - 76.86 = **23.14%.**

17. C

Explanation:

From getting on the bus to arriving to school takes:

45 + 10 = **55 minutes**

If Meg gets to school at 8:25am, the bus must have left the bus stop at:

8:25 - 55 minutes = **7:30**

Since there are buses every 25 minutes, the following buses will arrive at:

7:30 + 25 = **7:55**

7:55 + 25 = **8:20**

Arriving at 8:00 am at the bus station, Meg will catch the **8:20 bus**. Since the journey takes 55 minutes, she will arrive at school at **9:15 am.**

18. D

Explanation:

Time taken for Abigail to fetch the children and to reach home:

$(\frac{12}{20}) + (\frac{6}{60}) = 0.7\text{hrs} =$ **42 minutes**

Given that Olly has a 30 minutes delayed start, he will only have 12 minutes to complete the 12 miles journey home.

Hence, his speed would be:

$12 \div (\frac{12}{60}) =$ **60 mph**

Problem Solving

19. E

Explanation:

This question tests one's understanding of right-angled triangles. First, the question states that Arendelle is 10 miles northwest of Corona. In addition, it says that there are two other towns and that each town is due north, south, east or west by two other towns. Through these two statements, one should be able to infer that the four towns can form the vertices of an imaginary square or rectangle. However, given that the figures in the options are 6 or 8, one can gauge that the question is testing Pythagoras' Theorem, using a 6-8-10 right-angled triangle.

Once the above has been understood, one would be able to reason out each of the given statements. The diagram below is for a reference.

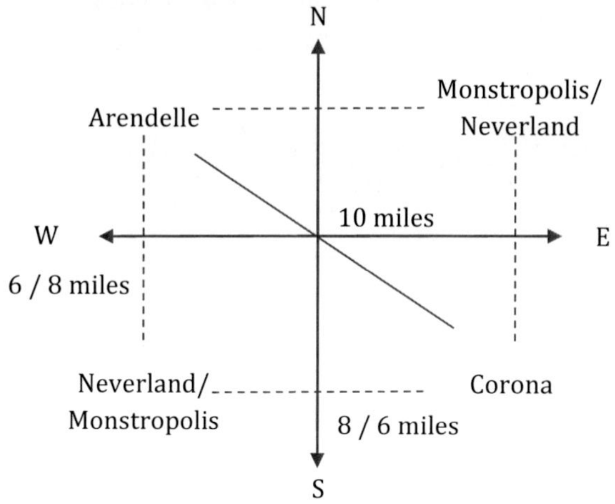

Option 'A' is incorrect since if Neverland is 8 miles south of Arendelle, then Monstropolis cannot be 8 miles east of Arendelle as well. One of the two distances must be 6 miles. **Option 'B' is incorrect** because if Monstropolis is 6 miles south of Arendelle, then Neverland must be 6 miles north of Corona. Similar to Option 'B', if Neverland is 8 miles west of Corona, then Monstropolis must be 8 miles east of Arendelle. Therefore, **Option 'C' is incorrect**. **Option 'D' is incorrect** since no town should be placed east of Corona.

Option 'E' is reasonable. If Neverland is 6 miles north of Corona and Monstropolis is 8 miles west of Corona, it gives a perfect rectangle that suits the description in the question.

20. C

Explanation:

200000 people were diagnosed and 0.7 (i.e., 140000) people were informed. Of these 140,000 people:

$\frac{3}{5}$ x 140000 = **84000 have tested themselves**

140000 - 84000 = **56000 partners who were informed but were not tested.**

(200000 x 4) - 140,000 = **660000 were not informed and were not tested.**

Hence:

660000 + 56000 = **716000 were not tested**.

If tested, 25% of the tests return with a positive result.

Therefore:

716000 ÷ 4 = **179000 people who were not tested are assumed to have gonorrhoea.**

21. D

Explanation:

There are 4 different types of meals. This means that the first student in each group to receive his/her meal can have any of the 4 meals. The second student can only have one of 3 meals as he/she will not be given the same meal that the first student received. This applies to the third and fourth students as well.

Hence, the different permutations of distributing the meals would be:

4 x 3 x 3 x 3 = **108 ways**

Given that the organiser exhausted all ways of distributing the meals. This means that there must have been a minimum of 108 groups.

Hence, the minimum number of participants at the camp is:

108 x 4 = **432**

22. E

Explanation:

Since the average of the eight chocolate bars is £1.50:

The sum of all eight chocolate bars:

8 x 1.5 = **£12**

In order to calculate the maximum possible value for the most expensive chocolate bar, assume that 7 bars were priced at 50 pence as well.

50 p x 7 = **£3.50**

Therefore, the maximum price of the eighth chocolate bar:

12 - 3.5 = **£8.50**

23. D

Explanation:

When the greatest house number along the street is known, one will be able to work out the number of houses along the street. For example, if 141 is the greatest number, the following houses are 139, 137, 135, ...

Once this is known, all that is left to know is the relative position of Finn's house. **For example, the 2nd highest, 3rd lowest, etc.**

24. E

Explanation:

There were 24 guppies initially - **9 male and 15 female**. Of two thirds of the guppies (i.e., $\frac{2}{3}$ x 24 = 16) died, $\frac{1}{2}$ x 16 = 8 were female and the rest (i.e., 8) are male. This means, there are **7 females and 1 male left**. Each female gave birth to 15 fries, but since only 40% survive, this means that, for each female, only 6 fries are successfully reproduced. Given that there are 7 females, that will be a total of 42 fries.

Therefore, the total number of fish in the tank would be:

42 + 7 + 1 = **50**

25. B; D

Explanation:

To approach questions like this, it's best to draw a table to work out the information given.

- First, it is given that Hainanese chicken came first place and Meeko came in third.
- Flit made *rendang* but did not come last. Hence, Flit has to be in second place.
- Given that Percy did better than one of the participants, he could not have come in last. Hence, Percy is in the first place and Roo is in the last place.
- The participant who made the braised chicken did better than Roo, hence, that participant has to be Meeko.
- Therefore, Roo made roasted chicken.

Percy	Hainanese	1st
Flit	Rendang	2nd
Meeko	Braised	3rd
Roo	Roasted	4th

From the above, **Options 'B' and 'D'** are incorrect as Percy made Hainanese chicken and Meeko made braised chicken.

26. B

Explanation:

Mean is given by the sum of the height of all students divided by the number of students.

Let the number sum of the height of the students be given as 's_1' and 's_2' for groups with 'b' and 'c' number of students respectively:

$s_1 = 96b$

$s_2 = 134c$

$s_1 + s_2 = 110(b + c)$

Rearrange the above equations:

$96b + 134c = 110b + 110c$

$134c - 110c = 110b - 96b$

$24c = 14b$

$\frac{c}{b} = \frac{7}{12}$

27. D

Explanation:

Baking goes at the rate of 40 buns per 20 minutes. Hence, it would take an hour for 120 buns (i.e., 3 batches of buns).

Problem Solving

Problem Solving

Cooling takes 15 minutes. However, bear in mind that the cooling for each batch will begin as soon as it is taken out of the oven. This means that the 15-minute cooling process of the first batch takes place simultaneously with the baking time of the second batch.

Packing takes 10 seconds per bun. This means for each batch (i.e., 40 buns), it would take Harvey 400 seconds which is equivalent to 6 minutes and 40 seconds. Even though it takes 15 mins + 6 mins 40 seconds = 21 mins 40 seconds to fully prepare the buns for delivery, the extra 1 min and 40 seconds of packing of the first batch can still take place when the second batch is cooling down. This applies to the second batch as well. However, you should be aware that 21 minutes 40 seconds is needed to cool down and pack the third batch of buns.

Hence, the total time needed to prepare the 3 batches of buns is 20 mins + 20 mins + 20 mins + 21 mins 40 seconds = 81 mins 40 seconds. Given that the answer options disregard the 'seconds' unit, this can be rounded up to 82 minutes (equivalent to 1 hour and 22 minutes)

Harvey needs to arrive at the school at 8:00 am after an estimated drive of 35 minutes.

This means that he has to leave his house at 7:25 am latest.

Therefore, he has to start baking the buns by:

7:25 am - 1 hour 22 mins = **6:03 am**.

---

28. E

Explanation:

This question deals with the different permutations of 3 songs from a selection of 15 songs.

The possible permutations are:

15 x 14 x 13 = 2,730

Since the question asks for 'how many other possible arrangements', it means that the arrangement described in the question itself should be excluded.

Therefore:

2,730 - 1 = 2,729

---

29. A

Explanation:

A negative, non-zero score only results from a combination of having at least a "1" in the pair of numbers.

The probability of getting a zero or positive score is:

1 - 0.64 = 0.36

This means the probability of getting two numbers that are not "1" is 0.36

Thus, the probability of getting a non-"1" number is:

$\sqrt{0.36} = 0.6$

Hence, the probability of spinning a "1" is:

1 - 0.6 = 0.4

---

30. A

Explanation:

The probability of getting "1" is 0.4.

Let 'B' be the factor of which "1" is bigger than the rest of the 5 sectors. Assume that the rest of the sectors are 1-unit area each.

Thus, "1" has:

B x 1 = B unit area.
$B \div (B + 5) = 0.4$
$B = 0.4B + 2$
$0.6B = 2$
$B = \frac{10}{3}$

31. D

Explanation:

This question is best approached by finding the probability of getting an odd product first.

Each dice has 6 faces, each numbered from 1 to 6.

Given that all the dice are independent, the number of possible outcomes is:

6 x 6 x 6 x 6 x 6 x 6 (or 6^6)

For the product to be an odd number, none of the 6 numbers can be even (i.e., all 6 numbers must be odd). The only odd numbers on a dice are 1, 3 and 5.

Hence, the number of possible outcomes that will give an odd product is:

3 x 3 x 3 x 3 x 3 x 3 (or 3^6)

Therefore, the probability of getting an odd product is:

$3^6 \div 6^6 = (\frac{1}{2})^6 = \frac{1}{64}$

Given that the product can only be odd or even, then the probability of getting an even product will be:

$\frac{63}{64}$

32. D

Explanation:

Mariana has the bottle (maximum capacity of **500 ml**) and the cup (maximum capacity of 300 ml) to use. To work out **300 ml**, she has to first use a full cup of water and pour it into the bottle. Then, she has to fetch another full cup of water to continue filling the bottle. When the bottle is full, there will be **100 ml of water** left in the cup. She then has to empty the bottle before adding the 100 ml of water from the cup to the bottle. Lastly, she fills the cup with 300 ml of water once more and adds this to the bottle to get **400 ml of water**. This process requires **900 ml** of water for the cup to be filled thrice.

33. C

Explanation:

Assume that $'x'$ is the cost per passenger:

Since the cost per passenger would have been £3 lower if there were 24 friends:

$16x = 24(x - 3)$
$16x = 24x - 72$
$8x = 72$
$x =$ **£9.00**

Since Becca pays with a £20.00 note:

20 - 9 = **£11.00**

34. A

This question tests one's ability to recognise the pattern.

"Each consonant moves forward to the next letter in the alphabet, each vowel moves backwards to the previous letter in the alphabet; vowel A moves backwards to become Z, vice versa".

Problem Solving

One should be able to get the code 'QIZTHDHZO' followed by 'RHAUIEIAN'.

Original	First Code	Second Code
P	Q	R
H	I	H
Y	Z	A
S	T	U
I	H	I
C	D	E
I	H	I
A	Z	A
N	O	N

35. C

Explanation:

Given that the bullet train travels four times faster than the regular train, this means that the time taken for it to complete the same journey is:

12 ÷ 4 = **3 mins**

If the bullet train travels a distance of 7 km in 3 mins, this means it can travel a distance of:

$7 \times \frac{60}{3}$ = **140 km in an hour**

Hence, the answer is **140 km/h.**

36. C

Explanation:

In **5 milliseconds, the third alarm will go off for 6 milliseconds**. At the point when it goes off, the other two alarms are still off.

37. B

Explanation:

To determine when all the alarms will come on together, work out the least common multiple of the intervals when the alarms will be on. The first alarm turns on every 8 milliseconds - it turns on again at 8 ms, 16 ms, 24 ms, and so on. The second alarm turns on every 10 milliseconds - 10 ms, 20 ms, 30 ms, and so on. The third alarm turns on every 12 milliseconds - 12 ms, 24 ms, 36 ms and so on. This means that they will all turn on at the same time at the least common multiple of 8, 10 and 12.

To find the least common multiple of 8, 10 and 12, break them down to their prime factors.

8 = **2 x 2 x 2**

10 = **2 x 5**

12 = **2 x 2 x 3**

Next, multiply each factor by the greatest number of times it occurs. The integers 3 and 5 have only occurred once whereas 2 has occurred thrice in the number 8.

Therefore, the Lowest Common Multiple is:

2 x 2 x 2 x 3 x 5 = **120 ms.**

Given that a millisecond has passed, the answer is **119 milliseconds.**

38. E

Explanation:

Let the age of the first and second corpses be 'F' and 'S' respectively.

Equation 1: <u>$F = S^2$</u>

Equation 2: <u>$F - 6 = 25(S - 6)$</u>

Substitute Equation 1 into Equation 2:

$S^2 - 6 = 25(S - 6)$; $S^2 - 6 = 25S - 150$; $S^2 - 25S + 144 = 0$; $(S - 16)(S - 9) = 0$

<u>$S = 16$ or $S = 9$</u>

If $S = 16$, then $F = 256$

If $S = 9$, then $F = 81$

Given that the current age of 'F' is an even number, then **<u>'F' and 'S' have to be aged 256 and 16 respectively.</u>**

Hence, their **<u>age difference is 140 years.</u>**

39. E

Explanation:

This question is best solved by quickly sketching a diagram of the family tree.

- Quinn has 1 son, Maddox, and 2 daughters, Neveah and Rylee.
- Maddox is married to Layla and they have a daughter named Priscilla.

Therefore, the only accurate answer is **<u>Option 'E'</u>**. **<u>Option 'A'</u>** is incorrect as Neveah is Priscilla's aunt. **<u>Option 'B'</u>** is incorrect because Quinn is Layla's father-in-law. **<u>Option 'C'</u>** is incorrect because Rylee is female and is Maddox's sister. **<u>Option 'D'</u>** is incorrect because Quinn is the grandfather of Priscilla.

40. D

Explanation:

Volume of concentrate:

1250 ml x 2 = **<u>2500 ml</u>**

Volume of juice after dilution:

(2 x 2 x 300) + (5 x 250) + (7 x 350) + 3850 = **<u>8750 ml</u>**

Volume of water used for dilution:

8750 - 2500 = **<u>6250 ml</u>**

Ratio of water to concentrate:

6250 : 2500 = **<u>5 : 2</u>**

41. B

Explanation:

Each day, Dalley saves a net total of two apples. At the end of the 5th day, he would have saved 10 apples. On the following morning (i.e., 6th day), he would pick five apples from the farm. This would give him **<u>15 apples in total</u>**, which is sufficient for him to bake the apple crumble.

42. A

Explanation:

This question can be confusing but it is made easier by summarising the information given in equations. Let 'my passcode' be denoted as 'M', 'my sister's passcode' be denoted as 'S', 'my brother's passcode' be denoted as 'B' and 'my cousin's passcode' be denoted as 'C'.

Equation 1: $S = 2M + 160$

Equation 2: $B = 2S + 160$

Equation 3: $C = 2B + 160$

Substituting Equation 1 into Equation 2:

$B = 2(2M + 160) + 160$

$B = 4M + 480$ → *Equation 4*

Substituting Equation 4 into Equation 3:

$C = 2(4M + 480) + 160$

$C = 8M + 1120$

$C = 8(M + 140)$ → *Equation 5*

From the equation above, 'C' is divisible by 8. The largest 4-digit number that is divisible by 8 is 9992.

Hence, substitute C = 9992 into the Equation 5:

M = 1109

43. C

Explanation:

This question requires a careful elimination of the options and to reason out the statements given. Considering that Xyla was told the month and Yale was told the day of Zion's birthday:

"Xyla: I don't know when Zion's birthday is, but I know that Yale doesn't know as well."

- The first part of the sentence *"Xyla: I don't know when Zion's birthday is"* is redundant. There is no way Xyla can tell when Zion's birthday is by just knowing the month.
- However, the second part *"I know that Yale doesn't know as well"* gives a clue. The only way Xyla knows that Yale doesn't know is that Xyla was told that the month is January or February. This is because all the possible dates in those two months, which are 12, 13, 14 and 15, are repeated in another month.
- In other words, the only way Yale could know the birthday is if he was told 16 or 17.

"Yale: I initially didn't know when Zion's birthday was, but I know now."

- By now, Yale should have deduced that Xyla was told either January or February.
- The fact that he can tell when Zion's birthday is means that he must have been told the number 13, 14 or 15 as they only appear once in those two months.
- If Yale had been told the number 12, he would still be as clueless about Zion's birthday.

"Xyla: In that case, I know when Zion's birthday is too."

- At this point, given that Yale was able to tell Zion's birthday, Xyla is down to 3 possible options - 13th of January, 15th of January or 14th of February.
- The only way for Xyla to say that she now knows Zion's birthday is that she was told February earlier.

Hence, Zion's birthday is on the **14th of February.**

44. D

Explanation:

Adanna is paying 6% tax, which can also be expressed as 106% (i.e., 1.06) of the price. With a 40% discount, she pays 60% (i.e., 0.60) of the price.

Given that 'd' is the total amount Adanna paid to the cashier, form the equation as below:

$d = s \times 1.06 \times 0.60$

$$s = \frac{d}{(0.60)(1.06)}$$

45. A

Explanation:

Option 'B' is true as the question states that sad people are unsuccessful. **Option 'C' is also correct** because all famous people are successful. **Option 'D' is true** because all famous people are successful, and all successful people are hardworking.

46. A

Explanation:

Let the flat rate for the packaging fee be 'F' and the rate per kilogram of durian be 'D':

Equation 1: $F + 4D = \underline{16.40}$

Equation 2: $F + 7D = \underline{26.90}$

Equation 2 - Equation 1:

$3D = 10.50$

$\underline{D = 3.50}$

Substitute D = 3.50 into Equation 1:

$F + 4(3.50) = 16.40$

$\underline{F = 2.40}$

Hence, for 9 kg of durian, the total cost of it would be:

$2.40 + 9(3.50) = \underline{\pounds 33.90}$

47. A

Explanation:

The volume of the final solution is:

$0.9 \times 200 = \underline{180 \text{ ml}}$

In this volume, 3 parts of it is water and 1 part of it is the partially diluted glucose. In other words, the partially diluted solution takes up $\frac{1}{4}$ of the beaker - i.e., $180 \times \frac{1}{4} = 45$ ml.

The original glucose concentrate was diluted using 19 parts water and 1-part concentrate. This means the concentrate is $\frac{1}{20}$ of 45ml - i.e.,

$45 \times \frac{1}{20} = \underline{2.25 \text{ ml}}$

48. D

Explanation:

After 1st minute: $0.8 \times 140 = \underline{112 \text{ cm}^3}$

After 2nd minute: $0.8 \times 112 = \underline{89.6 \text{ cm}^3}$

After 3rd minute: $0.8 \times 89.6 = \underline{71.68 \text{ cm}^3}$

After 4th minute: $71.68 \times 0.7 = \underline{50.176 \text{ cm}^3}$

After 5th minute: $50.176 \times 0.7 = \underline{35.1232 \text{ cm}^3}$

49. B

Explanation:

This question is best approached by looking at the events that occurred while keeping track of the number of people present in the laboratory.

Event	Number of people in the laboratory
There were 21 students and a teacher in a Chemistry laboratory.	22
Five students, who finished their work early, were about to leave for a break when one of them slipped and hit his head at the corner of the table.	22
The laboratory assistant, who had arrived from the preparation room (+1).	23
As the team of three paramedics arrived within the next 10 minutes (+3).	26
A third of the students, including the ones who were about to leave, had left the laboratory (-7).	19
Two of the school administrators had also arrived at the scene to speak with the teacher outside the laboratory (-1). This is because the school administrators did not enter the lab; instead, they talked to the teacher outside of the laboratory.	18
Thankfully, the paramedics were able to stabilise his neck and to mobilise him onto a stretcher.	<u>18</u>

50. D

Explanation:

First, establish that the number of right leg dominant players:

25 x 10 = **<u>250</u>**

Let the number of left leg dominant females be 'F' and the number of left leg dominant males be 'M'. *With this, form the equations below:*

Equation 1: F + M = <u>25</u>

Equation 2: 7F + 12M = <u>250</u>

Equation 1 can be rearranged to F = 25 - M. *Substitute this into Equation 2:*

7(25 - M) + 12M = 250

175 - 7M + 12M = 250

5M = 75

<u>M = 15</u>

Substitute M = 15 into F = 25 - M:

F = 25 - 15

<u>F = 10</u>

	Dominance	
Gender	Right Leg	Left Leg
Female	70	10
Male	180	15
Total	250	25

Thus, the probability of right leg dominant play being male is $\frac{\mathbf{180}}{\mathbf{250}}$ = **0.72.**

51. D

Explanation:

The best way to solve this question is to create a table representing all the information given in the question.

	Monday	Tuesday	Wednesday	Thursday	Friday	Saturday	Sunday
Timothy	/	/	X	/	/	/	X
Noah	/	/	/	X	X	/	X
Zachary	X	X	/	/	/	/	X

- Everyone works on Saturdays.
- No one works on Sundays.
- Zachary works four consecutive days; one of it is Saturday and not Sunday. Hence, it can be deduced that the other three working days for Zachary is Wednesday, Thursday and Friday.
- From the aforementioned statement, it can be deduced that Zachary will not be working on Monday and Tuesday. Given that there must be two employees on any weekday, Timothy and Noah will have to work on those days.
- Noah will not be available to work on Thursday and Friday. Given that he is also not working on Sunday, this means that he must work the rest of the days - Monday, Tuesday, Wednesday, Saturday.
- As a result, Timothy will not work on Wednesday and that he will work on Friday. Hence, Timothy works on Monday, Tuesday, Thursday, Friday and Saturday.

52. E

Explanation:

First, Reggie and Miso were either born in <u>January and March respectively or May and July</u>. However, given that Orsona (i.e., which has to be born in October) has her birthday five months after Miso's, it can be deduced that <u>Miso's birthday is in May and that Reggie's is in July</u>. The number of months between October to July in the following year is <u>9 months.</u>

53. D

Explanation:

There are **900 students in the school**. Given that the intake is consistent every year and that there are only 3 years of students, each year has 300 students. Of these 300, **150 are male and 150 are female**.

Of the 300 Year 2 students, **100 took French whilst 200 took Spanish**. A total of 75 students took Japanese whilst 225 took Korean. Thus, the maximum number of boys who took both Spanish and Korean is 150, as there are only 150 boys in the cohort. The minimum number of boys who took Spanish and Korean is 0. This is because it is possible if all girls take Spanish and Korean as well. As a result, of the 150 boys, **100 took French and 50 took Spanish, and 75 took Japanese and 75 took Korean**. It is possible that all 75 students who took Korean took French as well, leaving no boys who take the Spanish and Korean combination. Hence, the difference between the maximum and minimum is **150.**

54. C

Explanation:

A summary of Griffin's travel to work every day is shown below:

Home → (5 mins walk) → Ferry → Underground → (7 mins walk) → Central Station → (8 mins ride) → Bus Stop → (2 mins walk) → Factory

Griffin's walking time, as well as the ferry, the underground and the bus journeys, are all constant. However, the waiting times in between underground and ferry and at central station may vary. For him to save the most of his time, he should take the 7:59 am or 8:05 am ferry. This is so that he can catch the underground 4 minutes after leaving the ferry arrival terminal. He has two options – to arrive by underground at 8:30 am or 8:36 am. If he arrives at 8:30 am, he will walk and arrive at central station by 8:37 am, wait for 2 minutes and catch the 8:39 am bus. If he arrives at 8:36 am, he will arrive at central station at 8:43 am and he would have to wait for 6 minutes before catching the bus at 8:49 am.

Hence, Griffin should catch the 7:39 am ferry if he wants to arrive in his workplace with the shortest time possible.

His total travelling time, in minutes, would be:

5 (walk) + 12 (ferry) + 4 (wait) + 15 (underground) + 7 (walk) + 2 (wait) + 8 (bus) + 2 (walk) = 55 mins

55. B

Explanation:

Griffin plans to arrive at the office by **8:55 am**. This means he has to be at the bus stop by **8:53 am** and he has to be on the bus by 8:45 am. Hence, he has to take the **8:39 am** bus at the central station. He would then have to leave the underground arrival station at **8:32 am**, which works well for him if he takes the 8:15 am underground. Since the taxi takes 13 minutes to arrive at the ferry departure terminal, Griffin must leave his house by **8:02 am at the latest**.

56. C

Explanation:

In a year, Griffin works a total of:

(40 x 5) + 20 = 220 days a year

Each day, he spends:

2(2.40 + 1.50 + 0.60) = <u>£9 for a round trip</u>
(Bear in mind that the first line in the question stem states that he takes the same mode of transport to and from the office every day).
In a year, he spends: 9 x 220 = <u>£1980</u>
By purchasing the annual pass, Griffin saves:
1980 - 1250 = <u>£730</u>

57. D

Explanation:
27 km = <u>27000 m</u>
Time taken to drive to work:
27000 ÷ 20 = 1350 seconds <u>(22.5 mins)</u>
If he has to arrive at work by 9:00 am, he should leave his house by:
22.5 mins - 24 mins - 5 mins = <u>8:08 am</u>

58. F

Explanation:
The numbers are arranged in alphabetical order and all numbers in the series are of single digits. Therefore, the series goes as:
<u>Eight, Five, Four, Nine, One, Seven, Six, Three, Two, Zero.</u>

59. B

Explanation:
Intuitively, one might think that six slices are needed to achieve this. However, this number can be reduced if the cheese was cut along the horizontal plane twice first, followed by being cut vertically twice on its face. This will take **<u>four slices in total to give 12 equal blocks of cheese.</u>**

60. C

Explanation:
Consider Callum:
Money received for his age: 10 + 7(5) = **<u>£45</u>**
Money received for his grades: **<u>£12</u>**
Total money received: 45 + 12 = **<u>£57</u>**
Consider Suzie:
Total money received: 2(57) + 7 = **<u>£121</u>**
Money received for her age: 10 + 3(5) = **<u>£25</u>**
Money received for her grades: 121 - 25 = **<u>£96</u>**
Number of A+ achieved: 96 ÷ 12 = **<u>8</u>**
<u>Suzie achieved 7 more A+ compared to her brother, Callum.</u>

61. E

Explanation:
From the question, Benjamin finishes school first, **<u>Dominic finishes 40 minutes after Benjamin, and Christopher finishes 20 minutes after Dominic.</u>**
Time taken to reach home = Time of travel (in minutes) + Time of delay
Benjamin: $\frac{17}{8}$ x 60 = <u>127.5 mins</u>
Christopher: ($\frac{17}{15}$ x 60) + 60 = <u>128 mins</u>
Dominic: ($\frac{17}{12}$ x 60) + 40 = <u>125 mins</u>
Therefore, the order of them arriving home would be **<u>Dominic, Benjamin, Christopher.</u>**

62. A

Explanation:

Calculate the distance between X and Y:

52 x 3.5 = **182 km**

Calculate the distance travelled during the first two hours:

46 x 2 = **92 km**

Therefore, the distance travelled in the final 1.5 hours is:

182 - 92 = 90

90 ÷ 1.5 = **60 kilometres per hour**

Convert kilometres per hour into miles per hour:

60 x 0.6 = **36 miles per hour**

63. E

Explanation:

Joseph did 15 minutes of breaststroke and 15 minutes of freestyle.

The total distance travelled by Joseph is:

$(\frac{15}{60} \times 3) + (\frac{15}{60} \times 1) = \underline{1\ \text{mile}}$

Since they both cover the same distance, Daniel must have done the freestyle and breaststroke for **0.5 miles each**.

The time he would have taken is:

$(\frac{0.5}{3} + \frac{0.5}{1}) \times 60 = \underline{40\ \text{minutes}}$

64. D

Explanation:

Three pairs of shoes were purchased. Hence, **the discount for each pair of shoe is £9.**

Thus, the total cost would be:

2(150 - 9) + (90 - 9) = **£363**

65. D

Explanation:

Let the price per pair of shoes purchased be 'P'. The number of shoes purchased is 15, hence, the expression is **$15(P - 15^2)$.** From this, 'P' cannot be equal or any lesser than **15^2 (i.e., £225)**. Given that the owner wants to prevent making a loss, he should find a shoe that is £20 more than £225. Hence, the minimum price per pair of shoe that the owner would recommend is **£245**.

For 15 pairs, this would cost:

245 x 15 = **£3675**

66. C

Explanation:

Let the number of pairs of shoes purchased be 'N'. The cost of purchasing 'N' pairs of shoes is **$N(192 - N^2)$** and the cost of each pair of shoes will be **$192 - N^2$**. This means that **N^2 cannot be greater than 192**. The greatest squared product of an integer that is lesser than 192 is 13^2, which equals **169.**

67. C

Explanation:

This question can be approached through trial and error or, if one has background knowledge on differential calculus, it can be approached mathematically as well.

From the information given, construct the equation below:

$M = N(192 - N^2)$
$M = 192N - N^3$
$dM/dN = 192 - 3N^2$
When M is maximum, dM/dN = 0.
$192 - 3N^2 = 0$
$3N^2 = 192$
$N^2 = 64$
<u>N = 8</u>
This means that for the customer to have paid the greatest amount of money, 'M' at checkout, she must have purchased 8 pairs of shoes. This would amount to **<u>£1024.</u>**
For the rest of the options, the amount of which she would have paid are as below:
<u>If N = 2, M = 376</u>
<u>If N = 5, M = 835</u>
<u>If N = 11, M = 781</u>
<u>If N = 13, M = 299</u>

68. C

Explanation:
The spice costs **<u>£96 per kilogram</u>**. This means that it costs **<u>48 p per 5 grams</u>**. The initial rate is £2.40 per 10 grams. This means it is charged at £1.20 per 5 grams for the first 10 grams of spices added.
For a bowl of noodles with 15 grams, the chef charges an extra:
1.20 x 0.8 = **<u>96 p</u>**
At 20 grams, he charges:
96 x 0.8 = **<u>77 p</u>**
At 25 grams, he charges:
77 x 0.8 = **<u>62 p</u>**
At 30 grams, he charges:
62 x 0.8 = **<u>50 p</u>**
At 35 grams, he charges:
50 x 0.8 = **<u>40 p</u>**
This is lower than the cost per **<u>5 grams of spice, which is 48 p.</u>**
Hence, the maximum amount of spice he should add to a bowl of noodles is **<u>30 grams.</u>**

69. A

Explanation:
First, it is important to recognise that at any particular stop, students can get on or off the minibus. Hence, the minimum number of stops the bus could have had is 8 stops. Of these 8 stops, the minimum taken for 6 of them was 100 seconds ,whereas the minimum time taken for the rest of the 2 stops is 80 seconds.
This is an added duration of:
[(6 x 100) + (2 x 80)] = 760 s = **<u>12 mins 40 s (rounded up to 13 mins)</u>**
Estimated time of arrival:
8:00 am + 36 mins + 13 mins = **<u>8:49 am</u>**

70. B

Explanation:
Let 'x' be the price of Cake 1, 'y' be the price of Cake 2 and 'z' be the price of Cake 3:
$x + y = 4.9$ **<u>(Equation 1)</u>**

$x + z = 6.1$ **(Equation 2)**
$y + z = 4.5$ **(Equation 3)**
Subtract Equation 1 from Equation 2:
$-y + z = 1.2$ **(Equation 4)**
Add Equation 3 and Equation 4:
$2z = 5.7$
z = £2.85
Substitute z= 2.85 into Equation 3:
$y + 2.85 = 4.5$
y = £1.65
Substitute z= 2.85 into Equation 3:
$x + 2.85 = 6.1$
x = £3.25
The difference between the price of Cake 1 and Cake 3:
3.25 - 2.85 = **0.4 (40 pence)**

71. B

Explanation:

The median amount of money spent is 16. Given that there are 5 figures in the question, this has to be the 3rd term in the series. The mode is 25, hence, this means that more than one of the five terms must be 25. Given that 16 is the middle and 3rd term, this means that 25 is the 4th and 5th terms.

The mean of the 5 terms is 16. Hence, the total of the 5 terms is:
16 x 5 = **80**
Therefore, the sum of the 1st , 2nd and 3rd term (i.e., the total minus the 4th and 5th terms) must be:
80 - 25 - 25 = **30**
Therefore, the mean of the 3 smallest terms is:
30 ÷ 3 = **£10**

72. E

Explanation:

This question is quite straightforward, provided that one remembers that the question asks for what he has to purchase and not what he exactly needs for baking. Also, note that the recipe given is for 16 tarts, but Adrian is baking for 11 x 4 = 44 tarts this time. Hence, the quantity that needs to be purchased for each ingredient is as below.

Crumbled cookies: $\frac{500}{16} \times 44 =$ **1375 g**
(Since the cookies are sold in packs of 100 g, he needs to purchase 1,400 g)

Butter: $\frac{250}{16} \times 44 =$ **687.5 g**
(Since butter is sold in blocks of 250 g, he needs 3 x 250 = 750 g)

Lemon: $\frac{6}{16} \times 44 =$ **16.5** (this means he has to purchase 17 lemons)

Condensed milk: $\frac{2}{16} \times 44 =$ **5.5** (this means he has to purchase 6 cans).

Eggs: $\frac{4}{16} \times 44 =$ **11 eggs**

Alternatively, solve this question by eliminating unreasonable options. **Options 'B', 'C' and 'D'** can be eliminated at first sight as they have odd units of ingredients such as 5.5

cans of condensed milk. Hence, by calculating the number of cookies that is required, Option 'E' can be selected immediately.

73. B

Explanation:

If Badrul was telling the truth, then the rest of the four friends are not telling the truth. However, if Clyde isn't telling the truth, then what Klara says is true - that Clyde isn't telling the truth. This contradicts the first statement. **Hence, Badrul cannot be telling the truth.**

If Badrul isn't telling the truth, then that means Clyde is telling the truth. Hence, Klara isn't telling the truth. This means Naowarat is telling the truth. Jihyo would then not be telling the truth. **Therefore, 3 of them were not telling the truth.**

74. C

Explanation:

There are 50 adults in the group.

$0.48 \times 50 = \underline{24}$

A total of 24 adults of them go to the cinemas at least once a month. Hence, 26 go to the cinemas less than once a month.

$\frac{5}{6} \times 24 = \underline{\textbf{20 adults}}$

Exactly 20 adults go to the cinemas at least once a week.

Of these 20 adults:

0.35 x 20 = **7 of them do not subscribe Netflix at all.**

Of the 26 adults who go to the cinemas less than once a month:

$\frac{1}{2}$ x 26 = **13 of them subscribe to Netflix.**

The other 13 do not.

Hence, the percentage of adults who do not subscribe to Netflix is:

$\frac{(7+13)}{50} \times 100 = \underline{40\%}$

75. C

Explanation:

Wanli cannot work with Carven as they have worked together for the last five days. Hence, Option 'A' is incorrect. If Wanli works with Sashi, then Carven has to work with Anthony. As a result, **Option 'B' is incorrect**. Therefore, **Wanli has to work with Anthony.**

76. E

Explanation:

From the question, arrange the following students according to their test scores, in increasing order, with certainty:

Danyal, Karmen, Andre, Ciara

Firdaus scored higher than Danyal but his exact position compared to the rest of the students is not known. **Options 'A' and 'C'** are incorrect as Danyal scored lower than the rest of the students. **Options 'B' and 'D'** are incorrect as, although they may be possibilities, there is not sufficient information to be certain of their accuracy. **Option 'E'** is correct as the question mentions that Firdaus 'may' have attained a score lower than Karmen, which is a realistic possibility.

Problem Solving

77. A

Explanation:

Looking at the options, the date has to fall in December 1998. The date 12/1998 itself has 4 integers in it. Hence, the closest possible date would be 29/12/1998. This is 3 days before 01/01/1999.

78. A

Explanation:

The best way to solve this is to determine the prime factors to the numbers in the table.

	r	s
p	2 x 7 x 13	3 x 3 x 3 x 5 x 7
q	2 x 3 x 3 x 3 x 13	3 x 3 x 3 x 3 x 3 x 3 x 5

Once this is worked out, deduce what each integer represents.

Looking at the prime factors of 'pr' and 'ps', deduce that 7 is the only similar prime factor. Hence, 'p' must be 7.

Hence, r is:

2 x 13 = 26

(and s = 3 x 3 x 3 x 5 = 135)

If r = 2 x 13, then q must be 3 x 3 x 3 = 27

The values for 'q' and 's' correspond to the numbers shown in the table above.

Hence:

p + q + r + s = 7 + 27 + 26 + 135 = 195

79. D

Explanation:

From the following statements, produce the table shown below.

- Barnabe wore Number 3.
- Cheung finished first.
- Cheung doesn't belong to the house Topaz, nor did he wear a red shirt.
- Demetrius finished the race before Barnabe.
- Achille finished after Demetrius, but before the student who wore Number 3.

Student	Number	House Colour	Position
Achille			3rd
Barnabe	III		4th
Cheung		Green/ Blue	1st
Demetrius			2nd

It is known for sure that only one student finished the race in the same position as the number on his shirt. In addition, Achille is not that student as Number 3 has been taken up by Barnabe. Hence, that leaves two options:

Option 1: Cheung wears 4 and Demetrius wears 2, while Cheung wears 4

With the scenario above, the table would be:

A Lakshmi, T R Enoch, S Z Y Ooi. Doctors Academy Publications, Cardiff, UK, 2020.

Student	Number	House Colour	Position
Achille	I	Green/ Yellow	3rd
Barnabe	III	Green/ Yellow	4th
Cheung	IV	Blue	1st
Demetrius	II	Red	2nd

Option 2: Cheung wears 1 and Demetrius wears 4
With the scenario above, the table would be:
As a result, it has to be Option 2.
Therefore, from the table above, <u>**only Option 'D' is correct**</u> - the student who finished 3rd is from the Ruby house.

80. F

Explanation:

Assuming if Cindy had drunk Bubbleologist every day:
For each purchase, she would have collected 30 points, which is equivalent to 30 pence. At the start, Cindy would need 12 sets of 30 pence (i.e., 12 cups) to collect sufficient points for a free cup. When she redeems her free cup on the 13th day, she would have a remaining of (12 x 30) - 345 = 15 points in her card.
The 15 points would allow her to redeem a free cup after the next 11 purchases. This would get her 11 x 30 = 330 points; hence 11 purchases are sufficient to reach 345 points. When she redeems her free cup on the 25th day, she would have a remaining of 0 points in her card.
The remaining 6 days of December will not be enough for her to collect points to redeem another free cup. Hence, she purchases a cup a day for the rest of December.
In total, she spends:
(12 + 11 + 6) x 3.45 = **£100.05.**
Assuming if Cindy had drunk Bobastry every day:
For every 10 days, she would have spent the cost of 9 cups. For 30 days, she would have spent a total cost of 27 cups. Including the 31st day in December, the total cost would be:
28 x 3.80 = **£106.40**
The difference in the cost:
106.40 - 100.05 = **£6.35 (Bubbleologist costs less)**

81. D

Explanation:

There are 600 teeth in the initial set. He first removes all multiples of 4. From 1 to 600, the biggest multiple of 4 is 600. Hence, there are **600 ÷ 4 = 150 multiples of 4**. There are **600 - 150 = 450 teeth remaining**. He then removes all multiples of 8. However, given that 8 is a multiple of 4, this means that all multiples of 8 had been removed. The anthropologist removes one third of the remaining teeth - in other words, there are two thirds of 450 pieces of teeth left. This means there are 450 x $\frac{2}{3}$ = **300 teeth left in the display.**
The weight of each tooth is given by its density multiplied by its volume.
Volume of an average tooth: 0.3 x 0.4 x 0.5 = **0.06 cm^3**
Weight of an average tooth: 0.06 x 2 = **0.12 g**
Weight of all the remaining teeth: 0.12 x 300 = **36 g**

Problem Solving

Problem Solving

82. E

Explanation:

This question can be a little confusing, but the working can be made less tedious by finding the angles of each hand, using 1200 as a reference point of 0°. Sketching a diagram would help as well.

First, calculate the angle for the minute hand:

60 minutes → **<u>360°</u>**

26 minutes → $\frac{26}{60}$ x 360 = <u>156°</u> (in a clockwise direction from the 1200 mark)

Next, calculate the angle for the hour hand:

1 hour → $\frac{1}{12}$ x 360 = <u>30°</u>

This means that the hour hand at 11:00 is 330° in a clockwise direction from the 12:00 mark.

The proportion of this 30° that would have moved in the 26 minutes would be:

$\frac{26}{60}$ x 30 = <u>13°</u>

Hence, at 11:26, the hour hand is **<u>330 + 13 = 343° in a clockwise direction</u>** from the 12:00 mark.

<u>Summary:</u>

Hour hand - **<u>343° clockwise</u>**

Minute hand - **<u>156° clockwise</u>**

Angle between the two hands: 343 - 156 = <u>187°</u> (this has to be the larger angle as the supplementary angle is $<180^{\circ}$)

83. B

Explanation:

Consider School X:

Total percentage of students who play racquet sports:

15.80 + 9.40 + 13.80 = <u>39%</u>

Number of students who play racquet sports:

0.39 x 1,500 = <u>585</u>

Consider School Y:

Total percentage of students who play racquet sports:

16.25 + 17.50 + 13.25 = <u>47%</u>

Number of students who play racquet sports:

0.47 x 0.80 x 1,500 = <u>564</u>

Difference in the number of students who play racquet sports:

585 - 564 = <u>21</u>

84. C

Explanation:

This question can be approached by **<u>"fact-checking" each of the statements or by making a Venn diagram.</u>**

By the first method, one can infer from Huzah that **<u>Option 'C' is false</u>** as the question had stated that Huzah does not ski nor swim, whereas Harry skis.

85. E

Explanation:

This question requires one to assess the risk of each patient group in getting the disease. From the text, one should be able to derive the probabilities as below.

1 - overweight, below age of 60 - $\frac{1}{3}$

2 - overweight, equal or above age of 60 - $\frac{2}{3}$

3 - not overweight, below age of 60 - $\frac{1}{6}$

4 - not overweight, equal or above age of 60 - $\frac{1}{12}$

Group 2 already has a risk that is above 50% chance. Hence, they should not be given the drug. For the rest of the groups, multiplying $\frac{5}{4}$ (i.e., increase in 25% chance) to their original probabilities will give $\frac{5}{12}, \frac{5}{24}$ and $\frac{5}{48}$ for Groups 1, 3 and 4 respectively. All these probabilities are lesser than 50%. Hence, it is safe to prescribe them the drug.

86. D

Explanation:

The best way to solve this question is to create a table to match each individual to a genre.

- While Ankara and Berlin may enjoy accompanying their friend to jazz nights, they are both not matched to jazz as the friend would be the one to match to jazz.
- Cheyenne is not matched to country nor classical.
- Berlin is not matched to country music as well.
- Cheyenne doesn't like jazz.

With the information above, one can form the table below:

	Country	Jazz	Classical	Dubstep
Ankara		X		
Berlin	X	X		
Cheyenne	X	X	X	
Dakota				

- Cheyenne is matched to dubstep music. Hence, cross out dubstep for the rest of the group.
- With that, one can tell that Berlin likes classical music. Classical music can be crossed out for the rest of the group too.
- Next, match Ankara to country and lastly, Dakota to jazz.

With the information above, one should be able to get the table below:

	Country	Jazz	Classical	Dubstep
Ankara	/	X	X	X
Berlin	X	X	/	X
Cheyenne	X	X	X	/
Dakota	X	/	X	X

Problem Solving

87. C

Explanation:

Let the fixed rate be 'F' and let the half-hourly rate be 'R'.

Equation 1: F + 13R = 73.5

Equation 2: 3(F + 24R) = 385.50

Equation 2 can be simplified to:

F + 24R = £128.50 (Let this be Equation 3)

Equation 3 - Equation 1:

11R = 55

<u>R = 5</u>

Substitute R = 5 into Equation 1:

F + 13(5) = 73.5

<u>F = 8.5</u>

To rent 2 rods for 4.5 hours, it would cost:

2(F + 9R) = 2[8.5 + (9 x 5)] = **<u>£107</u>**

88. D

Explanation:

This question requires one to be able to quickly count the days of the month backwards. This goes by a general rule of:

- If the preceding month has 28 days, the day of the same corresponding date (i.e., 13th) will move backwards by 0 days.
- If the preceding month has 29 days (i.e., in February of a leap year), the day of the same corresponding date will move backwards by 1 day.
- If the preceding month has 30 days, the day of the same corresponding date (i.e., 13th) will move backwards by 2 days.
- If the preceding month has 31 days, the day of the same corresponding date will move backwards by 3 days.

Hence, the 13th of February 2020 (bear in mind that 2020 is a leap year) is on a Thursday (given that it moves backwards by 1 day). Therefore, the 13th of January 2020 will be a Monday by moving backwards by 3 days. As a result, the **<u>13th of December 2019 is a Friday.</u>**

89. E

Explanation:

Let the number of people who made a purchase be 'P' and the number of people who did not make a purchase be 'N'.

Form the equation:

<u>N + P = 2000</u>

Each 'P' is given 12 pairs and each 'N' is given 6 pairs. However, only half of 'P' accepted the samples. This means that the equation 0.5(12P) + 6N = T can be formed, where 'T' is the total number of pairs given out.

0.5(12P) + 6N = T

6P + 6N = T

T = 6(P + N)

T = 6(2,000)

<u>T = 12000</u>

90. B

Explanation:

This question can be solved in two ways. One way to solve it is to work it out mathematically using equations and the other is to solve it backwards. Both methods will be shown below.

Method 1:

Let the original number of vouchers on display be 'N_0' and every subsequent number of vouchers be N_1, N_2, and so on. Given that 1 in 5 vouchers are given out, that would mean that 4 in 5 are left. The fraction 4 in 5 is equivalent to 80% or 0.8.

$N_1 = 0.8N_0 + 25$

$N_2 = 0.8N_1 + 25$

$N_2 = 0.8(0.8N_0 + 25) + 25$

$N_2 = 0.64N_0 + 45$

$N_3 = 0.8N_2 + 25$

$N_3 = 0.8(0.64N_0 + 45) + 25$

$N_3 = 0.512N_0 + 61$

Given that $N_3 = 381$,

$381 = 0.512N_0 + 61$

$0.512N_0 = 320$

$\underline{N_0 = 625}$

Method 2:

After the start of the 3rd hour, there are 381 vouchers. This means, before adding the 25 vouchers, there were 356 vouchers. 356 represents 80% of the number vouchers of the previous hour.

Hence, the number of vouchers during the 2nd hour was:

$\frac{356}{4} \times 5 = \underline{445}$

Before 25 vouchers were added at the start of the second hour, there were 420.

Therefore, the number of vouchers during the 1st hour is:

$\frac{420}{4} \times 5 = \underline{525}$

Before 25 vouchers were added at the start of the first hour, there were 500.

As a result, the number of vouchers before the 1st hour is:

$\frac{500}{4} \times 5 = \underline{625}$

---

91. E

Explanation:

The quickest way to solve this question is to draw a diagram to arrange the students in order of their positions.

From the first statement, one can tell that the order from first to last goes as: John, Franklin, Sucre.

From the second statement, one can deduce: **John, Franklin, Theodore, Sucre/ David**. The slash (/) means that one cannot be certain of David's position relative to Sucre. This means he could have finished before or after Sucre.

Hence, the correct answer is **Option 'E'**, which states that David finishes after Franklin, John and Theodore bit not necessarily Sucre.

92. E

Explanation:

Total number of hours needed to build a robot:

(3 x 5) + 4] x 8 x 5 = **760 hours**

Therefore, with 8 students and 6 hours daily, the number of days needed would be:

760 ÷ 4 ÷ 10 = 19 days **(3 weeks 4 days)**

---

93. A

Explanation:

When Ginnie buys 3,000 shares at 45 pence per share, she pays:

3,000 x 0.45 x 1.1 = **£1485**

When Ginnie sells 3,000 shares at 58 pence per share, she receives:

3,000 x 0.58 x 0.9 = **£1566**

From the trade above, she makes a profit of:

1566 - 1485 = **£81**

When Ginnie buys 2,000 shares at 15 pence per share, she pays:

2,000 x 0.15 x 1.1 = **£330**

When Ginnie sells 1,000 shares at 33 pence per share, she receives:

1000 x 0.33 x 0.9 = **£297**

From the trade above, she makes a loss of:

330 - 297 = **£33**

Hence, the net profit made by Ginnie is:

81 - 33 = **£48**

---

94. E

Explanation:

Let his initial pay be 'P'. Given that Justin has only worked for 2 full years, the increment his pay has had was 10% and 20% in the last 2 years.

This means that £99,990 represents:

P x 1.1 x 1.2 = 1.32P

Hence, **P = £75,750**

---

95. D

Explanation:

The key to this whole code is *"phone number"*. The numbers 724-466 refers to the numbers on a typical phone keypad. The dots in the second letter states which of the letters of each the corresponding number mean. For example, 7 corresponds to 'PQRS' on the keypad. The 4 dots refer to the fourth letter which is an S. The number 2 corresponds to 'ABC'. The 1 dot refers to the first letter which is an A. **When the code is deciphered, it will read Saigon.**

---

96. A; F

Explanation:

The rate at which food is released is 0.4 kg/day.

Consider Mike:

Initial amount of food: **6 kg**

Amount of food left during a 'beep':

0.2 x 6 = **1.2 kg**

Amount of food that has been released when he receives a 'beep':

6 - 1.2 = **4.8 kg**

Time taken to get a 'beep':
4.8 ÷ 0.4 = <u>12 days</u>
Consider Sulley:
Initial amount of food: <u>8 kg</u>
Amount of food left during a 'beep':
0.2 x 8 = <u>1.6 kg</u>
Amount of food that has been released when he receives a 'beep':
8 - 1.6 = <u>6.4 kg</u>
Time taken to get a 'beep':
6.4 ÷ 0.4 = <u>16 days</u>
Considering the following options:
<u>Option 'A'</u> - This is correct as Mike receives a 'beep' after 12 days whereas Sulley receives a 'beep' after 16 days.
<u>Option 'B'</u> - If A is correct, B is incorrect.
<u>Option 'C'</u> - At the first 'beep', the amount of food released by both the feeders combined is 4.8 x 2 = 9.6 kg. Hence, this is incorrect.
<u>Option 'D'</u> - Within the first fortnight (i.e., 14 days), only Mike will receive the 'beep'. This is incorrect.
<u>Option 'E'</u> - Mike receives the 'beep' after 4.8 kg of food is released. This is incorrect.
<u>Option 'F'</u> - This is correct, as shown by the calculations above.

97. B

Explanation:

Initially, there were 7 cones. In the first round, she damaged $\frac{1}{3}$ of 6 cones, that is, 2 cones in total. Hence, there were 5 cones left at the end of the first round. In the second round, only one cone was damaged as it was accidentally stepped on by Merida's father. There are now 4 cones left. The father purchased an extra 6 cones, but when he returned, 50% (i.e., 2 cones) had been stolen by monkeys. As a result, 8 cones were used for the third round of practice. Given that Merida smashes half of the 8 cones, there will only be <u>4 cones left at the end of the three rounds.</u>

98. D

Explanation:

$\frac{7}{8}$ of a cup's full capacity is 175 ml.
Therefore, the cup's full capacity must be:

$175 \div (\frac{7}{8}) = \underline{200\text{ ml}}$

The total amount of mixed syrup prepared is 4 litres or 4000 ml. Given that 175 is not a factor of 4000, there will be some remaining syrup after the second last cup.

$4{,}000 \div 175 = \mathbf{22\frac{6}{7}}$.

The remaining $\frac{6}{7}$ is equivalent to 150 ml. Hence, the final cup will be filled at a proportion of:

$\frac{150}{200} \text{ x } 100 = \underline{75\%}.$

99. B

Explanation:

In the second option, one pays £25 for 9 months which will cost:
9 x 25 = <u>**£225**</u>

In the first option, one would pay 20 + 2N, where 'N' is the number of times one visits the gym in the 9 months.

Thus,

$20 + 2N > 225$

<u>$N > 102.5$</u>

Hence, one would have to visit the gym **<u>at least 103 times in 9 months</u>** to make it worth the money. Each month, one should visit the gym:

$103 \div 9 = 11.444...$ **<u>(12 times on average, when rounded up)</u>**

100. D

Explanation:

The individual who is telling the truth must be calculated. Hence, the quickest way to solve this is to calculate the probability in which all of them are lying and that it is not raining.

The probability of all three are lying is:

$\frac{2}{3} \times \frac{2}{3} \times \frac{2}{3} = \frac{8}{27}$

Hence, the probability of at least one of them telling the truth is:

$1 - \frac{8}{27} = \frac{19}{27}$

101. E

Explanation:

The teaspoons come in a box of 180 units. Each box allows the production of 90 tea sets. Each box costs £250.

The teacups come in a box of 300 units. Each box allows the production of 30 tea sets.

Each box costs:

250 x 3 = **<u>£750</u>**

The ink cartridge prints 120 logos which allows the production of:

$120 \div 12 =$ <u>6 tea sets</u>

Each cartridge costs:

$\frac{1}{5} \times 250 =$ **<u>£50</u>**

The lowest common multiple of 90, 30 and 6 is 90. Hence, for every 90 tea sets produced, one box of teaspoons, 3 boxes of teacups and 15 ink cartridges are needed. These would cost **<u>£250 (250 x 1), £2250 (750 x 3) and £750 (50 x 15)</u>** respectively.

The total would be:

250 + 2250 + 750 = **<u>£3250</u>**

With a budget of £26,000:

$26{,}000 \div 3250 = 8$ lots of 90 tea sets can be manufactured. That is a total of **<u>720 tea sets.</u>**

102. E

Explanation:

Let $'x'$ be the number of blueberries and $'y'$ be the number of blackberries. Let Bakery 'A' be 'A' and let Bakery 'B' be 'B'.

Bakery 'A': $2x + 3y$

Bakery 'B': $4x + y$

<u>$x = 282$</u>

$2A + 4B = 282$ →Equation 1:

<u>$y = 163$</u>

$3A + B = 163$

B = 163 - 3A →Equation 2
Substitute Equation 2 into Equation 1:
2A + 4(163 - 3A) = 282
2A + 652 - 12A = 282
-10A = -370
A = 37
Substitute A = 37 into Equation 2:
B = 163 - 3(37)
B = 52

103. D

Explanation:
Out of the 2000 hamsters:
0.42 x 2000 = 840 are males
Therefore:
2000 - 840 = 1160 are females
If the proportion of male and female red-eyed hamsters is the same, the number of red eyed hamsters will be:
$\frac{240}{840}$ x 1160 = 331 (approximately 330)

104. B

Explanation:
From the question, one should be able to work out their relative positions based on the individuals' weights.
Arranging in ascending order:
Delia, Ashlyn, Blair, Edeline and Courtney

105. C

Explanation:
Given that Brian plays a counterpunching game, this means that Dylan plays an aggressive baseliner game and, thus, Zian plays a counterpunching game. The only pairing that has yet to be arranged is Brian versus Jack.
Given that Brian has won against Dylan, who has won against Zian, who has won against Jack, one can expect **Brian to be the likely winner in his match against Jack.**

106. B

Explanation:
It will take two builders six days to build the kitchen. As a result, one builder will take:
2 x 6 = **12 days**
If they hire an extra worker, there will be three workers. The time taken would then be:
12 ÷ 3 = **4 days**
The work will finish:
6 – 4 = **2 days earlier**

107. B

Explanation:
The number of headbands of each pattern is irrelevant to this question, except for the fact that there is one plain white headband. Besides the plain white headband, there are four other patterns of headbands. Hence, as long as they draw out five headbands, they are guaranteed to get at least two of the same patterns. However, taking into account the plain white headband, **they would need to draw out six to guarantee a match.**

108. C

Explanation:

The figure 4750 represents 95% of the tickets sold.

This means:

4750 ÷ 0.95 = 5,000 tickets were sold and 5,000 - 4750 = **250 individuals bought tickets but did not attend the concert.**

Of the 5,000 tickets, $\frac{1}{8}$ x 5,000 = 625 are males and 5000 - 625 = **4375 are females.**

Given that men are four times more likely to miss concerts compared to women, this means that out of 250 no-shows, 200 would be men and 50 would be women. Hence, 4375 - 50 = **4325 females attended the concert.**

109. B

Explanation:

First, one has to understand how the wrapping process would occur for the sponge and bubble wraps. The sponge is 2 inches thick and a single layer is used to completely surround the object. This essentially adds 4 inches to each dimension, given that the sponge covers both sides to each dimension.

Hence, with the sponge wrap used, the dimensions of the object would now be:

6 x 14 x 8 inches

This would cost: 0.25 x 14 = **£3.50**

Next, the sponge-wrapped object is wrapped with bubble wrap. Given that 2 layers of 0.5-inch bubble wraps are used, this adds 1 inch to each side; therefore, this adds 2 inches to each dimension. Hence, with the bubble wrap surrounding the sponge wrap, the dimensions would be: **8 x 16 x 10 inches**

This would cost: 2 x 8 = **£16.00**

In total, the wrapping service would cost: £3.50 + £16.00 = **£19.50**

110. B

Explanation:

Using a bubble wrap on a 16 x 17 x 11-inch box would give the dimensions of:

18 x 19 x 13 inches

This would cost: 2 x 13 = **£26.00**

Using a sponge wrap on a 4 x 28 x 20-inch box would give the dimensions of:

8 x 32 x 24 inches

This would cost: 0.25 x 32 = **£8.00**

It would be: 26 ÷ 8 = **3.25 times more expensive**

111. D

Explanation:

For every increase in an inch of the dimensions of the box, the cost of the sponge wrap and bubble wrap would proportionally increase by 25 pence and £2. The total change would be an increase of £2.25 per inch.

Hypothetically, assume a "box" has dimensions of 0 x 0 x 0 inches. There will still be 4 inches of sponge wrap and 6 inches of bubble wrap around it.

This means that the starting price for a cubic box is: (0.25 x 4) + (2 x 6) = **£13**

Hence, if the box has dimensions of 1 x 1 x 1 inches, it would cost:

13 + 2.25 = **£15.25**

This allows the equation C = 13 + 2.25D to be formed, where 'C' is the cost of the wrapping and 'D' is the dimension of the cubic box.

Problem Solving

$50 = 13 + 2.25D$

$2.25D = 37$

<u>D = 16.4...</u>

It is not expected to get the actual value of 'D'; however, one should be able to approximate that the largest possible value for 'D' would be **<u>16 inches.</u>**

112. D

Explanation:

Let the number of times Mr Hidayat plays badminton be:

<u>3 + B</u>, where 3 represents the number of times he plays with his best friend and 'B' represents the number of training sessions he has with his students.

Let the number of students (excluding Sakura and siblings) Mr Hidayat coaches be 'C'.

With Sakura and her two brothers included, it would be:

<u>C + 3</u>

Bear in mind that Mr Hidayat provides one-to-one training. Therefore, for one student he coaches, it is considered an extra one time of him playing badminton. In other words, 'B' and 'C' increases proportionally.

In 20 weeks, if Sakura and siblings are not around, Mr Hidayat would restock his shuttlecocks four times. In 20 weeks, if Sakura and siblings are around, he restocks his shuttlecocks five times. This means, for a given length of time, Mr Hidayat increases his rate of restocking his shuttlecocks by 1.25 times when Sakura and siblings are around.

Thus, deduce the equation below:

$3 + B_{\text{with Sakura and siblings}} = 1.25(3 + B_{\text{without Sakura and siblings}})$

Substituting C and C + 3 into the Bs above:

$3 + C + 3 = 1.25(3 + C)$

$6 + C = 3.75 + 1.25C$

$0.25C = 2.25$

<u>C = 9</u>

With Sakura and siblings included, Mr Hidayat has a total of **<u>12 students.</u>**

113. E

Explanation:

This diagram can be approached with a Venn diagram to facilitate the fact-checking process. Otherwise, carefully reason out the options to check if they are accurate.

<u>One cannot be sure of any of the options given</u>. Whilst all children play the violin, there could also be students of other age groups (i.e., teenagers and young adults) who also play the violin. It is also uncertain if any of the teenagers play the violin. The **<u>question did not provide information</u>** as to whether a student can play both the violin and the piano, nor whether any student play the drums.

114. B

Explanation:

The original time taken for express service delivery is 2 weeks.

Given that Santorino opts for the regular service, this increases the time for delivery to:

2 x 1.25 = <u>2.5 weeks</u>

Moreover, the COVID-19 pandemic has caused all posting services to be delayed. *This further increases the delivery time to:*

2.5 x 1.3 = <u>3.25 weeks</u>

115. B

Explanation:

Let the adult entry fee be 'A' and the adult rate per 25g of food be 'R'.

Equation 1:

$(\frac{900}{25})R + A = 20.2$

<u>36R + A = 20.2</u>

Equation 2:

$(\frac{425}{25})R + A = 11.65$

<u>17R + A = 11.65</u>

Equation 1 - Equation 2:

19R = 8.55

<u>R = 45 pence</u>

Substitute R = 45 pence into Equation 2:

17(0.45) + A = 11.65

<u>A = £4</u>

Hence, for Flint's meal, it would cost her:

$4 + (\frac{0.45 \times 375}{25})$ = **<u>£10.75</u>**

116. D

Explanation:

Entry fee for children is half of that of the adult's, hence, it costs £2. Their rate per 25 grams of food is $\frac{2}{3}$ of the adult's; therefore, it costs 30 pence.

Melissa's meal will cost:

$(\frac{850}{25} \times 0.3) + 2$ = **<u>£12.20</u>**

117. E

Explanation:

The initial cost of Henry's meal is:

$(\frac{1175}{25} \times 0.45) + 4$ = **<u>£25.15</u>**

That means he managed to save:

25.15 - 17.95 = **<u>£7.20</u>**

Given that 50 grams of food costs 90 pence, this means Henry solved:

7.2 ÷ 0.9 = <u>8 cubes</u>

The average time taken per cube is:

10 ÷ 8 = <u>1.25 minutes</u> (1 min 15 s)

118. D

Explanation:

The weight of food received by each dog is expressed as below:

Smallest dog	W
Second smallest/ fourth largest dog	W + D
Third smallest/ third largest dog	W + 2D
Fourth smallest/ second largest dog	W + 3D
Largest dog	W + 4D

119. D

Explanation:

The total food received by the dogs is 5 kg. The sum of the five expressions from the table in the previous solution is:

$5W + 10D$

Hence, $5W + 10D = 5$

120. D

Explanation:

The sum of the expressions for the three largest dogs is:

$W + 2D + W + 3D + W + 4D = 3W + 9D$

This is equal to 8 times the sum of the expressions of the other 2 dogs, which is:

$W + W + D = 2W + D$

Hence, the overall equation is:

$8(2W + D) = 3W + 9D$

121. E

Explanation:

Simplify the equation from the previous question:

$8(2W + D) = 3W + 9D$

$16W + 8D = 3W + 9D$

$13W = D$

$W = \frac{D}{13}$

122. E

Explanation:

From Q119, 5 kg is expressed as:

$5W + 10D$

From Q121:

$W = \frac{D}{13}$

Substituting $W = \frac{D}{13}$ *into* $5W + 10D$:

$5(\frac{D}{13}) + 10D = \frac{135D}{13}$

123. E

Explanation:

From the question text, there are 12 pistachios, 4 cashews, 2 almonds and 18 hazelnuts. Instinctively, one might think that getting 2 hazelnuts would be of the greatest probability. However, this is not true.

The probability of getting 2 hazelnuts is:

$\frac{18}{36} \text{x} \frac{17}{35} = \mathbf{\frac{17}{70}}$

The probability of getting a hazelnut and a pistachio is greater as one can have hazelnut-pistachio or pistachio-hazelnut.

The probability of this phenomenon is:

$2 \text{ x} \frac{18}{36} \text{x} \frac{12}{35} = \mathbf{\frac{12}{35}}$

Hence, the answer is <u>hazelnut and pistachio.</u>

(In the interest of time, ignore calculating the denominators of the probabilities as they will all be the same, provided they are not simplified).

124. E

Explanation:

Combination 1 is impossible as there are only 2 almond nuts in the container. Hence, **<u>Option 'A' is incorrect.</u>**

The probability of Combination 2 is:

$\frac{4}{36} \text{x} \frac{2}{35} \text{x} \frac{1}{34}$ x 3, which will give a numerator of <u>24</u>

Bear in mind that the fractions must be multiplied by 3 because the order in which the cashew is drawn has 3 variations. (Again, in the interest of time, ignore calculating the denominators of the probabilities as they will all be the same, provided they are not simplified).

The probability of Combination 3 is:

$\frac{4}{36} \text{x} \frac{3}{35} \text{x} \frac{2}{34}$ x 3, which will give a numerator of <u>72</u>

The probability of Combination 4 is:

$\frac{4}{36} \text{x} \frac{3}{35} \text{x} \frac{2}{24}$, which will give a numerator of <u>24</u>

This means that the <u>probability of Combination 4 occurring is the same as that as Combination 2</u>. Both combinations have a probability of occurrence that is lesser than that of Combination 3. Hence, **<u>Option 'E' is the correct answer</u>**.

125. D

Explanation:

Of the 36 nuts, there are 18 hazelnuts, 12 pistachios, 4 cashews and 2 almonds. To approach this question, first consider the types of nuts present. In this case, there are 4. Given that the question is only interested in 3 types of nuts, first add the numbers of the two types of nuts with the greatest counts. In this case, that would be <u>hazelnuts (18) and pistachios (12)</u>. That gives an answer of 30. This means that if Nadia draws 30 nuts, she is guaranteed at least two types of nuts in her hand. It is important to consider that it is possible that all 30 nuts drawn consist of all the hazelnuts and pistachios. To make sure she gets three different types, she has to draw just one more nut - <u>this will give an answer of 31.</u>

126. B

Explanation:

Construct a map of the relative positions of the five towns:

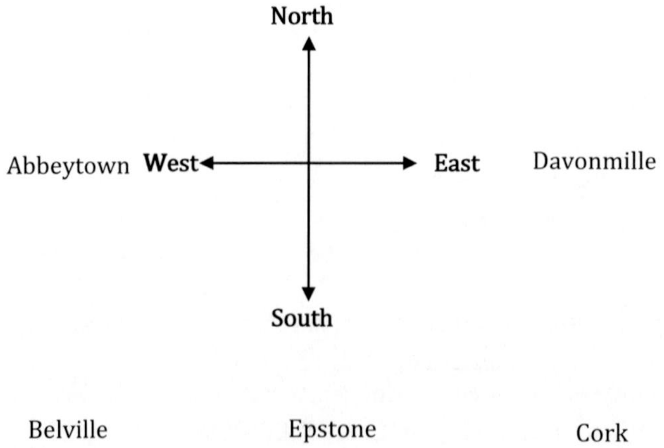

Consider the diagram above:

Option 'B' is incorrect because Belville is South West of Davonmille, and not East. As the above diagram indicates, all of the other Options are correct.

127. F

Explanation:

From the information:

1st - ? , red top; 2nd - ?; 3rd – Collin, ? top; 4th - ?

Alice was wearing a blue top and didn't come last. Therefore, she must have come second (1st and 3rd places are taken):

1st - ? , red top; 2nd – Alice, blue top; 3rd – Collin, ? top; 4th - ?

Bethany did better than the child in the green top. As a result, Bethany must have come first (can't be last because she ran quicker than the child in the green top):

1st - Bethany , red top; 2nd – Alice, blue top; 3rd – Collin, ? top; 4th - ?

The child who wore an orange top did better than Jacob. Therefore, Collin wore an orange top. Jacob came last and he wore a green top.

1st - Bethany, red top; 2nd – Alice, blue top; 3rd – Collin, orange top; 4th – Jacob, green top

Statements 1, 2 and 5 are correct. Statements 3 and 4 are incorrect. Therefore, Option 'F' is the correct answer.

128. A

Explanation:

Calculate the number of elderly patients with a positive test result:

1615 + 285 = 1900

The probability of an elderly patient with a positive test result having the disease: $\mathbf{\frac{1615}{1900}}$

The probability of an elderly patient with a positive test result not having the disease: $\mathbf{\frac{285}{1900}}$

Therefore, the difference in probability: $\frac{1615}{1900} - \frac{285}{1900} = \mathbf{\frac{1330}{1900}}$

129. D

Explanation:

On the first try, the child has **3 different colours** of marbles to choose from. For the next five attempts, the child has a choice of **2 different colours** because each marble chosen cannot be the same colour as the previous one.

Therefore, the final calculation would be:

3 x 2 x 2 x 2 x 2 x 2 = **96 different possibilities**

130. B

Explanation:

Suppose Alfie is telling the truth:

Bert states that Alfie is telling the truth.

When Dave says that Caitlin is not telling the truth, it implies that Bert is saying the truth.

Since both Bert and Alfie are claiming to say the truth, there is a contradiction and **Alfie is lying**. Consequently, **Bert is not telling the truth** as well.

Therefore, **Caitlin must be telling the truth** (she stated that Bert was lying about Alfie speaking the truth). **Dave and Ellie both contradict Caitlin**.

As a result, **Caitlin is the only one telling the truth**.

131. C

Explanation:

Consider Johnson:

He has an attendance of 97%. However, to be eligible for a holiday to Greece, he must have **less than** 3% absences (in other words, an attendance of **more than** 97%). Therefore, he is also not eligible for Spain (absences less than or equal to 1%). As a result, **Johnson is eliminated**.

Consider Dwayne:

He fulfils the criteria for attendance in order to qualify for the holiday to Greece. However, he needs a customer satisfaction rating of **more than 3**, and, therefore, he is not eligible for Greece. **Dwayne is eliminated**.

Consider Kristina:

She has an attendance of 99%, which is **less than or equal to 1% of absences** (fulfils criteria for holiday to Spain). Kristina has a customer rating of 3, while the holiday to Spain requires a rating of **4 or more**. The holiday to Greece requires a customer rating of **more than 3**, which she is also not eligible for. Therefore, **Kristina is not eligible for either holiday**.

Consider Carson:

He has an attendance of 98% (has **absences of less than 3%**). Therefore, he is eligible for a holiday to Greece but not to Spain (which requires **absences less than or equal to 1%**). He has a customer satisfaction rating of 5 (which exceeds the criteria of a 3) and has 20 complaints (which is less than 0.03 x 2000 = 60 complaints from the customers he has served). Therefore, **Carson is eligible for a holiday to Greece**.

Consider Molly:

She has an attendance of 98% (has **absences of less than 3%**). Therefore, she is eligible for a holiday to Greece but not to Spain (which requires **absences less than or equal to 1%**). She has a customer satisfaction rating of 4 (which exceeds the criteria of a 3) and

has 59 complaints (which is less than 0.03 x 2000 = 60 complaints from the customers she has served). Therefore, **Molly is eligible for a holiday to Greece**.
In conclusion, **only Molly and Carson** are eligible for a free holiday.

132. **A**

Explanation:

Find the ranges of number of sweets counted by each child:
Subtract and add 3 from each number of sweets counted:
7 sweets: Range- 4 to 10
9 sweets: Range – 6 to 12
11 sweets: Range – 8 to 14
Therefore, the minimum amount of sweets to satisfy all conditions: 8
The maximum amount of sweets to satisfy all conditions: 10
The range: 10 – 8 = 2

133. **D**

Explanation:

If an individual has Type II diabetes:
Risk of developing Disease P: 1 in 2 (8 ÷ 4 = 2)
If an individual smokes:
Risk of developing Disease P: 1 in 16 (8 x 2 = 16)
Each dose reduces the user's risk by half:
If individual has Type II diabetes and has one dose:
Risk of developing Disease P: 1 in 4 (2 x 2 = 4)
If individual has Type II diabetes and has two doses:
Risk of developing Disease P: 1 in 8 (4 x 2 = 8)
If individual has Type II diabetes and has three doses:
Risk of developing Disease P: 1 in 16 (8 x 2 = 16)
Therefore, an individual with Type II diabetes must have **3 doses** in order to have the same likelihood of developing Disease P as an individual who smokes (both ratios are 1 in 16).

134. **E**

Explanation:

Find the total number of people with brown eyes:
(0.35 x 160) + (0.3 x 150) + (0.15 x 80) + (0.6 x 110) = 179
Find the total number of people who were surveyed:
160 + 150 + 80 + 110 = 500
Therefore, the number of people who have blue eyes:
500 – 179 = 321
Percentage of all those surveyed who had blue eyes:

$$\frac{321}{500} = 64.2\%$$

Therefore, **Option 'E' is the closest percentage** – this is the correct answer.

135. **A**

Explanation:

Consider Statement 1:
If Judy has one of each cereal bar:
70 + 50 + 25 = 145 pence (£1.45)
If Judy had two of each cereal bar:

2(70) + 2(50) + 2(25) = 290 pence (£2.90)
If Judy had three of each cereal bar:
3(70) + 3(50) + 3(25) = 435 pence (£4.35)
Therefore, she cannot have an equal number of each bar to equal £3.50. **Statement 1 is correct**.
Consider Statement 2:
£3.50 can be spent on:
5 chocolate cereal bars,
7 caramel cereal bars or
14 honey cereal bars
Therefore, she doesn't have to buy a chocolate bar for the total to equal £3.50. **Statement 2 is incorrect**.
Consider Statement 3:
From Statement 2, the £3.50 can be spent on a single type of cereal bar which isn't chocolate.
Statement 3 is incorrect.
Consider Statement 4:
If she bought only chocolate cereal bars, Judy would buy 5 of them. Since the Statement states **more than 5**, **Statement 4 is incorrect**.
Therefore, only **Statement 1 is correct**.

---

136. C

Explanation:
Convert 0.2 hours to minutes:
0.2 x 60 = **12 minutes**
Find the Lowest Common Multiple of 20, 12 and 15:
20 x 3 = 60; 12 x 5 = 60; 15 x 4 = 60
Therefore, the children meet each other **every hour (60 minutes)**.
If the children were in the same position 5 minutes ago:
60 – 5 = **55 minutes**
The children will meet again in **55 minutes**.

---

137. D

Explanation:
From left to right:
For the first chair, there are **5 different children** who could sit. Assuming that the first chair is occupied, there are now **4 different children** who can sit. For the third chair, there are **3 different children**. For the second chair, there is only an option between **2 children**. As a result, the final chair will have the **remaining child**.
Therefore, the number of different arrangements:
5 x 4 x 3 x 2 x 1 = **120**
Since two arrangements have been stated:
120 – 2 = **118 other possible arrangements**

---

138. C

Explanation:
Calculate the number of people who were fined:
Employee 1: 30 minutes late - **£15 fine**
Employee 2: 35 minutes late - **£20 fine**

Employee 3: 30 minutes early - **no fine**
Employee 4: 5 minutes late – **no fine**
Employee 5: 34 minutes late - **£20 fine**
Employee 6: 2 minutes late - **no fine**
Employee 7: 10 minutes early - **no fine**
Employee 8: 11 minutes late - **£15 fine**
Therefore, total fines collected:
15 + 20 + 20 + 15 = **£70**
Money for the office upgrade:
0.2 x 70 = **£14**

---

139. D

Explanation:
Calculate the number of students who were supposed to attend:
36 students attended the Sixth Form, which was 90% of the number of pupils who were supposed to attend:
36 ÷ 0.9 = **40 students were supposed to attend**
1 in 4 are male students were supposed to attend:
40 ÷ 4 = **10 male students were supposed to attend**
Calculate the number of students who missed Wednesday:
40 – 36 = **4 students missed Wednesday**
Since men were three times as likely to miss Sixth Form:
3 males and 1 female missed Sixth Form on Wednesday
Given that out of 10 male students who were supposed to attend, 3 missed Wednesday:
10 – 3 = **7 male students attended Drewstring Sixth Form on Wednesday**

---

140. E

Explanation:
Since every one of the 60 students study 3 subjects:
120 x 3 = **360 subject choices available**
120 students study English (because all students study English).
Calculate the number of students who study Mathematics: 55% x 120 = **66**
Calculate the number of students who study Computer Science: 35% x 120 = **42**
Calculate the number of students who study French: 75% x 120 = **90**
Therefore, total number of subject choices taken up by Mathematics, Computer Science, English and French: 120 + 66 + 42 + 90 = **318**
Number of subject choices taken up by Physics: 360 – 318 = **42 subject choices from Geography**
Therefore, **42 students study Geography**.

---

141. D

Explanation
Since the trip comprises of 50% girls and 50% boys:
There are 30 girls and 30 boys.
The maximum number of girls who ordered a ham sandwich and a drink:
$\frac{2}{3}$ x 30 = **20** (since the two-thirds of girls who ordered a ham sandwich could have also ordered a drink)
The minimum number of girls who ordered a ham sandwich and a drink is as follows:

Problem Solving

Calculate the number of girls who didn't order a ham sandwich but could have ordered a drink:

$\frac{1}{3} \times 30 = 10$

In addition, all 30 boys could have ordered a drink.

$\frac{10+30}{60} = \frac{2}{3}$ (number of children in the class who could have overall ordered a drink)

Therefore, minimum number of girls with **ordered a ham sandwich and a drink is 0**.

Difference between maximum and minimum:

20 – 0 = **20**

---

142. C

Explanation:

Assume:

a = 1st digit; b = 2nd digit; c = 3rd digit; d= 4th digit; e = 5th digit

Since the second digit is the square of the first digit:

$b = a^2$

The sum of the first and the third digit is equivalent to 5 times the first digit:

$a + c = 5a$

$c = 5a - a$

$c = 4a$

The fourth digit is twice more than the square of the first digit:

$d = a^2 + 2$

The sum of the fifth and third digit is equivalent to 10 minus two times the first digit:

$e + c = 10 - 2a$

$e = 10 - 2a - c$

Substitute ***c = 4a*** *into c:*

$e = 10 - 2a - 4a$

$e = 10 - 6a$

The sum of all the digits is 57.

$a + b + c + d + e = 57$ **(Equation 1)**

Substitute all of the other equations into ***Equation 1:***

$a + a^2 + 4a + (a^2 + 2) + 10 - 6a = 57$

$2a^2 - a - 45 = 0$

$(2a + 9)(a - 5) = 0$

a = -4.5 or a = 5

Since the first digit cannot be negative, a = 5

---

143. B

Explanation:

Assume 'y' is the total money spent and 'x' is the number of adults:

In the original scenario, each adult contributes £26:

$y = 35x$ **(Equation 1)**

If 6 more friends had shared the cost:

$y = 21x + (10 \times 21)$ **(Equation 2)**

The two equations equal each other:

$35x = 21x + 210$

$14x = 210$

$x = 15$

Since each adult paid £35:
35 x 15 = **£525**

---

144. A

Explanation:

If the **difference** between two dates is a **multiple of seven**, the two dates will fall on the same day.

Consider Jacob and Jack:

Difference between 26th February 2020 and 27th May 2020 = **91 days**

91 ÷ 7 = 13 weeks

Therefore, Jacob and Jack are born on the same day.

Consider Jacob and Josh:

Difference between 21st November 2019 and 27th May 2020 = **195 days**

Since 195 is not divisible by 7, Jacob and Josh are not born on the same day. Consequently, Josh and Jack are not born on the same day (because Jack and Jacob are born on the same day).

Consider Jacob and Joe:

Difference between 10th March 2020 and 27th May 2020 = **78 days**

Since 78 is not divisible by 7, Jacob and Joe are not born on the same day. Consequently, Josh and Joe are not born on the same day (because Jack and Jacob are born on the same day).

Consider Josh and Joe:

Difference between 21st November 2019 and 10th March 2020 = **110 days**

Since 110 is not divisible by 7, Josh and Joe are not born on the same day.

Therefore, the only children born on the same day are **Jacob and Jack**.

---

145. B

Explanation:

Consider the increase in the number of students attending Choir between 2019 and 2020: 23 – 24 = -1 (decrease of 1)

Consider the increase in the number of students attending Hockey between 2019 and 2020: 12 – 9 = 3 (increase of 3)

Consider the increase in the number of students attending Chess between 2019 and 2020: 14 – 13 = 1 (increase of 1)

Consider the increase in the number of students attending Coding between 2019 and 2020: 18 – 6 = 12 (increase of 12)

Consider the increase in the number of students attending Orchestra between 2019 and 2020: 34 -15 = 19 (increase of 19)

Consider the increase in the number of students attending Journalism between 2019 and 2020: 16 – 19 = -3 (decrease of 3)

Consider the increase in the number of students attending Netball between 2019 and 2020: 10 – 2 = 8 (increase of 8)

Therefore, the highest to lowest increase between 2019 and 2020:

Orchestra, Coding, Netball, Hockey, Chess, Choir, Journalism

---

146. E

Explanation:

Calculate the number of visitors who were about to leave:

75% of visitors:

Problem Solving

(0.75 x 24) = **18 individuals**

50% of the visitors who were leaving, and all of the healthcare assistants left:

9 + 4 = **13 individuals**

Total number of 'living' people left in the room:

15 'living' patients (one patient pronounced dead)

5 doctors (3 doctors who were already in the room and 2 senior doctors who arrived upon hearing the commotion)

0 healthcare assistants (all healthcare assistants leave)

4 nurses

15 visitors (24 - 9)

6 members of the crash team

Therefore, total number of 'living' people:

15 + 5 + 0 + 4 + 15 + 6 = **45**

147. D

Explanation:

Convert Lola's and Graham's speed into kmph:

Lola: 10 x 1.6 = 16 kmph

Graham: 12.5 x 1.6 = 20 kmph

Calculate the time taken by each individual and multiply by 60 to find the time in minutes:

Jamal: $\frac{18}{15}$ x 60 = **72 minutes**

Lola: $\frac{18}{16}$ x 60 = **67.5 minutes**

Graham: $\frac{18}{20}$ x 60 = **54 minutes**

However, Jamal set off 5 minutes before Lola and 17 minutes before Graham:

Lola: 67.5 + 5 = **72.5 minutes**

Graham: 54 + 17 = **71 minutes**

Therefore, the order of arrivals at the destination would be:

Graham, Jamal, Lola

148. B

Explanation:

Calculate the number of hours worked by all three carpet fitters to carpet Hotel 'A':

$\frac{15}{60}$ x 288 = **72 hours**

Since all three carpet fitters work 6 hours a day:

72 ÷ 6 = 12 days work for all three carpet fitters

Therefore, there are:

12 x 3 carpet fitters = **36 total days of work**

If there were:

6 + 3 = **9 carpet fitters**,

It would take a fewer amount of days to complete the same amount of work.

Days of work:

36 ÷ 9 = **4 days work for all 9 carpet fitters**

149. E

Explanation:

This is an example of compound interest - the interest paid is dependent on the principal amount of money in the bank.

The multiplying factor is 103% (100% + 3%)
In Year 1: 8000 x 1.03 = **£8240**
In Year 2: 8240 x 1.03 = **£8487.20**
Consider Bank B:
The multiplying factor is 104% (100% + 4%)
In Year 1: 7500 x 1.04 = **£7800**
In Year 2: 7800 x 1.04 = **£8112**
Therefore, the difference in the value of the investment:
8487.20 - 8112 = **£375.20** (**£375** to the nearest pound)

150. E

Explanation:

Whilst all toy cars are sold in packs of three, other toys may also be sold in packs of three - **Option 'B'** is incorrect. The statement given by the toy shop employee does not illustrate the assertion that robots are sold in packs of three - it cannot be concluded for certain. Therefore, **Option 'C'** is eliminated. There is no information on whether some items are sold with batteries and in packs of three, nor if any toy car packs contain trucks. As a result, **Options 'A' and 'D'** are incorrect. **Option 'E'**, which states that none of the other Options are correct, is the right answer.

151. C

Explanation:

There are:
10 orange marbles (0.5 x 20)
1 blue marble (0.1 x 10)
1 maroon marble
8 lilac marbles (10 - 2)
Therefore, the most likely combination to draw will involve the **orange and lilac marbles.**
Probability of two orange marbles:

$$\frac{10}{20} \times \frac{9}{19} = \frac{9}{38}$$

Probability of one orange and one lilac marble:
Andy can draw one orange marble, followed by a lilac marble or one lilac marble, followed by an orange marble:

$$(\frac{8}{20} \times \frac{10}{19}) + (\frac{10}{20} \times \frac{8}{19}) = \frac{16}{38}$$

Therefore, the combination of an **orange and a lilac marble** is more likely.

152. E

Explanation:

Since there are the least number of blue and maroon marbles in the bag, the answer must involve either of these colours. Since the draw is taken without replacement, blue and blue or maroon and maroon is impossible. This is because there is **only one blue/maroon marble** in the bag.

153. H

Explanation:

There is only one maroon and one blue marble; therefore, it will be possible to take out 18 lilac and orange marbles. Therefore, **19 out of the 20** marbles would need to be taken out in order to be certain of getting the blue or maroon marble.

Problem Solving

154. D

Explanation:

Since nine printers take seven minutes to print the book, one machine will take:

9 x 7 = **63 minutes to print a book**

Six printers will take: 63 ÷ 6 = **10.5 minutes**

Therefore, it takes: 10.5 – 7 = **3.5 minutes longer to print one book**

Printing four books with six printers will take: 3.5 x 4 = **14 minutes more compared to nine printers**

155. A

Explanation:

Let trousers be 'x' and shoes be 'y':

Clare: $3x + 7y = 286$

Sophie: $5x + 2y = 227.75$

Multiply the first equation by 5:

$15x + 35y = 1430$

Multiply the first equation by 3:

$15x + 6y = 683.25$

Eliminate the $'x'$ term by subtraction the first equation from the second one:

$29y = 746.75$

$y = 25.75$

The price of the shoes is **£25.75.**

156. B

Explanation:

Each bracelet now uses 40% less beads than before. Therefore, the weight of the beads will be **240 g** (60% of 400 g).

From 3 kg which is 3000 g:

3000 ÷ 240 = **12.5 bracelets are made**

Since 0.5 of a bracelet is not possible, a total of **12 bracelets are made**.

As a result, the weight of the beads left over would be:

0.5 x 240 = **120 g**

157. B

Explanation:

There are at least two ways to solve this problem. One method would be to substitute each of the options until the correct answer is found, but this could be time consuming. Another method is to understand that for a house with six rooms, it could cost:

Cleaner 'A': **£25**

Cleaner 'B': £10 + (6 x £2) = **£22**

Therefore, it costs £3 more to hire Cleaner 'B'. The cost for each room after this £1 for Cleaner 'A' and £2 for Cleaner 'B'; **this is a difference of £1**.

Both the cleaners will charge the same for:

6 + (3 ÷ 1) = **9 rooms**

158. C

Explanation:

Since no consecutive number shared more than one common factor, all the common factors of the numbers should be found to identify numbers that cannot be adjacent to each other. The factors of each number are:

A Lakshmi, T R Enoch, S Z Y Ooi. Doctors Academy Publications, Cardiff, UK, 2020.

54 = 1, 2, 3, 6, 9, 18, 27, 54
63 = 1, 3, 7, 9, 21, 63
74 = 1, 2, 37, 74
83 = 1, 83
91 = 1, 7, 13, 91
All the number have a common factor of one. Therefore, they must not have any other common factor other than one if they are to be adjacent to each other. This means 54 cannot be near 63 (common factors of 3 and 9) or 74 (common factor of 2). This **eliminates Option 'A', 'B' and 'D'**. The integer 63 cannot be adjacent to 54 or 93 (common factor of 7). Therefore, **Option 'E' can be eliminated**. This leaves **Option 'C' as the correct answer**.

159. B

Explanation:
The cheapest option is to hire the care for a week, and then pay the hourly rent on the eighth day until 5pm. This will be:
£170 + (£2 x 9 hours) = **£188**
Paying for one whole day on the last day would bring the **total cost to £195, which is more expensive.**

160. E

Explanation:
Her mum will pay her:
£5 x 10 = **£50**
As she ran an extra 4 km after the 6 km, her grandparents will pay her:
£10 + (£2 x 4) = **£18**
Her three friends paid her a total of:
£10 x 3 = **£30**
This comes to a total of £98 at the end of her run.
Her dad will match this by paying her £98.
Therefore, in total she has raised:
£98 + £98 = **£196**

161. E

Explanation:
Draw a diagram with all the relative positions. The clothes shop is above the shoe shop and cookie store, but it is below the cinema. The food court is above all the other shops:

The cookie stall is below the food court, cinema and clothes shop. Therefore, the position of the stall relative to the shoe shop **cannot be determined from the information given.**

162. B

Explanation:

A 30-minute lesson costs £20 and a 60-minute lesson costs £35.

Therefore, the tutor charges:

£35 - £20 = **£15 for 30 minutes**

The rate per minute is:

15 ÷ 30 = **0.5**

He charges 50 pence per minute.

For 30 minutes the cost is:

30 x 0.5 = **£15**

However, the tutor charges £20; the base rate is:

£20 - £15 = **£5**

For a 4-hour lesson (4 x 60 = 240 minutes), it would cost:

(240 x 0.5) + 5 = **£125**

163. B

Explanation:

Every month her hair has a net growth of **1 cm**. At the end of the 16th month, her hair will be 16 cm longer. At the 17th month, it grows 4 cm more. Since it has now reached the 20 cm mark, she will not be cutting it at the end of this month. As a result, it will take **17 months to grow her hair to be 20 cm longer**.

164. C

Explanation:

If the original volume of the soap in the bottle is 'V' ml, it then increases by 25%:

V x 1.25 = 1.25V

Afterwards, it decreases by 15% from this volume. *Therefore, it will be:*

100 – 15 = **85% of the larger volume**

1.25V x 0.85 = **1.0625V**

The volume has **increased by 6.25%** compared to the original volume.

165. B

Explanation:

Option 'A' is not true since it is not known if there are grapes of other colour in the basket. This is because not all grapes are red and the fruits in the basket are not all red. **Option 'B' is true** as one of the statements states that not all the fruits in the basket are red. **Option 'C' may not be true** as it is not known if all apples are red, we only know that the apples in the basket are red. **Option 'D' may also not be true** as there isn't enough information to state that there are other fruits apart from apples and grapes. **Option 'E' may not be true** as it is not known if there are any grapes of a different colour in the basket.

166. A

Explanation:

Since the answers are in percentages and for ease of calculation, let the money Ria has to spend be £100. On the phone she spends £60 (60% of £100), leaving £40. Therefore, any answer above 40% can be eliminated. She spent 30% less than what she spent on the phone on the headphones; hence, the price of the headphones is 65% of that of the phone.

This is: 60 x 0.65 = **£39**

In total, she has spent: £60 + £39 = **£99**; 100 – 99 = **£1**
Therefore, **Ria has 1% of her money left over.**

167. B

Explanation:

The journey time is 8 hours to the nearest hour. Therefore, the minimum journey time is 7 hours 30 minutes and the maximum journey time would be 8 hours 29 minutes. This means that the **passengers can expect to arrive between 9:30 pm and 10:29 pm (BST).**

168. C

Explanation:

The bunch contains 11 hands each with 18 bananas. Therefore, there are:
11 x 18 = **198 bananas in the bunch**
The minimum weight of a banana would be 15 grams, since the weight is rounded to the nearest 10 grams
As a result, the minimum weight of the bunch is:
198 x 15 = **2970 grams**

169. E

Explanation:

Drawing a table with the information may make it easier to understand the content.

Activities at the Leisure Centre	TOWN			
	A	B	C	D
Hockey	Everyone			
Swimming	Some	Everyone		
Badminton		No - one	Some	
Football			Some	
Running	Everyone	Everyone	Everyone	Everyone

Option 'A' may not be true as it is not known for certain that there are people from Town C who like football and badminton. There is not sufficient information regarding people in Town C who like swimming or the activities that people in Town D like. Hence, **Option 'B' cannot be concluded.** There is **not enough information to conclude Option 'C'**, as it is not known if people from Town A like badminton. The passage states that everyone likes running, but it is not known if people from Towns B, C or D like hockey; therefore, **Option 'D' is not true. Option 'E' is true** as everyone in Town A plays hockey and likes running. Some people from Town A like to swim; hence, they must be involved in three activities at the leisure centre.

170. C

Explanation:

The current ratio of boys to girls is 81:2, this could be 81 boys and 2 girls. The number of boys had decreased by 40% in the last two terms. Therefore, the current number is 60% of the total number of boys two terms ago.
Let 'x' be the number of boys two terms ago:

$$\frac{81}{x} = \frac{60}{100}$$

$$x = \frac{8100}{60}$$

$\underline{\boldsymbol{x = 135}}$

The number of girls had tripled; hence, two terms ago it would have been $\frac{2}{3}$.

The ratio of boys to girls was:

$135{:}\frac{2}{3} = \underline{405{:}\,2}$

171. D

Explanation:

The total of £450 is 120% of the cost it took the company to make the washing machine, since they made 20% profit selling it at £450.

Therefore, the cost to make it is:

$$\frac{450}{x} = \frac{120}{100}$$

$$x = \frac{45000}{120}$$

$\underline{\boldsymbol{x = 375}}$

The original price of the washing machine before the 10% discount was:

£450 ÷ 0.9 = **<u>£500</u>**

Hence, they would make a profit of:

500 - 375 = **<u>£125 if it was sold at full price.</u>**

172. C

Explanation:

If Friedrich picks out **<u>seven marbles</u>** from the bag, he is guaranteed that **<u>at least two will be of the same colour</u>**. This is because there are only six different colours of marbles. The total number of all the colours does not affect the answer.

173. C

Explanation:

Charlie runs the last 5 km (9 km – 4 km = 5 km) at a speed of 2.5 km/h without Valentina.

This will take him:

Speed = distance ÷ time

Time = distance ÷ speed

Time = 5 ÷ 2.5

Time = 2 hours

<u>Time = 120 minutes</u>

Charlie will reach the end point in 2 hours. Valentina lost 30 minutes talking to her friend.

To reach the end of the race at the same time as Charlie, she must cover the last 5 km in:

120 – 30 = **<u>90 minutes (1.5 hours)</u>**

Therefore, her speed will be:

Speed = 5 ÷ 1.5

<u>Speed = 3.3..... km/h</u>

Problem Solving

174. D

Explanation:

Exactly 35% of the shoes are for children. *Therefore, 65% are for adults; this accounts for:*

2,500 x 0.65 = **1625 shoes**

A total of 65 of the 1625 shoes are from Vietnam; this accounts for:

$\frac{65}{1625} = \frac{1}{25}$, **which is 4% of all the adult shoes.**

The same proportion of children's shoes are also from Vietnam.

There are:

2,500 x 0.35 = **875 children's shoes**

875 x 0.04 = **35 are from Vietnam**

The total number of shoes from Vietnam are:

65 + 35 = **100**

Another approach to this question is to find 4% of 2,500 (after calculating that 65 is 4% of 1625). Since 4% of both adult and children's shoes are from Vietnam, one can calculate **4% of 2,500.**

175. B

Explanation:

Cost for four nights and five days stay:

Four nights: £25 + (£17x3) = **£76**

Walks: 5 x 8 = **£40**

Total: **£116**

Cost for the seven nights and eight days stay:

Seven nights: £25 + (£17 x 6) = **£127**

Walks: £50 + £8 = **£58**

Total: **£185**

Difference is: 185– 116 = **£69**

176. C

Explanation:

If Lucy was telling the truth, then this contradicts the passage as only one person can tell the truth according to her statement. If she is that one person, no-one else can tell the truth. If Lucy is correct, then Bill is lying. Therefore, Jose is telling the truth. This is already more than one person not lying. As a result, Lucy is lying. This means that Bill is telling the truth. However, Jose is lying. Bo is telling the truth and Amoli lied. Therefore, the **pupils who lied to the teacher are Lucy, Jose and Amoli.**

177. E

Explanation:

None of the options can be concluded as all the cakes have chocolate in them, and nothing is stated regarding fruit in cakes. There is no information regarding desserts that contain both chocolate and fruit. The shop could also sell some desserts with fruits that are not tarts; however, there is no information about this nor any information of how many fruits are used in each tart.

178. D

Explanation:

Write the information as a list:

Oldest

Iva

Stella

Nuru | Jamal

Peter

The relation of Peter's age compared to Nuru is not known; however, it is known that he is younger than Iva, Stella and Jamal. Therefore, **he is younger than Iva and Stella but not necessarily Nuru.**

179. B

Explanation:

Since less than 10% of the pupils had no pets, the remaining 90% of the population can overlap. To find the smallest possible overlap:

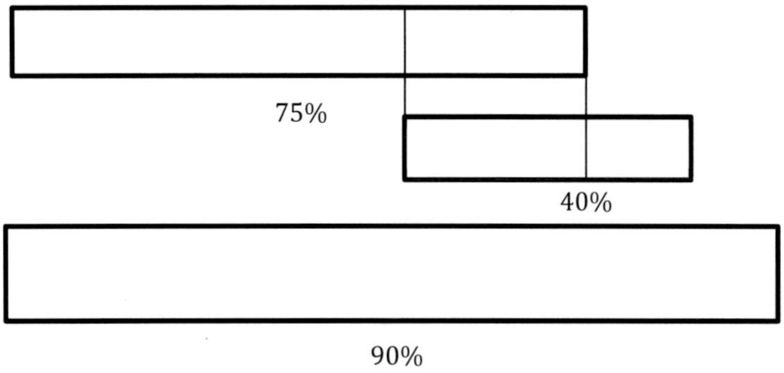

There is an overlap of **(40 +75) – 90 = 25%.** This is the minimum overlap if the number of children who owned no pets was 10%. However, since it is less than 10% of pupils who don't own a pet, the minimum overlap could be **25 – 10 = 15%.** This is the absolute lowest the overlap can be in the question.

The maximum overlap is calculated in a similar manner:

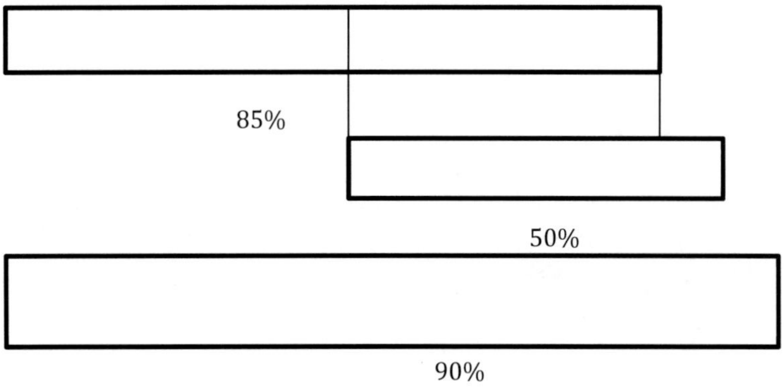

The maximum overlap is **(85 + 50) - 90 = 45%**

Therefore, the percentage of children owned both a cat and a dog are between:

15% - 45%

180. A

Explanation:

If there are 68 tails, there must be 68 Species of 'A' and 'B' in total.

Notice that:

6 x 66 = **396**

This leaves:

400 – 396 = **4 legs remaining**

Therefore, the last **4 legs are from 2 of the Species 'B' insects**, giving a total of 68 insects. The number of wings is irrelevant to the question.

181. C

Explanation:

For her first pick, she has a choice of 4 coins. After this, she only has 3 remaining types of coins that she could pick if she is to pick a coin that is not the same. The number of different ways that this can be done is:

4 x 3 x 3 x 3 x 3 x 3 = **972**

182. C

Explanation:

The answers are in kmh^{-1}; convert the time to hours:

15 minutes = 0.25 hours

Let the speed of the car be X kmh^{-1}; therefore, the relative speed will be 2X ms^{-1}. *Using speed = distance ÷ time:*

2X = 20 ÷ 0.25

2X = 80

X = 40 kmh^{-1}

Problem Solving

183. B

Explanation:

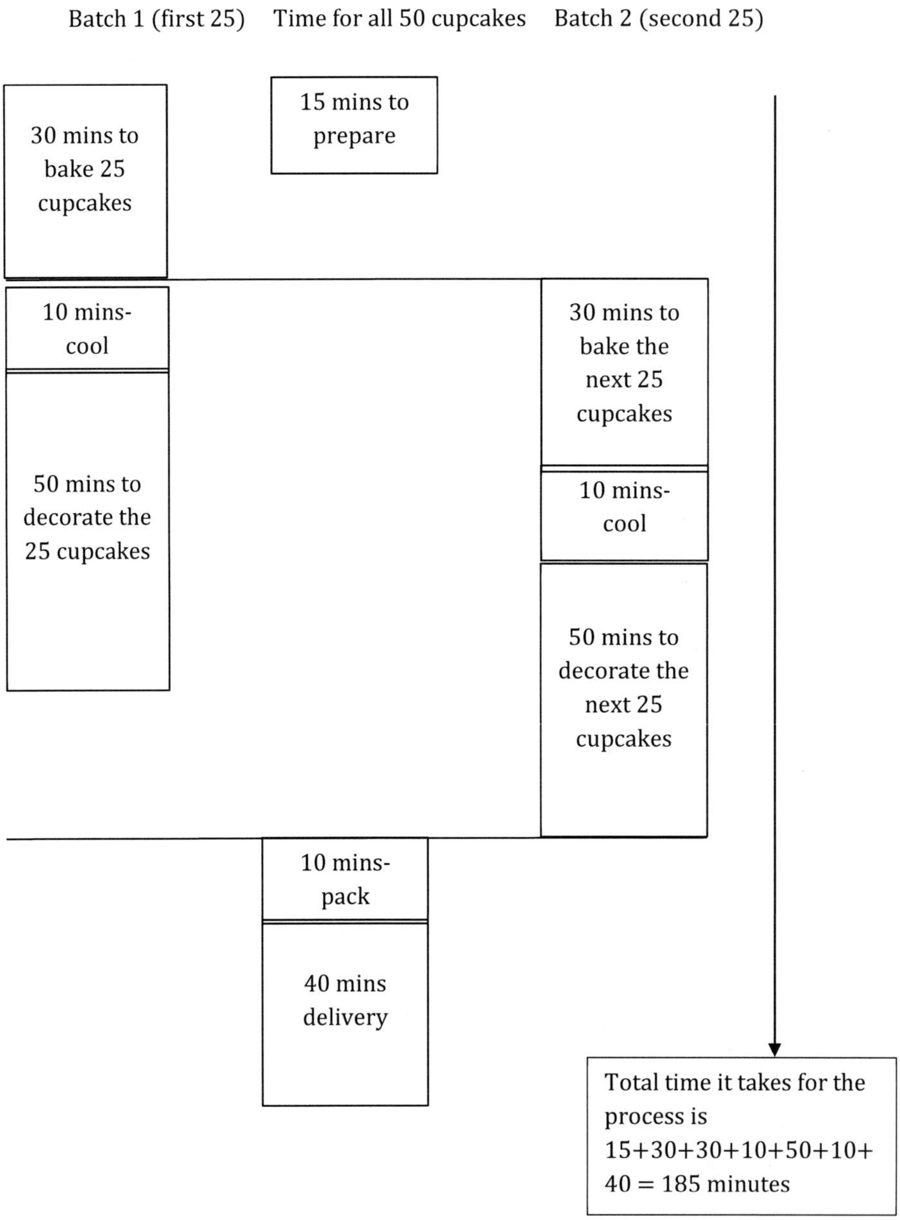

Ju can start baking the second set of 25 cupcakes as the first set starts to cool. She can then decorate these whilst the second set is still baking. Since the total time for the process is 185 minutes (3 hours 5 minutes) **she must start at 2:55 pm to ensure it is ready to be delivered to the client at 6 pm.**

184. D

Explanation:

Let x be the number of biscuits that his mother put in the tin. There are $\frac{3}{4}x$ biscuits remaining in the tin on the first day after he eats $\frac{1}{4}$ of the biscuits.

On the second day there are:

$\frac{3}{4} \times \frac{3}{4}x = \frac{9}{16}x$ **biscuits left.**

On the third day there are:

$\frac{3}{4} \times \frac{9}{16}x = \frac{27}{64}x$ **biscuits left.**

Therefore, $27 = \frac{27}{64}x$

<u>$x = 64$</u>

185. B

Explanation:

If there is a $\frac{2}{10}$ chance of picking a blue pen, then the probability of picking a red pen or black pen is $\frac{8}{10}$.

Let the number of red pens be x; therefore, the number of black pens are $2x$.

$\frac{8}{10} = 2x + x$

$\frac{8}{10} = 3x$

$x = \frac{8}{30}$

The probability of picking a blue pen is $\frac{2}{10}$, the probability of picking a red pen is $\frac{8}{30} = \frac{4}{15}$, and the probability of picking a black pen is $\frac{16}{30} = \frac{8}{15}$.

The lowest number of pens in the pencil case is 15.

Therefore, there is a:

$\frac{2}{10} \times \frac{1.5}{1.5} = \frac{3}{15}$ chance a blue pen is selected, meaning there are **<u>three blue, four red and eight black pens.</u>**

SECTION 2

Biology (B1) CELLS Specification

Topic	Objective	☺	😐	☹
B1.1	- Know and understand the structure and function of the main sub-cellular components of both animal and plant eukaryotic cells to include: o Cell Membrane o Cytoplasm o Nucleus o Mitochondrion o Cell Wall (Plant only) o Chloroplast (Plant only) o Vacuole (Plant Only)			
B1.2	- Know and understand the structure and function of the main sub-cellular components of prokaryotic cells (bacteria) to include: o Cell Membrane o Cytoplasm o Cell Wall o Chromosomal DNA/no 'true' nucleus e.g., plasmid DNA			
B1.3	- Know and understand the levels of organisation as: cells to tissues to organs to organ systems.			

Biology (B1) CELLS Questions

1. **Which one of the following statements regarding the cell membrane is incorrect?**
   A. The phospholipid bilayer consists of hydrophobic phosphate heads and hydrophilic fatty acid tails.
   B. The phospholipid bilayer is semi-permeable.
   C. It is a fluid mosaic of lipids, proteins and carbohydrates.
   D. Cholesterol regulates the fluidity of the cell membrane.

2. **The following structures relate to cell organelles:**
   1. Cell wall
   2. 80s ribosomes
   3. Cytoplasm
   4. Chloroplasts

   Which of these organelles are present in all fungal and bacterial cells?
   A. 1 only

B. 2 only
C. 3 only
D. 1 and 3 only
E. 1 and 4 only
F. 1, 2 and 3 only
G. 2, 3 and 4 only

3. Which amongst the following is present in all cells?

A. Mitochondria
B. Cell membrane
C. Vacuole
D. None of the above

4. Which row correctly identifies the approximate diameter of eukaryotic cell organelles?

	Nucleus	Mitochondria	Ribosomes	Chloroplasts
A.	20 μm	1 nm	5 nm	6 nm
B.	6 μm	1 μm	20 nm	5 μm
C.	6 nm	1 μm	20 μm	5 μm
D.	6 μm	1 nm	20 μm	5 nm

Biology

5. Which one of the following options correctly identifies the four main categories of tissue?

A. Muscle, Epithelial, Nervous and Connective
B. Muscle, Cardiac, Nervous and Epithelial
C. Muscle, Cardiac, Connective and Epithelial
D. Cardiac, Connective, Epithelial and Nervous

6. The following statements relate to the mitochondria:

1. Mitochondria are found in prokaryotic cells.
2. Mitochondria are only visible with an electron microscope.
3. It is an organelle that contains many enzymes for respiration.
4. Energy is released here in the form of ATP in respiration.

Which of these statement(s) is/are correct?

A. 2 only
B. 3 only
C. 4 only
D. 1 and 3 only
E. 3 and 4 only
F. 1, 2 and 3 only
G. 2, 3 and 4 only

7. **Blood from a patient was collected and centrifuged. The components settled into three layers as shown below.**

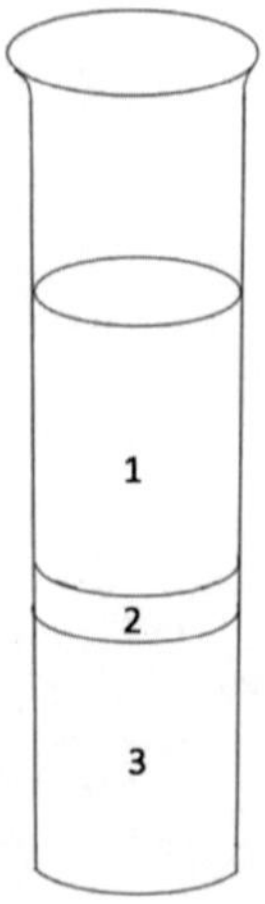

Which option represents Label 1?

A. Water, plasma proteins, nutrients and gases
B. Red blood cells, white blood cells and platelets
C. Water, hormones and red blood cells
D. Plasma proteins, gases and white blood cells
E. Water, white blood cells and platelets
F. Plasma proteins, white bloods and red blood cells

8. **What is the stored form of carbohydrates in animals?**

A. Glycogen
B. Glucose
C. Starch
D. Polypeptide
E. Polynucleotides
F. Lipids

9. **The diagram below shows an animal cell.**

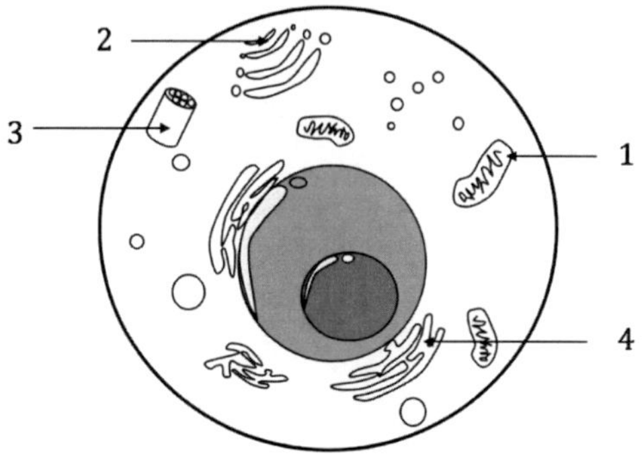

Which row correctly identifies the functions and features of the organelles labelled?

	Organelle 1	Organelle 2	Organelle 3	Organelle 4
A	Possesses ribosomes on the outer surface of the membrane.	Modifies proteins.	Place of occurrence for Krebs Cycle and Oxidative Phosphorylation.	Made from two centrioles.
B	Place of occurrence for Krebs Cycle and Oxidative Phosphorylation.	Involved in pulling chromatids apart in cell division.	Modifies proteins.	Its membrane is continuous with the outer nuclear membrane.
C	Its membrane is continuous with the outer nuclear membrane.	Made from two centrioles.	Modifies proteins.	Place of occurrence for Krebs Cycle and Oxidative Phosphorylation.
D	Modifies proteins.	Place of occurrence for Krebs Cycle and Oxidative Phosphorylation.	Made from two centrioles.	Involved in pulling chromatids apart in cell division.
E	Place of occurrence for Krebs Cycle and Oxidative Phosphorylation.	Modifies proteins.	Involved in pulling chromatids apart in cell division.	Its membrane is continuous with the outer nuclear membrane.

10. Which two monomers forms the disaccharide that is found in milk?

A. Glucose and fructose.
B. Glucose and galactose.
C. Maltose and glucose.
D. Sucrose and galactose.
E. Galactose and fructose.

11. Which row correctly identifies the role of the inorganic ions given below?

	Hydrogen ions	Sodium ions	Iron ions	Phosphate ions
A	Determines the pH in the bodily fluids.	Co-transport of glucose across the cell membrane.	Required for oxygen transport around the body.	Essential component in DNA and RNA.
B	Co-transport of glucose across the cell membrane.	Required for oxygen transport around the body.	Essential component in DNA and RNA.	Determines the pH in the bodily fluids.

Biology

C	Required for oxygen transport around the body.	Essential component in DNA and RNA.	Co-transport of glucose across the cell membrane.	Determines the pH in the bodily fluids.
D	Essential component in DNA and RNA.	Determines the pH in the bodily fluids.	Required for oxygen transport around the body.	Co-transport of glucose across the cell membrane.

Biology (B2) MOVEMENT ACROSS MEMBRANES Specification

Topic	Objective	☺	😐	☹
B2.1	- Know and understand the processes of diffusion, osmosis and active transport, including examples in living and non-living systems.			

Biology (B2) MOVEMENT ACROSS MEMBRANES Questions

12. The following statements relate to the movement of molecules across cell membranes:

1. Active transport requires channel proteins and energy from ATP.
2. Both diffusion and osmosis are passive processes.
3. Active transport and facilitated diffusion require channel and/or carrier proteins to assist in transport.
4. Particles stop moving across the cell membrane when equilibrium is reached.

Which statement(s) is/are correct?

A. 1 only
B. 2 only
C. 3 only
D. 1 and 3 only
E. 2 and 3 only
F. 1, 2 and 3 only
G. All of the above

---

13. Which one of the following factors does not affect the rate of simple diffusion into cells?

A. Concentration gradient
B. Temperature
C. Solubility of molecules
D. Number of carrier protein sites

14. Which row correctly describes the result of red blood cells in solutions of different tonicity?

	Hypertonic	Isotonic	Hypotonic
A	Turgid	Lysis	Plasmolysis
B	Shrivel	Ideal, no change	Plasmolysis
C	Shrivel	Ideal, no change	Lysis
D	Shrivel	Lysis	Ideal, no change

15. Which of the following processes cannot be an example of active transport?

A. Exchange of sodium and potassium using the sodium-potassium pump.
B. Uptake of glucose in small intestines of humans.
C. Uptake of mineral ions into root hair cells.
D. Exchange of oxygen and carbon dioxide in the alveoli.

16. An animal cell is placed in a dilute glucose solution. The cell is hypertonic compared to the solution. Glucose and water move into the cell.
What type of transport occurs for each of these molecules?

	Glucose	Water
A	Active transport	Diffusion
B	Facilitated diffusion	Osmosis
C	Active transport	Osmosis
D	Facilitated diffusion	Active transport

Biology (B3)	CELL DIVISION AND SEX DETERMINATION	Specification

Topic	Objective	☺	😐	☹
B3.1	**Mitosis and the cell cycle:** - Know and understand that the cell cycle includes interphase (the cell grows and DNA is copied) and mitosis (division leading to two daughter cells that have the same number of chromosomes so are genetically identical to each other and the parental cell). - Know and understand the role of mitosis in growth by increasing cell numbers, repair of tissues, replacement of worn out cells and asexual reproduction. - Understand that cancer is the result of changes in cells that lead to uncontrolled growth and division.			

B3.2	**Meiosis and the cell cycle:** - Know and understand the cell cycle includes interphase (the cell grows and DNA is copied) and meiosis (division that produces daughter cells, known as gametes, in which the chromosome number is halved from diploid to haploid, resulting in a single set of chromosomes). Each daughter cell will be genetically different. - Know and understand the role of meiosis in reducing the chromosome number and that the full chromosome complement is restored at fertilisation.			
B3.3	**Asexual and sexual reproduction:** - Know and understand that asexual reproduction involves one parent and that offspring are genetically identical when no mutations occur. - Know and understand that sexual reproduction involves two parents and that offspring are genetically different in relation to each other and the parents, leading to (increased) variation.			
B3.4	**Sex determination:** - Know that, in most mammals including humans, females are XX and males are XY. - Be able to establish the sex and ratio of offspring using genetic diagrams.			

Biology (B3)	CELL DIVISION AND SEX DETERMINATION	Questions

17. Which amongst the following processes does not occur during interphase?

A. DNA replication.
B. Synthesis of proteins.
C. Chromosomes becoming visible.
D. Duplicating of organelles.

18. The following statements relate to mitosis and meiosis:

1. Centrioles are found in the nucleus of the cell.
2. The number of chromosomes is doubled after mitosis.
3. DNA replication occurs in the prophase stage of mitosis.
4. The number of chromosomes remains the same after meiosis.

Which of the following statement(s) is/are correct?

A. 1 only
B. 2 only
C. 3 only
D. 1 and 3 only
E. 2 and 4 only
F. All of the above

G. None of the above

19. The following statements relate to cell division:

1. DNA replication takes place only during meiosis.
2. Spindle fibres from out of the centrosome.
3. Sister chromatids are homologous chromosomes.
4. Chromosomes are formed as a result of thickening of spindle fibres.

Which of the following statement(s) is/are correct?

A. 1 only
B. 2 only
C. 3 only
D. 1 and 3 only
E. 2 and 4 only
F. All of the above
G. None of the above

20. Which amongst the following statements regarding reproduction is incorrect?

A. Sexual reproduction requires two individual parents.
B. Some organisms are able reproduce both sexually and asexually.
C. Asexual reproduction has some advantages compared to sexual reproduction.
D. Binary fission is a type of asexual reproduction.

21. The following statements relate to mitosis:

1. Mitosis occurs in all eukaryotic cells.
2. Mitosis is required for the repair of tissues.
3. The phases of mitosis are discrete (separate) events.
4. Asexual reproduction relies on mitosis.

Which of the following statement(s) is/are incorrect?

A. 1 only
B. 2 only
C. 3 only
D. 1 and 3 only
E. 1, 2 and 4 only
F. All of the above
G. None of the above

22. Which amongst the following statements is true regarding benign tumours?

A. It can spread/metastasize to other organs.
B. It is characterised by a high mitotic index.
C. They have a high nuclear: cytoplasmic ratio.
D. Cells remain well-differentiated.

23. The following statements relate to the development of tumours:

1. It is a result of mutations in genes that regulate meiosis.
2. If mitosis is not regulated, it can lead to the uncontrollable division of cells.
3. Tumours could develop due to a mutation that leads to the silencing of a tumour suppressor gene.
4. Tumours could develop due to an oncogene mutation that resulted in DNA replication and mitosis being permanently activated.

Which of the following statement(s) is/are correct?

A. 1 only
B. 2 only
C. 3 only
D. 1 and 3 only
E. 2, 3 and 4 only
F. All of the above
G. None of the above

24. The following statements relate to meiosis:

1. Interphase is part of meiosis.
2. Meiosis occurs in all cells.
3. Meiosis is the same as sexual reproduction.
4. Meiosis produces four genetically identical cells.

Which of the following statement(s) is/are incorrect?

A. 1 only
B. 2 only
C. 4 only
D. 1 and 3 only
E. 2, 3 and 4 only
F. All of the above
G. None of the above

25. Which amongst the following statements regarding meiosis is true?

A. The chromosome number after meiosis occurs is the same.
B. Meiosis occurs in all cells.
C. Meiosis generates genetic variation in offspring.
D. Two cycles of DNA replication occur.

26. Which of the following is not an advantage of sexual reproduction?

A. Introduces variation into a population.
B. More energy efficient than asexual reproduction.
C. Selection of beneficial mutations.
D. Better adaptation to a fluctuating environment.

27. The following statements relate to an egg cell:

1. It contains twice as much genetic information as a normal body cell.
2. Fertilised eggs grow by mitosis.
3. Human egg cells contain 23 pairs of chromosomes.
4. It has the same number of chromosomes as a sperm cell.

Which of these statement(s) is/are correct?

A. 2 only
B. 3 only
C. 4 only
D. 2 and 4 only
E. 3 and 4 only
F. 1, 2 and 3 only
G. 2, 3 and 4 only

Biology (B4)	INHERITANCE	Specification

Topic	Objective	☺	😐	☹
B4.1	- Know the nucleus as a site of genetic material/chromosomes/genes in plant and animal cells.			
B4.2	- Know and understand the following genetic terms: o Gene o Allele o Dominant o Recessive o Heterozygous homozygous o Phenotype o Genotype o Chromosome			
B4.3	**Monohybrid crosses:** - Use and interpret genetic diagrams to depict monohybrid (single gene) crosses. - Use family trees/pedigrees. - Express outcome as ratios, numbers, probabilities and percentages. - Understand the concept of inherited conditions. - Know that most phenotypic features are the result of multiple genes rather than a single gene inheritance.			

Biology (B4)	INHERITANCE	Questions

28. The following statements relate to inheritance:

1. Genes solely determine phenotypes.
2. All mutations are harmful.
3. Dominant alleles are the most common in a population.
4. An allele is an alternate form of the same gene.

Which of the following statement(s) is/are incorrect?

A. 1 only
B. 2 only
C. 4 only
D. 1 and 3 only
E. 1, 2 and 3 only
F. All of the above
G. None of the above

29. Huntington's disease is an autosomal dominant condition. What is the difference in probability of a heterogenous father and a homogenous dominant mother having a child with this condition compared to a heterogenous mother and a homogenous recessive father?
    A. 25%
    B. 50%
    C. 75%
    D. 100%

30. Tay-Sachs is an autosomal recessive condition. The following family tree illustrates the individuals who are affected.

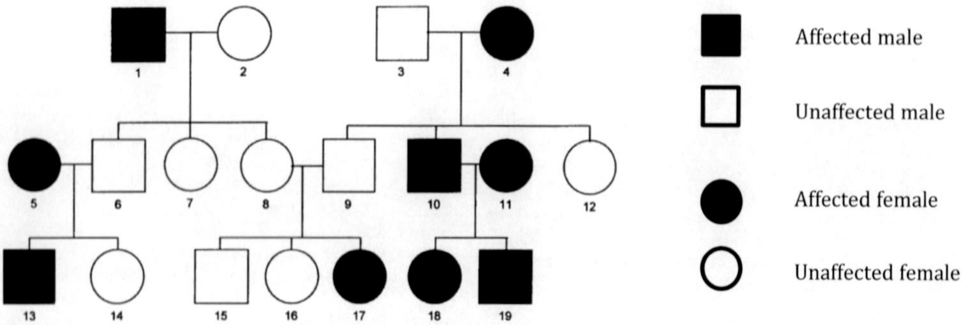

Assuming that the Tay-Sachs allele is modelled using 't', which row correctly identifies the genotypes of the following numbers?

	'2'	'6'	'10'
A	TT	Tt	Tt
B	tt	Tt	tt
C	Tt	TT	Tt
D	Tt	Tt	tt

31. The allele for Cystic Fibrosis, an inherited disorder caused by a recessive allele, is modelled using the letter 'c'. Both parents of a child are heterozygous for cystic fibrosis. Which row shows the correct probability of the child having each combination?

	Has Cystic Fibrosis:	Carrier of Cystic Fibrosis:	Does not have Cystic Fibrosis and is not a carrier:
A	50%	25%	25%
B	25%	25%	50%
C	25%	50%	25%
D	50%	50%	0%
E	25%	0%	75%

32. Individual 'A' has Sickle Cell Anaemia, a recessive disorder. Individual 'B' is homozygous dominant for the same trait. Consider the following genetic diagram:

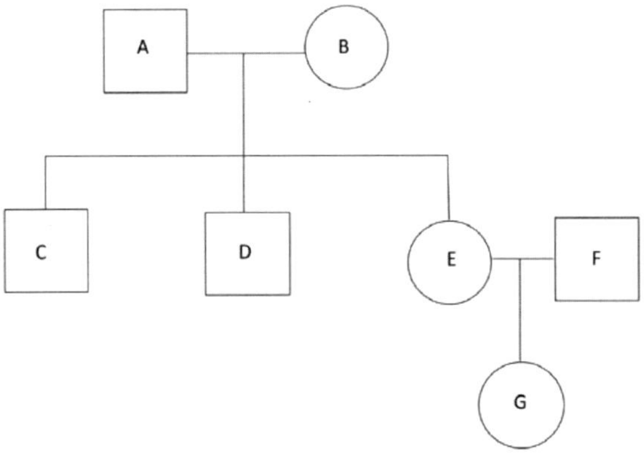

What is the probability of Individual 'G' having sickle cell anaemia if:

	F is homozygous dominant?	F is heterozygous?
A	0%	50%
B	25%	50%
C	50%	25%
D	0%	25%
E	25%	0%

33. Red-green colour blindness is an X-linked disorder. A boy has red-green colour blindness, but neither his parents nor his grandparents have this condition. Who is he most likely to have inherited this gene from?

A. Maternal grandmother
B. Paternal grandmother
C. Paternal grandfather
D. Maternal grandfather

Biology (B5)	DNA	Specification

Topic	Objective	☺	😐	☹
B5.1	**Understand that:** o The genome is the entire genetic material (DNA) of an organism. o Chromosomes contain DNA.			
B5.2	**Describe the structure of DNA:** - Know that DNA is a polymer made up of two strands forming a double helix. - Know that DNA is made from four different nucleotides, each consisting of a common sugar and phosphate group along with one of four different bases attached to the sugar. - Know the complementary pairs of bases – adenine (A) with thymine (T), guanine (G) with cytosine (C) – and that the sequence of these bases is the genetic code.			
B5.3	**Protein synthesis:** - Know and understand that genes carry the code for proteins. - Know and understand that the genetic code is 'read' as triplets, and that each triplet codes for an amino acid. - Understand that protein synthesis involves the production of proteins from amino acids.			
B5.4	**Gene mutations:** - Understand that a mutation is a change in the DNA. - Know that most mutations have no effect on the phenotype, some will have a small effect, whilst occasionally others will determine the phenotype.			

Biology

Biology (B5)	DNA	Questions

34. The diagram below shows two nucleotides:

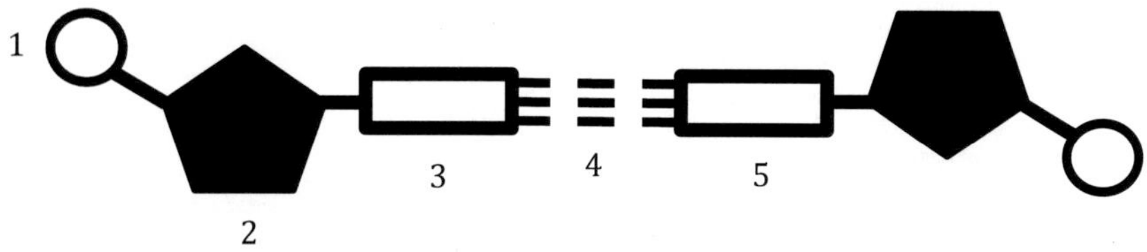

Which row correctly describes the above structure?

	1	2	3	4	5
A	Phosphorus Group	Deoxyribose	Guanine	Hydrogen Bond	Cytosine
B	Phosphate Group	Deoxyribose	Adenine	Phosphodiester Bond	Cytosine
C	Phosphate Group	Deoxyribose	Cytosine	Hydrogen Bond	Guanine
D	Phosphorus Group	Ribose	Thymine	Phosphodiester Bond	Adenine

35. Which statement regarding the coding of amino acids is correct?

A. Each DNA base codes for an amino acid.
B. Each mRNA codon codes for an amino acid.
C. Each tRNA codes for an amino acid.
D. None of the above.

36. Which sequence corresponds to the correct process of transcription in prokaryotes?

A. Hydrogen bonds break → Free DNA nucleotides pair with exposed template strand → Production of mRNA.
B. Hydrogen bonds break → Free DNA nucleotides pair with exposed template strand → Production of pre-mRNA → Splicing to remove introns.
C. Hydrogen bonds break → Free RNA nucleotides pair with exposed template strand → Production of mRNA.
D. Hydrogen bonds break → Free RNA nucleotides pair with exposed template strand → Production of pre-mRNA → Splicing to remove introns.

37. Which sequence corresponds to the correct process of translation?

A. mRNA attached to ribosome on smooth ER → tRNA brings complementary anti-codon with specific amino acid → Enzyme catalyses formation of peptide bonds between amino acids → Stop codon reached and peptide is released.
B. mRNA attached to ribosome on rough ER → tRNA brings complementary anti-codon with specific amino acid → Enzyme catalyses formation of peptide bonds between amino acids → Stop codon reached and peptide is released.
C. mRNA attached to ribosome on rough ER → tRNA brings complementary codon with specific amino acid → Enzyme catalyses formation of peptide bonds between amino acids → Stop codon reached and peptide is released.
D. mRNA attached to ribosome on smooth ER → tRNA brings complementary anti-codon with specific amino acid → Enzyme catalyses formation of phosphodiester bonds between amino acids → Stop codon reached and peptide is released.

38. Consider the following statements:

1. White blood cells and mature red blood cells in humans have the same number of chromosomes.
2. DNA in mitochondria is packed together to form a chromosome.
3. The major constituent of a chromosome is DNA.
4. Prokaryotic DNA is not associated with histones.

Which of these statement(s) is/are correct?

A. 1 only
B. 2 only
C. 3 only
D. 4 only
E. 1 and 4 only
F. 3 and 4 only
G. 1, 2 and 3 only
H. 2, 3 and 4 only

39. Identify the part labelled 'X' in the nucleotide shown below:

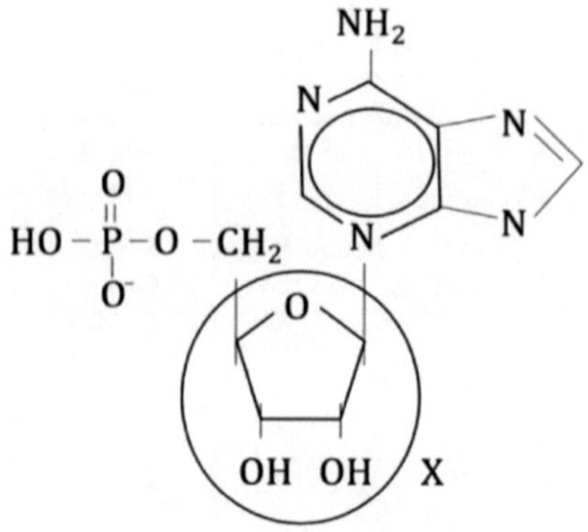

A. Ribose sugar
B. Deoxyribose sugar
C. Nucleotide base
D. Phosphate group
E. Hexose sugar

40. Listed below are different bases:

1. Adenine
2. Cytosine
3. Guanine
4. Thymine
5. Uracil

Which of the aforementioned bases are purine?

A. 1 and 2 only
B. 1 and 3 only
C. 2 and 4 only
D. 1, 3 and 5 only
E. 1, 2 and 3 only
F. 2, 4 and 5 only

41. An mRNA sequence is given below that codes to make amino acids to join together and form a protein:

AUGGGCCCGGUAAGGGCCCAGAUC

A deletion mutation occurred on the fifth nucleotide.

Using the table below, determine the change that has occurred on the third amino acid of the protein

2nd base in codon (columns); 1st base in codon (rows); 3rd base in codon (right)

	U	C	A	G	
U	Phe Phe Leu Leu	Ser Ser Ser Ser	Tyr Tyr STOP STOP	Cys Cys STOP Trp	U C A G
C	Leu Leu Leu Leu	Pro Pro Pro Pro	His His Gin Gin	Arg Arg Arg Arg	U C A G
A	Ile Ile Ile Met	Thr Thr Thr Thr	Asn Asn Lys Lys	Ser Ser Arg Arg	U C A G
G	Val Val Val Val	Ala Ala Ala Ala	Asp Asp Glu Glu	Gly Gly Gly Gly	U C A G

A. Changed from 'Arg' to 'Pro'.
B. Changed from 'Pro' to 'Gly'.
C. Changed from 'Gly' to 'Ala'.
D. Changed from 'Pro' to 'Arg'.
E. Changed from 'Val' to 'STOP'.

Biology (B6)	GENE TECHNOLOGIES	Specification

Topic	Objective	☺	😐	☹
B6.1	**Genetic engineering:** - Understand the process of genetic engineering to include: o taking a copy of a gene from (DNA/chromosomes of) one organism. o insertion of that gene into the DNA of another organism. the roles of restriction enzymes and ligases. - Recall examples of genetic engineering in different cell types. - Explain the benefits and risks of using genetic engineering in medical applications.			
B6.2	**Stem cells:** - Know that embryonic stem cells can give rise to any cell type. - Know that cells lose this ability as an animal matures. - Know the functions of stem cells including adult stem cells. - Explain the benefits and risks of using stem cells in medical applications.			
B6.3	**Selective breeding:** - Understand the impact of selective breeding on domesticated animals.			

Biology (B6)	GENE TECHNOLOGIES	Questions

42. Which sequence corresponds to the correct process of genetic engineering?

A. Selection of desired characteristic → Take copy of gene from DNA of one organism using restriction enzymes → Insertion of gene into DNA of another organism using ligase enzymes.

B. Selection of desired characteristic → Take copy of gene from DNA of one organism using ligase enzymes → Insertion of gene into DNA of another organism using restriction enzymes.

C. Selection of desired characteristic → Insertion of gene into DNA of another organism using restriction enzymes → Take copy of gene from DNA of organism using restriction enzymes.

D. Selection of desired characteristic → Insertion of gene into DNA of another organism using ligase enzymes → Take copy of gene from DNA of organism using restriction enzymes.

Biology

43. Which one of the following statements is not an example of genetic engineering?

A. Crop plants being modified to be resistant to certain herbicides.
B. The gene for human insulin being inserted into bacteria for the production of large quantities of insulin.
C. Selecting cows that produce a lot of milk in order to breed them.
D. Rice crops being modified to possess additional vitamins.

44. Which one of the following statements regarding stem cells is incorrect?

A. Stem cells are only harvested from embryos.
B. Embryonic stem cells can only give rise to certain cell types.
C. Cells maintain the ability to differentiate into any cell as an animal matures.
D. All of the above.

45. Which one of the following statements is not an impact of selective breeding?

A. It can result in an increased quality of livestock.
B. Reduced genetic diversity.
C. Inbreeding.
D. Transfer of the desired gene into other species.

46. The diagram below shows an overview of DNA recombination:

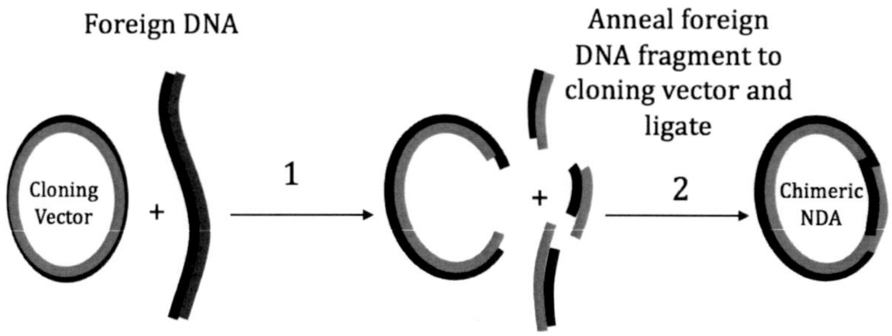

What enzymes are used for Steps 1 and 2?

	Step 1	Step 2
A	DNA Ligase	Restriction Endonuclease
B	DNA Helicase	DNA Polymerase
C	Restriction Endonuclease	DNA Polymerase
D	Restriction Endonuclease	DNA Ligase
E	DNA Helicase	Restriction Endonuclease
F	DNA Polymerase	DNA Ligase

Biology (B7) VARIATION Specification

Topic	Objective	☺	😐	☹
B7.1	**Natural selection and evolution:** - Know that there is usually extensive genetic variation within a population of a species. - Describe evolution as a change in the inherited characteristics of a population over time through a process of natural selection which may result in the formation of a new species. - Explain how evolution can occur through natural selection of variants that give rise to phenotypes best suited to their environment. - Understand antibiotic resistance and that it is an example of evolution through natural selection.			
B7.2	**Sources of variation:** - Understand that variation can be genetic/inherited, resulting in a range of phenotypes. - Understand that variation can also be environmental, which affects a range of phenotypes.			

Biology (B7) VARIATION Questions

47. Which statement correctly defines evolution?

A. A change in the inherited characteristics of a community over time through a process of natural selection, which may result in the formation of a new species.

B. A change in the inherited characteristics of a population over time through a process of natural selection, which may result in the formation of a new species.

C. A change in the inherited characteristics of a population over time through a process of natural selection, which will always result in the formation of a new species.

D. A change in the inherited characteristics of a population over time through a process of selective breeding, which may result in the formation of a new species.

48. Which sequence corresponds to the correct process of natural selection?

A. There is a wide range of variation for a particular characteristic in a species → Individuals with favourable chromosomes are more likely to survive and breed successfully → Favourable chromosomes are passed onto next generation.

B. There is a no variation for a particular characteristic in a species → Individuals with favourable alleles are more likely to survive and breed successfully → Favourable alleles are passed onto next generation.

C. There is a wide range of variation for a particular characteristic in a species → Individuals with favourable alleles are more likely to survive and breed successfully → Favourable alleles are passed onto next generation.
D. There is no range of variation for a particular characteristic in a species → Individuals with favourable chromosomes are more likely to survive and breed successfully → Favourable chromosomes are passed onto next generation.

49. Which one of the following statements regarding variation is correct?
A. Variation is always genetic.
B. Variation is always environmental.
C. Variation can be genetic and/or environmental.
D. None of the above.

50. Which one of the following statements regarding organisms of similar species is incorrect?
A. They breed to produce a hybrid.
B. They always look very similar.
C. They share a recent common ancestor.
D. They often tend to live in similar habitats.

Biology (B8) ENZYMES Specification

Topic	Objective	☺	😐	☹
B8.1	- Understand that enzymes are biological catalysts.			
B8.2	- Understand the mechanism of enzyme action including the active site and enzyme specificity.			
B8.3	- Understand the factors affecting the rate of enzyme action: o Temperature o pH			
B8.4	- Know the role of the amylases, proteases and lipases in digestion.			

Biology (B8) ENZYMES Questions

51. The following statements relate to amylase activity:
1. Both temperature and pH alter bonds in the tertiary structure of an enzyme.
2. Amylase is only produced in the pancreas and small intestine.
3. The optimal pH of amylase is acidic-neutral.
4. Amylase breaks down maltose to starch.

Which of the following statement(s) is/are incorrect?

A. 1 only
B. 2 only
C. 4 only
D. 1 and 3 only
E. 2 and 4 only
F. 1, 2 and 4 only
G. None of the above

52. The following statements relate to protease activity:

1. Protease is only found in animals and plants.
2. Protease is produced in the stomach, pancreas, gallbladder and small intestine.
3. Pepsin (stomach protease) and trypsin (pancreatic protease) both have an acidic optimum pH.
4. Protease hydrolyses amino acids to polypeptides.

Which of the following statement(s) is/are correct?

A. 1 only
B. 2 only
C. 4 only
D. 1 and 3 only
E. 2 and 4 only
F. 1, 2 and 4 only
G. None of the above

53. The following statements relate to lipase activity:

1. Lipase produced in the salivary glands have an acidic pH.
2. Lipase is produced in the pancreas and small intestine.
3. Lipase enzymes break down fat into fatty acids and glycerol.
4. All lipase enzymes have the same optimal pH and temperature.

Which of the following statement(s) is/are correct?

A. 1 only
B. 2 only
C. 4 only
D. 2 and 3 only
E. 2 and 4 only
F. 1, 2 and 3 only
G. 2, 3 and 4 only
H. None of the above

54. Which of the following factors do not affect enzyme activity?

A. pH
B. Temperature
C. Substrate concentration
D. Size of substrate

55. **The three curves below show the rate of reaction of three enzymes found in the digestive system at varying pH levels:**

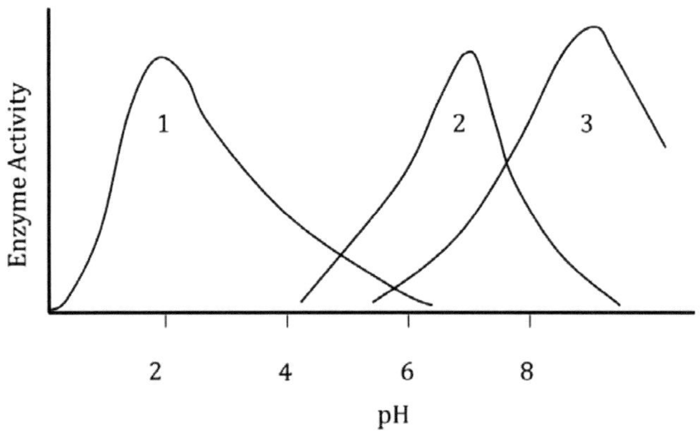

Which row correctly identifies the enzymes represented by these curves?

	1	2	3
A	Pepsin	Trypsin	Salivary Amylase
B	Salivary Amylase	Pepsin	Trypsin
C	Trypsin	Salivary Amylase	Pepsin
D	Pepsin	Salivary Amylase	Trypsin
E	Trypsin	Pepsin	Salivary Amylase
F	Salivary Amylase	Trypsin	Pepsin

Biology (B9) ANIMAL PHYSIOLOGY Specification

Topic	Objective	☺	😐	☹
B9.1	**Respiration:** - Understand the process of cellular respiration. - Understand the process of aerobic respiration, including the word equation. - Understand the process of anaerobic respiration in animals, including the word equation.			

B9.2	**Organ systems:** - <u>Nervous system:</u> o Understand that the central nervous system comprises of the brain and spinal cord. o Explain the structure and function of sensory neurones, relay neurones, motor neurones, synapses and the reflex arc. - <u>Respiratory system:</u> o Explain the structure and function of the respiratory system, including the structure of the thorax. o Understand the processes of ventilation and gas exchange. o Understand the importance of a high surface area : volume ratio for the gas exchange process. - <u>Circulatory system:</u> o Understand the structure and function of the circulatory system, including the heart, heart rate and ECGs, and the blood vessels (arteries, veins and capillaries). o Understand the composition and function of the blood (red blood cells carry oxygen; white blood cells are involved in antibody production and phagocytosis; platelets are involved in blood clotting; and plasma is involved both in the transport of blood components and other dissolved substances including hormones, antibodies, urea and carbon dioxide, and in the distribution of heat). o Understand the relationship with the gaseous exchange system. o Understand the need for exchange surfaces and a transport system in multicellular organisms in terms of surface area : volume ratio. - <u>Digestive system:</u> o Understand the structure and function of the digestive system. o Understand the processes of peristalsis, digestion, absorption and egestion. - <u>Excretory system:</u> o Understand the structure and function of the excretory system, including the kidney and the nephron. o Understand the role of the kidneys in homeostasis.			

Biology

B9.3	**Homeostasis:** - Know that homeostasis is the maintenance of a constant internal environment and appreciate its importance. - Understand the concept of negative feedback. - Understand the regulation of blood glucose levels, including the role of insulin and glucagon. - Understand Type 1 and Type 2 diabetes, and how Type 1 diabetes can be treated. - Understand the regulation of water content (including ADH) and the regulation of temperature.			
B9.4	**Hormones:** - Recall that hormones are released from specific endocrine glands and travel in the blood to their target structures. - Explain the roles of thyroxine and adrenaline in the body, including thyroxine as an example of a negative feedback system. - Describe the role of hormones in human reproduction including: o those in the menstrual cycle (FSH, LH, oestrogen and progesterone) o those in contraception, and the differences between hormonal and non-hormonal forms of contraception.			
B9.5	**Disease and body defence:** - <u>Communicable diseases:</u> o Know that communicable diseases are caused by pathogenic bacteria, viruses, protists and fungi. o Understand the transmission routes of sexually transmitted infections, including the effect on the immune system of HIV which results in AIDS. o Understand the treatment of disease, including the use of antibiotics, vaccines (role of dead and inactive pathogens, antibody production and formation of memory cells) and techniques to prevent the spread of pathogens including HIV. o Understand the process of discovery and development of new medicines including pre-clinical and clinical testing. - <u>Non-communicable diseases:</u> o Know that the following diseases are caused by the interaction of many factors: cardiovascular disease, many forms of cancer, some lung and liver diseases and diseases influenced by nutrition, including Type 2 diabetes.			

	o Know that cardiovascular disease can be treated/managed using life-long medication (including statins, anti-coagulants and anti-hypertensive drugs), surgical procedures (including stents and bypass for coronary heart disease), and lifestyle changes (including reducing smoking, more exercise and a balanced diet).			

Biology (B9) | ANIMAL PHYSIOLOGY | Questions

56. Which amongst the following statements regarding respiration is correct?

A. Plants respire only when they do not photosynthesise.
B. Respiration is an endothermic chemical reaction.
C. Humans expire CO_2 during respiration, while plants expire O_2 during respiration.
D. Both plants and animals can respire in terms of cellular respiration.

57. Which row displays the correct word equation for both aerobic and anaerobic respiration in humans?

	Aerobic	Anaerobic
A	glucose + oxygen → carbon dioxide + water (+energy)	glucose + enzymes →carbon dioxide and lactic acid
B	glucose + oxygen → carbon dioxide + water (+energy)	glucose + enzymes →carbon dioxide and ethanol
C	glucose + oxygen (+energy) → carbon dioxide + water	glucose + enzymes →carbon dioxide and lactic acid
D	glucose + oxygen (+energy) → carbon dioxide + water	glucose + enzymes →carbon dioxide and ethanol

58. Which sequence correctly describes the process that results in inspiration?

A. Diaphragm contracts → Internal intercostal muscles contract → Ribs move upwards and outwards → Expansion of thoracic cavity → Decrease in thoracic pressure.
B. Diaphragm contracts → External intercostal muscles contract → Ribs move upwards and outwards → Expansion of thoracic cavity → Decrease in thoracic pressure.
C. Diaphragm relaxes → External intercostal muscles contract → Ribs move upwards and outwards → Expansion of thoracic cavity → Decrease in thoracic pressure.
D. Diaphragm contracts → External intercostal muscles contract → Ribs move upwards and outwards → Expansion of thoracic cavity → Increase in thoracic pressure.

59. The following statements relate to factors that determine the rate of certain processes.

1. Concentration gradient
2. Surface area: volume ratio
3. Solubility of the gas
4. Width of the air-blood barrier

Biology

Which of the following factors influence gas exchange in the alveoli?

A. 1 only
B. 2 only
C. 4 only
D. 2 and 3 only
E. 2 and 4 only
F. 1, 3 and 4 only
G. All of the above
H. None of the above

60. The following statements relate to blood vessels.

1. Arteries have a wide lumen and thick muscular walls.
2. Only veins have valves.
3. Capillaries are one cell thick and have thin permeable walls.
4. Arteries typically transport blood under low pressure, while veins transport blood under high pressure.

Which of the following statement(s) is/are correct?

A. 1 only
B. 2 only
C. 3 only
D. 1 and 4 only
E. 2 and 3 only
F. 1, 2 and 4 only
G. None of the above

61. The following statements relate to the circulatory system.

1. The right ventricle has a thicker muscular wall compared to the left ventricle.
2. Blood is produced in the heart.
3. Platelets produce antibodies.
4. Blood is a tissue.

Which of the following statement(s) is/are correct?

A. 1 only
B. 2 only
C. 3 only
D. 4 only
E. 1, 2 and 3 only
F. 2, 3 and 4 only
G. None of the above

62. Which sequence corresponds to the correct order of the digestive system?

A. Peristalsis → Egestion → Deglutition → Absorption → Digestion
B. Deglutition → Peristalsis → Egestion → Absorption → Digestion
C. Deglutition → Peristalsis → Digestion → Absorption → Egestion
D. Peristalsis → Absorption → Deglutition → Digestion → Egestion
E. Deglutition → Peristalsis → Absorption → Digestion → Egestion

63. Which of the following statements regarding digestion is correct?

A. Digestion begins in the jejunum (small intestine).
B. The digestive system is regulated by voluntary smooth muscles.

C. The small intestine has a wider diameter than the large intestine.
D. The small intestine is longer than the large intestine.
E. The stomach receives its blood supply from the inferior vena cava.

64. Which sequence corresponds to the correct order of the structures through which urine flows in a nephron?

A. Bowman's capsule → Distal Convoluted Tubule → Loop of Henle →Proximal Convoluted Tubule → Collecting Duct.
B. Bowman's capsule → Proximal Convoluted Tubule → Loop of Henle → Distal Convoluted Tubule → Collecting Duct.
C. Bowman's capsule → Proximal Convoluted Tubule → Loop of Henle → Collecting Duct → Distal Convoluted Tubule.
D. Bowman's capsule → Proximal Convoluted Tubule → Distal Convoluted Tubule-Loop of Henle → Collecting Duct.

65. Which of the following processes is not an example of negative feedback?

A. Osmoregulation
B. Blood sugar regulation
C. Blood clotting
D. Control of blood pressure

66. The following statements relate to hormones involved in the menstrual cycle.

1. FSH, produced in the ovaries, causes an egg to mature in the ovary.
2. LH, produced in the pituitary gland, maintains the lining of the uterus for the second half of the menstrual cycle.
3. Oestrogen, produced in the ovaries, stimulates the pituitary gland to release LH.
4. Progesterone, produced in the ovaries, stimulates the ovaries to release oestrogen.

Which of the following statement(s) is/are correct?

A. 1 only
B. 2 only
C. 3 only
D. 4 only
E. 1, 2 and 3 only
F. 1, 2 and 4 only
G. None of the above

67. The following statements relate to the eye:

1. The cornea refracts light into the eye.
2. The lens focuses the light onto the retina.
3. The optic nerve carries impulses from the receptors to the brain.
4. Rods are sensitive to colour.

Which of these statement(s) is/are correct?

A. 1 only
B. 2 only
C. 4 only
D. 1 and 3 only
E. 1 and 4 only
F. 1, 2 and 3 only
G. 2, 3 and 4 only

68. Which sequence of events concerning the reflex arc is in the correct order?

A. Stimulus → Receptor → Motor Neurone →Relay Neurone →Sensory Neurone →Effector →Response.

B. Stimulus →Effector →Sensory Neurone →Relay Neurone→Motor Neurone →Receptor → Response.

C. Stimulus →Receptor →Sensory Neurone→Relay Neurone →Motor Neurone →Effector →Response.

D. Stimulus →Receptor →Sensory Neurone →Brain →Motor Neurone →Effector →Response

E. Stimulus → Receptor →Sensory Neurone →Motor Neurone →Effector →Response.

69. Which row correctly identifies the blood that runs through the following large vessels?

	Aorta	Vena Cava	Pulmonary Vein	Pulmonary artery
A	Deoxygenated	Deoxygenated	Deoxygenated	Oxygenated
B	Deoxygenated	Oxygenated	Oxygenated	Oxygenated
C	Deoxygenated	Oxygenated	Oxygenated	Deoxygenated
D	Oxygenated	Deoxygenated	Deoxygenated	Oxygenated
E	Oxygenated	Deoxygenated	Oxygenated	Deoxygenated

70. Which statement regarding bile is correct?

A. Bile is alkaline.

B. Bile is produced in the gallbladder.

C. Bile helps with digestion in the stomach.

D. Bile helps with the digestion of proteins.

E. Bile helps with the digestion of carbohydrates.

71. With regard to pathogens, which microbe causes each of the following diseases?

	HIV	Flu	Salmonella	Malaria
A	Virus	Virus	Bacteria	Protozoa
B	Virus	Bacteria	Bacteria	Fungi
C	Bacteria	Virus	Bacteria	Protozoa
D	Virus	Virus	Fungi	Protozoa
E	Fungi	Bacteria	Bacteria	Virus

72. Which row correctly matches each disorder with its cause?

	Type I Diabetes	Type II Diabetes	Scurvy	Anaemia
A	Lack of insulin being produced by the pancreas.	Body cells no longer respond to the insulin produced by the pancreas.	Lack of Vitamin D.	Lack of Iron.
B	Lack of insulin being produced by the pancreas.	Body cells no longer respond to the insulin produced by the pancreas.	Lack of Vitamin C.	Lack of Iron.
C	Body cells no longer respond to the insulin produced by the pancreas.	Lack of insulin being produced by the pancreas.	Lack of Vitamin C.	Lack of Iron.
D	Body cells no longer respond to the insulin produced by the pancreas.	Lack of insulin being produced by the pancreas.	Lack of Iron.	Lack of Vitamin C.

73. Consider the three oxygen dissociation curves below.

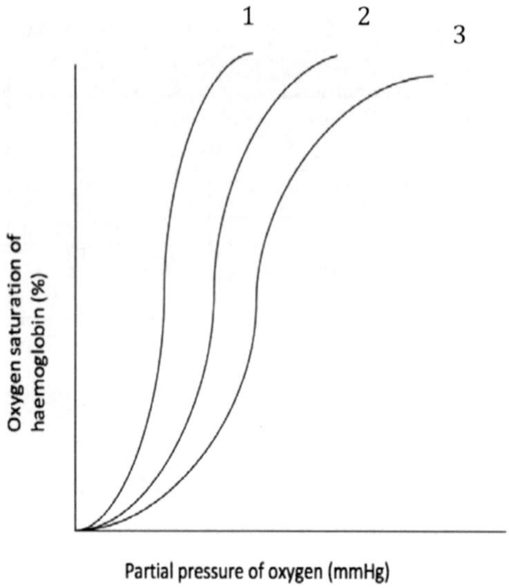

Which row best describes the species of animal that these curves belong to?

	Llama (a mammal that lives at high altitudes)	Dog	Mouse
A	1	2	3
B	1	3	2
C	2	1	3
D	3	2	1
E	2	3	1
F	3	1	2

A Lakshmi, T R Enoch, S Z Y Ooi. Doctors Academy Publications, Cardiff, UK, 2020.

74. The figure below shows a cardiac pressure-volume loop:

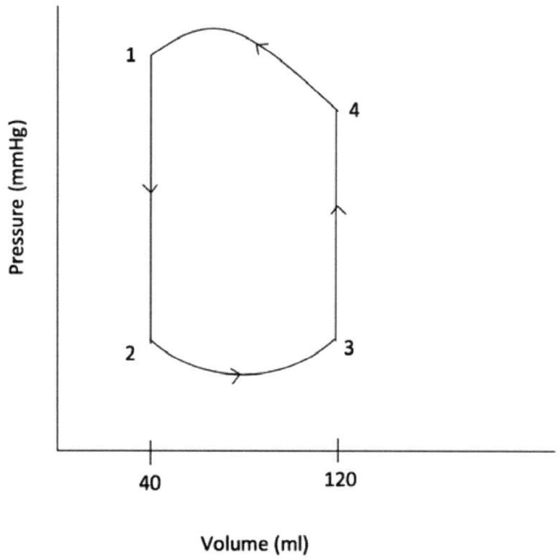

Which row best describes the process that occurs at each of the labelled stages?

	1	2	3	4
A	Mitral valve opens.	Mitral valve closes.	Aortic valve opens.	Aortic valve closes.
B	Mitral valve closes.	Aortic valve opens.	Aortic valve closes.	Mitral valve opens.
C	Aortic valve closes.	Mitral valve opens.	Mitral valve closes.	Aortic valve opens.
D	Aortic valve opens.	Aortic valve closes.	Mitral valve opens.	Mitral valve closes.
E	Mitral valve opens.	Aortic valve closes.	Mitral valve closes.	Aortic valve opens.
F	Mitral valve opens	Mitral valve closes	Aortic valve closes	Aortic valve opens

75. The following statements relate to the lungs:

1. Asbestosis increases the functional residual capacity of the lungs.
2. Emphysema increases the functional residual capacity of the lungs.
3. Fibrosis of the lungs decreases the function residual capacity.
4. Those suffering from emphysema have difficulty exhaling.
5. The energy required to breathe is decreased in a scarred lung.

Which of these statement(s) is/are correct?
A. 1, 2 and 3 only
B. 2, 3 and 4 only
C. 3, 4 and 5 only
D. 1, 2, 3 and 4 only
E. 2, 3, 4 and 5 only
F. All of the above

76. Within the renal system, Angiotensin II is a hormone that constricts the efferent arterioles more than the afferent arterioles.
Which row best describes the processes that occur?

	Amount of sodium filtered into the Bowman's capsule	The concentration of proteins in the capillaries after the glomerulus	Glomerular filtration rate	Renal blood flow
A	Increases	Decreases	Increases	Decreases
B	Decreases	Stays the same	Decreases	Decreases
C	Stays the same	Decreases	Stays the same	Decreases
D	Decreases	Increases	Decreases	Increases
E	Increases	Decreases	Increases	Stays the same
F	Increases	Increases	Stays the same	Decreases
G	Increases	Increases	Increases	Decreases

77. The following statements relate to the hormones that are involved in homeostasis:
1. Insulin reduces the blood glucose level.
2. Glucagon is released when the blood glucose levels are low.
3. Insulin is released by the beta cells of the pancreas.
4. ADH increases the reabsorption of water in the kidney.
5. ADH is released from the adrenal gland.

Which of these statement(s) is/are correct?
A. 1, 2 and 3 only
B. 2, 3 and 4 only
C. 3, 4 and 5 only
D. 1, 2, 3 and 4 only
E. 2, 3, 4 and 5 only
F. All of the above

78. Consider the following statements regarding the functions of the liver:
1. Metabolises fat
2. Produces bile
3. Detoxification
4. Stores vitamins
5. Releases glucagon

Which of these statement(s) is/are correct?
A. 1, 2 and 3 only

Biology

B. 2, 3 and 4 only
C. 3, 4 and 5 only
D. 1, 2, 3 and 4 only
E. 2, 3, 4 and 5 only
F. All of the above

79. Which option correctly represents the passage of food down the digestive system?

A. Mouth→Pharynx→Oesophagus→Stomach→Duodenum→Jejunum→ Ileum→Caecum→Ascending Colon→Transverse Colon→Descending Colon→Sigmoid Colon→Rectum→Anus.
B. Mouth→Oesophagus→Pharynx→Stomach→Duodenum→Jejunum → Ileum→ Caecum→ Ascending Colon→Transverse Colon→Descending Colon→Sigmoid Colon→Rectum→Anus.
C. Mouth→Oesophagus→Pharynx→Stomach→Duodenum→Jejunum→ Ileum→Caecum →Descending Colon→Transverse Colon→Ascending Colon→Sigmoid Colon→Rectum→Anus.
D. Mouth→Pharynx→Oesophagus→Stomach→Duodenum→ Ileum→Jejunum→Caecum→ Ascending Colon→ Transverse Colon→Descending Colon→Sigmoid Colon→Rectum→Anus.
E. Mouth→Pharynx→Oesophagus→Stomach→Duodenum→Jejunum→ Ileum→Sigmoid Colon → Ascending Colon→Transverse Colon→Descending Colon→Caecum→Rectum→Anus.

80. The diagram below shows an ECG. Identify the segment which is labelled as 3.

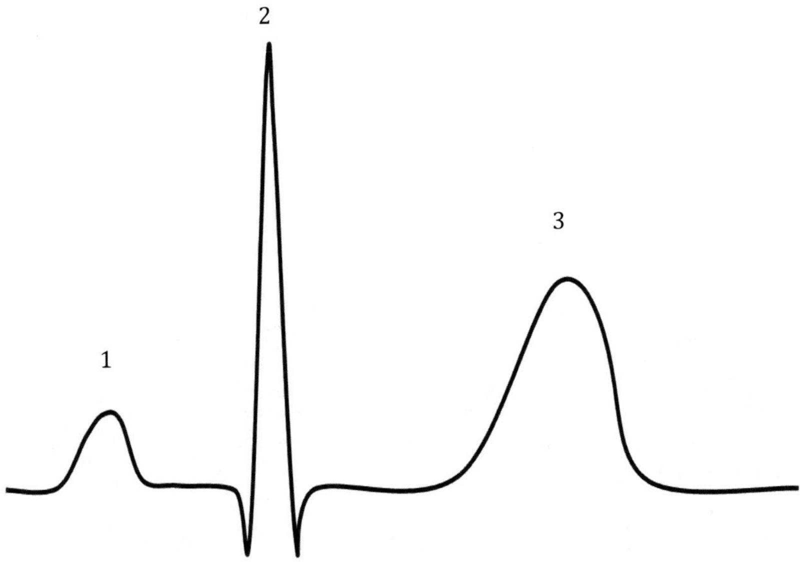

A. Ventricular depolarisation
B. Atrial depolarisation
C. Ventricular repolarisation
D. Atrial relaxation
E. Ventricular relaxation
F. Atrial contraction

Biology

81. The diagram below represents a spirometer trace. What is the volume labelled X?

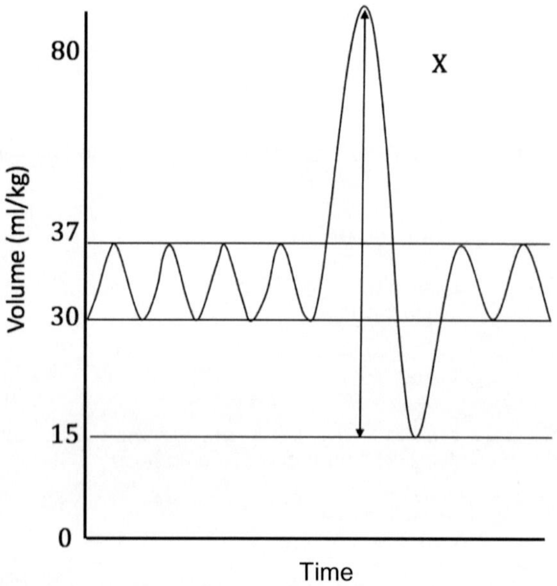

A. Inspiratory capacity + expiratory reserve volume
B. Inspiratory reserve volume + expiratory reserve volume
C. Total lung capacity – functional residual capacity
D. Vital capacity – expiratory reserve volume
E. Inspiratory reserve volume + tidal volume
F. Vital capacity – tidal volume

82. Which one of the structures listed below is not an organ?

A. Lungs
B. Roots
C. Stems
D. Kidney
E. Fruit
F. Leaves
G. Liver
H. Chlorophyll

83. Which amongst the following statements regarding the endocrine system is correct?

A. It has a faster action than the nervous system.
B. It has a long-lasting effect on the body.
C. It does not involve the brain.
D. It is not involved in homeostasis.

84. What substance does the brain mainly use to release energy when its main fuel source has been depleted?

A. Glucose
B. Ketone
C. Amino acid
D. Fatty acids

E. Glycerol
F. Minerals

85. Listed below are three different biological molecules:

1. Carbohydrates
2. Triglycerides
3. Proteins

Which of the aforementioned substances causes the pH levels to decrease when it is digested?

A. 1 only
B. 2 only
C. 3 only
D. 1 and 2 only
E. 1 and 3 only
F. 2 and 3 only
G. All of the above
H. None of the above

86. Listed below are different substances found in the human body:

1. Oxygen
2. Glucose
3. Carbon dioxide
4. Water
5. Lactic acid

Which of the aforementioned substances are involved in anaerobic respiration?

A. 1 and 2 only
B. 2 and 5 only
C. 1, 2 and 3 only
D. 2, 3 and 5 only
E. 2, 4 and 5 only
F. 2, 3, 4 and 5 only
G. 1, 2, 3, and 4 only
H. All of the above

87. Which one of the below statements regarding the nervous system is incorrect?

A. It involves chemicals.
B. The effect is localised.
C. It involves the brain.
D. Nerve impulses are only involuntary.
E. It helps to maintain a constant internal environment.

88. Which row correctly identifies the production and removal of waste substances found in the human body?

	Urea		Carbon dioxide	
	Site of production	The organ that removes it	Site of production	The organ that removes it
A	Alimentary Canal	Kidney	Lungs	All Cells
B	Liver	Rectum	Kidney	Lungs
C	Liver	Kidneys	All Cells	Lungs
D	Kidney	Liver	Heart	Lungs
E	Liver	Kidney	Muscle Cells	Lungs

89. What is the correct order through which sperm cells travel through from its site of production, in order to leave the body?

A. Testis, epididymis, sperm ducts and urethra
B. Sperm duct, testis, epididymis and urethra
C. Testis, sperm duct, epididymis and urethra
D. Epididymis, testis, sperm duct and urethra
E. Testis, sperm duct, urethra and epididymis

90. Which two hormones are required to maintain the lining of the uterus during the menstrual cycle?

A. Progesterone and FSH
B. FSH and LH
C. Oestrogen and LH
D. Oestrogen and Progesterone
E. FSH and Oestrogen
F. Progesterone and LH

91. Which one amongst the following hormones is not released from the pituitary gland?

A. Growth hormones
B. FSH
C. LH
D. Oxytocin
E. ADH
F. Adrenaline

92. Which one amongst the following is a possible adverse effect of treating diabetes?

A. Hyperglycaemia
B. Hypoglycaemia
C. Low blood pressure
D. High blood pressure
E. Ketoacidosis
F. Dehydration
G. Macrovascular disease

93. The graph below shows the levels of different hormones during the menstrual cycle.

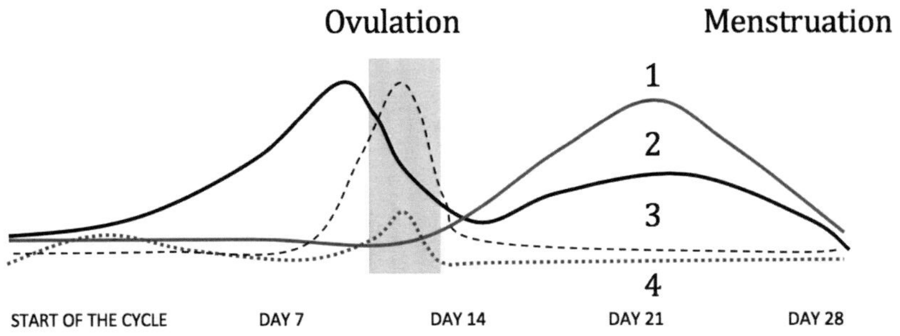

Identify the hormones represented by the four curves.

	1	2	3	4
A	Progesterone	Oestrogen	FSH	LH
B	Oestrogen	FSH	LH	Progesterone
C	LH	FSH	Progesterone	Oestrogen
D	FSH	Progesterone	Oestrogen	LH
E	Progesterone	Oestrogen	LH	FSH
F	Oestrogen	Progesterone	LH	FSH

94. During a traumatic injury, platelets cause the soluble fibrinogen to be converted to an insoluble fibre. This forms a mesh around the site of injury.
What is this fibre called?

A. Factor 8
B. Fibrin
C. Thrombin
D. Collagen
E. Elastin
F. Erythrocytes

95. Which one of the following statements is incorrect?

A. If type A agglutinins are present in a patient's blood, their blood group could be A.
B. Patients with blood group O have no agglutinins.
C. People with type B agglutinins would normally not produce anti-B antibodies.
D. O positive blood type is a universal donor.
E. Individuals with type AB blood do not have anti-A or anti-B antibodies.

96. Which one of the following statements is incorrect?

A. Thyroxine is a hormone that is secreted by the thyroid gland.
B. Thyroxine has a role in energy metabolism.
C. The hypothalamus and pituitary gland are involved in controlling and monitoring the thyroxine levels.
D. Low levels of thyroxine in the blood stream stimulate the hypothalamus to secrete Thyroid Stimulating Hormone (TSH).
E. Overactivity of the thyroid gland can cause hyperthyroidism.

Biology

Biology (B10) ECOSYSTEMS Specification

Topic	Objective	☺	😐	☹
B10.1	**Levels of organisation in an ecosystem:** - Describe the organisation of levels within an ecosystem from individuals through to populations, and from communities through to ecosystems. - Understand that communities are affected by abiotic and biotic factors. - Appreciate the factors that can cause a population to change in size. - Describe the importance of interdependence in ecosystems (relating to predation, mutualism and parasitism) and of competition in a community. - Know and understand that photosynthetic organisms are the primary producers of food in an ecosystem, and therefore biomass.			
B10.2	**Material cycling:** - Explain the importance of the carbon cycle to include the following processes: o photosynthesis o respiration o combustion o decomposition - Understand the importance of the water cycle to living organisms.			

Biology (B10) ECOSYSTEMS Questions

97. Which sequence correctly identifies the organisation of levels in ecology?

A. Individual species → Community → Population → Ecosystem → Biome → Biosphere
B. Individual species → Ecosystem →Population →Community →Biome →Biosphere
C. Individual species →Population →Community →Biome →Ecosystem →Biosphere
D. Individual species →Population →Community →Ecosystem →Biome → Biosphere

98. The following statements relate to material cycling.

1. The five stages of the water cycle are evaporation, transpiration, condensation, precipitation and collection.
2. Photosynthesis adds carbon to the atmosphere, while respiration, decomposition and combustion removes carbon from the atmosphere.

3. The starting point of the carbon cycle is photosynthesis, and the end point is respiration.
4. Water can only evaporate from oceans or lakes.

Which of the following statement(s) is/are correct?

A. 1 only
B. 2 only
C. 3 only
D. 4 only
E. 1, 2 and 3 only
F. 1, 2 and 4 only
G. None of the above

---

99. The diagram below shows part of the nitrogen cycle:

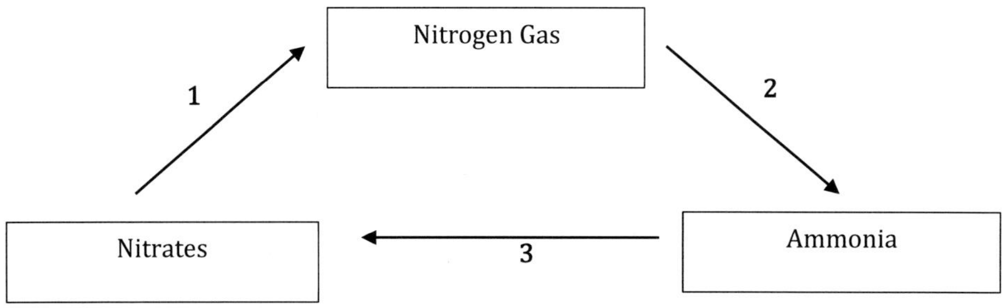

Which row correctly identifies the processes that occur at Labels 1, 2 and 3?

	1	2	3
A	Denitrification	Nitrogen fixation	Nitrification
B	Nitrification	Denitrification	Nitrogen fixation
C	Nitrogen fixation	Nitrification	Denitrification
D	Denitrification	Nitrification	Nitrogen fixation
E	Nitrogen fixation	Denitrification	Nitrification
F	Nitrification	Nitrogen fixation	Denitrification

---

100. Which one of the following statements best describes heterotrophs?

A. Feeders that must have a supply of complex organic molecules in their food, in order to make their own organic matter.
B. Self-feeders which use simple inorganic molecules from the environment to build complex organic molecules.
C. Feeders which obtain their energy from the light.
D. Feeders which obtain their energy from the oxidation of inorganic chemical compounds.

Biology(B1)	CELLS	Answers

1. A

Explanation:
Phosphate heads are polar and hydrophilic, while fatty acid tails are non-polar and hydrophilic. **Statement 'A' is incorrect** because it asserts that the phosphate heads are hydrophobic and fatty acid tails are hydrophilic. **Statement 'B' is correct** because the phospholipid bilayer is semi-permeable to allow the passage of small molecules, such as carbon dioxide and water. The cell membrane consists of lipids, proteins (such as glycoproteins and channel proteins), and carbohydrates - **Statement 'C' is correct**. Cholesterol binds fatty acid tails, which controls the fluidity of the cell membrane (**Statement 'D' is correct**).

2. D

Explanation:
Both fungal cells and bacterial cells possess **cell walls** and **cytoplasm**. However, since fungal cells are eukaryotic, they possess **80s ribosomes** while prokaryotic bacterial cells only have **70s ribosomes**. Neither fungal nor bacterial cells **possess chloroplasts**. Therefore, **Statements 1 and 3 are correct**.

3. B

Explanation:
Prokaryotic cells do not possess membrane-bound organelles, such as mitochondria. **Cell membranes** are present in all cells to control the entry and exit of materials, such as water, carbon dioxide and oxygen. A **vacuole** is only present in plant cells.

4. B

Explanation:
Since the nucleus is the largest organelle, it would have the largest diameter. As a result, **Options 'C' and 'D' can be eliminated**. Ribosomes are the smallest organelles in the table shown, which would **eliminate Option 'A'**. Therefore, **Option 'B' is the correct answer**.

5. A

Explanation:
Specialised cells that are grouped together with the same function are described as tissues. **Cardiac muscle is a sub-category of muscle**. Other muscle types include skeletal, striated and smooth. The major types of connective tissue are connective tissue proper, supportive tissue and fluid tissue. Nervous tissue is grouped into two main categories: neurons and neuroglia.
Neurons transmit electrical impulses, while neuroglia do not. Therefore, **Option 'A' is the correct answer**.

6. E

Explanation:
Statements 3 and 4 are correct. **Statement 1** is incorrect because mitochondria are not found in prokaryotes; these cells lack membrane-bound organelles. In addition, **Statement 2** is incorrect since mitochondria are visible with light microscopes.

7. A

Explanation:

Label 1 is the plasma containing water, plasma proteins and gases. **Label 2** represents white blood cells and platelets. **Label 3** illustrates the position of the red blood cells.

8. A

Explanation:

Carbohydrates are stored as glycogen in animals, and as **starch** in plants. **Polypeptides** are formed from amino acids, whereas **polynucleotides** consist of many nucleotides. **Lipids** are hydrolysed into glycerol and fatty acids.

9. E

Explanation:

Organelle 1 is the Mitochondria - this is where the Krebs cycle and Oxidative Phosphorylation (a stages of aerobic respiration) occurs. **Organelle 2** is the Golgi Apparatus and **Organelle 3** is the Centrosome. This consists of two centrioles that is involved in mitosis, in order to pull the chromatids apart. **Organelle 4** is the Rough Endoplasmic Reticulum, which possesses ribosomes on its outer surface. The membrane is continuous with the outer nuclear membrane.

10. B

Explanation:

The disaccharide found in milk is **lactose**. This is hydrolysed in the body to produce **glucose and galactose**.

11. A

Explanation:

Hydrogen ions determine the pH since pH is defined as the concentration of H+ ions that are present in a solution. **Sodium ions** are required to co-transport glucose and amino acids against their concentration gradient. **Iron ions** are part of the prosthetic group in haemoglobin; it binds to oxygen to transport it around the body. Finally, **phosphate ions** are components of RNA and DNA since each nucleotide has a phosphate group.

Biology (B2) | MOVEMENT ACROSS MEMBRANES | Answers

12. E

Explanation:

Statement 1 is incorrect since active transport only uses carrier proteins and not channel proteins. **Statement 2 is correct** as no energy from ATP is required for diffusion and osmosis. **Statement 3 is also correct** because proteins are required to assist in active transport and facilitated diffusion. **Statement 4 is incorrect** since particles will still be exchanged across the membrane, even when there is no net change. Therefore, **Option 'E' is the correct answer**.

13. D

Explanation:

Simple diffusion occurs through the phospholipid bilayer, and, therefore, it **does not rely on carrier or channel proteins**. Consequently, the number of carrier proteins would not affect the rate of simple diffusion. A **steeper concentration gradient** increases the rate of simple diffusion. An **increase in temperature** causes particles to have more energy and therefore a faster rate of diffusion. With regards to **solubility of molecules**, more lipid-soluble substances pass through the phospholipid bilayer at a faster rate.

14. C

Explanation:
Turgidity and plasmolysis are terms used to describe plant cells and not red blood cells - **Options 'A' and 'B' can be eliminated**. In a hypertonic solution, water moves out of the cell by osmosis, causing it to shrivel. In a hypotonic solution, water moves down a concentration gradient into the cell, causing it to burst (lysis). Therefore, **Option 'C' is the correct answer.**

15. D

Explanation:
The **sodium-potassium pump** requires energy from ATP, and, therefore, is a form of active transport. When **glucose concentrations are low in the small intestine**, active transport is used to move glucose against its concentration gradient. Since **mineral ions** are in higher concentrations inside root hair cells, active transport is required for the transport of these ions into the plant. **Carbon dioxide and oxygen** are gases that move along their relative concentration gradients; therefore, they rely on diffusion.

16. C

Explanation:
Water moves by **osmosis** across cell membranes. Osmosis is the movement of water particles from an area of high concentration to an area of low concentration across a partially permeable membrane. Since the cell contains a higher concentration of sugar compared to the surrounding solution, glucose has to move against the concentration gradient, in order to enter the cell. This requires energy; therefore, **active transport** occurs.

Biology (B3)	CELL DIVISION AND SEX DETERMINATION	Answers

17. C

Explanation:
Chromosomes become visible in prophase. All the other processes occur during interphase. During the **G1 phase of interphase**, the cell synthesises a variety of proteins that are needed for DNA replication. During the **S phase of interphase**, which follows the G1 phase, all of the chromosomes are replicated. Following replication, each chromosome now consists of two sister chromatids. The number and mass of organelles also double, in order for prophase to occur.

18. G

Explanation:
Centrioles are located in the cytoplasm, near the nuclear envelope. The number of chromosomes remain the same after mitosis and are halved after meiosis. DNA replication occurs during interphase, not during prophase. Therefore, **none of the statements are true**.

19. B

Explanation:

DNA replication is required for both meiosis and mitosis. Therefore, **Options 'A', 'D' and 'F' can be eliminated**. Since **Statement 2 is true**, the answer could be **either 'B' or 'E'**. However, chromosomes are formed from the condensing of chromatin and not from spindle fibres, and, therefore, **Option 'E' can be eliminated**. Homologous chromosomes are a pair of chromosomes, whereas two sister chromatids make up one chromosome. As a result, **Option 'C' can be eliminated**. Hence, **Option 'B' is the correct answer.**

20. A

Explanation:

Option 'A' is incorrect since some plants possess hermaphroditical characteristics (possesses both male pollen-producing stamens and female ovule-producing carpels). **Option 'B' is correct** because most fungi and some plants (such as daffodils or strawberries) are able to reproduce both sexually and asexually. Asexual reproduction has some advantages, including an increase in efficiency and a decrease in time to produce offspring – **Option 'C' is correct**. Binary fission, which only requires one parent, occurs in some single-celled eukaryotic organisms; therefore, **Option 'D' is correct**.

21. C

Explanation:

All eukaryotic cells require mitosis for cell growth and repair. Since asexual reproduction produces clones, it requires mitosis for genetically identical cells. As a result of the production of these identical cells, mitosis is used for tissue repair. The phases of mitosis are continuous, rather than discrete. Therefore, **Option 'C' is the correct answer**.

22. D

Explanation:

Options 'A', 'B' and 'C' describe the characteristics of malignant tumours. Since benign tumours do not metastasize, they remain well-differentiated. **The correct answer is therefore Option 'D'**. The other general characteristics of benign growths include: remains at the site of origin; grows slowly compared to malignant tumours; and, usually remains encapsulated within an outer tissue such as a connective tissue or epithelium. Features of malignant tumours, in addition to the facts presented in **Options 'A', 'B' and 'C'**, include: increased mitoses; abnormal mitosis (tripolar, tetrapolar, sunburst or bizarre); increased size of nucleus; pleomorphism (variation in size of nucleus and cell size); anaplasia - poor differentiation or lack of differentiation; coarse chromatin / hyperchromatism (increased nuclear DNA content with dark staining on hematoxylin and eosin staining); and, prominent nucleoli or multiple nucleoli.

23. E

Explanation:

Statement 1 is incorrect as tumours occur due to mitosis (uncontrolled cell division of genetically identical cells), rather than meiosis. Since all the other statements could all result in an uncontrolled cell division, the **correct answer is Option 'E'**.

24. F

Explanation:

Interphase is the stage that occurs prior to meiosis; therefore, **Statement 1 is incorrect**. Meiosis occurs in only reproductive cells; therefore, **Statement 2 is incorrect**. Sexual reproduction includes the fusion of gametes, and, therefore, it is not interchangeable with meiosis (Statement 3 is incorrect). Meiosis produces four genetically different cells. As a result, Statement 4 is incorrect. Therefore, **none of the statements are correct**.

25. C

Explanation:
Option 'C' is correct because the chromosome number after meiosis is halved. This creates genetic variation in offspring due to crossing over and independent segregation. Option 'A' is incorrect since the chromosome number after meiosis is halved. Meiosis only occurs in the gametes in order to produce a full set of chromosomes at fertilisation; therefore, Option 'B' is incorrect. Only one cycle of DNA replication occurs. As a result, Option 'D' is incorrect.

26. B

Explanation:
Since sexual reproduction requires both male and female gametes, it is not energy efficient. Option 'B' is correct. Options 'A' and 'C' are incorrect; both of these are advantages of sexual reproduction because it produces variation within a population. Due to sexual reproduction producing genetically different cells, it is better adapted to changing environments because there is an increase of genetic diversity. As a result, Option 'D' is incorrect.

27. D

Explanation:
An egg contains half as much genetic information as a normal body cell. Therefore, Statement 1 is incorrect. A human egg contains 23 chromosomes (rather than 23 pairs of chromosomes); Statement 3 is incorrect. Once the egg has been fertilised by the sperm to form a zygote, it undergoes mitosis – Statement 2 is correct. The egg contains the same number of chromosomes as a sperm cell because they are both haploid. Consequently, Statement 4 is correct.

Biology (B4) | INHERITANCE | Answers

28. E

Explanation:
Phenotypes can also be influenced by environmental factors, and, therefore, Statement 1 is incorrect. Some mutations may not influence the genotype due to the degenerate nature of the genetic code. Likewise, it may be advantageous and beneficial. As a result, Statement 2 is incorrect. The frequency of an allele in the population is not characterised by whether it is dominant or recessive; hence, Statement 3 is also incorrect. Statement 4 is correct. Therefore, Option 'E' is the correct answer.

29. B

Explanation:

Assume 'h' is the Huntington disease allele and draw a Punnett diagram for the two scenarios:

		Mother	
Father		**H**	**H**
	H	HH Huntington	HH Huntington
	h	Hh Huntington	Hh Huntington

From the Punnett diagram above, there is a **100% chance of the child having Huntington's disease**.

		Mother	
Father		**H**	**h**
	h	Hh Huntington	hh Not Huntington
	h	Hh Huntington	hh Not Huntington

From the Punnett diagram above, there is a **50% chance of the child having Huntington's disease**.

The difference in probability is therefore: 100%-50% = **50%**

30. D

Explanation:

Since Tay-Sachs is a **recessive condition**, one can expect that all affected individuals would possess **two recessive alleles (tt)**. Number '10' is an **affected male**, therefore, **Options 'A' and 'C' can be eliminated**. Since '2' is an unaffected female, she cannot possess two recessive alleles, and, therefore, **Option 'B' can be eliminated**.

31. C

Explanation:

Assume 'c' is the Cystic Fibrosis allele and draw a Punnett diagram for the given scenario:

Both parents are **heterozygous** - therefore, they must both be **'Cc'**.

		Mother	
Father		**C**	**c**
	C	CC Not Cystic Fibrosis	Cc Carrier
	c	Cc Carrier	cc Cystic Fibrosis

Biology

Therefore, the probability that the child does not have Cystic Fibrosis is and is not a carrier (CC):

$\frac{1}{4} = 25\%$

The probability that the child is a carrier (Cc):

$\frac{1}{2} = 50\%$

The probability that the child has Cystic Fibrosis (cc):

$\frac{1}{4} = 25\%$

The child will only develop cystic fibrosis if they **receive 2 alleles (cc)** since it is a recessive condition.

---

32. D

Explanation:

Assume 's' is the recessive allele for the Sickle Cell Anaemia allele and 'S' is the dominant allele.

Since Individual 'A' has the recessive condition sickle cell anaemia, their alleles are **'ss'**. Individual 'B' is homozygous dominant and, therefore, their alleles are **'SS'**. All of the children (Individuals 'C', 'D' and 'E') of Individuals 'A' and 'B' would therefore have the alleles **'Ss'**.

Draw a Punnett diagram for the given scenario:

If Individual 'F' were to be homozygous dominant:

		Individual F	
Individual E		**S**	**S**
	S	SS Not Sickle Cell Anaemia	SS Carrier
	s	Ss Carrier	Ss Carrier

For **Individual 'G'** to have sickle cell anaemia, she must have the allele 'ss'. From the above Punnett diagram, **the probability of this occurring is 0%.**

Draw a Punnett diagram for the given scenario:

If Individual 'F' were to be heterozygous:

		Individual F	
Individual E		**S**	**s**
	S	SS Not Sickle Cell Anaemia	SS Carrier
	s	Ss Carrier	ss Sickle Cell Anaemia

Individual 'G' to have sickle cell anaemia, she must have the allele 'ss'. From the above Punnett diagram, **the probability of this occurring is 25%.**

Therefore, the correct answer is **Option 'D'**.

33. A

Explanation:
Since no one in this child's family shows any signs of this disorder, none of his male relatives can carry the gene. Red-green colour blindness is an **X-linked condition**; therefore, the presence of the gene in men will cause it to be expressed. As a result, **neither of his grandfathers** can possess the gene. If the gene had been inherited from his paternal grandmother, his father would also have the condition. Since his parents do not have red-green colour blindness, the gene is from the **child's maternal grandmother**. She must have been a carrier of the gene and passed it onto the child's mother. They both did not have red-green colour blindness because it is a recessive condition.

Biology (B5)	DNA	Answers

34. C

Explanation:
Number '1' represents a phosphate group as opposed to a phosphorus group. Therefore, **Options 'A' and 'D' can be eliminated**. Since hydrogen bonds are present between two nucleotides on the two antiparallel strands, **Option 'C' is the correct answer**.

35. B

Explanation:
Three bases are required to code for one amino acid. This can be referred to as a DNA triplet, mRNA codon or a t-RNA anti-codon. **Option 'B'** is the only one that states a mRNA codon, and, therefore, it is the correct answer.

36. C

Explanation:
Transcription is the first part of protein synthesis, and, therefore, RNA nucleotides are required to produce mRNA. In prokaryotes, **transcription results directly in the production of mRNA**. Therefore, the sequence that correctly describes the process is **Option 'C'**.

37. B

Explanation:
Ribosomes are only present on the surface of rough Endoplasmic Reticulum (ER), therefore, **Options 'A' and 'D' can be eliminated**. Three bases present on tRNA are referred to as a complementary anti-codon, rather than a codon (used to describe mRNA). **Option 'C' can be eliminated**. Therefore, **Option 'B' is the correct answer.**

38. D

Explanation:
Mature red blood cells do not have a nucleus and, therefore, they do not have any chromosomes. In contrast, white blood cells have 23 pairs of chromosomes – **Statement 1** is incorrect. DNA in mitochondria is similar to prokaryotic DNA; both do not have chromosomes. As a result, **Statement 2** is wrong. A chromosome consists of approximately 70% proteins. Consequently, **Statement 3** is incorrect. **Statement 4** is correct - prokaryotic DNA is not associated with proteins.

39. A

Explanation:

This diagram illustrates an **RNA nucleotide**. The group labelled X is a **pentose sugar**. The OH group at Position 2 indicates that the **pentose sugar is a ribose sugar**, rather than deoxyribose.

40. B

Explanation:

Adenine and **Guanine** are purines. As a result, **Thymine**, **Cytosine** and **Uracil** are pyrimidines.

41. D

Explanation:

A deletion mutation in the mRNA sequence will cause a **frameshift mutation**, which moves every base after the mutation one position to the left. This will change the codons in the mRNA sequence, resulting in the coding of different amino acids.

Split the original mRNA into three bases to identify the codons:

AUG GGC CCG GUA AGG GCC CAG AUC

The codon for the third amino acid is CCG. Considering the given table of amino acids given, this codon codes for the amino acid **'Pro'**.

After the fifth base has been removed, the new mRNA sequence is:

AUG GCC CGG UAA GGG CCC AGA UC

The codon for the third amino acid is **CGG** (a frameshift mutation has occurred). Considering the given table of amino acids given, this codon codes for the amino acid **'Arg'**.

Therefore, the change that has occurred on the third amino acid is from **'Pro' to 'Arg'**.

Biology (B6) | GENE TECHNOLOGIES | Answers

42. A

Explanation:

In order for genetic engineering to take place, the desired gene must be isolated first using restriction enzymes. These restriction enzymes recognize and cut a specific DNA nucleotide sequence. **Options 'B' and 'D' can be eliminated**. Since **Option 'C'** mentions gene isolation after gene insertion, it is also incorrect. Consequently, **Option 'A' is the correct answer**.

43. C

Explanation:

Genetic engineering relies on the modification of the genome in order to produce desirable results. **Option 'C'** is an example of selective breeding, because humans are selecting the desired characteristics to breed for better quality offspring, rather than altering the genetic material of the cows. In **Options 'A', 'B' and 'D'**, genes are inserted into the organism to instantly modify the phenotype.

44. D

Explanation:

Stem cells can be harvested from many sites, including the placenta, bone marrow and circulating blood; therefore, **Option 'A' is eliminated**. Embryonic stem cells are pluripotent (able to differentiate into all cell types); therefore, **Option 'B' is eliminated**. As an animal matures, cells lose the ability to differentiate into other cell types, initially becoming multipotent (most adult stem cells) and later unipotent (adult skin cells); therefore, **Option 'C' is eliminated**. As a result, **Option 'D' is correct**.

45. D

Explanation:

Selective breeding has many advantages, such an increased quality of livestock or yield of crops. However, it has disadvantages such as a reduced genetic diversity (due to selection of desirable alleles) and inbreeding (two parents with desirable alleles may be bred despite being close relatives). **Option 'D' refers to a disadvantage regarding genetic engineering**, and, therefore, this is the correct answer.

46. D

Explanation:

Restriction Endonucleases are enzymes that recognise a particular sequence and cut DNA in a specific place. The same enzyme is used to cut the gene from the foreign DNA and the bacterial plasmid (the cloning vector) because it produces complementary sticky ends. **DNA Ligase** is used to join the two sticky ends together; it is used since DNA Ligase and the sticky ends form complementary base pairs.

Biology (B7) | VARIATION | Answers

47. B

Explanation:

From the BMAT specification, evolution is referred to as a **change in the inherited characteristics of a population over time through a process of natural selection, which may result in the formation of a new species**. A new species will only be formed if a species becomes isolated, resulting in different gene pools. If organisms are not able to breed to produce fertile offspring, they are different species.

48. C

Explanation:

Individuals within a species also show a wide range of phenotype variation due to mutations and sexual reproduction; **Options 'B' and 'D' can be eliminated**. All organisms within a species will have the same number and type of chromosomes; there are no 'favourable chromosomes' (**Option 'A' can be eliminated**). However, organisms may have alternate forms of the same gene (alleles), which may benefit an individual. Therefore, **Option 'C' is the correct answer**.

49. C

Explanation:

Variation can be influenced by both the genotype (DNA sequence in genome) and the environment (differences in the surroundings such as climate, diet and exercise); **Option 'C' is the correct answer.**

50. B

Explanation:
Organisms that are **closely related** and share a **common ancestor** may **not necessarily look similar**. This is due to **environmental variation** because they may have evolved in different environments to develop different features. Therefore, **Option 'B' is the correct answer**.

Biology (B8) ENZYMES Answers

51. E

Explanation:
Statement 1 is correct since both temperature and pH will alter hydrogen bonds present in the secondary and tertiary structure of an enzyme. **Statement 2 is incorrect** because amylase is produced in the salivary glands of the mouth, the pancreas and the small intestine. **Statement 3 is also correct** since salivary amylase has an optimal pH of 6.8, pancreatic amylase has an optimum pH of 6.7-7.0 and amylase in the small intestine has an optimum pH of 7.0. **Statement 4 is incorrect** as amylase hydrolyses starch to maltose (amylase is a catabolic enzyme, meaning it breaks down substances into smaller constituents).

Biology

52. G

Explanation:
Statement 1 is incorrect as protease is also found in bacteria, fungi, viruses and plants. **Statement 2 is incorrect** as protease isn't produced in the gallbladder. Since the pancreas is alkaline, trypsin has an alkaline optimum pH, so **Statement 3 is incorrect**. Protease is a catabolic enzyme, resulting in proteins broken down into amino acids; **Statement 4 is incorrect**.

53. D

Explanation:
Salivary glands have an optimum alkaline pH; therefore, **Statement 1 is incorrect**. Since lipase is produced in the pancreas and small intestine, **Statement 2 is correct**. **Statement 3 is also correct** as fat is hydrolysed into fatty acids and glycerol using lipase enzymes. Lipase enzymes are produced in the small intestine, pancreas and salivary glands, which each have their own optimal pH, therefore, **Statement 4 is incorrect**.

54. D

Explanation:
The **size of the substrate would not affect enzyme activity** because the enzyme's active site is complementary to the substrate. Consequently, the enzyme would be able to catalyse the substrate reaction, regardless of the size. The **pH alters the hydrogen bonds present** in the active site of the enzyme, which could increase or decrease enzyme efficiency. **An increase in temperature would increase enzyme activity** due to an increase in kinetic energy of the enzymes and substrates, resulting in an increase of enzyme-substrate complexes. However, after the optimum temperature is reached, hydrogen bonds present in the active site may break, leading to enzyme deformation and a sudden decrease in enzyme activity. **Increasing substrate concentration increases enzyme activity** due to an increase in the probability of enzyme-substrate complexes forming.

55. D

Explanation:

Pepsin is found in acidic conditions in the stomach; therefore, its optimum pH will be very low (at approximately pH 2). As a result, **Curve 1** is the pH curve for pepsin. Salivary amylase is found in the mouth; the optimum pH is approximately neutral at a pH of 7 – this is demonstrated in **Curve 2**. Trypsin is produced in the pancreas and released into the small intestine where the pH is alkaline. Consequently, its optimum pH would be greater than pH 7; this is illustrated in **Curve 3**.

Biology (B9)	ANIMAL PHYSIOLOGY	Answers

56. D

Explanation:

Option 'A' is incorrect since plant respiration occurs all the time (photosynthesis only occurs in the presence of sunlight). **Option 'B' is incorrect** because respiration produces energy; therefore, it is an exothermic reaction. **Option 'C' is also incorrect** as the products of respiration remain the same for all organisms (carbon dioxide and ethanol/lactic acid/water). **Option 'D' is correct**; all plants and animals undergo cellular respiration to provide cells with the energy to perform all the necessary functions to maintain life.

57. A

Explanation:

Aerobic respiration is an exothermic reaction (energy must be produced). Therefore, **Options 'C' and 'D' can be eliminated**. The question asks for anaerobic respiration in humans – the products are carbon dioxide and lactic acid (ethanol is produced in yeast – **Option 'B' can be eliminated**). As a result, **Option 'A' is the correct answer**.

58. B

Explanation:

In order for inspiration to occur, an **expansion in the thoracic cavity** must occur to **decrease the internal pressure**. This negative pressure will cause air to move down its concentration gradient from the surroundings into the lungs, causing inspiration. For an expansion in the thoracic cavity, the **diaphragm contracts** (flatten to increase volume), the **ribs move outwards** and the **external intercostal muscles contract** (to decrease pressure in the thoracic cavity). The answer which correctly describes the processes that occur prior to inspiration is **Option 'B'**.

59. G

Explanation:

Gas exchange in the alveoli relies on diffusion. The greater the difference in concentration, the more rapid the diffusion - **Statement 1 is correct**. The closer the distribution of the material gets to equilibrium, the slower will be the rate of diffusion. When there is more volume and less surface area, diffusion takes longer and is less effective. Therefore, **Statement 2 is correct**. The more soluble a gas is, the faster it will diffuse (**Statement 3 is correct**). The thicker the air-blood barrier, the slower the rate of gas exchange due to an increased diffusion pathway. **Statement 4 is correct**. As a result, all of the aforementioned factors influence gas exchange in the alveoli. **Option 'G' is the correct answer**.

60. C

Explanation:

Arteries have thick muscular walls to withstand high pressure, and, therefore, have a narrow lumen. **Statement 1 is incorrect**. Arteries do not usually have valves. However, two arteries originating from the left and right ventricles of the heart (aortic and pulmonary) have valves in order to prevent the backflow of blood into the ventricles. **Statement 2 is incorrect**. Capillaries are one cell thick in order to maximise efficient transport and exchange of substances including glucose, amino acids, oxygen, urea and carbon dioxide. **Statement 3 is correct**. **Statement 4 is the converse** (arteries typically transport blood under high pressure, while veins transport blood under low pressure).

61. D

Explanation:

The left ventricle has a thicker muscular wall compared to the right ventricle, due to the high forces required to pump blood around the whole body; therefore, **Statement 1 is incorrect**. Blood is produced in the bone marrow, rather than the heart; **Statement 2 is also incorrect**. White blood cells produce antibodies, whereas platelets aid in clotting. Therefore, **Statement 3 is incorrect**. Blood is defined as a tissue since it is a collection of similar, specialised cells that serve particular functions. As a result, **Statement 4 is correct**.

62. C

Explanation:

Deglutition is the action or process of swallowing, which occurs in the pharynx; as a result, this process occurs first in the digestive system. **Peristalsis** occurs next in the oesophagus, where a series of muscular contractions push food down into the stomach. In the stomach, **digestion** occurs in order to break down food molecules into smaller, soluble constituents using enzymes such as pepsin and trypsin. Useful digested food molecules are **absorbed** in the small intestine and undigested materials are **egested** in the faeces.

63. D

Explanation:

Digestion of certain molecules, such as carbohydrates, begin in the mouth, using enzymes present in saliva (e.g., salivary amylase); **Option 'A' is incorrect**. The digestive system is regulated by involuntary smooth muscle controlled by the autonomic nervous system; therefore, **Option 'B' is incorrect**. The large intestine is named as such due to its larger diameter, not its larger length, resulting in **Option 'C' being incorrect** and **Option 'D' being correct**. The stomach receives its blood supply from the aorta; as a result, **Option 'E' is incorrect.**

64. B

Explanation:

The filtrate enters a nephron through the **Bowman's capsule**, using ultrafiltration. Selective reabsorption of glucose occurs in the **Proximal Convoluted Tubule**, with water reabsorbed in the **descending limb of the Loop of Henle**. Sodium and chloride ions are reabsorbed in the **ascending limb of the Loop of Henle**, magnesium ions in the **Distal Convoluted Tubule** and ADH enables sufficient water to be conserved in the **collecting duct** (homeostatic control).

65. C

Explanation:

Negative feedback is the body's mechanism for reversing a change so that it returns back to the optimum. **Osmoregulation, blood sugar regulation and controlling blood pressure** are all examples of negative feedback. **Blood clotting** is an example of positive feedback because it causes changes that result in an even greater deviation from the norm.

66. C

Explanation:

Statement 1 is incorrect because Follicle Stimulating Hormone (FSH) is produced in the pituitary gland. **Statement 2 is incorrect** since Luteinising Hormone (LH) triggers ovulation, while progesterone maintains the uterus lining for the second half of the menstrual cycle. **Statement 3 is correct** - oestrogen also inhibits FSH. **Statement 4 is incorrect** as FSH stimulates the ovaries to release oestrogen.

67. F

Explanation:

Statements 1, 2 and 3 are correct. **Statement 4** is incorrect because rods cannot sense colour; they are sensitive to light intensity, whereas cones are sensitive to colour.

68. C

Explanation:

A **stimulus** is detected by a **receptor**. This sends an impulse along the **sensory neurone**, which is transmitted to the **relay neurone** in the spinal cord (because reflex arcs do not go through the brain). The impulse then travels down the **motor neurone** to the **effector**; the appropriate response is produced.

69. E

Explanation:

The aorta carries **oxygenated blood** away from the left ventricle of the heart and the vena cava returns **deoxygenated blood** from the body to the right atrium. The pulmonary artery carries **deoxygenated blood** from the right ventricle to the lungs and the pulmonary vein returns **oxygenated blood** to the left atrium of the heart.

70. A

Explanation:

Bile is alkaline (the usual pH range of the common duct bile is between 7.50 to 8.05) in order to neutralise the stomach acid; therefore, **Option 'A'** is correct. It is produced in the liver and stored in the gallbladder - **Option 'B'** is incorrect. Bile helps with the digestion of fats in the small intestine. As a result, **Options 'C', 'D' and 'E'** are incorrect.

71. A

Explanation:

HIV and Flu are caused by **viruses**. Salmonella is caused by **bacteria** and malaria is caused by **protozoa** (mosquitoes are the vector for this). An example of a disease caused by fungi is **Athlete's Foot**.

72. B

Explanation:

Type I Diabetes is caused by a lack of insulin being produced. In **Type II Diabetes**, insulin is produced by the pancreas, but the body cells do not respond to it effectively. As a result, there is an increase in blood glucose levels. **Scurvy** is caused by a lack of Vitamin C, and **anaemia** is due to a lack of iron.

73. A

Explanation:

Curve 1 is the oxygen dissociation curve for the llama because it lives at a high altitude. At high altitudes, there is a shortage of oxygen, and, therefore, there is a higher affinity for oxygen at lower partial pressures. The curve that is furthest to the left represents this. **Curve 3** represents a low affinity for oxygen. Comparing the dog and mouse, this curve must belong to the mouse since it has a larger Surface Area to Volume ratio. There is an increased heat loss in the mouse, due to the Surface Area to Volume ratio. As a result, the mouse has a higher metabolic rate than the dog. Consequently, **Curve 2** must represent the oxygen dissociation curve for a dog.

74. C

Explanation:

Cardiac pressure volume loops are a graphical representation of the cardiac cycle. Starting at **Label 2**, the ventricle has fully contracted and there is very little blood in the chamber. The pressure is also very low. The mitral valve opens at **Label 2** because the pressure in the atrium exceeds the pressure in the ventricle. The volume then starts to increase at **Label 3** because as the ventricle fills, there is little change in pressure. At **Label 3**, ventricular contraction begins; this causes the pressure to increase. As a result, the mitral valve closes. When the pressure of the ventricle exceeds the pressure of the arteries (aorta or pulmonary artery), the aortic valve will open – illustrated in **Label 4**. This causes the blood to leave the ventricle. The volume decreases because the aortic valves close when the ventricles begin to relax – this is demonstrated in **Label 1**.

75. B

Explanation:

Asbestosis causes the lungs to become stiffer; therefore, the Functional Residual Capacity (FRC) is reduced - **Statement 1** is incorrect. Emphysema causes the lungs to lose its elastic recoil properties. This means that less air can be exhaled out, which increases the FRC – **Statement 2** is correct. Fibrosis causes the lungs to become stiffer; therefore, the FRC is reduced – **Statement 3** is correct. Due to the loss of elastic recoil in emphysema, exhaling becomes more difficult – **Statement 4** is correct. More energy is required for breathing in a stiffer and more scarred lung – **Statement 5** is incorrect.

76. G

Explanation:

The **Glomerular Filtration Rate (GFR)** increases since there is a greater pressure in the glomerulus. This is due to the efferent arterioles constricting more than the afferent arterioles. The **amount of sodium filtered** also increases because the GFR increases. The **renal blood flow** decreases due to the efferent arterioles increasing the resistance to the blood flow. The **concentration of proteins** in the capillaries after the glomerulus increases; more water is filtered out at the Bowman's capsule, because there is an increase in GFR.

77. D

Explanation:

Insulin does reduce the blood glucose level in the body, while glucagon increases it. As a result, glucagon is released when the blood glucose levels are low – **Statements 1 and 2** are correct. Insulin is released by the beta cells in the pancreas and glucagon is released by the alpha cells - **Statement 3** is correct. **Statement 4** is also correct. **Statement 5** is incorrect because ADH is released form the pituitary gland.

78. D

Explanation:

Statements 1, 2, 3 and 4 correctly describe some of the main functions of the liver. **Statement 5** is incorrect since the alpha cells in the Islets of Langerhans of the pancreas release glucagon.

79. A

Explanation:

Food passes from the **mouth**, into the **pharynx**, down the **oesophagus** and into the **stomach**. Afterwards, it goes through the small intestine (which is divided into the **duodenum, jejunum and ileum**), which is followed by the large intestine (which is made up of the **caecum, ascending colon, transverse colon, descending colon and sigmoid colon**). Finally, it reaches the **rectum** where it is stored, until it is excreted through the **anus**.

80. C

Explanation:

Label 1 shows the depolarisation of the atria (atrial contraction); this is referred to as the 'P' wave. **Label 2** displays the 'QRS' complex, which is the depolarisation of the ventricles. **Label 3** is the 'T' wave; this illustrates the repolarisation of the ventricles.

81. A

Explanation:

The volume shown by arrow 'X' is the **vital capacity**. This is the **sum of the inspiratory capacity and the expiatory reserve volume**:

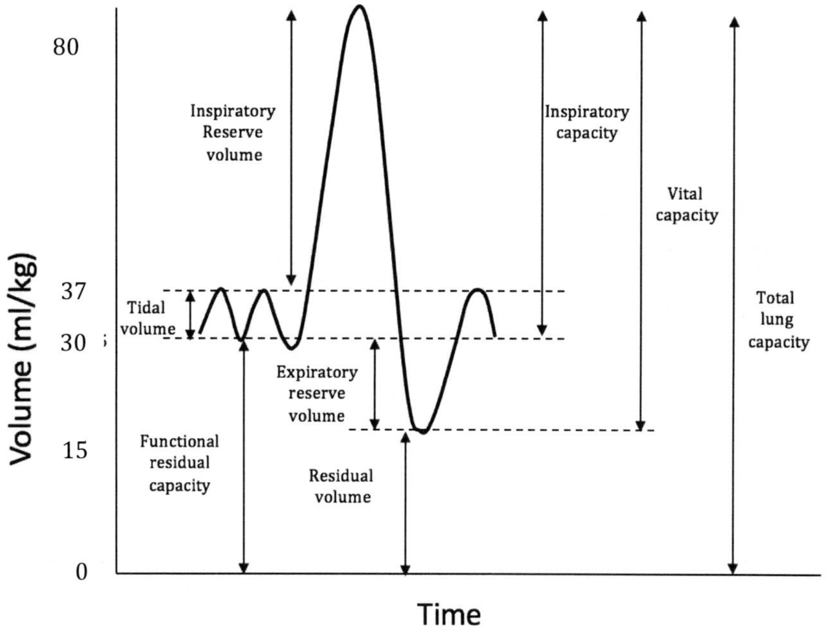

Biology

82. H

Explanation:

Chlorophyll is a photosynthetic pigment found in plants. The other structures are organs found in animals and plants.

83. B

Explanation:

A **nervous response is faster** than endocrine hormones; however, it is **not long-lasting**. The endocrine system **does involve the brain** since it is activated when changes in the body are detected by the brain. Therefore, it is also **involved in homeostasis**.

84. B

Explanation:

The **main fuel source for the brain is glucose**, which can be depleted during starvation. If this occurs, **ketones** act as the main reserve fuel for the brain.

85. F

Explanation:

The digestion of triglycerides produces glycerol and fatty acids; fatty acids **reduce the pH** of the mixture since it is acidic. The digestion of proteins produces amino acids; this also **reduces the pH**. Carbohydrates are hydrolysed into sugars - this **does not produce a pH change**.

86. B

Explanation:

Anaerobic respiration occurs when there is an insufficient supply of **oxygen**; as a result, **glucose** is broken down into **lactic acid**. **Water** and **carbon dioxide** are not produced in this reaction.

87. D

Explanation:

Nerve responses can either be **voluntary** (involving the brain) for the movement of skeletal muscles, or **involuntary** (not involving the brain) for reflexes. Therefore, **Option 'D'** is the correct answer.

88. C

Explanation:

Urea is produced in the **liver** and removed by the **kidneys**. Carbons dioxide is made by **all cells** (because they all respire) and is removed by the **lungs**.

89. A

Explanation:

Sperm cells are made in tubules within the **testis**; this is found in the scrotum. The sperm is then stored in the **epididymis**. It travels through the **sperm duct** to join the **urethra**, which opens at the tip of the penis.

90. D

Explanation:

Oestrogen is required for the lining of the uterus to thicken. When the egg is released, the ovary releases **progesterone**. This has the same effect as oestrogen; it maintains the thickness of the uterus lining. Luteinising Hormone (LH) and Follicle Stimulating Hormone (FSH) stimulate the ovary to release other hormones, including oestrogen. When the oestrogen levels increase, there is a rapid increase in the amount of LH released - this causes an egg to be released into the oviduct.

91. F

Explanation:

Adrenaline is produced in the adrenal medulla. **Growth hormones, FSH, LH, Oxytocin and ADH** are produced by the pituitary gland.

92. B

Explanation:

The treatment of diabetes involves lowering the blood glucose levels. However, the blood glucose levels may decrease too much; this may result in **hypoglycaemia**.

93. E

Explanation:

Curve 2 represents oestrogen because the concentration rises before ovulation and it falls after - this is due to oestrogen being required to build the lining of the uterus before ovulation occurs. **Curve 1** represents progesterone as this maintains the uterus lining, and, therefore, the levels only increase after the lining has built up. When the progesterone levels decrease, the uterus lining breaks down. **Curve 3** represents Luteinising Hormone (LH) because there is a rapid increase in the concentration of this hormone; this causes ovulation to occur. **Curve 4** represents Follicle Stimulating Hormone (FSH) because there is a slight increase of this hormone at the start of the menstrual cycle. This stimulates the ovaries to release oestrogen.

94. B

Explanation:

Fibrinogen is converted to a insoluble fibrous protein called **fibrin**. This forms a mesh around the site of injury. The mesh traps red blood cells to form a **clot**, which develops into a **scab** to protect the wound.

95. D

Explanation:

The universal donor blood group is O negative; it is not O positive blood. Therefore, **Option 'D'** is the correct answer. An individual with blood group O positive cannot donate blood to A negative, B negative, AB negative or O negative. This is because the Rh+ blood groups have the D antigen on the surface of their cell whereas Rh- blood groups do not have this antigen.

96. D

Explanation:

Low levels of thyroxine cause the hypothalamus to secrete **Thyrotropin Releasing Hormone (TRH)**. Therefore, **Option 'D'** is the correct answer. As a result, the pituitary gland is stimulated to release **Thyroid Stimulating Hormone (TSH)**, which causes the thyroid gland to release more thyroxine. Consequently, the thyroxine levels in the blood return to normal.

Biology (B10)	ECOSYSTEMS	Answers

97. D

Explanation:

A **species** is a group of organisms with similar characteristics that are able to interbreed to produce fertile offspring. A **population** is a number of organisms of the same species that live in a particular geographic area at the same time, with the capability of interbreeding. A **community** is an interacting group of different species in a common location. An **ecosystem** is a large community of living organisms (plants, animals and microbes) in a particular area. A **biome** is a community of plants and animals that have common characteristics for the environment they exist in but can be found over a range of continents. The **biosphere** is the zone of air, land and water where organisms exist, consisting of several layers including the atmosphere, the lithosphere and the hydrosphere.

98. A

Explanation:

Statement 1 is correct since the water cycle relies on evaporation, transpiration, condensation, precipitation and collection in order to function efficiently. **Statement 2 is incorrect** because photosynthesis removes carbon from the atmosphere (carbon dioxide and water → glucose and oxygen). The carbon cycle is a continuous process, and, therefore, there is no start or end point – **Statement 3 is incorrect**. Water can evaporate from any body of water, such as puddles, streams or soils. As a result, **Statement 4 is also incorrect**.

99. A

Explanation:

The process of converting nitrogen gas to ammonia is known as **nitrogen fixation**. Nitrification is the **conversion of ammonia to nitrates**. The conversion of nitrates to nitrogen gas is **denitrification**.

100. A

Explanation:

Option 'A' is the statement that best defines a heterotroph. **Option 'B'** describes an autotroph, **Option 'C'** describes a photoautotroph and **Option 'D'** describes a chemoautotroph.

Chemistry (C1)	ATOMIC STRUCTURE	Specification

Topic	Objective	☺	😐	☹
C1.1	- Describe the structure of the atom as a central nucleus (containing protons and neutrons) surrounded by electrons moving in shells/energy levels.			
C1.2	- Know the relative masses and charges of protons, neutrons and electrons, and recognise that most of the mass of an atom is in the nucleus.			
C1.3	- Know and be able to use the terms atomic number and mass number, together with standard notation (e.g., ${}^{12}_{6}C$), and so be able to calculate the number of protons, neutrons and electrons in any atom or ion.			
C1.4	- Use the atomic number to write the electron configurations of the first 20 elements in the Periodic Table (H to Ca) in comma-separated format (*e.g.,* 2,8,8,1 for a potassium atom).			
C1.5	- Know the definition of isotopes as atoms of an element with the same number of protons but different numbers of neutrons (so having different mass numbers). - Use data, including that from a mass spectrometer, to identify the number and abundances of different isotopes of elements.			
C1.6	- Know and use the concept of relative atomic mass, A_r, including calculating values from given data.			

Chemistry (C1)	ATOMIC STRUCTURE	Questions

1. Which row correctly identifies the relative masses of a proton, neutron and electron?

	Proton	Neutron	Electron
A	1	0	-1
B	1	1	$\frac{1}{1836}$
C	-1	$\frac{1}{1836}$	0
D	$\frac{1}{1836}$	1	1

2. **Which row correctly identifies the number of protons, neutrons and electrons in $^{36}_{17}Cl^{-}$?**

	Number of neutrons	Number of electrons	Number of protons
A	19	18	17
B	19	16	17
C	17	18	19
D	17	16	19

3. **Which of the following correctly illustrates the electron configuration in an O^{2-} ion?**
   A. 2, 6, 2
   B. 2, 6
   C. 2, 8, 2
   D. 2, 8

4. **Which of the following statements is not a property of an isotope?**
   A. Isotopes of the same element have the same chemical properties.
   B. All isotopes of the same element have the same atomic weight.
   C. Melting points and boiling points may differ between isotopes of the same element.
   D. Physical properties, such as radioactivity, may differ between isotopes of the same element.

5. **A sample of zinc is injected into a mass spectrometer. After the sample is vaporized and ionized, the ions $^{64}Zn^{2+}$, $^{66}Zn^{2+}$, $^{68}Zn^{2+}$ and $^{70}Zn^{2+}$ are detected. Which ion is deflected the most inside the spectrometer?**
   A. $^{64}Zn^{2+}$
   B. $^{66}Zn^{2+}$
   C. $^{68}Zn^{2+}$
   D. $^{70}Zn^{2+}$

Chemistry

6. **How many protons, neutrons and electrons are present in $^{8}_{16}O^{2-}$?**

	Protons	Neutrons	Electrons
A	8	8	10
B	6	8	8
C	8	8	6
D	8	10	6

7. **A potassium atom has an atomic number of 19 and mass number of 39. What is its electronic configuration?**
   A. 2, 8, 1
   B. 2, 8, 2
   C. 2, 8, 8, 1
   D. 2, 8, 6, 3
   E. 2, 8, 8, 2
   F. 2, 2, 6, 2, 6, 1

8. Using the mass spectrometer below, find the relative atomic mass of Boron.

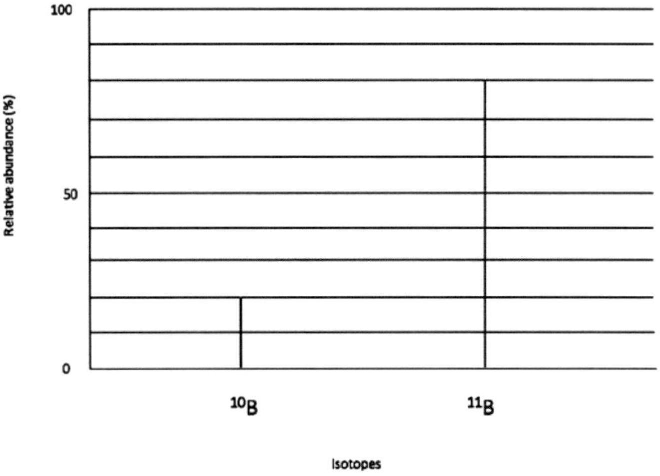

A. 10.2
B. 10.5
C. 10.7
D. 10.8
E. 10.9
F. 11.2

---

9. Cobalt has an atomic number of 27. The isotopes of cobalt are ^{56}Co, ^{57}Co, ^{59}Co and ^{60}Co. Which of the following statement(s) is/are correct?

1. The electronic configuration of the atoms is the same.
2. They all have the same chemical properties.
3. The number of neutrons in all of the isotopes are the same.
4. The number of protons is different in each isotope.

A. 1 only
B. 2 only
C. 3 only
D. 4 only
E. 1 and 2 only
F. 2 and 3 only
G. 3 and 4 only
H. 1, 2 and 3 only

Chemistry (C2) PERIODIC TABLE Specification

Topic	Objective	☺	😐	☹
C2.1	- Know that Periods are horizontal rows and Groups are vertical columns.			
C2.2	- Know that the elements are arranged in the order of increasing atomic number.			
C2.3	- Recall the position of metals and non-metals in the Periodic Table: alkali metals (Group 1), alkaline earth metals (Group 2), common non-metals in Group 16, the halogens (Group 17), the noble gases (Group 18) and the transition metals.			

C2.4	- Know and use the relationship between the position of an atom in the Periodic Table (Group and Period) and the electron configuration of the atom.			
C2.5	- Understand that elements in the same Group have similar chemical properties and reactivity increases down a metal Group, and it decreases down a non-metal Group.			

Chemistry (C2) PERIODIC TABLE Questions

10. The following statements relate to the Periodic Table.

1. Periods are vertical rows and Groups are horizontal columns.
2. Elements are arranged in order of only increasing atomic mass.
3. An element in Period 3 and Group 6 has three electrons in its outer shell.
4. Reactivity decreases going down a metal Group.

Which of the following statement(s) is/are correct?

A. 1 only
B. 2 only
C. 3 only
D. 4 only
E. 1, 2 and 3 only
F. 1, 2 and 4 only
G. None of the above

---

11. A Periodic Table Element X is in Group 2. Another Element Y is in Group 17 of the Periodic Table.
What is the likely formula of the ionic compound formed by X and Y?

A. X_2Y_3
B. X_3Y_2
C. XY_2
D. X_2Y
E. X_3Y_4
F. XY_3

Chemistry (C3)	CHEMICAL REACTIONS, FORMULAE AND EQUATIONS	Specification

Topic	Objective	☺	😐	☹
C3.1	- Understand that in a chemical reaction, new substances are formed by the rearrangement of atoms and their electrons, but no nuclei are destroyed or created.			
C3.2	- Know the chemical formulae of simple, common ionic and covalent compounds.			
C3.3	- Know and use state symbols: solid (s), liquid (l), gas (g), aqueous solution (aq).			
C3.4	- Be able to construct and balance a chemical equation, including ionic and half-equations.			
C3.5	- Understand that often chemical reactions can be reversible and do not go to completion. All reactants do not turn fully into the products but the reaction reaches a state of equilibrium in a closed system. - Know the factors that can affect the position of an equilibrium (concentration of reactants/products, temperature, overall pressure). - Predict the effect of changing these factors on the position of equilibrium.			

Chemistry (C3)	CHEMICAL REACTIONS, FORMULAE AND EQUATIONS	Specification

12. Below are different compounds.

1. CO_2
2. PH_3
3. $CuSO_4$
4. CH_3CH_2OH

Which of the above compounds are ionic?

A. CO_2, PH_3, CH_3CH_2OH
B. $CuSO_4$
C. $CuSO_4$, CH_3CH_2OH
D. PH_3, $CuSO_4$, CH_3CH_2OH

13. Which row correctly identifies the numbers required to balance the following equation?

a Al_2O_3 + b Fe → c Fe_3O_4 + d Al

	a	b	c	d
A	2	6	2	4
B	3	15	5	6
C	4	9	3	8
D	5	3	11	10

14. Which change will lead to a higher concentration of SO_2 in the reaction mixture?

$$2SO_{2(g)} + O_{2(g)} \rightleftharpoons 2SO_{2\,(g)} \quad \Delta H = -188kJmol^{-1}$$

A. Higher temperature
B. Lower pressure
C. Higher concentration of O_2
D. Use of a catalyst

15. The following statements relate to equilibrium:

1. A catalyst alters the final equilibrium position of the reaction.
2. Concentration of reactants/products, temperature and overall pressure can affect the equilibrium position.
3. When a system is at equilibrium and a change is made in the conditions, the rate of the favoured reaction increases but the rate of the unfavourable reaction decreases.
4. If a reaction is endothermic in the forward direction, and the temperature is raised, there will be an increased yield of products.

Which of the following statement(s) is/are incorrect?

A. 1 only
B. 2 only
C. 3 only
D. 4 only
E. 1 and 3 only
F. 2 and 4 only
G. 1, 2 and 4 only
H. None of the above

16. Balance the following equation:

a C_8H_{18} + **b** O_2 → **c** CO_2 + **d** H_2O

A. a= 1, b= 25, c= 16, d= 18
B. a= 2, b= 25, c= 16, d= 18
C. a= 2, b= 25, c= 16, d= 9
D. a= 2, b= 25, c= 8, d= 18
E. a= 1, b= 25, c= 8, d= 9

Chemistry

17. The forward reaction of the Haber process is exothermic. Below is the equation for this process.

$N_{2\,(g)} + 3H_{2(g)} \rightleftharpoons 2NH_{3\,(g)}$

The following changes are made to affect this reaction:

1. Add more nitrogen to the system.
2. Remove more hydrogen from the system.
3. Add ammonia to the system.
4. Increase the pressure.
5. Lower the temperature.
6. Add a catalyst.

Which of following actions would shift the position of the equilibrium to the right?

A. 1 and 4 only
B. 2 and 3 only
C. 1, 4 and 5 only
D. 2, 3 and 6 only
E. 1, 2 and 4 only
F. 2, 5 and 6 only
G. 1, 4, 5 and 6 only

18. A compound can be formed from the ions: Al^{3+}, H^{+} and CO_3^{2-}.
Which formula given below is a compound that the three different ions can form?

A. $AlHCO_3$
B. Al_2HCO_3
C. $Al(HCO_3)_2$
D. $AlH(CO_3)_2$
E. $Al_2H_2\,CO_3$

19. Consider the three addition reactions shown below.

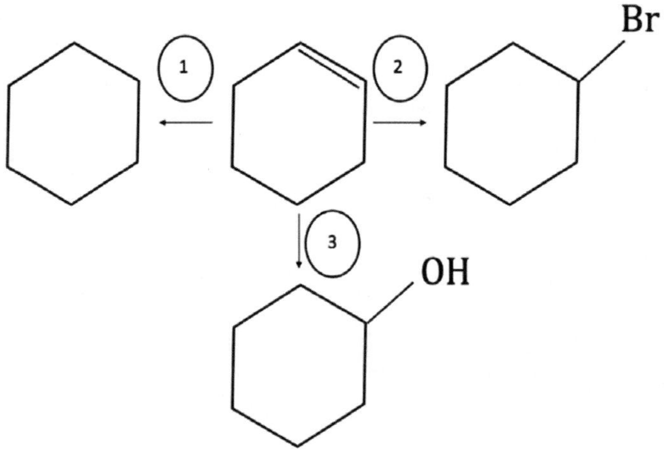

Chemistry

Which row correctly identifies the compounds that need to be added in each of the three reactions to produce the molecules shown?

	1	2	3
A	Hydrogen	Steam	Hydrogen bromide
B	Hydrogen	Bromine	Steam
C	Hydrogen	Hydrogen bromide	Steam
D	Steam	Hydrogen bromide	Methanol
E	Hydrogen	Bromine	Methanol

20. What is the oxidation number of nitrogen in N_2O_3?

A. +2
B. -2
C. +3
D. -3
E. +4
F. -4
G. +6
H. -6

Chemistry (C4) QUANTITATIVE CHEMISTRY Specification

Topic	Objective	☺	😐	☹
C4.1	- Use A_r values to calculate the relative molar mass, M_r			
C4.2	- Know that Avogadro's number gives the number of particles in one mole of a substance.			
C4.3	- Know that one mole of a substance is the A_r or M_r in grams and perform conversions of grams to moles and *vice versa* (including working in tonnes and kilograms). Know that the amount of a substance corresponds to the number of moles of a substance.			
C4.4	- Calculate the percentage composition by mass of a compound using the given A_r values.			
C4.5	- Know that the *empirical formula* is the simplest integer ratio of atoms in a compound. - Find the empirical formula of a compound from a variety of data, such as the percentage composition by mass of the elements present or reacting masses. - Find the molecular formula from the empirical formula if given the M_r value.			
C4.6	- Use balanced chemical equations to calculate the masses of			

	reactants and products, including if there is a limiting reactant present.			
C4.7	- Be able to construct balanced chemical equations from reacting masses or gas volumes data.			
C4.8	- Understand that (for an ideal gas) one mole of a gas occupies a set volume at a given temperature and pressure (for example, 24 dm^3 at room temperature and pressure [rtp]), and perform conversions of volumes to number of moles, and *vice versa*.			
C4.9	**Solutions:** - Understand that concentration can be measured in mol dm^{-3} or g dm^{-3} and be able to calculate the concentration given the number of moles (or mass) of solute and the volume of solution. - Know the term *saturated solution*, be able to calculate solubility and interpret solubility data.			
C4.10	- Use the concentrations of solutions (or find the concentrations from given data) and the reacting ratio of reactants from the balanced equation to perform titration calculations.			
C4.11	- Calculate the percentage yield of a reaction using the balanced chemical equation and the equation: percentage yield $= \frac{\text{actual yield (g)}}{\text{predicted yield (g)}} \times 100$			

Chemistry

Chemistry (C4) QUANTITATIVE CHEMISTRY Questions

21. What is the empirical formula for a compound that is 49% Carbon, 8% Hydrogen and 43% Oxygen? Assume Carbon has a mass number of 12, Hydrogen has a mass number of 1 and Oxygen has a mass number of 16.

A. CH_3O
B. CH_2O_4
C. $C_3H_5O_2$
D. $C_3H_6O_2$

22. The following reaction is performed with 2.00 g of MgCl2, which is the limiting reagent. A scientist isolates 1.80 g of the desired product, AgCl. Assume the mass number of Magnesium is 24, the mass number of Chlorine is 35 and the mass number of Ag is 110.

$$MgCl_{2\,(aq)} + AgNO_{3\,(aq)} \rightarrow AgCl_{\,(s)} + Ba(NO_3)_{2\,(aq)}$$

What is the percentage yield of the reaction?

A. 29.2%
B. 37.8%
C. 43.5%
D. 58.3%

A Lakshmi, T R Enoch, S Z Y Ooi. Doctors Academy Publications, Cardiff, UK, 2020.

23. What is the mass of potassium sulfate that can be produced from 240 g of potassium hydroxide? Assume that the amount of sulfuric acid is unlimited. The mass number of Potassium is 40, the mass number of Oxygen is 16, the mass number of Hydrogen is 1 and the mass number of Sulfur is 32.
    A. 360 g
    B. 371 g
    C. 739 g
    D. 645 g

24. How much more volume, in cm^3, does 150 g of ethane gas take up compared to 440 g of propane, at room temperature and pressure?
    A. 240000 cm^3
    B. 0.24 cm^3
    C. 240 cm^3
    D. 120 cm^3
    E. 340 cm^3
    F. 3.4 cm^3
    G. 120000 cm^3
    H. 0.12 cm^3

25. What is the number of hydrogen atoms in 0.5 moles of C_3H_7OH?
    A. 3.0110×10^{23}
    B. 2.4088×10^{24}
    C. 2.1077×10^{24}
    D. 3.7638×10^{22}
    E. 4.3014×10^{22}

26. A salt with the formula $Na_2CO_3 \bullet xH_2O$ has a molar mass of 196 g mol^{-1}.
    What is the value of x?
    (A_r values: Na = 23; C = 12; O =16; H = 1)
    A. 2
    B. 3
    C. 5
    D. 6
    E. 11
    F. 12

27. Exactly 12.5 cm^3 of sulphuric acid with a concentration of 0.15 $moldm^{-3}$ is neutralised by 20.0 cm^3 of sodium hydroxide.
    What is the concentration of the sodium hydroxide used?
    A. 0.0469 $moldm^{-3}$
    B. 0.0938 $moldm^{-3}$
    C. 0.188 $moldm^{-3}$
    D. 0.480 $moldm^{-3}$
    E. 188 $moldm^{-3}$

28. 3.85 g of calcium carbonate reacted completely with nitric acid.
    What is the volume of gas produced in this reaction at room temperature and pressure?
    (A_r values: Ca = 40; C = 12; O =16; H = 1; N = 14)
    A. 1.60 cm^3
    B. 462 cm^3
    C. 847 cm^3

D. 924 cm^3
E. 1850 cm^3

29. What mass of calcium oxide is formed when 3.2 g of calcium burns in oxygen?
(A_r values: Ca = 40; O =16)
A. 2.24 g
B. 2.29 g
C. 4.48 g
D. 5.60 g
E. 8.96 g

30. Hydrated copper sulphate of mass 0.25 g is heated until there was no further change in mass. The final mass measured was 0.10 g.
What was the formula for the hydrated copper sulphate?
(Ar: Cu = 63.5; S = 32; O = 16; H = 1)
A. $CuSO_4 \bullet 4H_2O$
B. $CuSO_4 \bullet 5H_2O$
C. $CuSO_4 \bullet 8H_2O$
D. $CuSO_4 \bullet 12H_2O$
E. $CuSO_4 \bullet 13H_2O$
F. $CuSO_4 \bullet 15H_2O$

31. A total of 100 cm^3 HCl solution with a concentration of 0.5 $moldm^{-3}$ needs to be made from a HCl solution of concentration 2 $moldm^{-3}$.
What is the ratio of 2 $moldm^{-3}$ HCl solution to water that is added together to dilute the solution?
A. 1:2
B. 1:3
C. 1:4
D. 2:3
E. 3:4

Chemistry

32. 0.5 g of magnesium was added to 100 cm^3 water. (A_r: Mg = 24; O = 16; H = 1)
What is the concentration of magnesium hydroxide produced?
A. 0.208 $moldm^{-3}$
B. 0.416 $moldm^{-3}$
C. 86.2 $moldm^{-3}$
D. 104 $moldm^{-3}$
E. 208 $moldm^{-3}$
F. 416 $moldm^{-3}$

33. Hydrogen peroxide (H_2O_2) undergoes photochemical decomposition to form water and oxygen.
What is the maximum volume of oxygen obtained at room temperature and pressure if 0.4 mol of hydrogen peroxide undergoes photochemical decomposition?
A. 4.4 dm^3
B. 4.8 dm^3
C. 8.9 dm^3
D. 9.6 dm^3
E. 17.8 dm^3
F. 19.2 dm^3

34. Exactly 200 cm^3 of 0.4 moldm^{-3} of $MgBr_2$ is mixed with 100 cm^3 of 0.5 moldm^{-3} NaBr. What is the total concentration of bromide ions in the mixture?

A. 0.4 moldm^{-3}
B. 0.5 moldm^{-3}
C. 0.6 moldm^{-3}
D. 0.7 moldm^{-3}
E. 0.8 moldm^{-3}
F. 0.9 moldm^{-3}

Chemistry (C5)	OXIDATION, REDUCTION AND REDOX	Specification

Topic	Objective	☺	😐	☹
C5.1	- Know that on a basic level, oxidation is the gain of oxygen and that reduction is the removal of oxygen.			
C5.2	- Know and be able to use the concept that oxidation and reduction are the transfer of electrons, i.e., reduction is the gain of electrons and oxidation is the loss of electrons.			
C5.3	- Determine and use the oxidation states of atoms in simple inorganic compounds.			
C5.4	- Identify any chemical equation that involves: oxidation only, reduction only, redox (both oxidation and reduction taking place), or no oxidation/reduction.			
C5.5	- Understand the concept of *disproportionation* and recognise reactions (or species) where this occurs.			
C5.6	- Understand the terms *oxidising agent* and *reducing agent* and be able to identify them in reactions.			

Chemistry (C5)	OXIDATION, REDUCTION AND REDOX	Questions

35. **Which row correctly identifies the oxidation states of the following chemical reaction?**

$$Fe_2O_{3\,(s)} + 3CO_{(g)} \rightarrow 2Fe_{(s)} + 3CO_{2\,(g)}$$

	Fe in Fe_2O_3	C in CO	Fe $_{(s)}$	C in CO_2
A	+3	-2	0	+2
B	+2	+3	+3	-2
C	+2	-3	+2	+3
D	+3	+2	0	+4

36. **Below are four different chemical reactions.**
    1. $2CuCl \rightarrow CuCl_2 + Cu$
    2. $CuSO_4 + Mg \rightarrow Cu + MgSO_4$
    3. $2H_2O_2 \rightarrow 2H_2O + O_2$
    4. $2NaOH + Cl_2 \rightarrow NaCl + NaClO + H_2O$

    Which of the above are not examples of disproportionation reactions?

    A. 1 only
    B. 2 only
    C. 3 only
    D. 2 and 3 only
    E. 1, 2 and 3 only
    F. 1, 2 and 4 only
    G. None of the above

37. **For the electrolysis of molten potassium chloride, what is the half equation at the anode?**

    A. $Cl^- - e^- \rightarrow Cl$
    B. $2Cl^- - 2e^- \rightarrow Cl_2$
    C. $K^+ + e^- \rightarrow K$
    D. $K - e^- \rightarrow K^+$
    E. $Cl + e^- \rightarrow Cl^-$

Chemistry

Chemistry (C6)	CHEMICAL BONDING, STRUCTURE AND PROPERTIES	Specification

Topic	Objective	☺	😐	☹
C6.1	- Define and understand the differences between elements, compounds and mixtures.			
C6.2	- Understand that atoms often react to form compounds which have the electron configuration of a noble gas (Group 18). Understand that the type of bonding taking place depends on the atoms involved in the reaction.			
C6.3	**Ionic bonding:** - Know that ions are formed by transfer of electrons from atoms of metals to atoms of non-metals, and that these ions (of opposite charge) attract to form ionic compounds. - Predict the charge of the most stable ions formed from elements in Groups 1, 2, 16 and 17 and aluminium by consideration of their electron configuration. - Know the chemical formulae of common compound ions, e.g., CO_3^{2-} and OH^- - Know that when an element can exist in more than one oxidation state, e.g., Cu, Fe, then Roman numerals are used to denote the one present, e.g., iron(III) chloride for $FeCl_3$. - Determine the formulae of ionic compounds from their constituent ions. - Understand the general physical properties of ionic compounds, such as melting point and conductivity.			
C6.4	**Covalent bonding:** - Know that a covalent bond is formed when atoms share one (or more) pair(s) of electrons, generally between non-metals. - Understand that covalently bonded substances can be small molecules (e.g., water, ammonia, methane) or giant structures (e.g., diamond, graphite, silicon dioxide). - Understand the general physical properties of substances composed of small molecules or of those that exist as giant covalent structures.			

Chemistry

C6.5	**Metallic bonding:** - Understand that solid metals exist as a giant structure of positively charged ions surrounded by delocalised (free) electrons. - Understand the general physical properties of metals, such as melting point and conductivity.			
C6.6	- Understand that intermolecular forces can exist between molecules and that these forces must be overcome in melting and boiling.			
C6.7	- Be able to relate structure and bonding to physical properties, such as melting point and conductivity.			

Chemistry (C6) — CHEMICAL BONDING, STRUCTURE AND PROPERTIES — Questions

38. The following statements relate to bonding.

1. Ions are always formed by transfer of electrons from atoms of non-metals to atoms of metals – these ions attract to form ionic compounds.
2. Only non-metals can form covalent bonds.
3. Solid metals exist as a giant structure of positively charged ions surrounded by delocalised electrons.
4. A covalent bond is formed when atoms share one or more pairs of electrons.

Which of the above statement(s) is/are incorrect?

A. 1 only
B. 2 only
C. 3 only
D. 4 only
E. 1 and 2 only
F. 3 and 4 only
G. None of the above

39. Listed below are some different properties related to bonding:

1. High melting and boiling points.
2. Malleable and ductile.
3. Electrical conductivity at all times.
4. Low melting and boiling points.
5. Do not conduct electricity.
6. Conduct electricity only when molten or dissolved in solution.

Which row correctly identifies each of the above properties with the correct type of structure?

	Metallic	Simple covalent	Giant covalent	Ionic
A	1, 2 and 3 only	4 and 5 only	1 only	1 and 6 only
B	2 and 3 only	1 and 4 only	1, 2 and 5 only	6 only
C	1 and 6 only	5 only	1 only	4 and 6 only
D	1, 5 and 6 only	4 only	3 only	2 and 3 only
E	1, 2 and 5 only	3 and 6 only	1 only	6 only

40. Iron (III) metal reacts with chlorine gas. What is the formula of the product formed?

A. $FeCl$
B. $FeCl_2$
C. $FeCl_3$
D. Fe_2Cl_3
E. Fe_3Cl_2

41. What is the formula for strontium nitride?

A. SrN
B. Sr_2N
C. SrN_2
D. Sr_2N_3
E. Sr_3N_2

42. What is the oxidation number of chromium in $Cr_2O_7^{2-}$?

A. +6
B. +7
C. +8
D. +12
E. +14
F. +16

43. What is the oxidation number of sulphur in sulphuric acid?

A. +2
B. +4
C. +5
D. +6
E. -2
F. -4
G. -5
H. -6

44. Which row correctly identities the bond in the molecules given below?

	Cl_2	NaCl	$CaCO_3$	H_2O	$CuCl_2$
A	Covalent	Ionic	Ionic	Covalent	Ionic
B	Covalent	Ionic	Ionic and Covalent	Covalent	Ionic
C	Ionic	Covalent	Ionic and Covalent	Covalent	Ionic
D	Covalent	Ionic	Ionic	Covalent	Covalent
E	Ionic	Covalent	Ionic	Ionic and Covalent	Ionic

Chemistry

45. **A chiral carbon is a carbon atom that is attached to four different atoms or groups. Chiral carbons have optical isomers which are non-super imposable mirror images. Consider the molecule $C_7F_{15}Br$. How many straight chain structural isomers does this molecule have which contains a chiral carbon?**
    A. 1
    B. 2
    C. 3
    D. 4
    E. 5
    F. 6
    G. 7

Chemistry (C7) GROUP CHEMISTRY Specification

Topic	Objective	☺	😐	☹
C7.1	- Know the physical and chemical properties of the alkali metals (Group 1), the halogens (Group 17) and the noble gases (Group 18).			
C7.2	- Describe the trends in chemical reactivity and physical properties of the alkali metals (Group 1) and make predictions based on those trends.			
C7.3	**The halogens (Group 17):** - Describe the trends in chemical reactivity and physical properties of the halogens and make predictions based on those trends. - Explain what is meant by a displacement reaction, in terms of reactivity competition, between halogens and halide ions.			

Chemistry

Chemistry (C7) GROUP CHEMISTRY Questions

46. **Below are statements relating to the alkali metals, the halogens or the noble gases.**
    1. This Group contains elements which are silvery, soft and not dense.
    2. This Group contains elements which are all odourless, colourless and monatomic.
    3. This Group all form acids when combined with hydrogen.
    4. This Group contains elements which must be stored in a mineral oil solution.

Which row below correctly matches the aforementioned properties to the relevant Group?

	Alkali metal	Halogen	Noble gas
A	1 and 4 only	3 only	2 only
B	1 only	3 and 4 only	2 only
C	4 only	3 only	1 and 2 only
D	1 and 4 only	2 only	3 only

---

47. Which row correctly identifies the properties of Fluorine?

	Colour	Group number	Physical state at room temperature
A	Yellow	16	Gas
B	Yellow	17	Liquid
C	Green	17	Gas
D	Yellow	17	Gas
E	Green	16	Gas

---

48. Element X has the electronic configuration 2, 8, 2.
Which of the statements below regarding Element X are true?

1. It is an Alkaline Earth Metal.
2. Element X reacts with chlorine to form XCl.
3. Element X reacts with water to form $X(OH)_2$.
4. It is in Period 2 of the Periodic Table.
5. It contains 12 protons.

A. 1 only
B. 5 only
C. 1 and 3 only
D. 1, 2 and 3 only
E. 1, 2 and 5 only
F. 1, 3 and 5 only
G. 1, 2, 3 and 5 only
H. 1, 3, 4 and 5 only

Chemistry (C8) SEPARATION TECHNIQUES Specification

Topic	Objective	☺	😐	☹
C8.1	- Know that chemical processes are required to displace constituent elements from their compounds.			
C8.2	- Know that physical processes are required to separate mixtures, including miscible/immiscible liquids and dissolved/insoluble solids.			

C8.3	- Know when to apply the following separation techniques: Simple/fractional distillation, paper chromatography (including use of Rf values), use of a separating funnel, centrifugation, dissolving, filtration, evaporation and crystallisation.			
C8.4	Know how to establish the purity of a substance using chromatography.			

Chemistry (C8) SEPARATION TECHNIQUES Questions

49. Below is a diagram illustrating a separation technique.

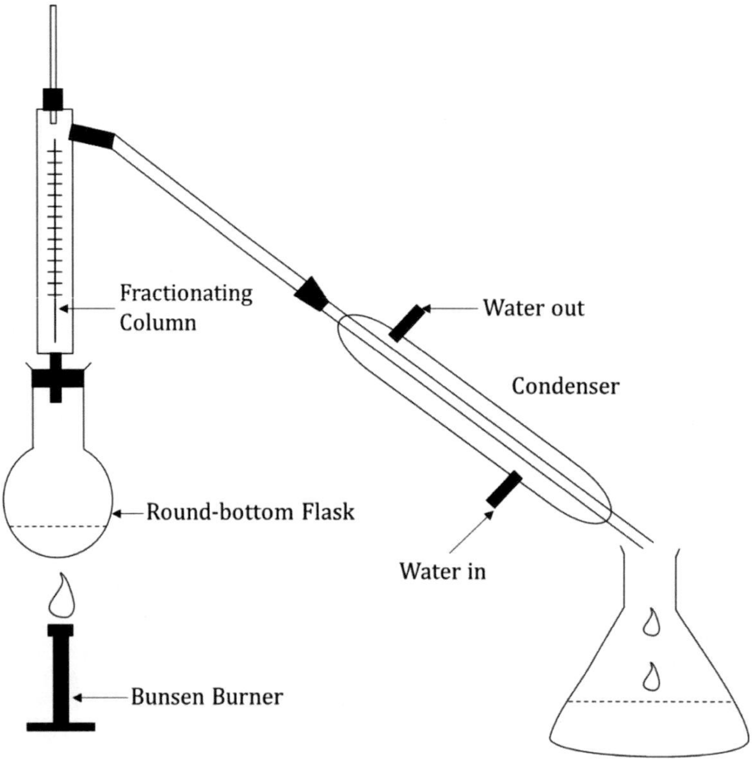

Which of the following reactions would the above separation technique be appropriate?

A. Purification of sea water.
B. Separation of crude oil.
C. Separation of sand from water.
D. Testing water sample to look for pollution in lakes and rivers.

50. Below is an image of a chromatogram.

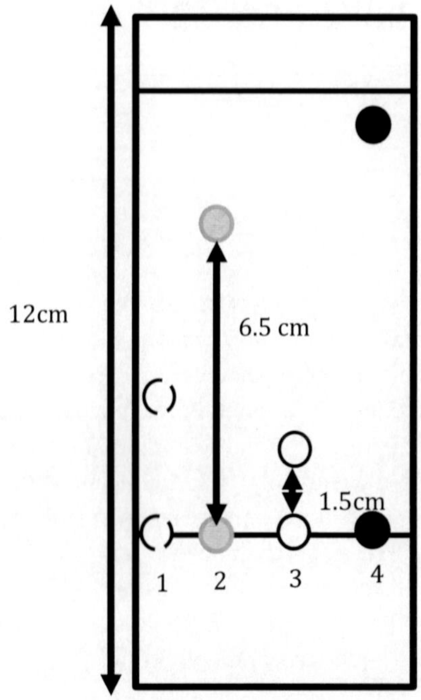

Which row correctly approximates the R_f values for the above spots?

	1	2	3	4
A	3.5	1.85	8	0.9
B	0.83	0.54	0.13	1
C	0.83	0.13	0.54	0.25
D	0.25	0.54	0.13	0.83

51. Which of these reactions do not occur?

A. $Cl_2 + 2I^- \rightarrow I_2 + 2Cl^-$

B. $Cl_2 + 2Br^- \rightarrow Br_2 + 2Cl^-$

C. $Br_2 + 2I^- \rightarrow I_2 + 2Br^-$

D. $I_2 + 2At^- \rightarrow At_2 + 2I^-$

E. $At_2 + 2Br^- \rightarrow Br_2 + 2At^-$

Chemistry (C9)	ACIDS, BASES AND SALTS	Specification

Topic	Objective	☺	😐	☹
C9.1	**Acids:** - Define an acid as a substance that can form $H^+(aq)$ ions or that is an H^+ donor. - Describe reactions with metals, carbonates, metal hydroxides and metal oxides in which salts are formed. - Understand the terms strong, weak, dilute and concentrated. - Know that some oxides of non-metals react with water to form acidic solutions. - Recall that pH is a measure of H^+ ion concentration and recall that a change of 1 on the pH scale corresponds to a change by a factor of 10 in H^+ ion concentration. - Know that one mole of some acidic substances is able to form/donate more than one mole of H+ ions, including the use of the terms mono-, di-, tri-, and polyprotic.			
C9.2	**Bases:** - Define a base as a substance that can form $OH^-(aq)$ ions or that is an H^+ acceptor. - Understand the terms strong, weak, dilute and concentrated. - Know that some oxides and hydroxides of metals react with water to form alkaline solutions.			
C9.3	- Know that the reaction of an acid with a base can lead to neutralisation and is often exothermic.			

Chemistry

Chemistry (C9)	ACIDS, BASES AND SALTS	Questions

52. Below are four definitions related to acids.

1. This acid completely dissociates into ions in solution.
2. This acid will undertake reversible reactions.
3. This acid is when the concentration of the water mixed into the acid is higher than the concentration of the acid itself .
4. An acid which is either in pure form or has a high concentration.

Which of the above statements correctly defines a strong acid?

A. 1 only
B. 2 only
C. 3 only
D. 4 only

E. 1 and 4 only
F. 2 and 3 only
G. 1, 2 and 3 only
H. None of the above

53. Listed below are six different reactions:

1. $MgO + H_2O \rightarrow Mg(OH)_2$
2. $SO_2 + H_2O \rightarrow H_2SO_3$
3. $BaO + H_2O \rightarrow Ba(OH)_2$
4. $NO_2 + H_2O \rightarrow HNO_3$
5. $ZnO + H_2O \rightarrow Zn(OH)_2$
6. $2NaOH + 2Na \rightarrow 2Na_2O + H_2$

Which of the above reactions form acidic solutions?

A. 1 only
B. 2 only
C. 4 only
D. 1 and 2 only
E. 2 and 4 only
F. 2 and 3 only
G. 5 and 6 only
H. 1, 3, 5 and 6 only
I. None of the above

54. After a chemical reaction, the pH of a solution changed from pH 7.3 to pH 8.3. By what factor did the hydrogen ion concentration of the solution change?

A. H+ concentration decreased by a factor of 2.
B. H+ concentration increased by a factor of 2.
C. H+ concentration decreased by a factor of 5.
D. H+ concentration increased by a factor of 5.
E. H+ concentration decreased by a factor of 10.
F. H+ concentration increased by a factor of 10.
G. H+ concentration decreased by a factor of 15.
H. H+ concentration increased by a factor of 15.

Chemistry (C10)	RATES OF REACTION	Questions

Topic	Objective	☺	😐	☹
C10.1	- Describe the qualitative effects on a rate of reaction of concentration, temperature, particle size, a catalyst and, for gases, pressure.			
C10.2	- Know that the rate of reaction can be found by measuring the loss of a reactant or the gain of a product, or by measurement of a physical property over time, and be able to identify which of these measurements can be used in a given situation.			
C10.3	- Interpret data in graphical form concerning the rate of a reaction.			
C10.4	- Use collision theory to explain changes in the rate of a reaction.			
C10.5	- Understand that particles must have sufficient energy when they collide to react, and that this energy is called the activation energy (E_a). Identify the activation energy on an energy level diagram.			
C10.6	**Know that catalysts:** - Are not used up in a reaction. - Are chemically unchanged at the end of a reaction. - Provide an alternative route (reaction mechanism) with a lower activation energy and interpret this effect on an energy level diagram. - Do not affect the position of an equilibrium.			

Chemistry (C10) | RATES OF REACTION | Specification

55. Below are three methods used for measuring the rate of a reaction.

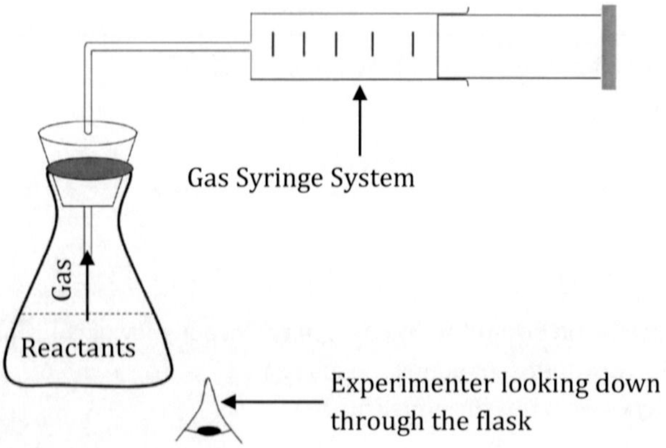

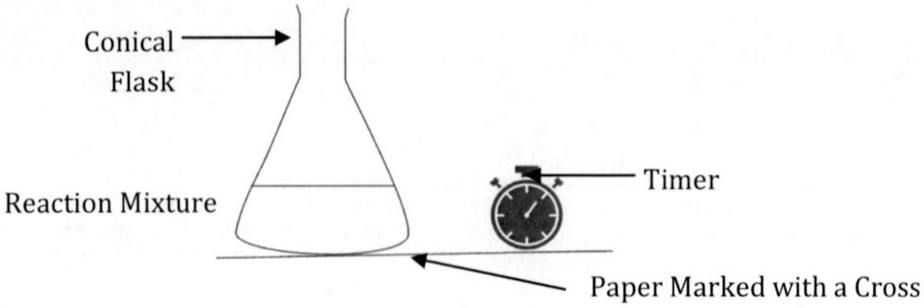

Four reactions are listed below:

1. Magnesium reacting with sulfuric acid.
2. Calcium carbonate reacts with hydrochloric acid.
3. Hydrogen peroxide decomposing in the presence of the manganese (IV) oxide catalyst.
4. $Na_2S_2O_{3\,(aq)} + HCl_{\,(aq)} \rightarrow NaCl_{\,(aq)} + SO_{2\,(aq)} + S_{\,(s)} + H_2O_{\,(l)}$

Which row correctly identifies the appropriate experiment set-up with each reaction?

	Reaction 1	Reaction 2	Reaction 3	Reaction 4
A	Y only	X only	X and Z only	Z only
B	X and Z only	Y only	X and Z only	Z only
C	X and Z only	X and Z only	X and Z only	Y only
D	Z only	X only	Y only	X and Z only

56. Below are factors that affect the rate of reactions:

1. Concentration
2. Temperature
3. Particle size (surface area)
4. Catalyst
5. Pressure

The rate of the reaction can be altered by changing the frequency of collisions or altering the number of particles with sufficient activation energy.
Which row correctly categorises the above factors?

	Alter collision frequency	Alter number of particles with sufficient activation energy
A	1, 3 and 5 only	2 and 4 only
B	1, 3 and 4 only	2 only
C	1, 2 and 5 only	4 only
D	2, 4 and 5 only	1, 3 and 5 only
E	1, 2, 3 and 5 only	2 and 4 only

57. Consider the following statements regarding catalysts.

1. They are not used up in a reaction.
2. They are chemically altered by the end of the reaction.
3. They provide an alternative route with a lower activation energy.
4. They alter the position of the equilibrium to favour the forward reaction.

Which of the aforementioned statement(s) is/are true?

A. 1 only
B. 2 only
C. 3 only
D. 4 only
E. 1 and 2 only
F. 1 and 3 only
G. 2 and 4 only
H. 1, 3 and 4 only
I. 2, 3 and 4 only

Chemistry (C11) | ENERGETICS | Specification

Topic	Objective	☺	😐	☹
C11.1	- Understand the concepts of an exothermic reaction, for which ΔH is negative (negative enthalpy change), and an endothermic reaction, for which ΔH is positive (positive enthalpy change).			
C11.2	- Know that if a reversible reaction is exothermic in one direction, it is endothermic in the other direction.			
C11.3	- Be able to interpret energy level diagrams.			
C11.4	- Be able to calculate energy changes from specific heat capacities and changes in temperature in calorimetry experiments.			
C11.5	- Know that bond breaking is endothermic and bond formation is exothermic and be able to use bond energy data to calculate energy changes.			

Chemistry (C11) | ENERGETICS | Questions

58. Below is an energy level reaction diagram:

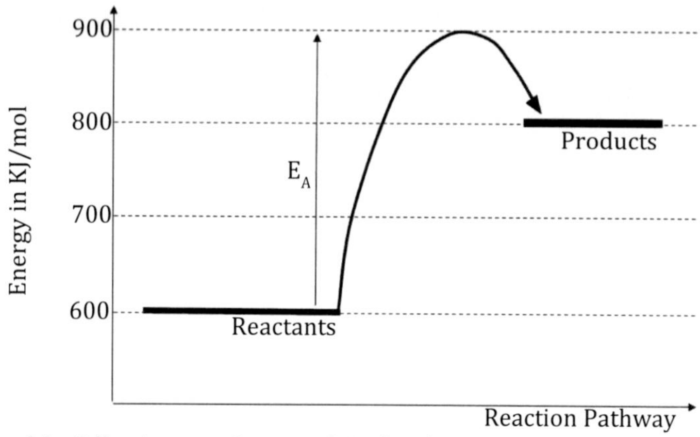

Which one of the following reactions result in the above energy change?

A. Combustion of fuels

B. Melting ice

C. Mixture of an acid and base

D. An oxidation reaction

59. The energy from burning 0.6 g of butane was transferred to 250 cm^3 of water, raising its temperature from 25°C to 65°C. Assuming that the specific capacity of water is 4180 J/kg°C, and that 1 cm^3 of water has a mass of 1 g, which one of the following is the energy change of the reaction?
 A. 41, 800 J
 B. 627 J
 C. 26,125 kJ
 D. 41,800 kJ
 E. 26,125 J
 F. 627 kJ
 G. 27,125 J

60. The complete combustion of propane, and the relevant approximate bond energy data, is demonstrated below:

$$CH_4 + 2O_2 \rightarrow CO_2 + 2H_2O$$

Bond	Bond enthalpy ($kJmol^{-1}$)
C-H	400
C-C	350
O-O	140
O=O	500
C-O	360
C=O	800
O-H	460

Chemistry

What is the energy change in the above reaction?
 A. -1560 $kJmol^{-1}$
 B. -840 $kJmol^{-1}$
 C. + 840 $kJmol^{-1}$
 D. -680 $kJmol^{-1}$

61. Consider the energy diagram below.

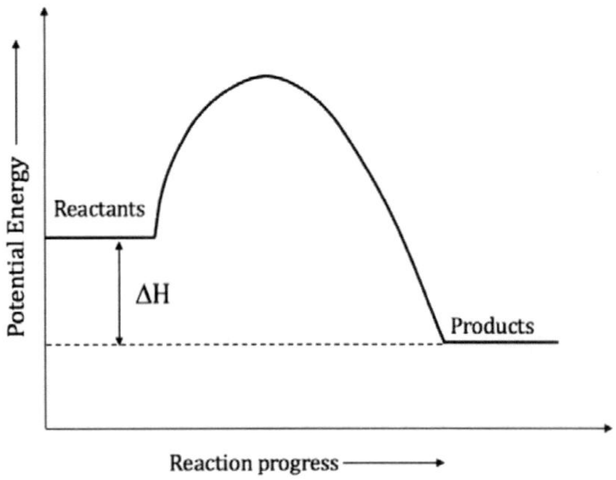

Which statement regarding the energy diagram is true?

A. ΔH is positive.
B. The products are more stable than the reactants.
C. Energy is absorbed from the surroundings.
D. The energy used to break the bonds in the reactants is greater than the energy released to form the bonds in the products.

62. What is the average bond enthalpy of the reaction given below?

Assume all the compounds are in their gaseous state.

$$C_2H_6 + Cl_2 \rightarrow C_2H_5Cl + HCl$$

Bond	Bond enthalpy ($kJmol^{-1}$)
C-C	348 kJ/mol
C-H	413 kJ/mol
Cl-Cl	242 kJ/mol
C-Cl	328 kJ/mol
H-Cl	431 kJ/mol
H-H	436 kJ/mol

A. - 104 kJ/mol
B. + 104 kJ/mol
C. - 452 kJ/mol
D. + 454 kJ/mol
E. + 332 kJ/mol

Chemistry

Chemistry (C12) ELECTROLYSIS Specification

Topic	Objective	☺	😐	☹
C12.1	- Understand the terms electrode, cathode (negative electrode), anode (positive electrode) and electrolyte.			
C12.2	- Understand why direct current (dc), and not alternating current (ac), is used in electrolysis.			
C12.3	- Understand that in electrolysis at the cathode, the cations (positively charged ions) receive electrons (reduction) to change into atoms or molecules, and at the anode, the anions (negatively charged ions) lose electrons to form atoms or molecules (oxidation).			

C12.4	- Understand and be able to predict the products of the electrolysis of the following: o aqueous solutions (including those of salts), including situations where more than one ion/molecule is attracted to a single electrode o molten binary compounds			
C12.5	- Be able to write half-equations for the processes taking place at each electrode.			
C12.6	- Explain how electrolysis is used to electroplate objects.			

Chemistry (C12) ELECTROLYSIS Questions

63. The diagram shows an electrolysis experiment.

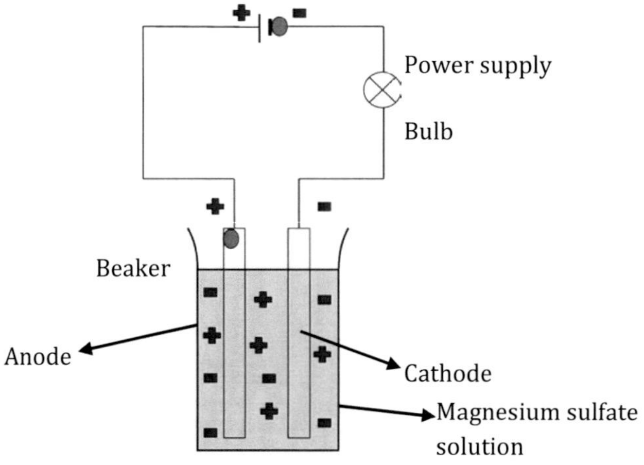

Which reaction occurs at the anode and which reaction occurs at the cathode for this experiment?

	Anode	Cathode
A	$2H^+ + 2e^- \rightarrow H_2$	$4OH^- \rightarrow 2H_2O + O_2 + 4e^-$
B	$Mg^{2+} + 2e^- \rightarrow Mg$	$2H^+ + 2e^- \rightarrow H_2$
C	$2H^+ + 2e^- \rightarrow H_2$	$Mg^{2+} + 2e^- \rightarrow Mg$
D	$4OH^- \rightarrow 2H_2O + O_2 + 4e^-$	$2H^+ + 2e^- \rightarrow H_2$
E	$SO_4^{2-} \rightarrow SO_2 + O_2 + 2e^-$	$2H^+ + 2e^- \rightarrow H_2$

64. Six statements related to electrolysis are listed below:

1. Cations receive electrons to change into atoms or molecules.
2. Reduction occurs.
3. Anions lose electrons to form atoms or molecules.

4. Oxidation occurs.
5. When copper is purified by electrolysis, this electrode loses mass as copper is dissolved.
6. In electroplating, this electrode is the object to be electroplated (e.g., a metal spoon or pan).

Which of the above statements directly relate to the cathode?

A. 1 only
B. 2 only
C. 3 only
D. 4 only
E. 1 and 2 only
F. 3 and 4 only
G. 1, 2 and 6 only
H. 1, 3 and 4 only
I. 1, 4 and 6 only
J. All of the above

65. Consider the metals given below:

1. Potassium
2. Copper
3. Iron
4. Zinc
5. Sodium
6. Magnesium

Which of these metals are extracted using electrolysis?

A. 1 and 2 only
B. 3 and 4 only
C. 1, 5 and 6 only
D. 2, 3 and 4 only
E. 1, 2 and 5 only
F. All of the above

66. When potassium sulphate solution is electrolysed, what ions are discharged at the cathode?

A. Potassium ions
B. Hydrogen ions
C. Hydroxide ions
D. Sulphate ions
E. Oxide ions

67. Which one amongst the following statements regarding electrolysis is incorrect?

A. The cathode is negatively charged.
B. DC current is used in electrolysis.
C. Metal ions move towards the cathode.
D. The ions that move to the anode are oxidised.
E. Bubbles of chlorine gas form at the cathode when electrolysing molten potassium chloride.

Chemistry (C13) CARBON/ORGANIC CHEMISTRY Specification

Topic	Objective	☺	😐	☹
C13.1	**General concepts:** - Know that crude oil is the main source of hydrocarbons and that it is separated into fractions by fractional distillation (names and uses of specific fractions not expected). - Understand the link between carbon chain length and the following trends in physical properties of hydrocarbons: boiling points, viscosity, flammability. - Know the use of longer chain alkanes in cracking to form shorter chain alkanes and alkenes and be able to write balanced chemical equations for these reactions. - Understand structural isomerism and be able to recognise examples. - Understand and be able to use the following terms: molecular formula, full structural formula (displayed structure) and condensed structural formula. - Understand and be able to use the terms complete combustion and incomplete combustion and be able to write balanced chemical equations for such reactions. - Know the IUPAC guidelines for the systematic naming of carbon compounds and apply the guidelines in order to be able to name all the compounds in this section of the specification. - Know and understand the terms homologous series and functional group.			
C13.2	**Alkanes (saturated hydrocarbons):** - Describe alkanes as a homologous series with the general formula of C_nH_{2n+2} - Be able to name, or recognise from the name, the C1 to C6 straight-chain alkanes.			

Chemistry

A Lakshmi, T R Enoch, S Z Y Ooi. Doctors Academy Publications, Cardiff, UK, 2020.

C13.3	**Alkenes (unsaturated hydrocarbons):** - Describe alkenes as a homologous series with a double bond and the general formula C_nH_{2n}. Be able to name, or recognise from the name, C2 to C6 straight-chain alkenes, including the position of the double bond. - Recognise and be able to use the test for unsaturation with bromine water. - Know that addition reactions take place with the following substances: hydrogen, halogens, hydrogen halides and steam. - Be able to write the balanced chemical equations for these reactions and recognise the formulae of the products formed. (Mechanisms and consideration of carbocation stability are not required.)			
C13.4	**Polymers:** Addition polymerisation, polyalkenes: - Know that alkenes or other molecules with a C=C bond may react with each other to form long-chain saturated molecules called polymers by addition reactions called polymerisation, and that the unsaturated molecules are called monomers. - If given an unsaturated monomer molecule, be able to recognise the structure of the polymer and vice versa. - Be able to recognise the repeating unit of these polymers. Condensation polymerisation, polyesters and polyamides (to include amino acids forming proteins): - If given the monomer molecules, be able to recognise the structure of the polymer and vice versa. - Be able to recognise the repeating unit of these polymers. - Understand the terms biodegradable and non-biodegradable when applied to polymers.			
C13.5	**Alcohols:** - Describe alcohols as a homologous series with the general formula $C_nH_{2n+1}OH$. - Be able to name, or recognise from the name, C1 to C6 straight-chain alcohols, including the position of the -OH group. - Describe the reaction of alcohols with sodium metal.			
C13.6	**Carboxylic acids:** - Describe carboxylic acids as a homologous series with the general formula $C_nH_{2n+1}COOH$. - Be able to name, or recognise from the name, C1 to C6 straight-chain carboxylic acids. - Describe the chemical properties of carboxylic acids as those of weak acids, and so be able to predict their reactions and determine the formulae of their salts. - Know that carboxylic acids react with alcohols in the presence of an acid catalyst to produce esters.			

Chemistry (C13) CARBON/ORGANIC CHEMISTRY Questions

68. Which row correctly describes the trends of boiling points, viscosity and flammability on decreasing hydrocarbon chain length?

	Boiling point	Viscosity	Flammability
A	Increase	Increase	Decrease
B	Decrease	Decrease	Increase
C	Increase	Decrease	Increase
D	Decrease	Increase	Increase

69. Fractional distillation is a process required to separate crude oil into its different fractions. Listed below are some of the key stages:

1. The crude oil enters a tall fractioning column, which has a temperature gradient (hotter at the bottom).
2. Different fractions have different boiling points; therefore, they condense at different heights up the fractioning column.
3. Vapours from the oil rise through the column.
4. Liquids/gases/solids are led out of the fractioning column at different heights .
5. The crude oil is heated to 350°C .

Which of the following correctly demonstrates the order of the fractional distillation process?

A. 5, 6, 3, 4,2
B. 1, 5, 3, 2, 4
C. 5, 1, 3, 2, 4
D. 1, 3, 4, 2, 5

70. Which of the following are structural isomers?

1.
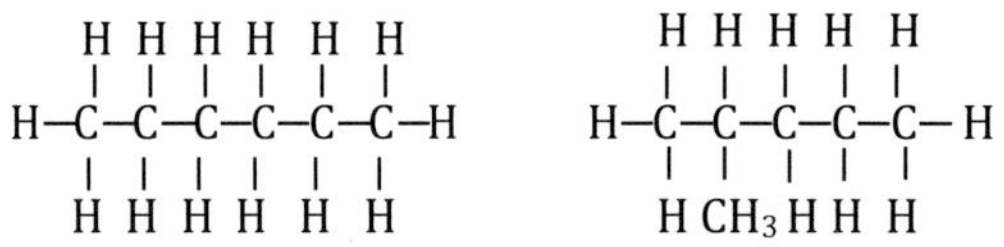

2.

3.

4.
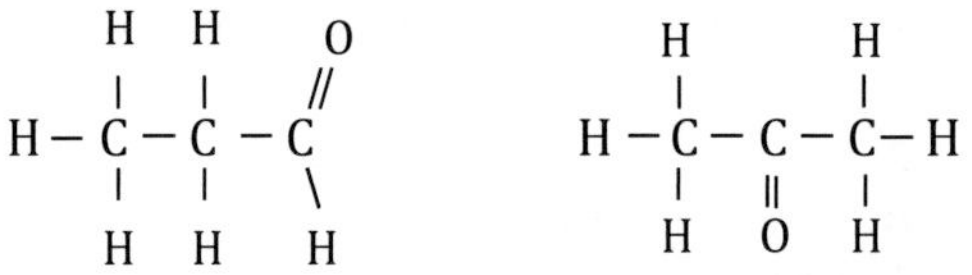

A. 1 only
B. 2 only
C. 3 only
D. 4 only
E. 1 and 4 only
F. 2 and 3 only
G. 1, 3 and 4 only
H. None of the above

71. Which of the following correctly identifies 2-hydroxypropanoic acid?

1. $CH_3CH_2(OH)COOH$
2. 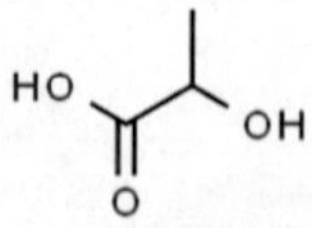

3. $C_3H_6O_3$
4. 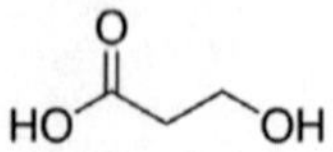

A. 1 only
B. 2 only
C. 3 only
D. 4 only
E. 1 and 4 only
F. 2 and 3 only
G. 1, 3 and 4 only
H. None of the above

72. Which one of the following equations is correctly balanced to represent incomplete combustion?

A. $2C_{10}H_{22} + 31O_2 \rightarrow 20H_2O + 22CO_2$
B. $2C_6H_{14} + 13O_2 \rightarrow 12CO + 14H_2O$
C. $2C_4H_{10} + 7O_2 \rightarrow 10\ H_2O + 4CO + 3C$
D. $C_7H_{16} + 15\ O_2 \rightarrow 14CO + 16H_2O$

73. Two alkanes, butane and hexane, are illustrated below.

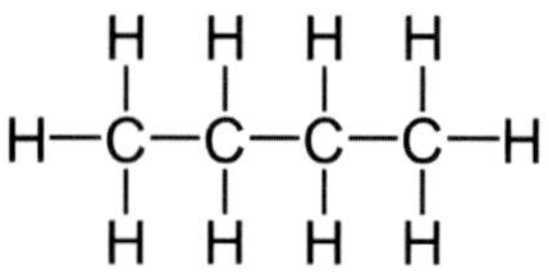
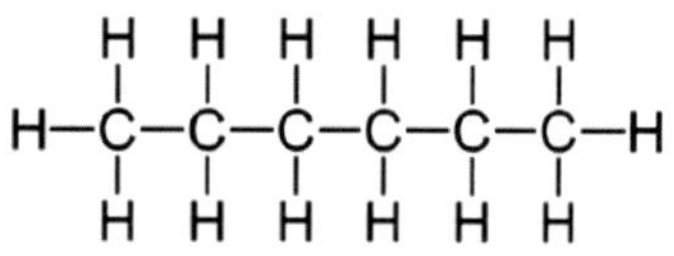

How many more structural isomers does hexane have compared to butane?

A. 1

B. 2

C. 3

D. 4

74. Which of the following molecules can be formed from the addition reaction with an alkene?

1. 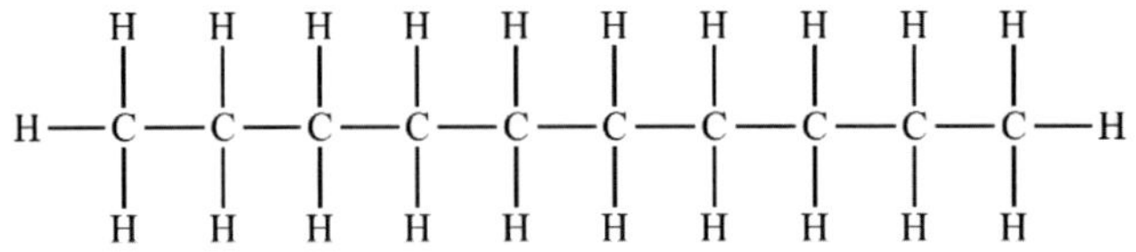

2. 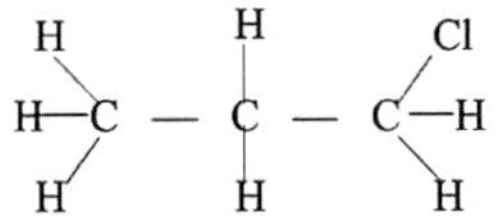

3. 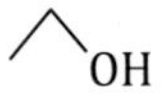

4. 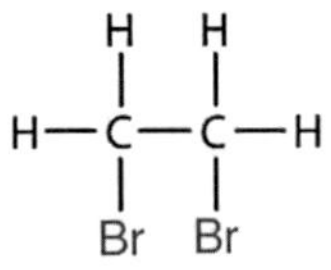

A. 1 only

B. 2 only

C. 3 only

D. 4 only

E. 1 and 4 only

F. 2 and 3 only

G. 1,2 and 3 only

H. 1,2 and 4 only

I. 1, 3 and 4 only

J. All of the above

75. Which one of the following structures could display the monomer unit for poly(pentene)?

A. 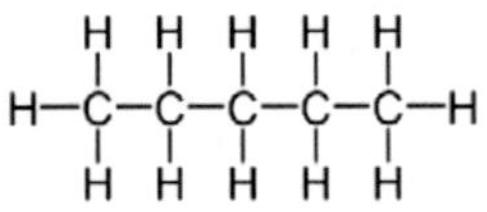

B. 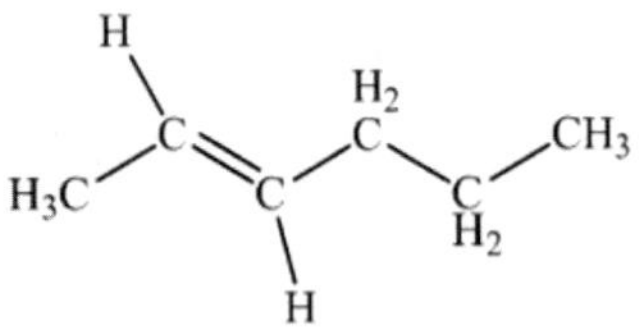

C. 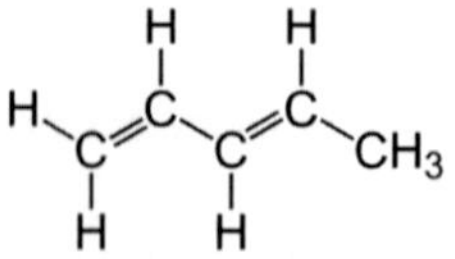

D. 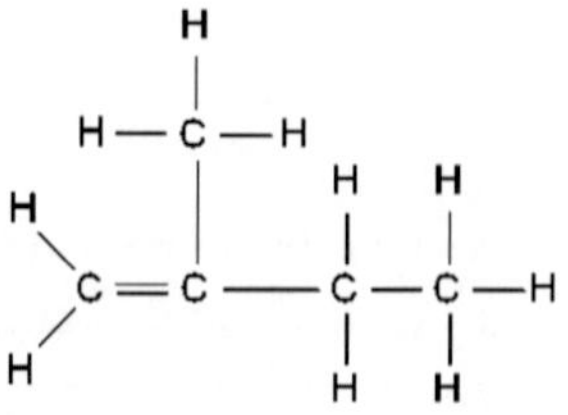

---

76. The following polyester is produced from two monomers:

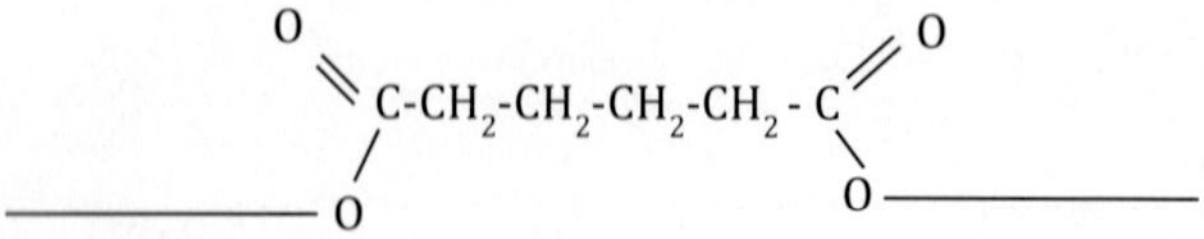

Which of the following two monomers could produce the above polymers?

A. $C_2H_4O_2$ 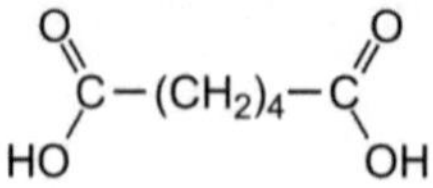

B. 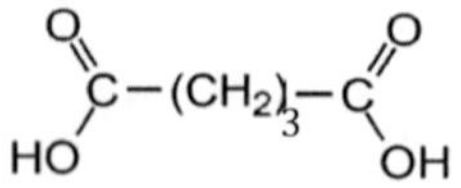 $HOCH_2CH_2OH$

C. 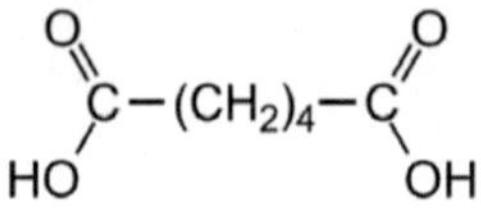 $C_2H_6O_2$

D. $HOCH_2CH_2OH$ 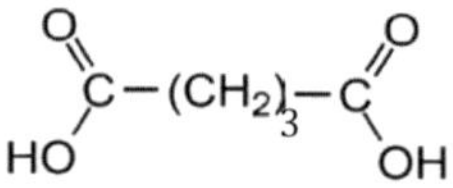

---

77. Nylon 6,6 is a polyamide produced from two monomers. The repeating unit of this polymer is shown below:

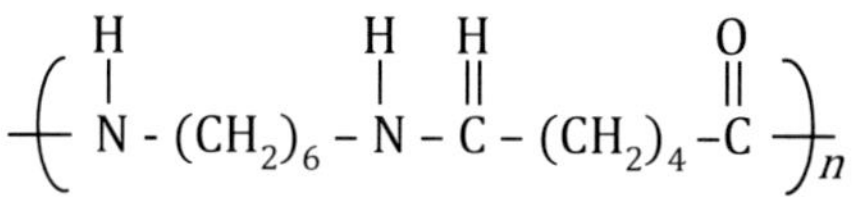

Which of the following two monomers could produce the above polymers?

A. $HN(CH_2)_6NH$, $CO(CH_2)_4CO$

B. $H_3NCH_2CH_2CH_2CH_2CH_2CH_2NH_3$, $(CH_2)_4(COOH)_2$

C. $(CH_2)_4(COOH)_2$, $H_2N(CH_2)_6NH_2$
D. $H_2NCH_2CH_2CH_2CH_2CH_2CH_2CH_2NH_2$, $(CH_2)_4(COOH)_2$

78. Which one amongst the following equations correctly illustrates the balanced reaction of sodium with butanol?

A. $2Na_{(s)} + 2C_4H_9OH_{(l)} \rightarrow 2C_4H_9ONa_{(l)} + H_{2(g)}$
B. $2Na_{(s)} + 2C_4H_9OH_{(l)} \rightarrow 2C_4H_9ONa_{(l)} + 2H_{2(l)}$
C. $2Na_{(s)} + 2C_4H_9OH_{(l)} \rightarrow C_4H_9ONa_{(l)} + H_{2(g)}$
D. $2Na_{(s)} + C_4H_9OH_{(l)} \rightarrow 2C_4H_9ONa_{(l)} + H_{2(l)}$

79. Molecule X partially ionises in solution. It decolourises bromine water and forms a white precipitate when an aqueous solution of silver nitrate is added in the presence of dilute nitric acid.

Which one of the following could represent Molecule X?

A. $CH_2OHCHCClCH_3$
B. $HOOCCHCClCH_2COOH$
C. $HOOCCH_2CHClCH2COOH$
D. $CH_3CH_2CHBrCOOH$

80. Consider the molecules below:

1. C_2F_4
2. $C_2H_2Cl_2$
3. C_8H_{18}
4. $C_{10}H_{20}$
5. $C_{13}H_{28}$
6. $C_{15}H_{30}$

Which molecule cannot undergo polymerisation?

A. 1 and 2 only
B. 3 and 5 only
C. 4 and 6 only
D. 1, 2 and 3 only
E. 1, 3 and 5 only
F. 1, 2, 4 and 6 only
G. 1, 2, 3 and 5 only

81. $HCOOC_3H_7$ is an ester.
Name the carboxylic acid and alcohol that it was made from.

A. Propanoic acid and methanol.
B. Methanoic acid and propanol.
C. Propanoic acid and ethanol.
D. Ethanoic acid and propanol.
E. Butanoic acid and methanol.
F. Methanoic acid and butanol.
G. Butanoic acid and ethanol.
H. Ethanoic acid and butanol.

Chemistry

82. **Aspirin is used as a painkiller. The structure of this compound is shown below.**

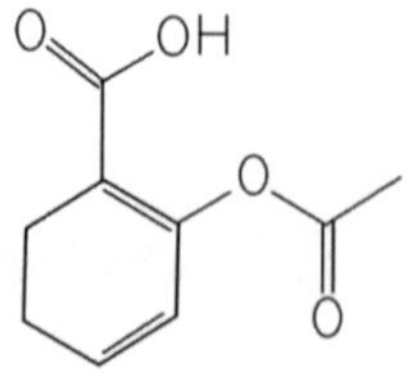

Listed below are different functional groups.

1. Alkene
2. Alcohol
3. Ketone
4. Aldehyde
5. Ester
6. Carboxylic acid

What are the functional groups present in aspirin?

A. 1 and 6 only
B. 1 and 3 only
C. 3 and 4 only
D. 5 and 6 only
E. 1, 3 and 6 only
F. 1, 4 and 5 only
G. 1, 5 and 6 only
H. 2, 3 and 5 only

---

83. **Which test confirms the presence of the functional group present in the following compound?**
$(CH_3)_2CCHCH_2C(CH_3)_3$

A. Bromine water turns colourless.
B. Bromine water turns orange.
C. Silver metal forms with Tollens reagent.
D. Gas production with HCl.
E. Iodine turns colourless.
F. Iodine turns purple.

---

84. **The diagram below shows the skeletal formula of four organic compounds.**

1. 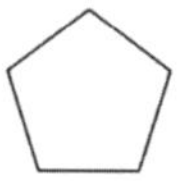

3. 

2. 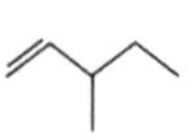

4. 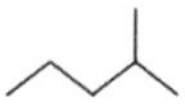

Which of the aforementioned compounds are isomers?

A. 1 and 2 only
B. 1 and 3 only

C. 1 and 4 only
D. 2 and 3 only
E. 2 and 4 only
F. 3 and 4 only

---

85. Identify the monomer that gives rise to the addition polymer shown below.

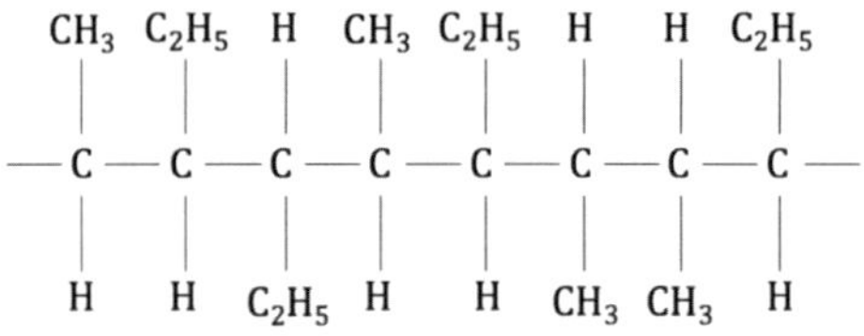

A. But-2-ene
B. Pent-2-ene
C. 2-methylbut-1-ene
D. 2-methylbut-2-ene
E. 3-methylbut-1-ene

Chemistry (C14)	METALS	Specification

Topic	Objective	☺	😐	☹
C14.1	- Understand that the reactivity of a metal is linked to its tendency to form positive ions and the ease of extraction of the metal.			
C14.2	- Be able to use displacement reactions to establish the order of reactivity of metals and vice versa.			
C14.3	- Describe how the uses of metals are related to their physical and chemical properties, e.g., Al, Fe, Cu, Ag, Au, Ti, and understand that alloys can be formed to produce materials with specific properties.			
C14.4	- Know that most metal ores are the oxides of the metal, and that the extraction of metals always involves reduction processes.			
C14.5	- Know that common properties of transition metals include: o they are able to form stable ions in different oxidation states. o they often form coloured compounds. they are often used as catalysts (as ions or atoms).			

Chemistry (C14)	METALS	Questions

86. Three metals - X, Y and Z - are being tested for reactivity. When Metal X is placed in a Metal Y sulfate solution, Metal X gradually disappears as it forms a solution. When Metal Y is placed in a Metal Z solution, Metal Y coats the surface of Metal Z. When Metal Z is placed in a Metal X solution, Metal Z gradually disappears to form a solution. Which one of the following demonstrates the reactivity of Metals X, Y and Z, in order of least to most reactive?
    A. Z ,X ,Y
    B. Z, Y, X
    C. Y, X, Z
    D. X, Y, Z

87. Three metals - 1, 2 and 3 - are being investigated in a laboratory. Metal 1 has a low density and a high thermal conductivity; hence, it is used for aeroplane bodies. Metal 2, once combined with tungsten or chromium, forms a hard alloy that it used for infrastructure, such as bridges. Metal 3 can also form alloys, such as brass, bronze and cupronickel.
    Which one of the following correctly identifies the three metals?

	Metal 1	Metal 2	Metal 3
A	Aluminium	Iron	Copper
B	Silver	Copper	Aluminium
C	Gold	Titanium	Copper
D	Copper	Iron	Aluminium

88. Listed below are a number of properties relating to metals:
    1. Often forms coloured compounds.
    2. High melting and boiling points.
    3. Often used as a catalyst.
    4. Conduct electricity.
    5. Solid at room temperature (apart from mercury).
    6. Conduct heat.
    7. Malleable and ductile.
    8. Form stable ions in different oxidation states.

    Two metals - aluminium and magnesium - are chosen. Which of the above properties will aluminium have that magnesium doesn't?
    A. 1 and 3 only
    B. 1, 4, 7 and 8 only
    C. 2, 4, 6 and 7 only
    D. 1 and 8 only
    E. 6, 7 and 8 only
    F. 1, 3 and 8 only
    G. 2, 4 and 6 only

89. Which one amongst the following statements is not a property of transition metals?

A. They often form coloured compounds.
B. They are often used as catalysts.
C. They are able to form stable ions in different oxidation states.
D. They cannot form stable complexes.

---

90. Which metal is used as a catalyst in catalytic converters on motor vehicles?

A. Rhodium
B. Copper
C. Aluminium
D. Silver
E. Titanium

Chemistry (C15) KINETIC/PARTICLE THEORY Specification

Topic	Objective	☺	😐	☹
C15.1	- Be able to describe the packing and movement of particles in the three states of matter: solid, liquid and gas.			
C15.2	- Understand the changes to the packing and movement of particles in the following changes of state: freezing, melting, boiling/evaporating, and condensing. - Understand that the energy required for these processes is related to the bonding and structure of the substance, including a consideration of intermolecular forces.			

Chemistry (C15) KINETIC/PARTICLE THEORY Questions

91. Nitrogen is an element with a melting point of 63K and a boiling point of 76K. Which row correctly identifies the states of nitrogen at different temperatures?

	56K	80K	-243°C	-208°C
A	Gas	Liquid	Solid	Solid
B	Solid	Gas	Solid	Liquid
C	Liquid	Solid	Liquid	Gas
D	Liquid	Solid	Gas	Liquid

Chemistry

Chemistry (C16)	CHEMICAL TESTS	Specification

Topic	Objective	☺	😐	☹
C16.1	- Know and recognise the following tests for gases: o hydrogen – explodes with a 'squeaky pop' when a burning splint is held at the open end of a test tube. o oxygen – relights a glowing splint. o carbon dioxide – limewater turns cloudy when shaken with the gas. o chlorine – damp blue litmus paper turns red and then is bleached (paper turns white).			
C16.2	- Know, recognise and describe the following tests for the anions: o carbonates – using a dilute acid. o halides – using an aqueous solution of silver nitrate in the presence of dilute nitric acid (chlorides form a white precipitate; bromides form a cream precipitate; iodides form a yellow precipitate). o sulfates – using an aqueous solution of barium chloride in the presence of dilute hydrochloric acid.			
C16.3	- Know and recognise the test for the following metal cations using aqueous sodium hydroxide: o Al^{3+}, Ca^{2+} and Mg^{2+} each form a white precipitate. o Cu^{2+} forms a blue precipitate. o Fe^{2+} forms a green precipitate. o Fe^{3+} forms a brown precipitate.			
C16.4	- Recall and recognise the flame test for the cations of the followingmetals: - Li (crimson red), Na (yellow-orange), K (lilac), Ca (red-orange), Cu (green)			
C16.5	- Know and recognise the test for the presence of water using anhydrous copper(II) sulfate (colour change from white to blue).			

Chemistry (C16)	CHEMICAL TESTS	Questions

92. Brine is a solution of sodium chloride (NaCl) and water. The process of electrolysis uses an electrical current to bring about a chemical change and produce three products. One of the products is NaOH; the other two are gases.
Considering that only these two gases are produced in this process, which two tests would confirm their presence?

A. 'Squeaky pop', Damp red litmus paper turning blue.
B. 'Squeaky pop', Damp blue litmus paper turning red.
C. Relighting a glowing splint, limewater turning cloudy.
D. Relighting a glowing splint, 'Squeaky pop'.

93. Three test tubes are filled with three unknown aqueous solutions:

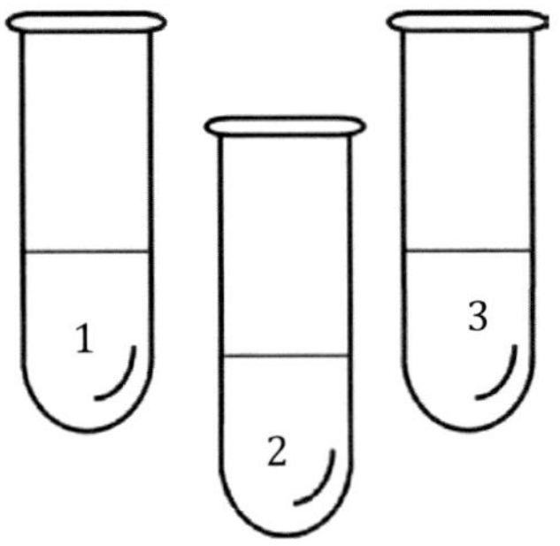

All three solutions change colour from white to blue in the presence of anhydrous copper (II) sulfate. Solution 1 and Solution 2 both form a white precipitate when aqueous sodium hydroxide is added. Solution 1 also forms a white precipitate when an aqueous solution of barium chloride is added in the presence of dilute hydrochloric acid. Solution 2 effervesces in the presence of dilute hydrochloric acid. Solution 3 forms a green precipitate in the presence of aqueous sodium hydroxide, and a cream precipitate from an aqueous solution of silver nitrate in the presence of dilute nitric acid. Which of the following could be each of the unknown solutions?

A. Solution 1 - Al_2CO_3, Solution 2 - $CaSO_4$, Solution 3 - $FeCl_3$
B. Solution 1- $CaBr_2$, Solution 2 - $MgSO_4$, Solution 3 - $CuBr_2$
C. Solution 1 - $MgSO_4$, Solution 2 - $CaCO_3$, Solution 3 - $FeBr_2$
D. Solution 1 - $CuSO_4$, Solution 2 - $MgCl_2$, Solution 3 - $FeCl_3$

94. Which row correctly identifies the flame test colours for each cation?

	Na	K	Cu	Li	Ca
A	Lilac	Crimson red	Red-orange	Yellow-orange	Green
B	Yellow-orange	Lilac	Green	Crimson red	Red-orange
C	Red-orange	Lilac	Crimson red	Green	Yellow-orange
D	Green	Yellow-orange	Red-orange	Crimson red	Lilac

95. Which one amongst the following is the test for ammonia?

A. Relights a glowing splint.
B. Produces a 'Squeaky pop' sound when a lighted splint is held to it.
C. Turns limewater cloudy when bubbled through it.
D. Turns damp red litmus paper blue.
E. Bleaches damp litmus paper to a white colour.

96. Consider the following metal cations:

1. Al^{3+}
2. Ca^{2+}
3. Mg^{2+}
4. Cu^{2+}
5. Fe^{2+}
6. Fe^{3+}

Which of these forms a white precipitate when they react with aqueous sodium hydroxide?

A. 1 only
B. 1 and 2 only
C. 1 and 4 only
D. 2 and 6 only
E. 1, 2 and 3 only
F. 2, 3 and 5 only
G. 1, 3 and 6 only
H. 1, 2, 3 and 4 only

97. The products of combustion can be tested with the experiment set-up shown below:

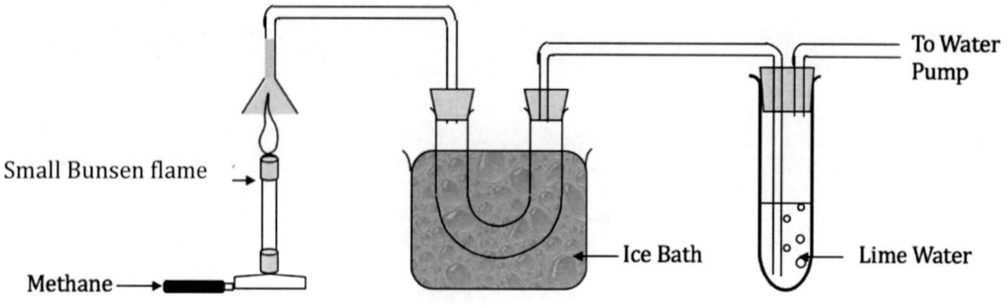

Which test confirms the presence of the product that forms in the U tube?

A. Anhydrous copper(II) sulphate changes colour from white to blue.
B. Anhydrous copper(II) sulphate changes colour from blue to white.
C. Cobalt chloride paper changes from pink to blue.
D. Cobalt chloride paper changes from pink to white.

Chemistry (C17)	AIR AND WATER	Specification

Topic	Objective	☺	😐	☹
C16.5	- Know and recognise the test for the presence of water using anhydrous copper(II) sulfate (colour change from white to blue).			
C16.5	- Know and recognise the test for the presence of water using anhydrous copper(II) sulfate (colour change from white to blue).			
C16.5	- Know and recognise the test for the presence of water using anhydrous copper(II) sulfate (colour change from white to blue).			
C16.5	- Know and recognise the test for the presence of water using anhydrous copper(II) sulfate (colour change from white to blue).			

Chemistry (C17)	AIR AND WATER	Questions

98. Which row correctly identifies the composition of dry air?

	Oxygen	Argon	Carbon dioxide	Nitrogen
A	21%	0.04%	0.04%	76%
B	22%	0.9%	0.04%	78%
C	22%	0.04%	0.9%	77%
D	21%	0.9%	0.04%	78%

---

99. Which one amongst the following statements regarding CFCs is correct?

A. They are compounds of chlorine and fluorine only.
B. They are not inert.
C. They have high boiling points.
D. They are soluble in water.
E. One CFC molecule can only cause the loss of three ozone molecules.
F. Free radicals are formed when a bond in the molecule is broken by UV radiation.
G. CFCs do not last a long time in the stratosphere.
H. They are extremely reactive.

100. Temporary hardness of water can be removed by boiling it. Temporary hard water contains calcium hydrogencarbonate. Softening the water produces three products. What is the name of the gas and precipitate produced?

A. Oxygen and calcium.
B. Carbon dioxide and calcium.
C. Hydrogen and calcium.
D. Oxygen and calcium oxide.
E. Carbon dioxide and calcium oxide.
F. Hydrogen and calcium oxide.
G. Oxygen and calcium carbonate.
H. Carbon dioxide and calcium carbonate.
I. Hydrogen and calcium carbonate.

Chemistry (C1)	ATOMIC STRUCTURE	Answers

1. B

Explanation:

Masses cannot be negative; **Options 'A' and 'C' can therefore be eliminated**. Electrons are the smallest sub-atomic particles; therefore, **Option 'B' is the correct answer**.

2. A

Explanation:

The atomic number (17) displays the number of protons present in the nucleus. As a result, **Options 'C' and 'D' can be eliminated**. The mass number (36) illustrates the number of protons and neutrons present in the nucleus. Consequently, by subtracting the atomic number from the mass number the number of neutrons can be found:

36-17=19

Usually, in atoms, the number of protons is equal to the number of electrons, since there is no overall charge. Since this chloride ion has a negative charge of -1, it has one more electron than protons present (electrons are negatively charged). The correct number of electrons is 17+1=18; hence, the **correct Option is 'A'**.

3. D

Explanation:

An oxygen atom usually has 8 electrons (the atomic number of oxygen is 8; atomic number is equal to the number of electrons in an atom since there is no overall charge). However, this ion has a negative charge of 2, resulting in 2 more electrons being present compared to the oxygen atom. Therefore, there are a total of 10 electrons. **Options 'C' and 'D' can be eliminated** as the numbers do not add up to 10. The first shell has 2 electrons, whereas the second shell has a maximum capacity of 8 (and not 6, hence, **Option 'A' is eliminated**). As a result, the **correct Option is 'D'**.

4. B

Explanation:

An isotope of the same element has the same number of protons and electrons, but a different number of neutrons. Since chemical properties are determined by electron arrangement, and all isotopes of the same element have the same electron arrangement, it follows that they will all have the same chemical properties. **Option 'A' can be eliminated**. Atomic weight is determined by the number of protons and neutrons in the nucleus. As isotopes have differing number of neutrons, they will also have differing atomic weights; **Option 'B' is not a property of isotopes and, therefore, is the correct answer**. Physical properties, including melting and boiling points, are determined by neutrons and protons. As a result, they may differ slightly between different isotopes due to the differing number of neutrons in the nucleus. As a result, **Options 'C' and 'D' can be eliminated**.

5. A

Explanation:

All four ions have the **same charge but differing masses**. The $^{64}Zn^{2+}$ has the lowest mass, and, therefore, it also would have the **lowest mass-charge ratio**. Since **the amount of**

Chemistry

deflection is inversely proportional to the mass-to-charge ratio, the $^{64}Zn^{2+}$ ion will be deflected more by the magnetic field inside the spectrometer.

6. A

Explanation:

The atomic number shows the number of protons in the nucleus (in this case, it is **eight**).

The number of neutrons is calculated using:

mass number – atomic number

16 – 8 = **8 neutrons**

Since the charge of the ion is 2-, there are 2 more electrons than protons - the **number of electrons is 10**.

7. C

Explanation:

Potassium has **19 electrons** (which is the same as the proton number). In an orbital, **two electrons** occupy the first shell, **eight in the second and third** and finally there is **one electron left to occupy the last shell**. The answers that do not add up to 19 can be quickly eliminated at the start such as **Options 'A', 'B' and 'E'**. Therefore, the correct answer is **Option 'C'**.

8. D

Explanation:

Calculate the relative atomic mass of Boron using the following formula:

[Sum of (Relative abundance x Mr) of each isotope] ÷ 100

[(20 x 10) + (80 x 11)] ÷ 100 = **10.8**

9. E

Explanation:

Isotopes have the **same electronic configuration** because they only differ due to the varying numbers of neutrons in the nucleus.

As a result, all isotopes of cobalt have **27 protons in its nucleus**.

Due to having the same electronic configuration, isotopes also have the **same chemical properties.** The number of neutrons is different in each isotope, resulting in different mass numbers but the same atomic number (because the number of protons remains constant).

Chemistry (C2) | PERIODIC TABLE | Answers

10. G

Explanation:

Statement 1 is incorrect – Periods are horizontal rows and Groups are vertical columns. **Statement 2 is incorrect** since elements are arranged in order of increasing atomic (proton) number to ensure that chemical properties appear in the correct Group and to allow for the presence of isotopes. Although atomic mass usually increases across the Periodic table, there are some notable exceptions, such as Cobalt (58.9332) and Nickel (58.6934), and Uranium (238.0289) and Neptunium (237.0482). **Statement 3 is incorrect** – a Period determines the number of orbitals, whereas a Group determines the number of electrons on the outer shell. **Statement 4 is incorrect** as reactivity increases going down a metal group but decreases going down a non-metal group. In metals, electrons are lost in order to produce ions. The attraction between the nucleus and the last electron gets weaker going down the group, which makes it easier for the atom to give up the electron; this increases its reactivity.

11. C

Explanation:
Element X has a **2+ charge** as an ion because it is in group 2. Element Y has a **1- charge** being in Group 17. Therefore, the ionic compound is **XY_2**. This is because **+2 + (-1 x 2) = 0**; two Ion Ys are needed to neutralise the +2 charge on Ion X.

Chemistry (C3)	CHEMICAL REACTIONS, FORMULAE AND EQUATIONS	Answers

12. B

Explanation:
A covalent bond is formed when atoms share one or more pairs of electrons, generally between non-metals. Since CO_2, PH_3 and CH_3CH_2OH are all non-metals, they must be covalently bonded. Ionic bonds form between metals (Cu is a transition metal) and non-metals (SO_4) - **Option 'B' is correct**.

13. C

Explanation:
In order to balance the chemical reaction, the number of each element on both sides must be equal. On the left-hand side, initially there are two aluminium atoms, three oxygen atoms and one iron atom. On the right-hand side, there are three iron atoms, four oxygen atoms and one aluminium atom. By process of elimination, **Option 'C'** results in the equation having equal numbers of aluminium, oxygen and iron atoms on either side.

14. C

Explanation:
The forward reaction is exothermic. If the temperature is increased, the system will try to **decrease the temperature** in order to oppose the change (Le Chatelier's Principle). More **endothermic reaction** will occur to decrease the temperature, which results in an **increased backward reaction** (reducing the yield). Similarly, a lower pressure will result in the equilibrium position shifting to the side with an increased number of moles to increase the pressure and opposing the change, reducing the yield. Adding a higher concentration of oxygen will cause the system to try to decrease the concentration due to Le Chatelier's Principle. As a result, the **equilibrium position will shift to the right** and **increase the yield**. A **catalyst does not affect the yield in an equilibrium mixture**, since it increases both the forward and backward reactions by the same amount.

15. E

Explanation:

Statement 1 is incorrect as a catalyst increases the forward and backward reactions by the same amount, thus, it doesn't change the equilibrium position. The concentration of reactants/products, temperature and overall pressure will affect the equilibrium position since the system will try to oppose the change produced (using Le Chatelier's Principle) – **Statement 2 is correct**. **Statement 3 is incorrect** since only the favourable reaction increases to oppose the change, whilst the unfavourable reaction proceeds at the same prior rate. **Statement 4 is correct**. The system will try to decrease the temperature in order to oppose the change, and, therefore, there is more endothermic reaction. Since the forward reaction is endothermic, there will be an increased yield of products.

16. B

Explanation:

Balance the carbon, hydrogen and oxygen in the combustion reaction.

Firstly, balance the carbon:

$C_8H_{18} + O_2 \rightarrow 8CO_2 + H_2O$

Balance the hydrogen:

$C_8H_{18} + O_2 \rightarrow 8CO_2 + 9H_2O$

Balance the oxygen:

$C_8H_{18} + 12.5\ O_2 \rightarrow 8CO_2 + 9H_2O$

Multiply by 2 to get whole numbers:

$\mathbf{2C_8H_{18} + 25O_2 \rightarrow 16CO_2 + 18H_2O}$

17. C

Explanation:

Adding more reactants causes the equilibrium to shift to the right, in order to decrease the concentration of the reactants – **Statement 1 is correct**. Increasing the pressure favours the side with fewer gas molecules; in this case, there are four gas molecules on the left-hand side and two on the right. As a result, the position of the equilibrium will shift to the right – **Statement 4 is correct**. As the forward reaction is exothermic, lowering the temperature would shift the equilibrium to the right, in order to increase the temperature – **Statement 5 is correct**. Removing more of the reactants and adding more product would shift the position of the equilibrium to the left – **Statements 2 and 3 are incorrect**. The catalyst has no effect on the position of equilibrium because it increases the rate of the reaction – **Statement 6 is incorrect**.

18. D

Explanation:

Since there are a combination of metal and non-metal ions, these three ions would join together with ionic bonds. The overall charge must be zero.

None of the compounds except Option 'D' have an overall charge of zero:

$(3+) + (1+) + (-2 \times 2) = \mathbf{0}$

Therefore, **Option 'D' is the correct answer.**

19. C

Explanation:

The compound that undergoes the three addition reactions is an alkene. **Reaction 1** shows an alkane forming. This requires hydrogen to react with the alkene. **Reaction 2** shows a halogenoalkane forming, which requires the addition of a hydrogen halide (hydrogen bromide in this case). If bromine was added, a dihalogenoalkane would form. Lastly, **Reaction 3** shows an alcohol. Steam added to an alkene with an acid catalyst forms an alcohol.

---

20. C

Explanation:

The oxidation number of oxygen is **-2.**

Since there are three oxygen ions the oxidation number becomes:

-2 x 3 = -6.

There is no overall charge in the molecule, therefore, the **charge of nitrogen must sum to +6.**

There are 2 nitrogen ions; as a result, the oxidation number of one ion is:

+6 ÷ 2 = +3.

Chemistry (C4)	QUANTITATIVE CHEMISTRY	Answers

21. D

Explanation:

The empirical formula is the simplest integer ratio of atoms in a compound. Assume that there are 100 g of the compound:

There would be 49 g of Carbon (49% of 100), 8 g of Hydrogen (8% of 100) and 43 g of Oxygen (43% of 100).

As a result, *moles of each element can be found using* **moles** $= \frac{\textbf{mass}}{\mathbf{M_r}}$:

Moles of Carbon: $\frac{49}{12}$ is approximately 4

Moles of Hydrogen: $\frac{8}{1} = 8$

Moles of Oxygen: $\frac{43}{16} = 2.6875$

In order to get the smallest whole number ratio, all three moles must be divided by the smallest number (in this case, 2.6875).

If the numbers are approximated for ease of calculation:

4 ÷2.6875 is approximately 1.5

8 ÷2.6875 is approximately 3.

2.6875 ÷2.6875 is approximately 1

Since 1.5 is not a whole number, times each ratio by 2:

1.5 x 2=3

3 x 2=6

1 x 2 = 2

Therefore, the empirical formula contains three carbons, 6 hydrogens and 2 oxygens (<u>$C_3H_6O_2$</u>).

22. A

Explanation:

Firstly, the equation given is not balanced. This is important to ensure that the number of atoms on each side is equal, which gives accurate masses of the compounds.

Balance the equation:

$MgCl_{2\,(aq)} + 2AgNO_{3\,(aq)} \rightarrow 2AgCl_{\,(s)} + Ba(NO_3)_{2\,(aq)}$

The limiting reagent is the one that is completely consumed; it limits the reaction from continuing because there is none left to react. Consequently, finding the moles of the limiting reagent allows an accurate mass of AgCl to be calculated.

Determine moles of limiting reagent:

Moles of $MgCl_2$:

$\frac{mass}{M_r} = \frac{2}{94}$ (approximately 0.02)

1 mole of $MgCl_2$ forms 2 moles of AgCl. Therefore, the number of moles must be doubled.

Ratio of $MgCl_2$: AgCl

1 : 2

0.02 x 2= <u>0.04</u>

mass of AgCl = moles x Mr

0.04 x 145 = <u>5.8 g</u>

Percentage yield:

$= \frac{\text{Actual yield}}{\text{Theoretical yield}} \times 100$

$= \frac{1.80}{5.80} \times 100$

Approximately $(\frac{2}{6}) \times 100 =$ <u>33%</u>

<u>Option 'A' is the percentage closest to 33%,</u> therefore, this is the correct answer.

23. B

Explanation:

Writing out the balanced equation:

$2KOH + H_2SO_4 \rightarrow K_2SO_4 + 2H_2O$

Approximate numbers in order to make it easier to calculate.

Calculate the moles of KOH:

Moles of KOH: $\frac{mass}{M_r} = \frac{240}{57}$ (approximately 4.2)

From the equation, 2 moles of KOH forms 1 mole of K_2SO_4, therefore, the number of moles must be halved.

Ratio of KOH : K_2SO_4 = 2:1

Moles of K_2SO_4:

$\frac{4.2}{2} =$ <u>2.1 moles</u>

Mass of K_2SO_4= moles x Mr

=2.1 x 176

= <u>369.6 g</u>

<u>Option 'B' is the closest to this answer</u>. Therefore, this is the correct option.

Chemistry

24. G

Explanation:

One mole of a gas occupies a set volume at a given temperature and pressure ($24dm^3$ at room temperature and pressure).

Firstly, the volume of ethane gas must be calculated:

M_r of C_2H_6:

2(12) +6 = 30

Number of moles $= \frac{\text{mass}}{M_r} = \frac{150}{30}$

= **5 moles**

Volume (dm^3) = number of moles x 24

= 5 x 24 = **$120\ dm^3$**

Secondly, the volume of propane gas must be calculated:

M_r of propane:

3(12) + 8 = **44**

Number of moles $= \frac{\text{mass}}{M_r}$

$= \frac{440}{44} =$ **10**

Volume (dm^3) = number of moles x 24

= 10 x 24 = **$240\ dm^3$**

Difference between the two volumes (in dm^3):

240-120 = **$120\ dm^3$**

The question states the volume to be in cm^3.

Convert dm^3 to cm^3: x1000

=120 x 1000 = **$120\ 000\ cm^3$**

Therefore, **Option 'G' is the correct answer**.

25. B

Explanation:

Number of atoms:

moles x number of atoms in the given formula x Avogadro's constant

Number of hydrogen atoms:

$0.5 \times 8 \times 6.022 \times 10^{23} =$ **2.4088×10^{24}**

26. C

Explanation:

The M_r of Na_2CO_3 is:

(23x2) + 12 + (16x3) = **106**

The molar mass of the water in the salt is:

196-106= **90**

The M_r of H_2O is:

(1x2) +16 =**18**

Therefore,

90 ÷ 18 = **5**

27. C

Explanation:

Write the balanced equation for the reaction:

$2NaOH + H_2SO_4 \rightarrow Na_2SO_4 + 2H_2O$

Consider the moles of sulfuric acid:

$0.15 \times 0.0125 = 3.75 \times 10^{-3}$

Using the ratios from the equation:

$3.75\times10^{-3} \xleftarrow{2:1} = 1.875 \times 10^{-3}$

Concentration = number of moles ÷volume

$c = 3.75\times10^{-3} \div 0.02$

$c = 0.1875$ moldm^{-3}

c = 0.188 moldm^{-3}

28. D

Explanation:

$CaCO_3 + 2HNO_3 \rightarrow Ca(NO_3)_2 + CO_2 + H_2O$

The gas produced in this reaction is **CO_2**.

Calculate the moles of CaCO3:

$3.85 \div 100 = 0.0385$

1:1 between $CaCO_3$ and CO_2

At room temperature and pressure:

$v = n \times 24$

$v = 0.0385 \times 24$

$v = 0.924$

v= 924 cm^3

29. C

Explanation:

$2Ca + O_2 \rightarrow 2CaO$

Use n = m ÷ Mr.

Moles of Ca:

$3.2 \div 40 = 0.08$

2:2 mole ratio:

$2Ca \rightarrow 2CaO$

Therefore, there are **0.08 moles of CaO**

$m = n \times Mr$

$0.08 \times (40 + 16) =$ **4.48 g**

30. E

Explanation:

The formula for the hydrated compound is $CuSO_4 \bullet x\, H_2O$:

	Anhydrous compound	Water of Crystallisation
Formula	$CuSO_4$	xH_2O
Mass	0.10	0.25 – 0.10 = 0.15
M_r	159.5	18
Moles (n = m ÷ Mr)	0.000626...	0.00833...
Divide both of the number of moles by the smallest value	0.000626 ÷ 0.000626 = **1**	0.00833 ÷ 0.000626 = **13.29**

Therefore, the value of x is 13;the formula for the water of crystallisation is $CuSO_4 \bullet 13\, H_2O$

Chemistry

31. B

Explanation:

The number of moles in the diluted solution is n = cv:

$n = 0.5 \times \frac{100}{1000}$

<u>**n = 0.05 mol**</u>

The volume of undiluted solution (that needs to be diluted) is 0.5 moldm^{-3}:

$v = \frac{n}{c}$

$v = \frac{0.05}{2}$; v= 0.025dm^3

<u>**v= 25cm^3**</u>

Exactly <u>**25 cm^3 of HCl solution**</u> with concentration 2 moldm^{-3} is used, and water is added to make it up to 100 cm^3.

Therefore, the volume of water added is:

100 - 25 = <u>**75 cm^3**</u>

The ratio will be <u>**25:75 = 1:3**</u>

32. A

Explanation:

$Mg + H_2O \rightarrow Mg(OH)_2 + H_2$

Calculate the moles of Mg:

n = m ÷ Mr

n = 0.5 ÷ 24

<u>**n= 0.0208...**</u>

Calculate the concentration of magnesium hydroxide:

c = n ÷ v

c= 0.0208 ÷ 0.1

<u>**c = 0.2083 moldm^{-3}**</u>

33. B

Explanation:

Write down the balanced equation for the reaction:

$2H_2O_2 \rightarrow 2H_2O + O_2$

If 0.4 mol of H_2O_2 is used, it would produce a maximum of <u>**0.2 mol**</u> of O_2 as the mole ratio is 2:1.

Since the volume obtained is at room temperature and pressure:

v = n x 24

v = 0.2 x 24

<u>**v = 4.8 dm^3**</u>

34. D

Explanation:

Use n = cv find the number of moles of Br$^-$ in MgBr$_2$ and NaBr:

MgBr$_2$:

n = 0.4 x 0.2 (convert 200cm^3 to 0.2dm^3)

<u>**n= 0.08 moles**</u>

There are 0.08 moles of MgBr$_2$, therefore, there must be:

0.08 x 2 = <u>**0.16 moles of Br$^-$**</u>

NaBr:

n = 0.5 x 01

Chemistry

n = 0.05 moles
There are **0.05 moles of NaBr** and, therefore, **0.05 moles of Br^-**.
There is only one bromide ion in each molecule of NaBr.
The total number of moles of Br^- is:
0.05 + 0.16 = **0.21 moles**
c= n ÷ v
Since the total volume is $100cm^3 + 200cm^3$:
c = 0.21 ÷ (0.1 + 0.2)
$c = 0.7 moldm^3$

Chemistry (C5)	OXIDATION, REDUCTION AND REDOX	Answers

35. D

Explanation:
Oxygen has an oxidation number of -2 (except in peroxides and F_2O).
In Fe_2O_3, there are three oxygen atoms, which gives an oxidation number of:
3(-2)=-6
Since Fe_2O_3 is an atom, two Fe atoms must be +6 to produce and overall neutral charge. As a result, **each Fe atom must be +3** in the first compound.
Similarly, **C in CO must be +2** to produce a neutral charge with the -2 oxidation state of oxygen. All **elements have an oxidation state of 0** (because they haven't been oxidised or reduced). Finally, **C in CO_2 must be +4** to balance out the
2(-2) = -4 oxidation state of the oxygen.

36. B

Explanation:
Disproportionation is a type of redox reaction where the same element is oxidised and reduced. **In Reaction 1**, copper is being oxidised from +1 (CuCl) to +2 ($CuCl_2$), whilst also being reduced from +1 (CuCl) to 0 (Cu). **Reaction 2 is a redox reaction**, but the same element isn't being oxidised and reduced, therefore, it is not a disproportionation reaction. **In Reaction 3**, oxygen is being oxidised from -1 (H_2O_2) to 0 (O_2), whilst also being reduced to -2 (H_2O). **In Reaction 4**, chlorine is being oxidised from 0 (Cl_2) to +1 (NaClO), whilst also being reduced to -1 (NaCl).

37. B

Explanation:
Chloride ions move to the anode and potassium ions to the cathode. Chloride ions lose electrons to become atoms. Chlorine atoms are always found in pairs as chlorine molecules. Therefore, the correct answer is **Option 'B'**. **Option 'C'** shows the half equation at the cathode.

Chemistry

Chemistry (C6)	CHEMICAL BONDING, STRUCTURE AND PROPERTIES	Answers

38. E

Explanation:
Statement 1 is incorrect because ions are formed by the transfer of electrons from metals to non-metals (metals donate electrons to non-metals since they generally have fewer electrons on their outer shells). Although covalent bonds are generally formed between non-metals, some transition metals in higher oxidation states can covalently bond. Therefore, **Statement 2 is incorrect. Statements 3 and 4 are correct** and are listed in the BMAT specification.

39. A

Explanation:
Metals have high melting and boiling points **(Statement 1)** due to their giant structures of positively charged ions surrounded by delocalised electrons. These metallic bonds require a lot of energy to overcome; therefore, they have high melting and boiling points. They are also malleable and ductile **(Statement 2)** due to the atoms' ability to slide past each other, without breaking the metallic bond. The delocalised electrons are able to move throughout the metallic layer, and from a positive terminal to a negative terminal, thus, being able to conduct electricity **(Statement 3)**. Simple covalent molecules have low melting and boiling points **(Statement 4)** due to weak intermolecular forces that are overcome when a substance is heated or melted. These intermolecular forces do not need much energy to overcome. Therefore, they have low melting and boiling points. Since simple covalent molecules have no delocalised electrons or ions (have no overall charge), they do not conduct electricity **(Statement 5)**. Giant covalent structures have a lattice of many strong covalent bonds, which require lots of energy to overcome (therefore, having high melting and boiling points). Although some giant covalent structures conduct electricity (such as graphite due to delocalised electrons within each layer), some do not (such as diamond because it has no delocalised electrons). Ionic structures have high melting and boiling points **(Statement 1)** because of the strong electrostatic attractions between the positively charged nucleus and negatively charged outer electrons that must be overcome. These structures can only conduct electricity when molten or dissolved in solution **(Statement 6)** because the ions are able to flow and move between positive and negative terminals.

40. C

Explanation:
Iron has a **valency of +3** as indicated by the Roman numeral. Chlorine is in Group 17; it has a **valency of -1**. Therefore, **three chloride ions are needed** for one Iron (III).

41. E

Explanation:
Strontium is a Group 2 metal; it has a **valency of +2**. A nitride ion is N^{3-}. As a result, **three strontium ions** are needed for every two nitride ions.

42. A

Explanation:

The oxidation number for oxygen is -2.

Since there are seven atoms, the total charge is:

7 x -2 = **-14**

There are two atoms of chromium.

Let '*y*' be its oxidation number.

Therefore, the overall equation is:

2*y* + (-14) = **-2**

y = +6.

The oxidation number of chromium is +6.

43. D

Explanation:

The formula for sulphuric acid is H_2SO_4. There is no overall charge in the compound; therefore, the **oxidation numbers must cancel out**. The oxidation state for **Hydrogen is +1 and for Oxygen is -2**. There are two Hydrogens, which results in a **charge of +2** and four Oxygens that produces a **charge of -8**. As a result, the overall charge is -6. Consequently, sulphur must have an oxidation state of **+6** for the molecule to be neutral.

44. B

Explanation:

Covalent bonds are the sharing of electrons between two atoms - these include Cl_2 and H_2O. Ionic bonds are the electrostatic attraction between oppositely charged ions. It involves the transfer of electrons. NaCl and $CuCl_2$ are examples of this. $CaCO_3$ includes both ionic and covalent bonds. The ionic bond is formed between the Ca^{2+} and CO_3^{2-} ions. The covalent bonds are found within the CO_3^{2-} ions.

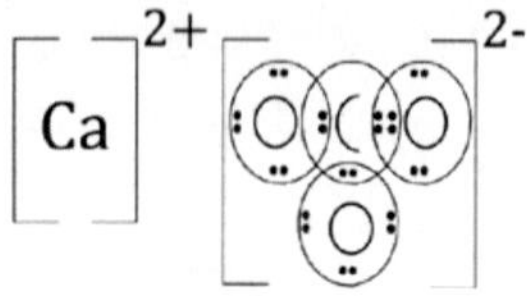

45. B

Explanation:

Since the question asks for straight chain isomers, it must be positional isomers (the position of the Br alters in each form). However, there are only **two possibilities** if there is a chiral carbon present. These are the two isomers that can form:

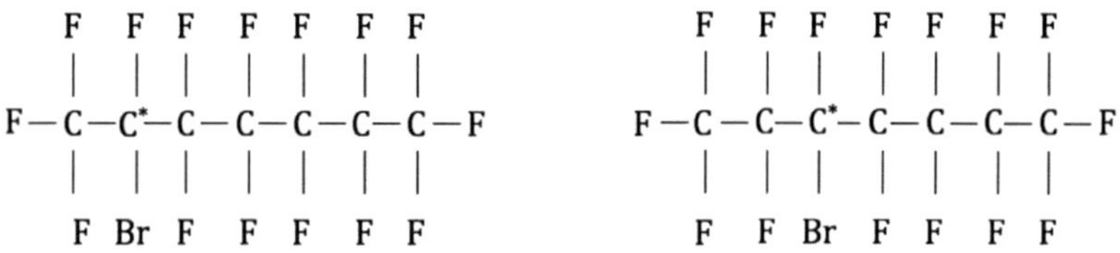

The chiral carbons have been marked with an asterisk. The **Br cannot be on Carbon one or four**, as this does not form a chiral carbon - the carbon atom will be attached to two of the same groups (two fluorine or two propyl groups respectively).

Chemistry (C7)	GROUP CHEMISTRY	Answers

46. A

Explanation:

Alkali metals have large atomic size with only one outer electron. Therefore, they have weak metallic bonding between the atoms. Due to the presence of weak metallic bonding, **alkali metals are soft and can be cut with a knife**. They get softer going down the group because the outermost electron is further away from the nucleus and the overall net force of attraction between the protons in the nucleus and the outermost electron decreases. The **noble gases are odourless, colourless and monatomic due to their electron configuration**. They have a full outer shell, resulting in noble gases remaining inert (unreactive). **The halogens react with hydrogen and produce acidic solutions due to covalent bonding**. Examples include hydrochloric acid (HCl), hydrobromic (HBr) acid hydroiodic acid (HI). The alkali metals must be stored in oil due to its reactivity, and its ability to react with oxygen in the air to produce metal oxides.

47. D

Explanation:

Fluorine is a **Group 17 halogen that is a yellow gas**. Other halogens include Chlorine (green gas), Bromine (orange liquid) and Iodine (grey solid).

48. F

Explanation:

Element X is in Group 2 since there are two electrons in its outer shell (it is an Alkaline Earth Metal) –**Statement 1** is correct. Chlorine is in Group 17 - it reacts by gaining one electron. Since Element X is in Group 2, it will lose two electrons; therefore, one atom of Element X will donate electrons to two chlorine atoms. As a result, the formula should be XCl_2 - **Statement 2** is incorrect. Element X has a valency of 2. Consequently, when it reacts with water it will produce $X(OH)_2$ – **Statement 3** is correct. The period number is the same as the number of electron shells, therefore, Element X is in Period 3 – **Statement 4** is incorrect. There are 12 electrons and 12 protons (the proton number is the same as the electron number). As a result, **Statement 5** is correct.

Chemistry (C8)	SEPARATION TECHNIQUES	Answers

49. B

Explanation:

The diagram illustrates **fractional distillation** (the only difference compared to simple distillation is the fractional column). Fractional distillation is used to separate liquids with similar boiling points. **Options 'A' and 'C' are separating water from solids** (salt or sand), therefore, **simple distillation or filtration** could be used. **Option 'D' requires chromatography** in order to assess the various substances present in the polluted water. Therefore, only **Option 'B'** would be appropriate for fractional distillation because all of the fractions would have similar boiling points.

50. D

Explanation:

Approximate the R_f of Spot '2':

$$\frac{6.5}{12} = 0.54...$$

Approximate the R_f of Spot '3':

$$\frac{1.5}{12} = 0.13....$$

Spot '4' would have the highest R_f, because it has travelled the furthest up the chromatogram during the same time period. Similarly, Spot '1' would have a R_f between Spots '2' and '3'. Considering the given options, only Option 'D' satisfies all of the criteria.

51. E

Explanation:

A more reactive halogen will displace a less reactive halide. The halogens get more reactive going down Group 17. Astatine (At) is less reactive than Bromine (Br); therefore, it cannot displace Br from its compound.

Chemistry (C9) | ACIDS, BASES AND SALTS | Answers

52. A

Explanation:

Statement 1 is the definition of a strong acid, Statement 2 is the definition of a weak acid (partially ionises in solution), Statement 3 is the definition of a dilute acid and Statement 4 is the definition of a concentrated acid. A strong acid may not necessarily be concentrated one. A strong acid indicates a low pH (number of H^+ ions present), whereas concentration refers to the amount of water added to the solution.

53. E

Explanation:

Oxides of non-metals react with water to form acidic solutions, while oxides and hydroxides of metals react with metal to form alkaline solutions. Reaction 1 contains magnesium (a metal), therefore, it will form an alkaline solution. Reaction 2 contains sulfur (a non-metal), therefore, it will form an acidic solution. Reactions 3, 5 and 6 all contain metal (Ba, Zn and Na), resulting in alkaline solutions. Reaction 4 contains nitrogen (a non-metal), which will produce an acidic solution. Therefore, Reactions 2 and 4 will produce an acidic solution.

54. E

Explanation:

The pH is a measure of the concentration of H^+ions. A change of one unit on the pH scale will change the H^+ concentration by a factor of 10. Since the pH increased from 7.3 to 8.3, there is a change of one unit and, therefore, the H^+ concentration changes by a factor of 10. The pH has increased, which makes the solution more alkaline and less acidic; as a result, the H^+ concentration would have decreased.

Chemistry (C10)	RATES OF REACTION	Answers

55. C

Explanation:

Experiment set-ups 'X' and 'Z' would be appropriate if a gas is produced. The volume of gas produced is measured in the gas syringe in Experiment X, while the difference in mass (due to gas evaporating into the environment) in Experiment Y can be recorded to measure the reaction rate. A cotton wool bud is placed over the conical flask in Y to prevent liquid spillages. **Experiment set-up 'Y' is appropriate if a precipitate is formed**. The time for the cross to disappear from view (due to the formation of a precipitate) is recorded and this can be used to determine the reaction rate. **Reaction 1** is between a metal and an acid, which always produces a salt and hydrogen. Since hydrogen gas is produced, either Experiment set-ups X or Y would be appropriate. **Reaction 2** would produce carbon dioxide gas; Experiment set-ups X or Y would be appropriate. In **Reaction 3**, hydrogen peroxide (H_2O_2) decomposes into water and oxygen gas, therefore, Experiment set-ups X or Y would be appropriate. Consider the state symbols in **Reaction 4**, which show that solid sulfur is produced (precipitate). Since no gas is produced, Experiment set-up Y would be most appropriate to calculate reaction rate.

56. E

Explanation:

An increase in **concentration, surface area or pressure** alters collision frequency since there are more particles in a given volume. These particles are more likely to collide and thus producing more successful frequent collisions. As **temperature** increases, both the collision frequency (particles have more kinetic energy and are more likely to collide above the required activation energy) and the number of particles with sufficient activation energy (since particles have increased kinetic energy, more of them will have the activation energy). A **catalyst** provides an alternative route with a lower activation energy; therefore, an increased number of particles will have the sufficient energy to react.

57. F

Explanation:

Catalysts are **not used up in a reaction** and are chemically unchanged at the end of the reaction. They do provide **an alternative route with a lower activation energy**, but they do not affect the position of equilibrium. Catalysts **increase the rate of the forward and reverse reactions equally**.

Chemistry (C11)	ENERGETICS	Answers

58. B

Explanation:

The energy level diagram indicates an **endothermic reaction** because the products are in a higher energy state than the reactants. This indicates that more energy has been taken in to form the product than to break the bonds of the reactants. **Combustion of fuels is an exothermic reaction** because it releases energy, usually in the form of heat. Similarly,

neutralisation (mixture of an acid and base) and **oxidation reactions** are also exothermic. **Melting ice** requires heat from the environment, therefore, it is an endothermic reaction.

59. A

Explanation:

Equation:

Energy change = mass x specific heat capacity x change in temperature

Consider the units of specific heat capacity, J/kg°C:

If the mass of the substance is in kg, the final answer will be in J.

Ignore the mass of butane burnt because the energy change is due to the rise in temperature of the water.

The mass must be converted from 250 cm^3 into 0.25 kg, because of the specific heat capacity units.

Energy change: 0.25 x 4180 x 40= **41800 J**

60. B

Explanation:

Bond breaking is endothermic and bond formation is exothermic. To calculate the overall energy change, the energy required to make bonds must be subtracted from the energy required to break them.

Bond breaking:

CH_4: 4 C-H bonds

$2O_2$: 2 O=O bonds (an oxygen molecule has a double bond)

Consider the bond enthalpy table:

4(400) + 2(500) = **2600**

Bond making:

CO_2: 2 C=O bonds (carbon dioxide has two double bonds)

$2H_2O$: 4 O-H bonds

Consider the bond enthalpy table:

2(800) + 4(460) = **3440**

Energy change = bonds broken - bonds made

= 2600 – 3440 = **- 840 kJmol^{-1}**

61. B

Explanation:

ΔH in exothermic reactions is negative (**Option 'A' is incorrect).**

ΔH = ∑ΔH (bonds broken) - ∑ΔH (bonds formed). In an exothermic reaction, energy is released into the surroundings. Therefore, **Option 'C' is incorrect.**

In exothermic reactions, the energy released when making the bonds is greater than the energy required to break the bonds; **Option 'D' is incorrect.** The products in the exothermic reaction are also more stable than the reactants as they have a lower energy level. As a result, **Option 'B' is the correct answer.**

62. A

Explanation:

ΔH = bonds broken – bonds made

Draw the displayed formula of the molecules to identify all the bonds:

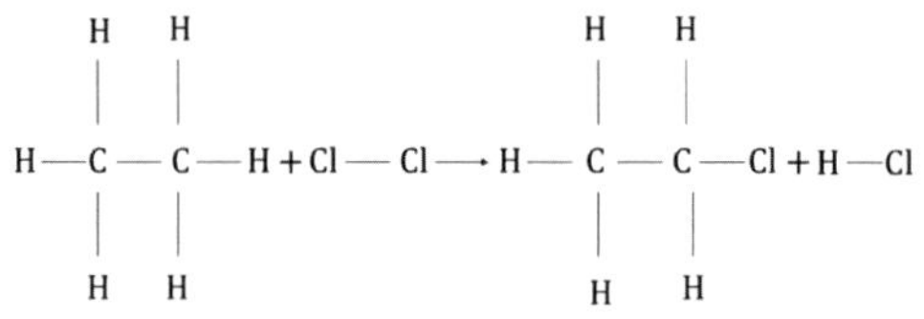

Bonds broken are:

1 x C-C = 348

6 x C-H = 6 x 413 = 2478

1 x Cl-Cl = 242

Total = 3068

Bonds made are:

1 x C-C = 348

5 x C-H = 5 x 413 = 2065

1 x C-Cl = 328

1 x H-Cl = 431

Total = 3172

ΔH:

3068 – 3172 = **- 104 kJ/mol**

Chemistry (C12) ELECTROLYSIS Answers

63. D

Explanation:

Two positive ions, Mg^{2+} and H^+ (from the solution) are attracted to the cathode. When the metal is more reactive than hydrogen (higher up in the reactivity series), hydrogen is produced. This is due to the hydrogen ions being more willing to accept electrons than a more reactive metal, such as magnesium. At the anode, oxygen is produced (from hydroxide ions), unless halide ions (chloride, bromide or iodide ions) are present. If halides are present, they lose their electrons before oxygen does in order to form the corresponding halogen.

64. G

Explanation:

Cations (positively charged ions) receive electrons from the negative charged electrode (cathode). Since they gain electrons, reduction occurs at the cathode. During the purification of copper, the anode is made of impure copper, while the cathode is made of pure copper. When current is passed through the cell, positively charged copper ions (Cu^{2+}) are pulled out of the anode into the liquid, and are attracted to the negative cathode, where they lose their positive charges and stick tightly as neutral atoms of pure copper metal. As a result, the cathode gains mass as the copper is deposited, while the anode loses mass as the copper dissolves. Similarly, in electroplating, the cathode should be the object that is electroplated, while the anode should be the metal that that will coat the object. As a result, the Statements that relate to the cathode are 1, 2 and 6.

65. C

Explanation:
The position of metals in the reactivity series determines how they are extracted. If they are more reactive than carbon, they are **extracted using electrolysis**. If they are below carbon, they are extracted by **reduction using carbon**.
Reactivity series: (from most reactive to least reactive)

I. Potassium
II. Sodium
III. Calcium
IV. Magnesium
V. Aluminium
VI. Carbon
VII. Zinc
VIII. Iron
IX. Tin
X. Lead
XI. Copper
XII. Silver
XIII. Gold
XIV. Platinum

66. B

Explanation:
When potassium sulphate is electrolysed, **hydroxide ions are discharged at the anode to form oxygen, and hydrogen ions are discharged at the cathode to form hydrogen gas.** Hydroxide ions and hydrogen ions are present in the water of the aqueous potassium sulphate solution. The electrolyte has two types of positive ions – potassium ions and hydrogen ions. Hydrogen ions gain electrons more easily compared to potassium; therefore, they are discharged at the cathode. There are two negative ions – sulphate ions and hydroxide ions. The hydroxide ions lose electrons more easily compared to the sulphate ions; this forms oxygen and water.

67. E

Explanation:
The **negative ions** in the electrolyte move to the **anode** (because it is the positive electrode). As a result, chloride ions move to the anode - they lose electrons to form chlorine gas.

Chemistry (C13) CARBON/ORGANIC CHEMISTRY Answers

68. B

Explanation:
Along decreasing carbon chain length, the **boiling points decrease** due to a reduced number of intermolecular forces required to overcome. **Viscosity also decreases** due to the reduced number of intermolecular forces present with a shorter carbon chain length. Smaller hydrocarbon chains have a **greater degree of flammability** because they have a higher proportion of carbon-hydrogen bonds compared to carbon-carbon bonds, for the same number of atoms.

69. C

Explanation:

Fractional distillation is used to separate substances with similar boiling points. Consequently, **crude oil must be heated** first in order to form a vapour. This is essential for the vapours to rise up the column and condense at its boiling point. Once heated, the crude oil **enters the fractioning column**, which has a temperature gradient to allow the different fractions to separate based on boiling point. The **vapours rise** through the column and, finally, **condense at different heights in the column**. As a result, the products are collected at **different heights within the fractioning column**.

70. E

Explanation:

Structural isomers possess the same molecular formula, but a different arrangement of atoms in space. There are three types - chain, position and functional group. Chain isomerism arises due to branching in the carbon chain (**Picture set 1 is an example**). In position isomerism, the basic carbon skeleton remains unchanged, but important groups are moved around on that skeleton. In functional group isomerism, the isomers contain different functional groups and have a different homologous series (**Picture set 4 is an example**). **Picture sets 2 and 3 are examples of stereoisomers**, the other form of isomer (differ in 3D orientation).

71. F

Explanation:

The molecular formula is **incorrect in Option 1** since the second carbon is bonded to five different groups (carbon can only form four bonds). The skeletal formula in **Option 2 is correct**; the COOH is on Carbon 1, with the alcohol (hydroxy-) group on Carbon 2. The correct molecular formula of 2-hydroxypropanoic acid is $CH_3CH(OH)COOH$ and condensing this further provides $C_3H_6O_3$; **Option 3 is correct**. **Option 4 is incorrect** because there are two COOH groups.

72. B

Explanation:

Incomplete combustion occurs when there is a reduced supply of oxygen; carbon monoxide or soot (particles of carbon) is produced rather than CO_2. **Option 'A' is incorrect** because it represents complete combustion (the products are CO_2 and H_2O). **Option 'B' is correct** since carbon monoxide and water are produced (products of incomplete combustion), and there is an equal number of carbons, hydrogens and oxygens on each side. **Options 'C' and 'D' are incorrect** due to the number of elements not being equally balanced on both sides.

73. C

Explanation:

Hexane has five structural isomers **- hexane, 2-methylpentane, 3-methylpentane, 2,2-dimethylbutane, and 2,3-dimethylbutane**. Butane has two isomers - **butane and 2-methylpropane**.

Therefore, the difference between the two alkanes is:

5 - 2 = **3**

Chemistry

74. J

Explanation:

Alkenes are more reactive than alkanes and cycloalkanes because they have a double bond. In an addition reaction, the double bond of the alkene partially breaks when the reactant molecule attacks and adds on across it. Alkenes undergo addition reactions with steam (produces an alcohol group), halogens (produces dihaloalkanes), hydrogen halides (produces haloalkanes) and hydrogen (produces alkanes). Since Option 1 is an alkane, Option 2 is a haloalkane, Option 3 is an alcohol and Option 4 is a dihaloalkane, all four can be produced from addition reactions with an alkene.

75. D

Explanation:

The monomer unit for poly(pentene) is pentene. The double bond of the monomer breaks during the addition polymerisation reaction, allowing the free bonds to form a polymer. As a result, the monomer cannot be Option 'A' due to the lack of double bonds. Option 'B' displays hexene (6 carbons) and Option 'C' has two double bonds (penta-1,3-diene). Only Option 'D' correctly illustrates pentene.

76. C

Explanation:

A polyester is produced from a dicarboxylic acid (two COOH group) and a diol (two alcohol groups). The dicarboxylic acid in the polyester has six carbons; Options 'B' and 'D' can be eliminated because the dicarboxylic acids have five carbon atoms. Water is lost between the dicarboxylic acid and the diol; one hydrogen from each end of the diol and one OH from each end of the dicarboxylic acid is combined to form the water. Therefore, Option 'A' is incorrect. Since two hydrogens are lost from the diol, the original number of hydrogens present were six (4+2=6); Option 'C' is correct.

77. C

Explanation:

A polyamide can be produced from a diamine and a dicarboxylic acid. Water is lost during the condensation process (H from each NH_2 and OH from COOH). Option 'A' is incorrect because the hydrogens lost during condensation have not been added back in (too few hydrogens present in both the diamine and the dicarboxylic acid). Option 'B' is incorrect because nitrogen has three bonds (binds to two hydrogens and a carbon) – if it binds to four, then there will be a positive charge. Option 'C' is correct because there are the correct numbers of carbon, oxygen, nitrogen and hydrogen. Option 'D' is incorrect since there are too many carbons in the diamine (seven rather than six).

78. A

Explanation:

Sodium and an alcohol forms hydrogen gas and sodium alkoxide. Options 'B' and 'D' can be eliminated since the state symbol of hydrogen shows liquid, rather than gas. Option 'C' is not balanced properly – number of sodium on each side are not equal. Option 'A' is correct because of the correct state symbols and the balanced equation.

79. B

Explanation:

Molecule X partially ionises in solution – indicates presence of a weak acid (due to a reversible reaction). Decolourisation of bromine illustrates presence of carbon-carbon double bond (addition reactions of alkenes). If a white precipitate is formed when an aqueous solution of silver nitrate is added in the presence of dilute nitric acid, it indicates the presence of chlorine ions. **Option 'A' does not have a weak acid present, Option 'C' does not have a double bond present between two carbons and Option 'D' does not have chlorine ions (has bromine ions instead).** Only **Option 'B' has all three characteristics** (the carbon double bond is between the second and the third carbon).

80. B

Explanation:

For addition polymerisation to occur, there must be a **double bond between the carbon-carbon atoms**. All of the options except **Molecules 3 and 5** have a double bond. Molecules 3 and 5 are alkanes (they are saturated); therefore, they cannot undergo addition polymerisation.

81. B

Explanation:

The ester shown is **propyl methanoate**. If the ester bond in the compound is broken, the alcohol it is made from is **C_3H_7OH** (propanol), and the carboxylic acid is **methanoic acid**.

82. D

Explanation:

The functional groups in aspirin consists of **carboxylic acids and esters**. The double bonds in the ring are not showing an alkene - the hexagonal structure represents benzene.

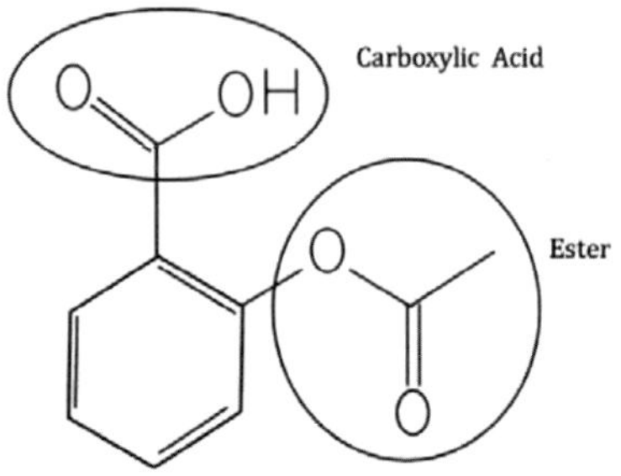

83. A

Explanation:

Draw the structure of the molecule:

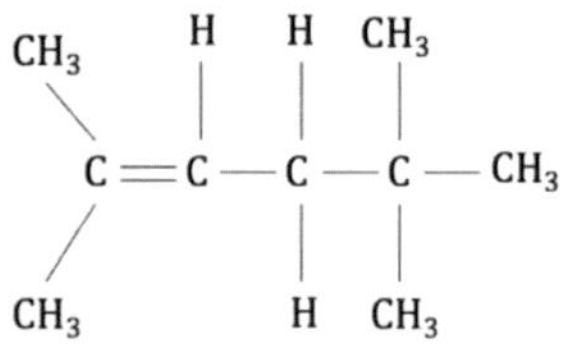

From the diagram, the functional group present is an **alkene group**. The test for alkenes uses orange bromine water (a positive result is indicated by the orange bromine water turning colourless).

A Lakshmi, T R Enoch, S Z Y Ooi. Doctors Academy Publications, Cardiff, UK, 2020.

84. D

Explanation:

Isomers have the **<u>same molecular formula but different arrangement of atoms</u>** (different structural formula).

Consider the molecular formula of each of the four compounds:

Compound 1 is **C_5H_{10}.**

Compound 2 is **C_6H_{12}.**

Compound 3 is **C_6H_{12}.**

Compound 4 is **C_6H_{14}.**

Therefore, **Compounds 2 and 3** are isomers as they both have the same molecular formulae (C_6H_{12}).

85. B

Explanation:

Identify the repeating unit of the polymer:

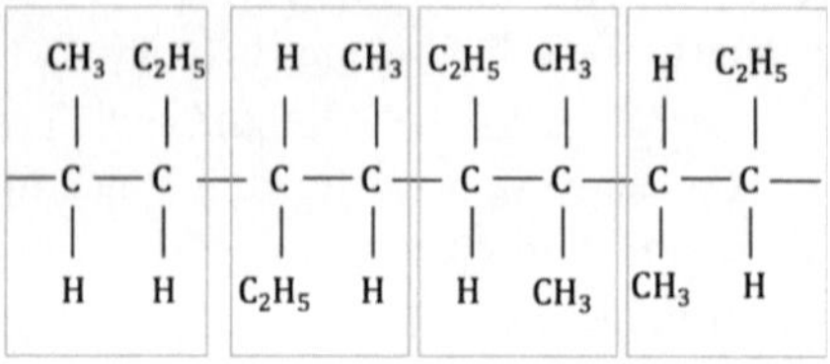

Secondly, add a double bond to the repeating unit to find the structure of the monomer:

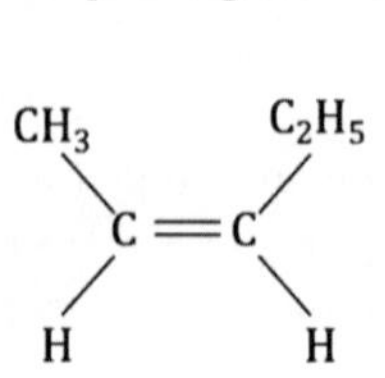

Therefore, the monomer is **Pent-2-ene (Option 'B').**

Chemistry (C14)	METALS	Answers

86. C

Explanation:

In a displacement reaction, a more reactive metal will displace a less reactive metal from its compounds. Displacement reactions are easily seen when a salt of the less reactive metal is in the solution. During the reaction, the more reactive metal gradually disappears as it forms a solution and the less reactive metal coats the surface of the more reactive metal. **Metal X is more reactive than Metal Y** since it displaces Metal Y in the sulfate solution (disappearing as it forms the sulfate solution). **Metal Z is more reactive than Metal Y** because Metal Y becomes displaced from the sulfate solution (therefore, it coats the surface of Metal Z). **Metal Z is more reactive than Metal X** since it displaces Metal X in the sulfate solution (disappearing as it forms the sulfate solution).

87. A

Explanation:

The range of properties that metals possess allow them to be used for a variety of purposes. Due to the **low density of aluminium**, **high thermal conductivity** and the **protection of a natural layer of aluminium oxide** that allows the metal to resist corrosion, it is the best metal for vessels, such as ships and aeroplanes. Iron can be combined with **carbon** (mild steel that is malleable and ductile), **tungsten** (tool steel that is hard and resistant to high temperatures) or chromium (stainless steel that is hard and resistant to rusting) in order to provide increased strength for infrastructure, such as bridges. An alloy is stronger than the pure element due to **distorted layers in the lattice**, which makes it harder for layers of atoms to slide past one another. Copper alloys include **bronze (copper and tin), brass (copper and zinc) and cupronickel (copper and nickel)**.

88. F

Explanation:

Aluminium is a **transition metal**, whilst magnesium is a **Group 2 metal**. Therefore, the only differences in properties will be the ones that are characteristic of transition metals – **forming coloured compounds, use as catalysts and forming stable ions in different oxidation states**. These characteristics are due to an incomplete sub-shell of electrons (d orbital), resulting in variable oxidation states, which allows electrons to jump between orbitals. The energy absorbed when an electron jumps from a lower energy orbital to a higher one corresponds to the frequency of light observed, which mostly lies in visible region.

89. D

Explanation:

Transition metals possess many unique characteristics - **they can form coloured compounds, be used as catalysts and can form stable ions in different oxidation states**. Since these metals can form stable complexes, **Option 'D'** is the correct answer.

90. A

Explanation:

A reaction between **nitrogen monoxide and carbon monoxide** occurs on a catalyst surface in order to form **nitrogen and carbon dioxide**. Rhodium is the best metal to use in a catalytic converter - **Option 'A' is the correct answer.**

Chemistry (C15) KINETIC/PARTICLE THEORY Answers

91. B

Explanation:

Firstly, converting -243 °C and -208 °C into Kelvin by adding 273:

This produces 30K and 65K respectively.

Since **56K is below the melting point of 63K**, nitrogen will be a solid. **A temperature of 80K is above the boiling point of 76K**, indicating that nitrogen is a gas at this temperature. **The temperature of 30 K is also below 63K**, demonstrating that nitrogen is a solid, but **65K is between the melting and boiling point**, indicating that nitrogen would be a liquid.

Chemistry

Chemistry (C16)	CHEMICAL TESTS	Answers

92. B

Explanation:
From sodium chloride, the chlorine negative ion (anion) will be attracted to the anode, **producing chlorine gas**. There are two positive ions (cations) – Na^+ and H^+. Since sodium is more reactive than hydrogen, **hydrogen gas is produced** at the cathode. This is due to the hydrogen ions being more willing to accept electrons than a more reactive metal, such as sodium. The test for hydrogen is a **'squeaky pop'** when a burning splint is held at the open end of a test tube) and the test for chlorine is **damp blue litmus paper turning red**, before being bleached to white.

93. C

Explanation:
A white precipitate when aqueous sodium hydroxide is added indicates the presence of either **Al^{3+}, Ca^{2+} or Mg^{2+} ions**. A green precipitate when aqueous sodium hydroxide is added indicates the presence of **Fe^{2+} ions**. The precipitates for **halides get darker going down the group** (chlorine-white, bromine-cream, iodine-yellow). **Sulfates form a white precipitate** when an aqueous solution of barium chloride is added in the presence of dilute hydrochloric acid. **Effervescence (fizzing)** in the presence of an acid indicates the presence of a carbonate.

94. B

Explanation:
These flame tests must be learnt from the BMAT specification **(page 333)**. If an atom or ion is excited by strong heating, electrons can be promoted from their normal unexcited state into higher orbitals. As they fall back down to lower levels (either in one go or in several steps), energy is released as light. Each of these jumps involves a specific amount of energy being released as light energy, and each corresponds to a particular wavelength (or frequency). As a result of all these jumps, a spectrum of lines will be produced, some of which will be in the visible part of the spectrum. The colour seen will be a combination of all these individual colours.

95. D

Explanation:
Option 'D' illustrates the test for ammonia. **Option 'A'** is the test for oxygen **Option 'B'** is the test for hydrogen, **Option 'C'** is the test for carbon dioxide and **Option 'E'** is the test for chlorine.

96. E

Explanation:
Cations 1, 2 and 3 form a **white precipitate** with aqueous sodium hydroxide. The Cu^{2+} ion forms a **blue precipitate**, the Fe^{2+} ion forms a **green precipitate** and the Fe^{3+} ion forms a **brown precipitate**.

97. A

Explanation:
Water from combustion **condenses in the U tube**. Cobalt chloride paper can also be used to test for water, but the correct colour change is **blue to pink**.

Chemistry

Chemistry (C17)	AIR AND WATER	Answers

98. D

Explanation:

Nitrogen is the most abundant gas in the atmosphere because it is a noble gas, and, therefore, is unreactive. **Oxygen** is the next abundant, at 21%, in order for respiration to occur. **Carbon dioxide** (required for photosynthesis) is present in smaller quantities than the noble gas **argon**, which is also relatively inert. This is because carbon dioxide could be poisonous in larger amounts.

99. F

Explanation:

CFCs are compounds of **chlorine, fluorine and carbon**. They are **inert, have a low boiling point and are insoluble in water**. One CFC molecule can cause the **loss of many ozone molecules** and CFCs remains in the stratosphere for **a long time** as they are **very unreactive**.

100. H

Explanation:

When temporary hard water is boiled, the calcium hydrogencarbonate undergoes **thermal decomposition**.

Calcium hydrogencarbonate → carbon dioxide + water + calcium carbonate

The gas produced is **carbon dioxide** and the precipitate is **calcium carbonate**.

Mathematics (M1)	UNITS	Specification

Topic	Objective	☺	😐	☹
M1.1	- Use standard units of mass, length, time, money and other measures. - Use compound units such as speed, rates of pay, unit pricing, density and pressure, including using decimal quantities where appropriate.			
M1.2	- Change freely between related standard units (e.g., time, length, area, volume/capacity, mass) and compound units (e.g., speed, rates of pay, prices, density, pressure) in numerical and algebraic contexts.			

Mathematics (M1)	UNITS	Questions

1. **A student invests £200 in a savings account which pays 6% interest per annum. How much money will be in her account after 3 years?**
   A. £166.12
   B. £212.00
   C. £236.00
   D. £238.20
   E. £252.49

2. **How many degrees does the hour hand of a clock change from 02:00 to 03:45 hours?**
   A. 22.5°
   B. 30°
   C. 52.5°
   D. 60°
   E. 630°

Mathematics (M2)	NUMBER	Specification

Topic	Objective	☺	😐	☹
M2.1	- Order positive and negative integers, decimals and fractions. Understand and use the symbols: $=, \neq, <, >, \leq, \geq$.			
M2.2	- Apply the four operations (addition, subtraction, multiplication and division) to integers, decimals, simple fractions (proper and improper) and mixed numbers – any of which could be positive and negative. - Understand and use place value.			
M2.3	- Use the concepts and vocabulary of prime numbers, factors (divisors), multiples, common factors, common multiples, highest common factor, lowest common multiple, and prime factorisation (including use of product notation and the unique factorisation theorem).			
M2.4	- Recognise and use relationships between operations, including inverse operations. Use cancellation to simplify calculations and expressions. - Understand and use the convention for priority of operations, including brackets, powers, roots and reciprocals.			
M2.5	- Apply systematic listing strategies. (For instance, if there are m ways of doing one task and for each of these tasks there are n ways of doing another task, then the total number of ways the two tasks can be done in order is $m \times n$ ways.)			
M2.6	- Use and understand the terms: square, positive and negative square root, cube and cube root.			
M2.7	- Use index laws to simplify numerical expressions, and for multiplication and division of integer, fractional and negative powers.			
M2.8	- Interpret, order and calculate with numbers written in standard index form (standard form); numbers are written in standard form as $a \times 10^n$, where $1 \leq a < 10$ and n is an integer.			
M2.9	- Convert between terminating decimals, percentages and fractions. Convert between recurring decimals and their corresponding fractions.			

M2.10	- Use fractions, decimals and percentages interchangeably in calculations. Understand equivalent fractions.			
M2.11	- Calculate exactly with fractions, surds and multiples of π. - Simplify surd expressions involving squares, e.g. $\sqrt{12} = \sqrt{4 \times 3} = \sqrt{4}\sqrt{3} = 2\sqrt{3}$ and rationalise denominators; for example, candidates could be asked to rationalise expressions such as: $\frac{3}{\sqrt{7}}, \frac{5}{3+2\sqrt{5}}, \frac{7}{2-\sqrt{3}}, \frac{3}{\sqrt{5}-\sqrt{2}}$.			
M2.12	- Calculate with upper and lower bounds and use in contextual problems.			
M2.13	- Round numbers and measures to an appropriate degree of accuracy, e.g. to a specified number of decimal places or significant figures. - Use inequality notation to specify simple error intervals due to truncation or rounding.			
M2.14	- Use approximation to produce estimates of calculations, including expressions involving π or surds.			

Mathematics (M2) NUMBER Questions

3. The symbol ¤ defines a binary operation such that $r ¤ s = rs/s^r$ for all positive integers. What is the value of (2 ¤ 4) ¤ 2?

A. $\frac{1}{\sqrt{2}}$

B. $\frac{8}{3}$

C. 1

D. $2\sqrt{9}$

E. $\frac{\sqrt{3}}{7}$

4. Evaluate:

$$\sqrt{\frac{3 \times 10^4 + 6 \times 10^3}{\frac{53400}{267} + \frac{27000}{15}}}$$

A. 18

B. $\frac{3\sqrt{5}}{2}$

C. $2\sqrt{9}$

D. $\sqrt{2}$

E. $\sqrt{38}$

F. $3\sqrt{2}$

G. $\sqrt{29}$

Mathematics

5. **Which one of the following is equivalent to $\frac{2}{1+\frac{1}{\sqrt{5}}}$?**

A. $\frac{5+\sqrt{5}}{2}$

B. $\frac{5-\sqrt{5}}{2}$

C. $\frac{10-\sqrt{5}}{4}$

D. $\frac{5+\sqrt{10}}{4}$

E. $\frac{5-\sqrt{10}}{4}$

F. $\frac{10-\sqrt{5}}{4}$

---

6. **Evaluate:**

$$\sqrt[3]{\frac{(0.9 \text{ x } 10^6)(12 \text{ x } 10^2)}{\frac{4}{100}}} - \sqrt{(1.25 \text{ x } 10^3)(5 \text{ x } 10^3)} + \sqrt{(3 \text{ x } 10^3) + (6 \text{ x } 10^2)}$$

A. 3500
B. 2500
C. 550
D. 560
E. 2758
F. 460

---

7. **Which one of the following is equivalent to $(\sqrt{8} - 6)^3$?**

A. $115\sqrt{8}$ -360
B. $116\sqrt{2}$ -330
C. $232\sqrt{2}$ -360
D. $230\sqrt{2}$ -330
E. $232\sqrt{8}$ -360
F. $232\sqrt{8}$ -330

---

8. **Evaluate:**

$$\frac{4}{\sqrt{8}+3\sqrt{2}} + \frac{3}{3\sqrt{2}-\sqrt{8}}$$

A. $19\sqrt{2}$

B. $\frac{18\sqrt{8}}{10}$

C. $\frac{19\sqrt{6}}{10}$

D. $\frac{19\sqrt{2}}{6}$

E. $\frac{19\sqrt{2}}{10}$

F. $\frac{19\sqrt{2}}{8}$

Mathematics

9. 'P' represents a geometric sequence.
   Given that $(2\sqrt{x} - 3)$, 3 and $(2\sqrt{x} + 3)$ are the first three terms of 'P', what is the value of x?
   A. 0.5
   B. 1.0
   C. 1.5
   D. 2.5
   E. 3.5
   F. 4.5
   G. 5.5

---

10. Evaluate:
   $9(0.\dot{5}\dot{2} - 0.\dot{3})$
   A. $\frac{19}{11}$
   B. $\frac{9}{11}$
   C. $\frac{19}{99}$
   D. $\frac{19}{9}$
   E. $\frac{9}{19}$
   F. $\frac{9}{99}$

---

11. $'x'$ is a positive integer, where 360 and 1500 are both divisors of $'x'$.
   If $x = 2^a \times 3^b \times 5^c$, where a, b and c are positive integers, what is the least possible value of a x b x c?
   A. 6
   B. 8
   C. 18
   D. 30
   E. 36
   F. 49

---

12. What is the smallest possible integer of $'y'$ such that 39375 multiplied by 'y' is a perfect square?
   A. 2
   B. 3
   C. 4
   D. 5
   E. 7
   F. 9

---

13. Rationalise $\frac{3}{4+\sqrt{7}}$, giving the answer in its simplest form.
   A. $\frac{(4+\sqrt{7})}{3}$
   B. $\frac{(4-\sqrt{7})}{3}$

Mathematics

C. $\frac{(12-3\sqrt{7})}{9}$

D. $\frac{(4-3\sqrt{7})}{3}$

E. $\frac{(12+3\sqrt{7})}{23}$

14. Solve:

$8 - \frac{6(x+3)}{2x-4} = 2$

A. 4
B. 7
C. 8
D. 14
E. 17

15. Solve the inequality: $x^2 > 4x - 3$

A. $x > 1 \; and \; x > 3$
B. $x < 1 \; and \; x < 3$
C. $x < 1 \; and \; x > 3$
D. $x > 1 \; and \; x < 3$
E. $x = 1 \; and \; x = 3$

16. Evaluate $3125^{\frac{3}{5}}$

A. 5
B. 25
C. 125
D. 225
E. 625

17. In the equation $\sqrt{2} + \sqrt{32} + \sqrt{8} = \sqrt{x}$ where $'x'$ is a positive integer. What is the value of $'x'$?

A. 28
B. 36
C. 42
D. 58
E. 72
F. 98
G. 128
H. 269

18. Write 300^2 as a product of its prime factors.

A. $2^2 \text{ x } 3 \text{ x } 5^2$
B. $2^3 \text{ x } 3 \text{ x } 5^2$
C. $2 \text{ x } 3^2 \text{ x } 5^2$
D. $2^2 \text{ x } 3^2 \text{ x } 5$
E. $2^4 \text{ x } 3^2 \text{ x } 5^4$

19. If $\frac{990 \text{ x } 10^A}{3 \text{ x } 10^B} \text{ x } 2 \text{ x } 10^C = 6.6 \text{ x } 10^{-6}$, what is A – B + C equal to?

A. -8
B. -6

Mathematics

C. -3
D. 2
E. 7

20. Evaluate:

$(\sqrt{17} - \sqrt{21})^2 (\sqrt{17} + \sqrt{21})^2$

A. 2
B. 4
C. 16
D. 152
E. $38 - 2\sqrt{357}$
F. $38 + 2\sqrt{357}$

21. Evaluate $2(2\sqrt{7} + 3\sqrt{13})^2 + 1$

A. 290
B. 291
C. $145 + 12\sqrt{91}$
D. $146 + 12\sqrt{91}$
E. $290 + 24\sqrt{91}$
F. $291 + 24\sqrt{91}$

22. Express $512^5 \times 2^{18}$ **in the form** 8^n

A. 8^{17}
B. 8^{21}
C. 8^{23}
D. 8^{24}
E. 8^{26}

Mathematics (M3) RATIO AND PROPORTION Specification

Topic	Objective	☺	😐	☹
M3.1	- Understand and use scale factors, scale diagrams and maps.			
M3.2	- Express a quantity as a fraction of another, where the fraction is less than 1 or greater than 1.			
M3.3	- Understand and use ratio notation.			
M3.4	- Divide a given quantity into two (or more) parts in a given *part: part* ratio. Express the division of a quantity into two parts as a ratio.			
M3.5	- Apply ratio to real contexts and problems, such as those involving conversion, comparison, scaling, mixing and concentrations. - Express a multiplicative relationship between two quantities as a ratio or a fraction.			

M3.6	- Understand and use proportion. - Relate ratios to fractions and to linear functions.			
M3.7	- Identify and work with fractions in ratio problems.			
M3.8	- Define percentage as 'number of parts per hundred'. - Interpret percentages and percentage changes as a fraction or a decimal, and interpret these multiplicatively. - Express one quantity as a percentage of another. - Compare two quantities using percentages. - Work with percentages greater than 100%. - Solve problems involving percentage change, including percentage increase/decrease, original value and simple interest calculations			
M3.9	- Understand and use direct and inverse proportion, including algebraic representations. Recognise and interpret graphs that illustrate direct and inverse proportion. - Set up, use and interpret equations to solve problems involving direct and inverse proportion (including questions involving integer and fractional powers). - Understand that x is inversely proportional to y is equivalent to x is proportional to $\frac{1}{y}$			
M3.10	- Compare lengths, areas and volumes using ratio notation. - Understand and make links to similarity (including trigonometric ratios) and scale factors.			
M3.11	- Set up, solve and interpret the answers in growth and decay problems, including compound interest, and work with general iterative processes.			

Mathematics (M3) RATIO AND PROPORTION Questions

23. The ratio of girls to boys in a class is 5:19. When 23 boys are added, the ratio becomes 10:61. What is the total number of children in the class after the boys are added?

A. 10
B. 18
C. 23
D. 48
E. 63
F. 71
G. 83
H. 92

24. Jenny collected money for charity from her cupcake sales. At the end of the year, the total collected was divided among three charities, 'X', 'Y' and 'Z' in the ratio $1:\frac{3}{5}:\frac{5}{6}$. Charity 'Z' received £1200.
What was the total amount collected for charity during the year?
A. £2154
B. £2304
C. £2920
D. £3504
E. £3620
F. £4554

25. An ice-cream shop sells only three different flavours – chocolate, strawberry and vanilla. The ratio of vanilla to strawberry is 2 : 1.6. The ratio of strawberry to chocolate is 9.6 : 8. Assuming that there are the least number of ice creams available in the shop, what is the probability of choosing one chocolate ice cream?
A. $\frac{2}{5}$
B. $\frac{10}{37}$
C. $\frac{15}{37}$
D. $\frac{48}{100}$
E. $\frac{1}{5}$
F. $\frac{5}{11}$

26. A bag contains red, yellow and blue marbles. The bag contains equal numbers of red and blue marbles. Joseph takes out 5 red, 15 yellow and 25 blue marbles from the bag. The ratio of red to yellow marbles remaining in the bag is 15 : 8. The ratio of yellow to blue marbles remaining in the bag is 4 : 5.
How many marbles were originally in the bag?
A. 45
B. 130
C. 94
D. 112
E. 177
F. 224

27. Four people share some money. Alice and Becky share their money in the ratio 2 : 3. Carlos and Darcy share five times as much money as Alice and Becky share. Alice and Becky share their money in the ratio 7 : 8.
What is the minimum amount of money that the four people share?
A. £5
B. £10
C. £15
D. £20
E. £25
F. £30
G. £35

Mathematics

28. The ratio of pupils in three schools 'A', 'B' and 'C' is $1 : \frac{2}{7} : \frac{4}{5}$
School 'B' has 420 students.
What is the total number of pupils in all the three schools?
A. 636
B. 1176
C. 1470
D. 2646
E. 3066

29. 'X' is inversely proportional to the cube root of 'Y'. When 'X' is 2, 'Y' is 512.
Find the value of 'Y' when 'X' is 8.
A. 4
B. 8
C. 16
D. 64
E. 512

30. Emily buys red and white paint in the ratio of 3:2. Each litre of red paint costs £5.46 and each litre of white paint costs £3.21. Emily bought 18 litres of red paint.
How much did she spend in total on paint?
A. £38.52
B. £98.28
C. £123.30
D. £136.80
E. £156.40

31. The area of a field is in the ratio 8:15. The length of its diagonal is 102 m.
What is the area of the field?
A. 2304 m^2
B. 4320 m^2
C. 4890 m^2
D. 9180 m^2
E. 10404 m^2

32. The vertices of the two shaded triangles that are inscribed within the square bisect its sides. Find the ratio of the area of the large square to the area of one of the shaded triangles.

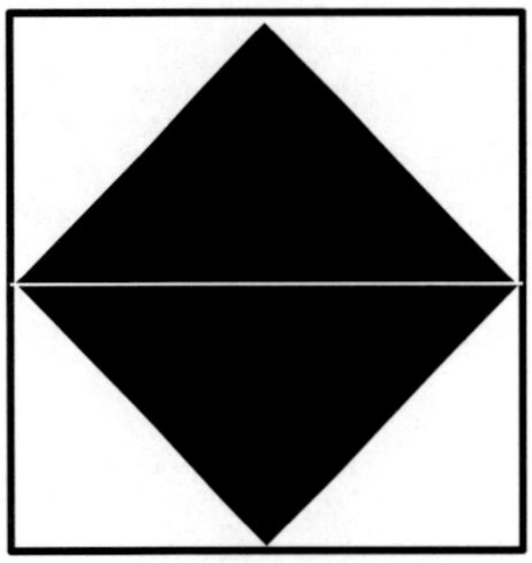

A. 2 : 1
B. 3 : 1
C. 4 : 1
D. 3 : 2
E. 4 : 3
F. 7 : 5

33. The ratio of boys to girls in a school with 756 students is 11:17. How many more girls are there compared to boys?
A. 27
B. 162

Mathematics

C. 168
D. 297
E. 459

Mathematics (M4)	ALGEBRA	Specification

Topic	Objective	☺	😐	☹
M4.1	- Understand, use and interpret algebraic notation; for instance: o ab in place of a × b ; 3y in place of y + y + y and 3× y; a^2 in place of a × a; a^3 in place of a × a × a; a^2b in place of a × a × b; $\frac{a}{b}$ in place of a÷b.			
M4.2	- Use index laws in algebra for multiplication and division of integer, fractional, and negative powers.			
M4.3	- Substitute numerical values into formulae and expressions, including scientific formulae.			
M4.4	- Collect like terms, multiply a single term over a bracket, take out common factors, and expand products of two or more binomials.			
M4.5	- Factorise quadratic expressions of the form x^2+bx+c, including the difference of two squares.			
M4.6	- Simplify expressions involving sums, products and powers, including the laws of indices. - Simplify rational expressions by cancelling or factorising and cancelling. - Use the four rules on algebraic rational expressions.			
M4.7	- Rearrange formulae to change the subject.			
M4.8	- Understand the difference between an equation and an identity. - Argue mathematically to show that algebraic expressions are equivalent.			
M4.9	- Work with coordinates in all four quadrants.			
M4.10	- Identify and interpret gradients and intercepts of linear functions $(y = mx + c)$ graphically and algebraically. - Identify pairs of parallel lines and identify pairs of perpendicular lines, including the relationships between gradients. - Find the equation of the line through two given points, or through one point with a given gradient.			

M4.11	- Identify and interpret roots, intercepts and turning points of quadratic functions graphically. - Deduce roots algebraically, and turning points by completing the square.			
M4.12	- Recognise, sketch and interpret graphs of: o linear functions o quadratic functions o simple cubic functions o the reciprocal function: $y = \frac{1}{x}$ with $x \neq 0$ o the exponential function: y = k for positive values of k o trigonometric functions (with arguments in degrees): $y = \sin x$, $y = \cos x$, $y = \tan x$ for angles of any size			
M4.13	- Interpret graphs (including reciprocal graphs and exponential graphs) and graphs of non-standard functions in real contexts to find approximate solutions to problems, such as simple kinematic problems involving distance, speed and acceleration.			
M4.14	- Calculate or estimate gradients of graphs and areas under graphs (including quadratic and other non-linear graphs), and interpret results in cases such as distance–time graphs, speed–time graphs and graphs in financial contexts.			
M4.15	- Set up and solve, both algebraically and graphically, simple equations including simultaneous equations involving two unknowns; this may include one linear and one quadratic equation. Solve two simultaneous equations in two variables (linear/linear or linear/quadratic) algebraically. - Find approximate solutions using a graph. - Translate simple situations or procedures into algebraic expressions or formulae; for example, derive an equation (or two simultaneous equations), solve the equation(s) and interpret the solution.			
M4.16	- Solve quadratic equations (including those that require rearrangement) algebraically by factorising, by completing the square, and by using the quadratic formula. - Know the quadratic formula $x = \frac{-b \pm \sqrt{b^2 - 4ac}}{2a}$ - Find approximate solutions of quadratic equations using a graph			
M4.17	- Solve linear inequalities in one or two variables. - Represent the solution set on a number line, or on a graph, or in words.			
M4.18	- Generate terms of a sequence using term-to-term or position-to-term rules.			
M4.19	- Deduce expressions to calculate the nth term of linear or quadratic sequences.			

Mathematics (M4)	ALGEBRA	Questions

34. The average weight of a group of girls is 50 kgs. After a girl weighing 58 kgs joins the group, the average weight of the group goes up by 1 kg.
What is the total number of girls in the group after the new girl was added?
A. 5
B. 6
C. 7
D. 8
E. 9
F. 10

35. Rearrange the formula $\frac{x}{y} = \frac{q}{r} + \frac{s}{t}$ to make 't' the subject:

A. $t = \frac{qry}{qx-sy}$
B. $t = \frac{sqy}{qx-sy}$
C. $t = \frac{sqy}{qx}$
D. $t = \frac{qy+sy}{rx}$
E. $t = \frac{qy+ty-rx}{x}$
F. $t = \frac{rsy}{rx-qy}$

36. Simplify:
$\frac{4x+5}{4x-5} + \frac{4x-5}{4x+5} - 3$

A. 0
B. $\frac{2(4x-5)}{(4x+5)(4x-5)}$
C. $\frac{16x^2}{(4x+5)(4x-5)}$
D. $\frac{8x-125}{(4x+5)(4x-5)}$
E. $\frac{-16x^2+125}{(4x+5)(4x-5)}$
F. $\frac{12}{4x-5}$

37. The equation gives 'y' in terms of 'x'.
$y = 6(\frac{x}{3} - 5)^2 + 12$
Rearrange the equation to give an expression for 'x' in terms of 'y'.

A. $\frac{\pm 3\sqrt{y-12}}{\sqrt{6}} + 15$

Mathematics

B. $\frac{\pm 3\sqrt{y-12}}{\sqrt{6}} - 15$

C. $\frac{\pm 3\sqrt{y+12}}{\sqrt{6}} + 15$

D. $\frac{\pm 3\sqrt{y-72}}{\sqrt{6}}$ - 15

E. $\frac{\pm 3\sqrt{y-12}}{\sqrt{6}} + 5$

38. Simplify:

$4x\ (2\ x^{-1/5})^5$

A. $\frac{1}{10}$

B. 128

C. 1

D. $\frac{1}{128}$

E. x^2

F. $128x^2$

39. The graphs of the following equations are drawn:

1. y= $2x$ -1
2. y= $x^2 + 5x$
3. y= $x^2 + 6x + 4$
4. y= -4

Which pairs of graphs do not intersect?

A. 1 and 2

B. 1 and 3

C. 2 and 3

D. 2 and 4

E. 3 and 4

40. The mean time for running a race by a group of 30 people was 47 seconds. The mean speed for these people was 6 ms^{-1}. The mean distance for a second group of people was added and the value of the mean increased by 10 metres.

Which formula represents the relationship between the number of people in the second group, 'P', and the mean distance of the second group, 'D'?

A. P= $\frac{300}{D-292}$

B. P= $\frac{300}{D-282}$

C. P= $\frac{8460}{D-282}$

D. P= $\frac{8460}{D-292}$

E. P= $\frac{8460}{D-282}$ - 30

Mathematics

41. Given that a= 1.6 x 10^5 and b=4 x 10^4, what is the value of $\frac{\sqrt{a} \text{ x } 3b}{5b\sqrt{a}}$?

A. $\frac{3}{8}$
B. $\frac{1}{2}$
C. $\frac{3}{5}$
D. $\frac{10}{7}$
E. $\frac{30}{6}$

42. Simplify:

$8 - \frac{x^4(1-36x^2)}{(6x+1)(4x^5)}$

A. $\frac{26x-1}{4x}$
B. $\frac{38x+1}{4x}$
C. $\frac{26x-1}{2x}$
D. $\frac{26x+1}{4x}$
E. $\frac{38x-1}{4x}$

43. Which one of the following is a simplification of $\frac{1.6\,x^{-5}y^5}{12.8\,x^{-3}y^8}$?

A. $\frac{1}{8}x^{-2}y^{-3}$
B. $\frac{1}{8}x^2y^3$
C. $\frac{3}{8}x^{-2}y^{-3}$
D. $\frac{3}{8}x^{-8}y^{-3}$
E. $\frac{3}{8}x^2y^3$
F. $8x^2y^3$
G. $8x^{-8}y^3$

44. A shop has £10225 in its till. The till only has £5, £10 and £50 notes. It has 25 more £20 notes compared to £5 notes, and four times as many £50 notes compared to £20 notes. How many notes are there altogether in the till?

A. 137
B. 182
C. 203
D. 238
E. 251
F. 306

Mathematics

45. **Which of the following is a simplification of $\frac{x}{x+2}$ - $\frac{(x+4)^2}{2x^2+3x-20}$?**

A. $\frac{x^2-9x-8}{x^2-x+10}$

B. $\frac{x^2-11x-8}{2x^2-x-10}$

C. $\frac{x^2+8x-11}{2x^2+x-10}$

D. $\frac{x^2+11x+8}{x^2-x-10}$

E. $\frac{x^2-10x-8}{2x^2+x+10}$

F. $\frac{3x^2+x-8}{2x^2-x-10}$

46. **Using the formula $x = y^3z^2$:**

Calculate the value of 'z' when:

$x = 3.2 \times 10^7$

$y = 2.0 \times 10^2$

A. 2

B. 4

C. 6

D. 200

E. 400

47. **The curve y = f(x) is transformed to y = f(x-3) + 5. Describe this transformation.**

A. Vertical translation of 5 units up and a horizontal translation of 3 units right.

B. Vertical translation of 5 units down and a horizontal translation of 3 units right.

C. Vertical translation of 5 units up and a horizontal translation of 3 units left.

D. Vertical translation of 5 units down and a horizontal translation of 3 units left.

48. **Simplify:**

$\frac{a^8 \times a^6}{\sqrt{a^4}} \div a^{\frac{1}{2}}$

A. a^{12}

B. $a^{\frac{9}{2}}$

C. $a^{\frac{19}{2}}$

D. $a^{\frac{23}{2}}$

E. $a^{\frac{13}{2}}$

Mathematics

49. What is the equation of the graph shown below?

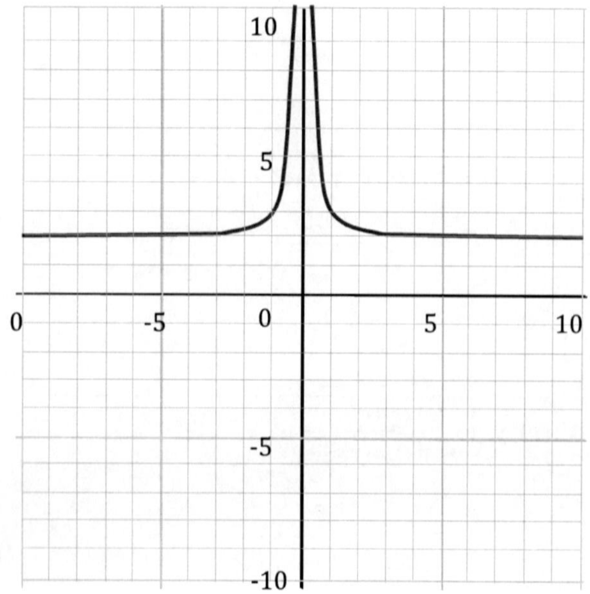

A. $y = \frac{1}{x}$

B. $y = \frac{1}{x} + 2$

C. $y = \frac{1}{x^2}$

D. $y = \frac{1}{x^2} + 2$

E. $y = \frac{1}{x^3}$

F. $y = \frac{1}{x^3} + 2$

G. $y = 2x$

50. Consider the graph below.

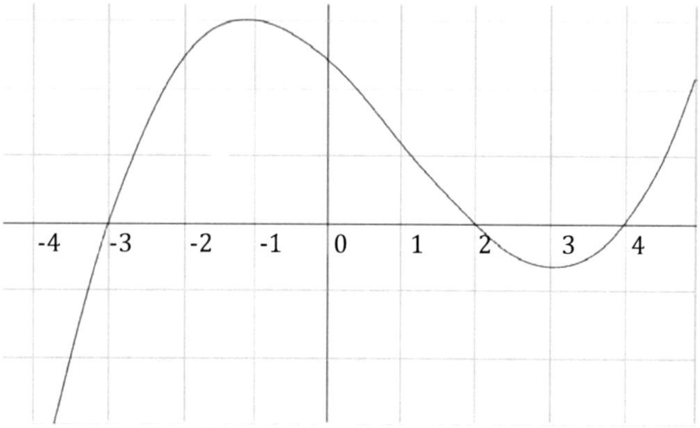

What are the coordinates of the point where the curve crosses $x=1$?

A. (1, 6)
B. (6, 1)
C. (1, 12)
D. (12, 1)
E. (1, -30)

51. **What is the minimum point of the curve $y = x^2 - 8x + 24$?**

A. (0, 24)
B. (4, 8)
C. (-4, 8)
D. (4, 16)
E. (4, 24)
F. (-4, 24)

52. **Simplify the fraction fully: $\frac{42b^2 x\, ab}{24a^3 \div (16a - 12a)}$**

A. 7b³
B. $\frac{7b^3}{a}$
C. $\frac{7b^3}{6a}$
D. $\frac{7b^2}{a}$
E. $\frac{7b^2}{6}$

53. **Rearrange $\frac{8}{\frac{x}{7}-6} - 6 = 18y$ to make $'x'$ the subject:**

A. $x = 7\left(\frac{4}{8y+3}\right) + 42$
B. $x = 7\left(\frac{8}{9y+3} + 42\right)$
C. $x = 7\left(\frac{4}{8y+3}\right) + 6$
D. $x = 7\left(\frac{4}{8y+3} + 6\right)$
E. $x = 7\left(\frac{4}{9y+3}\right) + 6$
F. $x = 7\left(\frac{4}{9y+3} + 6\right)$

54. **Simplify $\frac{2x^2+4x-6}{x^2+5x+6}$:**

A. $\frac{2(x-1)}{(x+2)}$
B. $\frac{(2x-1)}{(x+2)}$
C. $\frac{(2x-1)(2x+3)}{(x+2)(x+3)}$
D. $\frac{2(x-1)}{(x+3)}$
E. $\frac{2(x+1)}{(x+2)}$

Mathematics

F. $\frac{2(x-1)}{(x-2)}$

---

55. Write $\frac{3}{x}+\frac{7}{y}$ as a single fraction:

A. $\frac{10}{xy}$

B. $\frac{10}{x+y}$

C. $\frac{3y+7x}{x+y}$

D. $\frac{3x+7y}{x+y}$

E. $\frac{3y+7x}{xy}$

F. $\frac{3x+7y}{xy}$

---

56. Find the range for the function $f(x) = x^2 + 2x - 9$:

A. $f(x) \geq 9$
B. $f(x) \geq -9$
C. $f(x) \leq 9$
D. $f(x) \leq -9$
E. $f(x) \geq 10$
F. $f(x) \geq -10$
G. $f(x) \leq 10$
H. $f(x) \leq -10$

---

57. Rearrange the equation below to give 'x' in terms of 'y'.

$$y = \frac{4}{5}\left(\frac{x}{4}+7\right)^2 + 2$$

A. $7 \mp 4\sqrt{\frac{5y-10}{4}}$

B. $-7 \mp 4\sqrt{\frac{5y-10}{4}}$

C. $28 \mp 4\sqrt{\frac{5y-10}{4}}$

D. $-28 \mp 4\sqrt{\frac{5y-10}{4}}$

E. $-28 \mp 4\sqrt{\frac{5y+10}{4}}$

Mathematics (M5)	GEOMETRY	Specification

Topic	Objective	☺	😐	☹
M5.1	- Use conventional terms and notation: points, lines, line segments, vertices, edges, planes, parallel lines, perpendicular lines, right angles, subtended angles, polygons, regular polygons and polygons with reflection and/or rotational symmetries.			
M5.2	- Recall and use the properties of angles at a point, angles on a straight line, perpendicular lines and opposite angles at a vertex. - Understand and use the angle properties of parallel lines, intersecting lines, triangles and quadrilaterals. - Calculate and use the sum of the interior angles, and the sum of the exterior angles, of polygons.			
M5.3	- Derive and apply the properties and definitions of special types of quadrilaterals, including square, rectangle, parallelogram, trapezium, kite and rhombus. - Derive and apply the properties and definitions of various types of triangle and other plane figures using appropriate language.			
M5.4	- Understand and use the basic congruence criteria for triangles (SSS, SAS, ASA, RHS).			
M5.5	- Apply angle facts, triangle congruence, similarity, and properties of quadrilaterals to results about angles and sides.			
M5.6	- Identify, describe and construct congruent and similar shapes, including on coordinate axes, by considering rotation, reflection, translation and enlargement (including fractional and negative scale factors). - Describe the changes and invariance achieved by combinations of rotations, reflections and translations. - Describe translations as 2-dimensional vectors.			
M5.7	- Know and use the formula for Pythagoras' theorem: $a^2 + b^2 = c^2$ - Use Pythagoras' theorem in both 2 and 3 dimensions.			
M5.8	- Identify and use conventional circle terms: centre, radius, chord, diameter, circumference, tangent, arc, sector and segment (including the use of the terms minor and major for arcs, sectors and segments).			

M5.9	- Apply the standard circle theorems concerning angles, radii, tangents and chords, and use them to prove related results: o angle subtended at the centre is twice the angle subtended at the circumference o angle in a semicircle is 90° o angles in the same segment are equal o angle between a tangent and a chord (alternate segment theorem) o angle between a radius and a tangent is 90° o properties of cyclic quadrilaterals			
M5.10	- Solve geometrical problems on 2-dimensional coordinate axes.			
M5.11	- Know the terminology faces, surfaces, edges and vertices when applied to cubes, cuboids, prisms, cylinders, pyramids, cones, spheres and hemispheres.			
M5.12	- Interpret plans and elevations of 3-dimensional shapes.			
M5.13	- Use and interpret maps and scale drawings. Understand and use three-figure bearings.			
M5.14	- Know and apply formulae to calculate: o the area of triangles, parallelograms, trapezia o the volume of cuboids and other right prisms.			
M5.15	- Know the formulae: o circumference of a circle = $2\pi r = \pi d$ o area of a circle = πr^2 o volume of a right circular cylinder = $\pi r^2 h$ - Formulae relating to spheres, pyramids and cones will be given if needed. Use formulae to calculate: o perimeters of 2-dimensional shapes, including circles o areas of circles and composite shapes o surface area and volume of spheres, pyramids, cones and composite solids			
M5.16	- Calculate arc lengths, angles and areas of sectors of circles.			
M5.17	- Apply the concepts of congruence and similarity in simple figures, including the relationships between lengths, areas and volumes.			
M5.18	- Know and use the trigonometric ratios: $\sin\theta = \frac{\text{opposite}}{\text{hypotenuse}}$ $\cos\theta = \frac{\text{adjacent}}{\text{hypotenuse}}$ $\tan\theta = \frac{\text{opposite}}{\text{adjacent}}$ - Apply these to find angles and lengths in right-angled triangles and, where possible, general triangles in 2- and 3-dimensional figures. - Know the exact values of $\sin\theta$ and $\cos\theta$ for θ = 0°, 30°, 45°, 60°, 90°. Know the exact values of $\tan\theta$ for θ = 0°, 30°, 45°, 60°. Candidates are not expected to recall or use the sine or cosine rules.			
M5.19	- Apply addition and subtraction of vectors, multiplication of vectors by a scalar, and diagrammatic and column representations of vectors. - Use vectors to construct geometric arguments and proofs.			

Mathematics

Mathematics (M5)	GEOMETRY	Questions

58. Points 'P', 'Q' and 'T' are on the circumference of a circle, centre 'O'. The line 'ATB' is the tangent at 'T' to the circle.

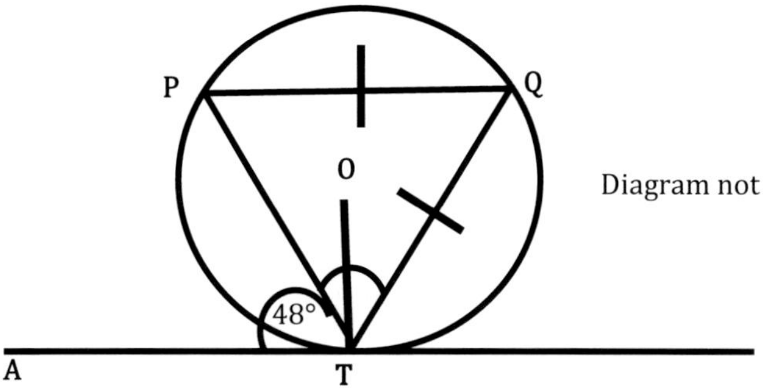

Diagram not drawn to scale

PQ= TQ

What is the size of angle 'OTQ'?

A. 10°
B. 18°
C. 19°
D. 20°
E. 21°
F. 24°
G. 33°

59. 'A' and 'B' are points on the circumference of a circle, centre 'O'.

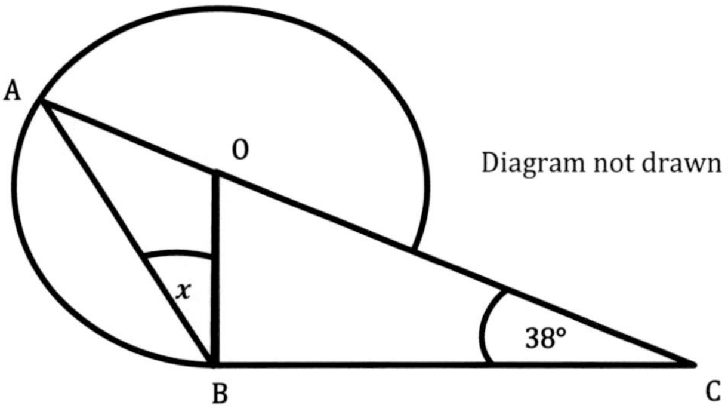

Diagram not drawn to scale.

'BC' is a tangent to the circle.
'AOC' is a straight line.

What is the size of the angle marked 'x'?

A. 24°
B. 26°
C. 29°
D. 33°
E. 52°
F. 63°

60. 'ABC' is an isosceles triangle in which AB=AC = 10cm and BC=8cm
What is the value of the tangent angle 'ABC'?

A. $\frac{\sqrt{29}}{2}$
B. $\frac{\sqrt{21}}{2}$
C. $\frac{3}{2}$
D. $\frac{2}{\sqrt{29}}$
E. $\frac{2}{3}$

61. A cube has length sides of 4cm. What is the length of a line joining the vertex to the midpoint of one of the opposite faces (the dashed line in the diagram below)?

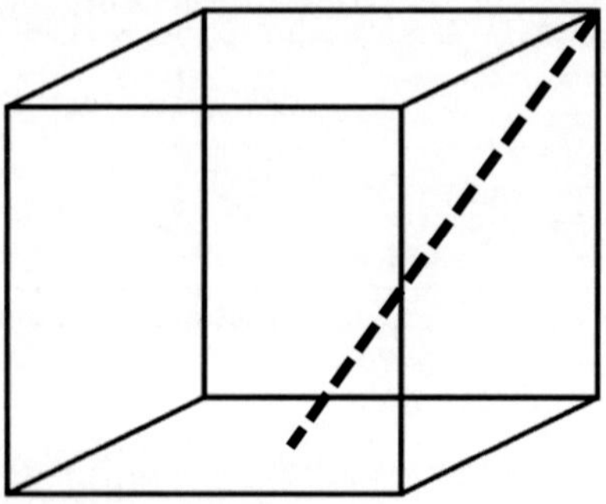

A. $2\sqrt{6}$
B. $\sqrt{2}$
C. $2\sqrt{5}$
D. $4\sqrt{2}$
E. $\sqrt{5}$

62. The total surface area of a cylinder is numerically the same as three times the volume of a right circular cone. The radius of both is 'r'cm, the height is 'h'cm.
Express 'h'in terms of 'r'.

Volume of a right circular cone $= \pi r^2 \frac{h}{3}$

A. $h = \frac{3r^2 - 2r}{2r^2}$
B. $h = \frac{2r^2}{3r^2 - 2r}$
C. $h = \frac{3r^2 - 2r}{2r^2}$

D. $h=\frac{2r^2}{3r^2 - 2r}$

E. $h=\frac{2r^2-3r^3}{3r^2+2r}$

63. **A design is set up by joining the points which are one quarter of the way along the sides of a square. This forms a second square as shown.**

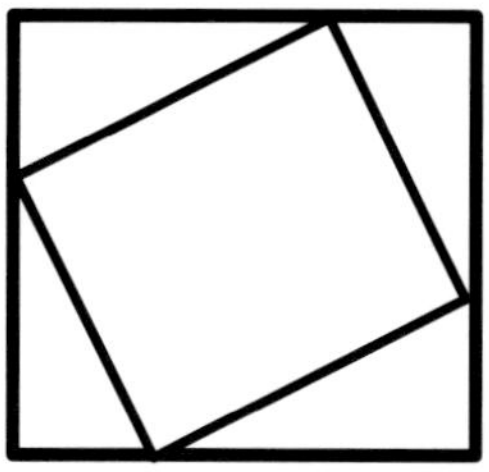

The process is repeated.

Calculate the area of the fourth square as a fraction of the original square.

A. $\frac{25}{64}$

B. $\frac{5}{8}$

C. $\frac{125}{512}$

D. $\frac{5}{64}$

E. $\frac{75}{1024}$

64. **If you look at a clock and the time is 08:15, what is the angle between the hour and the minute hands?**

A. 0°

B. 7.5°

C. 90°

D. 157.5°

E. 240°

F. 247.5°

65. **The diagram shows three similar right-angled triangles.**

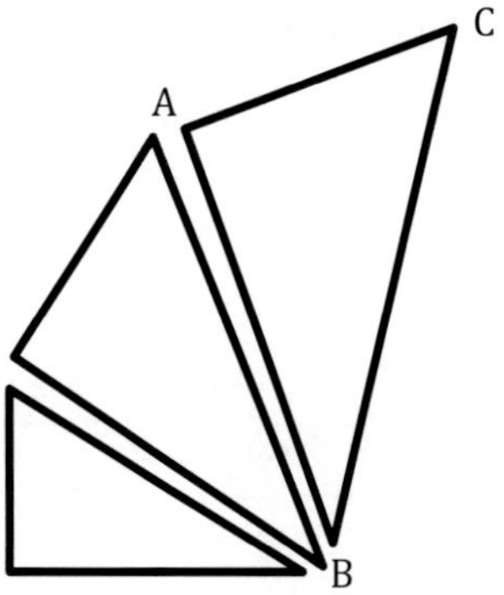

Given that:

$AC = \frac{17}{16}$cm

$AB = \frac{17}{4}$ cm

What is the area of the smallest triangle?

A. $\frac{289}{128}$ cm^2
B. $\frac{17}{4}$ cm^2
C. $\frac{17}{8}$ cm^2
D. 3 cm^2
E. $\frac{17}{16}$ cm^2
F. 2 cm^2

---

66. Four circles of equal size are inscribed in a square. Inside of the four circles is a smaller square tangent to each of the four circles.

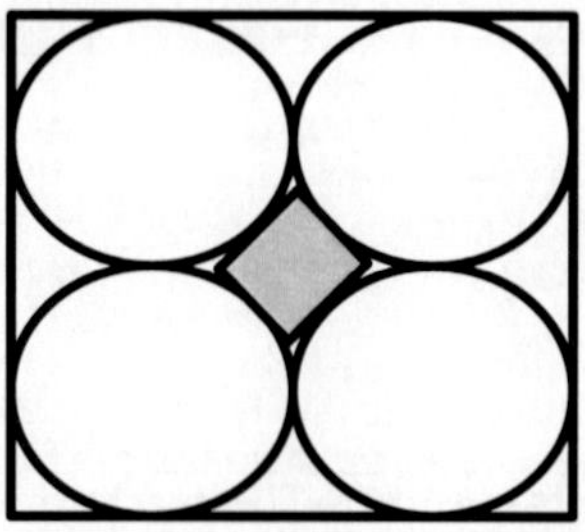

If the large square has a side equal to 6cm, what fraction of the large square is taken up by the small square?

A. $\frac{1}{2}$
B. $\frac{9-6\sqrt{2}}{4}$
C. $\frac{3\sqrt{2}}{4}$
D. $\frac{3}{4}$
E. $\frac{3-2\sqrt{2}}{4}$

---

67. A triangle with sides 6cm, 8cm and 10cm is placed within a square as shown below:

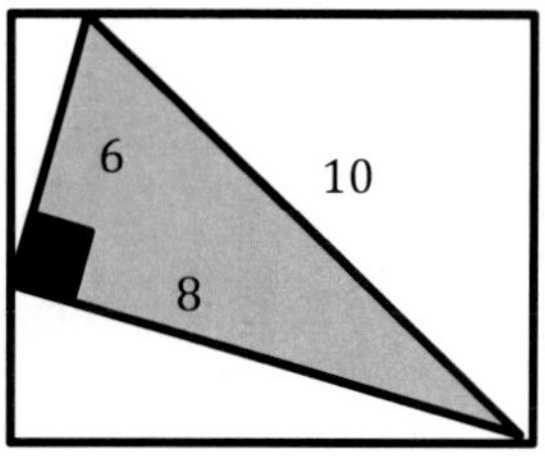

What is the length of one side of the square?

A. $\frac{32\sqrt{17}}{17}$

B. $\frac{1}{\sqrt{5}}$

C. $\frac{8\sqrt{3}}{3}$

D. $\sqrt{5}$

68. Find the angle $'x'$ in the diagram.

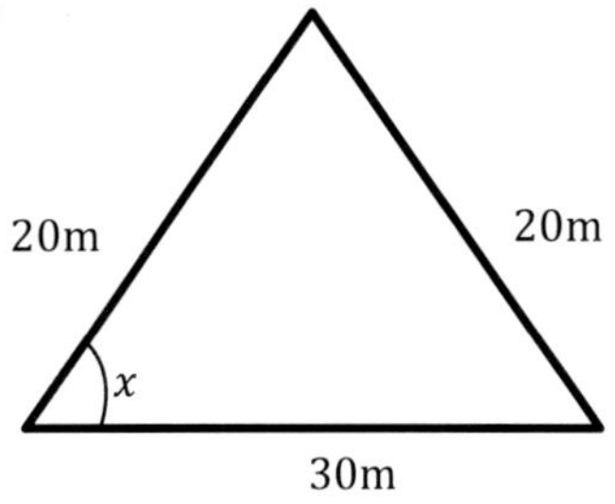

A. $Cos^{-1}(\frac{1}{2})$

B. $Cos^{-1}(\frac{3}{4})$

C. $Cos^{-1}(\frac{2}{3})$

D. $Cos^{-1}(\frac{1}{3})$

E. $Cos^{-1}(1)$

69. 'A', 'B' and 'C' are 3 supermarkets in a town. The bearing of 'A' from 'B' is 045°. The bearing of 'C' from 'A' is 135°. Supermarkets 'A' and 'B' are $3\sqrt{3}$ kms apart and the distance between 'A' and 'C' is 3 kms.

What is the bearing of supermarket 'B' from 'C'?

A. 30°

B. 60°

C. 75°

D. 255°

E. 300°

70. Point 'A' has coordinates (3,7) and point 'B' has coordinates (9, -13). What is the length of line 'AB'?

A. $6\sqrt{2}$

B. $2\sqrt{109}$

C. $4\sqrt{34}$

D. $6\sqrt{5}$

E. 72

F. 436

Mathematics

71. **The sector shown below has an area of $2cm^2$.**

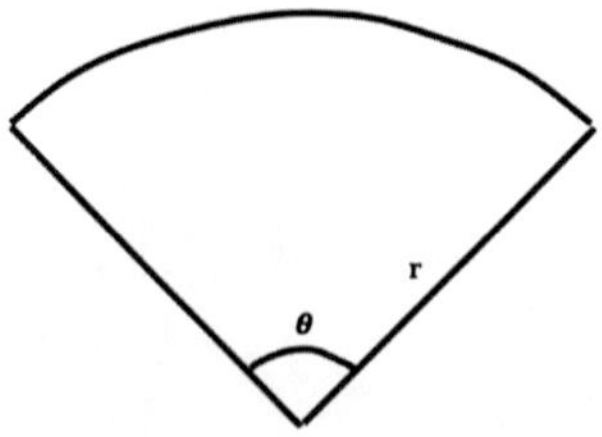

Given that r = 4, what is the perimeter of the arc?

A. 0.25 cm
B. 1 cm
C. 5 cm
D. 8 cm
E. 9 cm
F. 11 cm

72. **Length 'EA' = 3cm, 'AB' = 4cm and 'BC'= 12cm.**

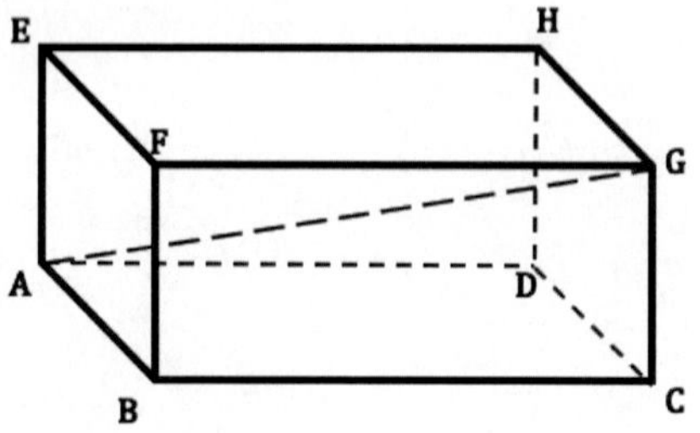

What is the length of the side 'AG'?

A. 5 cm
B. $4\sqrt{10}$ cm
C. $3\sqrt{17}$ cm
D. 13 cm
E. 153 cm
F. 169 cm

73. **The line 'AB' is the diameter of a circle. 'A' is (1,2) and 'B' is (2,4). What is the equation of the circle?**

A. $(x-1)^2 + (y-2)^2 = 5$
B. $(x-\frac{3}{2})^2 + (y-3)^2 = 5$
C. $(x-1)^2 + (y-2)^2 = \frac{\sqrt{5}}{4}$
D. $(x-\frac{3}{2})^2 + (y-3)^2 = \frac{\sqrt{5}}{4}$
E. $(x-\frac{3}{2})^2 + (y-3)^2 = \frac{5}{4}$
F. $(x-\frac{3}{2})^2 + (y-3)^2 = \sqrt{5}$

Mathematics

74. Find the volume of this square based pyramid.

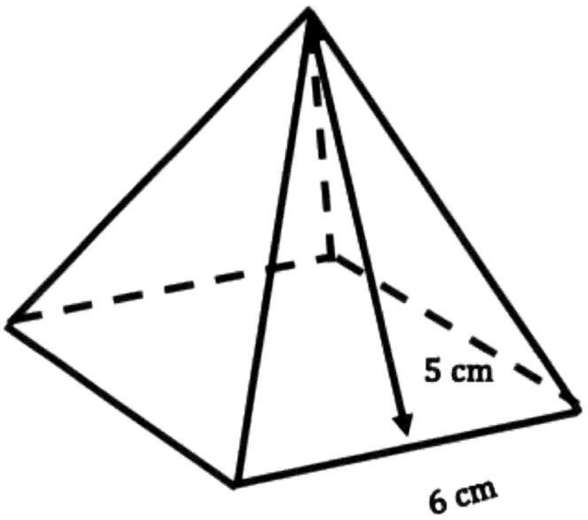

A. 32 cm^3
B. 48 cm^3
C. 50 cm^3
D. 60 cm^3
E. 62 cm^3

75. Given that sin (A+B) = sin(A) cos(B) + cos(A) sin(B), what is the exact value of sin 75°?

A. $\frac{(2+\sqrt{2})}{2\sqrt{2}}$
B. $\frac{(2-\sqrt{2})}{2\sqrt{2}}$
C. $\frac{(1+\sqrt{2})}{\sqrt{2}}$
D. $\frac{(\sqrt{6}+\sqrt{2})}{4}$
E. $\frac{(\sqrt{6}+\sqrt{2})}{2\sqrt{2}}$

76. The perimeter of a rectangle is 24 cm^2. Its length is $2xy$ and its width is $x + y$. Which equation correctly represents y in terms of x?

A. $y = \frac{12-x}{2x+1}$
B. $y = \frac{12+x}{2x+1}$
C. $y = \frac{12-2x}{2x+2}$
D. $y = \frac{12-x}{2x-1}$
E. $y = \frac{24-x}{2x+1}$

77. Given that cos (A+B) = cos(A) cos(B) - sin(A) sin(B), what is the exact value of cos 15°?

A. $\frac{(2-\sqrt{2})}{2\sqrt{2}}$
B. $\frac{(2+\sqrt{2})}{2\sqrt{2}}$

C. $\frac{(1+\sqrt{2})}{\sqrt{2}}$

D. $\frac{(\sqrt{6}+\sqrt{2})}{4}$

E. $\frac{(\sqrt{6}+\sqrt{2})}{2\sqrt{2}}$

78. Consider the triangles below.

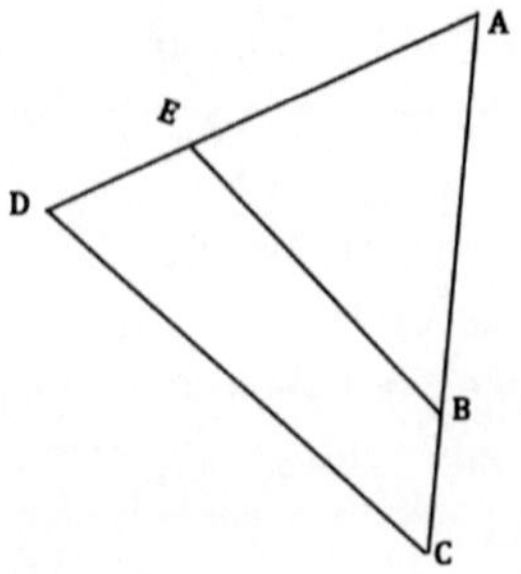

'AB' is 6cm, 'BC' is 2cm and 'DC' is 1.5 times longer than 'AB'. 'EB' is parallel to 'DC'. Find the length of 'EB'.

A. 3cm
B. 5.3cm
C. 6.75cm
D. 12cm
E. 27cm

Mathematics (M6)	STATISTICS	Specification

Topic	Objective	☺	😐	☹
M6.1	- Interpret and construct tables, charts and diagrams, including: o two-way tables, frequency tables, bar charts, pie charts and pictograms for categorical data o vertical line charts for ungrouped discrete numerical data o tables and line graphs for time series data o know the appropriate use of each of these representations.			

M6.2	- Interpret and construct diagrams for grouped discrete data and continuous data: o histograms with equal and unequal class intervals o cumulative frequency graphs - Know the appropriate use of each of these diagrams. - Understand and use the term frequency density.			
M6.3	- Calculate the mean, mode, median and range for ungrouped data. - Find the modal class; calculate estimates of the range, mean and median for grouped data, and understand why these are estimates. - Describe a population using statistics. - Make simple comparisons. - Compare data sets using like-for-like summary values. - Understand the advantages and disadvantages of summary values. - Calculate estimates of mean, median, mode, range, quartiles and interquartile range from graphical representation of grouped data. - Use the median and interquartile range to compare distributions.			
M6.4	- Use and interpret scatter graphs of bivariate data. - Recognise correlation and know that it does not indicate causation. - Draw estimated lines of best fit. - Interpolate and extrapolate apparent trends whilst knowing the dangers of so doing.			

Mathematics (M6)	STATISTICS	Questions

79. A school wants to investigate the preferred mode of transport for its students. A total of 200 students were surveyed. The pie chart below shows the results.

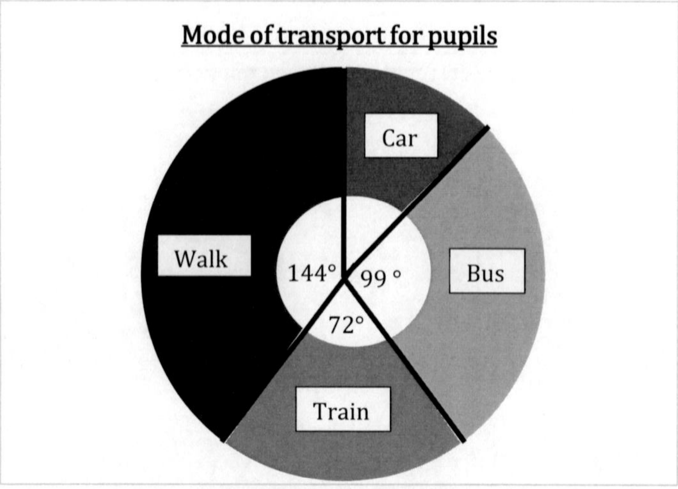

How many more children walk to school compared to those travelling by car?

A. 25
B. 30
C. 40
D. 55
E. 80

80. This histogram shows the diameter of marble balls in mm. Thirty-four marbles measured 35 mm or less.

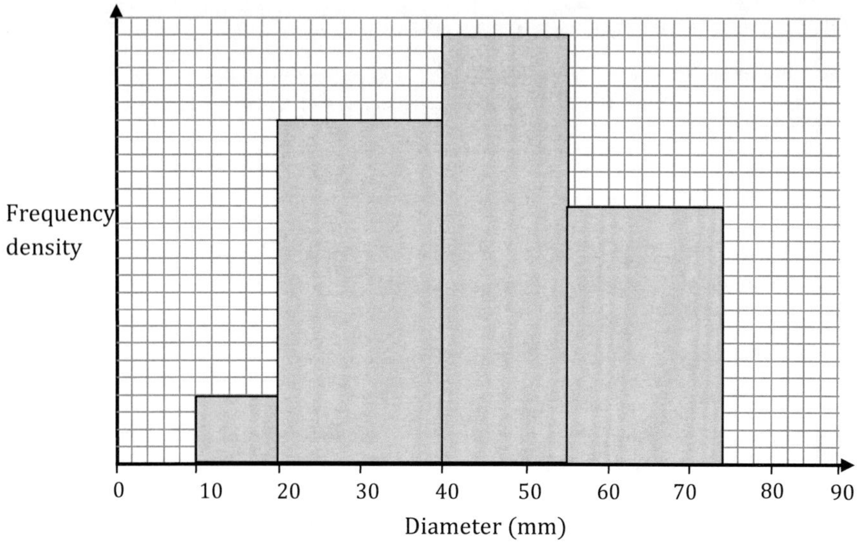

What was the difference in marbles that had a diameter of more than 64 mm compared to a diameter of less than 20 mm?

A. 2
B. 4
C. 7
D. 15
E. 11
F. 26
G. 32

81. The following graph shows the correlation between temperature and the length of a type of shoot in a greenhouse:

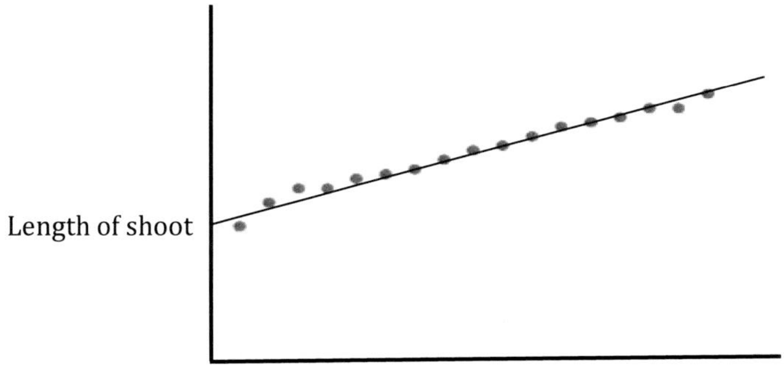

Which amongst the following statements can be proved using the above graph?

A. Temperature and length of the shoot are directly proportional to each other.
B. The positive correlation shows that temperature is the only variable that affects the length of the shoot.
C. There is a positive gradient, which suggests a correlation between temperature and length of shoot.
D. There is a weak negative correlation between temperature and length of shoot.
E. At high temperatures, enzymes become denatured, and, therefore, the length of the shoot decreases.
F. All shoot lengths increase with temperature.

82. Consider the table below representing the height of some pupils in a class:

Height (cm)	135 - 140	141 -145	146 - 150	151 -155	156 -160
Number of pupils	4	4	6	7	2

The centre of gravity on the human body is approximately 55% of an individual's height from the ground. Which of the options below represents the estimated mean height of the centre of gravity in the class?

A. 74 cm
B. 81 cm
C. 95 cm
D. 148 cm
E. 156 cm

83. The summary statistics given below are from data of the number of minutes 35 customers spent in a coffee shop.

$\Sigma fx = 2485$

$\Sigma fx^2 = 400\ 435$

Find the standard deviation.

A. 1 hour 11 minutes
B. 1 hour 20 minutes
C. 1 hour 35 minutes
D. 2 hours 17 minutes
E. 2 hours 23 minutes

84. Consider the graph below showing the relationship between the value and age of cars.

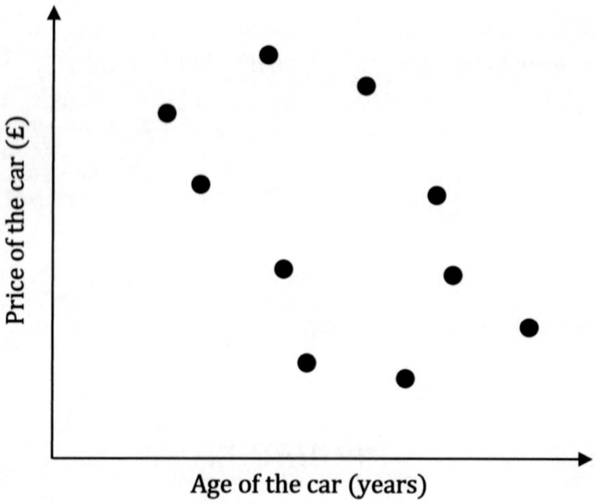

What can be concluded from this data?

1. There is a strong positive correlation.
2. There is a weak positive correlation.
3. There is a non-linear relationship.
4. There is a strong negative correlation.
5. There is a weak negative correlation.
6. The as the age of the car increases, it causes the price to decrease.

A. 1 only
B. 2 only
C. 3 only
D. 4 only
E. 5 only
F. 3 and 4 only
G. 3 and 5 only
H. 1 and 6 only
I. 2 and 6 only
J. 5 and 6 only
K. 3, 5 and 6 only

85. The mean weight of 9 people in a lift was 597 kgs. Another individual enters the lift and the mean decreased by 9%.
How much does this individual weigh?
A. 53.73 kg
B. 54.33 kg
C. 56.70 kg
D. 59.70 kg
E. 61.32 kg

86. A list of the length of several fish sampled from a pond is given below:

13.2 cm, 16.7 cm, 16.8 cm, 14.3 cm, 17.9 cm, 12.1 cm, 9.8 cm, 18.9 cm, 15.3 cm

In this data, outliers are considered to be mean $\mp$ IQR.
IQR is the interquartile range.
How many fish from the data sampled are considered to be outliers?
A. 0
B. 1
C. 2
D. 3
E. 4
F. 5
G. 6
H. 7

Mathematics (M7) PROBABILITY Specification

Topic	Objective	☺	😐	☹
M7.1	- Analyse the frequency of outcomes of probability experiments using tables and frequency trees.			
M7.2	- Apply ideas of randomness, fairness and equally likely events to calculate expected outcomes of multiple future experiments. - Understand that if an experiment is repeated, the outcome may be different.			
M7.3	- Relate relative expected frequencies to theoretical probability, using appropriate language and the '0 to 1' probability scale.			
M7.4	- Apply the property that the probabilities of an exhaustive set of outcomes sum to one. - Apply the property that the probabilities of an exhaustive set of mutually exclusive events sum to one.			

M7.5	- Enumerate sets and combinations of sets systematically, using tables, grids, Venn diagrams and tree diagrams. Candidates are not expected to know formal set theory notation.			
M7.6	- Construct theoretical possibility spaces for single and combined experiments with equally likely outcomes and use these to calculate theoretical probabilities.			
M7.7	- Know when to add or multiply two probabilities and understand conditional probability. - Calculate and interpret conditional probabilities through representation using expected frequencies with two-way tables, tree diagrams and Venn diagrams. - Understand the use of tree diagrams to represent outcomes of combined events: o when the probabilities are independent of the previous outcome o when the probabilities are dependent on the previous outcome.			

Mathematics (M7) | PROBABILITY | Questions

87. A teacher wanted to assess her students' preferences for two sports – football and tennis. A student can like football but not tennis, tennis but not football, both football and tennis or neither football nor tennis.
Within the school:
40% of people liked football but not tennis.
24% of people liked tennis but not football.
16% of people liked neither football nor tennis.
20% of people liked football and tennis.
A student, chosen at random, likes tennis. What is the probability that the student likes both tennis and football?

A. $\frac{1}{5}$

B. $\frac{1}{4}$

C. $\frac{5}{6}$

D. $\frac{3}{25}$

E. $\frac{5}{11}$

88. A bag contains 25 beads. The beads are identical in all respects except colour. 16 of the beads are blue and the remainder are white. A bead is taken from the bag and not replaced. A second bead is then taken at random from the bag.
What is the probability that both beads are white?
A. $\frac{3}{28}$
B. $\frac{1}{4}$
C. $\frac{37}{56}$
D. $\frac{3}{25}$
E. $\frac{9}{25}$
F. $\frac{1}{3}$

89. A bag contains 'p' pink balls, 'g' green balls and 'r' red balls . One ball is taken out at random and replaced. Following this, a second ball is taken out at random and replaced.
If the balls are identical in all respects except colour and are well mixed, what is the probability that the first ball was pink and the second green?
A. $\frac{pg}{(p+g+r)^2}$
B. $\frac{p+g}{(p+g+r)^2}$
C. $\frac{pg}{(p+g+r)(p+r)}$
D. $\frac{p+g}{(p+g+r)}$
E. $\frac{pg}{(p+r)(g+r)}$

90. I have two six-sided dice, each with faces numbered from 1 to 6. One of the dice is fair, but the other is not – it will land on numbers 1 to 5 with equal probability, but lands on 6 with a different probability.
When I roll the dice the probability that I get a total of 12 is $\frac{1}{42}$.
What is the probability that I get a total of 3 when I roll each of the dice once?
A. $\frac{1}{35}$
B. $\frac{2}{35}$
C. $\frac{1}{7}$
D. $\frac{1}{56}$
E. $\frac{3}{70}$

91. In a fairground game there are two bags, each of which contains 4 coloured balls. There is a total of 4 blue balls, 3 pink balls and 1 yellow ball. The player chooses one of the bags and removes two balls without replacing them. If the two balls are of the same colour, then the player wins. The player is equally likely to choose either of the bags. In Scenario 1, the balls are arranged to give the largest possible probability for the player to win, while in Scenario 2, the balls are arranged to give the smallest possible probability for the player to win.
What is the difference in probability between the two Scenarios that the player will win?
A. $\frac{1}{4}$

B. $\frac{3}{4}$
C. $\frac{1}{2}$
D. $\frac{5}{8}$
E. $\frac{1}{3}$

92. A bag contains 7 red and 3 yellow balls. Three balls are chosen at the same time at random from the bag.
What is the probability that exactly two of the balls are the same colour?

A. $\frac{7}{10}$
B. $\frac{7}{12}$
C. $\frac{14}{30}$
D. $\frac{7}{8}$
E. $\frac{7}{30}$
F. $\frac{7}{30}$
G. $\frac{3}{8}$

93. Students in a school were asked their favourite language to study. There are 82 students in the school.
A total of 39 students liked French.
A total of 50 students liked English.
A total of 39 students liked Spanish.
A total of 21 students liked French and English.
A total of 18 students liked English and Spanish.
A total of 19 students liked French and Spanish.
A total of 8 students liked none of the languages.
How many students liked all of the three languages?

A. 2 students
B. 4 students
C. 6 students
D. 8 students
E. 10 students
F. 12 students

94. A company has developed a new pregnancy test that can detect pregnancies at an earlier stage. It has a false positive rate of 5% and a false negative rate of 20%. Assuming that 10% of all women who take this pregnancy test are pregnant, a woman is randomly selected.
Given that this woman tests positive, what is the probability that she is actually pregnant?

A. 25%
B. 32%
C. 36%
D. 50%
E. 64%
F. 98%

95. A child plays two games. He wins Game 1 if he chooses a red marble from the bag. The child wins Game 2 if he chooses a blue marble from another bag. Playing Game 1 and Game 2 are independent events. The probability of the child winning both games is 0.8. The probability of the child winning Game 2 is five times more than the probability of him losing Game 1.
What is the probability that the child wins only one of the two games he plays?
A. 0
B. 0.2
C. 0.4
D. 0.6
E. 0.8
F. 1

96. In Jacob's wallet there are three £10 notes and two £5 notes only.
He needs £25 to purchase a scooter.
If he picks three notes at random from his wallet, what is the probability that he has picked the exact money to buy the scooter?
A. $\frac{1}{5}$
B. $\frac{3}{10}$
C. $\frac{9}{10}$
D. $\frac{3}{5}$
E. $\frac{9}{20}$

97. There are 30 pupils in a class; 9 students are new to the school. Amongst the new students, 2 want to study Medicine at University. The probability of wanting to study Medicine, given that the pupil is not new is $\frac{1}{7}$.
What is the probability that a pupil who wants to study Medicine is new to the school?
A. $\frac{2}{9}$
B. $\frac{2}{5}$
C. $\frac{2}{63}$
D. $\frac{23}{63}$
E. $\frac{1}{15}$

98. The following information show the sports that a group of 100 people regularly play each week:
A total of 43 individuals played tennis.
A total of 56 individuals played badminton.
A total of 53 individuals played football.
A total of 25 individuals played tennis and badminton.
A total of 22 individuals played badminton and football.
A total of 20 individuals played tennis and football.
A total of 15 individuals participate in all three sports.

Given that a person plays badminton, what is the probability that he or she plays tennis but not football?

A. $\frac{25}{56}$

B. $\frac{5}{12}$

C. $\frac{5}{28}$

D. $\frac{10}{43}$

E. $\frac{5}{23}$

99. Lisa and her brother bought a packet of sweets. In the packet there are $'x'$ strawberry flavoured sweets, $'y'$ that are blueberry flavoured and $'z'$ that are raspberry flavoured. Lisa randomly picks a sweet and eats it. Her brother then picks a sweet after her. What is the probability that a strawberry and raspberry sweet are removed from the packet?

A. $\frac{xz}{(x+y+z)}$

B. $\frac{2xz}{(x+y+z)}$

C. $\frac{xz}{(x+y+z)(x+y+z-1)}$

D. $\frac{2xz}{(x+y+z)(x+y+z-1)}$

E. $\frac{x+z}{(x+y+z)(x+y+z-1)}$

100. The table below shows the information found on the back of a packet of flower seeds.

Seed type	Number of seeds	Colour of the flower
Sunflower	27	Yellow
Marigold	43	Yellow
Sokol breadseed poppy	23	White
Aftermidnight breadseed poppy	12	Dark purple
Snapdragon	39	Pink

A gardener decides to plant each seed separately in seed trays. A seed is taken out of the packet and planted. Then a second seed is removed and planted in the seed tray as well. What is the probability that both the seeds the gardener picks produce yellow flowers?

A. $\frac{805}{3432}$

B. $\frac{3}{88}$

C. $\frac{301}{3456}$

D. $\frac{1225}{5184}$

E. $\frac{1849}{20736}$

F. $\frac{9}{256}$

Mathematics

Mathematics (M1) | UNITS | Answers

1. D

Explanation:

This is an exponential growth question, *the equation that can be used is:*

$N = N_0(1 + \frac{r}{100})^n$

Where <u>N is the amount after a certain time, N_0 is the initial amount, r is the percentage change and n is the number of years/ days/ hours</u>.

$N = 200(1 + \frac{6}{100})^3$

<u>**N = £238.20**</u>

2. C

Explanation:

From 02:00 to 03:00 hours, the hour hand moves:

$\frac{360}{12} = \underline{30°}$

At 03:45 hours, the hour hand will be $\frac{3}{4}$ of the way between 3 and 4.

Therefore, it moves:

$30° \times \frac{3}{4} =$ <u>22.5° from 3:00 to 3:45.</u>

In total the hour hand has moved $\underline{\mathbf{30° + 22.5° = 52.5°}}$

Mathematics (M2) | NUMBER | Answers

3. A

Explanation:

Assuming that 'r' is 2 and 's' is 4:

$2 ¤ 4 = \frac{2 \times 4}{4^2}$

$2 ¤ 4 = \frac{8}{16}$

$\mathbf{2 ¤ 4 = \frac{1}{2}}$

Assuming that 'r' is now ½ and 's' is 2:

$(2 ¤ 4) ¤ 2 = \frac{1}{2} \times \frac{2}{2^{0.5}}$

$(2 ¤ 4) ¤ 2 = \frac{\mathbf{1}}{\mathbf{\sqrt{2}}}$

4. F

Explanation:

Ignore the square root at first.

The numerator: $3000 + 600 = \underline{36000}$

The denominator: $\frac{53400}{267} + \frac{27000}{15}$

$\frac{534}{267} = 2$, therefore, $\frac{53400}{267} = \underline{200}$

$\frac{27000}{15} = \underline{1800}$

Therefore, $\frac{53400}{267} + \frac{27000}{15}$:

$1800 + 200 = \underline{2000}$

Numerator/denominator $= 36000 \div 2000$

$= \underline{18}$

Square root answer: $\sqrt{18} = \sqrt{9}\ x\sqrt{2}$

$= \underline{3\sqrt{2}}$

---

5. B

Explanation:

Consider the denominator:

$1 + \frac{1}{\sqrt{5}} = \frac{\sqrt{5}}{\sqrt{5}} + \frac{1}{\sqrt{5}}$

Therefore:

$\frac{2}{\frac{\sqrt{5}+1}{\sqrt{5}}} = 2 \div (\frac{\sqrt{5}+1}{\sqrt{5}})$

Dividing by a fraction is equivalent to multiplying by the inverse fraction:

$2 \text{ x } \frac{\sqrt{5}}{\sqrt{5}+1} = \frac{\mathbf{2\sqrt{5}}}{\mathbf{\sqrt{5}+1}}$

Rationalise the denominator:

$\frac{2\sqrt{5}}{\sqrt{5}+1} \text{ X } \frac{\sqrt{5}-1}{\sqrt{5}-1} = \frac{\mathbf{10-2\sqrt{5}}}{\mathbf{4}}$

Divide the numerator and denominator by 2:

$= \frac{\mathbf{5-\sqrt{5}}}{\mathbf{2}}$

---

6. D

Explanation:

Consider the first cube root:

$$\sqrt[3]{\frac{(0.9\ x\ 10^6)(12\ x\ 10^2)}{\frac{4}{100}}} = \sqrt[3]{\frac{10.8\ x\ 10^8}{4\ x\ 10^{-2}}}$$

$= \sqrt[3]{2.7 \text{ x } 10^{8-(-2)}}$

$= \sqrt[3]{2.7 \text{ x } 10^{10}}$

$\underline{=3000}$

Consider the second square root:

$\sqrt{(1.25 \text{ x } 10^3)(5 \text{ x } 10^3)}$:

$\sqrt{6.25 \text{ x } 10^6} = \underline{2500}$

Looking at the third square root:

$\sqrt{(3 \text{ x } 10^3) + (6 \text{ x } 10^2)} = \sqrt{3000 + 600}$

$\sqrt{3000 + 600} = \sqrt{3600}$

$= \underline{60}$

Combing all three answers:

$$\sqrt[3]{\frac{(0.9 \text{ x } 10^6)(12 \text{ x } 10^2)}{\frac{4}{100}}} - \sqrt{(1.25 \text{ x } 10^3)(5 \text{ x } 10^3)} + \sqrt{(3 \text{ x } 10^3) + (6 \text{ x } 10^2)}$$

$= 3000 - 2500 + 60$

$= \underline{560}$

7. C

Explanation:

Expand the brackets:

$(\sqrt{8} - 6)\ (\sqrt{8} - 6)\ (\sqrt{8} - 6)$

Consider the first two brackets:

$(\sqrt{8} - 6)\ (\sqrt{8} - 6) = 8 - 6\sqrt{8} - 6\sqrt{8} + 36$

$= \underline{\mathbf{44 - 12\sqrt{8}}}$

Multiply 44 - 12$\sqrt{8}$ by $\sqrt{8}$ – 6:

$(\sqrt{8} - 6)\ (44 - 12\sqrt{8}) = 44\sqrt{8} - 96 - 264 + 72\sqrt{8}$

$= \underline{\mathbf{116\sqrt{8} - 360}}$

Simplify 116$\sqrt{8}$:

$116\sqrt{8} = 116\sqrt{4 \text{ x } 2}$

$= 116 \text{ x } 2 \text{ x } \sqrt{2}$

$= \underline{\mathbf{232\sqrt{2}}}$

Therefore, the final answer:

$= \underline{\mathbf{232\sqrt{2} - 360}}$

8. E

Explanation:

Multiply both fractions together to produce a common denominator:

$$\frac{4(3\sqrt{2} - \sqrt{8}) + 3(\sqrt{8} + 3\sqrt{2})}{(\sqrt{8} + 3\sqrt{2})(3\sqrt{2} - \sqrt{8})}$$

Expand the numerator brackets:

$4(3\sqrt{2} - \sqrt{8}) + 3(\sqrt{8} + 3\sqrt{2}) = 12\sqrt{2} - 4\sqrt{8} + 3\sqrt{8} + 9\sqrt{2}$

$= 21\sqrt{2} - \sqrt{8}$

$= 21\sqrt{2} - \sqrt{4}\sqrt{2}$

$= 21\sqrt{2} - 2\sqrt{2}$

$= \underline{19\sqrt{2}}$

Expand the denominator brackets:

$(\sqrt{8} + 3\sqrt{2})(3\sqrt{2} - \sqrt{8}) = 3\sqrt{16} - 8 + 18 - 3\sqrt{16}$

$= \underline{10}$

Therefore, the overall fraction is:

$$\mathbf{\frac{19\sqrt{2}}{10}}$$

Mathematics

9. F

Explanation:

A geometric sequence has the same ratio (can multiply by the same number) between consecutive terms.

As a result, the ratio between the second and first term is equal to the ratio between the third and second term:

$$\frac{3}{2\sqrt{x}-3} = \frac{2\sqrt{x}+3}{3}$$

$9 = (2\sqrt{x} - 3)\,(2\sqrt{x} + 3)$

$9 = 4x + 6\sqrt{x} - 6\sqrt{x} - 9$

$4x = 18$

$\underline{x = 4.5}$

10. A

Explanation:

Consider $0.\dot{5}\dot{2}$*:*

Let:

$x = 0.525252.....$ <u>(Equation 1)</u>

Therefore,

$100\,x = 52.5252....$ <u>(Equation 2)</u>

Subtract Equation 1 from Equation 2:

$99x = 52$

$x = \frac{52}{99}$

Consider $0.\dot{3}$*:*

Let:

$x = 0.3333333.....$ <u>(Equation 1)</u>

Therefore,

$10\,x = 3.33333333....$ <u>(Equation 2)</u>

Subtract Equation 1 from Equation 2:

$9x = 3$

$x = \frac{3}{9}$

$x = \frac{1}{3}$

Therefore,

$9\left(\frac{52}{99} - \frac{3}{9}\right) = 9\left(\frac{52}{99} - \frac{33}{99}\right)$

$9\left(\frac{19}{99}\right) = \frac{19}{11}$

Mathematics

11. C

Explanation:

Consider the prime factors of 360 and 1500:

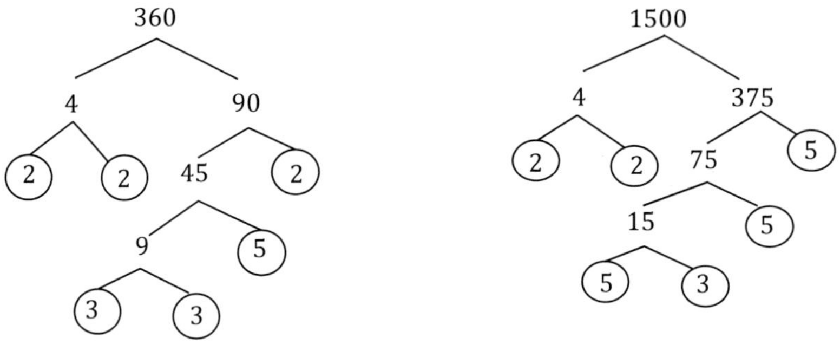

360 = <u>2^3 x 3^2 x 5</u>
1500 = <u>2^2 x 3 x 5^3</u>
Calculate the LCM (Lowest Common Multiple) of 360 and 1500:
This can be done by finding the highest number of repeats in each set (the 360 set and the 1500 set):
2^3 x 3^2 x 5^3
Therefore, <u>a = 3, b= 2 and c=3</u>
a x b x c : 3 x 2 x 3 =<u>18</u>

---

12. E

Explanation:

Consider the factors of 39375:

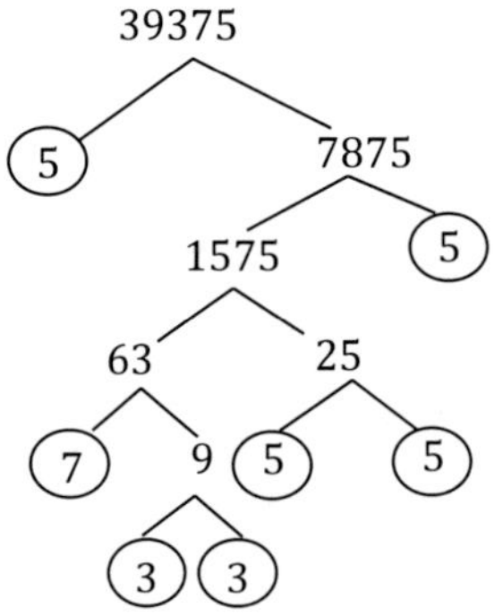

39375 = <u>3^2 x 5^4 x 7</u>
In order to make a square number, all of the powers must be even. Since 3 and 5 have even powers, '*y*' <u>must equal 7</u> (in order to produce 7^2, which has an even power).

13. B

Explanation:

$\frac{3}{4+\sqrt{7}}$ X $\frac{4-\sqrt{7}}{4-\sqrt{7}}$

$=\frac{12-3\sqrt{7}}{16-7}$

$=\frac{(12-3\sqrt{7})}{9}$ (this must be simplified by **dividing by 3**)

$=\frac{4-\sqrt{7}}{3}$

14. B

Explanation:

$8 - \frac{6(x+3)}{2x-4} = 2$

$\frac{6(x+3)}{2x-4} = 6$

$\frac{(x+3)}{2x-4} = 1$

$x + 3 = 2x - 4$

$x = 7$

Alternatively, **substitute each option into the equation** to see which gives the correct answer.

15. C

Explanation:

$x^2 > 4x - 3$

$x^2 - 4x + 3 > 0$

Factorise:

$x^2 - 4x + 3 = 0$:

$(x - 1)(x - 3) = 0$

$x = 1$ or $x = 3$

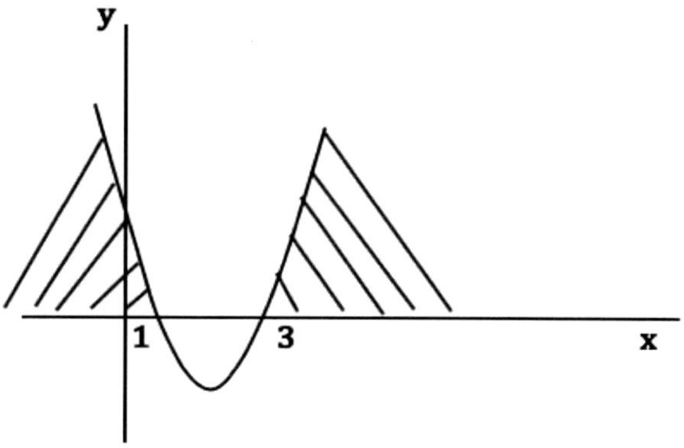

$x^2 + 4x - 3 > 0$ represents the area above the x-axis as it greater than 0.

Therefore, the values of x are **$x < 1$ and $x > 3$**

Mathematics

16. C

Explanation:

$\sqrt[5]{3125} = 5$

$5^3 = 125$

17. F

Explanation:

Simplify the equation:

$\sqrt{2} + 4\sqrt{2} + 2\sqrt{2} = \sqrt{x}$

$\sqrt{x} = 7\sqrt{2}$

$\sqrt{x} = \sqrt{49} \text{ x } \sqrt{2}$

$\sqrt{x} = \sqrt{98}$

$x = 98$

18. E

Explanation:

Find the prime factors of 300.:

(A prime factors tree can be used for this)

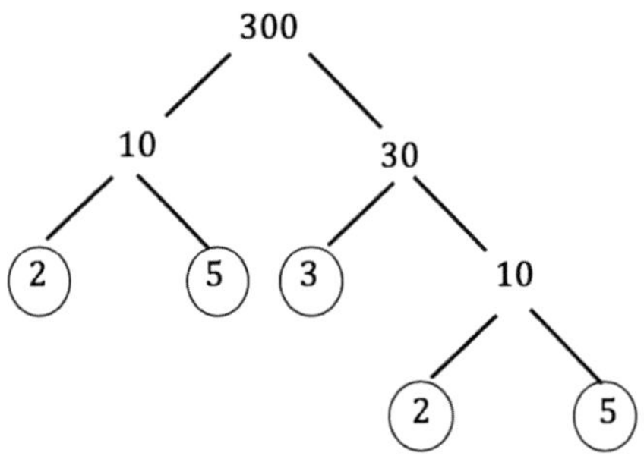

Mathematics

$300 = 2^2 \text{ x } 3 \text{ x } 5^2$

$300^2 = (2^2 \text{ x } 3 \text{ x } 5^2)^2$

$300^2 = 2^4 \text{ x } 3^2 \text{ x } 5^4$

19. A

Explanation:

$\frac{990 \text{ x } 10^A}{3 \text{ x } 10^B} \text{ x } 2 \text{ x } 10^C = 6.6 \text{ x } 10^{-6}$

Simplify this equation:

$330 \text{ x } 10^{A-B} \text{ x } 2 \text{ x } 10^C = 6.6 \text{ x } 10^{-6}$

$660 \text{ x } 10^{A-B+C} = 6.6 \text{ x } 10^{-6}$

$660 \text{ x } 10^{A-B+C} = 6.6 \text{ x } 10^{-6}$

$100 \text{ x } 10^{A-B+C} = 10^{-6}$

$10^{A-B+C} = 10^{-8}$

$\mathbf{A - B + C = -8}$

20. C

Explanation:

$(\sqrt{17} - \sqrt{21})^2(\sqrt{17} + \sqrt{21})^2$

This can be written as:

$[(\sqrt{17} - \sqrt{21})(\sqrt{17} + \sqrt{21})]^2$

This the difference between two squares :

$(a + b)\ (a - b) = a^2 - b^2$

$([\sqrt{17} - \sqrt{21})(\sqrt{17} + \sqrt{21})]^2 = (17 - 21)^2$

$= (-4)^2$

$= 16$

---

21. F

Explanation:

$2(2\sqrt{7} + 3\sqrt{13})^2 + 1$

$=2\left[(2\sqrt{7})^2 + 2(2\sqrt{7} \times 3\sqrt{13}) + (3\sqrt{13})^2\right] + 1$

$= 2[28 + 12\sqrt{91} + 117] + 1$

$= 2[145 + 12\sqrt{91}] + 1$

$= 290 + 24\sqrt{91} + 1$

$= \mathbf{291 + 24\sqrt{91}}$

---

22. B

Explanation:

Consider 512:

$512 = 8^3$

$512^5 = (8^3)^5$

$512^5 = 8^{15}$

Consider 2:

$2^3 = 8$

$2^{18} = 2^{(3 \times 6)}$

$2^{18} = (2^3)^6$

$2^{18} = 8^6$

Therefore, $512^5 \times 2^{18}$:

$8^{15} \times 8^6 = 8^{21}$

Mathematics

Mathematics (M3)	RATIO AND PROPORTION	Answers

23. F

Explanation:

Let 'g' be girls and 'b' be boys.

Expressing the initial ratio as a fraction: $\frac{g}{b} = \frac{5}{19}$ (Equation 1)

Expressing the second ratio as a fraction:

(b+23 since 23 new boys have been added): $\frac{g}{b+23} = \frac{10}{61}$

Rearranging the above:

$g = \frac{10(b+23)}{61}$

$61g = 10b + 230$

$g = \frac{10b}{61} + \frac{230}{61}$ (Equation 2)

From (Equation 1):

$\frac{g}{b} = \frac{5}{19}$

$g = \frac{5}{19}b$ (Equation 3)

(Equation 3) = (Equation 2):

$\frac{5b}{19} = \frac{10b}{61} + \frac{230}{61}$

Divide both sides by $\frac{5}{19}$:

$b = \frac{38b}{61} + \frac{874}{61}$

$b - \frac{38b}{61} = \frac{874}{61}$

Therefore, $\frac{23b}{61} = \frac{874}{61}$

$b = 38$

Using (Equation 3):

$g = \frac{5}{19} \times 38$

$g = 10$

Therefore, at the start, there were **48 children.**

As a result, 48+23=**71 children** were present after the boys were added.

24. D

Explanation:

$\frac{5}{6}$ of the total sale was given to Charity 'Z'.

Let 'a' be the amount of money produced:

$\frac{5}{6}a = 1200$

$a = \frac{6}{5} \text{ x } 1200$

$a = \underline{\mathbf{1440}}$

Therefore, Charity 'X' received £1440 (1 x 1440), Charity 'Y' received £864 ($\frac{3}{5}$ x 1440)

and Charity 'Z' received £1200 ($\frac{5}{6}$ x 1440).

Total amount = **1200 + 1440 + 864**

= **£3504**

25. B

Explanation:

Ratio of vanilla to strawberry is 2:1.6

Ratio of chocolate to strawberry is 8: 9.6

The number of strawberries should be equal in order to combine the two ratios:

Multiply the ratio of vanilla to strawberry by 6:

12 : 9.6

Therefore, the ratio of vanilla to strawberry to chocolate is:

12 : 9.6 : 8

To find the smallest number of ice cream flavours, the ratio must be the smallest whole number possible:

(12 : 9.6 : 8) x 5 = **60 : 48 : 40**

Therefore, total number of ice cream flavours:

60 + 48 + 40 = **148**

Probability of choosing a chocolate ice cream:

$\frac{40}{148} = \frac{\mathbf{10}}{\mathbf{37}}$

26. E

Explanation:

Assume:

Red = x marbles

Blue = x marbles (same number of red and blue marbles)

Yellow = x marbles

Once Joseph removes the specific number of marbles:

Red = x - 5

Blue = x - 25

Yellow = x - 15

The ratio of marbles remaining are:

Red : Yellow = 15 : 8

Yellow : Blue = 4 : 5

Multiply the Yellow : Blue ratio by 2 to have the same number of yellow marbles (enables the two ratios to be combined):

Yellow : Blue = 8 : 10

Therefore, combined ratio:

Red : Yellow : Blue = 15 : 8 : 10

Red : Blue = 15 : 10

$\frac{\text{Red}}{\text{Blue}} = \frac{15}{10}$

<u>Red = 1.5 x Blue</u>

Since Blue = x-25:

Red = 1.5 x (x-25)

Red = x -5 :

Combining these two equations:

x -5 = 1.5 (x-25)

2x -10 = 3x - 75

$x = 65$

Red : Yellow = 15 : 8

Originally, there were 65 red marbles.

However, 5 were removed by Joseph:

60 : y -15 = 15 : 8

$$\frac{60}{y-15} = \frac{15}{8}$$

Invert the fraction:

$$\frac{y-15}{60} = \frac{8}{15}$$

y – 15 = 32

y =47

Original number of marbles in the bag:

65 + 65 + 47 = **177**

---

27. F

Explanation:

Assume Alice and Becky have £x.

The ratio 2 : 3 has 2 +3 = 5 parts

Therefore,

Alice = $\pounds\frac{2}{5}x$

Becky = $\pounds\frac{3}{5}x$

Assume Carlos and Darcy have £ 5x <u>(share five times as much money as Alice and Becky):</u>

The ratio 7 : 8 has 7 +8 = 15 parts

Therefore,

Carlos = $\pounds\frac{7}{15}$ x $5x$

Darcy = $\pounds\frac{8}{15}$ x $5x$

Simplifying Carlos and Darcy's ratios:

Carlos = $\pounds\frac{7}{3}x$

Darcy = $\pounds\frac{8}{3}x$

Therefore, the ratio of Alice : Becky : Carlos : Darcy is:

$$\frac{2}{5}x : \frac{3}{5}x : \frac{7}{15}x : \frac{8}{15}x$$

To find the minimum amount of money, find the smallest whole number ratio (multiply the ratio by 15):

6 : 9 : 7 : 8

Therefore, the minimum amount of money is:

6 + 9 + 7 + 8 = **£30**

28. E

Explanation:

420 is simplified to $\frac{2}{7}$ in the ratio.

The multiplying factor is:

$420 \times \frac{7}{2} = \underline{1470}$

Consider School 'A':

1 x 1470 = **1470**

Consider School 'C':

$\frac{4}{5} \times 1470 = \underline{1176}$

Since School 'B' had 420 students, the total is:

1470 + 420 + 1176=**3066**

29. B

Explanation:

$X \propto \frac{1}{\sqrt[3]{Y}}$ This is written as $X = \frac{k}{\sqrt[3]{Y}}$

Substitute the values given in the question:

$2 = \frac{k}{\sqrt[3]{512}}$

$2 = \frac{k}{8}$

$\underline{16 = k}$

Now, use this value of k to find 'Y' when 'X' is 8:

$8 = \frac{16}{\sqrt[3]{Y}}$

$\sqrt[3]{Y} = 2$

$Y = 2^3$

$\underline{Y = 8}$

30. D

Explanation:

The proportion of red paint she needs is $\frac{3}{5}$.

Therefore, the total amount of paint she needs is:

$18 \div \frac{3}{5} =$ **30 litres**

30 – 18 = **12 litres**

18 litres of red paint will cost:

18 x 5.46 = **£98.28**

12 litres of white paint will cost:

12 x 3.21 = **£38.52**

Therefore, the total expenditure is **£136.80.**

Mathematics

31. B

Explanation:

If the ratio of the length and width is 8:15, then ratio of the length, width and diagonal is:

<u>**8:15:17**</u>, because 8, 15, and 17 is a Pythagorean triple ($8^2 + 15^2 = 17^2$).

<u>The length of the diagonal is 102 m.</u>

102÷17 = <u>**6.**</u>

Therefore, the length and width are:

8 x 6 = <u>**48 m**</u>

6 x 15 = <u>**90 m.**</u>

The area of the field is:

90 x 48 =<u>**4320 m²**</u>

32. C

Explanation:

Let the sides of the large square be 2x:

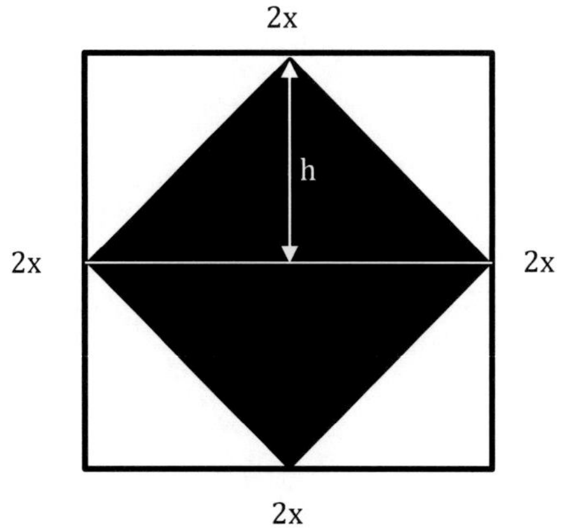

The length of the base of the triangle is $2x$ and the height is x. The area of the black triangle is $\frac{1}{2}bh$:

$= \frac{1}{2} \text{ x } 2x \text{ x } x$

$= \frac{1}{2} \text{ x } 2x^2$

$= \underline{\boldsymbol{x^2}}$

The area of the large square is $2x$ x $2x$ = $\boldsymbol{4x^2}$

Ratio of the large square to the black triangle is:

<u>$\boldsymbol{4x^2 : x^2}$</u>

<u>**4:1**</u>

33. B

Explanation:

<u>**11 + 17 = 28**</u>

756 ÷ 28 = <u>**27**</u> (one part is equal to 27 pupils)

The difference in the parts is:

17 – 11 = 6

Therefore, there will be 6 x 27 = **162** more girls than boys.

An alternative method would be to find the number of boys and girls, then find the difference between the two.

Boys: 11 x 27 = **297**

Girls: 17 x 27 = **459**

459 – 297 = **162**

Mathematics (M4)	ALGEBRA	Answers

34. D

Explanation:

Let the initial number of girls be 'n'.

Average weight = 50

Total weight = **50n**

After a girl of weight 58kg joins the group:

Total weight = 50n + 58

New average $= \frac{\mathbf{50n+58}}{\mathbf{n+1}}$

Given that the average weight of the group goes up by 1 kg:

$50+1 = \frac{50n+58}{n+1}$

$51 = \frac{50n+58}{n+1}$

51n+51=50n+58

N = 7

The initial number of girls =7

The number of girls after the addition= **7+1 = 8**

35. F

Explanation:

$\frac{x}{y} = \frac{q}{r} + \frac{s}{t}$

Make the right-hand side have a common denominator of 'rt':

$\frac{x}{y} = \frac{qt+rs}{rt}$

Invert fraction:

$\frac{y}{x} = \frac{rt}{qt+rs}$

Multiply the right-hand side by 'y' and the left-hand side by 'x':

$rtx = qty + rsy$

All expressions with t are on the left-hand side:

$rtx - qty = rsy$

Take 't' out as a common factor:

$t(rx - qy) = rsy$

$t = \frac{\mathbf{rsy}}{\mathbf{rx-qy}}$

36. E

Explanation:

$$=\frac{(4x+5)(4x+5) + (4x-5)(4x-5) - 3(4x+5)(4x-5)}{(4x-5)(4x+5)}$$

$$=\frac{16x^2 + 20x + 25 + 16x^2 - 20x + 25 - 3(16x^2 - 25)}{(4x-5)(4x+5)}$$

$$=\frac{16x^2 + 20x + 25 + 16x^2 - 20x + 25 - 48x^2 + 75}{(4x-5)(4x+5)}$$

$$=\frac{-16x^2 + 125}{(4x-5)(4x+5)}$$

37. A

Explanation:

Rearrange:

$$y - 12 = 6(\frac{x}{3} - 5)^2$$

$$\frac{y-12}{6} = (\frac{x}{3} - 5)^2$$

Square root both sides:

$$\pm\frac{\sqrt{y} - \sqrt{12}}{\sqrt{6}} = \frac{x}{3} - 5$$

Arrange all of the 'x' on one side:

$$\pm\frac{\sqrt{y} - \sqrt{12}}{\sqrt{6}} + 5 = +\frac{x}{3}$$

Multiply both sides by 3:

$$+3\,(\pm\frac{\sqrt{y-12}}{\sqrt{6}} + 5) = x$$

$$x = \frac{\pm 3\sqrt{y-12}}{\sqrt{6}} + 15$$

38. B

Explanation:

Solve the brackets first due to BODMAS (Brackets Order Division Multiplication Addition Subtraction)

$$(2x^{-1/5})^5 = 2^5 \times x^{-1}$$

$$=\frac{2^5}{x}$$

Multiply 4x by $\frac{2^5}{x}$*:*

$$= 4x \times \frac{2^5}{x}$$

$$=\frac{4x \times 32}{x}$$

$$=\frac{128x}{x}$$

$$=\underline{128}$$

Mathematics

39. B

Explanation:

To find the graphs that do intersect, the two equations can be rearranged to equal each other (since they are all y=.....):

The discriminant can then be tested to indicate if the two graphs have real roots (they intersect):

$b^2 - 4ac > 0$ (2 points of intersection)

$b^2 - 4ac = 0$ (1 point of intersection)

$b^2 - 4ac < 0$ (0 points of intersection)

A. $2x - 1 = x^2 + 5x$

$x^2 + 3x + 1 = 0$

Discriminant (**$b^2 - 4ac$**): $3^2 - 4(1)(1) = 5$

(discriminant is positive; therefore, these two graphs intersect)

B. $2x - 1 = x^2 + 6x + 4$

$x^2 + 4x + 5 = 0$

Discriminant (**$b^2 - 4ac$**): $4^2 - 4(5)(1) = \underline{-4}$

(discriminant is negative; therefore, these two graphs do not intersect because there are no real roots)

C. $x^2 + 5x = x^2 + 6x + 4$

$-x = 4$

$x = -4$ (intersection at $x = -4$)

D. $x^2 + 5x = -4$

$x^2 + 5x + 4 = 0$

Discriminant (**$b^2 - 4ac$**): $5^2 - 4(4)(1) = 9$

(discriminant is positive; therefore, these two graphs intersect)

E. $x^2 + 6x + 4 = -4$

$x^2 + 6x + 8 = 0$

Discriminant (**$b^2 - 4ac$**): $6^2 - 4(8)(1) = 4$

(discriminant is positive; therefore, these two graphs intersect)

40. A

Explanation:

For the first group:

Mean distance ran = speed x time

= 47 x 6

= <u>282 m</u>

Total distance = 282 x 30

= <u>8460 m</u>

For the second group:

Mean distance ran = 282 +10

= <u>292 m</u>

Total distance: P x D = PD

The mean is calculated by the total distance, divided by the total number of people. Therefore, the mean of both groups is:

$$\frac{(8460 + PD)}{30 + P} = 292$$

$8460 + PD = 292(30 + P)$

$8460 + PD = 8760 + 292P$

PD – 292P = 8760 – 8460

P (D-292) = 300

$P = \frac{\mathbf{300}}{\mathbf{D-292}}$

41. C

Explanation:

Consider the numerator:

$\sqrt{a}$ x 3b= $\sqrt{1.6 \text{ x } 10^5}$ x 3(4 x 10^4)

= **<u>4.8 x 10^7</u>**

Consider the denominator:

$5b\sqrt{a} = 5(4 \text{ x } 10^4)\sqrt{1.6 \text{ x } 10^5}$

= **<u>8 x 10^7</u>**

Dividing the numerator by the denominator:

$\frac{4.8 \text{ x } 10^7}{8 \text{ x } 10^7} = \frac{48}{80} = \frac{\mathbf{3}}{\mathbf{5}}$

42. E

Explanation:

Consider:

$(1 - 36x^2)$ = -$(6x + 1)$ $(6x - 1)$

Therefore,

$8 - \frac{x^4(1-36x^2)}{(6x+1)(4x^5)} = 8 + \frac{x^4(6x+1)(6x-1)}{(6x+1)(4x^5)}$

The '6x +1' can be cancelled out:

$= 8 + \frac{x^4(6x-1)}{4x^5}$

The 'x' can be cancelled out:

$= 8 + \frac{(6x-1)}{4x}$

<u>A common denominator of $4x$ can be established:</u>

Convert 8 into a fraction with denominator $4x$:

$8 = \frac{32x}{4x}$

Therefore,

$\frac{32x+6x-1}{4x} = \frac{\mathbf{38x-1}}{\mathbf{4x}}$

43. A

Explanation:

Consider the numbers first:

$\frac{1.6}{12.8} = \frac{16}{128}$

$\frac{16}{128} = \frac{\mathbf{1}}{\mathbf{8}}$

Consider the 'x':

$\frac{x^{-5}}{x^{-3}} = x^{-5-(-3)}$

$= \underline{\mathbf{x^{-2}}}$

Consider the 'y':

Mathematics

A Lakshmi, T R Enoch, S Z Y Ooi. Doctors Academy Publications, Cardiff, UK, 2020.

$\frac{y^5}{y^8} = x^{5\text{-}8}$

$= \underline{y^{-3}}$

Therefore, combining the three constituents:

$\boldsymbol{\frac{1}{8}x^{-2}y^{-3}}$

44. E

Explanation:

Let x be the number of £20 notes:

Number of £5 notes = (x-25)

Number of £20 notes = x

Number of £50 notes= 4x

$5(x\text{-}25) + 20x + 50(4x) = 10225$

$5x - 125 + 20x + 200x = 10225$

$225x = 10350$

$x = 46$

Number of £20 notes = **46**

Number of £5 notes = 46 – 25 = **21**

Number of £50 notes= 4(46) = **184**

Therefore, total number of notes:

21 + 184 + 46 = **251**

45. B

Explanation:

Consider $\frac{(x+4)^2}{2x^2+3x-20}$*:*

Factorise the denominator.

$\frac{(x+4)^2}{(x+4)(2x-5)}$

Divide the numerator and denominator by $x + 4$*:*

$\frac{x+4}{2x-5}$

$\frac{x}{x+2} - \frac{x+4}{2x-5}$

Common denominator of $(x + 2)(2x - 5)$*:*

$\frac{x(2x-5)-(x+4)(x+2)}{(x+2)(2x-5)} = \frac{2x^2-5x-x^2-6x-8}{(x+2)(2x-5)}$

$= \boldsymbol{\frac{x^2-11x-8}{2x^2-x-10}}$

46. A

Explanation:

$z^2 = \frac{3.2 \times 10^7}{(2.0 \times 10^2)^3}$

$z^2 = 4$

$z = 2$

47. A

Explanation:

y = f(x)+ a is a **vertical translation** of 'a' units up if it is positive and down if 'a' is negative

y = f(x - b) is a **horizontal translation** of 'b' to the right.

y= f(x + b) is a **horizontal translation** of' 'b' to the left.

48. D

Explanation:

$$\frac{a^8 x\, a^6}{\sqrt{a^4}} \div a^{\frac{1}{2}}$$

$$= \frac{a^{14}}{\sqrt{a^4}} \div a^{\frac{1}{2}}$$

$$= \frac{a^{14}}{a^2} \div a^{\frac{1}{2}}$$

$$= a^{12} \div a^{\frac{1}{2}}$$

$$= a^{11.5}$$

$$= \boldsymbol{a^{\frac{23}{2}}}$$

49. D

Explanation:

The graph showing $y = \frac{1}{x^2}$ *is:*

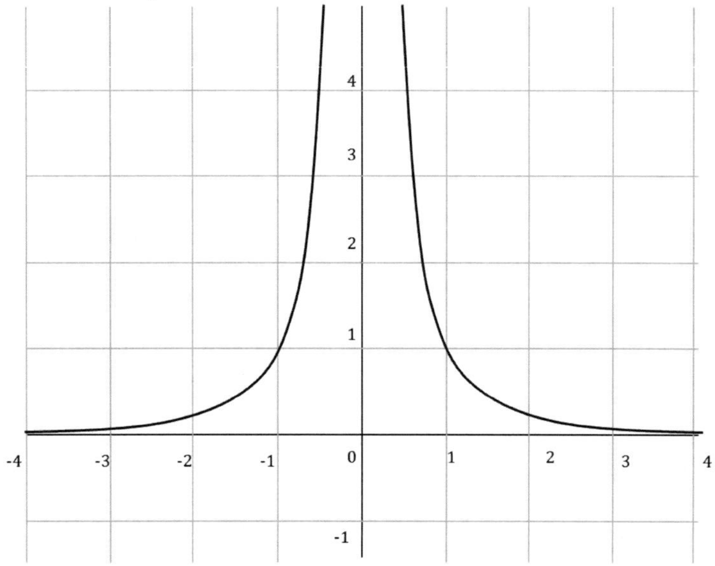

Here where $x = 1, y = 1$.

However, in the graph in the question when $\boldsymbol{x = 1, y = 3.}$

Therefore, it has been translated up by 2 units; hence the answer is **Option 'D'**.

The general shape of the graph should be recognised initially as $\mathbf{y = \frac{1}{x^2}}$.

50. C

Explanation:

This is a cubic curve and has 3 roots.

The roots (where the curve crosses the x-axis) are:

x =-3, x = 2 and x = 4

Therefore, the equation of the curve is:

$y = (x+3)(x-2)(x-4)$.

Substitute $x=1$ into the equation:

$y = (1+3)(1-2)(1-4)$

$y = 4 \times -1 \times -3$

$y = 12$

The coordinates are (1,12)

---

51. B

Explanation:

Complete the square:

$y = (x-4)^2 - 16 + 24$

This is simplified to:

$\mathbf{y = (x-4)^2 + 8}$

Therefore, the **minimum point is (4, 8)**

---

52. B

Explanation:

The numerator and denominator should be calculated separately.

The numerator becomes:

$42ab^3$

In the denominator, the bracket must be calculated before the division is completed:

$24a^3 \div 4a = 6a^2$

Therefore, the fraction is now simplified to:

$$\frac{42ab^3}{6a^2}$$

This is further simplified to $\frac{7b^3}{a}$

---

53. F

Explanation:

$$\frac{8}{\frac{x}{7}-6} - 6 = 18y$$

$$\frac{8}{\frac{x}{7}-6} = 18y + 6$$

$$\frac{8}{18y+6} = \frac{x}{7} - 6$$

$$\frac{4}{9y+3} = \frac{x}{7} - 6$$

$$\frac{4}{9y+3} + 6 = \frac{x}{7}$$

$$7\frac{4}{9y+3} + 6 = x$$

Mathematics

54. A

Explanation:

$$\frac{2x^2+4x-6}{x^2+5x+6}$$

Factorise out the 2:

$$=\frac{2(x^2+2x-3)}{x^2+5x+6}$$

Factorise the quadratics:

$$=\frac{2(x-1)(x+3)}{(x+2)(x+3)}$$

$$=\frac{\mathbf{2(x-1)}}{\mathbf{(x+2)}}$$

---

55. E

Explanation:

<u>The lowest common multiple of $'x'$ and $'y'$ is $'xy'$:</u>

$$=\frac{3}{x}+\frac{7}{y}$$

$$=\frac{\mathbf{3y+7x}}{\mathbf{xy}}$$

---

56. F

Explanation:

The range is the **<u>set of all the points on which the function maps</u>**.

Complete the square to find the turning point:

$= x^2 + 2x - 9$

$= (x + 1)^2 - 1 - 9$

$= (x + 1)^2 - 10$

Therefore, the turning point is at **<u>(-1, -10).</u>**

Since x^2 is positive the curve will be **<u>U shaped</u>**. Therefore, **<u>(-1, -10) is the minimum point.</u>**

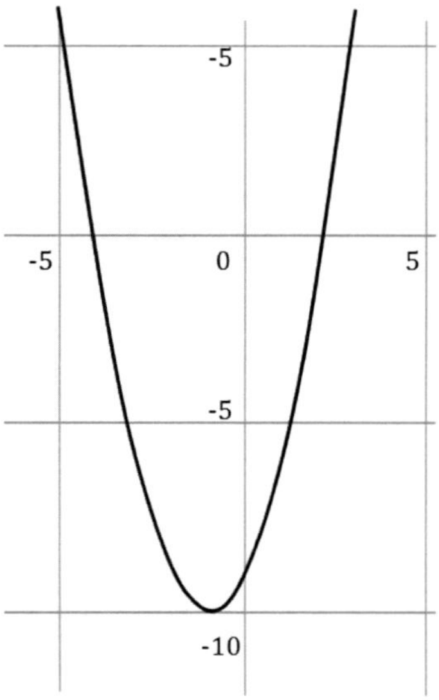

The range will be **<u>f(x) ≥ -10</u>**

57. D

Explanation:

$y = \frac{4}{5}\left(\frac{x}{4} + 7\right)^2 + 2$

$y - 2 = \frac{4}{5}\left(\frac{x}{4} + 7\right)^2$

$\frac{5y-10}{4} = \left(\frac{x}{4} + 7\right)^2$

$\mp\sqrt{\frac{5y-10}{4}} = \frac{x}{4} + 7$

$\mathbf{-28 \mp 4\sqrt{\frac{5y-10}{4}} = x}$

Mathematics (M5)	GEOMETRY	Answers

58. F

Explanation:

Alternate segment theorem:

Angle TQP = **48°**

Due to same base angles in an isosceles triangle:

Angle QPT = Angle PTQ

Angle QPT:

$\frac{180-48}{2}$ = **66°**

Angle OTP + Angle OTQ = 66°

Since tangent and radius are at 90°:

Angle OTP:

90° – 48° = **42°**

Angle OTQ = 66° - Angle OTP:

OTQ = 66° – 42°

= **24°**

59. B

Explanation:

Since the tangent and the radius meet at 90° on the circumference of the circle:

Angle CBO = **90°**

Angles in a triangle add up to 180°, therefore, angle COB can be found using subtraction:

Angle COB:

180° – (90°+38°) = 180°-128°

= **52°**

Angles on a straight line add up to 180°:

Angle BOA:

180°-52°= **128°**

Triangle OBA is isosceles because both radii are equal (OA=OB); therefore:

Angle OAB=Angle ABO

Angles in a triangle add up to 180°:

$128° + 2x = 180°$

$2x = 52°$

$\underline{x = 26°}$

60. B

Explanation:

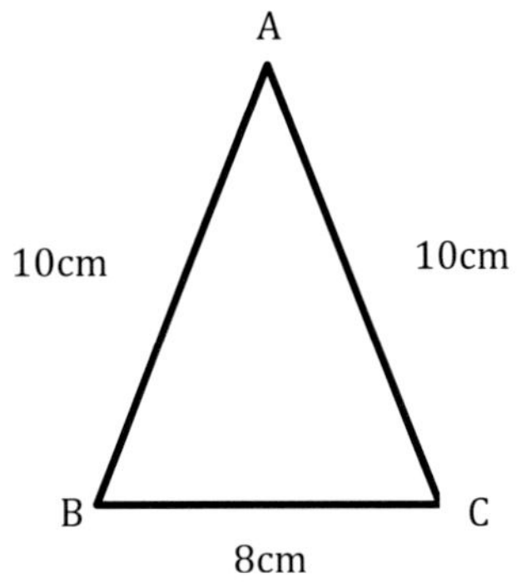

In order to use Pythagoras Theorem, a right angle must be formed.

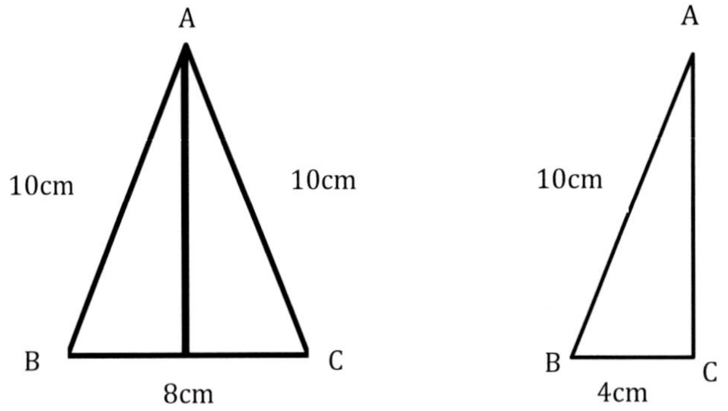

The length of AC is calculated using Pythagoras Theorem:

$AC^2 = 10^2 - 4^2$

$AC = \underline{\mathbf{2\sqrt{21}}}$

$\tan ABC = \dfrac{\text{opposite of B}}{\text{adjacent of B}}$

$= \dfrac{2\sqrt{21}}{4}$

$= \dfrac{\mathbf{\sqrt{21}}}{\mathbf{2}}$

61. A

Explanation:

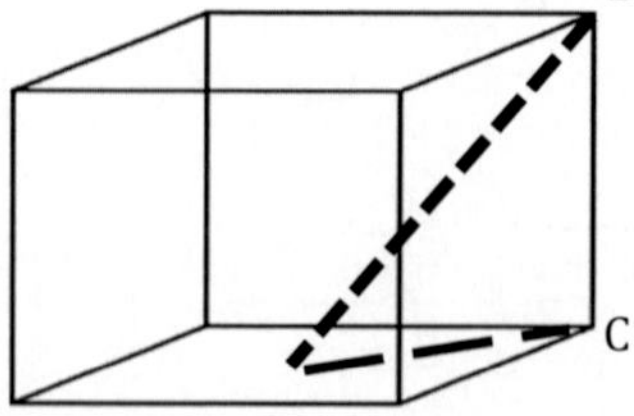

First, form a triangle and label is as ABC:

The length of AC must be found to find AB:

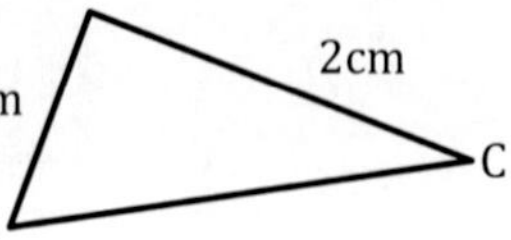

The shorter sides are both 2cm because the vertex is joined at the midpoint of the bottom face ($\frac{4}{2}=2$).

$AC = \sqrt{2^2 + 2^2}$

$AC = \underline{2\sqrt{2}}$

The length of AB can now be found using Pythagoras:

AC = $2\sqrt{2}$ and **BC = 4** (cube has length sides of 4cm)

$AB^2 = AC^2 + BC^2$

$AB = \sqrt{2\sqrt{2}^{\,2} + 4^2}$

$AB = \sqrt{8 + 16}$

$AB = \sqrt{24}$

$AB = \sqrt{4} \times \sqrt{6}$

$AB = \underline{\mathbf{2\sqrt{6}}}$

62. B

Explanation:

The surface area of a cylinder $= 2\pi r^2 + 2\pi rh$

The volume of a cone $= \pi r^2$

Since the **surface area of the cylinder = 3 (volume of cone)**:

$2\pi r^2 + 2\pi rh = 3(\pi r^2)$

Mathematics

$2\pi r^2 + 2\pi rh = 3\pi r^2 h$

Divide both sides by π:

$2r^2 + 2rh = 3r^2h$

Collect all 'h' on one side:

$2r^2 = 3r^2h - 2rh$

$2r^2 = h(3r^2 - 2r)$

Therefore, $h = \dfrac{2r^2}{3r^2 - 2r}$

63. C

Explanation:

Assume that the original square has sides of 1 unit:

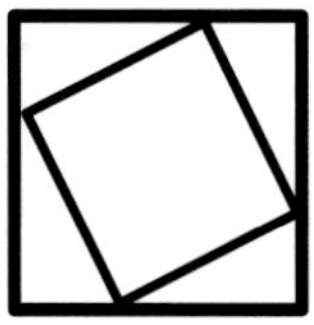

The triangle formed has sides $\frac{1}{4}$ (due to square being placed ¼ of the way into the larger square) and $\frac{3}{4}$ (because the square extends ¾ of the way down the larger square):

Find the hypotenuse of this triangle (using Pythagoras) to find the length of the smaller square:

Length of second square:

$$\sqrt{\frac{1}{4}^2 + \frac{3}{4}^2} = \frac{\sqrt{10}}{4}$$

Therefore, the length of the second square is $\frac{\sqrt{10}}{4}$

For the third square, the two sides are:

$$x = \frac{1}{4} \text{ x } \frac{\sqrt{10}}{4}$$

$$x = \frac{\sqrt{10}}{16}$$

$x = \frac{3}{4} \text{ x } \frac{\sqrt{10}}{4}$

$\boldsymbol{x = \frac{3\sqrt{10}}{16}}$

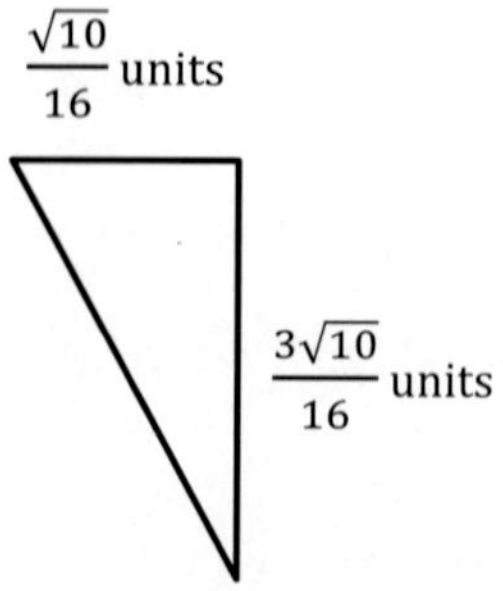

The hypotenuse is the same as the length of the third square:
Length of third square:

$\sqrt{\frac{\sqrt{10}}{16}^2 + \frac{3\sqrt{10}}{16}^2} = \boldsymbol{\frac{5}{8}}$

For the fourth square, the two sides are:

$x = \frac{1}{4} \text{ x } \frac{5}{8}$

$\boldsymbol{x = \frac{5}{32}}$

$x = \frac{3}{4} \text{ x } \frac{5}{8}$

$x = \frac{15}{32}$

The hypotenuse is the same as the length of the fourth square:

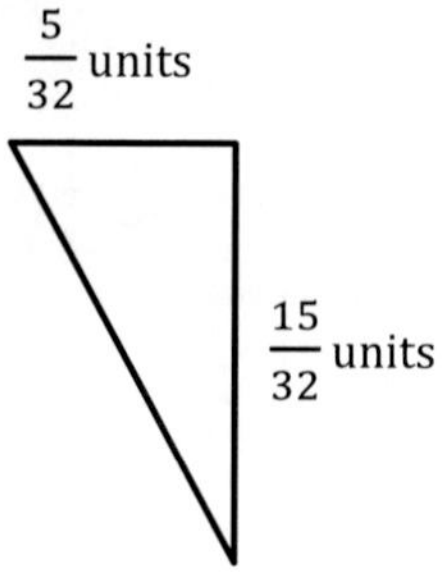

Length of fourth square”

$\sqrt{\frac{5}{32}^2 + \frac{15}{32}^2} = \sqrt{\frac{25+225}{1024}}$

$= \sqrt{\frac{125}{512}}$

Area of fourth square:

$\sqrt{\frac{125}{512}} \text{ x } \sqrt{\frac{125}{512}} = \boldsymbol{\frac{125}{512}}$

Mathematics

64. D

Explanation:

A circular clock always contains 360°.

Since there are 60 minutes on a clock, a minute hand moves 6°a minute:

= 6° a minute

Since there are 12 hours on a clock, an hour hands moves 30° an hour:

= 30° an hour

The minute hand points to 15 minutes:

15 x 6 = 90°

The hour hand at 08:00, has travelled for 8 hours:

30 x 8 = 240°

However, the hour hand will actually be between 08:00 and the 09:00, because it is not at an absolute hour mark. Fifteen minutes is equal to one-fourth of an hour.

In a quarter of an hour, the hour hand would have travelled:

0.25 x 30° = 7.5°

Therefore, total degree that the hour hand has travelled:

7.5° + 240° = 247.5°

Difference between the hour and minute hand:

247.5° - 90° = **157. 5°**

65. F

Explanation:

Label each triangle as 'X', 'Y' and 'Z':

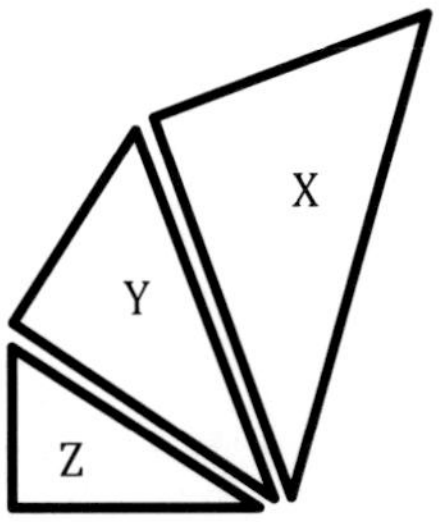

Looking at Triangle X:

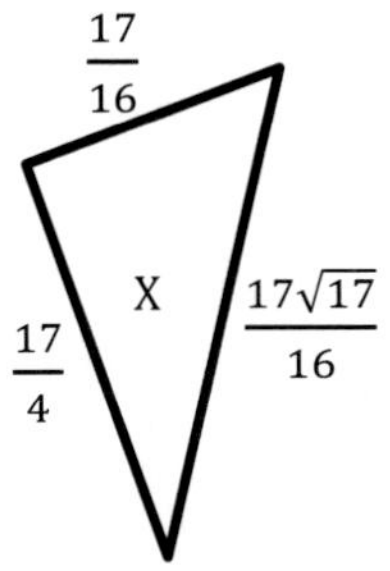

Using Pythagoras: the hypotenuse is: $= \sqrt{\frac{17^2}{16} + \frac{17^2}{4}}$

$= \frac{17\sqrt{17}}{16}$

Looking at Triangle Y:

From the given diagram, the $\frac{17}{4}$ cm of Triangle 'X' is the hypotenuse of Triangle 'Y'.

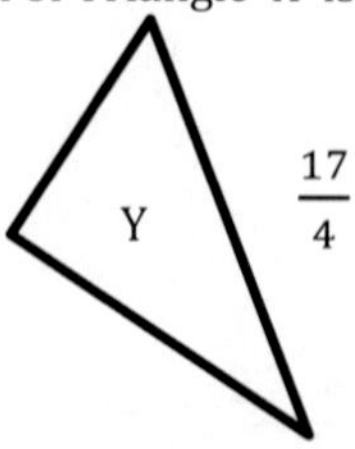

Since the triangles are similar, the ratio between the two hypotenuses are equal to the ratio between either two corresponding sides: $\frac{17\sqrt{17}}{16} \div \frac{17}{4} = \frac{\sqrt{17}}{4}$

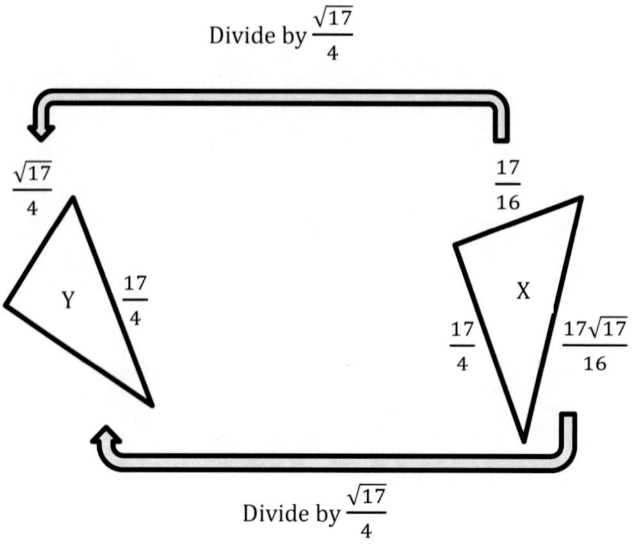

The missing side for Triangle 'Y' is : $\frac{17}{4} / \frac{\sqrt{17}}{4} = \underline{\boldsymbol{\sqrt{17}}}$

Looking at Triangle Z:

The $\sqrt{17}$ of Triangle 'Y' is the hypotenuse of Triangle 'X'.

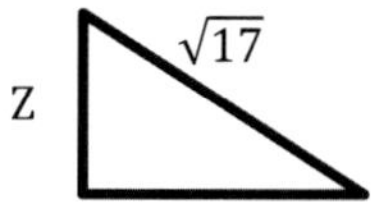

Since Triangle 'Y' and 'Z' are similar, the ratio between the two hypotenuses are equal to the ratio between either two corresponding sides: $\frac{17}{4} \div \sqrt{17} = \frac{\sqrt{17}}{4}$

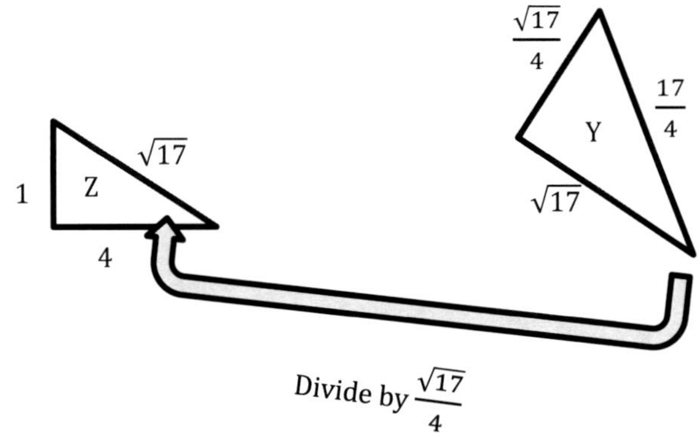

$= \frac{\sqrt{17}}{4} \div \frac{\sqrt{17}}{4}$

$= \underline{1}$

$\sqrt{17} \div \frac{\sqrt{17}}{4}$

$\underline{= 4}$

Area of Triangle 'Z' $= \frac{1}{2}$ x 4 x 1

$= \underline{2\ cm^2}$

---

66. E

Explanation:

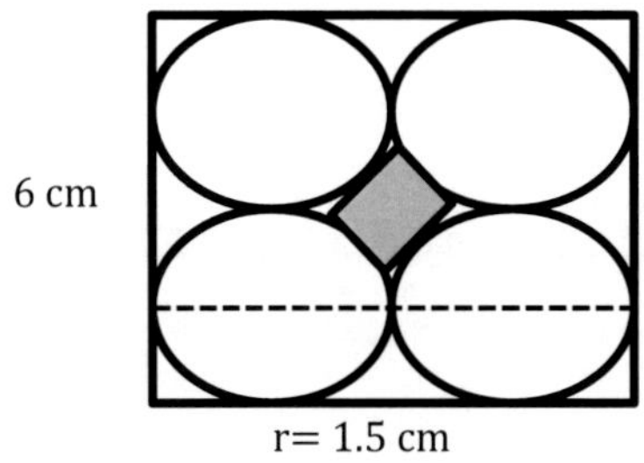

The large square's side is equal to 4 times the length of the radius of a single circle. Therefore, each circle has a radius:

<u>r = 1.5</u>

Form a triangle between the centres of 3 circles:

Let x be the length of the square:

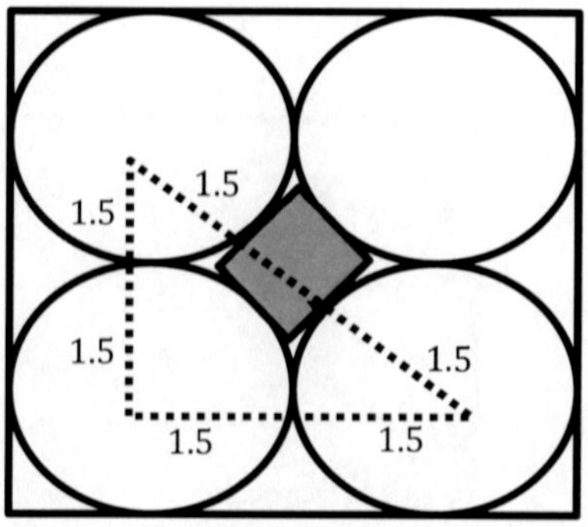

The two sides of the triangle have length 3cm, and the hypotenuse is equal to:

$3 + x$

Using Pythagoras:

'x' is: $\sqrt{3^2 + 3^2} = 3\sqrt{2}$

Therefore, the hypotenuse is $3 + x = 3\sqrt{2}$

$x = 3\sqrt{2} - 3$

Area of the small square : $(3\sqrt{2} - 3)^2 =$ **$27 - 18\sqrt{2}$ cm**

Area of the large square: $6 \times 6 =$ **36 cm**

Fraction of large square that is taken up by small square:

$= \frac{27 - 18\sqrt{2}}{36}$

$= \frac{\mathbf{3 - 2\sqrt{2}}}{\mathbf{4}}$

67. A

Explanation:

The triangle is a multiple of the 3,4,5 ($3^2 + 4^2 = 5^2$) triangle, therefore, there is a right angle between the 6cm and the 8cm:

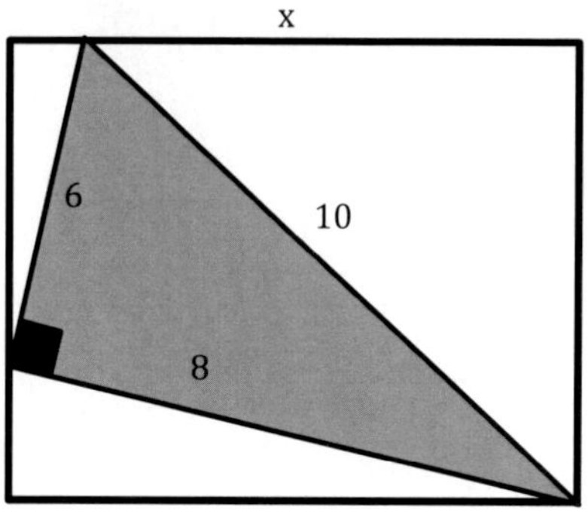

Consider the other two triangles:

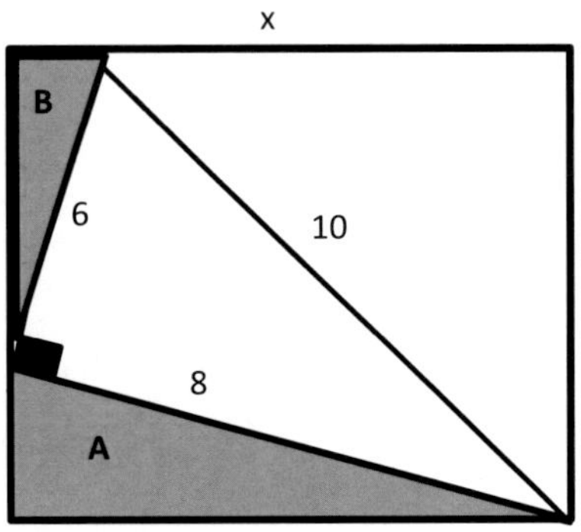

Consider Triangle A:

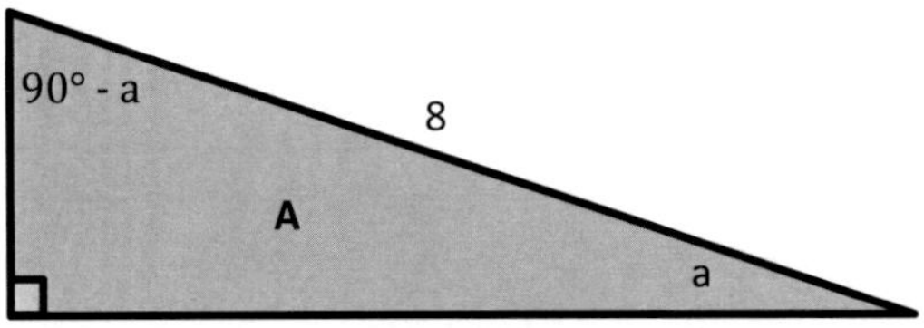

There is a right angle (due to square shape).
Let 'a' be one angle.
Since triangles have 180°, the third angle will be:
180° - (90° + a) = **<u>90° - a</u>**

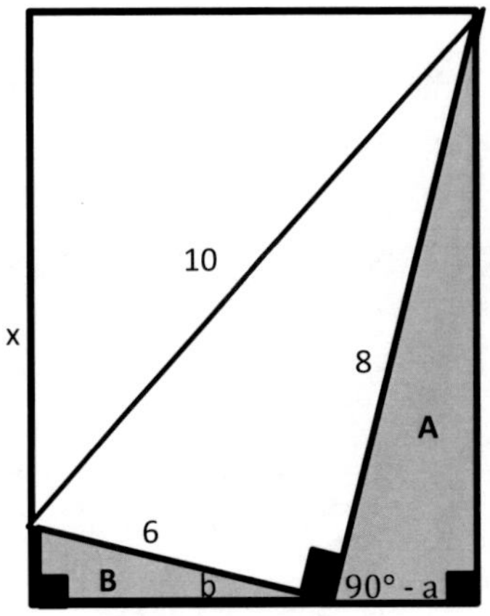

Since angles on s straight line equal to 180°:
b = 180° - 90° - (90° -a)
<u>b= a</u>

Consider Triangle B:

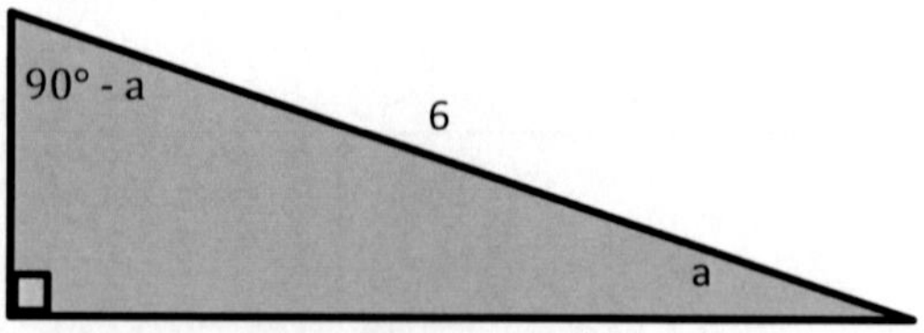

There is a right angle (due to square shape).
'a' is one angle (calculated from the previous diagram).
Since triangles have 180°, the third angle will be:
180° - (90° + a) = **<u>90° - a</u>**
<u>Therefore, Triangles A and B are similar (because they have three of the same angles)</u>
Since they are similar, the ratio of their sides is equal to each other:

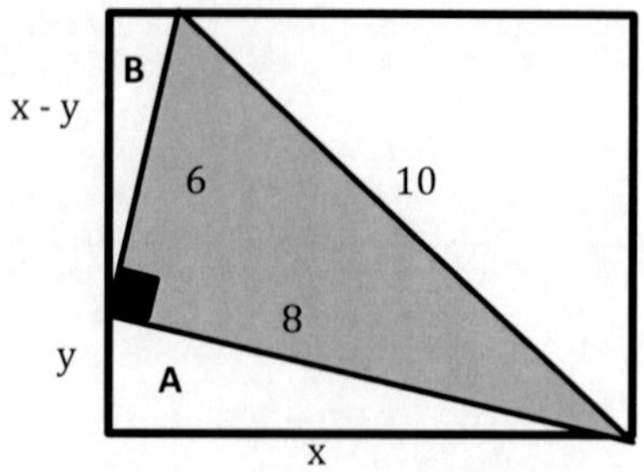

$\frac{x-y}{6} = \frac{x}{8}$

$8(x-y) = 6x$

$8x-6x = 8y$

$2x = 8y$

$x= 4y$

$\mathbf{y = \frac{x}{4}}$

Consider Triangle A:

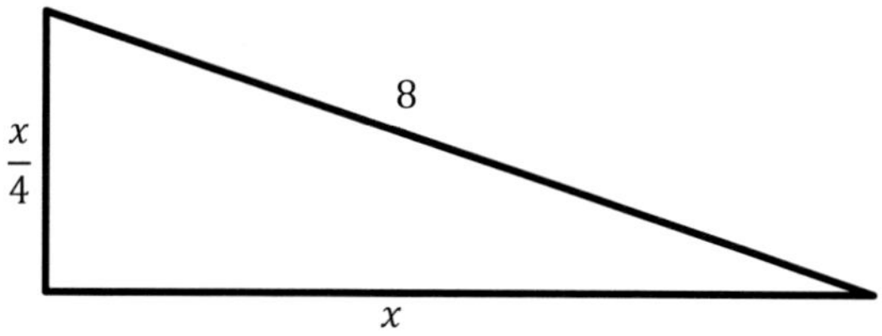

Pythagoras can be used to find x :

$8^2 = \frac{x^2}{4} + x^2$

$$64 = \frac{17}{16}x^2$$
$$x^2 = \frac{1024}{17}$$
$$x = \frac{32\sqrt{17}}{17}$$

68. B

Explanation:
Split the isosceles triangle into 2 right angle triangles.

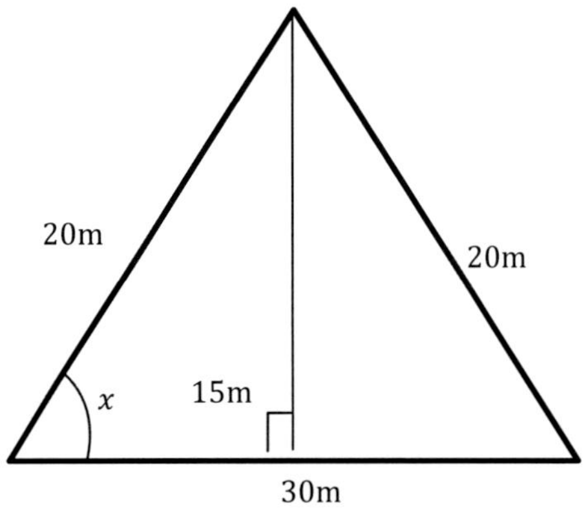

$$\cos x = \frac{adjacent}{hypotenuse}$$
$$\cos x = \frac{15}{20}$$
$$\cos x = \frac{3}{4}$$
$$x = \cos^{-1}\left(\frac{3}{4}\right)$$

69. D

Explanation:
Draw a diagram of the 3 supermarkets.

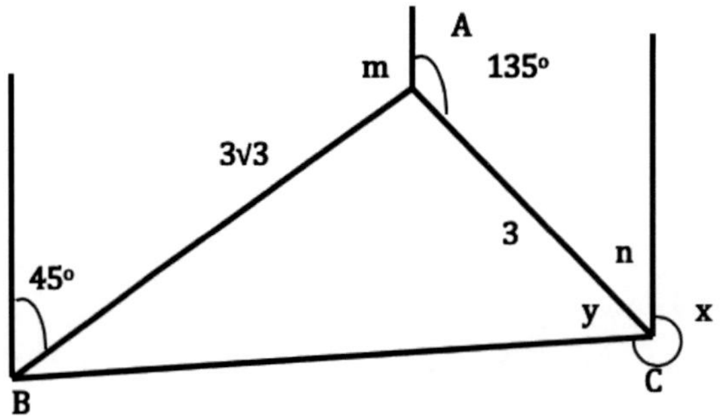

Mathematics

Angle BAC is a right angle as **interior angles add up to 180°:**
Angle 'm' is:
180 – 45 = 135°
Angles around a point sum to 360°
Angle BAC is:
360 – (135 + 135) = **90°**

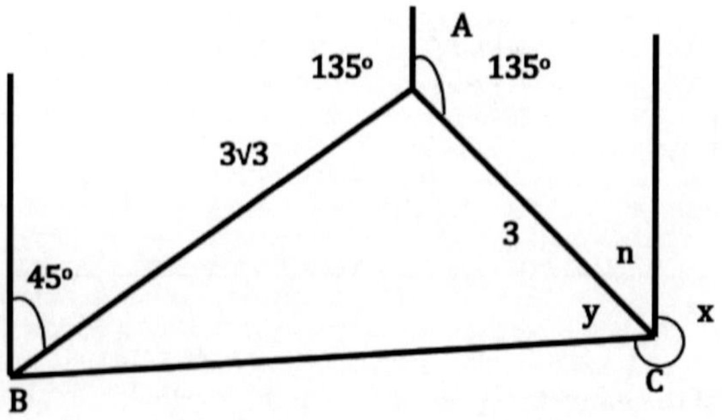

Angle x is the bearing of B from C (what needs to be found):
$\text{Tan } y = \frac{3\sqrt{3}}{3}$
$\text{Tan } y = \sqrt{3}$
y= 60°
Angles around a point sum to 360°:
x : **360 – (60 + n)**
Angle n is 45° as interior angels sum to 180° *(180 – 135 = 45)*
Therefore:
x : 360 – 105 =**255°**

Mathematics

70. B

Explanation:
To find the distance between the two points:
$\sqrt{(x_2 - x_1)^2 + (y_2 - y_1)^2}$
$= \sqrt{(3-9)^2 + (7 - -13)^2}$
$= \sqrt{(-6)^2 + (20)^2}$
$= \sqrt{436}$
$= \mathbf{2\sqrt{109}}$

71. E

Explanation:
Area of the sector is given by:
$\textbf{Area} = \frac{1}{2} r^2 \theta$
$2 = \frac{1}{2} \times 4^2 \times \theta$

$\theta = \frac{1}{4}$

Arc length = r θ

Arc length = 4 x $\frac{1}{4}$

Arc length = 1

Perimeter:

4 + 4 + 1= <u>9 cm</u>

72. D

Explanation:

To find the length of the diagonal (d):

d $= \sqrt{x^2 + y^2 + z^2}$

d $= \sqrt{3^2 + 4^2 + 12^2}$

d $= \sqrt{169}$

<u>d = 13</u>

73. E

Explanation:

<u>The midpoint of the diameter is the centre of the circle.</u>

Midpoint of AB:

$(\frac{1+2}{2}, \frac{2+4}{2}) = (\frac{3}{2}, 3)$

The diameter of the circle:

$\sqrt{(2-1)^2 + (4-2)^2} = \sqrt{5}$

The radius is half of that of the diameter:

$r = \frac{\sqrt{5}}{2}$

$r^2 = \frac{5}{4}$

The equation of the circle is:

$\left(x - \frac{3}{2}\right)^2 + (y-3)^2 = \frac{5}{4}$

74. B

Explanation:

The formula for the volume of a pyramid:

$\frac{1}{3}$ x base area x height

As it is a square based pyramid the base area is:

6 x 6 = <u>36</u>

The Pythagoras theorem has to be used to find the height:

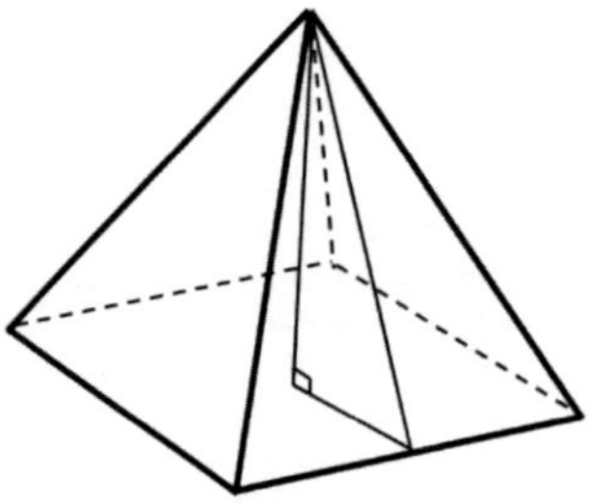

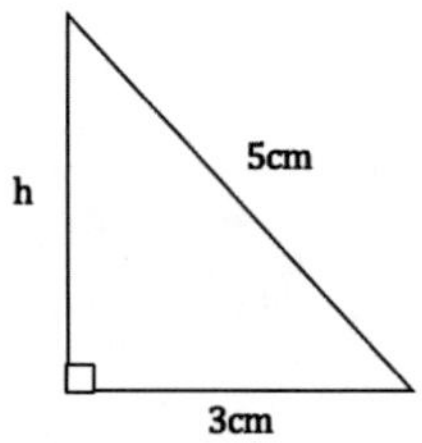

Since the base of the pyramid has a length of <u>**6 cm**</u>, the base of the triangle is half of this so (<u>**3 cm**</u>).

Using Pythagoras theorem, the height is:

$h^2 + 3^2 = 5^2$

$h^2 = 16$

<u>**h = 4 or -4**</u>

<u>**h = 4**</u> since it is a length it cannot be a negative number

The volume of the pyramid is:

$\frac{1}{3} \times 36 \times 4 = \underline{\mathbf{48\ cm^3}}$

75. D

Explanation:

Given that sin (A+B) = sin(A) cos(B) + cos(A) sin(B):

sin75 = sin (45 + 30)

= <u>sin45 cos 30 + cos45 sin30</u>

Using the exact values of cos and sin (need to be memorised):

$= \left(\frac{1}{\sqrt{2}} \times \frac{\sqrt{3}}{2}\right) + \left(\frac{1}{\sqrt{2}} \times \frac{1}{2}\right)$

$= \frac{\sqrt{3}+1}{2\sqrt{2}}$

$= \frac{\sqrt{3}+1}{2\sqrt{2}} \times \frac{\sqrt{2}}{\sqrt{2}}$

$= \frac{\sqrt{6}+\sqrt{2}}{4}$

76. A

Explanation:

Consider the following rectangle:

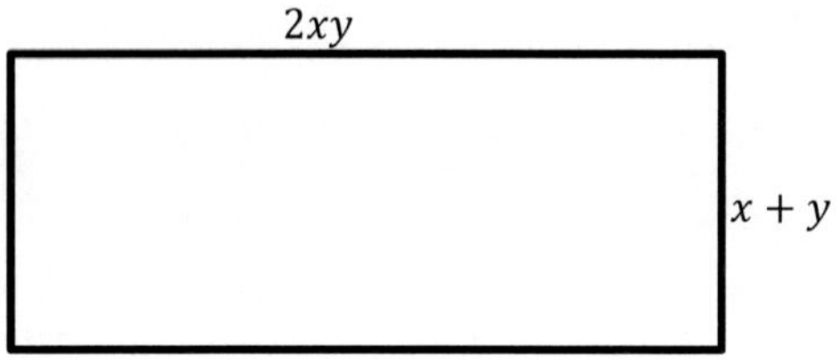

Perimeter is the 2(length + width):

$24 = 2(2xy + x + y)$

$12 = 2xy + x + y$

$12 - x = 2xy + y$

$12 - x = y\ (2x + 1)$

$y = \frac{12 - x}{2x+1}$

77. D

Explanation:

Given that cos (A+B) = cos(A) cos(B) - sin(A) sin(B), cos15 = cos (45+ (-30)):

cos 15 = cos(45)cos(-30) – sin(45)sin(-30)

Consider the following graph:

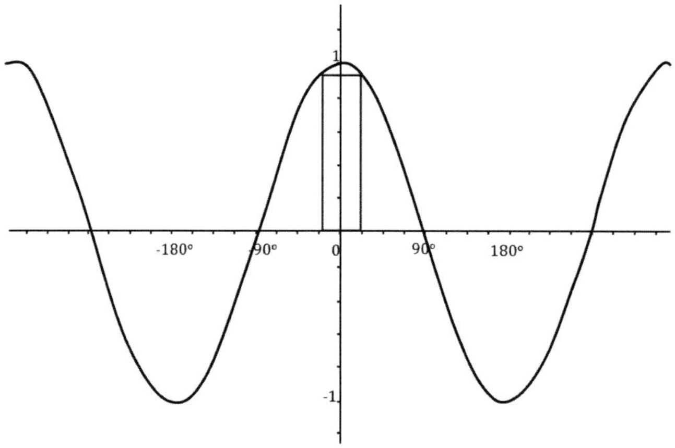

Therefore, from the above graph, **cos 30 = cos (-30)**

Consider the following graph:

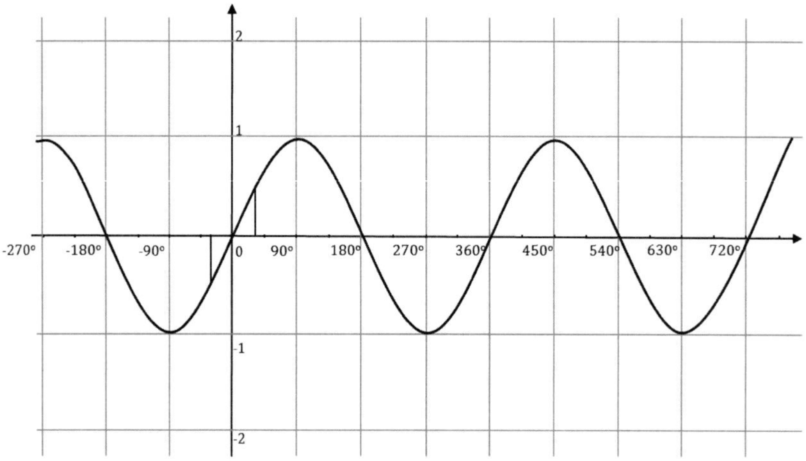

Therefore, from the above graph, - **sin30 = sin (-30)**

cos 15 = cos(45)cos(-30) – sin(45)sin(-30)

cos 15 = cos(45)cos(30) - sin(45) (-sin(30))

cos 15 = cos(45)cos(30) + sin(45)sin(30)

$$\cos 15 = \left(\frac{1}{\sqrt{2}} \text{ x } \frac{\sqrt{3}}{2}\right) + \left(\frac{1}{\sqrt{2}} \text{ x } \frac{1}{2}\right)$$

$$\cos 15 = \frac{\sqrt{3}+1}{2\sqrt{2}}$$

$$= \frac{\sqrt{3}+1}{2\sqrt{2}} \text{ x } \frac{\sqrt{2}}{\sqrt{2}}$$

$$= \mathbf{\frac{\sqrt{6}+\sqrt{2}}{4}}$$

78. C

Explanation:

<u>All the 3 angles in Triangles ABE and ACD are the same</u>; therefore, they are **<u>similar triangles.</u>**

This means that:

$\frac{AC}{DC} = \frac{AB}{EB}$

DC is:

1.5 x 6 = <u>9</u>

AC is AB + BC:

6 + 2 = <u>8cm</u>

$\frac{8}{9} = \frac{6}{EB}$

<u>EB = 6.75</u>

Mathematics (M6)	STATISTICS	Answers

79. D

Explanation:

First, find the angle of the pie chart for 'Car":

Angles in a circle add up to 360°

Therefore, the car angle is:

360° - (144° + 99° + 72°) = **<u>45°</u>**

Find the number of degrees that correspond to one person:

$\frac{360°}{200} = 1.8°$ per person

Number of people who travel by car:

$\frac{45°}{1.8} =$ **<u>25</u>**

Number of people who walk:

$\frac{144°}{1.8} =$ <u>80</u>

Therefore, difference in number of people who walk compared to travel by car:

80 – 25 = <u>55</u>

80. E

Explanation:

First, find the scale of the frequency density in order to find the number of marbles:

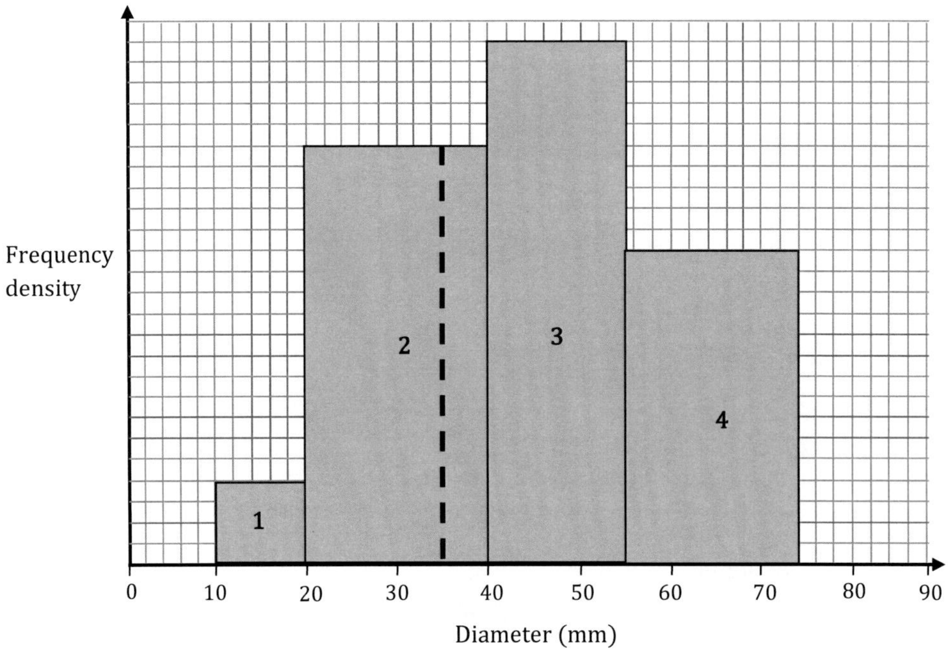

Consider Bar 1:

It has a length of 5 (from 10 to 20 in 5 squares) and a height of 4 squares.

Therefore, it represents:

5 x 4 = **20 squares**

Consider Bar 2 (prior to 35, which is represented by a dashed line):

It has a length of 7.5 (from 20 to 35 in 7.5 squares) and a height of 20:

Therefore, it represents:

7.5 x 20 = **150 squares**

150 squares + 20 squares = 34 marbles

170 squares = 34 marbles

1 square = **0.2 marbles**

Consider a diameter of more than 64 mm:

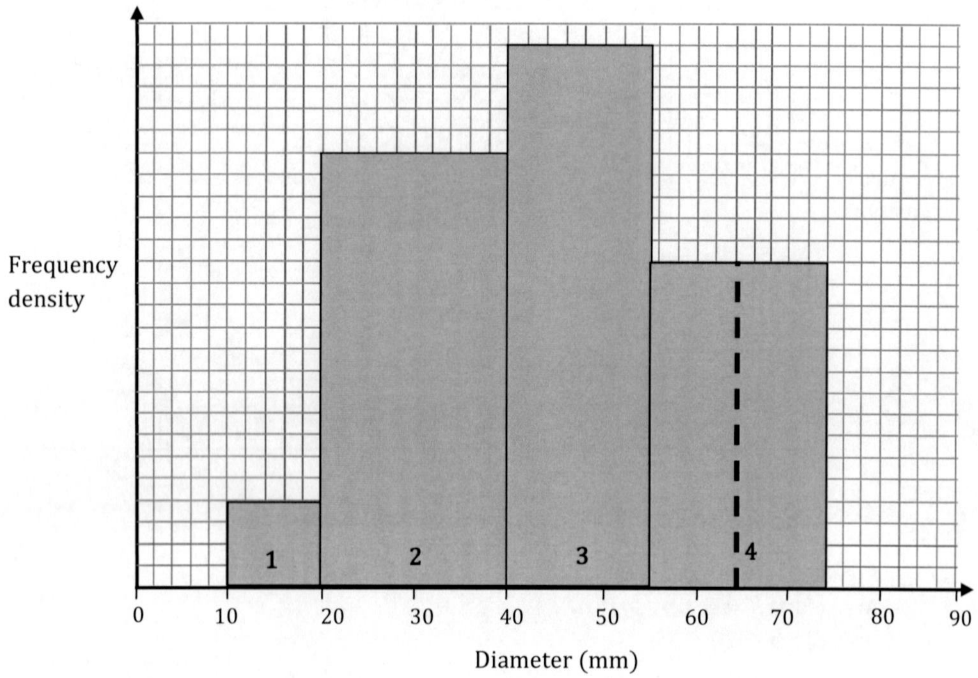

Area of bar: width x height

Area of bar: 5 x 15

Area of bar = <u>75</u>

To find number of marbles, multiply 75 by the number of marbles that one square represents:

75 x 0.2 = **<u>15 marbles</u>**

Consider a diameter of less than 20 mm:

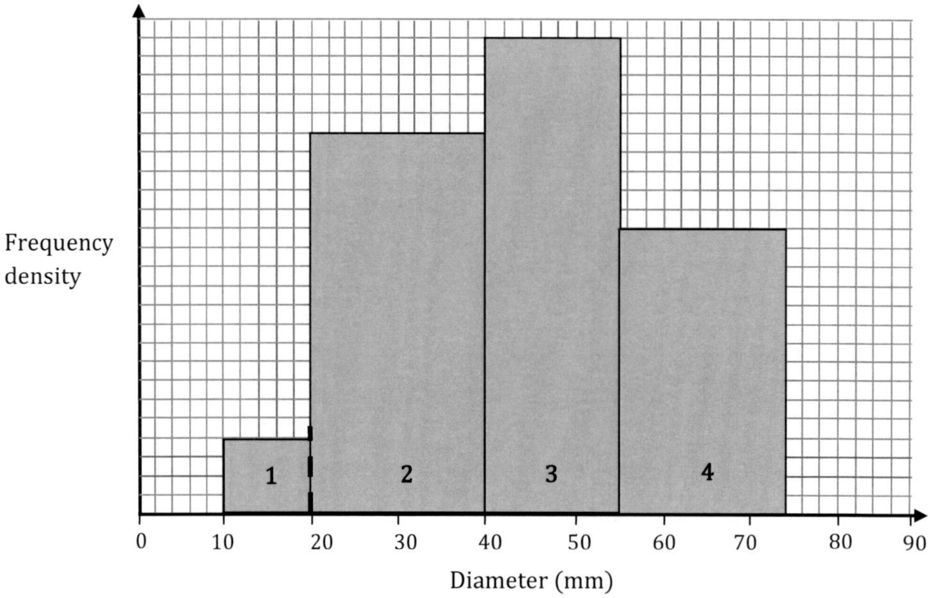

Area of bar: width x height

Area of bar: 5 x 4

Area of bar = **<u>20</u>**

To find number of marbles, multiply 20 by the number of marbles that one square represents:

20 x 0.2 = **<u>4 marbles</u>**

Therefore, the difference in the number of marbles:

15- 4 = **<u>11 marbles</u>**

81. C

Explanation:

If two variables are directly proportional, the resulting line of best fit will have a positive gradient and will <u>go through the origin</u>. Therefore, **<u>Statement 'A' is incorrect</u>**. Correlation does not equal causation. As a result, another factor other than temperature may affect the length of the shoot – there is not enough information in the question to assume that temperature is the only variable to affect shoot length. **<u>Statement 'B' is incorrect</u>**. **<u>Statement 'C' is correct</u>** because it <u>suggests</u> a correlation without explicitly implying that there is a definite correlation between temperature and length of shoot. The positive gradient of the graph implies a strong positive correlation; therefore, **<u>Statement 'D' is incorrect</u>**. There is insufficient evidence for **<u>Statement 'E'</u>** (from the graph, there seems to be a continuous positive gradient with no indication of the shoot length decreasing). This graph is for a particular shoot. Consequently, the graph cannot be generalised for all shoots – **<u>Statement 'F' is incorrect</u>**.

82. B

Explanation:

First find the mean height in the class, because 55% of this value is the answer to the question.

Mid-point	f	ft
137.5	4	550
143	4	572
148	6	888
153	7	1071
158	2	316
	$\Sigma f = 23$	$\Sigma ft = 3397$

Mean $= \frac{\Sigma ft}{\Sigma f}$ *, where t is the midpoint of each group:*

Calculate the mean:

$3397 \div 23 =$ **147.696**

This is approximately **148 cm** (mean height of the pupils in the class).

Find 55% of 148 to find the mean height of the centre of gravity on a body from the ground:

148 x 0.55 = **81 cm**

83. B

Explanation:

Standard deviation $= \sqrt{\frac{\Sigma fx^2}{n} - \left(\frac{\Sigma fx}{n}\right)^2}$ *, where n is the total number of customers.*

Insert the numbers into this equation: standard deviation :

$$\sqrt{\frac{400\,435}{35} - \left(\frac{2485}{35}\right)^2}$$

Standard deviation $= \sqrt{11\,441 - 71^2}$

Standard deviation $= \sqrt{6400}$

Standard deviation = 80 minutes

80 minutes = **1 hour 20 minutes**

84. E

Explanation:

The negative gradient on the curve shows that there is a negative correlation. If the points are not close to the line of best fit, the correlation is weak. It is a linear relationship. **Statement 6 is false** as it cannot be concluded from the data; a correlation does not necessarily mean that there is a causation.

85. D

Explanation:

The total weight of the 9 people in the lift is:

597 x 9 = **5373 kg**

The new mean is 9% less:

91% of 597kg = **543.27 kg**

The total weight of all 10 people is 5432.7 kg:

Mathematics

The weight of the last person is the difference between the two totals:
5432.7 – 5373 = **59.7 kg.**

86. B

Explanation:

$$\text{Mean} = \frac{13.2+16.7+16.8+14.3+17.9+12.1+9.8+18.9+15.3}{9}$$

$$\text{Mean} = \frac{135}{9}$$

Mean = 15

Put the numbers in order:

9.8, 12.1, 13.2, 14.3, 15.3, 16.7, 16.8, 17.9, 18.9

Lower quartile is the $\frac{9+1}{4} = \mathbf{2.5^{th}\ value}$

The 2.5th value is halfway between 12.1 and 13.2, which is **12.65.**

The upper quartile is the $\frac{3(9+1)}{4} = \mathbf{7.5^{th}\ value}$

This is halfway between 16.8 and 17.9, which is **17.35.**

The IQR= 17.35 – 12.65

= 4.7

The outliers at the lower end will be less than (mean – IQR)

= 15 – 4.7

=10.3

Therefore, any values **below 10.3 cm is an outlier**.

The outliers at the upper end will be greater than mean + IQR

= 15 + 4.7

= 19.7

Outliers will be greater than 19.7cm.

The **only outlier in the sampled data is 9.8cm.**

Mathematics (M7) | PROBABILITY | Answers

87. E

Explanation:

Assume that there are 100 pupils:

40 like football but not tennis (40%)

24 like tennis but not football (24%)

16 like neither tennis nor football (16%)

20 people like both football and tennis (20%)

Given that the student likes tennis, the denominator must be:

20+24 = **44**

20 people only like tennis, and 24 people like both tennis and football. Out of these 44 students, 20 like both football and tennis.

Therefore, the probability of a student liking tennis, given that they already like football is:

$$\frac{20}{44} = \frac{\mathbf{5}}{\mathbf{11}}$$

88. D

Explanation:

The number of white beads in the original bag:

25-16 = 9

There are 25 beads in the bag:

Probability of getting a white bead on the first try = $\frac{9}{25}$

This question is regarding **dependent probability** because the bead is not replaced.

Probability of getting a white bead on the second try = $\frac{8}{24}$

(There is one less white bead because it was taken in the first try, and there are 24 beads in the bag as one has been removed in the first try).

Final probability:

$$\frac{9}{25} \times \frac{8}{24} = \frac{3}{25}$$

89. A

Explanation:

This is an example of **independent probability**, where the outcome of the first colour doesn't influence the outcome of the second.

The total number of balls is the sum of pink, red and green balls:

$p + g + r$

The probability of the first ball being pink is:

$$\frac{p}{p+g+r}$$

The probability of the second ball being green is:

$$\frac{g}{p+g+r}$$

Therefore, the probability of both of them occurring:

$$\frac{p}{p+g+r} \times \frac{g}{p+g+r} = \frac{pg}{(p+g+r)^2}$$

90. B

Explanation:

The probability of the fair dice landed on 6 is $\frac{1}{6}$ (six different faces have an equal probability of being landed on)

The only possibility of a total of 12 being rolled is 6 from the first dice and 6 from the second dice.

Looking at the second dice:

Assume x is the probability of landing on a 6:

$$\frac{1}{6} \times x = \frac{1}{42}$$

$$x = \frac{1}{7}$$

Therefore, there is a $\frac{1}{7}$ chance of rolling a 6 on the second die.

Consequently, there is a $1 - \frac{1}{7} = \frac{6}{7}$ chance of landing between 1 and 5.

Since it will land on numbers 1 to 5 with equal probability,

Mathematics

$\frac{6}{7} / 5 = \frac{6}{35}$ chance of landing on 1,2,3,4 or 5.

A total of 3 can be made by rolling:

A 2 on the first dice and an 1 on the second dice

OR

An 1 on the first dice and a 2 on the second dice

Probability (2 on the first dice, 1 on the second dice) $= \frac{1}{6} \text{ x } \frac{6}{35} = \frac{1}{35}$

Probability (1 on the first dice, 2 on the second dice) $= \frac{1}{6} \text{ x } \frac{6}{35} = \frac{1}{35}$

Therefore, the total probability: $\frac{1}{35} + \frac{1}{35} = \mathbf{\frac{2}{35}}$

91. C

Explanation:

Consider Scenario 1:

The balls are arranged to give the largest possible probability for the player to win. Therefore, in Bag 1 there must be 4 blue balls, and in Bag 2 there must be 3 pink balls and 1 yellow ball.

There is a $\mathbf{\frac{1}{2}}$ **chance** of choosing either bag (the player is equally likely choose either bag)

Bag 1 probability of choosing two same coloured balls:

$\frac{1}{2} \text{ x } 1 \text{ x } 1 = \mathbf{\frac{1}{2}}$ (all balls are the same colour)

Bag 2 probability of choosing two same coloured balls:

$\frac{1}{2} \text{ x } \frac{3}{4} \text{ x } \frac{2}{3} = \mathbf{\frac{1}{4}}$

Adding both probabilities:

$\frac{1}{2} + \frac{1}{4} = \frac{3}{4}$

Consider Scenario 2:

The balls are arranged to give the smallest possible probability for the player to win. Therefore, in Bag 1 there must be 2 blue balls and 2 pink balls, and in Bag 2 there must be 2 blue balls, 1 pink ball and 1 yellow ball. There is a $\frac{1}{2}$ chance of choosing either Ball (the player is equally likely choose either bag)

Bag 1 probability of choosing two same coloured balls:

$(\frac{1}{2} \text{ x } \frac{2}{4} \text{ x } \frac{1}{3}) + (\frac{1}{2} \text{ x } \frac{2}{4} \text{ x } \frac{1}{3}) = \mathbf{\frac{1}{6}}$ (can choose either two blue balls or two pink balls)

Bag 2 probability of choosing two same coloured balls:

$\frac{1}{2} \text{ x } \frac{2}{4} \text{ x } \frac{1}{3} = \mathbf{\frac{1}{12}}$

Adding both probabilities:

$\frac{1}{12} + \frac{1}{6} = \frac{1}{4}$

Difference in probabilities between Scenario 1 and 2:

$\frac{3}{4} - \frac{1}{4} = \mathbf{\frac{1}{2}}$

Mathematics

92. A

Explanation:

Consider the 7 red balls:

The chance of choosing two red balls and 1 yellow ball is:

$\frac{7}{10} \times \frac{6}{9} \times \frac{3}{8} = \frac{7}{40}$

However, there are three different orders in choosing the three balls:

1 red, 1 yellow, 1 red

1 red, 1 red, 1 yellow

1 yellow, 1 red, 1 red

Therefore, $3(\frac{7}{40}) = \mathbf{\frac{21}{40}}$

Consider the 3 yellow balls:

The chance of choosing two yellow balls and 1 red ball is:

$\frac{3}{10} \times \frac{2}{9} \times \frac{7}{8} = \frac{7}{120}$

However, there are three different orders in choosing the three balls:

1 yellow, 1 red, 1 yellow

1 yellow, 1 yellow, 1 red

1 red, 1 yellow, 1 yellow

Therefore, $3(\frac{7}{120}) = \mathbf{\frac{7}{40}}$

Adding up these probabilities:

$\frac{7}{40} + \frac{21}{40} = \mathbf{\frac{7}{10}}$

93. B

Explanation:

Draw a Venn diagram:

Assume 'F' is French 'E' is English, and 'S' is Spanish. Let 'x' be all three subjects:

Students who like French and English = 21

Students who like French and Spanish = 18

Students who like French and Spanish = 19

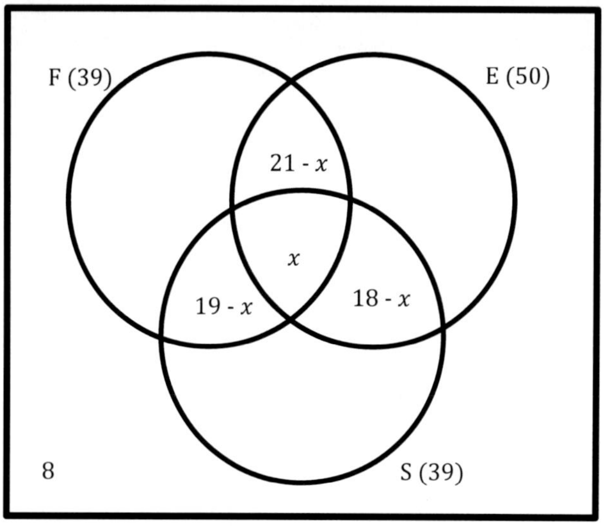

Students who like only French:

$39 - (21 - x + x + 19 - x)$

$= 39 - (40 - x)$

$= 39 - 40 + x$

$= \underline{\mathbf{-1 + x}}$

Students who like only Spanish:

$39 - (19 - x + x + 18 - x)$

$= 39 - (37 - x)$

$= 39 - 37 + x$

$= \underline{\mathbf{2 + x}}$

Students who like only English:

$50 - (21 - x + x + 18 - x)$

$= 50 - (39 - x)$

$= 50 - 39 + x$

$= \underline{\mathbf{11 + x}}$

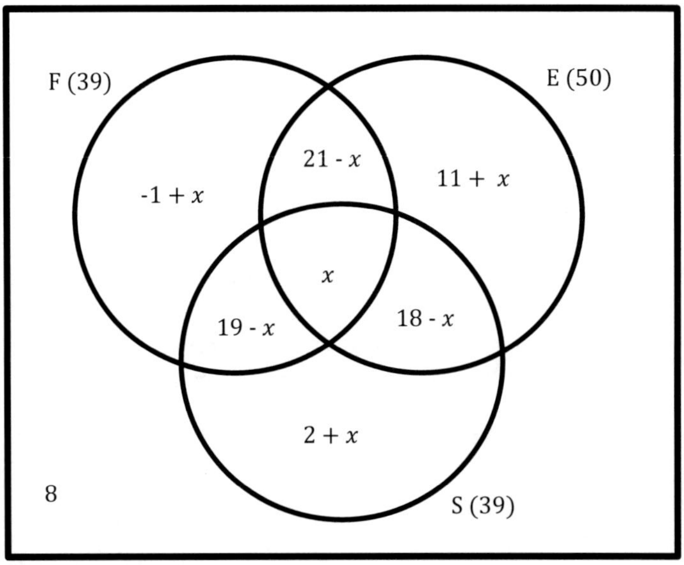

Since there are a total of 82 students:

$1 + x + 21 - x + 11 + x + 19 - x + x + 18 - x + 2 + x + 8 = 82$

$x + 78 = 82$

$\underline{\mathbf{x = 4}}$

Therefore, **<u>4 students like all three languages</u>**.

94. E

Explanation:

Draw a tree diagram. Assume that there are 10000 women.

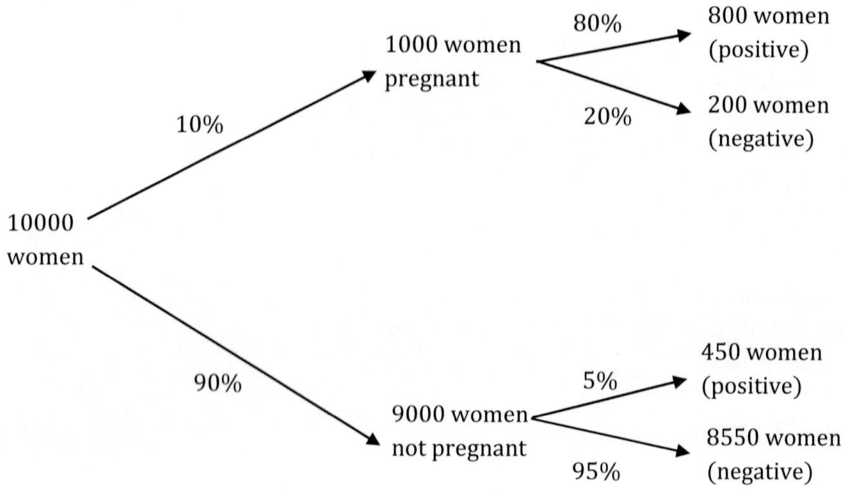

Given that the women test positive, the denominator must be:

$800 + 450 = 1250$

Therefore, the probability that the woman is actually pregnant:

$\frac{800}{1250} = \frac{16}{25} = \underline{64\%}$

95. B

Explanation:

Consider the following equations:

Assume 'P' is the probability.

P (winning Game 1) x P (winning Game 2) = 0.8 <u>(Equation 1)</u>

P (winning Game 2) = P (losing Game 1) x 5 <u>(Equation 2)</u>

P (winning Game 2) cannot be greater than 1, P (losing Game 1) must be **<u>less than or equal to 0.2</u>**. (0.2 x 5 = 1, which is the maximum probability of an event occurring).

P (losing Game 1) = 1 – P (winning Game 1) <u>(Equation 3)</u>

P (winning Game 2) = 5 x (1- P (winning Game 1)) <u>(Equation 4)</u>

Assume the probability of winning Game 1 is 'x'

P (winning Game 1) = x

Combine Equation '1' and Equation '4':

$x \times (5 \times (1 - x)) = 0.8$

$5x - 5x^2 = 0.8$

$x - x^2 = 0.16$

$x^2 - x + 0.16 = 0$

$(x - 0.8)(x - 0.2) = 0$

<u>$x = 0.8$ or $x = 0.2$</u>

Since P (losing Game 1) must be less than or equal to 0.2, **$x = 0.2$**

The probability of winning Game 1 must be:

P (winning Game 1) = 0.8

P (losing Game 1) = 0.2

P (winning Game 2) = P (losing Game 1) x 5

P (winning Game 2) = 5 x 0.2 = 1

P (losing Game 2) = 0

Probability of only winning one game:

P (winning Game 1) and P (losing Game 2) **= 0.8 x 0 = 0**

P (losing Game 1) and P (winning Game 2) **= 0.2 x 1 = 0.2**

Final probability:

0.2 + 0 = **0.2**

96. D

Explanation:

In order for Jacob to pick exactly £25, he could pick:

£10, £10, £5

or

£10, £5, £10

or

£5, £10, £10

The probability of choosing £10, £10, £5:

$\frac{3}{5} \times \frac{2}{4} \times \frac{2}{3} = \frac{1}{5}$

The probability of choosing £10, £5, £10:

$\frac{3}{5} \times \frac{2}{4} \times \frac{2}{3} = \frac{1}{5}$

The probability of choosing £5, £10, £10:

$\frac{2}{5} \times \frac{3}{4} \times \frac{2}{3} = \frac{1}{5}$

Therefore, adding the three probabilities:

$\frac{1}{5} + \frac{1}{5} + \frac{1}{5} = \frac{3}{5}$

97. B

Explanation:

Make a tree diagram with all the given information:

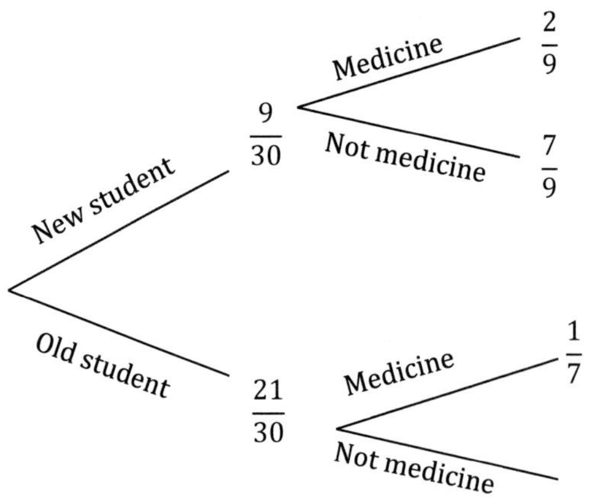

Mathematics

The probability the student wants to study medicine given they are not new to the school is $\frac{1}{7}$

<u>This is a seventh of 21, therefore it is 3 students.</u>

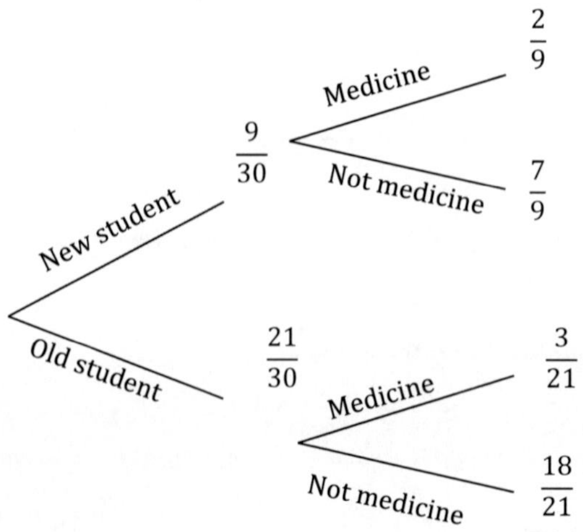

Therefore, the number of pupils **<u>who want to study medicine is 5</u>** and the **<u>number of new students in this group is 2</u>**.

The probability is $\frac{2}{5}$.

98. C

Explanation:

Draw a Venn diagram with the given information.

<u>Start with intersections (fill in the centre of the Venn diagram with the 15 people who do all 3 sports, then work outwards).</u>

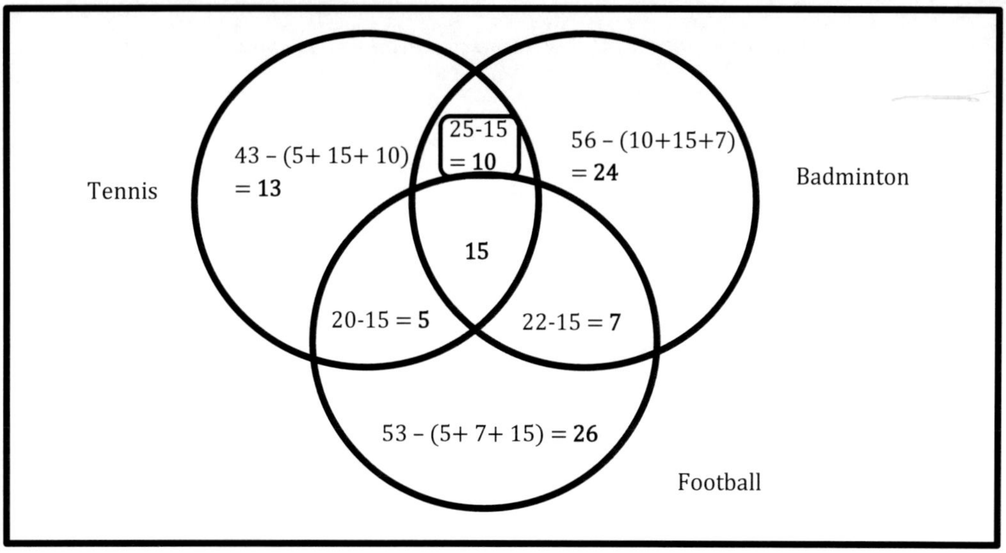

The total number of people playing badminton is **<u>56 people.</u>**
The number who play tennis and not football within this is **<u>10</u>** *(shown by the rectangle).*
Therefore, the probability is:
$$\frac{10}{56}$$
Simplify:
$$\frac{5}{28}.$$

99. D

Explanation:
The probably of picking a strawberry flavoured sweet is:
$$\frac{x}{x+y+z},$$
Picking a raspberry flavoured sweet is:
$$\frac{z}{x-1+y+z}$$
Since the first sweet is not replaced, the total number of sweets in the packet decreases.
This then becomes:
$$\frac{xz}{(x+y+z)(x+y+z-1)}$$
Picking a raspberry sweet then a strawberry one has the same probability of:
$$\frac{xz}{(x+y+z)(x+y+z-1)}.$$
These two events are added to find the overall probability:
$$\frac{2xz}{(x+y+z)(x+y+z-1)}.$$

100. A

Explanation:
<u>The total number of seeds is 144.</u>
The number of seeds that produce yellow flowers is:
$27+43 =$ <u>70.</u>
The probability of picking a seed that produces a yellow flower first is:
$$\frac{70}{144}$$
Since the removed seed is not replaced, the probability of picking a seed that makes a yellow flower the second time becomes:
$$\frac{69}{143}.$$
The two probabilities are multiplied together:
$$\frac{70}{144} \times \frac{69}{143} = \frac{805}{3432}$$

Mathematics

Physics (P1)	ELECTRICITY	Specification

Topic	Objective	☺	😐	☹
P1.1	**Electrostatics:** - Know and understand that insulators can be charged by friction. - Know and understand that charging is caused by gain or loss of electrons. - Know and understand that like charges repel and unlike charges attract. - Understand applications and hazards associated with electrostatics, including the role of earthing.			
P1.2	**Electric circuits:** - Know and recognise the basic circuit symbols and diagrams, including cell, battery, light source, resistor, variable resistor, ammeter, voltmeter, switch, diode. - Understand the difference between alternating current (ac) and direct current (dc). - Understand the difference between conductors and insulators and recall examples of each type. - Know and be able to apply: $\text{current}=\frac{\text{charge}}{\text{time}}, I=\frac{Q}{t}$ - Know and understand the use of voltmeters and ammeters, voltage V - Know and be able to apply: $\text{resistance}=\frac{\text{voltage}}{\text{current}}, R=\frac{V}{I}$ - Recall and interpret V–I graphs for a fixed resistor and a filament lamp. - Know the properties of NTC (negative temperature coefficient) thermistors, LDRs (light-dependent resistors) and ideal diodes. - Know and understand the current and voltage rules for series and parallel circuits. - Calculate the total resistance for resistor combinations in series. - Understand that the total resistance of a parallel combination is less than that of any individual resistor. - Know and be able to apply: $\text{voltage}=\frac{\text{energy}}{\text{charge}}, V=\frac{E}{Q}$			

Physics

	- Know and be able to apply: power = current × voltage, $P = IV = I^2R$ - Know and be able to apply: energy transfer = power × time, $E = VIt$			

Physics (P1) ELECTRICITY Questions

1. **Which of the following is not a correct unit of current?**
   A. Coulomb per second
   B. Joules per volt
   C. Volts per ohm
   D. Watts per volt

2. **A set of decorative lights is made from nine identical lamps connected in series. The set uses a current of $\frac{1}{18}$ A and is plugged directly into the 230 V mains electricity supply. What is the resistance of two of the lamps?**
   A. 2.84 Ω
   B. 284 Ω
   C. 460 Ω
   D. 320 Ω
   E. 920 Ω

3. **A filament lamp contains a thin coil of wire that heats up and produces light when an electric current passes through it.
   Which of the following graphs correctly demonstrates the relationship between voltage and current in the filament lamp?**

A.
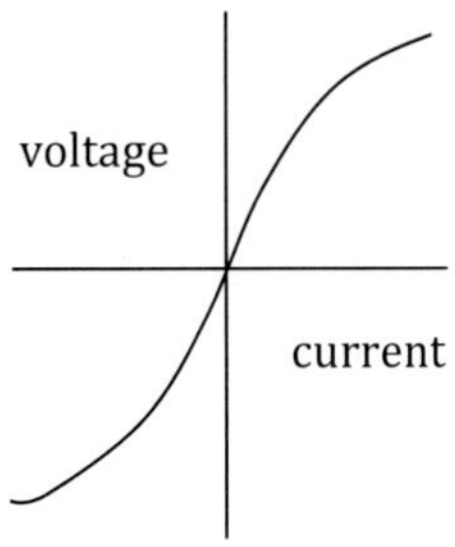

B.
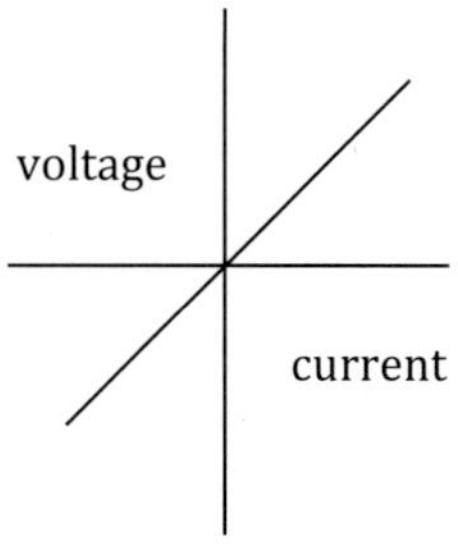

C.

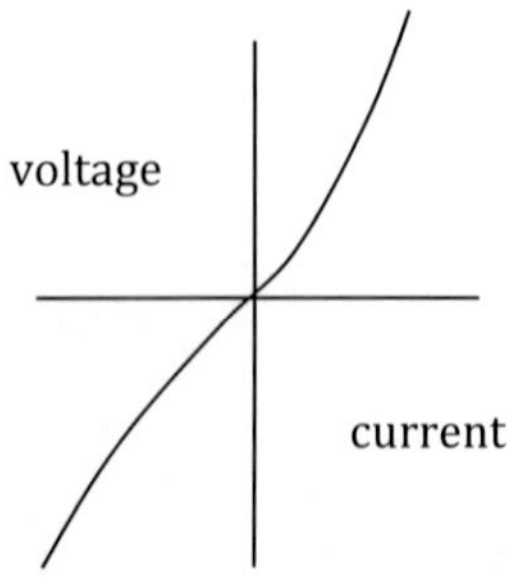

D.

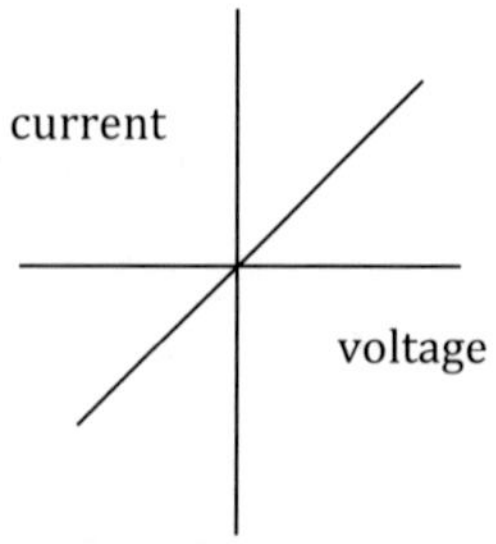

4. **The following statements relate to thermistors, LDRs or ideal diodes:**
   1. At low light levels, the resistance of the LDR is high and little current can flow through it.
   2. At low temperatures, the resistance of the thermistor is low and more current can flow through it.
   3. At high temperatures, the resistance of the thermistor is high and lots of current can flow through it.
   4. The diode has a very high resistance in one direction, and therefore, current can only flow in one direction.
   5. At high light levels, there is a high resistance in the LDR.

   Which of the above statements are true?
   A. 1 only
   B. 4 only
   C. 1 and 3 only
   D. 1 and 4 only
   E. 1, 3 and 4 only
   F. 1, 2, 3 and 4 only

5. **What is the correct unit for resistance?**
   A. Joule per Second
   B. Amp per Volt
   C. Volts per Amp
   D. Ohm per Second
   E. Watt per Amp

6. **A hairdryer with a power of 1.6k W is plugged into the 230 V mains supply. What is the current flowing through the hairdryer?**
   A. 0.00696 A
   B. 0.696 A
   C. 6.96 A
   D. 368 A
   E. 368,000 A

7. **A voltage of 8.0 V is applied across a series circuit with a bulb that has a resistance of 6 Ω and a variable resistor with a minimum resistance of 2 Ω. Given that the difference between the largest and smallest current possible in this circuit is 0.5 A, what is the maximum resistance of the variable resistor?**
   A. 2.5 Ω
   B. 4 Ω
   C. 10 Ω

D. 12 Ω
E. 16 Ω

8. Consider this electronic component.

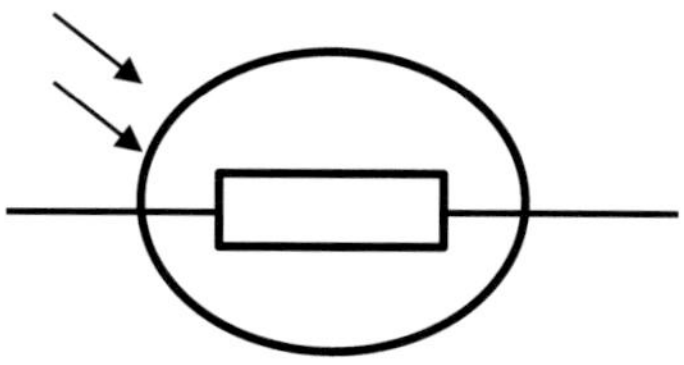

What causes the resistance to change in this component and how does it change?

A. Resistance increases as light increases.
B. Resistance decreases as light increases.
C. Resistance increases as temperature increases.
D. Resistance decreases as temperature increases.

9. Component X is heated gently. What happens to the brightness of the bulb and how is the resistance in the circuit affected?

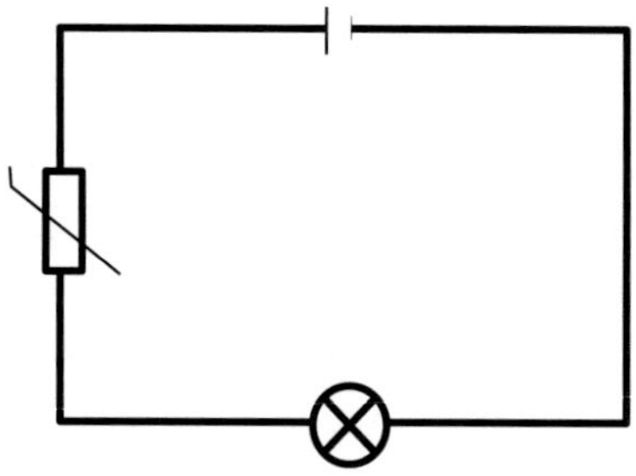

A. The brightness increases and the resistance decreases.
B. The brightness decreases and the resistance increases.
C. The brightness increases and the resistance increases.
D. The brightness decreases and the resistance decreases.
E. The brightness does not change but the resistance increases.
F. The brightness does not change but the resistance decreases.
G. The brightness increases and the resistance does not change.
H. The brightness decreases and the resistance does not change.

10. Consider the circuits below.

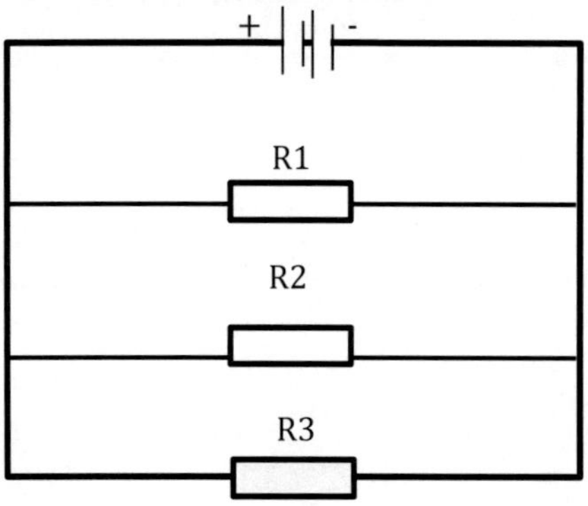

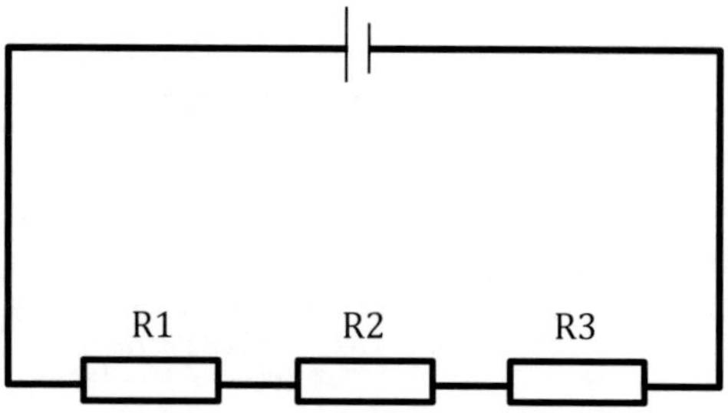

R1 is 10 Ω, R2 is 20 Ω, R3 is 30 Ω

What is the difference between the resistance of both the circuits?

A. $\frac{3589}{60}$ Ω

B. $\frac{600}{11}$ Ω

C. $\frac{11}{60}$ Ω

D. 60 Ω

E. $\frac{720}{11}$ Ω

F. $\frac{3611}{60}$ Ω

11. Which row correctly identifies the type of energy stored in each of the energy resources?

	Energy resource	Energy stored
A	Bio-fuel	Kinetic
B	Sun	Nuclear
C	Nuclear fuels	Chemical
D	Fossil fuels	Nuclear
E	Wind	Chemical

12. The circuit shown below has an input voltage of 12V.

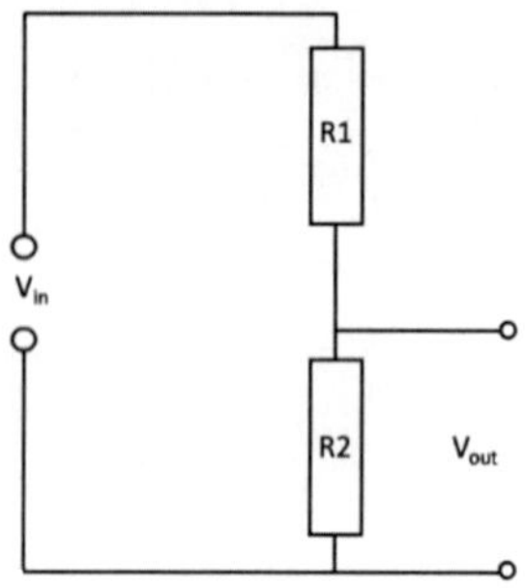

R_1 has a resistance of 10 Ω and R_2 has a resistance of 30 Ω. What is the output voltage?

A. 3 V

B. 9 V

C. 10 V

D. 12 V

E. 36 V

13. Circuit 'A' has 3 resistors in parallel, each with a resistance of Z Ω. Circuit 'B' has 3 resistors in series each with a resistance of Z Ω. Which circuit would need a greater voltage to ensure that the current is the same in both the circuits?

A. Circuit 'A'.

B. Circuit 'B'.

C. They would both have the same voltage.

D. More information is required.

14. Which one of these is not a unit for current?

A. Cs^{-1}

B. $\sqrt{\frac{W}{\Omega}}$

C. $\frac{\text{Volts}}{\Omega}$

D. JC^{-1}

Physics (P2)	MAGNETISM	Specification

Topic	Objective	☺	😐	☹
P2.1	**Properties of magnets:** - Know and be able to use the terms north pole, south pole, attraction and repulsion. - Know the magnetic field pattern around a bar magnet (including direction). - Understand the difference between soft and hard magnetic materials (e.g., iron and steel). - Qualitatively understand induced magnetism.			
P2.2	**Magnetic field due to an electric current:** - Know and understand the magnetic effect of a current. - Know the magnetic field patterns around current-carrying wires (including direction) for straight wires and coils/solenoids. - Know and understand the factors affecting magnetic field strength around a wire. - Understand the difference between permanent magnets and electromagnets.			
P2.3	**The motor effect:** - Know that a wire carrying a current in a magnetic field can experience a force. - Know the factors affecting the direction of a force on a wire in a magnetic field (including the left-hand rule). - Know the factors affecting the magnitude of the force on a wire in a magnetic field. - Know and be able to apply F = BIL for a straight wire at right angles to a uniform magnetic field. - Know and understand the construction and operation of a dc motor, including factors affecting the magnitude of the force produced. - Understand applications of electromagnets.			

P2.4	**Electromagnetic induction:** - Know and understand that a voltage is induced when a wire cuts magnetic field lines, or when a magnetic field changes. - Know the factors affecting the magnitude of an induced voltage. - Know the factors affecting the direction of an induced voltage. - Understand the operation of an ac generator, including factors affecting the output voltage. - Interpret the graphical representation of the output voltage of a simple ac generator. - Understand applications of electromagnetic induction.			
P2.5	**Transformers:** - Know and understand the terms step-up transformer and step-down transformer. - Know and use the relationship between the number of turns on the primary and secondary coils, and the voltage ratio: $\frac{V_p}{V_s} = \frac{n_p}{n_s}$ - Know that a consequence of 100% efficiency is total transfer of electrical power, and that this gives rise to the following relationship: $V_pI_p = V_sI_s$. Know and use this relationship to solve problems. - Understand power transmission, including calculating losses during transmission and the need for high voltage.			

Physics (P2)	MAGNETISM	Questions

15. Listed below are factors that influence the magnitude or direction of induced voltage in electromagnetic induction:

1. Decreasing the strength of the magnetic field.
2. Reversing the direction in which the wire, coil, or magnet is moved.
3. Turning the coil slower.
4. Adding more turns to the coil.

Which line in the table correctly categories the above factors into increasing the magnitude, decreasing the magnitude and altering the direction of the induced voltage?

	Increases magnitude	Decreases magnitude	Alters direction of induced voltage
A	2 only	1 only	3 and 4 only
B	1 and 4 only	3 only	2 only
C	4 only	2 only	1 and 3 only
D	4 only	1 and 3 only	2 only
E	2 and 3 only	1 only	4 only

16. A student makes two electromagnets. Electromagnet 'A', with a magnetic flux density of 10 T, experiences a force of 5 N when a wire of 25 cm is placed in the field. Electromagnet 'B', with a magnetic field strength of 0.5 T, experiences a force of 0.15 N when a wire of 50cm is placed in the field.
What is the difference in the current produced between the two electromagnets?

A. 0.4 A
B. 0.6 A
C. 1.2 A
D. 1.4 A
E. 2.0 A
F. 2.2 A

17. Electromagnets can be used in many applications for everyday life. Which of the following is not a use of electromagnets?

A. Electric bells and buzzers
B. Motors and generators
C. Cathode-ray tubes
D. Loudspeakers
E. Transformers
F. None of the above

18. A primary coil, with a resistance of 48 Ω and a current of 5 A, has 500 turns. A secondary coil has 25 turns. Assuming that the transformer has an efficiency of 100%, what is the voltage of the secondary transformer?

A. 2.4 V
B. 6 V
C. 12 V
D. 120 V
E. 240 V

19. **A primary coil has a voltage of 14 V and 7 turns. A secondary coil has a voltage of 75 V. Assume that the transformer has an efficiency of 100%.**
    Which line in the table correctly states the number of turns in the secondary coil and the type of transformer used?

	Number of turns in secondary coil	Type of transformer
A	37.5	Step-up
B	7.5	Step-up
C	24.5	Step-up
D	24.5	Step-down
E	37.5	Step - down

20. **A primary coil has a resistance of 25 Ω and a current of 8 A. a secondary coil has a voltage of 9 V and 90 turns. Assume that the transformer has an efficiency of 90%.**
    How many turns are in the primary coil?
    A. 1000
    B. 1200
    C. 1500
    D. 1800
    E. 2000

21. **Transformer 'A' has a primary coil of voltage 25 V and current 3 A, and a secondary coil of current 2.5 A. Transformer 'B' has a primary coil of voltage 30 V and current 15 A, and a secondary coil of current 5 A.**
    How many times larger is the secondary coil voltage in Transformer 'B' compared to the secondary coil voltage in Transformer 'A'?
    A. $\frac{1}{3}$
    B. $\frac{1}{2}$
    C. $\frac{3}{8}$
    D. 2
    E. 3

22. **The following statements relate to magnetic materials:**
    1. This material retains magnetism and is easy to demagnetise.
    2. They have a larger magnetic energy store.
    3. This material is used to create permanent magnets.
    4. This material can only be temporarily magnetised.
    5. This material can be permanently magnetised.

    Which of the above statements relate to a hard-magnetic material?
    A. 2, 3 and 5 only
    B. 1, 2 and 5 only
    C. 1 and 5 only
    D. 2 and 4 only
    E. 1, 2, 3 and 5 only
    F. 1 and 5 only

23. **An electron moving towards east enters a uniform magnetic field directed downwards. A proton moving vertically upwards enters a uniform magnetic field directed to the east. What is the direction of the force on the proton and the electron?**

	Electron	Proton
A	North	South
B	South	North
C	North	North
D	South	South
E	East	West

24. **Listed below are factors that relate to the production of a magnetic field due to an electrical current:**
1. Nature of core material
2. Temperature
3. Strength of current passing through the core
4. Reversing the direction of the wire
5. Number of turns of the wire
6. Shape and size of core

Which of the above factors do not influence the strength of an electromagnet?

A. 1 only
B. 3 only
C. 4 only
D. 4 and 5 only
E. 5 and 6 only
F. 1, 3 and 4 only
G. 1, 2, 4 and 6 only

25. **This wire carries a current of 5 A. What is the force acting on the wire?**

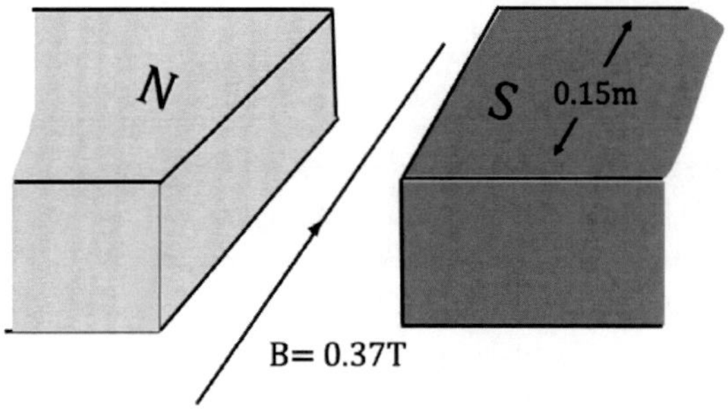

A. 0.75 N
B. 0.056 N
C. 0.28 N
D. 1.9 N
E. 0.56 N

26. **A transformer has twice as many turns on the secondary coil than the primary coil. If the output voltage is 500V, what would be the input voltage?**
    A. 50 V
    B. 100 V
    C. 250 V
    D. 750 V
    E. 1000 V

Physics (P3)	MECHANICS	Specification

Topic	Objective	☺	😐	☹
P3.1	**Kinematics:** - Know and understand the difference between scalar and vector quantities. - Know and understand the difference between distance and displacement and between speed and velocity. - Know and be able to apply: $\text{speed} = \frac{\text{distance}}{\text{time}}$ $\text{velocity} = \frac{\text{change in displacement}}{\text{time}}$ - Know and be able to apply: $\text{acceleration} = \frac{\text{change in velocity}}{\text{time}}$ - Interpret distance–time, displacement–time, speed–time and velocity–time graphs. - Perform calculations using gradients and areas under graphs. - Know and be able to apply: $\text{average speed} = \frac{\text{total distance}}{\text{total time}}$ - Know and be able to apply the equation of motion: $v^2 - u^2 = 2as$			
P3.2	**Forces:** - Understand that there are different types of forces, including weight, normal contact, drag (including air resistance), friction, magnetic, electrostatic, thrust, up thrust, lift and tension. - Know and understand the factors that can affect the magnitude and direction of the forces in 3.2. - Draw and interpret force diagrams. - Qualitatively understand resultant force, with calculations in one dimension.			

Physics

P3.3	**Force and extension:** - Interpret force–extension graphs. - Understand elastic and inelastic extension, and elastic limits. - Know and be able to apply Hooke's law (F = kx) and understand the meaning of the limit of proportionality. - Understand energy stored in a stretched spring as: $E = \frac{1}{2}Fx = \frac{1}{2}Fx^2$			
P3.4	**Newton's laws:** - Know and understand Newton's first law as: 'a body will remain at rest or in a state of uniform motion in a straight line unless acted on by a resultant external force'. - Understand mass as a property that resists change in motion (inertia). - Know and understand Newton's second law as: - force = mass × acceleration - Know and understand Newton's third law as: 'If body A exerts a force on body B then body B exerts an equal and opposite force of the same type on body A'.			
P3.5	**Mass and weight:** - Know and understand the difference between mass and weight. - Know and be able to apply gravitational field strength, g, approximated as $10Nkg^{-1}$ on Earth. - Know and be able to apply the relationship between mass and weight: w = mg - Understand free-fall acceleration. - Know the factors affecting air resistance. - Understand terminal velocity and the forces involved.			
P3.6	**Momentum:** - Know and be able to apply: momentum = mass × velocity, p = mv - Know and be able to use the law of conservation of momentum in calculations in one dimension. - Know and be able to apply: force = rate of change of momentum			
P3.7	**Energy:** - Know and be able to apply: - work = force × distance moved (in direction of force) - Understand work done as a transfer of energy. - Know and be able to apply: - gravitational potential energy = m x g x h, where h is the difference in height of the object. - Know and be able to apply : kinetic energy $= \frac{1}{2}mv^2$ - Know and be able to apply : power $= \frac{\text{energy transfer}}{\text{time}}$			

Physics

	- Know and be able to use in calculations the law of conservation of energy. - Understand the concepts of useful energy and wasted energy. - Know and be able to apply: $\text{percentage efficiency} = \frac{\text{useful output}}{\text{total input}} \times 100$			

Physics (P3)	MECHANICS	Questions

27. **Two parachutists, 'A' and 'B', experience different forces shown in the diagram. Parachutist 'A' has a mass of 55 kg, and Parachutist 'B' has a mass of 80 kg.**

Parachutist 'A' — Drag (air resistance) = 715 N

Parachutist 'B' — Drag (air resistance) = 1120 N

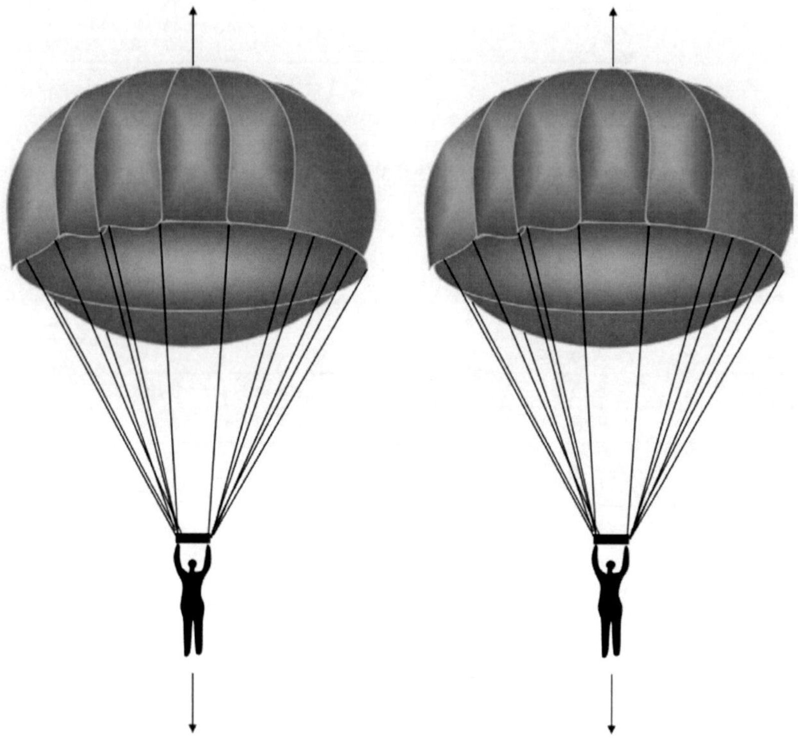

Weight = 550 N — Weight = 800 N

Which one of the following is the difference in the size of the acceleration between the two parachutists?

A. 1 ms^{-2}

B. 2 ms^{-2}

C. 3 ms^{-2}

D. 4 ms^{-2}

E. 5 ms^{-2}

28. The graph represents the motion of a vehicle during part of a journey.

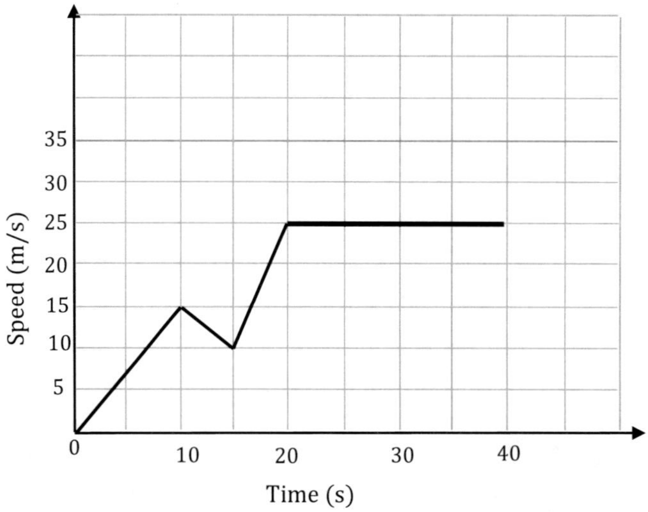

Which line correctly describes the vehicle's distance travelled in the first 40 seconds and acceleration in the first 10 seconds?

	Distance travelled (m)	Acceleration (ms^{-2})
A	700	0.66
B	725	0.15
C	525	0.60
D	525	1.25
E	725	1.50

Physics

29. A runner reaches a speed of 8 ms^{-1} after accelerating at 2.5 ms^{-2} whilst travelling a distance of 11 m.

What was the initial speed of the runner?

A. 2.1 ms^{-1}

B. 2.7 ms^{-1}

C. 3.0 ms^{-1}

D. 5.6 ms^{-1}

E. 7.8 ms^{-1}

F. 9.0 ms^{-1}

30. An object travels down a slide. At the top of the slide, the object initially travels at a speed of 5 ms^{-1}, and at the bottom it reaches a speed of 11 ms^{-1}. Its acceleration down the slide was 2.5 ms^{-2}.

How long is the slide?

A. 6.8 m

B. 10.4 m

C. 16.8 m

D. 19.2 m

E. 23.8 m

F. 38.4 m

31. Listed below are several examples of vectors and scalars.

1. Velocity
2. Mass
3. Displacement
4. Momentum
5. Temperature
6. Acceleration
7. Area
8. Force

Which line in the table correctly categorises the above examples into vector and scalar examples?

	Vector	Scalar
A	1, 4, 6 and 8 only	2 and 5 only
B	1, 3, 4, 6 and 8 only	2, 5 and 7 only
C	1, 3, 4 and 8 only	2 only
D	1 and 8 only	2 and 5 only
E	1, 4, 6 and 8 only	2, 3, 5 and 7 only

32. A leftward force is applied to a book in order to move it across a desk at constant velocity.

Ignoring air resistance, which force diagram best represents this scenario?

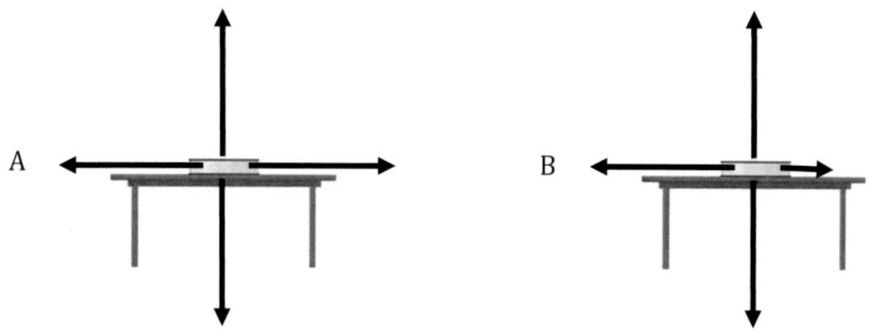

Physics

C

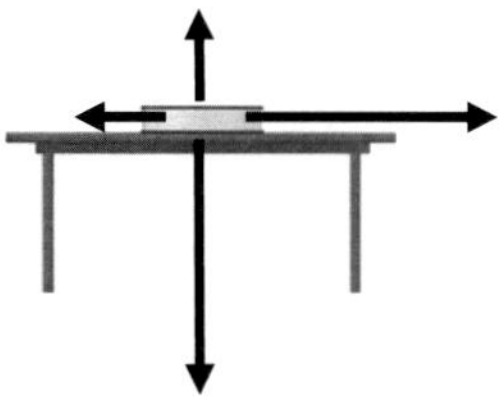

D

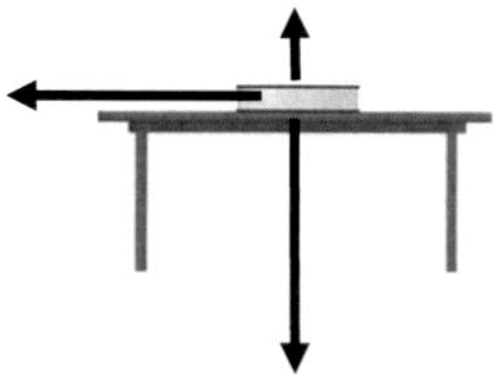

---

33. Below are three force–extension graphs:

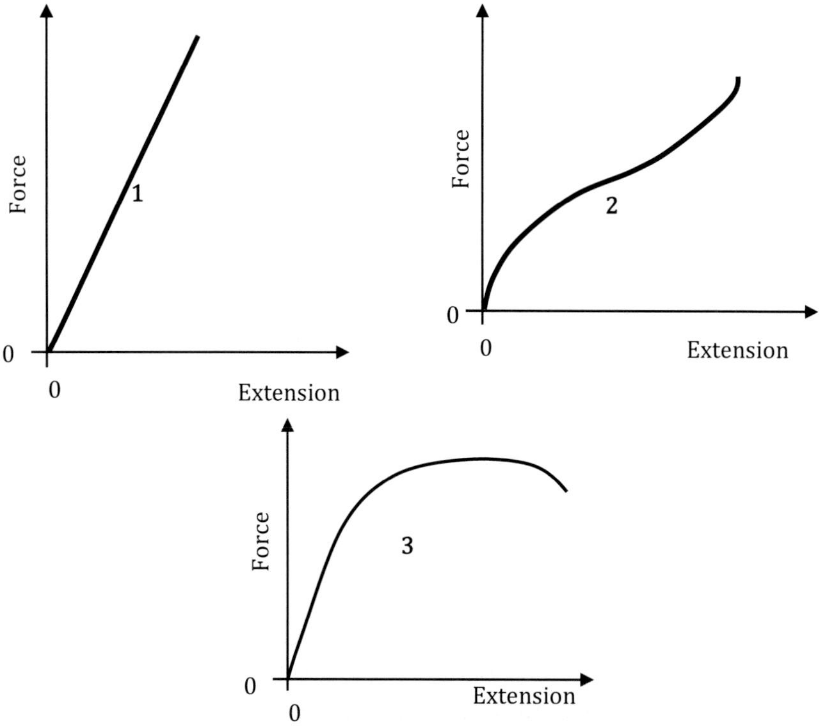

Which line in the table correctly matches the graph to the substance?

	Copper	Rubber	Glass
A	2	3	1
B	3	1	2
C	3	2	1
D	3	1	2
E	1	2	3

34. Spring 'A' of 30 cm is extended to 35 cm when a 2 kg mass hangs from it. Spring 'B' of 20 cm extends to 70 cm when a 5 kg mass hangs from it. What is the difference in the value of the rate constant, 'k', between the two springs?

A. 50 Nm^{-1}
B. 100 Nm^{-1}
C. 200 Nm^{-1}
D. 300 Nm^{-1}
E. 400 Nm^{-1}

35. Which of the following factors do not affect air resistance?

1. Mass of object
2. Shape of object
3. Density of air
4. Speed
5. Cross–sectional area of object

A. 1 only
B. 2 only
C. 3 only
D. 1 and 2 only
E. 2 and 3 only
F. 1, 3 and 5 only
G. All of the above
H. None of the above

36. A van of mass 1500 kg is travelling at a speed of 30 ms^{-1}. The van collides with a stationary car of mass 1000 kg. Both the van and the car continue to move together. What is the velocity of both the van and the car after the collision?

A. 10 ms^{-1}
B. 12 ms^{-1}
C. 15 ms^{-1}
D. 18 ms^{-1}
E. 25 ms^{-1}
F. 30 ms^{-1}

37. Two cars, 'Q' and 'R', start on the same level. Car 'Q' has a mass of 500 kg, while Car 'R' has a mass of 1000 kg. Car 'Q' moves at a constant speed of 5 ms^{-1} up a hill to a height of 10m in a time of 30 seconds. Car 'R' moves at a constant speed of 10 ms^{-1} up a hill to a height of 10 m in a time of 20 seconds.

What are the kinetic energies of the cars while they are travelling up the hills, and what are their gravitational potentials energies once they have reached the top?

	Kinetic energy	Gravitational potential energy
A	Car 'R' has 8 times as much as Car 'Q'	Car 'R' has twice as much as Car 'Q'
B	Car 'R' has 8 times as much as Car 'Q'	Car 'R' has four times as much as Car 'Q'
C	Car 'R' has 4 times as much as Car 'Q'	Car 'R' has twice as much as Car 'Q'
D	Car 'R' has 4 times as much as Car 'Q'	Car 'R' has four times as much as Car 'Q'

38. An object of mass 300 g is thrown with a velocity of 100 ms^{-1}. It hits a wall and after travelling 15 cm into the wall comes to rest.

What is the average stopping force of the wall on the object?

A. 100 N
B. 1000 N
C. 10000 N
D. 100000 N
E. 10000000 N

39. A 3500 kg van accelerates from rest to a velocity of 40 ms^{-1}. This takes 50 seconds. A 1500 kg car accelerates from 15 ms^{-1} to travelling 600m in 30 seconds. This take 100 seconds. What is the difference in the force required for the van compared to the car?

A. 75 N
B. 100 N
C. 225 N
D. 2575 N
E. 2725 N
F. 2800 N

40. A car of mass 200 kg travels at a velocity of 30 ms^{-1} on a level road. It comes to a stop using its brakes in 0.75 minutes. Assume that 90% of the energy is transferred to the brakes.

What is the power, in Watts, of the brakes?

A. 180 W
B. 200 W
C. 1800 W
D. 2000 W
E. 108000 W

41. A non-uniform beam 'AB' is 5m long. It has a weight of 50 N. The centre of mass is 3m from 'A'. Calculate the reaction force at 'B'.

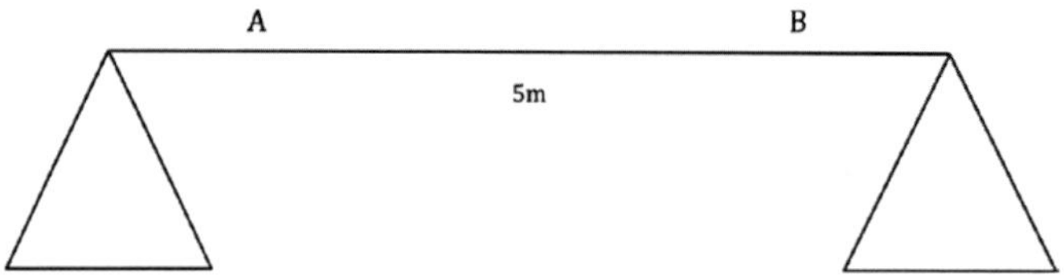

A. 20 N
B. 25 N
C. 30 N
D. 40 N

E. 50 N
F. 60 N

42. A pebble is dropped from the top of a cliff into the sea. When it hits the water, it is travelling at 10 ms^{-1}. The mass of the pebble is 0.03 kg. Assume that g= 10 N/kg.
What is the height of the cliff?
A. 0.5 m
B. 1.0 m
C. 1.5 m
D. 3.0 m
E. 5.0 m
F. 50 m

43. A spring has a spring constant of 4 Nm^{-1}. It is stretched from a length of 20 cm to 70 cm. Calculate the elastic potential energy stored by the spring, assuming that it is not stretched beyond the limit of proportionality.
A. 0.08 J
B. 0.50 J
C. 0.98 J
D. 1.00 J
E. 9800 J
F. 5000 J

44. A spring with a spring constant of 100 Nm^{-1} is attached to a ball of mass 0.5 kg. The ball is pushed into the spring with a force of 20 N. What is the final velocity after the force is removed?
A. $50\sqrt{2}$ ms^{-1}
B. $2\sqrt{10}$ ms^{-1}
C. 8 ms^{-1}
D. $2\sqrt{2}$ ms^{-1}
E. 16 ms^{-1}

45. A lift has a mass of 200 kg and there are 3 passengers in the lift, each with a mass of exactly 100 kg. The lift accelerates upwards at 3 ms^{-2}. Assume that g = 10 ms^{-2}

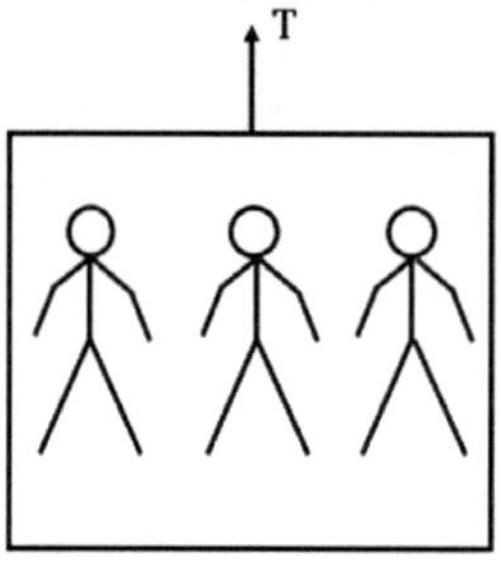

What is the tension in the cable?
A. 2000 N
B. 2600 N
C. 3500 N
D. 4500 N
E. 6500 N

Physics

46. What is the speed of the object between 0 and 4 seconds?

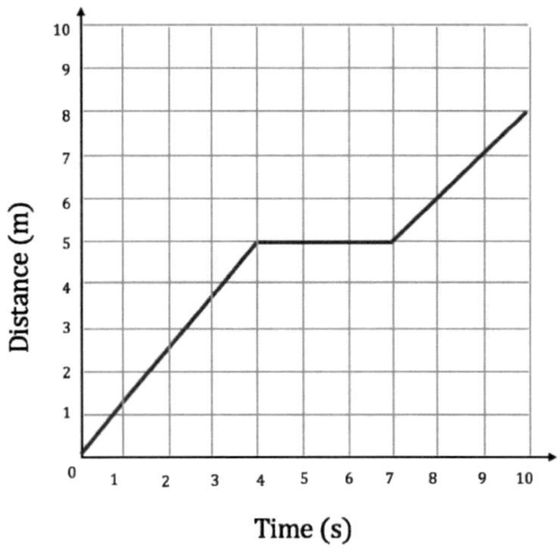

A. $\frac{5}{4}$ ms^{-1}
B. $\frac{4}{5}$ ms^{-1}
C. 10 ms^{-1}
D. 20 ms^{-1}
E. 25 ms^{-1}

---

47. A car accelerates uniformly from rest to reach a speed of 27 ms^{-1} in 9 seconds. What is the acceleration of the car?

A. -2 ms^{-2}
B. 2 ms^{-2}
C. -3 ms^{-2}
D. 3 ms^{-2}
E. -13.5 ms^{-2}
F. 13.5 ms^{-2}
G. -40.5 ms^{-2}
H. 40.5 ms^{-2}

---

48. Consider the following forces.

1. Gravitational force
2. Electrostatic force
3. Air resistance
4. Tension
5. Magnetic force
6. Friction

Which of these forces are contact forces?

A. 1 and 2 only
B. 4 and 6 only
C. 1, 2 and 3 only
D. 2, 4 and 6 only

E. 3, 4 and 6 only
F. 1, 3, 5 and 6 only
G. 3, 4, 5 and 6 only

49. A kettle is 85% efficient. If 9000 J of heat is given out into the room, what is the total electrical energy supplied to the kettle?

A. 1350 J
B. 7650 J
C. 10588 J
D. 36000 J
E. 60000 J
F. 180000 J

50. A particle accelerates uniformly from 6.25 ms^{-1} to 13.75 ms^{-1} in 2.5 seconds. What is the distance travelled by the particle?

A. 4 m
B. 8 m
C. 25 m
D. 50 m
E. 75 m

**51. Fuel burns at a rate of 0.2 kg/s and leaves the car at a speed of 80 ms^{-1}.
What thrust does the car provide?**

A. 14 N
B. 16 N
C. 250 N
D. 400 N
E. 500 N

52. Orbital period of a satellite is 180 minutes. How many orbits will this satellite complete in a week?

A. 8
B. 28
C. 42
D. 56
E. 112

53. A 200 g marble is rolled across the carpet with a forward force of 4.0 N. There is a frictional force of 2.6 N between the marble at the carpet. What is the acceleration of the marble?

A. 0.007 ms^{-2}
B. 7 ms^{-2}
C. 13 ms^{-2}
D. 20 ms^{-2}
E. 24 ms^{-2}

**54. A stone is thrown horizontally with an initial velocity of 7 ms^{-1}, from the top of a cliff that is 45 m high. Acceleration due to gravity = 10 ms^{-2}.
How long does it take to reach the foot of the cliff?**

A. 2 s
B. 3 s
C. 5 s
D. 9 s
E. 18 s

55. A 1500 kg car travelling at 40 ms^{-1} suddenly brakes with a braking force of 3000 N when the driver sees a cat run across the road. The driver has a reaction time of 0.4 s. Calculate the total distance the car travels from when the driver first saw the cat to when the car fully stops.
    A. 16 m
    B. 400 m
    C. 416 m
    D. 800 m
    E. 816 m

---

56. A space probe has a weight of 5000 N on earth. It is sent to another plant where it has a weight of 2000 N. It travels at a speed of 5 ms^{-1}. The gravitational field strength on Earth is 10 N/kg.
    What is the kinetic energy of the probe on the new planet?
    A. 500 J
    B. 1250 J
    C. 2500 J
    D. 6250 J
    E. 25.0 kJ
    F. 62.5 kJ

---

57. A cannon is set up to shoot 5 kg cannon balls vertically upwards. A cannon ball is shot every second to a height of 4 m. A new cannon is bought which is 9 times more powerful than the present one. This also shoots the same cannon balls every second. Assume that $g = 10ms^{-2}$.
    What height does the cannon ball reach when it is shot from the new cannon?
    A. 36 m
    B. 50 m
    C. 360 m
    D. 200 m
    E. 1800 m

---

58. Which of the following statement(s) regarding velocity is/are correct?
    1. The velocity of two cars travelling at a speed of 30 ms^{-1} in opposite directions is different.
    2. Velocity is a scalar quantity.
    3. Velocity = distance ÷ time.
    4. A satellite orbiting around earth at a constant speed has a constant velocity.

    A. 1 only
    B. 2 only
    C. 3 only
    D. 4 only
    E. 1 and 2 only
    F. 2 and 3 only
    G. 3 and 4 only
    H. 1 and 4 only

Physics (P4) | THERMAL PHYSICS | Specification

Topic	Objective	☺	😐	☹
P4.1	**Conduction:** - Know and understand thermal conductors and insulators, with examples - Know and be able to apply factors affecting rate of conduction.			
P4.2	**Convection:** - Understand and be able to apply the effect of temperature on density of fluid. - Understand and be able to apply fluid flow caused by differences in density.			
P4.3	**Thermal radiation:** - Understand thermal radiation as electromagnetic waves in the infrared region. - Know and be able to apply absorption and emission of radiation. - Know and be able to apply factors affecting rate of absorption and emission of thermal radiation.			
P4.4	**Heat capacity:** - Understand the effect of energy transferred to or from an object on its temperature. - Know and be able to apply: $\text{specific heat capacity} = \frac{\text{thermal energy}}{\text{mass x temperature change}}$ where temperature is measured in °C and specific heat capacity, c, is measured in $Jkg^{-1}°C^{-1}$			

Physics

Physics (P4) | THERMAL PHYSICS | Questions

59. What is the difference in energy, in kJ, required to raise the temperature of 100 g of water from 20°C to 50°C compared to raising the temperature of 250 g of water from 37°C to 87°C? Assume that the specific heat capacity of water is 4200 $Jkg^{-1}°C^{-1}$.

A. 6.2 kJ
B. 12.6 kJ
C. 39.9 kJ
D. 52.5 kJ
E. 105.0 kJ

60. Which one of the following statements relating to thermal physics is true?

A. Conduction in insulators is only caused by collisions between delocalised electrons and metal ions.

B. Metals are good conductors only due to the metal ions present in the lattice.

C. Conduction by passing vibrations between atoms is faster than conduction by collisions between delocalised electrons and metal ions.

D. When water is heated in convection, it becomes denser and rises.

E. Convection currents can occur in both liquids and gases.

F. Conduction in conductors is only caused by passing vibrations between atoms.

G. All types of radiation require the vibration of movement of particles.

61. A metal cooling tin is designed to transfer heat energy from the inside of the tin quickly to the surroundings. Which line in the table correctly identifies the properties of the tin that would enable it to transfer energy quicker to the surroundings?

	Surface colour	Surface texture	Surface area
A	Dark	Matt	High
B	Light	Shiny	High
C	Dark	Matt	Low
D	Light	Matt	Low
E	Dark	Shiny	High
F	Light	Shiny	Low

62. A metal block of mass 0.2 kg is heated using a heater that supplies 12600 J of energy. The temperature of the metal block doubles to reach 60°C. What is the specific heat capacity of the metal (assuming that very little heat is lost)?

A. 21 $Jkg^{-1}°C^{-1}$

B. 10.5 $Jkg^{-1}°C^{-1}$

C. 15.75 $Jkg^{-1}°C^{-1}$

D. 1050 $Jkg^{-1}°C^{-1}$

E. 1575 $Jkg^{-1}°C^{-1}$

F. 2100 $Jkg^{-1}°C^{-1}$

G. 4200 $Jkg^{-1}°C^{-1}$

63. Which statement regarding energy transfer is false?

A. Liquids and gases conduct heat more slowly than solids.

B. Gas becomes less dense as it is heated.

C. To reduce convention, the movement of fluid should be stopped.

D. Radiation can occur in vacuum.

E. Convection occurs in liquids, gases and solids.

F. The surface colour and texture have an effect on how much radiation is absorbed or emitted from an object.

64. What colour should a wood burning stove be painted to cause it to radiate as much heat as possible?

A. Matt black

B. Glossy black

C. Matt white

D. Glossy white

E. Matt silver

F. Glossy silver

65. A radiator heats 2 litres of water to increase its temperature from 16°C to 22°C in 100 seconds. It receives a supply of 240 V. The specific heat capacity of water is 4200 Jkg-1°C-1. What is the resistance of the radiator?

A. $\frac{10}{21}\,\Omega$

B. $\frac{800}{7}\,\Omega$

C. $\frac{8}{7}\,\Omega$

D. $504\,\Omega$

E. $\frac{800}{9}\,\Omega$

Physics (P5)	MATTER	Specification

Topic	Objective	☺	😐	☹
P5.1	**States of matter:** - Know the characteristic properties of solids, liquids and gases. - Know and be able to apply particle models of solids, liquids and gases. - Know and be able to explain properties of solids, liquids and gases in terms of particle motion and the forces and distances between the particles.			
P5.2	**Ideal gases:** - Be able to explain pressure and temperature in terms of the behaviour of particles. - Understand and be able to apply the effect of pressure (P) on gas volume (V) at constant temperature, i.e., $PV =$ constant.			
P5.3	**State changes:** - Understand the terms *melting point* and *boiling point*. - Know and understand the terms latent heat of fusion and latent heat of vaporisation. - Know and be able to apply specific latent heat calculations.			
P5.4	**Density:** - Know and be able to apply: $\text{density} = \frac{\text{mass}}{\text{volume}}, \ p = \frac{m}{v}$ - Understand the experimental determination of densities. - Be able to compare the densities of solids, liquids and gases.			

Physics

P5.5	**Pressure:** - Know and be able to apply : $\text{pressure} = \frac{\text{force}}{\text{area}}$ - Know and be able to apply : hydrostatic pressure = *hpg*, where h is the height or depth of the liquid.			

Physics (P5) **MATTER** **Questions**

66. Water has a mass of 250 kg and a volume of 0.25 m^3. A toy is dropped into the lake. Assume that the gravitational field strength is 10 Nkg^{-1}.
What is the increase in pressure on the toy caused by the water when it sinks from 2 m deep to 8 m deep?

A. 20000 Pa
B. 40000 Pa
C. 60000 Pa
D. 80000 Pa
E. 100000 Pa

67. Five experiments are used to investigate the relationship between pressure and gas volume in ideal gases. The same temperature was used for four of the experiments, while one experiment was conducted at a different temperature. Assume the same gas with the same mass is used in each experiment.

1. Experiment 1 was conducted at pressure 150 Pa and a volume of 3 m^3.
2. Experiment 2 was conducted at pressure 450 Pa and a volume of 1 x 10^6 cm^3.
3. Experiment 3 was conducted at pressure 45 Pa and a volume of 10 m^3.
4. Experiment 4 was conducted at pressure 50 Pa and a volume of 8 m^3.
5. Experiment 5 was conducted at pressure 75 Pa and a volume of 6 m^3.

Which experiment was conducted at a different temperature?

A. Experiment 1
B. Experiment 2
C. Experiment 3
D. Experiment 4
E. Experiment 5

68. How many times greater is the energy required to change 500 g of ice into water at 0°C compared to 350 g of water into steam at 100°C?
Assume the specific latent heat of water is 20 x 10^5 Jkg^{-1} for vaporisation and 35 x 10^5 Jkg^{-1} for fusion.

A. 0.5
B. 1.0
C. 1.5
D. 2.0
E. 2.5
F. 3.0
G. 3.5

69. **A girl has a mass of 58 kg and her feet have a total area of 290 cm^2. A boy has a mass of 37000 g and his feet have a total area of 74 cm^2. Assume that the gravitational field strength is 10 Nkg^{-1}.**
Which line in the table correctly identifies the pressure, in Ncm^{-2}, exerted on the ground by the girl and boy?

	Pressure exerted by the girl/ Ncm^{-2}	Pressure exerted by the boy/ Ncm^{-2}
A	2	5
B	0.5	0.2
C	5	2
D	0.2	0.5
E	2.5	5.2

70. **Mercury is an element with a melting point of -39°C and a boiling point of 360°C. Which row correctly identifies the states of mercury at different temperatures?**

	213 K	473K	-40°C	340°C
A	Gas	Gas	Solid	Liquid
B	Solid	Liquid	Solid	Liquid
C	Gas	Solid	Gas	Liquid
D	Liquid	Solid	Gas	Liquid

71. **A pebble is dropped into a swimming pool. The density of the water is 1000 kg/m^3 and the gravitational field strength is 10 N/kg. What is the hydrostatic pressure when it sinks from a depth of 2 m to 7 m?**
A. 2000 Pa
B. 5000 Pa
C. 7000 Pa
D. 9000 Pa
E. 20000 Pa
F. 50000 Pa
G. 70000 Pa
H. 90000 Pa

72. **Which statements regarding the life cycle of stars is incorrect?**
1. Stars begin as clouds of dust and gas.
2. The Sun is a small star.
3. A black dwarf will eventually become a black hole.
4. A white dwarf becomes a black dwarf.
5. Big stars will eventually explode in a supernova.

A. 1 only
B. 2 only
C. 3 only
D. 4 only
E. 5 only
F. 1 and 2 only

G. 2 and 4 only
H. 3 and 5 only

73. Which of the following statements explain why atmospheric pressure decreases as height above the ground level increases?

1. The number of air molecules increases.
2. The number of air molecules decreases.
3. The weight of the air increases.
4. The weight of the air decreases.
5. There is a higher proportion of oxygen as height increases.

A. 1 and 3 only
B. 1 and 4 only
C. 2 and 3 only
D. 2 and 4 only
E. 1, 3 and 5 only
F. 1,4 and 5 only
G. 2, 3 and 5 only
H. 2, 4 and 5 only

Physics (P6) | WAVES | Specification

Topic	Objective	☺	😐	☹
P6.1	**Wave properties:** - Understand the transfer of energy without net movement of matter. - Know and understand transverse and longitudinal waves. - Know and understand the terms: *peak, trough, compression* and *rarefaction.* - Recall examples of waves, including electromagnetic waves and sound. - Know and be able to use the terms: *amplitude, wavelength, frequency* and *period* - Know and be able to apply: frequency $= \frac{1}{\text{period}}$, $f=\frac{1}{T}$ - Know and be able to apply: wave speed = distance time - Know and be able to apply: wave speed = frequency × wavelength, $v = f\lambda$			

Physics

P6.2	**Wave behaviour:** - Know and understand reflection at a surface. - Know and understand refraction at a boundary. - Know and understand the effect of reflection and refraction on the speed, frequency, wavelength and direction of waves. - Know and understand the analogy of reflection and refraction of light with that of water waves. - Know and understand the Doppler effect.			
P6.3	**Optics:** - Draw and interpret ray diagrams to describe reflection in plane mirrors. - Know and be able to apply: angle of incidence = angle of reflection - Draw and interpret ray diagrams for refraction at a planar boundary. - Know and be able to interpret angle of incidence and angle of refraction. - Know and understand the effect of refraction on a wave.			
P6.4	**Sound waves:** - Understand the production of sound waves by a vibrating source. - Understand the need for a medium. - Understand qualitatively the relation of loudness to amplitude and pitch to frequency. - Know and understand longitudinal waves. - Understand that reflection causes echoes. - Recall that the range of human hearing is 20 Hz to 20 kHz. - Know and understand ultrasound and its uses (sonar and medical scanning).			
P6.5	**Electromagnetic spectrum:** - Know and understand the nature and properties of electromagnetic waves (they are transverse waves and travel at the speed of light in a vacuum). - Recall the component parts of the spectrum (radio waves, microwaves, IR, visible light, UV, X-rays, gamma). - Understand the distinction of the component parts by different wavelengths and/or frequencies. - Recall the order of the component parts by wavelength and/or frequency. - Understand applications and hazards of the component parts of the electromagnetic spectrum.			

Physics (P6)	WAVES	Questions

74. The first graph shows the variation of the displacement of particles with distance along a wave at a particular instant in time.
The second graph shows the variation with time of the displacement of a particular particle in this wave.

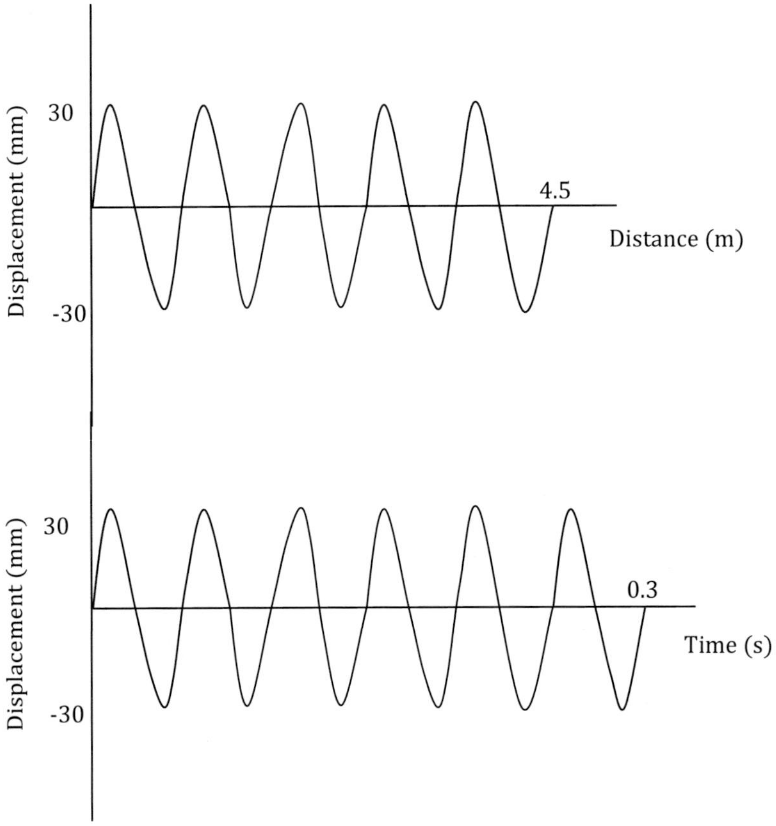

What is the speed of the wave?

A. 15 ms^{-1}
B. 18 ms^{-1}
C. 23 ms^{-1}
D. 45 ms^{-1}
E. 90 ms^{-1}

75. **The height of a wave varies with time as shown in the graph:**

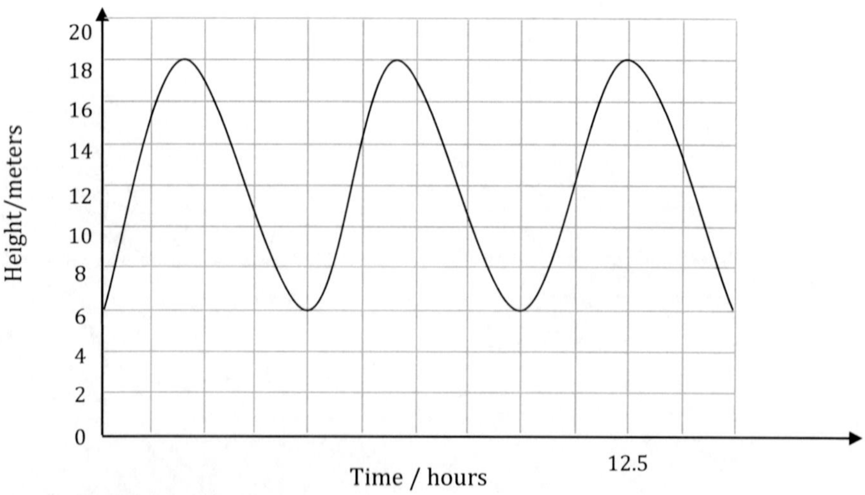

What is the amplitude and frequency of this wave?

	Amplitude/ metres	Frequency / hertz
A	12	$\frac{1}{18000}$
B	6	$\frac{1}{90000}$
C	18	$\frac{1}{1500}$
D	6	$\frac{1}{18000}$
E	6	$\frac{1}{90000}$
F	18	$\frac{1}{15000}$
G	12	$\frac{1}{18000}$

76. **A light ray travels through water at a speed of 3.0 x 108 ms-1 and a wavelength of 750 nm (1 nm = 10-9m).**
What could be the speed, frequency and wavelength of this light ray when travelling through air?

	Speed/ ms^{-1}	Frequency/ Hz	Wavelength/nm
A	3.0×10^8	2.5×10^{14}	750
B	3.0×10^8	2.5×10^{14}	850
C	3.0×10^8	4.0×10^{14}	750
D	3.0×10^8	4.0×10^{14}	850
E	4.0×10^8	2.5×10^{14}	750
F	4.0×10^8	2.5×10^{14}	850
G	4.0×10^8	4.0×10^{14}	750
H	4.0×10^8	4.0×10^{14}	850

77. **Which of the following diagrams correctly illustrate the ray diagram for refraction when a light ray crosses a boundary from air to glass?**

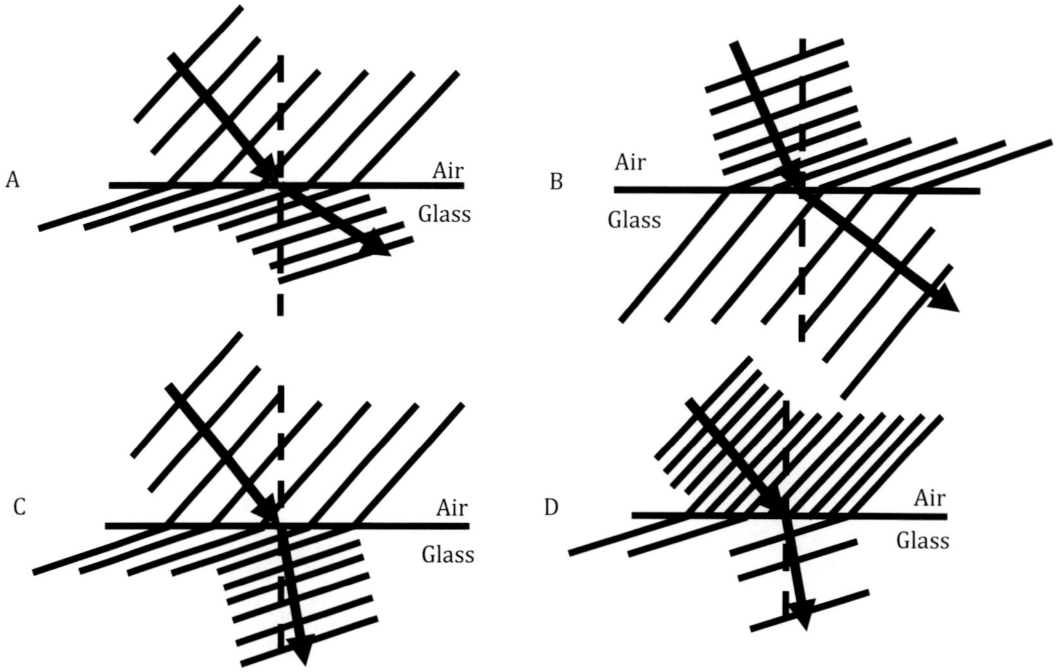

78. **Which one of the following diagrams is a correct illustration of reflection of a light wave at a plane mirror boundary?**

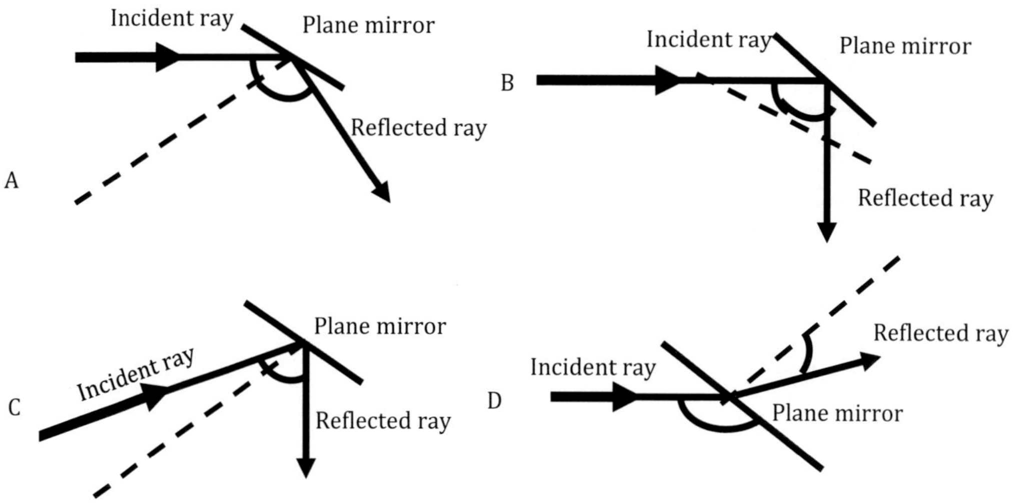

Physics

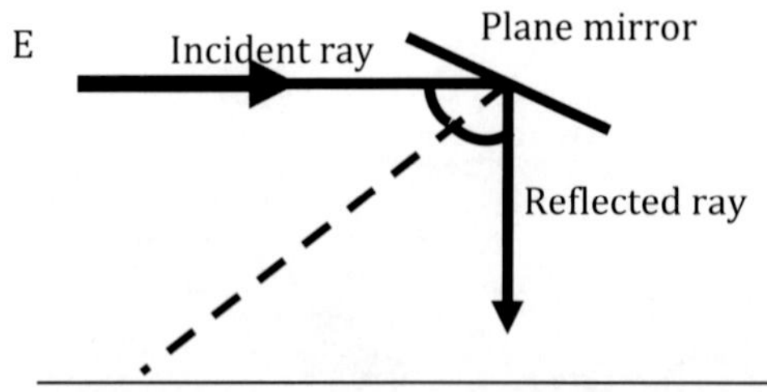

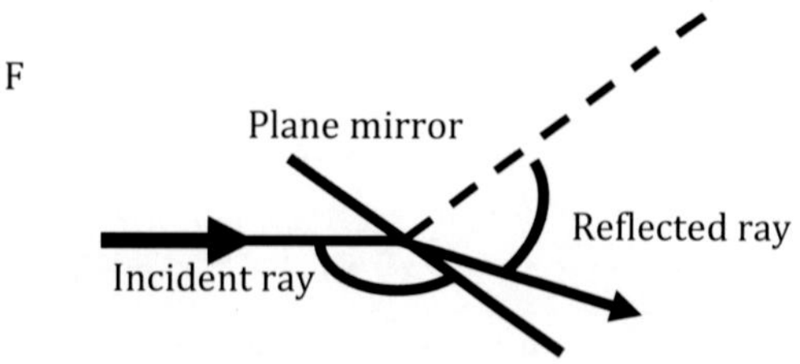

79. Which one of the following statements regarding waves is incorrect?

A. Sound waves are longitudinal, and they require a medium.
B. The range of human hearing is from 20 Hz to 20 MHz.
C. In the electromagnetic spectrum, radio waves have the lowest frequency, while gamma rays have the highest energy.
D. All electromagnetic waves are transverse and travel at the same speed of 3.0×10^8 ms^{-1} in a vacuum.
E. The longer wavelengths of radio waves are used in broadcasting and communications because they can travel further into Earth's atmosphere.
F. X-rays and gamma rays can cause cell mutations.
G. Microwaves can cause internal heating of body tissues.

80. Which one of the following statements regarding wave properties is correct?

A. When the wave oscillations are perpendicular to the direction of energy transfer, it is a longitudinal wave.
B. The time period of a wave is the time taken to complete a wave cycle, measured from peak to trough on adjacent waves.
C. The amplitude is the distance between the maximum and minimum points on a wave.
D. When the wave oscillations are parallel to the direction of energy transfer, it is a transverse wave.
E. Frequency can be measured in Hertz, which is equivalent to one wave per second.
F. All waves travel at 3.0 x 108 ms^{-1}.
G. The frequency and period of a wave are directly proportional.

81. The Doppler effect is a phenomena caused by a change in frequency and wavelength, while the speed of the wave remains constant. It can be calculated using the following formula:

$$F_o = F_s \left(\frac{v}{v \pm v_s}\right)$$

F_o = observed frequency from observer (Hz)
F_s = frequency of source (Hz)
V_s = speed of source (ms^{-1})
V = speed of sound (ms^{-1})
The plus or minus on the denominator is dependent on the source travelling away or towards the observer.

Physics

A police car is travelling away from Person 'B' and towards Person 'A'. The car is travelling at 100 ms^{-1} and sounds a siren with a frequency of 500 Hz. Assume that both Persons 'A' and 'B' remain stationary and the speed of sound is 300 ms^{-1}.

Which line in the table correctly identifies the frequencies heard by Persons 'A' and 'B'?

	Frequency heard by Person A (Hz)	Frequency heard by Person B (Hz)
A	750	375
B	375	730
C	800	400
D	400	800
E	250	500

82. Listed below are four statements regarding electromagnetic radiation.

1. Infrared radiation has a smaller wavelength than ultraviolet radiation.
2. Infrared radiation has a heating effect that can burn the skin.
3. Ultraviolet radiation can be used to disinfect water.
4. Radio waves can cause mutations in genes if absorbed.

Which of these statement(s) is/are correct?

A. 2 only
B. 3 only
C. 4 only
D. 2 and 3 only
E. 3 and 4 only
F. 1, 2 and 3 only
G. 2, 3 and 4 only

83. What is the frequency range of human hearing?

A. 10 Hz – 20 Hz
B. 20 Hz – 100 Hz
C. 20 Hz – 20 kHz
D. 20 kHz – 50 kHz
E. 20 kHz – 150 kHz

84. Consider the following statements about waves.

1. In transverse waves, the vibrations are in the same direction as the wave is travelling.
2. Light waves are transverse waves.
3. Longitudinal waves cannot be diffracted.
4. Refraction of sound waves cause echoes.

Which of these statement(s) is/are correct?

A. 1 only
B. 2 only
C. 4 only
D. 1 and 3 only
E. 3 and 4 only
F. 1, 2 and 3 only
G. 2, 3 and 4 only

85. Which row correctly identifies what happens to a wave when it travels from the air into water?

	Wavelength	Speed	Frequency
A	Increases	Stays the same	Increases
B	Increases	Increases	Stays the same
C	Stays the same	Increases	Decreases
D	Decreases	Decreases	Stays the same
E	Decreases	Decreases	Increases
F	Increases	Decreases	Stays the same
G	Increases	Decreases	Increases

86. This diagram represents a light ray entering a glass medium.

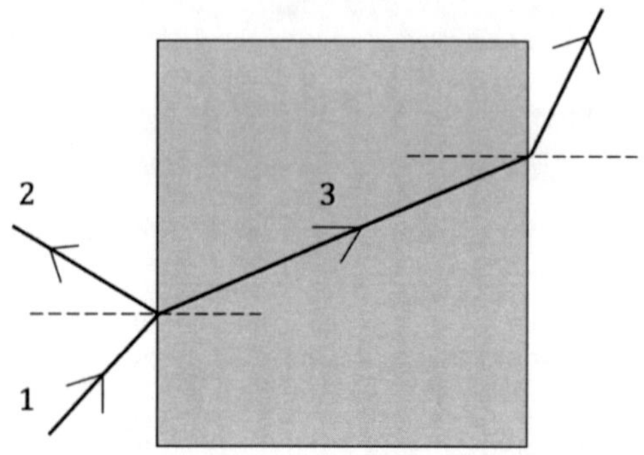

Which row correctly identifies each of the rays labelled 1, 2 and 3 in the diagram?

	Ray 1	Ray 2	Ray 3
A	Incident ray	Reflected ray	Refracted ray
B	Reflected ray	Incident ray	Refracted ray
C	Incident ray	Refracted ray	Reflected ray
D	Refracted ray	Reflected ray	Refracted ray
E	Incident ray	Refracted ray	Reflected ray

87. What is the definition of a light year?

A. The distance the light travels through a vacuum in one year.
B. The average speed at which the light travels in one year.
C. The time it takes for light to travel from one galaxy to another.
D. The distance the light travels on Earth in one year.
E. The time it takes for light to travel from Earth to another object in space.

88. **Waves at a speed of 3 ms^{-1} pass a seagull that is sitting on the seawater. The waves are 20 m long.**
How many times do the seagulls rise up and down as it floats on the sea in a minute?
A. 0.15 times
B. 1 time
C. 7 times
D. 9 times
E. 12 times

Physics (P7) RADIOACTIVITY Specification

Topic	Objective	☺	😐	☹
P7.1	**Atomic structure:** - Understand the atom in terms of protons, neutrons and electrons. - Know and be able to apply the nuclear model of atomic structure. - Know the relative charges and masses of protons, neutrons and electrons. - Understand and be able to use the terms atomic number and mass number. - Know and understand the term isotope. - Know and understand the term nuclide and use nuclide notation. - Understand that ionisation is caused by the gain/loss of electrons.			
P7.2	**Radioactive decay:** - Know and understand that emissions arise from an unstable nucleus. - Know and understand the random nature of emissions. - Know and understand the differences between alpha, beta and gamma emission. - Know and understand the nature of alpha and beta particles, and gamma radiation. - Be able to use and interpret nuclear equations. - Know the effect of decay on atomic number and mass number.			

A Lakshmi, T R Enoch, S Z Y Ooi. Doctors Academy Publications, Cardiff, UK, 2020.

P7.3	**Ionising radiation:** - Know the relative penetrating abilities of alpha, beta and gamma radiation. - Know the relative ionising abilities of alpha, beta and gamma radiation. - Understand qualitatively the deflection of alpha, beta and gamma radiation in electric or magnetic fields. - Know and appreciate the existence of background radiation. - Understand the applications and hazards of ionising radiation.			
P7.4	**Half-life:** - Be able to interpret graphical representations of radioactive decay (including consideration of decay products). - Understand the meaning of the term half-life. Understand and be able to apply half-life calculations.			

Physics (P7) RADIOACTIVITY Questions

89. It is known that a radioactive source emits a single type of radiation. Detectors are placed in the two positions shown. The graph shows how the readings change over time.

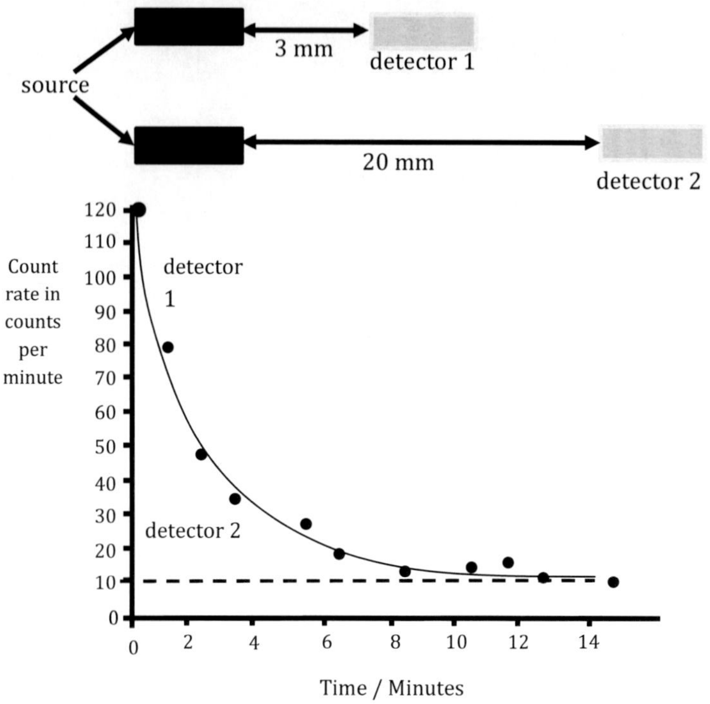

Which type of radiation does the source emit and what is its half-life?

	Type of radiation	Half-life (seconds)
A	Alpha	2
B	Alpha	120
C	Beta	2
D	Beta	130
E	Gamma	2
F	Gamma	135

90. Two substances, $^{235}_{92}U$ and $^{14}_{6}C$, decay by different types of radiation. $^{235}_{92}U$ decays by alpha radiation, while $^{14}_{6}C$ decays by beta radiation. Which line in the table correctly predicts the products formed?

	Alpha decay of $^{235}_{92}U$	Beta decay of $^{14}_{6}C$
A	$^{231}_{90}Th$	$^{14}_{7}N$
B	$^{235}_{90}U$	$^{15}_{7}N$
C	$^{232}_{94}Pu$	$^{15}_{6}C$
D	$^{235}_{94}Pu$	$^{13}_{7}N$
E	$^{235}_{90}Th$	$^{14}_{6}C$

91. The table below describes how the mass of Carbon–14 present in a sample varies with time from the start of the experiment.

Time / min	Mass of C- 14 /mg
0.0	0.0
1.6	8.3
3.2	16.0
4.8	17.8
6.4	18.6
8.0	22.7
9.6	26.6
11.2	28.0
12.8	31.6
14.4	31.7
16.0	32.0

Using information in the table, approximately what is the half-life of Carbon-14?

A. 1.6 minutes
B. 2.8 minutes
C. 3.2 minutes
D. 8.3 minutes
E. 14.4 minutes
F. 22.7 minutes

92. $^{75}_{34}Se$ is an unstable radioactive isotope that decays in a reaction that includes the emission of two alpha particles, three beta particles and five gamma particles, before reaching a stable isotope.
What are the atomic and mass numbers of the resulting stable isotope?

	Mass number	Atomic number
A	83	30
B	74	37
C	67	35
D	75	30
E	83	30
F	67	33
G	74	37

93. Which one of the following statements regarding nuclear physics is correct?
A. The half-life of a sample is half the time taken for the activity to halve.
B. Alpha radiation contains the same number of particles as a helium atom.
C. During beta radiation, an electron is emitted from the electron shell surrounding the nucleus.
D. Nuclear fusion is the splitting of a large atomic nucleus into smaller nuclei.
E. Gamma radiation can be stopped by a thin sheet of aluminium.
F. Alpha radiation is the most ionising and least penetrating compared to beta and gamma radiation.

94. Two radioactive sources 'P' and 'Q' have half-lives of 15 minutes and 12 minutes respectively. Both decay directly to form only stable isotopes.
The activity of the sample of the source 'P' was measured by a detector as 128 counts per second, and simultaneously the radioactivity of the source 'Q' was measured as 192 counts per second. The two samples were immediately measured.
What was the difference in count rate when the activity of 'P' and 'Q' was measured an hour later? Assume that all readings in this question have been corrected for background radiation.
A. 1 count per second
B. 2 counts per second
C. 4 counts per second
D. 6 counts per second
E. 8 counts per second
F. 10 counts per second
G. 12 counts per second

Physics

95. With regards to radioactive decay, which row is correct?

	Alpha particles	Beta particles	Gamma emissions
A	Penetrates through metal	Penetrates through paper	Blocked by thick lead
B	Blocked by paper	Penetrates through thin metal	Penetrates through skin
C	Blocked by metal	Blocked by paper	Penetrates through thin metal
D	Blocked by paper	Blocked by thick lead	Penetrates through thin metal
E	Penetrates through paper	Blocked by thin metal	Penetrates through thick lead

96. Three different radioactive sources emitting alpha, beta and gamma rays are used. The nuclear radiation is measured using a sensor. Metal sheets of varying thickness is placed between the source and sensor.

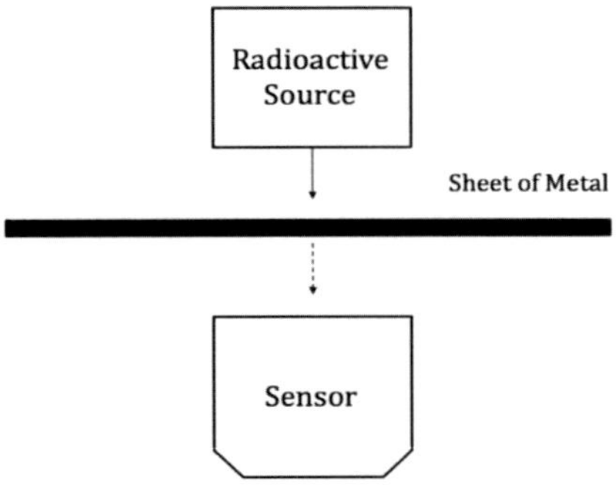

Thickness of the sheet of metal (mm)	Average count from Source 1 (counts per second)	Average count from Source 2 (counts per second)	Average count from Source 3 (counts per second)
0.0	72	66	34
0.2	36	14	32
0.4	25	6	35
0.6	15	1	31
0.8	8	0	33
1.0	2	0	30
1.2	0	0	32
1.4	1	1	29

Identity the radiation that are emitted from Sources 1, 2 and 3.

	Source 1	Source 2	Source 3
A	Alpha	Beta	Gamma
B	Gamma	Alpha	Beta
C	Beta	Gamma	Alpha
D	Beta	Alpha	Gamma

Physics

97. Consider the statements below about the electron arrangement in atoms.

1. When an atom absorbs electromagnetic radiation, the electrons move further away from the nucleus.
2. When an atom absorbs electromagnetic radiation, the electrons move closer to the nucleus.
3. When an atom absorbs electromagnetic radiation, the electrons move to a lower energy level.
4. When an atom emits electromagnetic radiation, the electrons move to a lower energy level.

Which of the aforementioned statements are false?

A. 1 and 3 only
B. 1 and 4 only
C. 2 and 3 only
D. 2 and 4 only
E. 1, 3 and 4 only
F. 2, 3 and 4 only

98. What are the constituents of an alpha particle?

A. 2 protons and 2 neutrons
B. The constituents are the same as that of a hydrogen nucleus
C. 4 neutrons and 2 protons
D. 4 protons and 2 neutrons
E. 1 electron

99. A radioactive element has a count rate of 60 after it was found 15 weeks ago. This element has a half-life of 5 days.

What was its original count rate?

A. 720
B. 1,048, 576
C. 2,097,152
D. 62,914,560
E. 125,829,120

100. The radioactivity of an element has decreased from 1472 counts to 23 counts in 114 hours. What is its half-life?

A. 2 hours
B. 5 hours
C. 19 hours
D. 22 hours
E. 64 hours

Physics (P1)	ELECTRICITY	Answers

1. **B**

Explanation:

Consider the following equations that relate to current in electricity:

1. $\text{current} = \dfrac{\text{charge}}{\text{time}}$

2. $\text{resistance} = \dfrac{\text{voltage}}{\text{current}}$

3. $\text{current} = \dfrac{\text{power}}{\text{voltage}}$

4. $\text{voltage} = \dfrac{\text{energy}}{\text{charge}}$

Consider equation 1:

$$\text{current} = \frac{\text{charge}}{\text{time}}$$

Replacing the equation with units:

$$\text{Amperes} = \frac{\text{Coulomb}}{\text{Second}}$$

Therefore, a correct unit for current is coulomb per second.

Consider equation 2:

$$\text{resistance} = \frac{\text{voltage}}{\text{current}}$$

Rearranging:

$$\text{current} = \frac{\text{voltage}}{\text{resistance}}$$

Replacing the equation with units:

$$\text{Amperes} = \frac{\text{Volts}}{\text{Ohm}}$$

Therefore, a correct unit for current is volts per ohm.

Consider equation 3:

$$\text{current} = \frac{\text{power}}{\text{voltage}}$$

Replacing the equation with units:

$$\text{Amperes} = \frac{\text{Watts}}{\text{Volts}}$$

Therefore, a correct unit for current is watts per volt.

Consider equation 4:

$$\text{voltage} = \frac{\text{energy}}{\text{charge}}$$

Substitute charge= current x time into charge:

$$\text{voltage} = \frac{\text{energy}}{\text{current x time}}$$

Rearranging the equation:

$$\text{current} = \frac{\text{energy}}{\text{voltage x time}}$$

Physics

$$\text{Amperes} = \frac{\text{Joules}}{\text{Volts x Seconds}}$$

Therefore, joules per volt is not a correct unit (since time is also at the denominator).

2. E

Explanation:

Equation:

V (voltage) = I (current) x R (resistance)

$$R = \frac{\text{voltage}}{\text{current}}$$

$$R = \frac{230}{\frac{1}{18}}$$

R = 230 x 18; R = **4140 Ω**

If the total resistance is 4140Ω, then each lamp has a resistance of:

$$\frac{4140}{9} = \underline{460\ \Omega}$$

Therefore, the resistance of two lamps is: 460 Ω x 2 = **920 Ω**

3. C

Explanation:

As the potential difference across a filament lamp increases, the current increases. This results in a higher temperature, which increases the resistance of the filament. The collision between the delocalised electrons and the lattice ions increases due to more rigorous vibration of the lattice ions. Resistance is proportional to voltage; therefore, on a voltage-current graph, the gradient (which demonstrates resistance because $R = \frac{V}{I}$) should steepen to indicate an increase in resistance. Consequently, Graph C is correct rather than Graph A (which has a reducing resistance at a higher current and voltage). Graphs B and D demonstrate a wire at constant temperature because the voltage and current remain directly proportional to each other.

4. D

Explanation:

Consider thermistors:

Thermistors have a range of uses, including temperature sensors and electronic thermometers. Its resistance decreases as the temperature increases. This allows an increase of current to flow at higher temperatures. Thermistors can be used in fire alarms (they will trigger a relay circuit which rings an alarm when sufficient current passes through it due to decreased resistance at increased temperatures). At low temperatures, the thermistor has a high resistance and little current can flow through it (Statement 2 is incorrect). At high temperatures the resistance of the thermistor is low and more current flows through it. Therefore, **Statement 3 is incorrect**.

Consider LDRs (Light- Dependent Resistors):

LDRs can be used in security lights since their resistance decreases as the light intensity increases. In the dark, the LDR resistance is high, resulting in less current flowing through it (Statement 1 is correct). However, at high light levels, current must pass through in order to switch the security lights on. Therefore, the resistance must be low (Statement 5 is incorrect).

Consider diodes:

These electrical components are used to regulate the potential difference in circuits.

As a result, it has a high resistance in one direction to ensure that the current only travels in one direction (**Statement 4 is correct**).

5. C

Explanation:

Ohm's Law is **V=IR:**, therefore, **$R = \frac{V}{I}$.**

The unit for this is **volts per amp**, which is **ohms**.

6. C

Explanation:

Power = current x voltage

Current $= \frac{\text{power}}{\text{voltage}}$.

First, convert 1.6k W to W:

1.6 x 1000 = **1600 W**

Current:

$\frac{1600}{230} = \underline{6.96\ A}$

7. C

Explanation:

Ohm's Law V= IR can be rearranged to $I = \frac{V}{R}$.

Maximum current flow is possible when there is minimum resistance.

Let the maximum resistance of variable resistor = X

Maximum current:

$\frac{8}{6+2} = \underline{1\ A.}$

Minimum current:

$\frac{8}{6+X} = \underline{Y\ A.}$

Difference between the highest and lowest current is:

1-Y = 0.5

Y= 0.5

Therefore,

$\frac{8}{6+X} = 0.5$

X = 10

8. B

Explanation:

The electronic component shown is an **LDR**. Therefore, **resistance decreases when the level of light increases.**

9. A

Explanation:

Component X is a **thermistor**, as it is heated the **resistance decreases** and the **brightness of the lamp increases** as the **current increases**.

10. B

Explanation:

The resistance of the parallel circuit is **$1/R_T = 1/R_1 + 1/R_2 + 1/R_3$**

$1/R_T = \frac{1}{10} + \frac{1}{20} + \frac{1}{30}$

Physics

$1/R_T = \frac{11}{60}$

$R_T = \frac{60}{11}\ \Omega$

The total resistance in a **series circuit is the sum of the individual resistances.**

So, the total for the series circuit is:

$10 + 20 + 30 = \mathbf{60\ \Omega}$

The difference is therefore $60 - \frac{60}{11} = \mathbf{\frac{600}{11}}\ \Omega$

11. B

Explanation:

Bio-fuel stores **chemical energy.**

Nuclear fuels store it as **nuclear energy.**

Fossil fuels store **chemical energy.**

Wind stores **kinetic energy.**

12. B

Explanation:

The diagram shows a **potential divider circuit.**

The equation to calculate the output voltage (V_{out}) is:

$V_{out} = \frac{R2}{R1 + R2} \times V_{in}$

$V_{out} = \frac{30}{10 + 30} \times 12$

$V_{out} = \underline{9\ V}$

13. B

Explanation:

The series circuit has a total resistance of:

$Z + Z + Z = \mathbf{3Z\Omega}$

The parallel circuit would have a total resistance of:

$\frac{1}{\text{total resisatnce.}} = \frac{1}{Z} + \frac{1}{Z} + \frac{1}{Z}$

Total resistance $= \mathbf{\frac{Z}{3}\ \Omega}$

The resistance in the parallel circuit is smaller than that in the series circuit.

$V = IR$

$I = \frac{\mathbf{V}}{\mathbf{R}}$

Since the current is the same in both of the circuits, the **voltage in Circuit B must be greater than in Circuit A** as there is a greater resistance in circuit B.

14. D

Explanation:

Option 'A' is correct as current = charge ÷ time.

Option 'B' is correct as it is derived from the equation : Power = current^2 x resistance

Option 'C' is derived from V = IR.

Therefore, **Option 'D' is incorrect**.

Physics

Physics (P2)	MAGNETISM	Answers

15. D

Explanation:

Decreasing the strength of the magnetic field:

This will decrease the magnitude of an induced voltage because the wire will cut through a weaker magnetic field. Consequently, there will be a **weaker induced voltage produced.**

Reversing the direction in which the wire, coil, or magnet is moved:

This **alters the direction** of the induced voltage as a result of the wire, coil or magnetic moving in the opposite direction.

Turning the coil slower:

As the coil rotates between the poles of the magnet, the sides of the coil cuts through the magnetic field; therefore, a current flows in a coil. Since current is proportional to voltage, the voltage is also altered by the speed of the coil turning. If the coil is turned slower, the coil cuts the magnetic field less frequently, resulting in a reduced current and, therefore, a **reduced induced voltage.**

Adding more turns to the coil:

This increases the number of field lines, which makes the electromagnet stronger. Therefore, turning the coil will result in an increase in frequency of the wire cutting the magnetic field line. This will increase the current produced, and because current is proportional to induced voltage, there is an **increase in the induced voltage.**

---

16. D

Explanation:

Consider Electromagnet A:

Equation: F = BIL

F (force) = 5 N

B (magnetic flux density/magnetic field strength) = 10 T

I = ?

L = 0.25 m

$$I = \frac{F}{BL}$$

$$I = \frac{5}{10 \times 0.25}$$

I = **2 A**

Consider Electromagnet B:

Equation: F = BIL

F (force) = 0.15 N

B (magnetic flux density/magnetic field strength) = 0.5 T

I = ?

L = 0.5 m

$$I = \frac{F}{BL}$$

$$I = \frac{0.15}{0.5 \times 0.5}$$

Physics

I = **0.6 A**

Therefore, the difference in current produced:

2 – 0.6 = **1.4 A**

---

17. C

Explanation:

The main advantages of an electromagnet are that they can be turned on and off and the strength of the magnetic field can be varied.

Electric bells and buzzers:

When an electrical current flows through a rod in the buzzer, the rod becomes magnetic and attracts a piece of iron attached to the clapper. As a result, this hits the bell to make it ring.

Motors and generators:

A magnetic field is produced when a current flows through the coil, causing the motor to move.

Cathode-ray tubes:

This is a type of vacuum tube for focusing electrons. They use permanent magnets in order to aim at a specific target. A ring of permanent magnets, alternating north and south poles, is on the end of an electron gun's yoke, and these ringed magnets can be rotated to focus the beam for better reception or tighter focus.

Loudspeakers:

When a fluctuating electric current flows through the coil, it becomes a temporary electromagnet. It is attracted and repelled by a permanent magnet. As the coil moves, it moves the cone back and forth to produces sound waves into the air.

Transformers:

They use electromagnetic induction to change the voltage of alternating currents.

---

18. C

Explanation:

First, find the primary voltage:

V = I x R

V = 48 x 5

V = **240 V**

To find the voltage in the secondary transformer, use the equation:

$$\frac{V_P}{V_S} = \frac{n_P}{n_S}$$

$$\frac{240}{Vs} = \frac{500}{25}$$

Invert fractions:

$$\frac{V_S}{240} = \frac{25}{500}$$

$$V_s = \frac{25}{500} \times 240$$

V_s = **12 V**

Physics

19. A

Explanation:

First, find the number of turns using:

$\frac{V_p}{V_s} = \frac{n_p}{n_s}$

$\frac{14}{75} = \frac{7}{n_s}$

Invert the fractions:

$\frac{75}{14} = \frac{n_s}{7}$

$N_s = \frac{75}{14} \times 7$

$N_s =$ **<u>37.5 turns</u>**

If the number of turns in the secondary coil is larger than the number of turns in the primary coil, it is a **<u>step-up transformer</u>**. A step- up transformer increases the voltage by the increased number of coils, resulting in an increased in induced voltage.

20. D

Explanation:

Find the voltage in the primary coil:

V= I x R

V = 25 x 8

V = **<u>200 V</u>**

If the transformer has 100% efficiency:

$\frac{V_p}{V_s} = \frac{n_p}{n_s}$

$\frac{200}{9} = \frac{n_p}{90}$

$N_p = \frac{200}{9} \times 90$

$N_p =$ **<u>2000 turns</u>**

However, the transformer has an efficiency of 90%:

2000 x 0.9 = **<u>1800</u>**

Therefore, there would be **<u>1800 turns</u>** in the primary coil with an efficiency of 90%.

21. E

Explanation:

Consider Transformer 'A':

<u>Equation:</u> $V_p I_p = V_s I_s$

$V_p = 25$ V

$I_p = 3$ A

$V_s = ?$

$I_s = 2.5$ A

$V_p I_p = V_s I_s$

$V_s = \frac{25 \times 3}{2.5}$

$V_s =$ **<u>30 V</u>**

Consider Transformer 'B':

<u>Equation:</u> $V_p I_p = V_s I_s$

$V_p = 30$ V

$I_p = 15$ A
$V_s = ?$
$I_s = 5$ A
$V_p I_p = V_s I_s$
$V_s = \frac{30 \times 15}{5}$
$V_s =$ <u>90 V</u>

Therefore, the secondary coil voltage in Transformer 'B' is $\frac{90}{30}$ = <u>3 times larger</u>

22. A

Explanation:

A hard-magnetic material retains its magnetism, which makes it harder to demagnetise. Hard magnetics have a high coercivity (measures a material's resistance to becoming demagnetised), allowing them to retain their magnetism in the absence of a magnetic field. Therefore, **Statement 1 is incorrect**. Due to its ability to retain magnetism, hard magnetic materials have a high energy magnetic energy store; **Statement 2 is correct**. Since hard magnetic materials are able to stay magnetic without a magnetic field, they are used as a permanent magnet (can be permanently magnetised) – **Statements 3 and 5 are correct**. **Statement 4** relates to soft-magnetic materials.

23. B

Explanation:

Using Fleming's Left-Hand rule:
Thumb – direction of force
First finger – Direction of magnetic field (North to South)
Second finger – Current pointing from positive to negative

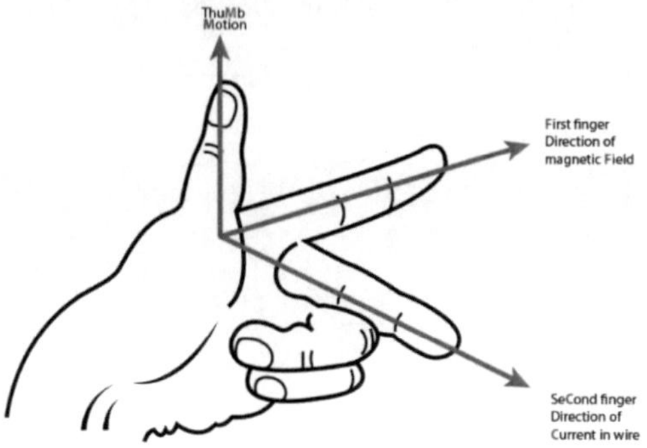

Consider the electron:
Thumb: ?
First finger – points downwards (magnetic field is directed downwards)
Second finger: points left (to the West) – electrons are negatively charged particles, therefore, current is moving in the opposite direction (as current moves from positive to negative).
Aligning the left hand properly, **the thumb points to the South.**
Consider the proton:
Thumb: ?
First finger – points towards right (magnetic field is directed to the east)

Second finger: points upwards – protons are positively charged particles, therefore, current is moving in the same direction (as current moves from positive to negative).

Aligning the left hand properly, **the thumb points to the North.**

24. C

Explanation:

Consider the core (material, shape and size):

The metal inside the coil of wire can magnify or reduce the magnetic field produced, which in turn will **alter the strength of the electromagnet**. An iron core will produce a strong electromagnet, while a steel core will produce a weak electromagnet. An increased size will also magnify the magnetic field, while various shapes may alter the current and magnetic fields produced.

Consider temperature:

A magnet subjected to heat **experiences a reduction in its magnetic field** because the particles within the magnet are moving at an increasingly faster and more disordered rate. Therefore, the current-carrying ability of wire decreases with high temperatures.

Consider strength of current passing through the core:

The magnetic field is caused by the current flowing in the wire. The bigger the current the stronger the magnetic field and hence **the stronger the electromagnet.**

Consider the number of turns of the wire:

Increasing the number of coils adds more magnetic field lines and makes the **electromagnet stronger**. Turning coils around and passing a current through them will make a much stronger electromagnet.

Consider reversing the direction of the wire:

This has **no effect on the strength of an electromagnet** as the same current will be produced (reversing the wire direction will influence the direction of induced voltage in electromagnetic induction).

25. C

Explanation:

F= BIL can be used for a straight wire at right angles to a uniform magnetic field.

F = 0.37 x 5 x 0.15

F = 0.2775

F = 0.28 N

Physics

26. C

Explanation:

The ratio between the number of turns in the coils of the transformer is the same as the ratio of voltages:

$$\frac{\text{Primary voltage}}{\text{secondary voltage}} = \frac{\text{turns on primary}}{\text{turns on secondary}}$$

Let the turns on the primary coil be x and the secondary coil be 2x. $\frac{\text{Primary volatge}}{500} = \frac{x}{2x}$; *The 'x' will cancel out:*

$$\frac{\text{Primary voltage}}{500} = \frac{1}{2}$$

Primary voltage = **250V**

A Lakshmi, T R Enoch, S Z Y Ooi. Doctors Academy Publications, Cardiff, UK, 2020.

Physics (P3)	MECHANICS	Answers

27. A

Explanation:

Consider parachutist 'A':

Equation: **Resultant force= mass x acceleration**

Resultant force: 715 – 550 = 165N

$$\text{Acceleration} = \frac{\text{resultant force}}{\text{mass}}$$

$$\text{Acceleration} = \frac{165}{55}$$

Acceleration = <u>3 ms^{-2}</u>

Consider parachutist 'B':

Equation: **Resultant force= mass x acceleration**

Resultant force: 1120 – 800 = 320N

$$\text{Acceleration} = \frac{\text{resultant force}}{\text{mass}}$$

$$\text{Acceleration} = \frac{320}{80}$$

Acceleration = <u>4 ms^{-2}</u>

Therefore, difference in size of acceleration:

4 - 3 = <u>1 ms^{-2}</u>

28. E

Explanation:

Consider the distance travelled first:

Distance travelled = area under speed time graph

Split the graph into four sections to find the area:

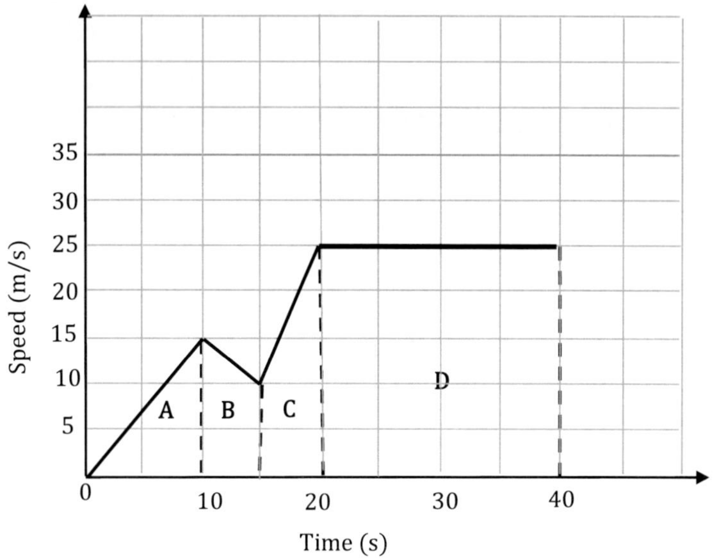

Area A: Area of a triangle

$$\text{Area} = \frac{1}{2} \times 10 \times 15$$

Area = **75 m**

Area B: Area of a trapezium

Area $= \frac{1}{2}(15 + 10) \times 5$

Area = **62.5 m**

Area C: Area of a trapezium

Area $= \frac{1}{2}(10 + 25) \times 5$

Area = **87.5 m**

Area D: Area of a rectangle

Area = 20 x 25

Area = **500 m**

Total area = 500 + 87.5 + 62.5 + 75

= **725 m**

Consider the acceleration travelled:

Acceleration $= \frac{\text{speed}}{\text{time}}$

Acceleration $= \frac{15}{10}$

Acceleration = **1.5 ms^{-2}**

---

29. C

Explanation:

Equation: $\mathbf{v^2 - u^2 = 2as}$

(final speed) v = 8 ms^{-1}

(initial speed) u = ?

(acceleration) a = 2.5 ms^{-2}

(distance) s = 11 m

Rearranging: $v^2 - u^2 = 2as$

$8^2 - u^2 = 2\,(2.5)(11)$

$u^2 = 8^2 - 2(2.5)(11)$

$u^2 = 9$

u = 3 ms^{-1} (although $u = \pm 3$, initial speed cannot be negative).

---

30. D

Explanation:

Equation: $\mathbf{v^2 - u^2 = 2as}$

(final speed) v = 5 ms^{-1}

(initial speed) u = 11 ms^{-1}

(acceleration) a = 2.5 ms^{-2}

(distance) s = ?

Rearranging: $v^2 - u^2 = 2as$

$11^2 - 5^2 = 2\,(2.5)\,(s)$

$S = \frac{11^2 - 5^2}{2(2.5)}$

S= 19.2 m

Physics

31. B

Explanation:

A **vector quantity has both magnitude (size) and direction**. It is specified by a number, a direction and a unit. Vector quantities include velocity (speed in a given direction), displacement (distance in a given direction), momentum, acceleration and force.

A **scalar quantity has magnitude (size) but no direction**. It is specified by a number and a unit. Quantities that do not depend on magnitude are mass, temperature and area.

32. B

Explanation:

A leftward force is applied, which causes the book to **move to the left**. This means that the leftward force must be greater than the frictional forces (right arrows) that oppose the motion of the book. Therefore, the **left arrow must be greater than the right arrow** (**Options 'A' and 'C' can be eliminated**). Since the book is remaining on the desk, (it is in vertical equilibrium) the **weight of the book and the reaction force must be equal**. Therefore, **Option 'B'** illustrates the correct force diagram.

33. C

Explanation:

Consider copper:

Copper is a ductile metal (can be stretched into wires). Once it reaches its limit of proportionality and then its elastic limit, it will retain its new shape before, eventually, snapping. Therefore, the extension starts to decrease after its elastic limit since it is retaining a different shape; as a result, **Graph 3** represents copper.

Consider rubber:

Rubber does not follow Hooke's Law and will remain elastic until it breaks. It becomes fully stretched and very difficult to stretch further when it has been lengthened considerably (resulting in a curve rather than a straight-line gradient). If it is released before it reaches its limit of proportionality, it will regain its original shape. Therefore, **Graph 2** represents this.

Consider glass:

Glass is brittle and it follows Hooke's Law (force is directly proportional to extension) until it snaps. This results in a straight line through the origin (**Graph 1**).

34. D

Explanation:

Consider Spring 'A':

x (extension): 0.35 -0.3 = **0.05 m**

Force = mass x gravitational field strength (assume gravitational field strength is 10 Nkg^{-1})

F = m x g

F = 2 x 10

F = **20 N**

Since $E = \frac{1}{2} F x = \frac{1}{2} kx^2$:

$F x = kx^2$

Divide each side by 'x':

$F = kx$

$k = \frac{F}{x}$

$k = \frac{20}{0.05}$

$k =$ **400 Nm⁻¹**

Consider Spring 'B':

x (extension): 0.7 -0.2 = **0.5 m**

Force = mass x gravitational field strength (assume gravitational field strength is 10 Nkg^{-1})

F = m x g

F = 5 x 10

F = **50 N**

Since $E = \frac{1}{2} F x = \frac{1}{2} kx^2$:

$F x = kx^2$

Divide each side by 'x':

$F = kx$

$k = \frac{F}{x}$

$k = \frac{50}{0.5}$

$k =$ **100 Nm^{-1}**

Therefore, difference in rate constant:

400 Nm^{-1} – 100 Nm^{-1} = **300 Nm^{-1}**

35. A

Explanation:

Mass is a scalar quantity; therefore, it is not affected by direction. **Objects with different masses also have different momentums**, which results in a different change in velocity. The **change in motion due to air resistance** gets bigger as the mass becomes smaller. All objects have the **same gravitational field strength on Earth** (10Nkg^{-1}) regardless of mass – **air resistance is influenced by weight (vector quantity) rather than mass**.

36. D

Explanation:

Consider the momentum of the van before collision:

Momentum = mass x velocity

Momentum = 1500 x 30

Momentum = 45000 kg ms^{-1}

Consider the momentum of the car before collision:

Momentum = mass x velocity

Momentum = 0 x 800

Momentum = 0 kg ms^{-1}

Therefore, total momentum before collision:

0 + 45000 = **45000 kg ms^{-1}**

Momentum is always conserved. In a closed system, the total momentum before an event is equal to the total momentum after an event.

Consider the momentum after the collision:

Momentum = mass x velocity

Momentum: 60000 kg ms^{-1}

Physics

Mass: 1000 + 1500 = **2500 kg**

Velocity: ?

$$\text{Velocity} = \frac{\text{momentum}}{\text{mass}}$$

$$\text{Velocity} = \frac{45000}{2500}$$

Velocity = **18 ms^{-1}**

37. A

Explanation:

Consider Car 'Q':

Kinetic energy: $\frac{1}{2}$ x m x v^2

Kinetic energy: $\frac{1}{2}$ x 500 x 5^2

Kinetic energy: **6250 J**

Assume that gravitational field strength(g) is10 Nkg^{-1}:

Gravitational Potential Energy: m x g x h

Gravitational Potential Energy: 500 x 10 x 10

Gravitational Potential Energy: **50000 J**

Consider Car 'R':

Kinetic energy: $\frac{1}{2}$ x 1000 x v^2

Kinetic energy: $\frac{1}{2}$ x 1000 x 10^2

Kinetic energy: **50000 J**

Assume that gravitational field strength(g) is10 Nkg^{-1}:

Gravitational Potential Energy: m x g x h

Gravitational Potential Energy: 1000 x 10 x 10

Gravitational Potential Energy: **100000 J**

Consider both kinetic energies:

$\frac{50000}{6250} = 8$ **(Car 'R' has 8 times more kinetic energy than Car 'Q')**

Consider both kinetic energies:

$\frac{100000}{50000} = 2$ **(Car 'R' has 2 times more gravitational potential energy than Car 'Q')**

38. C

Explanation:

Consider the following equations:

Work done = Force x Distance

Kinetic energy = $\frac{1}{2}$ x mass x velocity^2

Since Kinetic energy is one for of work done, the two equations equal each other:

$$F \times d = \frac{1}{2} \times m \times v^2$$

$$F = \frac{\frac{1}{2} \times m \times v^2}{d}$$

Convert 300g into 0.3 kg and 15cm into 0.15m:

$$F = \frac{\frac{1}{2} \times 0.3 \times 100^2}{0.15}$$

F = **10000 N**

Physics

39. E

Explanation:

Consider the van:

$$\text{Force} = \frac{\text{change in momentum}}{\text{time taken}}$$

First, calculate the change in momentum:

Change in velocity: 40 – 0 = 40 ms^{-1}

Mass: 3500

Therefore, change in momentum:

3500 x 40 = **140000 $kgms^{-1}$**

Calculate the force:

$$\text{Force} = \frac{\text{change in momentum}}{\text{time taken}}$$

$$\text{Force} = \frac{140000}{50}$$

Force = **2800 N**

Consider the car:

$$\text{Force} = \frac{\text{change in momentum}}{\text{time taken}}$$

First, calculate the final velocity:

$$\frac{600}{30} = 20$$

Calculate the change in momentum:

Change in velocity: 20 – 15 = **5 ms^{-1}**

Mass: 1500

Therefore, change in momentum:

1500 x 5 = **7500 $kgms^{-1}$**

Calculate the force:

$$\text{Force} = \frac{\text{change in momentum}}{\text{time taken}}$$

$$\text{Force} = \frac{7500}{100}$$

Force = **75 N**

Therefore, the difference in force:

2800– 75 = **2725 N**

40. C

Explanation:

Calculate the kinetic energy of the car initially:

$$KE = \frac{1}{2} \times m \times v^2$$

$$KE = \frac{1}{2} \times 200 \times 30^2$$

KE = **90000 J**

The law of conservation of energy states that energy cannot be created or destroyed, but only changed from one form into another or transferred between objects.

Since 90% of the kinetic energy is transferred to the brakes, the energy transfer is:

0.9 x 90000 = **81000 J**

$$\text{Power (W)} = \frac{\text{energy transfer (J)}}{\text{time (s)}}$$

Convert 0.75 minutes into seconds:

0.75 x 60 = 45 seconds

$$\text{Power} = \frac{81000}{45}$$

Power = **1800 W**

41. C

Explanation:

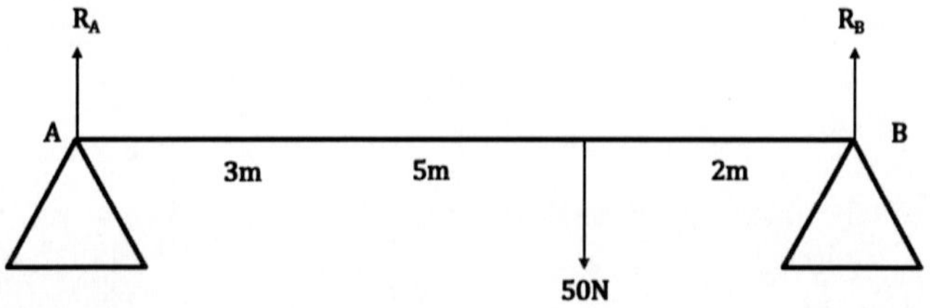

R↑:

$R_A + R_B =$ **50N**

Moments about 'A':

Clockwise = anticlockwise

3 x 50 = 5 x R_B

R_B = 30 N

42. E

Explanation:

GPE = mgh

= 0.03 x 10 x h

As the pebble is dropped from a height, **the total amount of GPE at the top is converted to KE at the bottom of the cliff.**

KE = GPE and $KE = \frac{1}{2}mv^2$

$KE = \frac{1}{2} \times 0.03 \times 10^2$

= **1.5 J**

GPE = 1.5

1.5 = 0.03 x 10 x h

h = 5 m

43. B

Explanation:

Elastic Potential Energy = $\frac{1}{2}kx^2$

Where k = 4 and x = 70 -20, therefore, **x = 50** (as it is extended by 50cm).

However, x should be in meters so $x = 50 \div 100 = 0.5$

$EPE = \frac{1}{2} \times 4 \times 0.5^2$

EPE = 0.5 J

44. D

Explanation:

Conservation of energy means that the potential energy of the spring is converted to kinetic energy:

$\frac{1}{2}\boldsymbol{kx^2} = \frac{1}{2}\boldsymbol{mv^2}$

Hooke's law: F = kx

20 = 100 x x

x = 0.2

$\frac{1}{2}$ x 100 x $0.2^2 = \frac{1}{2}$ x 0.5 x v^2

2 = 0.25 v^2

8 = v^2

v = 2√2 ms^{-1}

---

45. E

Explanation:

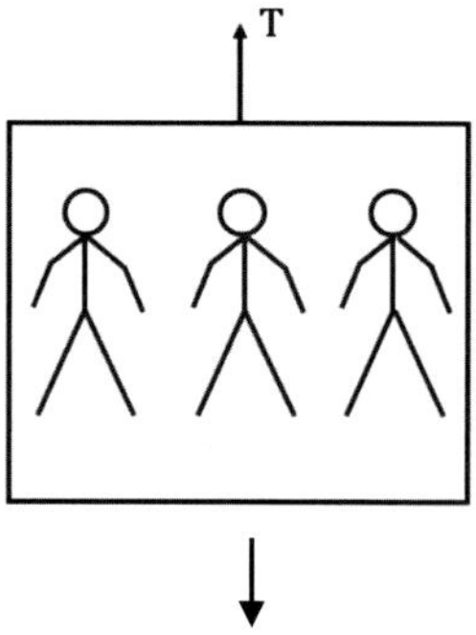

F = ma

The resultant force is **T minus the weight.**

T- 5000 = 500 x 3

T – 5000 = 1500

T = **6500N**

[200 + (100 x 3)]

= 500 kg

= 5000N

---

46. A

Explanation:

Speed is the gradient of the graph.

Gradient:

$\frac{\text{difference in y}}{\text{difference in x}} = \frac{\mathbf{5}}{\mathbf{4}}$ **ms^{-1}**

---

47. D

Explanation:

This question involves the **SUVAT equations**. Since the car started from rest, the initial speed is 0 ms^{-1}.

U = 0

V = 27

A = ?

T = 9

v = u + at (select the SUVAT equation without 'S')

27 = 0 + a x 9

a = 3 ms^{-2}

---

48. E

Explanation:

Friction, air resistance and tension are contact forces.

Gravitational force, electrostatic force and magnetic force are all non-contact forces.

---

49. E

Explanation:

If 9000J is given out into the room, then this is the wasted energy.

The useful energy accounts for 85%, so the wasted energy is:

15% (100 -85) of the total energy.

Physics

A Lakshmi, T R Enoch, S Z Y Ooi. Doctors Academy Publications, Cardiff, UK, 2020.

The total energy supplied to the kettle is:
9000 ÷ 0.15 = **60 000J**

50. C

Explanation:

This question involves the **SUVAT equations.**
S = ?
U = 6.25
V = 13.75
A
T = 2.5

$s = \frac{u+v}{2} \times t$ (select the SUVAT equation without 'A')

$s = \frac{6.25 + 13.75}{2} \times 2.5$

s = 25 m

51. B

Explanation:

The momentum gained by the fuel in one second is:
Change in momentum = mass x velocity
Change in momentum = 0.2kg x 80 ms^{-1}
Change in momentum = 16 $kgms^{-1}$
The force provided by the car is
Force = change in momentum ÷ time
Force = 16 ÷ 1
Force = 16 N

52. D

Explanation:

180 minutes is **3 hours.**
Work out the number of hours in a week:
7 days x 24 hours per day = **168 hours**
It takes 3 hours to complete one orbit. Therefore, in 168 hours, the satellite completes:
168 ÷ 3 = **56 orbits.**

53. B

Explanation:

Draw a diagram with the information provided:

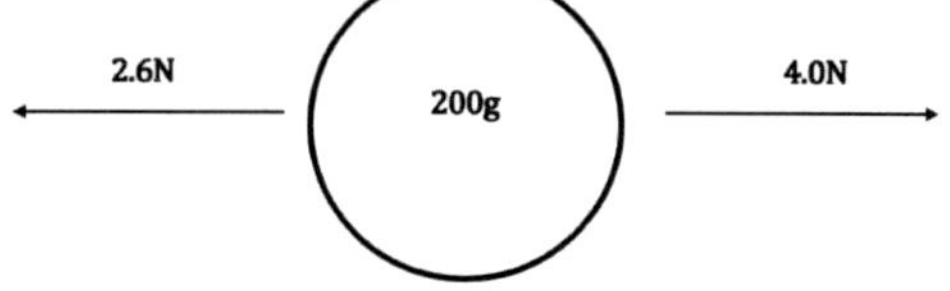

Notice that the mass is in grams; convert this into kilograms:
200g is **0.2kg.**
Find the resultant force of the marble:
4.0 – 2.6 =**1.4N.**
F = ma
Acceleration = resultant force ÷ mass

Physics

Acceleration = 1.4 ÷ 0.2

Acceleration = 7 ms^{-2}

---

54. B

Explanation:

This question involves the **SUVAT equations**.

We are trying to find the time it takes for the stone to fall 45m, so the initial vertical velocity is $0ms^{-1}$.

The initial horizontal velocity is $7ms^{-1}$ - this is not the same as the vertical velocity.

S = 45m

U = $0ms^{-1}$

V

A = $10ms^{-2}$

T = t

$s = ut + \frac{1}{2} at^2$

$45 = 0 \times t + \frac{1}{2} \times 10 \times t^2$

$45 = 5t^2$

$9 = t^2$

$t = 3$

The stone takes 3s to the reach the foot of the cliff.

---

55. C

Explanation:

This question is asking for the stopping distance.

Stopping distance = thinking distance + braking distance.

Thinking distance = speed x time

= 40 x 0.4

= 16 m

(this is the distance that the car travels in the time that it takes the driver to notice the cat and start applying the brakes)

Braking distance:

Work done = braking force x distance

Work is done to remove all the kinetic energy of the car to bring it to a stop.

Work done = kinetic energy

$= \frac{1}{2} mv^2$

$\frac{1}{2} mv^2$ = braking force x distance

$\text{Distance} = \frac{\frac{1}{2} \times 1500 \times 40^2}{3000}$

Distance = **400 m**

The car travels **400 m** from when the driver applies the brakes to when the car fully stops.

The total distance the car travels (stopping distance) is:

16 + 400 = 416 m

56. D

Explanation:

The weight of the probe is **5000 N**.

Therefore, its mass must be:

5000 ÷ 10 = 500 kg.

The mass of the object does not change on another planet, only the weight changes.

$KE = \frac{1}{2} mv^2$

$KE = \frac{1}{2} \times 500 \times 5^2$

KE = 6250 J

---

57. A

Explanation:

The force that the cannon shoots the ball can be found using **F = ma**, where a is $10ms^{-2}$ as the cannon ball is shot vertically upwards.

F = 5 x 10

F = **50 N.**

The work done by the cannon is found using:

Work done = Force x Distance

= 50 x 4

Work done = **200 J.**

Power = Work done ÷ Time.

Since a cannon ball is shot every second the time is 1 second:

Power = 200 ÷ 1

Power = **200 W.**

The new cannon is 9 times more powerful, so its power is:

200 x 9 = **1800 W.**

Work done = power x time:

1800 x 1 = **1800 J.**

The force is the same in both cannons as they both shoot the same cannon balls every second.

Distance = Work done ÷ Force.

Distance = 1800 ÷ 50

Distance = **36 m.**

The cannon ball reaches a height of 36 m.

---

58. A

Explanation:

Statement 1 is true as velocity is a vector quantity so two cars travelling in opposite directions have different velocities despite their speed being the same. **Statement 2** is false as velocity is a vector quantity. **Statement 3** is wrong as velocity = displacement ÷ time. **Statement 4 is incorrect** as the velocity of the satellite is always changing because the direction is changing.

Physics (P4)	THERMAL PHYSICS	Answers

59. C

Explanation:

Consider the equation:

Thermal energy (J) =

specific heat capacity ($Jkg^{-1}°C^{-1}$) x mass (kg) x temperature change (°C)

Consider 100 g of water:

Thermal energy = 4200 x 0.1 x 30

Thermal energy = **12600 J**

Consider 250 g of water:

Thermal energy = 4200 x 0.25 x 50

Thermal energy = **52500 J**

Therefore, difference in thermal energy:

52500 – 12600 = **39900 J**

Convert into kJ:

$$\frac{39900}{1000} = \underline{39.9\ kJ}$$

60. E

Explanation:

Conduction in insulators is only caused by passing vibrations between atoms (insulators do not have delocalised electrons), while conduction in conductors are caused by collisions between delocalised electrons and metal ions. As a result, **Statements 'A' and 'F' are incorrect**. Conductors are able to transfer heat quicker than insulators due to the collisions between the delocalised electrons and the metal ions. Therefore, **Statement 'C' is incorrect**. Metals are good conductors because they contain delocalised electrons, which are able to travel within the layer and transfer heat from one end to the other. **Statement 'B' is incorrect**. When water is heated in convection, it rises since it becomes less dense. An increase in density results in an more particles in a unit volume, which would cause the water particles to sink. Consequently, **Statement 'D' is incorrect**. Convection can occur in liquids (boiling water causes the hot water to rise while the cooler water sinks to replace it) or gases (air close to a radiator will rise due to a reduced density and colder air will replace it). **Statement 'E' is correct**. Infrared radiation, a type of heat transfer, is an electromagnetic wave and, therefore, can travel through a vacuum. Therefore, **Statement 'G' is incorrect**.

61. A

Explanation:

In order to transfer heat energy to the surroundings, the cooling tin must be a good emitter of heat. **Black, matt surfaces** absorb almost all light (therefore, they appear black). As a result of absorbing more light, they also emit more heat. These surfaces are good absorbers and good emitters of infra-red radiation. On the other hand, light and shiny surfaces are good reflectors (but poor absorbers and poor emitters). A **larger surface area** will also increase the rate of infrared emission due to an increase in area for the thermal energy to exit the metal cooling tin.

62. F

Explanation:

Specific heat capacity $= \frac{\text{thermal energy}}{\text{mass x temperature change}}$

The <u>thermal energy is 12 600J</u>, <u>mass is 0.2kg</u> and the <u>temperature change is 30°C.</u>

SHC $= \frac{12600}{0.2 \times 30} =$ <u>2100 $Jkg^{-1}°C^{-1}$</u>

---

63. E

Explanation:

<u>Option 'A'</u> is true as the particles in liquid and gas aren't held tightly together which slows down conduction. <u>Option 'B'</u> is true as gas expands and becomes less dense as it is heated. <u>Options 'C', 'D' and 'F'</u> are true. <u>Option 'E'</u> is false - convections cannot occur in solids as the particles can't move (they can only vibrate in their position).

---

64. A

Explanation:

More radiation is absorbed and emitted by <u>matt black surfaces</u>. <u>Light and glossy</u> coloured objects are poor absorbers and emitters of radiation, but they can reflect radiation.

---

65. B

Explanation:

Energy transferred to the radiator is calculated using:

<u>Q = mcΔT</u>

Q = 2 x 4200 x (22-16)

<u>Q = 50400 J</u>

Power = work done ÷ time

Power = 50 400 ÷ 100

<u>Power = 504 W</u>

Power = current x voltage

Current = voltage ÷ resistance

Therefore:

<u>Power = $voltage^2$ ÷ resistance</u>

Resistance = $240^2 \div 504$

Resistance $= \frac{800}{7}\ \Omega$

Physics (P5)	MATTER	Answers

66. C

Explanation:

First, find the density of water:

density $= \frac{\textbf{mass}}{\textbf{volume}}$

density $= \frac{250}{0.25}$

<u>density = 1000 kgm^{-3}</u>

Consider the following equation:

Hydrostatic pressure = height x density x gravitational field strength

Change in height: 8-2 = 6 m

Density: 1000 kgm^{-3}

Gravitational field strength: 10 Nkg^{-1}

Therefore,

Hydrostatic pressure = 6 x 1000 x 10

Hydrostatic pressure = **60000 Pa**

67. D

Explanation:

For a fixed mass of an ideal gas kept at a constant temperature, the **pressure and volume are inversely proportional:**

Assume 'k' is the constant:

$P = k \times \frac{1}{V}$

k = PV

Therefore, all experiments at the same temperature will have the **same rate constant**.

Consider Experiment 1:

k = 150 Pa x 3 m^3

k = **450**

Consider Experiment 2:

k = 450 Pa x 1 m^3

k = **450**

Consider Experiment 3:

k = 45 Pa x 10 m^3

k = **450**

Consider Experiment 4:

k = 50 Pa x 8 m^3

k = **400**

Consider Experiment 5:

k = 75 Pa x 6 m^3

k = **450**

Therefore, **Experiment 4 has a different rate constant**. This shows that it was **conducted at a different temperature**.

68. E

Explanation:

Consider the equation:

E_h (J) = m(kg) x l (Jkg^{-1})

E_h (energy required to change state)

m (mass)

l (specific latent heat of vaporisation/fusion)

Consider the melting of ice into water:

Specific latent heat of fusion is the amount of heat required to change a unit mass of the substance from solid to liquid state at its melting point, without any change in temperature.

Therefore, energy required to change state is:

E = 0.5 x (35 x 10^5)

E = **1.75 x 10^6 J**

Consider the transition of water into steam:

Specific latent heat of vaporisation is the amount of heat required to change a unit mole of the substance from liquid to gas state at its boiling point, without any change in temperature.

Therefore, energy required to change state is:

$E = 0.35 \times (20 \times 10^5)$

$E = \underline{0.7 \times 10^6 \text{ J}}$

Divide the two energies by one another:

$$\frac{1.75 \times 10^6}{0.7 \times 10^6} = \underline{2.5}$$

Therefore, 2.5 times more energy is required to convert 500g of ice into water compared to 350g of water into steam.

69. A

Explanation:

Considering the girl:

Equation:

Weight (N) = mass (kg) x gravitational field strength (10 Nkg^{-1})

Weight = 58 x 10

Weight = **580 N**

To find the pressure:

$$\text{Pressure } (Ncm^{-2}) = \frac{\text{Force (N)}}{\text{Area } (cm^2)}$$

$$\text{Pressure} = \frac{580}{290}$$

Pressure = **2 Ncm^{-2}**

Considering the boy:

Equation:

Weight (N) = mass (kg) x gravitational field strength (10 Nkg^{-1})

Weight = 37 x 10

Weight = **370 N**

To find the pressure:

$$\text{Pressure } (Ncm^{-2}) = \frac{\text{Force (N)}}{\text{Area } (cm^2)}$$

$$\text{Pressure} = \frac{370}{74}$$

Pressure = **5 Ncm^{-2}**

70. B

Explanation:

Firstly, convert Kelvin to °C:

213 K: 213 – 273 = **-60°C**

473 K: 473 – 273 = **200°C**

Since -60°C and -40°C are below the melting point of -39°C, **mercury will be a solid**. The temperatures of 200°C and 340°C are between the melting and boiling point of mercury. This implies that **mercury is a liquid at 200°C and 340°C** .

71. F

Explanation:

Use the equation:

Physics

hydrostatic pressure = hρg

The change in the depth is:

7-2 = 5 m

= 5 X 1000 X 10

= 50000 Pa

72. C

Explanation:

Option 'C' is the only false statement. Stars begin as clouds of dust and gas – Statement 1 is correct. Statement 2 is correct because the Sun possesses similar characteristics to small stars. A black dwarf is the final structure that a small star forms at the end of its life cycle. A neutron star becomes a black hole - this is the last stage of the life cycle of a large star. Therefore, **Statements 4 and 5** are correct.

73. D

Explanation:

Atmospheric pressure is caused by **air molecules colliding with a surface.** At higher levels above the ground, there are less air molecules within the atmosphere. As a result, the weight of the air also decreases. **Statements 2 and 4** are the only correct answers.

Physics (P6) | WAVES | Answers

74. B

Explanation:

To find the speed, the distance and time of each wave must be calculated.

Looking at the first graph:

There are 5 complete waves in 4.5 m. Therefore, each wave:

$\frac{4.5}{5} = 0.9$ m

Looking at the second graph:

There are 6 complete waves in 0.3 s. Therefore, each wave:

$\frac{0.3}{6} = 0.05$ s

The speed of the wave;

$\frac{0.9}{0.05} = 18$ ms^{-1}

75. D

Explanation:

Consider the amplitude:

The amplitude of the wave is the maximum positive from the undisturbed position. The wave has a maximum height of 18 and a minimum height of 6; therefore, its undisturbed position is:

$\frac{18+6}{2} = 12$

The maximum height from the undisturbed position:

18 – 12 = **6**

Therefore, the amplitude is **6 metres**.

Physics

Consider the frequency:

The frequency is the number of waves each second. It can be calculated by $\frac{1}{T}$, where 't' is the wave period. The wave period is the distance passing through a stationary point, in seconds. From the graph, 10 increments on the 'x' axis is 12.5 hours, therefore, 1 increment is 1.25 hours. Each wave takes 4 squares; it therefore takes 4(1.25) = 5 hours to pass. The hours must be converted into seconds in order to be put into the equation.

Converting 5 hours into seconds:

5 x 60 x 60 = 18000 seconds.

Therefore, the frequency is $\mathbf{\frac{1}{18000}}$

76. H

Explanation:

Consider the following equation:

Wave speed = frequency x wavelength

For a given frequency of light, the wavelength is proportional to wave speed. The wave is crossing a medium from water to air, therefore, the light ray is entering a less dense material (since air has fewer particles per unit volume compared to water). Since there are less particles in the air, the **wave speed will increase**. Consequently, the **wavelength will also increase**. The **frequency remains the same**, therefore, becoming a constant in the wave speed equation. This is because frequency depends on the source of the light, rather than the density of the material it is travelling through.

Find the frequency:

$v = f \times \lambda$

$f = \frac{v}{\lambda}$

$f = \frac{3 \times 10^8}{750 \times 10^{-9}}$

f = **4×10^{14} Hz**

77. C

Explanation:

As waves travel from a less dense (air) to a more dense (glass) medium, the wave speed decreases (becomes more difficult for the light ray to pass through the denser medium). As a result, the wavelength also decreases for a given frequency of light because the wavelength is proportional to wave speed. **The wave fronts become closer together** in the dense medium and **light bends towards the medium** since light rays travel more slowly in a denser medium. Therefore, **Option 'C'** is the correct diagram. In **Option 'A'**, the arrow indicates the light rays moving away from the normal in glass, which is incorrect. In **Options 'B' and 'D'**, the wave fronts are further apart in glass, which would indicate that the light rays are moving at a faster speed in a denser medium.

78. E

Explanation:

In reflection, the angle of incidence equals the angle of reflection (the incident and reflected rays will be reflected at the same angle from the plane mirror). In addition, the normal (dashed line) is always perpendicular to the surface of reflection (in this case, the plane mirror). In Diagrams 'A' and 'C', the incident ray is reflected at a smaller angle compared to the reflected ray (the angle of incidence is not equal to the angle of reflection). Therefore, **Diagrams 'A' and 'C' are incorrect**. **Diagram 'B' is incorrect** because the normal is parallel to the plane mirror, rather than perpendicular. **Diagrams 'D' and 'F' are incorrect** since the reflected ray goes through the plane mirror, rather than be reflected at the same angle as the angle of incidence. Therefore, **Diagram 'E' is correct** because the normal is perpendicular to the plane mirror, and the angle of incidence equals the angle of reflection.

79. B

Explanation:

Longitudinal waves are when the wave oscillations are parallel to the direction of energy transfer. Sound needs a material medium for their propagation to travel because the molecules present in a solid, liquid or gas can carry sound waves from one point to another. Sound cannot progress through the vacuum because the vacuum has no molecules which can vibrate and propagate the sound waves. Therefore, **Statement 'A' is correct**. The range of human hearing is from 20 Hz to 20 kHz (not 20 MHz) – **Statement 'B' is incorrect**. Radio waves have the longest wavelength, the lowest energy and the lowest frequency, while gamma rays have the shortest wavelength, the highest energy and the highest frequency. **Statement 'C' is correct**. Transverse waves have oscillations that are perpendicular to the direction of energy transfer. All electromagnetic have the same speed of 3.0×10^8 ms^{-1} in a vacuum. Consequently, **Statement 'D' is correct**. **Statements 'E', 'F' and 'G' relate to the uses and hazards of the electromagnetic waves – they are all correct**.

80. E

Explanation:

A longitudinal wave occurs when the wave oscillations are parallel to the direction of energy transfer (**Statement 'A' is incorrect**), while a transverse wave occurs when the wave oscillations are perpendicular to the direction of energy transfer (**Statement 'D' is incorrect**). The time period is measured between the same points on two adjacent waves (either between two peaks or two troughs), therefore, **Statement 'B' is incorrect**. The amplitude is the maximum distance from the mean undisturbed position, rather than the distance between the peak and the trough. As a result, **Statement 'C' is incorrect**. **Statement 'E' is correct** because frequency is the number of waves that pass a fixed point per second. All electromagnetic waves travel at 3.0×10^8 ms^{-1}, but other waves, such as sound waves, travel at 340 ms^{-1}; therefore, **Statement 'F' is incorrect**. The frequency and period of a wave are inversely proportional – as the number of waves that pass a fixed-point increase, the time taken for one wave cycle to be completed decreases. As a result, **Statement 'G' is incorrect**.

81. A

Explanation:

Consider the equation:

$$F_o = F_s \left(\frac{v}{v \pm v_s}\right)$$

$F_o = ?$

$F_s = 50$ Hz

$V_s = 100$ ms^{-1}

$V = 300$ ms^{-1}

When a source is travelling towards the observer, the **frequency of the sound increases**. Therefore, V_s must be subtracted to make the denominator smaller (thus, giving a larger frequency). When a source is travelling away from the observer, the frequency of the sound decreases. Therefore, V_s must be added to make the denominator larger (thus, giving a smaller frequency).

Consider Person 'A':

Since the source is travelling towards Person 'A', V_s must be subtracted.

$$F_o = F_s\left(\frac{V}{V - V_S}\right)$$

$$F_o = 500\left(\frac{300}{300 - 100}\right)$$

F_o = **750 Hz**

Consider Person 'B':

Since the source is travelling away Person 'B', V_s must be added.

$$F_o = F_s\left(\frac{V}{V + V_S}\right)$$

$$F_o = 500\left(\frac{300}{300 + 100}\right)$$

F_o = **375 Hz**

82. D

Explanation:

Infrared radiation has a **larger wavelength** than ultraviolet radiation -**Statement 1** is incorrect. Radio waves do not cause damage if they are absorbed by the human body - **Statement 4** is false.

83. C

Explanation:

Human hearing is between **20 Hz – 20 kHz**. Therefore, **Option 'C'** is the correct answer.

84. B

Explanation:

Statement 1 is incorrect as the vibrations in transverse waves are 90° to the direction of travel. **Statement 2 is correct**. All waves can be diffracted, reflected and refracted – **Statement 3 is incorrect**. Reflection of sound waves causes echoes – **Statement 4 is incorrect**

85. D

Explanation:

When a wave travels from a less dense medium (air) to a denser medium (water), it **slows down** and the **wavelength decreases**. The **frequency stays the same** despite the speed decreasing, as the wavelength has decreased.

86. A

Explanation:

The angle the light hits the medium is the **angle of incidence (Ray 1)**. The wave is **reflected (Ray 2)** when it bounces off the medium. The wave is **refracted (Ray 3)** when it goes through the glass medium, but it changes direction.

87. A

Explanation:

Light year is a **measure of distance and not time**. It is defined as a unit of astronomical distance equivalent to the distance that light travels in one year, which is 9.4607 ×

10^{12} km. According to the International Astronomical Union, a light-year is the distance that light travels in vacuum in one Julian year.

88. D

Explanation:

The wave equation should be used for this question:

$v = f\lambda$.

$f = v \div \lambda$

$f = 3 \div 20$

f = 0.15 Hz

The seagull rises up and down **0.15 times per second.**

There are **60 seconds in a minute:**

Therefore, in one minute the seagull rises up and down:

0.15 x 60 = **9 times.**

Physics (P7)	RADIOACTIVITY	Answers

89. B

Explanation

Consider the two sources:

Detector 1, at 3 mm away, is detecting the count rate successfully (count rate is decreasing on the graph). This implies that the radiation from the source is reaching Detector 1. However, at Detector 2 (20 mm away), the count rate is constant, suggesting that the radiation is not reaching it. The only type of radiation that does not travel more than 2 cm in air is **alpha radiation**. Therefore, **Options 'C', 'D', 'E' and 'F'** can be eliminated.

Consider the half-life:

One of the definitions of half-life is the time it takes for the count rate to half. Initially, the count rate is 120 counts per minute; therefore, half would be 60 counts per minute.

Reading off the graph from 60 count rate, the time is 2 minutes.

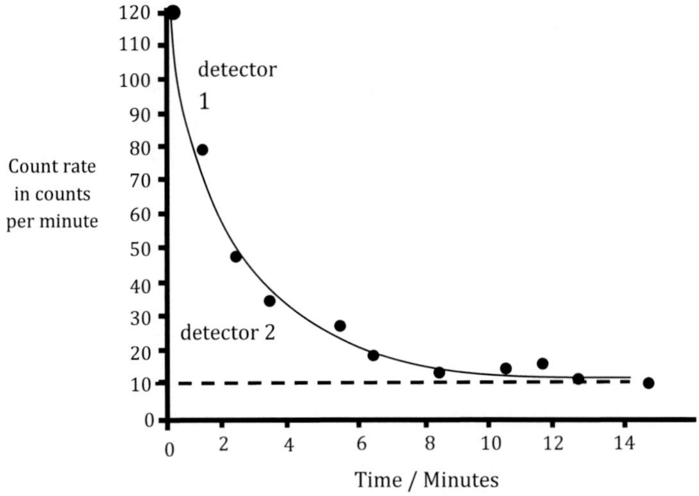

Convert 2 minutes into seconds: 2 x 60 = **120 seconds**

90. A

Explanation:

Consider alpha decay:

This decay consists of two protons and two neutrons. Therefore, when it is emitted from a substance, it will **decrease the atomic (proton number) by 2 and the mass number by 4.** Consequently, the alpha decay of $^{235}_{92}U$ will result in $^{231}_{90}Th$.

Consider beta decay:

This occurs when a nucleus contains too many neutrons. As a result, a neutron will change into a proton and emit an electron. Therefore, the **atomic (proton) number will increase by 1 but the mass number will remain the same** (since the mass of a proton is the same as the mass of a neutron). Consequently, the beta decay of $^{14}_{6}C$ will result in $^{14}_{7}N$.

91. C

Explanation:

One of the definitions of half-life is the time taken for the mass of a substance to halve. Looking at the table, the final mass of C-14 is 32mg. Half of the final mass is 16mg, which is reached at 3.2 minutes. Therefore, the approximate half–life of C-14 is 3.2 minutes.

92. F

Explanation:

Alpha decay consists of two protons and two neutrons. Therefore, when it is emitted from a substance, it will decrease the atomic (proton number) by 2 and the mass number by 4. If two alpha particles are emitted, the **atomic number decreases by 4** and the **mass number by 8**.

Beta decay occurs when a nucleus contains too many neutrons. As a result, a neutron will change into a proton and emit an electron. Therefore, the atomic (proton) number will increase by 1 but the mass number will remain the same (since the mass of a proton is the same as the mass of a neutron). If three beta particles are emitted, the **atomic number increases by 3** and the **mass number remains the same**. Gamma decay releases energy as gamma rays, and therefore, there is no change to the mass number or atomic number.

Therefore, the overall change is a **decrease of 1 in the atomic number** and a **decrease of 8 in the mass number**.

93. F

Explanation:

The half-life of a sample is the time taken for the half of the sample to decay, the activity of the sample to halve or the count rate to halve (not half the time taken for the activity to halve) – **Statement 'A' is incorrect.**

A helium atom contains 2 protons, 2 neutrons and 2 electrons, whereas alpha radiation only contains 2 protons and 2 neutrons. Alpha radiation has the same number of particles as a helium nucleus; therefore, **Statement 'B' is incorrect**.

During beta radiation, a neutron splits into a proton and an electron (the electron is emitted from the nucleus rather than the shells surrounding the nucleus). **Statement 'C' is incorrect.**

Nuclear fission is used in power stations in order to produce energy. It involved splitting a large nucleus into many smaller nuclei. Nuclear fusion is the converse – it is combining many small nuclei into a large nucleus. Therefore, **Statement 'D' is incorrect**.

Gamma radiation is most penetrating due to its mass (has the smallest mass because it is composed of high energy rays compared to sub-atomic particles present in alpha and beta radiation). As a result, it travels the furthest distances compared to alpha or beta radiation. Alpha radiation can stop in the air, beta radiation can be stopped by a thin sheet of aluminium and gamma radiation can only be stopped by many metres of concrete. As a result, **Statement 'E' is incorrect**.

Alpha radiation is the most ionising (has a positive charge of +2 due to the presence of two protons). However, because it has the largest mass of 2 protons and 2 neutrons, alpha particles have the greatest mass compared to beta or gamma radiation. This mass causes it to be the least penetrative. Consequently, **Statement 'F' is correct**.

94. B

Explanation:

Consider Source 'P':

In one hour:

$\frac{60}{15} = \underline{4}$ (the activity will half 4 times in an hour)

If the count rate is 128 counts per second, this will halve 4 times (equivalent to 2^4).

$\frac{128}{2^4} = \underline{\textbf{8 counts per second}}$

Consider Source 'Q':

In one hour:

$\frac{60}{12} = \underline{5}$ (the activity will half 5 times in an hour)

If the count rate is 192 counts per second, this will halve 5 times (equivalent to 2^5).

$\frac{192}{2^5} = \underline{\textbf{6 counts per second}}$

Therefore, the difference in count rate:

8 – 6 = **2 counts per second**

95. D

Explanation:

Alpha particles are blocked by **paper, skin, thin metal and lead**.

Beta particles can **penetrate through paper and skin,** but it is **blocked by thin metal and lead**.

Gamma emissions can **penetrate through skin, paper and metal** but it is **blocked by thick lead**.

96. D

Explanation:

Gamma rays are not stopped by metal sheets. Therefore, there wasn't a noticeable change in its count rate – hence it is from **Source 3**. Alpha particles cannot penetrate through metal; as a result, it showed the greatest decrease in its count rate. Consequently, alpha particle are emitted from **Source 2**. Finally, beta particles are more penetrating than alpha particles, but it is also stopped by metals, therefore, it is from **Source 1**.

A Lakshmi, T R Enoch, S Z Y Ooi. Doctors Academy Publications, Cardiff, UK, 2020.

97. C

Explanation:

When an **atom absorbs electromagnetic radiation**, the electrons move further away from the nucleus and they move to a higher level. When **electromagnetic radiation is emitted**, the electrons move to a lower energy level and closer to the nucleus. Therefore, **Statements 2 and 3** are false.

98. A

Explanation:

Alpha particles have **2 protons and 2 neutrons** - its nucleus is the same as that of a **helium atom**. Therefore, **Option 'A'** is the correct answer. Beta particles consist of one electron and gamma radiation contains gamma rays.

99. E

Explanation:

The count rate of this element would halve every 5 days.

15 weeks is equivalent to:

15 x 7 = **105 days.**

105 ÷ 5 = **21** *(the number of half-lives that have passed).*

Therefore, the original count rate is **60 x 2^{21}** *(because the count rate must have halved 21 times).*

$2^{21} = 2^5 \times 2^5 \times 2^5 \times 2^5 \times 2$

= 32 x 32 x 32 x 32 x 2

= **2,097,152**

60 x 2,097,152 = **125,829,120**

100. C

Explanation:

$$\frac{1472}{23} = 64$$

$= 2^6$

The element has gone through **6 half-lives in 114 hours.**

114 ÷ 6 = **19 hours**

Therefore, its half-life is **19 hours.**

Physics

SECTION 3

Section 3	Writing Task	Task 1

If A Patient Dies After A Routine Operation Or Procedure, It Is A Case Of Medical Error.

Explain what you think is meant by the statement. Present a counter-argument. To what extent do you agree with the argument?

Due to the enhanced standard of modern healthcare, mortality rates during surgery have reduced. Comprehensive risk assessments and protocol guidance have been implemented to reduced human error. In addition, new technologies, such as laparoscopic surgery, have been designed to minimise the length of hospital stays and the risk of wound infections. Consequently, one may contend that mortality from a routine operation is a direct contribution of negligence and error.

However, due to a myriad of complexities and confounding factors, one cannot ascertain the precise effects of surgery on a particular individual. There is a myriad of risks that doctors cannot account for, due to the vagaries of the interaction between medicine and human physiology. These include wound infections, excess bleeding, haematomas and pulmonary embolisms. Patients who are unaware of suffering from sex-linked disorders, such as haemophilia, could have excessive bleeding during surgery. Complications, for example malignant hypothermia, could arise mid-surgery, due to an adverse reaction to anaesthesia. Alternatively, a patient could suffer from a previously unknown allergy to a certain medication, resulting in an anaphylactic shock. Lastly, the fragility and vulnerability of a patient may increase their risk of mortality; older patients are more at risk of death after a routine operation.

In conclusion, despite the advancement of technology and implementation of protocols, one cannot predict the consequences of a particular surgery. There are many risks associated with surgery, including equipment failure and unknown allergies, that could contribute to an individual's mortality. As a result, no surgery is completely safe.

Section 3	Writing Task	Task 2

Extreme Sport Injuries Should Not Be Treated Under A Publicly Funded Health Service.

Explain the reasoning behind this statement. Suggest an argument against this statement. To what extent do you agree with the argument?

This statement implies that injuries sustained due to extreme sports are self-inflicted; individuals have decided to take risks and participate. Since this is a lifestyle choice, an individual has the capacity or ability to avoid dangerous sports.

As a result, one may contend that a public health service should not cater to these individuals. Due to the increased demand on the National Health Service (NHS) without a proportionate increase in supply, there is a lack of sufficient resources. Consequently, one may assert that the NHS should prioritise treating illnesses that patients cannot control. Genetic diseases, such as Neurofibromatosis or Tay-Sachs disease, and autoimmune diseases, including rheumatoid arthritis and multiple sclerosis, detrimentally impact an individual's quality of life. Since these diseases are not self-inflicted, only these individuals should be able to access free healthcare.

In contrast to the aforementioned argument, the NHS, founded in 1948, was designed to be free at the point of delivery. In addition to this, it should not discriminate based on an individual's circumstances; any injury or illness should be treated without bias. Alternatively, following the same reasoning, one may assert that other diseases that are a result of lifestyle choices should not be treated under the NHS. For example, liver cirrhosis is associated with excessive alcohol consumption and a sedentary lifestyle could lead to obesity and Type II diabetes. However, not treating these diseases under the NHS reduced distributive justice, which is a core tenet of the NHS.

Therefore, the statement does not justify that extreme sports, which is considered a choice, should not be treated by a publicly funded health service because many illnesses treated by the NHS are due to an individual's lifestyle choice.

Section 3	Writing Task	Task 3

Doctors Are The Most Difficult Patients To Treat.

What do you understand about this statement? Give examples of how doctors can be good patients and terrible patients. What does this suggest about a doctor's empathy towards their patients?

When doctors become patients themselves, their high expectations of the medical profession often leaves them unsatisfied with the care, leading them to be quite uncooperative and hence the most difficult patients. Doctors may have already diagnosed themselves before visiting their own physician, this leaves them with hoping for high standards of care and a flawless diagnosis. With the high expectations, they are often left displeased and this breaks down the doctor-patient relationship. It may also be unusual for the physician to swap roles to become the patient which again has an impact on building trust in the relationship with their doctor. Moreover, a placebo effect can often be created when there is a good doctor-patient relationship that is built on trust, this leads to the treatment that is given to be more effective. Provided that, a lack of this trust and good relationship makes the physician the worst patient to treat.

On the other hand, doctors may sometimes make the best patients due to the level of understanding they have of the limitations of a doctor, the healthcare system and their medical knowledge. For example, if a tumour was removed in surgery and it later recurred, the doctor would understand it was not in the control of the treating doctor and be more cooperative.

Furthermore, explaining complex medical terms would be easier, they don't need to be too simplified. On the contrary, they often do make bad patients due to the confidence their own medical knowledge provides them to reject or disagree with their doctor. If the physician, as a patient, was offered a hip replacement as the best means to reduce their pain by their Orthopaedic surgeon, and the physician believed that a hip resurfacing was a better option, then this leads to a lack of satisfaction with the care. Therefore, the all-important and effective doctor-patient relationship deteriorates.

Doctors treat patients with empathy, but when they themselves have been patients at some point, they experience what a patient goes through and this makes them better doctors, as the empathy they would then feel is truly genuine. They are then able to built on their compassion towards their patients after understanding their needs and expectations. Thus, the doctor-patient relationship improves and they are able to provide high-quality care in a holistic manner.

Section 3	Writing Task	Task 4

The Human Body Should Be Regarded As A Complex Mechanism.

Explain what you think is meant by the statement. Present a counter-argument. To what extent do you agree with the argument?

In this context, the noun 'mechanism' implies that the body is a system of parts which work in collaboration with each other. This statement therefore suggests that, while the human body might be complex, the way in which it functions is predictable.

It could be argued, on the one hand, that categorising the human body as a mechanism, albeit a complex one, is over-simplifying the interactions that occur within it. Indeed, if the human body is a machine and its processes are anticipated, scientists should be able to ascertain the precise effects of certain medications. Yet, we know that this is not true: due to the vagaries of the human genome, scientists cannot predict how an individual will react to various medications. One may thus contend that regarding the body as a mechanism is insufficient in treating patients.

On the other hand, however, certain physiological processes are comparable between humans. By treating the body as a mechanism, scientists can assess fundamental activities that occur in all individuals, allowing certain notions to be understood in greater detail. Processes such as peristalsis and egestion can be analysed thoroughly in order to gain a greater insight into the human body in general.

In conclusion, I concur that the body should be regarded as a complex mechanism because this allows us to continue to enhance our biological understanding. However, this notion should be approached with caution, and it should always be contextualised appropriately. Scientists must consider that differences between individuals will always exist and that these prohibit the conceptualisation of the human body as one complex mechanism.

Section 3	Writing Task	Task 5

Death Is Ultimately Inevitable. Healthcare Professionals Must Realise This When Treating Patients.

What do you think this statement means? What are the issues of healthcare professionals not always accepting that, on occasions, a patient's death cannot be prevented?

The human body is constructed in such a way that, at a certain point in every individual's life, it starts to physically deteriorate. No matter what medical interventions have been put in place to try to decelerate this physical decay, death is ultimately a natural and inevitable process. Healthcare professionals must realise this truth when attempting to prolong a patient's life, and they should act in the manner that suits the patient's condition and outcome. There is no one-size-fits-all approach, and healthcare professionals should realise this.

The inability of healthcare professionals to accept that a patient's death is drawing near may compromise the quality of care with which that individual is provided. The patient might be offered an incorrect or less effective care plan, and this may ultimately reduce his or her quality of life. A pertinent example is that it may be preferable for a doctor to not operate on a patient with a highly malignant brain tumour due to the risk of the surgery resulting in life-long paralysis. Rather, the patient might find greater comfort in a holistic approach to alleviate the effects of this terminal illness. However, this approach can only be actioned once the doctor has realised that it is beyond his or her power to quash the natural process of death.

The healthcare professional's ability to acknowledge that, on occasions, death cannot be prevented can provide the patient with enhanced care; understanding that a patient's death is near allows doctors and nurses to alter the care plan to ensure that it suits his or her condition. If an elderly lady is diagnosed with Stage Four lung cancer, doctors must know which actions to take and which actions to avoid in order to improve the patient's quality of life and demonstrate beneficence. This positions the patient's care as the doctor's primary concern.

In conclusion, it is important for healthcare professionals to appreciate that life has a natural end and to recognise when this is imminent. It is crucial to provide treatment that befits the patient's condition. This could be the moment in which it is realised that a patient in palliative care is close to death. Despite their potential to cause addiction, stronger painkillers could then be administered in order to reduce the patient's pain and keep him or her comfortable; the side effects of the drug are unimportant at this stage in the patient's life. In essence, doctors must always prioritise the care, wishes and comfort of their patients. They should endeavour to treat the person rather than simply attempt to cure the disease.

Section 3	Writing Task	Task 6

Doctors Must Always Offer Help In Emergency Situations Within Clinical Settings Or In The Community.

Explain what you understand by this statement. Argue to the contrary. To what extent do you agree with the statement?

The General Medical Council (GMC) states that, as a doctor, it is one's duty to provide assistance to anyone in danger or in a health-related emergency. After five to six years in medical school, as well as further specialised training within a clinical environment, a doctor will often be the most appropriate, and perhaps the only, person who can provide aid in an emergency. Doctors arguably possess a sound understanding of the mechanisms of the human body and the specific actions to take in certain situations, and it can therefore be deemed their responsibility to offer help during an emergency.

However, there are certain factors that should be considered to ensure that the most suitable action is taken to assist the patient. These include the safety of the environment, the competence of the doctor, and the immediate availability of necessary resources. It must be safe for the doctor to intervene; he or she should take particular caution in the case of a fire, for example. Putting oneself at risk and endangering one's own life might culminate in two patients instead of one. In addition, a doctor should limit his or her assistance when he or she is not competent to help the patient or not in a suitable physical and/or mental condition to provide care. If an emergency occurs in a restaurant and the doctor is heavily under the influence of alcohol, he or she should not carry out any medical procedures. This could result in more harm than good, and we must remember that one of the pillars of medical ethics is non-maleficence. The doctor should therefore seek assistance by calling the emergency services.

In my opinion, a doctor should always be willing to offer help in an emergency, but he or she should also take into consideration the abovementioned issues and make an appropriate decision that will provide the best care for the patient. Each situation should be assessed, and a balanced decision should be taken to offer maximum assistance that complies with the doctor's knowledge but simultaneously recognises his or her limitations.

Section 3	Writing Task	Task 7

A Surgeon's Mortality Rates Should Not Be Published. This Prevents Doctors Taking On Challenging Cases.

What is meant by this statement? Argue to the contrary. To what extent do you think publishing mortality rates affect the work of a surgeon?

According to the statement, publishing mortality rates of surgeons might deter them from taking on cases that are considered high-risk due to the fear of having a high mortality rate associated with their name. It is probable that a surgeon who routinely takes on complicated cases, especially in the context of patients with associated co-morbidities, would have a higher mortality rate than his or her colleagues who perform only routine, and relatively "safe", cases. In addition, such data varies from surgical specialty to surgical specialty. A pertinent example is that a complex cardiovascular or neurosurgical procedure is likely to carry a higher risk of death than a simple operation on the hand. If mortality rates are made public without a comprehensive delineation of the peripheral details, patients can formulate an ill-placed conceptualisation of a particular surgeon, and this might dissuade surgeons from accepting high-risk cases for fear of being projected as incompetent. This can result in fewer skilled surgeons taking on complex cases.

On the contrary, open discussion in Morbidity and Mortality (M&M) meetings within departments and the publication of morbidity and mortality rates of all surgeons is the most appropriate way to maintain transparency. Since complete analysis of the data in such publications will illuminate factors that lead to negative outcomes, it is a beneficial process which will advance the wider medical field. A multitude of factors come into play in these circumstances, and the primary cause for which the patient was operated is not the only aspect that is considered. For example, if a patient who recently had a myocardial infarction undergoes emergency abdominal surgery, the risk of death during the operation is significant due to the underlying cardiac condition. The co-morbidities of the patient, anaesthetic risks, and the stage of the disease (particularly in the case of cancer) are factors that can be assessed prior to the procedure and adequate preparation can be taken . It should also be remembered that mortality may, on occasions, be completely unrelated to the procedure. The surgery might have had a positive outcome, but the patient could die due to an underlying and undiagnosed disease.

In conclusion, the publication of adequate data and an analysis of the influence of particular variables on the final outcomes reveals the factors that underlie mortality rates. These can then be addressed appropriately in subsequent cases to improve the standard of care provided. The benefits of publishing such data outweigh the disadvantages as, when conducted in the correct manner, it proves an apt method of measuring, assessing and improving clinical care.

Section 3 | Writing Task | Task 8

Patients Who Are Most Likely To Survive Following Treatment Should Be Prioritised.

Explain the reasoning behind this statement. Argue to the contrary. To what extent do you agree with the statement?

This policy was adopted by the National Health Service (NHS) during the COVID-19 pandemic. Due to a dearth of resources, certain patients were prioritised for care, such as given ventilators, in an attempt to save those who were most likely to survive. The limited resources within the NHS must often be allocated according to various criteria. The overstretched budget and a lack of staff prompt patients to be triaged and prioritised in such a way that allows those with a greater chance of survival to be helped. This might mean that a young patient with liver cirrhosis caused by alcoholism is accepted for a liver transplant rather than an elderly patient with liver cancer due to the fact that the younger patient has higher chance of survival. This method thus encourages patients who have a longer life expectancy and who will arguably respond well to treatment to be prioritised.

On the other hand, doctors should not consider a patient's likelihood of survival alone. They must also consider the patient's quality of life after treatment to ensure beneficence. A physically fit patient undergoing a complex neurosurgical procedure might have a greater chance of survival compared to an elderly patient with a BMI of above 35 who needs a hip replacement under general anaesthetic. However, the neurosurgical procedure carries a risk of paralysis, whilst a successful hip replacement has a smaller overall risk and would potentially improve the patient's quality of life. If resources must be allocated to one patient over another, the quality of each individual's life and the results of the treatment must be contemplated; the patient's chance of survival should not be the only factor considered.

In conclusion, I believe that doctors must try to envisage each patient's life after any procedure and allocate resources to those who will benefit. The measure 'quality-adjusted life years' can provide further information for doctors and aid them to make appropriate decisions that are in the best interest of the patient. Resources must be allocated in a suitable and timely manner to maximise the benefit to patients.

Section 3	Writing Task	Task 9

Curing Diseases Is Expensive And A Waste Of Money.

What do you think is meant by this statement? Argue to the contrary. To what extent do you agree that it is a waste of money to cure diseases?

The National Health Service (NHS) accounts for a large proportion of the UK's government budget. It might be argued that this money could be allocated to other sectors of the country. Rather than spending billions of pounds on the NHS each year to reduce the population's ailments, the country could attribute money to businesses and increase the productivity of its economy. This would allow the UK to prosper and compete on a global scale. Moreover, encouraging economic growth by increasing the UK's productive capacity would bring more revenue into the country, which would arguably improve the quality of life of its citizens. This statement therefore suggests that the expense afforded to the eradication of diseases could be better in order to enhance a country's development.

On the contrary, we might question how a country can progress if its citizens are unhealthy. Indeed, the workforce can function optimally only if it is free from disease. If people are unable to work for extensive periods of time or, even, at all due to sickness, economic retardation would ensue. It is, in fact, a vicious circle: if a country does not provide the resources to maintain the health of its citizens, they will simply become sicker, and this will hinder the economic output even further. It can be argued that money invested in health is never a detrimental investment in terms of excellent returns from a healthy population whose output is efficient and outlook is positive. Investment in the NHS therefore indirectly contributes to economic progress.

While the eradication of disease prompts the economy to become more productive due to a strong workforce, its effects also touch many other areas. If a country helps its citizens to fight diseases, the citizens will be not only physically healthy but also mentally healthy. If the country appears to abandon its population for economic benefits, individuals might become frustrated, angry and upset. If we consider the issue in a humane and benevolent manner, curing diseases cannot be "a waste of money", however expensive it might be. As doctors and humans, the fact that every life matters should be firmly positioned at the forefront of our minds.

In conclusion, I do not believe that it is a waste of money to cure diseases. On the contrary, an unhealthy population would place even greater pressure on the economy. Keeping citizens healthy contributes to a productive workforce, better output from employees, and, perhaps more importantly, a happier nation.

Task 1:

If A Patient Dies After A Routine Operation Or Procedure, It Is A Case Of Medical Error.

Explain what you think is meant by the statement. Present a counter-argument. To what extent do you agree with the argument?

Due to the enhanced standard of modern healthcare, mortality rates during surgery have reduced. Comprehensive risk assessments and protocol guidance have been implemented to reduced human error. In addition, new technologies, such as laparoscopic surgery, have been designed to minimise the length of hospital stays and the risk of wound infections. Consequently, one may contend that mortality from a routine operation is a direct contribution of negligence and error.

Comment [A1]: Verb is incorrectly conjugated.

However, due to a myriad of complexities and confounding factors, one cannot ascertain the precise effects of surgery on a particular individual. There is a myriad of risks that doctors cannot account for, due to the vagaries of the interaction between medicine and human physiology. These include wound infections, excess bleeding, haematomas and pulmonary embolisms. Patients who are unaware of suffering from sex-linked disorders, such as haemophilia, could have excessive bleeding during surgery. Complications, for example malignant hypothermia, could arise mid-surgery, due to an adverse reaction to anaesthesia. Alternatively, a patient could suffer from a previously unknown allergy to a certain medication, resulting in an anaphylactic shock. Lastly, the fragility and vulnerability of a patient may increase their risk of mortality; older patients are more at risk of death after a routine operation.

Comment [A2]: Repetition. Try to use synonyms since they will enhance the quality of your writing.

Comment [A3]: Check the way in which you use prepositional verbs. Here, the phrase should be:

'risks for which doctors cannot account'

Comment [A4]: Check syntax.

Comment [A5]: Check syntax.

Comment [A6]: No need for comma here.

Comment [A7]: Since you are referring to 'a patient' (singular), it would be better to use the singular pronoun here.

In conclusion, despite the advancement of technology and implementation of protocols, one cannot predict the consequences of a particular surgery. There are many risks associated with surgery, including equipment failure and unknown allergies, that could contribute to an individual's mortality. As a result, no surgery is completely safe.

Comment [A8]: 'which'

Examiner Comments:

While the response addresses the first two parts of the statement, the candidate does not discuss the extent to which he/she agrees with the argument. The response also fails to allude to the idea of "medical error", but this forms an important part of the statement.

The counterargument provides relevant examples. Yet, the candidate fails to elaborate on these examples: he/she cites them but does not demonstrate why these particular examples allow him/her to challenge the statement.

While the conclusion alludes to the idea that operations are never entirely "safe", it is not entirely convincing as it only states that "no surgery is safe". It does not expand on this, it does not refer back to the idea of medical errors, and it does not offer an opinion.

Mark: 2.5B

Task 2:

Extreme Sport Injuries Should Not Be Treated Under A Publicly Funded Health Service.

Explain the reasoning behind this statement. Suggest an argument against this statement. To what extent do you agree with the argument?

This statement implies that injuries sustained due to extreme sports are self-inflicted; individuals have decided to take risks and participate. Since this is a lifestyle choice, an individual has the capacity or ability to avoid dangerous sports.

Comment [A9]: This verb is left "hanging". It is a prepositional verb (*participate in*).

As a result, one may contend that a public health service should not cater to these individuals. Due to the increased demand on the National Health Service (NHS) without a proportionate increase in supply, there is a lack of sufficient resources. Consequently, one may assert that the NHS should prioritise treating illnesses that patients cannot control. Genetic diseases, such as Neurofibromatosis or Tay-Sachs disease, and autoimmune diseases, including rheumatoid arthritis and multiple sclerosis, detrimentally impact an individual's quality of life. Since these diseases are not self-inflicted, only these individuals should be able to access free healthcare.

In contrast to the aforementioned argument, the NHS, founded in 1948, was designed to be free at the point of delivery. In addition to this, it should not discriminate based on an individual's circumstances; any injury or illness should be treated without bias. Alternatively, following the same reasoning, one may assert that other diseases that are a result of lifestyle choices should not be treated under the NHS. For example, liver cirrhosis is associated with excessive alcohol consumption and a sedentary lifestyle could lead to obesity and Type II diabetes. However, not treating these diseases under the NHS reduced distributive justice, which is a core tenet of the NHS.

Therefore, the statement does not justify that extreme sports, which is considered a choice, should not be treated by a publicly funded health service because many illnesses treated by the NHS are due to an individual's lifestyle choice.

Comment [A10]: Incorrectly conjugated verb.

Comment [A11]: Incorrect verb conjugation. This is the singular form of the verb, but the subject to which reference is made (*extreme sports*) is plural.

Comment [A12]: Try to avoid double negatives. They confuse and deflate your argument.

Examiner Comments:

This response starts well, and the second paragraph is particularly strong. It explains the reasoning behind the statement, using appropriate examples to support its claims.

The counterargument is weak. It does not discuss or detail why extreme sport injuries **should** be treated under the NHS. The conclusion does not draw together the response or the primary aspects of the statement.

The candidate has failed to answer the final part of the question and does not suggest if he/she agrees with the statement.

Mark: 2.5B

Task 3:

Doctors Are The Most Difficult Patients To Treat

What do you understand about this statement? Give examples of how doctors can be good patients and terrible patients. What does this suggest about a doctor's empathy towards their patients?

When doctors become patients themselves, their high expectations of the medical profession often leaves them unsatisfied with the care, leading them to be quite uncooperative and hence the most difficult patients. Doctors may have already diagnosed themselves before visiting their own physician, this leaves them with hoping for high standards of care and a flawless diagnosis. With the high expectations, they are often left displeased and this breaks down the doctor-patient relationship. It may also be unusual for the physician to swap roles to become the patient which again has an impact on building trust in the relationship with their doctor. Moreover, a placebo effect can often be created when there is a good doctor-patient relationship that is built on trust, this leads to the treatment that is given to be more effective.

Comment [A13]: Incorrect verb conjugation. You are referring to 'their high expectations', which is plural. The verb should thus be conjugated to agree with this.

Comment [A14]: Commas are absent.

Comment [A15]: Check punctuation and syntax. A comma cannot be used here. You could write:

'...visiting their own physician. This leaves them...'

OR

'...visiting their own physician, which leaves them...'

Comment [A16]: Check this. Grammatically incorrect.

Comment [A17]: Awkward syntax.

Comment [A18]: Comma required after 'displeased'.

Comment [A19]: Commas are absent. This should be written as:

'...which, again, has...'

Comment [A20]: You have used the plural possessive pronoun, but you have referred to a singular subject (*the physician*). It would be better to use the singular possessive pronoun here.

Comment [A21]: This needs to be two sentences, separated with a full stop.

Comment [A22]: Awkward syntax.

Provided that, a lack of this trust and good relationship makes the physician the worst patient to treat.

Comment [A23]: Awkward syntax. These two words cannot be used here this manner.

On the other hand, doctors may sometimes make the best patients due to the level of understanding they have of the limitations of a doctor, the healthcare system and their medical knowledge. For example, if a tumour was removed in surgery and it later recurred, the doctor would understand it was not in the control of the treating doctor and be more cooperative.

Furthermore, explaining complex medical terms would be easier, they don't need to be too simplified. On the contrary, they often do make bad patients due to the confidence their own medical knowledge provides them to reject or disagree with their doctor. If the physician, as a patient, was offered a hip replacement as the best means to reduce their pain by their Orthopaedic surgeon, and the physician believed that a hip resurfacing was a better option, then this leads to a lack of satisfaction with the care. Therefore, the all-important and effective doctor-patient relationship deteriorates.

Comment [A24]: This should be a colon rather than a comma.

Comment [A25]: Try to avoid contractions. These are informal and not enhance the quality of your writi

Comment [A26]: Awkward syntax

Comment [A27]: Please see comm above on the use of possessive pronc

Comment [A28]: As above.

Doctors treat patients with empathy, but when they themselves have been patients at some point, they experience what a patient goes through and this makes them better doctors, as the empathy they would then feel is truly genuine. They are then able to built on their compassion towards their patients after understanding their needs and expectations. Thus, the doctor-patient relationship improves and they are able to provide high-quality care in a holistic manner.

Comment [A29]: Incorrectly conjugated.

Examiner Comments:

The response addresses all aspects of the question, offering appropriate examples to support its arguments. The arguments are rational, and there is evidence of a balanced consideration of the statement.

It is unfortunate that the quality of English dilutes the strength of the response. While the ideas are arranged in a coherent manner, the syntax and grammar cause the arguments to, on occasions, become ambiguous. The tone is rather informal.

Mark: 3.5B

<u>Task 4:</u>

The Human Body Should Be Regarded As A Complex Mechanism.

Explain what you think is meant by the statement. Present a counter-argument. To what extent do you agree with the argument?

In this context, the noun 'mechanism' implies that the body is a system of parts which work in collaboration with each other. This statement therefore suggests that, while the human body might be complex, the way in which it functions is predictable.

It could be argued, on the one hand, that categorising the human body as a mechanism, albeit a complex one, is over-simplifying the interactions that occur within it. Indeed, if the human body is a machine and its processes are anticipated, scientists should be able to ascertain the precise effects of certain medications. Yet, we know that this is not true: due to the vagaries of the human genome, scientists cannot predict how an individual will react to various medications. One may thus contend that regarding the body as a mechanism is insufficient in treating patients.

On the other hand, however, certain physiological processes are comparable between humans. By treating the body as a mechanism, scientists can assess fundamental activities that occur in all individuals, allowing certain notions to be understood in greater detail. Processes such as peristalsis and egestion can be analysed thoroughly in order to gain a greater insight into the human body in general.

In conclusion, I concur that the body should be regarded as a complex mechanism because this allows us to continue to enhance our biological understanding. However, this notion should be approached with caution, and it should always be contextualised appropriately. Scientists must consider that differences between individuals will always exist and that these prohibit the conceptualisation of the human body as *one* complex mechanism.

Examiner Comments:

This response answers all aspects of the question in a logical and coherent manner. It presents a sound counterargument which subsequently enables the candidate to reach a conclusion.

It is clear, simple and focused, using sensible and relevant examples to support its arguments and offering a balanced view of the statement.

Mark: 4.5A

Task 5:

Death Is Ultimately Inevitable. Healthcare Professionals Must Realise This When Treating Patients.

What do you think this statement means? What are the issues of healthcare professionals not always accepting that, on occasions, a patient's death cannot be prevented?

The human body is constructed in such a way that, with ageing, the vital organs fail to perform in an optimal manner, the agility diminishes and the cognition declines. No matter what medical interventions are put in place to try and decelerate this deterioration, death is ultimately a natural and inevitable process. Healthcare professionals must realise this sombre fact when attempting to prolong a patient's life, and they should act in the manner that suits the patient's condition and outcome. There is no one-size-fits-all approach, and it is imperative for the healthcare professionals to appreciate this.

The inability of healthcare professionals to accept that a patient's death is drawing near may compromise the quality of care with which that individual is provided. The patient might be offered an incorrect or less effective care plan, and this may ultimately reduce his or her quality of life. A pertinent example is that it may be preferable for a doctor to not operate on a patient with a highly progressive brain tumour due to the risk of the surgery resulting in life-long paralysis. Rather, the patient might find greater comfort in a holistic approach to assuage the effects of this terminal illness. However, this approach can only be actioned once the doctor has realised that it is beyond his or her power to negate the natural process of death.

The healthcare professional's ability to acknowledge that, on occasions, death cannot be prevented can provide the patient with enhanced care; understanding that a patient's death is near allows doctors and nurses to alter the care plan to ensure that it suits his or her condition. If an elderly lady is diagnosed with Stage IV lung cancer, doctors must know which actions to take and which actions to avoid in order to improve the patient's quality of life and demonstrate beneficence. This positions the patient's care as the doctor's primary concern.

In conclusion, it is important for healthcare professionals to appreciate that life has a natural end and to recognise when this is imminent. It is crucial to provide treatment that befits the patient's condition. This could be the moment in which it is realised that a patient in palliative care is close to death. Stronger painkillers, despite their propensity to cause addiction, could then be administered in order to alleviate the patient's pain and keep him or her comfortable; the side effects of the drug are unimportant at this stage in the patient's life. In essence, doctors must always prioritise the care, wishes and comfort of their patients. They should endeavour to treat the person rather than simply attempt to cure the disease.

Examiner Comments:

This response has a clear and coherent structure which is guided by the components of the question. It commences by demonstrating a sound understanding of the statement, and it is evident that the candidate has understood the question.

Simple, yet relevant, examples are used to draw the definite conclusion that healthcare professionals should recognise that they cannot control death. All aspects of the question are addressed in a convincing manner, and the conclusion successfully brings together a balanced consideration of the statement.

It is written in a fluent manner and exhibits a sound use of grammar and vocabulary.

Mark: 4.5A

Task 6:

Doctors Must Always Offer Help In Emergency Situations Within Clinical Settings Or In The Community.

Explain what you understand by this statement. Argue to the contrary. To what extent do you agree with the statement?

The General Medical Council (GMC) states that, as a doctor, it is one's duty to provide assistance to anyone in danger or in a health-related emergency. After five to six years in medical school, as well as further specialised training within a clinical environment, a doctor will often be the most appropriate, and perhaps the only, person who can provide aid in an emergency. Doctors arguably possess a sound understanding of the mechanisms of the human body and the specific actions to take in certain situations, and it can therefore be deemed their responsibility to offer help during an emergency.

However, there are certain factors that should be considered to ensure that the most suitable action is taken to assist the patient. These include the safety of the environment, the competence of the doctor, and the immediate availability of necessary resources. It must be safe for the doctor to intervene; he or she should take particular caution in the case of a fire, for example. Putting oneself at risk and endangering one's own life might culminate in two patients instead of one. In addition, a doctor should limit his or her assistance when he or she is not competent to help the patient or not in a suitable physical and/or mental condition to provide care. If an emergency occurs in a restaurant and the doctor is heavily under the influence of alcohol, he or she should not carry out any medical procedures. This could result in more harm than good, and we must remember that one of the pillars of medical ethics is non-maleficence. The doctor should therefore seek assistance by calling the emergency services.

In my opinion, a doctor should always be willing to offer help in an emergency, but he or she should also take into consideration the abovementioned issues and make an appropriate decision that will provide the best care for the patient. Each situation should be assessed, and a balanced decision should be taken to offer maximum assistance that complies with the doctor's knowledge but simultaneously recognises his or her limitations.

Comments:
The response addresses all aspects of the question, approaching the statement in a balanced and thoughtful manner. The counterargument is strong, and appropriate examples have been used to support its claims.

The arguments are rational, and the response follows a simple structure that allows an easy and convincing reading. It is evident that the candidate has understood the question.

Mark: 4.5A

Section 3 | Writing Task | Examiner Comments

Task 7:

A Surgeon's Mortality Rates Should Not Be Published. This Prevents Doctors Taking On Challenging Cases.

What is meant by this statement? Argue to the contrary. To what extent do you think publishing mortality rates affect the work of a surgeon?

According to the statement, publishing mortality rates of surgeons might deter them from taking on cases that are considered high-risk due to the fear of having a high mortality rate associated with their name. It is probable that a surgeon who routinely takes on complicated cases, especially in the context of patients with associated co-morbidities, would have a higher mortality rate than his or her colleagues who perform only routine, and relatively "safe", cases. In addition, such data varies from surgical specialty to surgical specialty. A pertinent example is that a complex cardiovascular or neurosurgical procedure is likely to carry a higher risk of death than a simple operation on the hand. If mortality rates are made public without a comprehensive delineation of the peripheral details, patients can formulate an ill-placed conceptualisation of a particular surgeon, and this might dissuade surgeons from accepting high-risk cases for fear of being projected as incompetent. This can result in fewer skilled surgeons taking on complex cases.

On the contrary, open discussion in Morbidity and Mortality (M&M) meetings within departments and the publication of morbidity and mortality rates of all surgeons is the most appropriate way to maintain transparency. Since complete analysis of the data in such publications will illuminate factors that lead to negative outcomes, it is a beneficial process which will advance the wider medical field. A multitude of factors come into play in these circumstances, and the primary cause for which the patient was operated is not the only aspect that is considered. For example, if a patient who recently had a myocardial infarction undergoes emergency abdominal surgery, the risk of death during the operation is significant due to the underlying cardiac condition. The co-morbidities of the patient, anaesthetic risks, and the stage of the disease (particularly in the case of cancer) are factors that can be assessed prior to the procedure and adequate preparation can be taken. It should also be remembered that mortality may, on occasions, be completely unrelated to the procedure. The surgery might have had a positive outcome, but the patient could die due to an underlying and undiagnosed disease.

Comment [A1]: Is this always the case? Note that the final sentence of this paragraph contradicts this.

Writing Task

In conclusion, the publication of adequate data and an analysis of the influence of particular variables on the final outcomes reveals the factors that underlie mortality rates. These can then be addressed appropriately in subsequent cases to improve the standard of care provided. The benefits of publishing such data outweigh the disadvantages as, when conducted in the correct manner, it proves an apt method of measuring, assessing and improving clinical care.

Comments:
The first prompt ('what is meant by this statement?') is answered in sufficient detail, and it is evident that the candidate understands the connotations of the statement. He/She has articulated a sound argument in the first paragraph, which benefits from the use of appropriate examples.

The counterargument, however, is not convincing. It deviates from the statement and does not explicitly highlight why a surgeon's mortality rates **should** be published.

The final prompt has not been addressed. The response does not outline the candidate's opinion and the extent to which he/she believes that the publication of mortality rates affects the work of the surgeon.

The conclusion is weak, and it fails to adequately draw together the main ideas of the response.

Mark: 2.5A

<u>Task 8:</u>

Patients Who Are Most Likely To Survive Following Treatment Should Be Prioritised.

Explain the reasoning behind this statement. Argue to the contrary. To what extent do you agree with the statement?

This policy was adopted by the National Health Service (NHS) during the COVID-19 pandemic. Due to a dearth of resources, certain patients were prioritised for care, such as given ventilators, in an attempt to save those who were most likely to survive. The limited resources within the NHS must often be allocated according to various criteria. The overstretched budget and a lack of staff prompt patients to be triaged and prioritised in such a way that allows those with a greater chance of survival to be helped. This might mean that a young patient with liver cirrhosis caused by alcoholism is accepted for a liver transplant rather than an elderly patient with liver cancer due to the fact that the younger patient has higher chance of survival. This method thus encourages patients who have a longer life expectancy and who will arguably respond well to treatment to be prioritised.

Comment [A2]: This is rather contentious, and perhaps a different example is required here. This raises a discussion of ethics that must be unpacked if this example is to be used.

It is also important to consider that, if a patient with cancer is considered for a transplant, it is very likely that he/she will have a reasonable chance of survival.

On the other hand, doctors should not consider a patient's likelihood of survival alone. They must also consider the patient's quality of life after treatment to ensure beneficence. A physically fit patient undergoing a complex neurosurgical procedure might have a greater chance of survival compared to an elderly patient with a BMI of above 35 who needs a hip replacement under general anaesthetic. However, the neurosurgical procedure carries a risk of paralysis, whilst a successful hip replacement has a smaller overall risk and would potentially improve the patient's quality of life. If resources must be allocated to one patient over another, the quality of each individual's life and the results of the treatment must be contemplated; the patient's chance of survival should not be the only factor considered.

In conclusion, I believe that doctors must try to envisage each patient's life after any procedure and allocate resources to those who will benefit. The measure 'quality-adjusted life years' can provide further information for doctors and aid them to make appropriate decisions that are in the best interest of the patient. Resources must be allocated in a suitable and timely manner to maximise the benefit to patients.

Comment [A3]: This sentence is redundant.

Comments:

The candidate shows a sound understanding of the meaning of the statement and is able to explain this in a convincing manner. The first paragraph could, however, be enhanced with more thoughtful and more appropriately-positioned examples.

The counterargument is good and is reinforced by a relevant example. The candidate has expressed his/her thoughts here in a simple yet persuasive manner.

The final prompt has not been addressed. The response does not illustrate the extent to which the candidate agrees with the statement.

The conclusion is weak and does not address the aim of the response. The final sentence is redundant.

Mark: 3.5A

Task 9:

Curing Diseases Is Expensive And A Waste Of Money.

What do you think is meant by this statement? Argue to the contrary. To what extent do you agree that it is a waste of money to cure diseases?

The National Health Service (NHS) accounts for a large proportion of the UK's government budget. It might be argued that this money could be allocated to other sectors of the country. Rather than spending billions of pounds on the NHS each year to reduce the population's ailments, the country could attribute money to businesses and increase the productivity of its economy. This would allow the UK to prosper and compete on a global scale. Moreover, encouraging economic growth by increasing the UK's productive capacity would bring more revenue into the country, which would arguably improve the quality of life of its citizens. This statement therefore suggests that the expense afforded to the eradication of diseases could be better in order to enhance a country's development.

On the contrary, we might question how a country can progress if its citizens are unhealthy. Indeed, the workforce can function optimally only if it is free from disease. If people are unable to work for extensive periods of time or, even, at all due to sickness, economic retardation would ensue. It is, in fact, a vicious circle: if a country does not provide the resources to maintain the health of its citizens, they will simply become sicker, and this will hinder the economic output even further. It can be argued that money invested in health is never a detrimental investment in terms of excellent returns from a healthy population whose output is efficient and outlook is positive. Investment in the NHS therefore indirectly contributes to economic progress.

While the eradication of disease prompts the economy to become more productive due to a strong workforce, its effects also touch many other areas. If a country helps its citizens to fight diseases, the citizens will be not only physically healthy but also mentally healthy. If the country appears to abandon its population for economic benefits, individuals might become frustrated, angry and upset. If we consider the issue in a humane and benevolent manner, curing diseases cannot be "a waste of money", however expensive it might be. As doctors and humans, the fact that every life matters should be firmly positioned at the forefront of our minds.

In conclusion, I do not believe that it is a waste of money to cure diseases. On the contrary, an unhealthy population would place even greater pressure on the economy. Keeping citizens healthy contributes to a productive workforce, better output from employees, and, perhaps more importantly, a happier nation.

Comments:

The response addresses each aspect of the question in a clear and coherent manner. The counterargument is convincing, but it could benefit from a concrete example; this would strengthen it.

The conclusion neatly draws together the main points of the response.

The response could be enhanced by addressing a little more closely the claim that curing diseases is expensive. This is not discussed in the response.

Mark: 4A

MOCK TESTS

Mock Test 1	Thinking Skills (Section 1)	Questions

1. An analogue clock reads as 10:25. What is the largest angle between the hour and the minute hands at this time?
   A. 75°
   B. 150°
   C. 158.5°
   D. 162.5°
   E. 197.5°
   F. 210°

2. When a dead body is found, forensic scientists must attempt to determine the time and cause of death. At the moment, they often use simple temperature measurements to determine the time of death, but a new mathematical model could provide more accurate answers. This new method uses skin temperature data collected from the scene where a body is found to create a 3D computer simulation. This new mathematical model provides the most accurate time of death by estimating the temperature change of the body since death, which can be used to calculate the elapsed time. The team of scientists found that the mathematical model, which used skin temperature data from 8 human corpses, was within 38 minutes of the true time elapsed since death, whereas the standard method gives estimates within 3 to 7 hours for the post-mortem interval (PMI).

   Which one of the following best states an assumption made in this argument?
   A. It assumes that simple temperature measurements are not as accurate as this new mathematical model.
   B. It assumes that the cause of death can be identified using the same 3D computer simulation.
   C. It assumes that the difference in skin temperature since death is an accurate way of determining a reliable time of death.
   D. It assumes that the 3D computer simulation only uses skin temperature data in order to identify a time of death.
   E. It assumes that 38 minutes within the true time elapsed since death is the closest time that this new mathematical model can estimate.

3. The average price of eight different types of chocolate bars in a given shop is £1.50, with the cheapest chocolate bar priced at 50 pence. What is the maximum possible value for the most expensive chocolate bar?
   A. £1.00
   B. £2.50
   C. £6.50
   D. £7.00
   E. £8.50
   F. £9.50
   G. £10.00

4. Nanoparticles, acting as drug carriers to deliver toxic payloads to target cells, are used in therapeutics. Thermal energy is emerging as an important form of therapy, and many gold nanomaterials can convert photons into thermal energy for targeted photothermal therapy.

Furthermore, magnetic nanoparticles are also attractive for their ability to mediate heat induction. Many other subfields have advanced by the recent developments in nanomedicine, including tissue engineering, regenerative medicine, medical devices, and vaccines; nanomedicine will have a tremendous impact on health care and the practice of clinical medicine.

Which of the following best expresses the main conclusion of the passage above?

A. Nanoparticles can convert photons into thermal energy for targeted photothermal therapy.
B. Magnetic nanoparticles can attract heat and electricity induction.
C. Currently, only tissue engineering, regenerative medicine, medical devices, and vaccines rely on nanomedicine.
D. Therapeutics act as drug carriers that can deliver toxic payloads to target cells.
E. In the future, nanomedicine will have many uses in clinical medicine.

5. **Body mass index (BMI) is a tool that doctors use to assess if a person is of an appropriate weight for their age, gender, and height. The measurement uses an individual's height and weight to assess health. A BMI between 25 and 29.9 indicates that a person might be overweight. A BMI of 30 or over suggests that a person may be obese. If a person is overweight or obese, it can increase his/her risk of developing a number of complications, including metabolic syndrome, arthritis and certain types of cancer. Metabolic syndrome involves a plethora of conditions, such as high blood pressure, Type II diabetes and cardiovascular disease. Therefore, preventing obesity by maintaining a healthy weight will reduce the risk of developing certain diseases and its associated complications.**

Which of the following best illustrates the main conclusion of the passage?

A. A BMI between 25 and 29.9 indicates that a person might be overweight.
B. A number of complications, such as arthritis and certain forms of cancer, can develop due to obesity.
C. Preventing obesity by maintaining a healthy weight will reduce the risk of developing certain diseases and its associated complications.
D. BMI is an accurate tool for assessing an individual's health.
E. BMI is an accurate tool in detecting obese individuals.

6. **The typical symptoms of Salmonella include diarrhoea, fever and stomach cramps. Symptoms usually begin six hours to four days after infection. Infections usually resolve in three to seven days, and mild cases often do not require treatment. Antibiotics are only used to treat severe cases. If not treated, the Salmonella infection can spread from the intestines to the blood stream, leading to sepsis and then death. Johnny started having a high fever and diarrhoea three days after he ate some uncooked meat; consequently, he was prescribed antibiotics. After two weeks, he became much better. Therefore, it can be concluded that Johnny suffered from Salmonella in the period of time specified above.**

Which of the following best illustrates a flaw in this reasoning?

A. It ignores the fact that one symptom of Salmonella is stomach cramps; Johnny did not have this.
B. It ignores the fact that antibiotics can be used on any bacterial infection and not just Salmonella.
C. It assumes that all severe Salmonella cases require antibiotics.

D. It assumes that Salmonella is the only infection to include symptoms of a fever and diarrhoea.

E. It assumes that all Salmonella infections spread from the intestines to the blood stream.

7. **In a factory, 40% of cars produced do not function properly. During quality control, 85% of the faulty cars are identified and rejected, but, unfortunately, in error, 10% of non-faulty cars are also rejected. If all of the cars that are not rejected are then sold, what percentage of the cars sold by the factory are faulty?**

A. 0.01%

B. 0.05%

C. 0.1%

D. 0.15%

E. 0.25%

F. 1.0%

8. **Everyone who wants to have tennis lessons at the sports centre needs to buy an annual membership for £40. Each lesson then costs £5. At the local tennis club, no membership needs to be bought and the tennis lessons cost £30 per term. There are six terms per year. After how many classes at the sports centre is the annual cost for lessons more expensive than at the tennis club?**

A. 28

B. 29

C. 30

D. 32

E. 37

9. **'Q' and 'P' are brothers. 'D' is the daughter of 'C', who is the mother of 'Q'. 'L' is the son of 'P' and the grandson of 'G'.**
Which of the following statements could be reliably concluded from the information given?

A. 'G' and 'C' are the parents of 'D'.

B. 'P' is the father of 'G'.

C. 'Q' is the paternal aunt of 'L'.

D. 'D' is the maternal aunt of 'L'.

E. 'G' and 'Q' are cousins.

10. **There are five numbers with a mean of 9. The median is 10 and the mode is 12. The range of these numbers is 8. What is the second biggest number?**

A. 4

B. 5

C. 7

D. 9

E. 10

11. **Abraham and Katherine own different coloured marbles. They put all their marbles in a bag. The table shows the details of the marbles in the bag. Some information in the table is missing.**

Colour of the Marble	Abraham's	Katherine's	TOTAL
Red	4	2	6
Blue		5	8
Yellow			
White			10

Mock Test

Green	4		9
TOTAL		26	40

The probability that a yellow marble belongs to Abraham is 1 in 7.

What is the probability that a yellow marble selected at random does not belong to Abraham?

A. 1 in 7
B. 2 in 7
C. 5 in 7
D. 2 in 14
E. 5 in 26

---

12. **Bacteria evolve to become antibiotic resistant by picking up free-floating genetic material from their environments. They then incorporate the scavenged genes into their own DNA. In this way, bacteria can collect genes shed from microbes that are already resistant, and thus, gain resistance themselves. However, bacteria aren't able to catch wayward bits of DNA without the right equipment; they must first enter a state called 'competence' to build the machinery required to scoop genetic material from their surroundings. Now, a new study of the bacteria Streptococcus pneumoniae has highlighted a potential drug that stops bacteria from becoming competent in the first place. This new drug will prevent antibiotic resistance.**

Which one of the following best states the main assumption made in this argument?

A. It assumes that all bacteria collect resistant genes from microbes.
B. It assumes that a drug can prevent a bacterium from becoming competent.
C. It assumes that bacteria will not become antibiotic resistant if they are prevented from becoming competent.
D. It assumes that all bacteria have the same mechanisms as Streptococcus pneumoniae.
E. It assumes that bacteria will not be able to divide by binary fission and pass on their resistant gene.

---

13. **It's important to note that hand sanitizer isn't the first strategy to prevent infection. According to the Centre for Disease Control and Prevention, frequent and thorough hand-washing with soap (for at least 20 seconds) is the best method for reducing hand germs and curbing disease transmission, because it kills the most bacteria. When soap and water aren't available, hand sanitizers can be used as an alternative. The alcohol in hand sanitizers facilitates them to kill microbes, and the CDC recommends that sanitizers contain 60% to 95% alcohol in order to eradicate germs. According to CNN, hand sanitizers can also curb microbe exposure — but only as long as they have the correct ratio of alcohol to other ingredients.**

Which one of the following would most weaken this argument?

A. An increase of alcohol in hand sanitisers kills a lower percentage of bacteria.
B. In a recent study, using hand sanitisers destroyed 98% of bacteria, while hand washing only destroyed 96% of bacteria.
C. Hand sanitisers should only be used if hand-washing with soap is not available.
D. Recently, it has been proven that hand sanitisers killed less than half of the bacteria that hand-washing with soap would.
E. The correct ratio of alcohol to other ingredients will determine the strength of the hand sanitiser.

14. Journalism has three main functions: to inform the citizenry, apply scrutiny to power and, in the broadest sense, to enlighten a culture, through the spread of ideas and ideals. It has been recently reported that many appalling attacks on journalists across the world have occurred. From America to Australia, journalists are being silenced, punched or hit with truncheons for trying to chronicle events. Most journalists are decent, public-spirit folk, neither rich nor famous, who want simply to get at the truth. We shall miss them if they disappear.

Which of the following best expresses the main conclusion of the passage above?

A. Journalism has three main functions: to inform the citizenry, apply scrutiny to power and to enlighten a culture.
B. Journalism may disappear due to the way they are treated for seeking the truth.
C. There have been many attacks on journalists around the world.
D. There have been more journalist attacks in America and Australia compared to the rest of the world.
E. Journalists are decent, individuals who are neither rich nor famous, simply wanting to uncover the truth.

---

15. A group of 16 friends hired a limousine for their school prom. The cost of the limousine was shared equally amongst them.
If there had been 24 friends sharing the cost, the cost per passenger would have been £3 lower. Becca, one of the friends in the original group of 16, pays with a £20 note. How much change would she expect to receive?

A. £6.00
B. £9.00
C. £11.00
D. £13.00
E. £15.00
F. £17.00

---

16. A new wearable robotic arm has been developed that uses hydraulics and is capable of picking up items weighing up to 5 kg. The waist-mounted device weighs about as much of a human arm and has been shown completing a variety of tasks. Researchers view this robot as being a co-worker when doing chores because it increases productivity by freeing up the user to make decisions based on creativity or judgment. The arm has three degrees of freedom when it comes to movement but is designed in such a manner that it can't swing back and accidentally hit its operator in the face. Therefore, wearable technology allows humans to perform more complex tasks that require creativity or judgement.

Which of the following best illustrates a flaw in this reasoning?

A. It ignores the fact that the robotic arm can only perform repetitive and tedious tasks.
B. It assumes that all humans require wearable technology in order to perform more tasks in a shorter period of time.
C. It assumes that the strength of the robotic arm is required in everyday tasks.
D. It ignores the fact that other wearable technology may be more useful in enabling humans to perform other tasks.
E. It assumes that all wearable technology allows humans to perform other tasks.

17. Two different cubes are illustrated below.

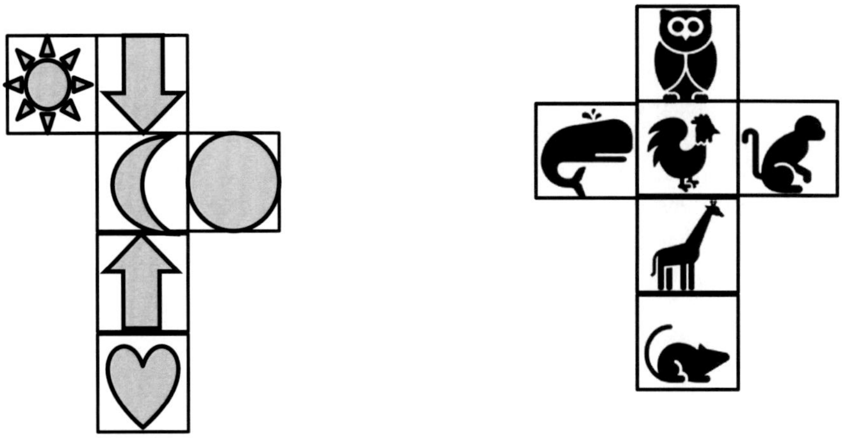

Which one of the following sets of cubes can be made from the nets above?

A

B

C

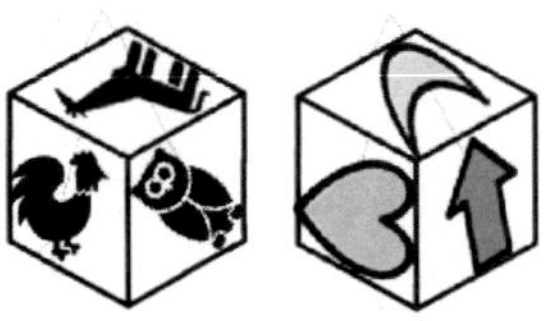

D

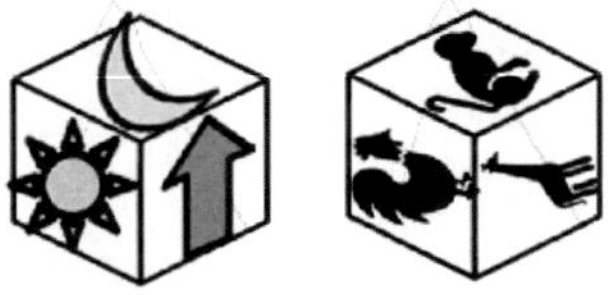

E

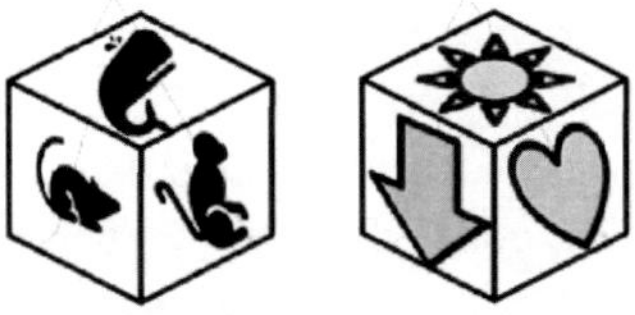

18. A survey conducted by the Royal Society for Public Health asked 13 to 24-year olds in the UK how social media platforms impacted their health and wellbeing. The survey results found that Snapchat, Facebook, Twitter and Instagram all led to increased feelings of depression, anxiety, poor body image and loneliness. Offline, the gold standard advice for helping kids build a healthy self-esteem is to get them involved in an activity that they're interested in. When kids are able to feel proud of their own accomplishments, they're happier and better prepared for success in real life. As a result, children and young adults should not be encouraged to use social media because it is detrimental to their health.

Which one of the following best states an assumption made in this argument?

A. The downsides of social media outweigh the benefits.

B. Children under the age of 13 who use social media are not impacted negatively by social media.
C. Snapchat, Facebook, Twitter and Instagram are the only social media platforms that can lead to depression.
D. Depression, anxiety, poor body image and loneliness can be caused by social media.
E. All kids will be happier without social media.

19. A packet of biscuits comes in three different sizes. The smallest packet contains mini biscuits, the medium packet contains the standard sized biscuits and the large packet contains jumbo biscuits.

The weight of each packet is given below:

- Small – 100 grams
- Medium – 260 grams
- Large – 420 grams

The company decides to add 25% biscuits to each packet. As a special offer, if two medium sized packets are bought, the customer will get a small packet for free. If a customer buys 2 medium packets in the special offer, what is the additional percentage of biscuits that they have compared to what they would get before the offer?

A. 19%
B. 30%
C. 36%
D. 49%
E. 74%

20. There are 24 square tiles on a bathroom wall forming the pattern shown below. All the tiles are of the same size.

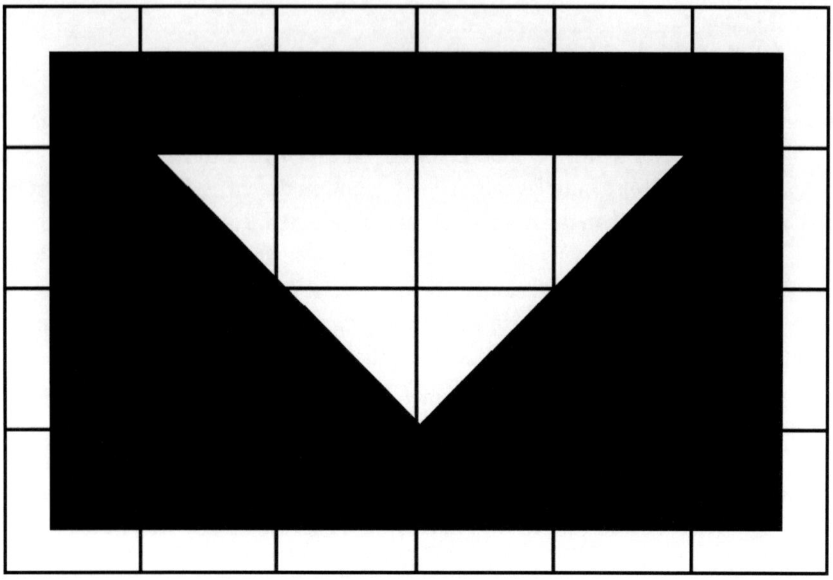

How many different patterns of tiles are used to make this pattern?

A. 4
B. 5
C. 6
D. 7
E. 8

21. A bag contains different coloured marbles. Some marbles are made of glass and the others are made of plastic. There are three different colours – red, blue and yellow. There is a total of 150 marbles of which a third are plastic. There is a 2 in 5 chance that a glass marble is blue. The number of yellow marbles is twice that of the red marbles. There are the same number of blue marbles as yellow marbles.

What is the chance of a blue marble picked at random being made of plastic?

A. 1 in 3
B. 1 in 2
C. 2 in 3
D. 4 in 15
E. 2 in 15

22. A group of 15 friends are having a picnic at a park. They have each been allocated to buy a particular food item for everyone. Max is bringing crisps for everyone. He wants to ensure that everyone gets two packets of crisps of a flavour of their choice. He buys three different types of flavours – ready salted, salt & vinegar and cheese & onion. What is the minimum number of packets he must buy to ensure that everyone gets 2 packets of crisps in the flavour of their choice?

A. 15 packets
B. 30 packets
C. 45 packets
D. 60 packets
E. 90 packets

23. At the end of March, individuals in the UK focused on whether the country could meet its end-of April target of conducting 100,000 tests for coronavirus a day. While increasing testing capacity is important for countries that failed to contain the virus, the way the test results are used is more important than the number of tests conducted. To reduce the spread of the virus, many researchers think that countries need to move to testing those without any signs of disease, instead of focusing on those with symptoms. "A good strategy would be to devote part of the resources for identifying those who are asymptomatic, starting with random testing in the population," says Giulia Giordano at the University of Trento in Italy. "People with mild symptoms can be isolated without wasting a test that could be instead used for identifying hidden outbreaks," she says.

Which of the following best expresses the main conclusion of the above argument?

A. The way the test results are used is more important than the number of tests conducted.
B. People who do not have symptoms should only be tested now.
C. Testing people with symptoms is wasting the tests available.
D. Everyone should be tested once a week to reduce the spread of the virus.
E. Random testing should be done to identify asymptomatic people as well.

24. **Ana drew a bar chart below to represent the sales of different cakes in her café on Wednesday and a Thursday last week:**

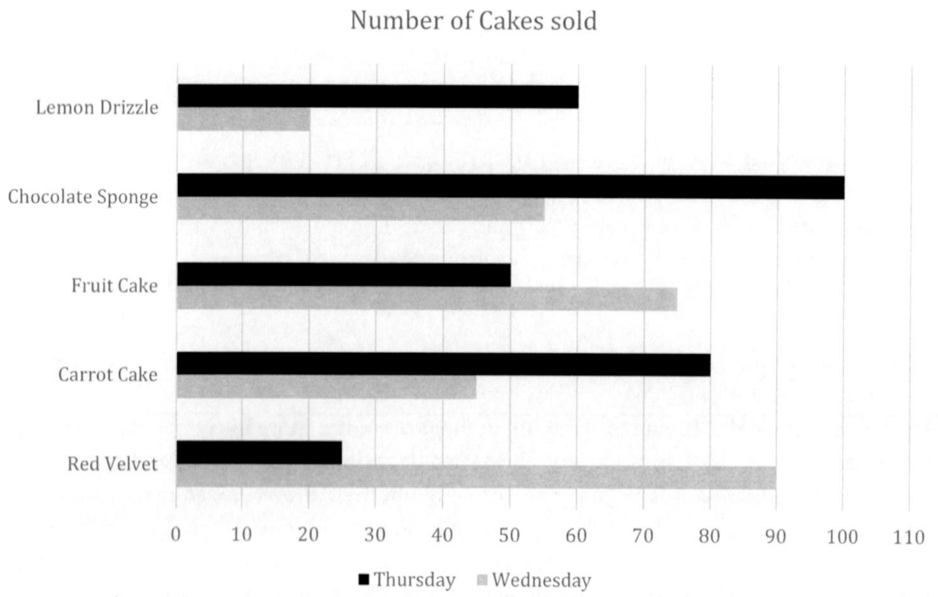

She also drew a type of pie chart for one of the days, but she only labelled one section and forgot to include one type of cake.

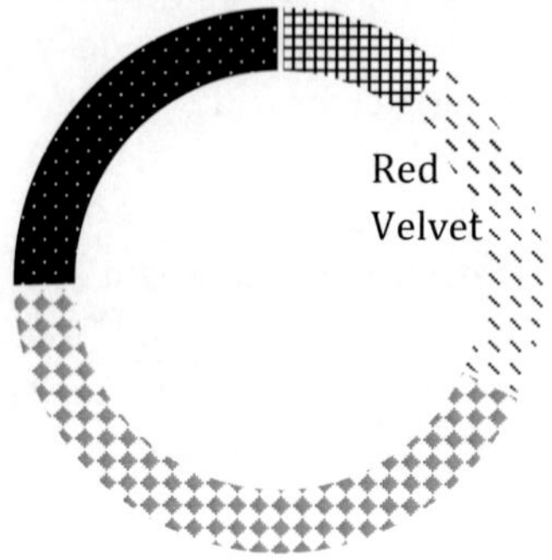

Which cake was missed out from the pie chart?

A. Lemon Drizzle
B. Chocolate Sponge
C. Fruit Cake
D. Carrot Cake
E. Red Velvet

25. **According to new research, children from wealthier families are spending more time each day studying during the coronavirus lockdown. A survey of families in England suggests that better-off children would have studied for around seven days more than their poorer peers by next month. A study of more than 4,000 families, carried out for the Institute for Fiscal Studies**

(IFS), found the gap in time spent on education activities was slightly bigger for primary age children than older pupils. When schools reopen, children from poorer backgrounds will need more support to catch up compared with children from wealthier families.

Which of the following best illustrates a flaw in this reasoning?

A. It ignores the fact that 4000 families are not a representative sample of the whole of England.

B. It assumes that children from poor backgrounds will require support because they have all spent less time studying during the coronavirus lockdown.

C. It assumes that children from wealthier backgrounds are able to study better at home compared to children from poorer backgrounds.

D. It ignores the fact that some children are able to work better at home compared to at school.

E. It assumes that older pupils spend more time on educational activities compared to primary age children.

26. Researchers found that flamingos with pinker hues are much more likely to initiate aggressive encounters and to fight. In a variety of species, from birds to fish, animals with brighter carotenoid-based colours have superior foraging abilities; they recover more quickly from diseases, and overall have better body conditions. Experiments with house finches have also shown that males with the reddest breast feathers are faster at taking flight and escaping from predators. Furthermore, male sex hormones such as testosterone have been shown to work with carotenoids in male zebra finches, which increases the red hue of their beaks and makes the birds more aggressive. Therefore, animals that possess brighter colours have an advantage that will enable them to all survive for a longer period of time.

Which one of the following best states an assumption made in this argument?

A. It assumes that the ability of an animal to fight determines its likelihood of survival.

B. It assumes that testosterone increases the red hue of beaks, which makes birds more aggressive.

C. It assumes that animals with superior foraging abilities are more likely to survive.

D. It assumes that the colour of an animal determines survival rate.

E. It assumes that only colour influences an animal's likelihood to survive.

27. Meg's journey from her house to school involves walking to the bus station and taking a bus to school. The bus leaves the station at 25-minute intervals and the bus journey takes 45 minutes.

The school which Meg attends is a 10-minute walk from the bus stop where she gets off. If she arrives at the bus stop at 7:15 am, she gets to school at 8:25 am.

At what time wills she get to school if she arrives at the bus stop at 8:00 am?

A. 8:50 am

B. 9:05 am

C. 9:15 am

D. 9:25 am

E. 9:35 am

F. 9:45 am

28. A recent study reveals that dogs share certain metabolic conditions - such as obesity - with their human owners. Thus, learning more about dogs' gut microbiota and how they are affected by diet could help humans to understand how best to tackle eating habits. Similarly,

dogs can also develop some forms of cancer. Dogs can get brain tumours to a similarly destructive effect; as a result, learning the genes that predispose canines to brain tumours may also be translated into cancer research for human patients. Moreover, a serious form of canine cancer could shed light into how certain types of cancers develop in humans.

Which one of the following cannot be reliably concluded from the passage above?

A. Learning how dogs are affected by diet could help humans to prevent obesity.
B. Genes may predispose dogs to brain tumours.
C. Dogs' gut microbiota could potentially be affected by diet.
D. Dogs can get tumours to a similarly destructive effect as humans.
E. Cancer research for human patients may be aided by studying brain tumours in dogs.

29. Abby decides to host a party in order to celebrate her 10th birthday. She asks her friends to vote for their favourite party theme. After she counted $\frac{1}{5}$ of the votes, $\frac{2}{5}$ suggested a circus theme and $\frac{3}{5}$ suggested a winter wonderland theme. What percentage of the remaining votes must be in favour of the circus theme so that the total count will result in a vote of 3:2 in favour of this theme?

A. 5%
B. 25%
C. 45%
D. 65%
E. 85%

30. According to a new report, a teen who ate only junk food for years slowly went blind as a result of his poor diet. The case demonstrates a little-known fact about poor diets: in addition to being tied to obesity, heart disease and cancer, poor diets can also permanently damage the nervous system, particularly vision. The teen's problems began at age 14, when he went to the doctor complaining of tiredness. However, by age 15, he developed hearing loss and visual problems, but the doctors couldn't find the cause — results from an MRI and eye exam were normal. Over the next two years, the teen's vision got progressively worse. When he was 17, an eye test showed that his vision was 20/200 in both eyes, the threshold for being "legally blind" in the United States. After ruling out other possible causes for his vision loss, he was diagnosed with nutritional optic neuropathy, or damage to the optic nerve that results from nutritional deficiencies.

Which of the following best expresses the main conclusion of the passage above?

A. A poor diet could permanently damage the nervous system, particularly vision.
B. A poor diet can lead to obesity, heart disease and cancer.
C. Nutritional deficiencies can lead to optic nerve damage.
D. Most teenagers become blind due to poor diets.
E. Optic nerve damage only occurs due to nutritional deficiencies.

31. Using data collected by Japan's Kaguya lunar orbiter over a year and a half, Shoichiro Yokota and his colleagues at Osaka University in Japan have discovered that the moon emits carbon ions across almost its entire surface. Some areas, such as the moon's large basaltic plains, emit more carbon ions than other regions, such as the highlands. According to Yokota, these plains are made of younger material, and as such, emit more carbon because they have been exposed to space for a shorter period of time. Older regions have been exposed to more space

weathering, and, therefore, have already lost much of their carbon. The researchers compared the moon's carbon emissions with estimates of the carbon supplied by two external sources – the solar wind and collisions with micrometeoroids. They found that they didn't match up. Yokota states that the emission is a bit larger than the supply from outer space, which is why the team believes the moon has its own carbon supply.

Which of the following best expresses the main conclusion of the above argument?

A. The moon's large ballistic plain is the main emitter of carbon ions.
B. The plains emit more carbon as they have been exposed to space for a shorter period of time.
C. The moon has its own carbon supply.
D. The emission from the moon is larger than the supply from outer space.
E. Older regions of the moon have lost a lot of their carbon.

32. The pie chart below shows the number of people who were involved in car accidents from different age groups.

Car accidents across different age groups

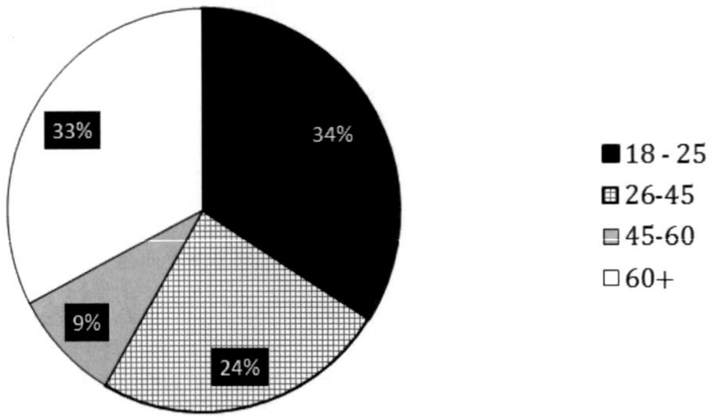

Which amongst the following statement(s) can be concluded from the data given above?

1. Young drivers tend to be the most dangerous.
2. Accidents are more severe and dangerous in the 60+ age group.
3. The largest proportion of accidents occur in the age group between 18-25.
4. A total of 24% of all the drivers aged 26-45 are involved in car accidents.

A. 1 only
B. 3 only
C. 1 and 3 only
D. 2 and 4 only
E. 1, 2 and 3 only

Mock Test 1	Thinking Skills (Section 1)	Answer Sheet

BioMedical Aptitude Test

SECTION 1 Thinking Skills

BMAT candidate number

B					

Centre number

Date of birth (DD MM YYYY)

First name (s)

Surname / Family name

Fill in the appropriate circle for your chosen answer e.g.

A B C D E
○●○○○

Use a soft pencil. If you make a mistake, erase thoroughly and try again.

1. A B C D E F ○ ○ ○ ○ ○ ○
2. A B C D E ○ ○ ○ ○ ○
3. A B C D E F G ○ ○ ○ ○ ○ ○ ○
4. A B C D E ○ ○ ○ ○ ○
5. A B C D E ○ ○ ○ ○ ○
6. A B C D E ○ ○ ○ ○ ○
7. A B C D E F ○ ○ ○ ○ ○ ○
8. A B C D E ○ ○ ○ ○ ○
9. A B C D E ○ ○ ○ ○ ○
10. A B C D E ○ ○ ○ ○ ○
11. A B C D E ○ ○ ○ ○ ○
12. A B C D E ○ ○ ○ ○ ○
13. A B C D E ○ ○ ○ ○ ○
14. A B C D E ○ ○ ○ ○ ○
15. A B C D E F ○ ○ ○ ○ ○ ○
16. A B C D E ○ ○ ○ ○ ○
17. A B C D E ○ ○ ○ ○ ○
18. A B C D E ○ ○ ○ ○ ○
19. A B C D E ○ ○ ○ ○ ○
20. A B C D E ○ ○ ○ ○ ○
21. A B C D E ○ ○ ○ ○ ○
22. A B C D E ○ ○ ○ ○ ○

23 A B C D E ○ ○ ○ ○ ○

24 A B C D E ○ ○ ○ ○ ○

25 A B C D E ○ ○ ○ ○ ○

26 A B C D E ○ ○ ○ ○ ○

27 A B C D E F ○ ○ ○ ○ ○ ○

28. A B C D E ○ ○ ○ ○ ○

29. A B C D E ○ ○ ○ ○ ○

30. A B C D E ○ ○ ○ ○ ○

31. A B C D E ○ ○ ○ ○ ○

32. A B C D E ○ ○ ○ ○ ○

Mock Test 1	Scientific Knowledge and Applications (Section 2)	Questions

1. **Which line in the table correctly balances the following equation?**

$p\,Cu_{(s)} + q\,HNO_{3\,(aq)} \rightarrow r\,Cu(NO_3)_{2\,(s)} + s\,NO_{(g)} + t\,H_2O_{(l)}$

	p	*q*	*r*	*s*	*t*
A	4	8	4	2	3
B	3	8	3	2	4
C	2	4	2	1	2
D	5	2	5	3	1
E	8	2	4	4	8

2. **A circuit contains two different light bulbs (Lamp 'A' and Lamp 'B') of unknown resistance that are shown in the diagram. The power output of the circuit is 36 W.**

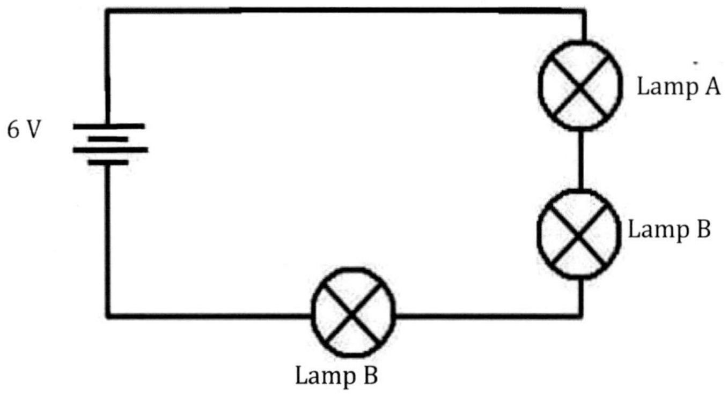

Lamp 'A' has twice the resistance of Lamp 'B'. What is the overall resistance of the circuit when two of Lamp 'A' and one of Lamp 'B' are added to this circuit?

A. 0.25 Ω
B. 1 Ω
C. 1.25 Ω
D. 1.5 Ω
E. 2 Ω
F. 2.25 Ω
G. 2.5 Ω
H. 2.75 Ω

3. What is the value of x in the following equation?

$$\frac{2x+2}{1.6} + \frac{10x+5}{15} = \frac{15}{12}$$

A. $\frac{4}{23}$
B. $\frac{8}{23}$
C. $-\frac{4}{23}$
D. $-\frac{8}{23}$
E. $-\frac{16}{23}$
F. $\frac{23}{36}$

4. Listed below are four different reactions:

A. The formation of a carboxylic acid and an alcohol from an ester.
B. The formation of calcium hydroxide and hydrogen gas from calcium.
C. The fermentation of glucose.
D. Hydrolysis of a triglyceride to form glycerol and fatty acids.

Which of the above reactions require water as a reactant?

A. 1 only
B. 3 only
C. 4 only
D. 1 and 2 only
E. 3 and 4 only
F. 2 and 4 only
G. 1 and 4 only
H. 1, 2 and 4 only
I. 2, 3 and 4 only
J. All of the above
K. None of the above

5. Assume that eye colour is determined by a single allele. The 'B' allele is dominant and results in brown eyes. The 'b' allele is recessive for blue eyes. Katie, who has blue eyes, and Jack, who has brown eyes, are having a baby boy. What is the probability that he will have blue eyes?

A. 0% only
B. 25% only
C. 50% only
D. 0% or 25% only
E. 0% or 50% only
F. 25% or 50% only

6. A car travels 50 metres in 2.5 seconds. If 2 people, one weighing 56 kg and another weighing 24 kg, each jump out of the car, by how much does the kinetic energy change?

A. -8000 J
B. -16,000J
C. 0 J
D. 8000J
E. 16,000J

7. **Which row in the table correctly describes the processes that occur when the external temperature increases?**

	Temperature change detected by	**Hair muscles**	**Blood flow in capillaries**	**Sweat gland secretion**	**Arterioles near skin**	**Heat loss from skin**
A	Hypothalamus	Relax	Increases	Increases	Vasodilate	Increases
B	Cerebral Cortex	Constrict	Increases	Decreases	Vasodilate	Decreases
C	Hypothalamus	Relax	Decreases	Decreases	Vasodilate	Decreases
D	Hypothalamus	Relax	Increases	Increases	Vasoconstrict	Increases
E	Cerebral Cortex	Constrict	Decreases	Decreases	Vasoconstrict	Decreases

8. **Sulfur trioxide can be formed in the Contact Process at 723K using the following equation:**

$$2SO_{2\,(g)} + O_{2\,(g)} \rightleftharpoons 2SO_{3\,(g)} \quad \Delta H = -196\ kJmol^{-1}$$

Which line in the table correct shows the effect of increasing the temperature to 860K and using a catalyst in the above reaction?

	Increasing Temperature		**Using a catalyst**	
	Equilibrium Position	**Reaction Rate**	**Equilibrium Position**	**Reaction Rate**
A	Moves to right	Decreases	Moves to left	Increases
B	Moves to left	Decreases	No change	Increases
C	Moves to left	Increases	Moves to left	Increases
D	Moves to left	Increases	No change	Increases
E	Moves to right	Decreases	Moves to left	Increases
F	Moves to right	Increases	No change	Increases

9. **'A' is inversely proportional to the cube root of 'B'. When A = 9, B = 216. The square root of 'C' is inversely proportional to 'D'. When C = 324, D = 3. What is the value of 'B' when 'A' is 6 and what is the value of 'C' when 'D' is 8?**

	Value of B	**Value of C**
A	81	$4\sqrt{3}$
B	729	$8\sqrt{3}$
C	729	$4\sqrt{3}$
D	81	$8\sqrt{3}$
E	729	$8\sqrt{3}$

10. **A toy tyre, on a flat surface, travelled 24 metres in 1.6 seconds. It then reaches a slope that is 30 m high. After it rolls down the slope, its speed reduces by 60%. The diameter of the toy tyre is 60 mm. Take π to be 3.1. What would be the approximate speed of the tyre in revolutions per second at the bottom of the slope?**

A. 16 revolutions per second

Mock Test

B. 18 revolutions per second
C. 32 revolutions per second
D. 36 revolutions per second
E. 64 revolutions per second
F. 72 revolutions per second

11. Jacob buys three laptops, Laptop 'X', Laptop 'Y' and Laptop 'Z', from a store. The total price of all three laptops was £950. However, he must pay 20% of Laptop X's price for additional features, 45% of Laptop Y's price for additional features and 25% of Laptop Z's price for additional features. This totals to £300. Considering that the price of Laptop 'X' is three times less than the price of Laptop 'Z', which line in the table correctly identifies the prices of all three laptops?

	Laptop X	Laptop Y	Laptop Z
A	£50	£750	£150
B	£125	£450	£375
C	£140	£390	£420
D	£150	£350	£450
E	£200	£150	£600
F	£225	£50	£675

12. An analysis of a rock found in the soil shows that it contains 86% of Substance 'A' and 8% of Substance 'B' by mass. Substance 'B' is formed from the decay of Substance 'A' with no loss of mass and is not normally found on a rock.
The half-life of Substance 'A' is 650 years. What is the approximate age of the rock?

A. 500 years
B. 650 years
C. 1000 years
D. 1300 years
E. 1950 years
F. 2600 years
G. 3000 years
H. 3900 years

13. Which one of the following depicts the correct sequence of structures for the flow of urine?

A. Urethra → Urinary bladder → Ureter → Collecting duct → Convoluted tubules
B. Convoluted tubules → Collecting duct → Ureter → Urinary bladder → Urethra
C. Collecting duct → Urinary bladder → Convoluted tubules → Ureter → Urethra
D. Convoluted tubules → Ureter → Collecting duct → Urethra → Urinary bladder
E. Urethra → Ureter → Convoluted tubules → Urinary bladder → Collecting duct
F. Convoluted tubules → Collecting duct → Urethra → Urinary bladder → Ureter

14. A compound contains carbon (M_r of 12) , oxygen (M_r of 16), nitrogen (M_r of 14) and hydrogen only (M_r of 1). It contains 57% carbon, 10% nitrogen and 27% oxygen by mass. What is the molecular formula of this compound?

A. $C_{14}H_{18}N_2O_5$
B. $C_7H_9NO_3$
C. $C_7H_9NO_2$

D. $C_{14}H_{16}N_2O_4$
E. $C_{12}H_{18}NO_5$

15. Kelly is planning on long road trip between 2430 to 6800 miles. The cost of petrol will be between 80 pence to £1.60 per litre across the different states and her car will average 20 to 30 miles per gallon. Assume that 1 gallon = 4.5 litres.
What is the difference between the maximum and minimum cost of petrol that she would incur for the trip?
A. £2911.60
B. £1138.60
C. £1238.40
D. £2156.40
E. £3138.60
F. £3911.40

16. Transformer 'A' has a primary coil of voltage 60 V and current 5 A, and a secondary coil of current 1.2 A. Transformer 'B' has a primary coil of voltage 30 V and current 5 A, and a secondary coil of current 20 A.
How many times larger is the secondary coil voltage in Transformer 'B' compared to the secondary coil voltage in Transformer 'A'?
A. 0.06
B. 0.12
C. 0.24
D. 4
E. 8
F. 16

17. Which line in the table correctly identifies the oxidising and reducing agents in the following redox equation?

$$8H_3O^+ + Cr_2O_7^{2-} + 3NO_2^- \rightarrow 2Cr^{3+} + 3NO_3^- + 12H_2O$$

	Oxidising agent	Reducing agent
A	NO_2^-	Cr
B	Cr	NO_3^-
C	Cr	N
D	O_2	H_2O
E	Cr	NO_2^-
F	NO_3^-	H

18. A two-tiered cake is made from two different flavours - red velvet and vanilla. The red velvet cake is made from cocoa powder, plain flour and brown sugar. It contains $\frac{1}{5}$ cocoa powder, $\frac{7}{20}$ of brown sugar and 742.5 grams of plain flour. The vanilla cake is made from plain flour, white sugar and vanilla extract. It contains double the amount of plain flour as the chocolate cake, $\frac{9}{20}$ of vanilla extract and $\frac{2}{5}$ of white sugar.
What is the total mass of the two cake mixtures?
A. 1580 grams
B. 1650 grams
C. 3230 grams
D. 9900 grams

Mock Test

E. 13130 grams
F. 11550 grams

19. A total of 200 grams of Iron (III), with an Mr of 160, and 182 grams of Chlorine gas, each with an Mr of 35, react together to form Iron (III) Chloride. Which reactant is in excess, and approximately how many grams of it would be left over?

	Excess Reactant	Number of grams in excess
A	Chlorine	13
B	Chlorine	26
C	Iron	26
D	Chlorine	51
E	Iron	51

20. The reading of a water wave produced in a ripple tank is shown below. Each wave has a wavelength of 15 cm.

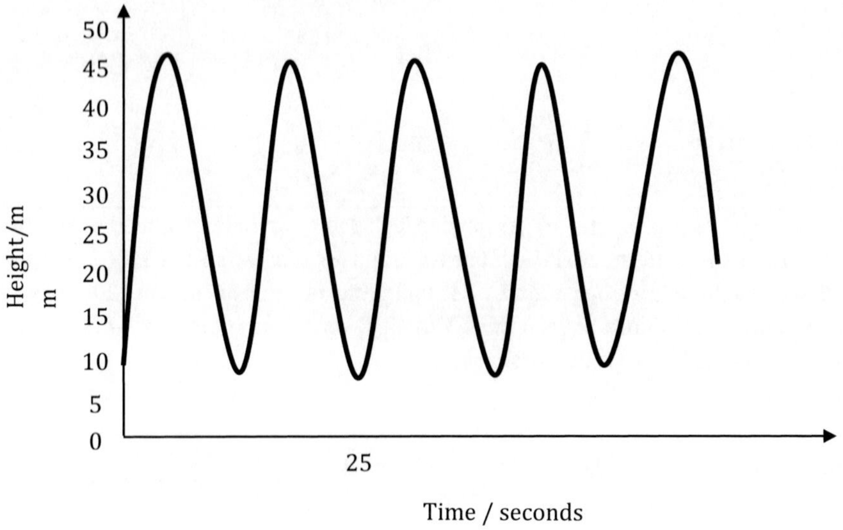

There are four statements regarding this wave:

1. The waves have an amplitude of 22.5 mm.
2. There are 5 complete wavelengths shown.
3. Each wave has a frequency of 0.04 Hz.
4. Each wave has a speed of $0.012ms^{-1}$.

Which amongst the aforementioned statement(s) is/are correct?

A. 1 only
B. 2 only
C. 3 only
D. 4 only
E. 1 and 2 only
F. 2 and 4 only
G. 2 and 3 only
H. 1 and 4 only

I. 1, 2 and 3 only
J. 1, 2 and 4 only

21. The DNA of Organism A contains 4.5 billion bases, where 28% are adenine. The DNA of Organism B contains 6 billion bases, where 36% are thymine. What is the difference in the number of guanine bases present in the DNA of Organism A compared to the DNA of Organism B?

A. 0.05 billion
B. 0.1 billion
C. 0.15 billion
D. 0.2 billion
E. 0.25 billion
F. 0.3 billion
G. 0.35 billion

22. In the formula, $A = \frac{1}{3(0.6B)^3}$, if B is divided by 3, by which factor is A multiplied by?

A. 3
B. 9
C. 27
D. $\frac{1}{3}$
E. $\frac{1}{9}$
F. $\frac{1}{27}$

23. Patient X's tidal volume (the volume of gas inhaled/exhaled by an individual in one breath at rest) is 800 cm^3. He takes 18 breaths per minute. Patient Y's tidal volume is 15% lower than Patient X. She takes 20 breaths per minute. Assuming the air inhaled contains 20% oxygen, approximately how much more oxygen does Patient X inhale compared to Patient Y in 2 minutes if their breathing rates remained constant?

A. 0.32 dm^3
B. 0.64 dm^3
C. 0.96 dm^3
D. 1.6 dm^3
E. 3.2 dm^3
F. 6.4 dm^3
G. 9.6 dm^3

24. Two children, of mass 15 kg and 10 kg respectively, are sitting on the floor of a lift. The lift accelerates downwards at 5 ms^{-2}. Assume that g= 10 Nkg^{-1}.
What would be the combined weight of the two people (in N) if measured in the lift?

A. 25 N
B. 50 N
C. 125 N
D. 150 N
E. 250 N
F. 275 N
G. 300 N

25. The following diagram illustrates the reflex arc that occurs when an individual touches a sharp pin:

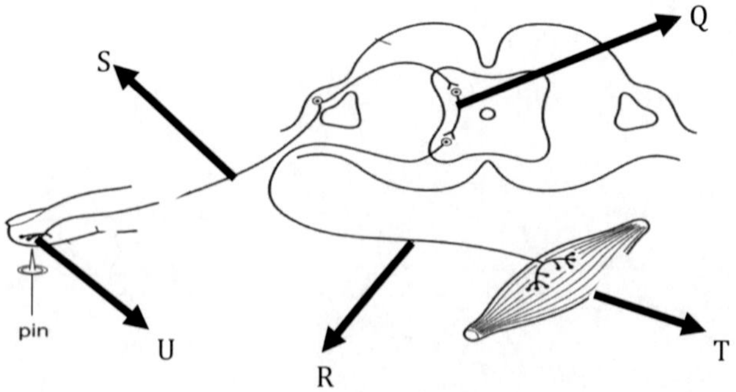

Which line in the table correctly identifies the letters shown in the diagram above?

	Motor Neurone	Receptor	Sensory Neurone	Effector	Relay neurone
A	U	T	S	R	Q
B	U	S	Q	R	T
C	R	U	S	Q	T
D	S	T	R	U	Q
E	R	U	S	T	Q
F	R	S	T	Q	U

26. Which of the following reactions listed below are endothermic?

1. The reaction between hydrochloric acid and potassium hydroxide.
2. The formation of ice cubes from water.
3. Nuclear fission.
4. Photosynthesis.
5. Aerobic respiration.
6. The decomposition of calcium carbonate to calcium oxide and carbon dioxide.

A. 1 and 2 only
B. 3 and 5 only
C. 4 and 6 only
D. 1, 2 and 3 only
E. 2, 3 and 5 only
F. 4, 5 and 6 only
G. 1, 2, 3 and 5 only
H. 2, 4, 5 and 6 only
I. All of the above
J. None of the above

27. Which of the following statement(s) relating to the digestive system is/are correct?

1. The liver receives blood from the intestine and the heart.
2. The liver stores bile before releasing it into the duodenum.
3. Bile contains sodium hydrogen carbonate, which is an acid.
4. Carbohydrates are digested in the mouth, stomach and pancreas.

A. 1 only
B. 3 only
C. 4 only
D. 1 and 2 only
E. 3 and 4 only
F. 2 and 4 only
G. 1 and 4 only
H. 1, 3 and 4 only
I. 2, 3 and 4 only
J. All of the above
K. None of the above

Mock Test 1	Scientific Knowledge and Applications (Section 2)	Answer Sheet

BioMedical Aptitude Test

SECTION 2 Scientific Knowledge and Applications

Fill in the appropriate circle for your chosen answer e.g.

A B C D E
○●○○○

Use a soft pencil. If you make a mistake, erase thoroughly and try again.

BMAT candidate number: B

Centre number

Date of birth (DD MM YYYY)

First name (s)

Surname / Family name

1. A B C D E
2. A B C D E F G H
3. A B C D E F
4. A B C D E F G H I J K
5. A B C D E F
6. A B C D E
7. A B C D E
8. A B C D E F
9. A B C D E
10. A B C D E F
11. A B C D E F
12. A B C D E F G H
13. A B C D E F
14. A B C D E
15. A B C D E F
16. A B C D E F
17. A B C D E F
18. A B C D E F
19. A B C D E
20. A B C D E F G H I J
21. A B C D E F G
22. A B C D E F
23. A B C D E F G
24. A B C D E F G
25. A B C D E F
26. A B C D E F G H I J
27. A B C D E F G H I J K

Mock Test

Mock Test 1	Writing Task (Section3)	Questions

YOU MUST COMPLETE ONLY ONE OF THE FOLLOWING TASKS

Each of the tasks consists of a statement in bold followed by three prompts. It is important that you address all three parts of your chosen task.

Task 1 - **If the facts do not fit the theory, change the facts.**

Explain the reasoning behind this statement. Argue that the theory must be altered rather than the facts. To what extent do you agree with the argument?

Task 2 - **All essential prescription medicines should be provided to patients free of charge.**

Explain what you think is meant by the statement. Present a counter-argument. To what extent do you agree with the argument?

Task 3 - **The art of healing only requires scientific knowledge in order to improve a patient's health.**

Explain what you think is meant by the statement. Present a counter-argument. To what extent do you agree with the argument?

Mock Test 2	Thinking Skills (Section 1)	Questions

1. An online cake shop has 600 regular customers. To celebrate its 25th year in business, the cake shop decides to bake a special cake; the flavour is decided via an online poll. In the poll, 300 of the regular customers voted for a chocolate and caramel flavour, and the rest voted for a strawberry and vanilla flavour. If the voters indicated a preference for the chocolate and caramel flavour over the strawberry and vanilla flavour in the ratio of 8:6, what was the percentage of regular customers who took part in the online poll?
   A. 87.5 %
   B. 88 %
   C. 88.5 %
   D. 89 %
   E. 89.5 %
   F. 90 %
   G. 90.5 %

2. Approximately three quarters of British universities– including top institutions such as Oxford and University College London (UCL) – have seen a decline in their international league table rankings. According to a 2021 university guide compiled by publishing firm Quacquarelli Symonds (QS), a total of 62 out of 84 UK institutions witnessed their world ranking been downgraded for the fourth consecutive year. According to the data, 66 UK universities saw a drop in their staff to student ratio, while 59 had fewer research citations. Many attribute the decline in ranking due to poorer teaching and declining research opportunities. Furthermore, the number of international students enrolling on courses in the UK had fallen at 51 universities. As a result, UK universities must employ more staff and encourage students to conduct more research in order to improve their rankings on an international level.

   Which one of the following best states the main assumption made in this argument?
   A. The decline in international rankings was only due to the reduced staff to student ratio and the amount of research conducted.
   B. Fewer research citations indicate a reduction in research opportunities.
   C. The reduction in international students is due to the decline in the international rankings of UK universities.
   D. Oxford and UCL are the only top institutions in the UK.
   E. A drop in the staff to student ratio has resulted in fewer research citations.

3. A martial arts academy organises a state-wide karate competition. The competition is organised in such a manner that there is a group stage followed by a knockout stage. The group stage is structured in a round-robin format where each participant is set up a match with every other participant in their group of five. The participant who wins the most matches in each group proceeds to the next round, which is the knockout round. In this round, each participant is randomly paired with another and the winner of each match proceeds to the next round. This goes on until there are only two participants left in the final round, who compete for the first and second place. The two losing semi-finalists will compete with each other for the third-place. The competition received an overwhelming response and the

registration was full within two days. Given that 176 matches took place in total, how many participants registered for the competition?

A. 90
B. 85
C. 80
D. 70
E. 60

4. A new algorithm has been designed by a team in Canada that may be able to prevent online bullying and predict the likelihood of suicidal behaviours. The team trained a machine learning algorithm to spot words and phrases associated with bullying on 'Ask FM', a social media site that allows users to ask and answer questions. It managed to detect and block almost two-thirds of insults within almost 114,000 posts in English and was more accurate than a simple keyword search. Likewise, scientists at the Vanderbilt University Medical Centre and Florida State University trained machine learning algorithms to look at the health records of patients who self-harm. The algorithms were able to predict with an accuracy of 92%, whether a patient would attempt to end his/her life in the week following an instance of self-harm. As a result, additional algorithms could be developed that rely only on data already collected routinely at the point of care to predict the risk of suicidal thoughts and behaviours.

Which of the following best expresses the main conclusion of the passage above?

A. The new algorithm can detect keywords at a faster rate compared to a keyword search.
B. Exactly 92% of the results from this new algorithm is accurate.
C. Algorithms can predict online bullying more accurately compared to human intervention.
D. This new algorithm could prevent online bullying and suicidal behaviours.
E. Algorithms can be used in a variety of ways in order to aid individuals in everyday life.

5. The five fruits and vegetables a day campaign has been around since 2003. However, in the last 17 years, there has hardly been any change in the amount of fruits and vegetables people consume. More funding should be allocated to this campaign in order to raise awareness of the benefits of eating five fruits and vegetables a day. Adults under 65 are eating around four portions a day on average. Older adults and children are consuming even less. The five-a-day campaign is based on advice from the World Health Organization, which recommends eating a minimum of 400 grams of fruit and vegetables a day to lower the risk of serious health problems, such as heart disease, stroke and some types of cancer. Five-a-day was chosen because it was viewed as realistic. Research has suggested that to get maximum benefit, individuals should be eating twice that amount.

Which of the following best illustrates a flaw in this reasoning?

A. It ignores the fact that heart disease, stroke and some types of cancer could be caused by other risk factors.
B. It assumes that increased awareness through extra funding will result in more people eating five a day.
C. It assumes that eating ten fruits and vegetables a day would reduce the risk of developing serious health problems.
D. It assumes that individuals listen to the advice given by the Government regarding fruit and vegetable consumption.

E. It ignores the fact that consuming ten fruits and vegetables a day is more beneficial than consuming only five.

6. **With the global paralysis induced by the coronavirus, levels of pollution and carbon emission are dropping everywhere — leaving bluer skies, visible mountains, splendid wildflowers. Venice's famously murky canals are running clear. After decades of industry and the Government slow-walking the climate issue, for some, it is proof that effective action can be achieved.**

   However, nature's revival has come at enormous cost, with Europe's economy projected to decline 7.4 percent this year. Therefore, for many, such as the suddenly unemployed, concerns about climate — which seemed urgent just a few months ago — seems less so now. Those competing camps are now locked in debate over how and what to rebuild — between those who want to get the economy moving again, no matter how, and those who argue that the crisis is a chance to accelerate the transition to a cleaner economy.

   Which one of the following statements is best supported by the above passage?

   A. A cleaner economy is more important than economic growth.
   B. Concerns about the climate are no longer important.
   C. Rebuilding the economy is the priority now.
   D. The improvement in the environment shows that effective actions can be taken.
   E. It is not possible to maintain a clean environment and get the economy moving again.

7. **University researchers in Switzerland and the United States examined how the brain responded to different types of dreams. They found that bad dreams improved the effectiveness of the brain in reacting to frightening experiences when awake. The neuroscientists, from the University of Geneva and the University of Wisconsin in the USA, have suggested that dreams could be used as a form of therapy for anxiety disorders. With more than 250 electrodes attached to 18 subjects - and with another 89 people keeping diaries of their sleeping and dream patterns - the researchers examined how the emotions experienced during dreams were connected with feelings when awake. It suggested that bad dreams were a way of preparing people for fear in their waking lives.**

   Which of the following best expresses the main conclusion of the passage above?

   A. Dreams are used as a form of therapy for anxiety disorders.
   B. Bad dreams may aid people to deal with frightening experiences when they are awake.
   C. Emotions experienced during dreams are connected to feelings when awake.
   D. Bad dreams improve the effectiveness of the brain compared to extensive cognitive exercises.
   E. Bad dreams are the only way of preparing people for fear in their waking lives.

8. Shown below is a net of a cube.

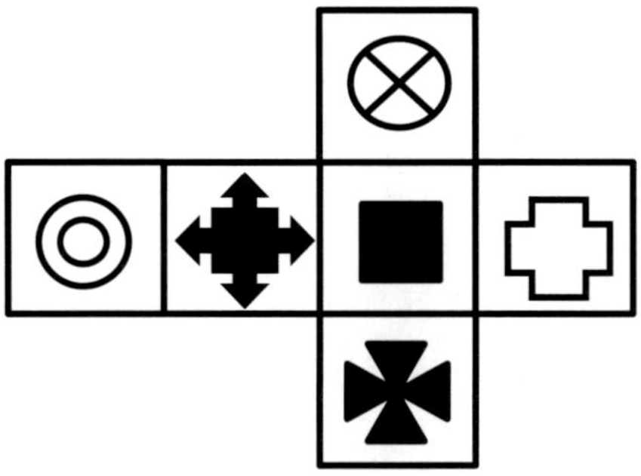

Which one of the following nets would produce the same cube when folded up as the net shown above?

A.

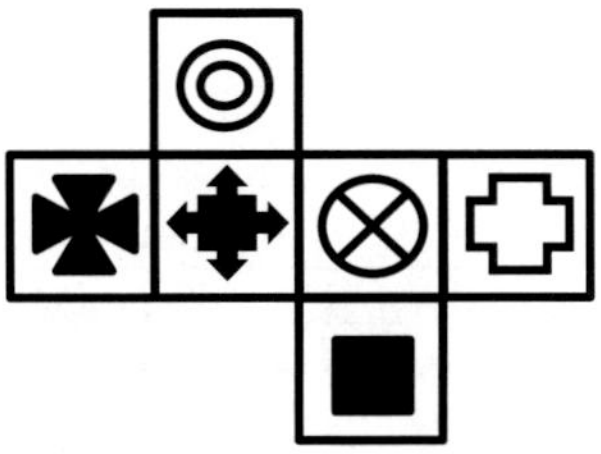

B.

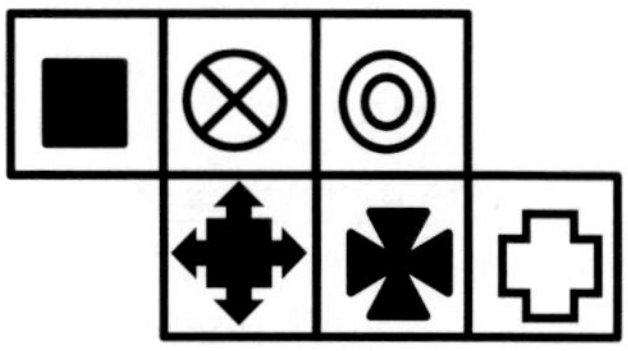

C.

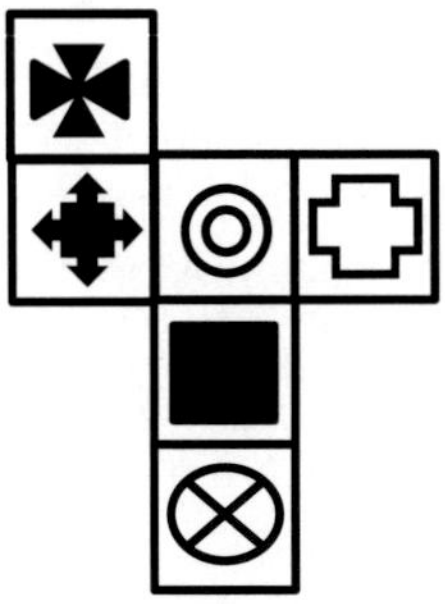

D.

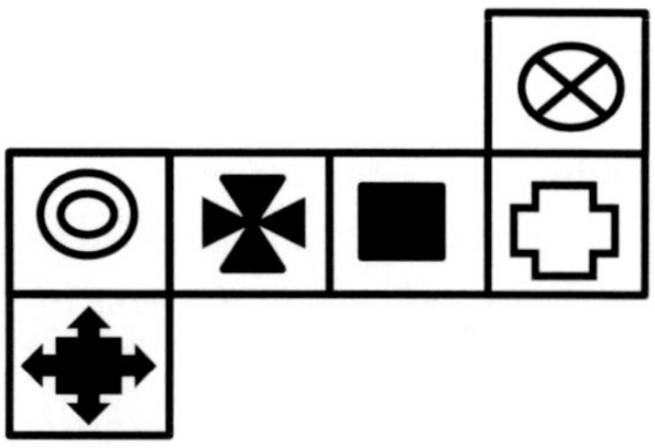

E.

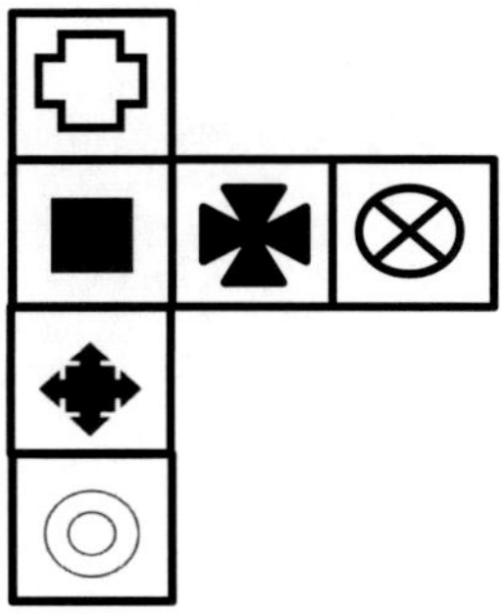

9. Five types of flowers have been planted in a row in Timothy's garden – roses, lilies, tulips, poppies and sunflowers. The roses are found to the left of the tulips, which are found on the right of the poppies. The lilies are planted to the right of the roses and to the left of the sunflowers.

The sunflowers are found to the right of:

A. Poppies and lilies, but not necessarily the tulips.
B. Roses, lilies and poppies, but not necessarily the tulips.
C. Tulips and poppies, but not necessarily the roses.
D. Roses and lilies, but not necessarily the tulips or poppies.
E. Lilies and tulips, but not necessarily the poppies.

10. The table below shows the number of pupils who are involved in different sports activities.

Sports	Girls	Boys
Tennis	65	76
Badminton	78	72
Netball	88	32
Football	56	57
Rugby	45	59
Swimming	72	35
Rowing	35	98
Cricket	61	21
TOTAL	500	450

Which of the following sporting activities does the pie chart shown below represent?

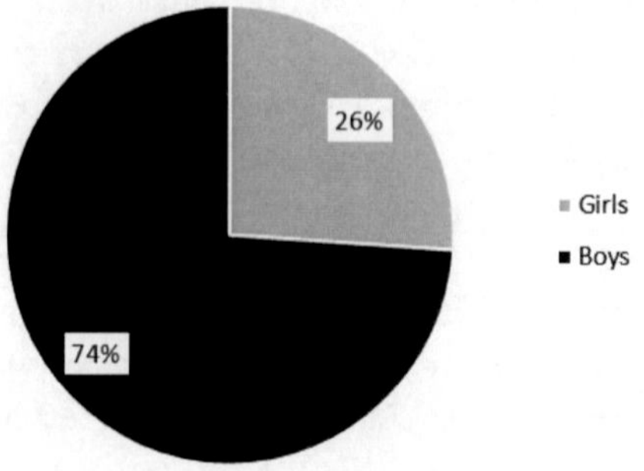

A. Cricket
B. Rowing
C. Swimming
D. Netball
E. Tennis

11. Two friends create a code language with symbols. "ø¥† µ°√ π^∑œ" means "keep looking above" and "ç√¥ ¬∂Δ π^∑œ" means "keep the keys". Which of the following symbols represent the word 'keys'?

A. ¬∂Δ
B. ç√¥
C. ø¥†
D. ¬∂Δ or ø¥†
E. ¬∂Δ or ç√¥

Mock Test

12. **Travis lives 5 km away from Ruby and 2 km away from Joe. Ruby and Joe leave their houses at the same time and run to Travis' house at a constant speed. Ruby runs at a speed of 1.25 km/hr and Joe runs at a speed of 1.5 km/hr.**

    What is the difference in the time taken for both of them to reach Travis' house?
    A. 1 hour 20 minutes
    B. 1 hour 44 minutes
    C. 2 hours 40 minutes
    D. 3 hours 15 minutes
    E. 4 hours

13. **Current evidence indicates that children are less likely than adults to acquire the coronavirus infection after exposure, less likely to test positive for SARS-CoV-2 at the population-level, and potentially less likely to transmit the infection to others. However, the latter conclusion is based on research performed during a period in which schools have generally been closed, and, therefore, isn't necessarily reflective of the true infectivity of children. The disease in children seems to follow a milder course than in adults, with many cases being asymptomatic. However, critical cases have also been described and there are rare instances of a serious post-infection hyperinflammatory syndrome.**

    What is the main conclusion of this passage?
    A. There will be fewer children infected compared to teenagers.
    B. Children are less likely to have severe symptoms and less likely to transmit the coronavirus; this is based on information collected after schools have closed.
    C. Many children who had coronavirus still tested negative for SARS-CoV-2.
    D. Transmission between children are low because schools have closed.
    E. Children are less likely to acquire the infection because they are in quarantine since schools have been shut for many months.

14. **In IVF, women under 30 had a 44% chance of a live birth in their first cycle; women aged 30-34 had only marginally lower rates than these. Women aged 40-44 had an 11% chance of a live birth in their first cycle. From the data above, women who started IVF before they turned 35 had the highest success rates. As a result, a new technique, called spindle transfer, has been developed for older women. It is used to remove faulty mitochondrial DNA in these women and replace it with the nucleus from a donor mother's egg. Women aged 40-44 who have undergone this procedure have a 18% chance of a live birth in their first cycle. Therefore, this spindle transfer technique, which utilises mitochondrial replacement therapy, is better for age-related infertility.**

    Which one of the following is an assumption made in this passage?
    A. Mitochondria in the eggs of women aged 40 – 44 are at fault in some cases of infertility.
    B. Women under 30 had a 44% chance of being infertile.
    C. Spindle transfer is only successful for older women.
    D. Women who started IVF before they turned 35 had the highest success rates.
    E. Women aged 40 – 44 can only become fertile due to IVF and spindle transfer.

15. **According to the latest research, reading is the best form of cognitive exercise. A growing body of research indicates that reading could alter the neural pathways in the brain. Using MRI scans, researchers have confirmed that reading involves a complex network of circuits and signals in the brain. As reading ability matures, these networks become stronger and**

more sophisticated. Brain scans showed that throughout the process of reading and for days afterward, brain connectivity increased, especially in the somatosensory cortex, the part of the brain that responds to physical sensations such as movement and pain. Research shows that regular reading can improve brain connectivity, increase vocabulary and comprehension, reduce stress, lower blood pressure and heart rate, and combat symptoms of depression.

Which of the following best illustrates a flaw in this reasoning?

A. It assumes that the neural pathways in the brain are only changed by daily reading.
B. It ignores the fact that other cognitive exercises can also alter neural pathways in the brain.
C. It assumes that the advantages of reading outweigh any other cognitive exercise.
D. It assumes that the MRI scans are an accurate way of assessing brain signals.
E. It assumes that reading alone can lower blood pressure and combat symptoms of depression.

16. **Walking is an underrated and important form of exercise. It improves fitness, cardiac health, alleviates depression and fatigue, improves one's mood and creates less stress on joints by reducing pain. When comparing the results of the most recent National Runners' Health Study with the National Walkers' Health Study, researchers found that the energy used for moderate-intensity walking and vigorous-intensity running resulted in similar reductions in risk for high blood pressure, high cholesterol, diabetes and heart disease over the study's six year period. Past studies have supported this notion, finding that a daily walk can reduce the risk of stroke in both men and women, reduce the days spent in a hospital each year and can even lower the risk of death by up to 39% (when compared with no leisure-time physical activity).**

Which one of the following cannot be reliably concluded from the passage above?

A. Walking improves fitness, cardiac health and alleviates depression and fatigue.
B. Walking is a better form of exercise compared to running.
C. Walking lowers the risk of death by up to 39% compared to no leisure time physical activity.
D. Walking can result in similar reductions in risk for high blood pressure and high cholesterol compared to running.
E. Walking can reduce the risk of a stroke in both men and women.

17. **Mr and Mrs Gonville and their family of six children are going on a road trip in their 8-seater car, made of three rows in a 2-3-3 fashion. Seb and Tia are twins, but they always quarrel with each other; therefore, they will try to distance themselves as far as possible. Pam is the oldest sibling and is the most caring. She is overprotective of her youngest sibling, Una who is a 1-year-old and sits in a baby car seat. To ensure that the other siblings do not bully Una, Pam makes sure that she is the only one who sits next to her. Roe particularly likes sitting in the centre of the middle row as she feels that that seat is where she can directly get the cool air from the air-conditioner. Both parents sit in the front row. Mrs Gonville who sits on the left side of the car reads her book throughout the entire journey. At one point of the trip, Pam reaches to the back part of the car to grab some packed crisps for everyone to snack on. Tia, being the closest in distance to her mother passes her a packet of crisps.**
Who is seated the furthest from the driver?

A. Pam
B. Roe

C. Seb
D. Tia
E. Una
F. The sixth child

18. The population of Africa is expected to roughly double by 2050. Population growth rates continue to pose lingering challenges to development efforts on the continent. The average woman in Africa today has about 4.7 children. This varies significantly from 2.5 in southern Africa to between 5.5 and 5.8 in central and western Africa. The average in other parts of the world is 2.2 or less, with a global average of 2.5 children per woman. One of the reasons why women in Africa still have so many children is that the average age at which they become mothers for the first time is more than 4 years earlier than the global average of 26. In addition, the adolescent birth rates are very high. In central and western Africa, for example, it is almost three times the global average. Addressing these statistics may help to significantly slow population growth rates globally.

Which one of the following best states the main assumption made in this argument?

A. Women in Africa have the most children.
B. Women in Africa are more likely to have children at a younger age compared to women in Asia.
C. The population of Africa will double by 2050.
D. Africa is a major contributor to overpopulation on the planet.
E. Overpopulation will become a major issue in the future.

19. In a sports club there are 175 members. A total of 40% of the members are children or teenagers. Of the adult members, 60% are females. If $\frac{1}{7}$ of the male adult members decide to stop their membership, what percentage of the total do all the male adults with a membership represent?

A. 20%
B. 21%
C. 24%
D. 34%
E. 36%

20. The chart below shows the movie genre that 80 men and 80 women prefer.

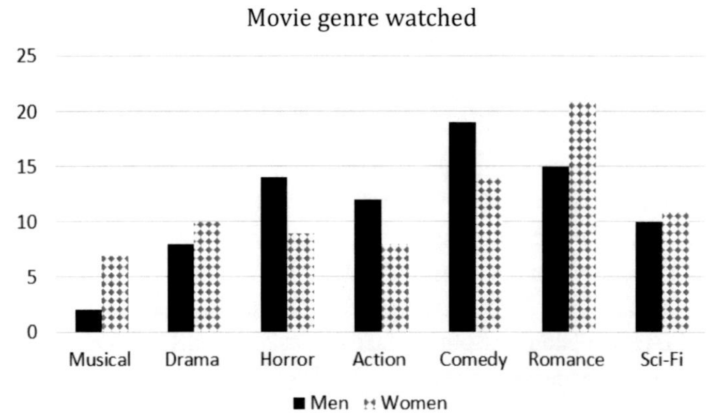

Which of the following pie charts correctly represents the information about the genre that women like?

A

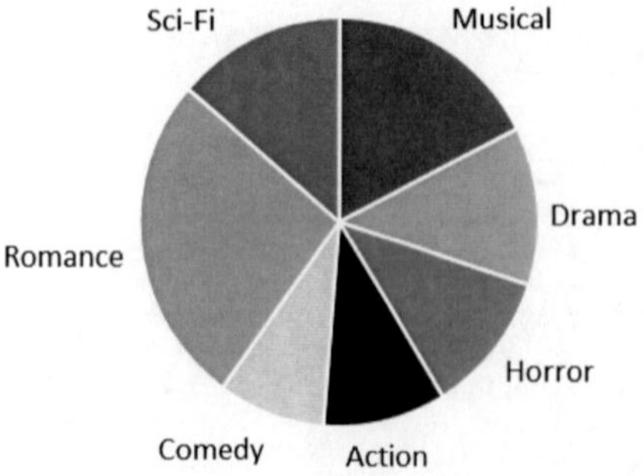

B

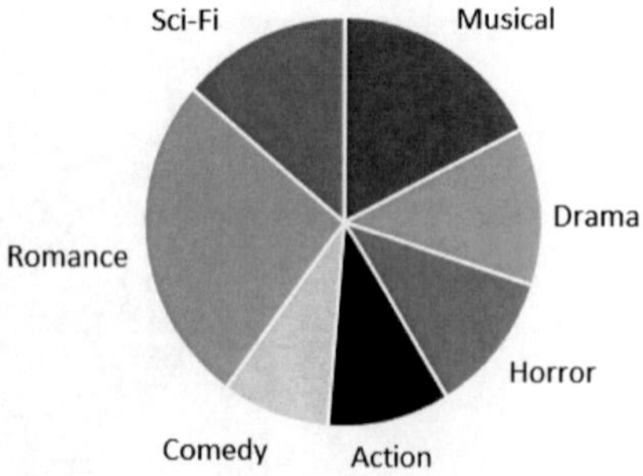

C

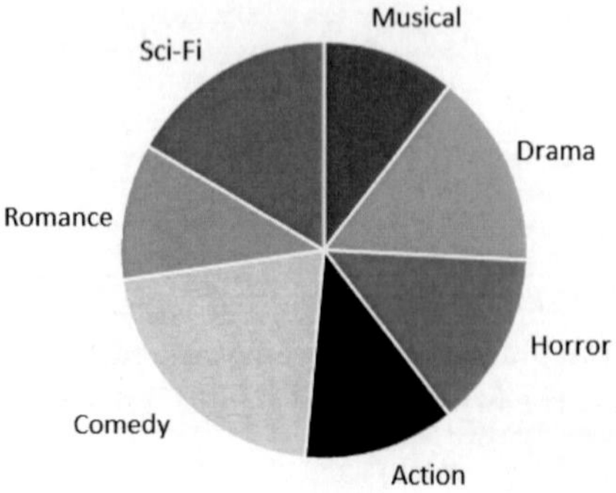

D

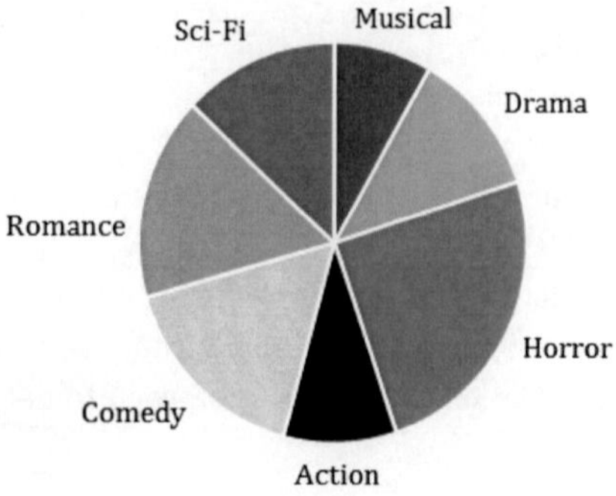

E

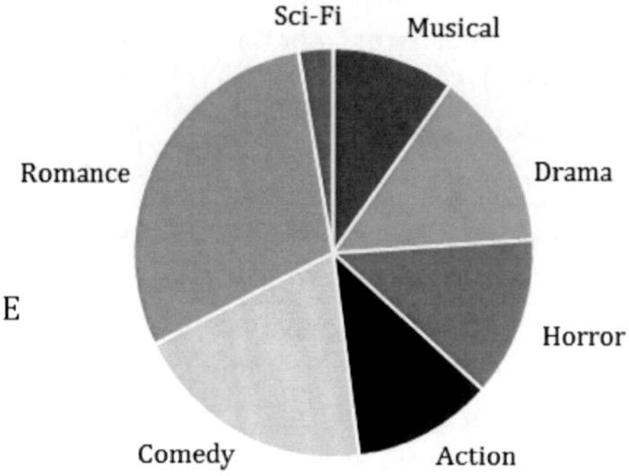

21. **The table below shows the time each student spent doing their homework for each subject in a week.**

Subject	Victoria	Isabella	Paula	Hekla	Katla
Biology	30	25	30	60	60
Chemistry	60	25	30	40	30
Maths	120	75	90	60	60
Physics	30	50	60	120	120

The pie chart below represents the information about the time spent on each subject by one of the students.

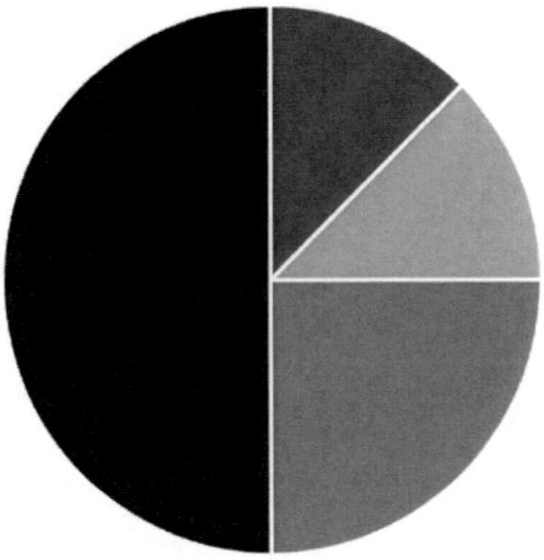

Which student does the chart represent?

A. Victoria
B. Isabella
C. Paula
D. Hekla
E. Katla

22. **Pamela buys a new bookshelf for her revision folders. She places the red folder above the white folder, which is below the black folder. The blue folder is below the red folder and above the black folder. The green folder is below the black folder which is above the grey folder.**

The grey folder is below:

A. Blue folder, red folder but not necessarily below the black folder.
B. Red folder, black folder but not necessarily below the blue folder.
C. Blue folder, red folder and black folder.
D. Red folder, black folder and white folder.
E. Red folder, black folder and green folder but not necessarily below the white folder.

23. **Individuals need to stop focussing so much attention on the dangers of vaping. In 2019, there were only 66 deaths directly linked to vaping, while there were 146,383 deaths from strokes in the USA. As a result, people must think about proportionality since these statistics show that anti-vaping campaigns are not necessary in comparison with the dangers from strokes. This clearly implies that vaping is not as dangerous as it is perceived to be.**

Which of the following statements identify a weakness in the above argument?

1. More people may die from vaping if there were no anti-vaping campaigns that highlight the dangers of vaping.
2. There may be more people who are at risk of a stroke compared with those who vape.
3. The particulates in aerosols are dangerous due to the inhalation of oxidising agents, which could affect the circulatory and respiratory system.

 A Lakshmi, T R Enoch, S Z Y Ooi. Doctors Academy Publications, Cardiff, UK, 2020.

A. 1 only
B. 2 only
C. 3 only
D. 1 and 2 only
E. 1 and 3 only
F. 2 and 3 only
G. All of the above

24. A flat pyramid shape has 5 horizontal rows. The number of bricks in a row is 2 less than the number of bricks in the row immediately below. If there are 115 bricks and 5 rows in total, how many bricks does the top row contain?

A. 11
B. 13
C. 15
D. 17
E. 19
F. 21

25. In England, researchers from the University of Exeter Medical School recently analysed mental health data from 10,000 city dwellers. They used high-resolution mapping to track where the subjects had lived over 18 years. They found that people living near more green space reported less mental distress, even after adjusting for income, education, and employment (all of which are also correlated with health). In 2009 a team of Dutch researchers found a lower incidence of 15 diseases—including depression, anxiety, heart disease, diabetes, asthma, and migraines—in people who lived within about a half mile of green space. In addition, in 2015, an international team overlaid health questionnaire responses from more than 31,000 Toronto residents onto a map of the city, block by block. Those living on blocks with more trees showed a boost in heart and metabolic health equivalent to what one would experience from a £20,000 gain in income. Lower mortality and fewer stress hormones circulating in the blood have also been connected to living close to green space.

Which one of the following cannot be reliably concluded from the passage above?

A. Individuals who lived near more green space reported less mental distress compared to those who didn't.
B. Individuals who live within half a mile of green space will not suffer from depression and anxiety.
C. Those living on blocks with more trees in Canada showed a boost in heart and metabolic health.
D. Lower mortality and fewer stress hormones circulating in the blood have also been connected to living close to green space.
E. Individuals are less likely to suffer from asthma and migraines if they live approximately half a mile from green space.

26. There is recent research that finds evidence of lasting positive effects of video games on basic mental processes—such as perception, attention, memory and decision-making. Most of the research involves effects of action video games—that is, games that require players to move rapidly, keep track of many items at once, hold a good deal of information in their mind at once, and make split-second decisions. The best evidence that gaming improves these abilities comes from experiments in which all the participants are initially non-gamers, and then some,

but not others, are asked to play a particular video game for a certain number of hours per day and a certain number of days. In these experiments, the typical finding is that those who play the video game improve on measures of basic perceptual and cognitive abilities while those in the control group do not. Therefore, all children should be encouraged to play video games in order to improve certain skills.

Which of the following best illustrates a flaw in this reasoning?

A. It assumes that perception, attention, memory and decision-making can only be improved by playing video games.
B. It ignores the fact that video games can have a detrimental impact on children's health.
C. It assumes that video games are the only way of developing vital skills required in everyday life.
D. It ignores the fact that many gamers may have developed these skills prior to playing video games.
E. It assumes that the advantages of children playing video games outweigh the drawbacks.

---

27. Quon and Ruth want to know how old Skye is. Their conversation goes as follows.
Skye: I rear two pet tortoises whose ages are younger than mine. If you multiplied all of our ages (i.e., my age and the age of my two tortoises) together, you would get 144. To keep things simple, I can assure you that I'm only using whole numbers for our ages.
Quon: That doesn't help much! What else can you tell us?
Skye: If you added up all of our three ages, you would get the number on Quon's football jersey.
Ruth: All of us know Quon's jersey number, but we still can't work out your age. Skye: Did I mention that my tortoises are of the same age?
Quon and Ruth: I see! Now we know your age.

Which of the following could be the number on Quon's football jersey?

A. 15
B. 16
C. 36
D. 40
E. 44

---

28. Carlisle, an anaesthetic in the NHS, has developed statistical methods that can identify fraud in medical research. For example, Yoshitaka Fujii, a clinician, published results from a series of randomised controlled clinical trials (RCTs) investigating medicines to prevent nausea and vomiting in patients after surgery. Carlisle showed that it was extremely unlikely that some of the patterns in Fujii's data had occurred by chance. Due to this incident and further investigations, Fujii lost his university job. In addition, 183 of his papers were retracted, which is more retractions than any other individual has had. As a result, it follows that the statistical methods that Carlisle used to identify medical fraud in Fujii's work can be used for all medical fraud suspicions. In 2017, Carlisle produced an analysis of over 5,000 clinical trials. Most were published in journals in his own field, anaesthetics, but he also included two top-ranking American medical journals, the Journal of the American Medical Association (JAMA) and the New England Journal of Medicine (NEJM). He found suspect data in about 90 papers.

Which one of the following best illustrates a flaw in the reasoning?

A. It assumes that Fujii lost his university job due to Carlisle's statistical methods.
B. It assumes that Fujii's papers were only retracted due to Carlisle's statistical methods.
C. It proves that Carlisle's method uses measures of discrepancies between the groups called p-values, which is then combined in a trial into a single measure.
D. It assumes that all fraudulent medical research can be identified using Carlisle's statistical methods.
E. It asserts that all of the data from the 90 papers were fraudulent.

29. **Consider the following statements:**
Those who like netball like hockey.
Those who like football like cricket.
Those who like cricket do not like hockey.
If all of the above statements are true, which of the following statements must also be true?

1. Those who like football do not like netball.
2. Those who like netball like football.
3. Those who like netball do not like cricket.
4. Those who like hockey do not like football.
5. Those who like football like hockey.

A. 1, 2 and 3 only
B. 1, 3 and 4 only
C. 3, 4 and 5 only
D. 1 and 5 only
E. 3 and 4 only
F. 1, 2, 3 and 4 only
G. None of the above

30. **According to a joint study from the Global Commission on Aging and Transamerica Centre for Retirement Studies, travelling can keep an individual healthy. The study found that women who vacation at least twice a year show a significantly lower risk of suffering a heart attack than those who only travel every six years or so. The same is true for men. Men who do not take an annual vacation show a 20 percent higher risk of death and 30 percent greater risk of heart disease. In addition, according to one study, three days after taking a vacation, travellers report feeling less anxious, more rested and in a better mood. Interestingly, these benefits tend to linger for weeks after the trip has ended. Therefore, travelling is essential in order to reap a number of important health benefits.**

Which of the following best illustrates a flaw in this reasoning?

A. It assumes that all individuals have enough money to go travelling.
B. It ignores the fact that travelling could have some downsides to health and wellbeing.
C. It assumes that all travellers feel less anxious, more rested and in a better mood after taking a vacation.
D. It assumes that travelling is the only way to reap health benefits.
E. It ignores the fact that heart disease can be prevented using methods other than travelling.

31. All of Lola's books with a green sticker on the spine are non-fiction books and all the non-fiction books she has are from the library. No fiction book has a green sticker on the spine. Which one amongst the following statements is true?

A. Some of the fiction books are from the library.
B. She owns all the fiction books.
C. She does not have any non-fiction books without the green sticker.
D. None of the fiction books have a sticker on the spine.
E. No book with a green sticker on the spine is a fiction.

32. The number of hours five students watched TV on one day was recorded. The time that they first switched the TV on and then turned it off was recorded on Saturday.

	On	Off	On	Off	On	Off
Charlie	11:51	13:50	14:15	19:00	20:30	23:04
Madhav	8:55	10:57	12:23	19:37	20:15	23:16
Nuan	12:18	16:21	18:33	20:32	20:59	22:04
Kwame	13:22	14:02	17:56	19:12	20:05	22:40
Anton	6:55	7:55	15:46	17:14	19:16	20:37

From the data collected, the number of hours spent watching TV between 19:00 to 21:00 was analysed.
Which student watched TV for the longest amount of time during this two-hour period?

A. Charlie
B. Madhav
C. Nuan
D. Kwame
E. Anton

Mock Test

A Lakshmi, T R Enoch, S Z Y Ooi. Doctors Academy Publications, Cardiff, UK, 2020.

Mock Test 2 | Thinking Skills (Section 1) | Answer Sheet

BioMedical Aptitude Test

SECTION 1 Thinking Skills

BMAT candidate number: B

Centre number

Date of birth (DD MM YYYY)

First name (s)

Surname / Family name

Fill in the appropriate circle for your chosen answer e.g.

A B C D E
○ ● ○ ○ ○

Use a soft pencil. If you make a mistake, erase thoroughly and try again.

1. A B C D E F G
2. A B C D E
3. A B C D E
4. A B C D E
5. A B C D E
6. A B C D E
7. A B C D E
8. A B C D E
9. A B C D E
10. A B C D E
11. A B C D E
12. A B C D E
13. A B C D E
14. A B C D E
15. A B C D E F
16. A B C D E
17. A B C D E F
18. A B C D E
19. A B C D E
20. A B C D E
21. A B C D E
22. A B C D E

23 A B C D F F G

24 A B C D E F

25 A B C D E

26 A B C D E

27 A B C D E

28. A B C D E
29. A B C D E F G
30. A B C D E
31. A B C D E
32. A B C D E

Mock Test 2	Scientific Knowledge and Applications (Section 2)	Questions

1. **The graph below represents the distance travelled in a straight line by a car.**

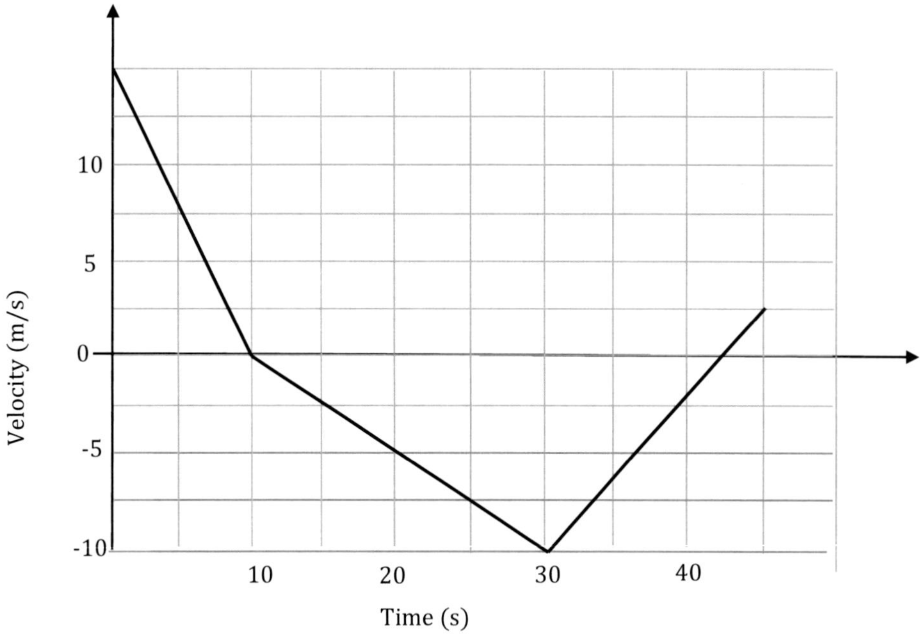

What is the total distance travelled by the car from t=0 to t=45 seconds?

A. 137.5 metres
B. 337.5 metres
C. 350 metres
D. 420 metres
E. 435.5 metres
F. 445.5 metres

2. **Which line in the table correctly identifies the processes that occur during expiration?**

	External intercostal muscles	Diaphragm	Lung volume	Internal intercostal muscles	Air pressure inside lungs
A	Contract	Relax	Decrease	Relax	Increase
B	Contract	Relax	Decrease	Contract	Increase
C	Relax	Relax	Decrease	Contract	Increase
D	Contract	Contract	Decrease	Relax	Increase
E	Relax	Contract	Decrease	Relax	Increase
F	Relax	Contract	Decrease	Contract	Increase

A Lakshmi, T R Enoch, S Z Y Ooi. Doctors Academy Publications, Cardiff, UK, 2020.

3. **Consider a graph representing $y = (x-9)^3 + 3(x-2)^2 - 5(x-3) - 10$ and a Point X (4, -125). Assume that each unit is a millimetre. Point X is:**
   A. More than 5mm above the curve
   B. Less than 5 mm above the curve
   C. On the curve
   D. More than 5 mm below the curve
   E. Less than 5 mm below the curve

4. **Which line in the table correctly matches the flame test colour to the metal cations?**

	Green	Crimson Red	Yellow-orange	Lilac	Red Orange
A	Sodium	Lithium	Calcium	Potassium	Copper
B	Copper	Sodium	Lithium	Potassium	Calcium
C	Calcium	Lithium	Sodium	Potassium	Copper
D	Calcium	Sodium	Lithium	Potassium	Copper
E	Copper	Lithium	Sodium	Potassium	Calcium
F	Lithium	Sodium	Calcium	Potassium	Copper

5. **Tommy lifts up a 900-gram book from the table to a height of 4 metres. Assume that gravity is 10 ms-2.**
   How much work has he done and how much work is required to hold the book at this height?

	Work done (J)	Work on holding (J)
A	36	36
B	36,000	0
C	36,000	36,000
D	36	18
E	36,000	18,000
F	36	0

6. **The different types of stationary sold in a shop is represented by a pie chart. A total of 44.8% of their sales are from black biros, 26.9% are from 30 cm rulers, 6.7% are from pencil cases, 3.6% are from felt tip sets and the rest are from pencils. How many degrees of the pie chart circle are used to represent the sales from pencils?**
   A. 32.6°
   B. 32.8°
   C. 64.2°
   D. 64.6°
   E. 64.8°
   F. 65.2°

7. **Which row displays the correct word equation for anaerobic respiration in humans and in yeast?**

	Anaerobic respiration in yeast	Anaerobic respiration in humans
A	glucose + oxygen → carbon dioxide + water (+energy)	glucose + enzymes →carbon dioxide and lactic acid
B	glucose + enzymes →carbon dioxide and lactic acid	glucose + enzymes →carbon dioxide and ethanol
C	glucose + enzymes →carbon dioxide and ethanol	glucose + enzymes →carbon dioxide and lactic acid
D	glucose + oxygen (+energy) → carbon dioxide + water	glucose + enzymes →carbon dioxide and ethanol

8. **Jess makes two electromagnets. Electromagnet X, with a magnetic flux density of 50 T, experiences a force of 2.5 N when a wire of 10 cm is placed in the field. Electromagnet Y, with a magnetic field strength of 5.5 T, experiences a force of 16.5 N when a wire of 40 cm is placed in the field.**
What is the total amount of current produced in the two electromagnets?
A. 6 A
B. 6.5 A
C. 7 A
D. 7.5 A
E. 8 A
F. 8.5 A

9. **The symbol § defines a binary operation such that the following equation applies for all positive integers: $j \S k = j^{-1}/kj^{-k}$**
What is the value of 1 § (3 § 4)?
A. $\frac{2}{27}$
B. $\frac{2}{9}$
C. $\frac{1}{9}$
D. $\frac{4}{27}$
E. $\frac{5}{9}$
F. $\frac{16}{27}$

10. The diagram shows an electrolysis experiment.

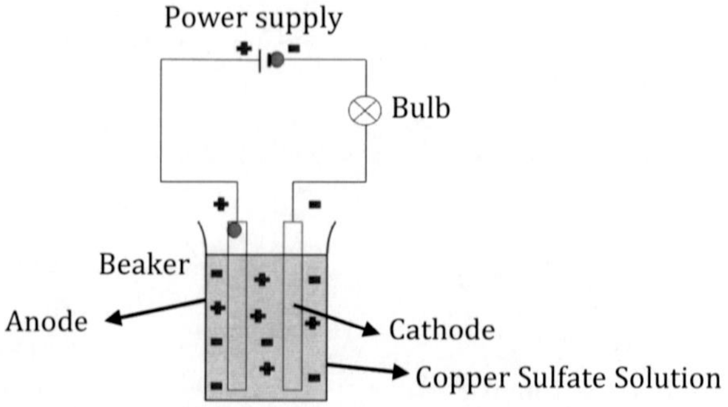

In this experiment, which reaction occurs at the anode and which reaction occurs at the cathode?

	Anode	Cathode
A	$2H^+ + 2e^- \rightarrow H_2$	$4OH^- \rightarrow 2H_2O + O_2 + 4e^-$
B	$Cu^{2+} + 2e^- \rightarrow Cu$	$2H^+ + 2e^- \rightarrow H_2$
C	$4OH^- \rightarrow 2H_2O + O_2 + 4e^-$	$Cu^{2+} + 2e^- \rightarrow Cu$
D	$4OH^- \rightarrow 2H_2O + O_2 + 4e^-$	$2H^+ + 2e^- \rightarrow H_2$
E	$SO_4^{2-} \rightarrow SO_2 + O_2 + 2e^-$	$2H^+ + 2e^- \rightarrow H_2$

11. The table below shows the heart rate, respiratory rate, temperature and blood pressure of five different mammals:

	Heart rate (beats per minute)	Respiratory rate (inhalations per minute)	Temperature (°C)	Blood pressure (mmHg)
1	56	91	34.6°	92
2	30	83	36.2°	113
3	63	130	38.7°	102
4	90	154	35.9°	97
5	10	50	39.2°	80

Which of the following correctly ranks the mammals in descending order of surface area per unit volume of the body?

A. 1>4>2>3>5
B. 5>2>1>3>4
C. 5>1>4>3>2
D. 5>3>2>4>1
E. 4>3>1>2>5
F. 2>3>4>1>5

Mock Test

12. A primary coil, with a resistance of 16 Ω and a current of 0.8 A, has 5 turns. A secondary coil has 120 turns. Assume that the transformer has an efficiency of 100%.
Which line in the table correctly identifies the voltage of the secondary transformer and the type of transformer used?

	Secondary Voltage (V)	Type of Transformer
A	53	Step-Up
B	307.2	Step-Up
C	106.8	Step-Up
D	53	Step-Down
E	307.2	Step-Down
F	106.8	Step-Down

13. Evaluate:
999(0.8 – 0 625)

A. 163
B. 164
C. 165
D. 166
E. 263
F. 264
G. 265
H. 266

14. Which of the following options shows the correct order of electromagnetic waves, from the highest to the lowest wavelength?

A. Radio waves - Microwaves - Optical - X-rays - Gamma rays
B. Gamma rays - Ultraviolet rays - Optical - Infrared - Microwaves - Radio waves
C. Gamma rays - X-rays - Optical - Ultraviolet - Infrared - Microwaves - Radio waves
D. X-rays - Ultraviolet - Optical - Microwaves - Infrared - Radio waves
E. Radio waves - Microwaves - Optical - Ultraviolet - X-rays - Gamma rays
F. Microwaves - Infrared - Optical - Ultraviolet - X-rays - Gamma rays

15. Which of the following processes add carbon to the atmosphere?

1. Respiration
2. Decomposition
3. Combustion
4. Photosynthesis

A. 1 only
B. 3 only
C. 4 only
D. 1 and 3 only
E. 2 and 3 only
F. 3 and 4 only
G. 1, 2 and 3 only
H. 2, 3 and 4 only
I. All of the above

16. Which line in the table correctly identifies the properties of methane at room temperature?

	Melting and Boiling Points	Electrical conductivity	State at room temperature
A	High	When dissolved in solution	Gas
B	Low	None	Gas
C	Low	Always	Gas
D	High	None	Solid
E	Low	When dissolved in solution	Solid
F	High	Always	Solid

17. The following diagram shows a circle with two tangents, WY and WX. Angle XWY is 58°. What is the size of angle XZY?

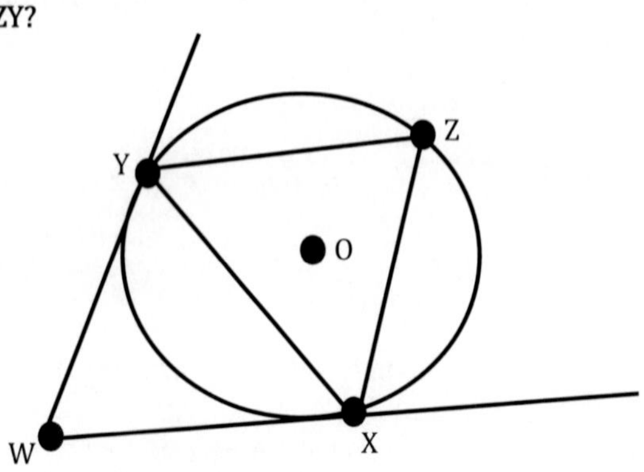

A. 30°
B. 61°
C. 126°
D. 58°
E. 238°
F. 119°

18. What is the combined volume, in cm³, that 345 grams of ethanol gas and 272 grams of ammonia gas require, at room temperature and pressure?

A. 282,000 cm^3
B. 0.282 cm^3
C. 564 cm^3
D. 564,000 cm^3
E. 0.564 cm^3
F. 2.82 cm^3
G. 1.41cm^3
H. 5.64 cm^3

19. The following structures relate to the large and small intestines:

1. Appendix
2. Sigmoid colon
3. Jejunum
4. Ileum
5. Caecum
6. Rectum

Which of the above are not regions of the large intestine?

A. 1 only
B. 2 and 3 only
C. 3 and 4 only
D. 1 and 6 only
E. 1, 3 and 4 only
F. 1, 3 and 6 only
G. 2, 5 and 6 only
H. All of the above
I. None of the above

20. Two passengers, one of 80 kg and the other of 45 kg, are in a car. The car travels 5.4 kilometres in 2 minutes. The car suddenly decelerates to 10 ms^{-1} in 5 seconds. What is the combined force that acts on the two passengers?

A. 315 N
B. 470 N
C. 685 N
D. 875 N
E. 925 N
F. 1015 N

21. Which row correctly identifies the numbers required to balance the following equation?

$$a\ MoS_2 + b\ O_2 \rightarrow c\ MoO_3 + d\ SO_2$$

	a	b	c	d
A	2	6	2	3
B	1	7	1	4
C	3	7	3	2
D	2	7	2	4

22. What is the difference in energy, in kJ, required to raise the temperature of 25 grams of vegetable oil from 15°C to 75°C compared to raising the temperature of 30 grams of water from 36°C to 61°C?

Assume that the vegetable oil remains in the same state. The specific heat capacity of vegetable oil is 1800 $Jkg^{-1}°C^{-1}$ and the specific capacity of water is 4200 $Jkg^{-1}°C^{-1}$.

A. 0.45 kJ
B. 0.5 kJ
C. 0.55 kJ
D. 0.6 kJ
E. 0.65 kJ
F. 0.7 kJ

23. **A bag contains only 36 marbles. The marbles are identical in all respects except colour. Exactly 10 marbles are purple, 12 are red and the remainder are pink. A random marble is taken from the bag and not replaced. A second random marble is then taken from the bag. What is the probability of getting one pink and one purple marble from the bag?**

A. $\frac{1}{3}$

B. $\frac{1}{6}$

C. $\frac{1}{9}$

D. $\frac{2}{9}$

E. $\frac{2}{13}$

F. $\frac{1}{12}$

24. **Which row correctly identifies the number of protons, neutrons and electrons in $^{97}_{35}Br^{-}$?**

	Proton	Neutron	Electron
A	35	36	35
B	35	62	36
C	62	35	36
D	62	36	35

25. **The following structures relate to plant and animal cells:**
   1. Cell membrane
   2. Chromosomal DNA
   3. Vacuole
   4. Chloroplasts
   5. Mitochondria
   6. Cell wall

Which of the above structures are found exclusively in animal cells?

A. 1 only
B. 1 and 2 only
C. 1 and 5 only
D. 2 and 5 only
E. 1, 2 and 5 only
F. All of the above
G. None of the above

26. **The following statements relate to pentane and propane.**
   1. Pentane has a higher boiling point compared to propane.
   2. Propane is less viscous compared to pentane.
   3. Propane is more flammable compared to pentane.

Which amongst the aforementioned statement(s) is/are incorrect?

A. 1 only

B. 2 only
C. 3 only
D. 1 and 2 only
E. 2 and 3 only
F. 1 and 3 only
G. All of the above
H. None of the above

27. Which line in the table correctly identifies the effect of various hormones secreted by the body?

	Adrenaline	FSH	Thyroxine	Progesterone
A	Stimulates conversion of glycogen to glucose in liver cells	Inhibits LH production	Increases metabolism	Stimulates oestrogen release
B	Stimulates conversion of glycogen to glucose in liver cells	Stimulates oestrogen release	Increases metabolism	Inhibits LH production
C	Increases metabolism	Stimulates oestrogen release	Stimulates conversion of glycogen to glucose in liver cells	Inhibits LH production
D	Increases metabolism	Inhibits LH production	Stimulates conversion of glycogen to glucose in liver cells	Stimulates oestrogen release
E	Stimulates oestrogen release	Stimulates conversion of glycogen to glucose in liver cells	Inhibits LH production	Increases metabolism

Mock Test 2	Scientific Knowledge and Applications (Section 2)	Answer Sheet

BioMedical Aptitude Test

SECTION 2 Scientific Knowledge and Applications

BMAT candidate number

B

Centre number

Date of birth (DD MM YYYY)

First name (s)

Surname / Family name

Fill in the appropriate circle for your chosen answer e.g.

A B C D E
○●○○○

Use a soft pencil. If you make a mistake, erase thoroughly and try again.

1. A B C D E F
○ ○ ○ ○ ○ ○

2. A B C D E F
○ ○ ○ ○ ○ ○

3. A B C D E
○ ○ ○ ○ ○

4. A B C D E F
○ ○ ○ ○ ○ ○

5. A B C D E F
○ ○ ○ ○ ○ ○

6. A B C D E F
○ ○ ○ ○ ○ ○

7. A B C D
○ ○ ○ ○

8. A B C D E F
○ ○ ○ ○ ○ ○

9. A B C D E F
○ ○ ○ ○ ○ ○

10. A B C D E
○ ○ ○ ○ ○

11. A B C D E F
○ ○ ○ ○ ○ ○

12. A B C D E F
○ ○ ○ ○ ○ ○

13. A B C D E F G H
○ ○ ○ ○ ○ ○ ○ ○

14. A B C D E
○ ○ ○ ○ ○

15. A B C D E F G H I
○ ○ ○ ○ ○ ○ ○ ○ ○

16. A B C D E F
○ ○ ○ ○ ○ ○

17. A B C D E F
○ ○ ○ ○ ○ ○

18. A B C D E F G H
○ ○ ○ ○ ○ ○ ○ ○

19. A B C D E F G H I J
○ ○ ○ ○ ○ ○ ○ ○ ○ ○

20. A B C D E F
○ ○ ○ ○ ○ ○

21. A B C D E
○ ○ ○ ○ ○

22. A B C D E F
○ ○ ○ ○ ○ ○

23. A B C D E F
○ ○ ○ ○ ○ ○

24. A B C D
○ ○ ○ ○

25. A B C D E F G
○ ○ ○ ○ ○ ○ ○

26. A B C D E F G H
○ ○ ○ ○ ○ ○ ○ ○

27. A B C D E
○ ○ ○ ○ ○

Mock Test 2 | Writing Task (Section 3) | Questions

YOU MUST COMPLETE ONLY <u>ONE</u> OF THE FOLLOWING TASKS

Each of the tasks consists of a statement in bold followed by three prompts. It is important that you address all three parts of your chosen task.

Task 1 - Rich individuals should not be able to buy better medical treatment.

Explain what you think is meant by the statement. Present a counter-argument. To what extent do you agree with the argument?

Task 2 - Life has a natural end, and doctors and healthcare professionals need to recognise that the point may come in the progression of a patient's condition where death is drawing near. - ***UK General Medical Council, Good Practice***

Explain what you think is meant by the statement. Present a strong argument to illustrate the above quote. To what extent do you agree with the argument?

Task 3 - In the next 15 years, biological sciences will be less useful in medicine compared to data sciences and software.

Explain what you think is meant by the statement. Present a counter-argument. To what extent do you agree with the argument?

Mock Test 3	Thinking Skills (Section1)	Questions

1. Cindy bought ingredients from Supermarket 'A' for a smoothie. She bought some bananas, strawberries and orange juice. The price for the bananas and the strawberries were in the ratio 4:3 and the cost of the orange juice was £2.50. The next week, she shopped in Supermarket 'B'. In this supermarket, the price of the bananas was 25% greater than in Supermarket 'A' and the price of the strawberries was 10% greater. The cost of the orange juice is halved.
If she had spent £6 in Supermarket 'A', how much did it cost her to buy the ingredients from Supermarket 'B'?
   A. £4.75
   B. £5.25
   C. £5.33
   D. £5.40
   E. £6.65

2. There are 6 chocolate bars in a packet with 2 different flavours - 3 caramel and 3 white chocolate. The chocolates are picked out of the packet until it is empty.
What is the probability that the 2 flavours will be picked out in an alternating sequence? (For example, caramel - white chocolate - caramel... or white chocolate - caramel - white chocolate...)
   A. $\frac{1}{10}$
   B. $\frac{2}{10}$
   C. $\frac{1}{20}$
   D. $\frac{2}{30}$
   E. $\frac{1}{35}$

3. Adolescence (the age between 10 and 24 years) is a period of life characterised by heightened sensitivity to social stimuli and the increased need for peer interaction. The physical distancing measures mandated globally to contain the spread of COVID-19 are radically reducing adolescents' opportunities to engage in face-to-face social contact outside their household. Studies have shown the importance of peer acceptance and peer influence during adolescence. Animal research has shown that social deprivation and isolation have unique effects on brain and behaviour in adolescence compared with other stages of life. However, the decrease in adolescent face-to-face contact might be less detrimental due to widespread access to digital forms of social interaction through technologies. The findings reviewed highlight how physical distancing might have a disproportionate effect on an age group for whom peer interaction is a vital aspect of development.

   Which of the following best expresses the main conclusion of the above argument?
   A. Physical distancing has been put in place due to the global pandemic.

B. Social distancing could have an effect on the development of adolescence, but the use of social media are reducing the negative impact that self-isolation could have as it provides a platform to allow communication.
C. Teenagers are more sensitive to social stimuli and need more peer interaction.
D. Peer interaction is a vital part of the development of teenagers.
E. Many adolescents are suffering from mental health issues due to a lack of face-to-face contact.

4. **Masks should be used as part of a comprehensive strategy of measures to suppress transmission and save lives; the use of a mask alone is not sufficient to provide an adequate level of protection against COVID-19. One should also maintain a minimum physical distance of at least one metre from others, frequently wash hands and avoid touching the face or the mask. Medical masks can protect people wearing the mask from getting infected, as well as can prevent those who have symptoms from spreading them.**

What is the main conclusion that can be drawn from this passage?
A. Masks will stop the spread of COVID-19.
B. The use of masks and social distancing is sufficient to prevent the spread of the virus.
C. Masks and social distancing provide increased protection from people getting infected and spreading the virus.
D. Everyone should wear a mask.
E. Medical masks are more effective than fabric masks.

5. **There are 150 rooms in a Holiday Inn Hotel. A family of five tries to book a room a week before their holiday. All the suite rooms are fully booked. Only 40 family rooms and a number of single rooms are available at the moment. The ratio of family to single rooms that are currently available is 4:7. What percentage of rooms in the hotel are available to book?**
A. 27%
B. 36%
C. 47%
D. 63%
E. 73%

6. **It takes three days for five builders to assemble and build a new kitchen in House A. The builders get recruited to build another kitchen in House B identical to the one they made in House A. However, two of the builders become ill and can't come to work. How much longer does it take to build the kitchen in House B compared to House A?**
A. 1 day
B. 2 days
C. 3 days
D. 4 days
E. 5 days

7. **Jatin and Maria are both feeling unwell. Jatin visits the GP surgery. He was prescribed some antibiotics as his GP said he has a bacterial infection. Jatin starts to feel better after a week. Maria thinks that she would feel better if she also got prescribed the same antibiotic. She decides to meet and request her GP to prescribe her antibiotics, since she has proof that Jatin is getting better.**
What is a flaw in the above argument?
A. The GP may not believe Maria that Jatin got better.

B. Maria assumes that she has the exact same illness as Jatin and, therefore, the antibiotics would work.
C. Maria and Jatin did not get sick at the same time; therefore, it could be that Maria's symptoms are only getting worse now, whereas Jatin has already passed this phase.
D. Maria should have visited her GP when Jatin did; as a result, she would have improved by now.
E. Maria and Jatin have different GP surgeons; therefore, they may not get prescribed the exact same medication.

8. A new test was introduced into the healthcare to test for patients with a particular disease. The sensitivity of a test is the proportion of true positives that are correctly identified. The new test is compared with the Gold Standard Test and the results are shown below:

		Gold Standard Test		
		Positive	Negative	Total
New Test	Positive	12	4	16
	Negative	6	24	30
	Total	18	28	46

What is the sensitivity of this test?

A. $\frac{1}{3}$
B. $\frac{2}{3}$
C. $\frac{1}{2}$
D. $\frac{6}{43}$
E. 3

9. All men above the age of 55 in a particular country are invited for a bowel screening test every 2 years. The patients at Iechyd Surgery are invited for their first screening at some point between their 55th and 57th birthday. Should they fail to show up for their appointment, reminders will be sent out to them every 4 months. Should a patient accept the invitation or the reminder, their screening appointment will be set exactly two weeks from the date of acceptance. Patients are invited for the next screening exactly 2 years after their previous screening. Mr Leblanc lives alone and manages his daily activities himself. Given that he always accepts the screening on the second reminder, at what age, in years, will he be able to receive his 5th screening earliest?

A. 63
B. 64
C. 65
D. 66
E. 67

10. Puppies should be trained from a young age if they are to become obedient and gentle dogs. They will learn more if they are trained early and if the owners often revisit the tricks that they have taught their puppies. The more training a puppy receives, he or she will be more obedient. This is because the dog will always follow instructions given by the owner.

What is a flaw in the above argument?

A. Dogs can be trained to become obedient even if they weren't trained as a puppy.
B. Some violent dogs were trained well when they were puppies.
C. Even if a dog received a lot of training as a puppy, it does not mean that he or she will always follow instructions and be gentle; the training may not have been successful.
D. Some dogs are inherently gentle without training.
E. Training a puppy early may not be possible if the owner only got the puppy after he or she is a couple of months old.

11. A local crisps company buys 10 kg of potatoes. When these potatoes are prepared and made into crisps, the final weight of the crisps is only half of that of the original weight of the potatoes. They divide these into packets where each packet is identical and contains 140 grams of crisps. The company decides to increase the number of packets that they sell; therefore, they decrease the content of the crisps in each packet by 15%. What is the weight of the crisps that is left over after the maximum number of crisp packets are filled?

A. 2 grams
B. 21 grams
C. 42 grams
D. 65 grams
E. 119 grams

12. A car rental company charges a base rate and a cost per mile. Travelling 30 miles would cost a customer £45. A customer travelling 70 miles would be charged £80. How much would it cost to travel 120 miles?

A. £105.00
B. £123.75
C. £137.14
D. £180.00
E. £190.00

13. All the students in a class who swim also play hockey, but not all of the hockey players swim. Some of the students who play hockey also play football. Not all the students in the class play hockey.

Which statement below is definitely true?

A. Some students in the class do not play any sports.
B. Some students only play hockey.
C. Some students in the class do at least two sports.
D. Some students only play football.
E. Some students in the class play all three sports.

14. The new machines that were bought by the factory are much more efficient and makes fewer mistakes compared to the workers there. The company would save a lot of money by replacing their workers with the machines. This will increase their profits.

Which one of the following statements weakens the argument?

A. The workers can do a variety of different jobs that the machines cannot.
B. The initial cost of the machines is extremely high. Therefore, replacing all the workers will not be cost-effective.
C. The machines are much faster than the workers.
D. The machines will break down more often than the workers taking sick leave.
E. The quality of the work done by the machines is poorer compared to the workers.

15. **Wesley believes involving pupils in more extracurricular activities such as playing a musical instrument or being a part of a sports team will improve their concentration in class. He believes that this will then lead to better examination grades. He states that schools that involve more extracurricular activities into the timetable have shown better examination results and higher pass rates.**
    Which one of the following statements is an underlying assumption of the argument above?
    A. Pupils who are involved in too many extracurricular activities may not have enough time to study.
    B. Examination results and pass rates are a reliable method of determining how well the pupils concentrate.
    C. Pupils who take part in more extracurricular activities tend to be the students who concentrate better in class.
    D. Extracurricular activities help the pupils relax and allows them to focus more.
    E. Not all schools can afford to include many extracurricular activities in their timetable.

16. **Clara downloaded two new apps on her phone. The first app runs in the background and uses up 1.5% of her battery from full charge (100%) every half an hour. The second app uses 20% of the total the first app uses in a whole day (24 hours). Clara fully charges her phone in the morning. What percentage of battery life will her phone have exactly at the same time the next day, if she does not recharge her phone? Assume that the battery life consumed by other apps on her phone is negligible.**
    A. 0.0%
    B. 13.6%
    C. 28.0%
    D. 85.6%
    E. 86.4%

17. **Two different flavours of popcorn - salted and caramel - are sold at the cinema. These have already been arranged into packets. At the end of the day, the ratio of salted to caramel is 15:17. The number of packets of salted popcorn decreased by 25% from the start of the day and there were half the number of packets of caramel flavoured popcorn compared to the start of the day. What was the ratio of salted to caramel flavoured popcorn at the start of the day?**
    A. 17:30
    B. 30:17
    C. 10:17
    D. 17:10
    E. 17:40

18. **There are three different biscuits in a tin - digestives, custard cream and shortbreads. A third of the biscuits are custard cream. There are twice as many digestives as there are shortbreads. What is the minimum number of custard cream biscuits in the tin?**
    A. 1
    B. 2
    C. 3
    D. 4
    E. 9

19. **Due to high competition, the physics teachers at a particular school require a PhD qualification in order to be recruited. Therefore, teachers without a PhD should not apply for a job at this school.**

What is the flaw in the above argument?

A. Some teachers without a PhD are better at teaching than those with a PhD.
B. It assumes that a PhD is sufficient to be recruited as a physics teacher.
C. It generalises the requirements for the physics teacher for all teachers.
D. Many teachers at the school do not have a PhD.
E. All of the applicants for the job have a PhD.

20. In 1651, English philosopher Thomas Hobbes startled the world with Leviathan, an account of the good and evil lurking in human nature. Hobbes argued that people, when left to their own devices, were naturally vicious. Fortunately, they were also gregarious, and it was through their groups, societies and civilisations that people expressed their best selves.

What is the assumption of this passage?

A. Being sociable creatures is what has prevented humans from becoming uncivilised and unable to live in as a society.
B. Laws and rules have prevented humans from becoming vicious.
C. If rules didn't exist in society, there would be chaos.
D. Humans who show vicious behaviours, such as committing murder, are punished by the society.
E. Humans have a naturally tendency to become violent.

21. Soap bubbles that deliver pollen to flowers could offer an alternative way of fertilising plants as bee populations decline, while being more delicate than other methods. There is a lot of interest in developing new approaches to fertilise flowers, because about 90 percent of flowering plants depend on insect pollinators, such as bees, whose populations are falling due to climate change and pesticide use.

What is the conclusion of this passage?

A. Soap bubbles delivering pollen seems to be a promising method to fertilise flowers in the future as bee populations decline.
B. Pesticide use should be reduced to prevent the decrease in the bee population.
C. Other methods of pollination are harsher.
D. Insect pollinators are essential for fertilising flowers.
E. Pesticide use is threatening to the insect population.

22. In a supermarket, all fruits are imported, and all imported items are expensive. Most of the vegetables are also imported.

Which one amongst the following statements is true?

A. Every expensive item in the shop is imported.
B. None of the vegetables are expensive.
C. A food item is not a fruit unless it is imported.
D. Some fruits are expensive.
E. If a vegetable is grown locally, it is sold at a low price.

23. In a bag of marbles, a third of the marbles are removed every minute for four minutes. At the end of the fourth minute, there are 32 marbles left.

How many marbles were in the bag at the beginning?

A. 48
B. 81
C. 96
D. 162
E. 192

24. Lola has a drawer full of scarves; she has many scarves of each colour. The colours she has are red, blue, green, pink, grey, black and white. If she takes out a scarf at random each day for a week, how many different ways can she pick her scarves out of her drawer so that she does not wear the same colour on consecutive days?

A. 720

B. 5040

C. 279,936

D. 326,592

E. 823,543

---

25. To become a successful music teacher, one requires a natural talent, dedication to his/her work and patience. Layla is a very talented singer and has always been hardworking and dedicated to her work. She has also demonstrated a lot of patience during her training. Therefore, she would be a successful music teacher.

What is a flaw in the above argument?

A. It does not mention how long Layla has been training.

B. It only mentions Layla has a talent in singing but not any other musical talents.

C. It assumes Layla wants to become a music teacher.

D. It assumes that all music teachers require a natural talent.

E. It only states what is necessary to become a music teacher; this does not mean that these factors are sufficient.

---

26. A fruit was weighed on three different weighing scales. Each of these weighing scales has an accuracy that is 4 grams above or below the weight they read. The three scales read 99 grams, 102 grams, and 101 grams.

What is the minimum range of the actual weight of the fruit?

A. 95 g - 101 g

B. 96 g - 106 g

C. 97 g - 101 g

D. 98 g - 103 g

E. 99 g - 102 g

---

27. There are five pirates of different levels of seniority. The oldest pirate is given the priority to distribute 100 gold coins amongst the five pirates including himself. After the oldest pirate has announced his allocation, all the pirates (including the most senior pirate) will vote to accept or reject the allocation. If 50% or more of the pirates agree to the allocation, then the allocation is accepted. This means that a tie (e.g., a 2-2 vote) is enough to pass the allocation. If less than 50% of the pirates agree, the oldest pirate is killed, and the 100 gold coins are passed to the second oldest pirate. If the second oldest pirate is killed, the gold coins will be passed to the third oldest pirate, and so on.

Assuming that all five pirates are rational but greedy, what is the maximum number of coins the oldest pirate can get?

A. 99 coins

B. 98 coins

C. 97 coins

D. 35 coins

E. 34 coins

28. A company produces newspapers, all of which have a number of pages which is a multiple of 24. A newspaper can have 24, 48, 72, ... pages. The front cover is always counted as page 1. The centre of the newspapers could have pages numbered as:
    A. 13 and 14
    B. 23 and 24
    C. 46 and 37
    D. 71 and 72
    E. 96 and 97

29. Mr Bebb and his daughter, Mari, live in a small town near Cardiff. The town is a car ride away from Mari's school. Every Wednesday, Mr Bebb consistently leaves his house at a particular time to drive, at a constant speed, to Mari's school to pick her up at exactly 4:30 pm when her student council meetings end. Immediately, Mr Bebb and Mari return home together at the same constant speed Mr Bebb had initially driven. One day, Mari did not feel well and decided to leave her meeting early to go home on foot. Mari had been walking for 30 minutes - on the same route her father drives - when she bumped into her father. Mr Bebb picked her up where they met, and they arrived home 20 minutes earlier than they usually do. How early did Mari leave her student council meeting?
    A. 20 minutes
    B. 30 minutes
    C. 40 minutes
    D. 50 minutes
    E. 60 minutes

30. Judith and her now-deceased husband have been together since they were teenagers. On her 20th birthday and every decade after, her husband gets her a short chain, each made of five gold links. Judith, who recently celebrated her 70th birthday alone, found out that her husband had prepared for her one last chain for this birthday. She realises that if she combines all of them into one big loop of 30 links, she would get a necklace. She brings it into a jeweller, who tells her that the cost of making the necklace will be £5 for each link that is broken and then resealed.
    What is the minimum cost Judith would need to pay to the jeweller?
    A. £20
    B. £25
    C. £30
    D. £35
    E. £40

31. A total of 500 sweets are divided amongst six children. No two children have the same number of sweets, and each has at least 30 sweets.
    What is the greatest number of sweets the child with the third highest number of sweets can have?
    A. 85
    B. 133
    C. 134
    D. 135
    E. 136

32. Divansh is at the bank and he is waiting at the sitting area for his number to be called. When a number is called, it also appears on a board which displays the numbers in their common digital form. He quickly notices that the number in the unit place (last digit) does not

correspond to the number called by the system as some of the light elements are faulty. If the board is currently showing the number '4501', what are the possible numbers that can be called out by the system?

A. 4501, 4503, 4504, 4505, 4507, 4508
B. 4500, 4503, 4504, 4507, 4508, 4509
C. 4500, 4503, 4504, 4505, 4507, 4508, 4509
D. 4500, 4501, 4503, 4504, 4507, 4508, 4509
E. 4501, 4502, 4504, 4505, 4506, 4507, 4508, 450

Mock Test 3 | Thinking Skills (Section 1) | Answer Sheet

BioMedical Aptitude Test

SECTION 1 Thinking Skills

BMAT candidate number

B					

Centre number

Fill in the appropriate circle for your chosen answer e.g.

A B C D E
○●○○○

Use a soft pencil. If you make a mistake, erase thoroughly and try again.

Date of birth (DD MM YYYY)

First name (s)

Surname / Family name

1.	A ○	B ○	C ○	D ○	E ○
2.	A ○	B ○	C ○	D ○	E ○
3.	A ○	B ○	C ○	D ○	E ○
4.	A ○	B ○	C ○	D ○	E ○
5.	A ○	B ○	C ○	D ○	E ○
6.	A ○	B ○	C ○	D ○	E ○
7.	A ○	B ○	C ○	D ○	E ○
8.	A ○	B ○	C ○	D ○	E ○
9.	A ○	B ○	C ○	D ○	E ○
10.	A ○	B ○	C ○	D ○	E ○
11.	A ○	B ○	C ○	D ○	E ○
12.	A ○	B ○	C ○	D ○	E ○
13.	A ○	B ○	C ○	D ○	E ○
14.	A ○	B ○	C ○	D ○	E ○
15.	A ○	B ○	C ○	D ○	E ○
16.	A ○	B ○	C ○	D ○	E ○
17.	A ○	B ○	C ○	D ○	E ○
18.	A ○	B ○	C ○	D ○	E ○
19.	A ○	B ○	C ○	D ○	E ○
20.	A ○	B ○	C ○	D ○	E ○
21.	A ○	B ○	C ○	D ○	E ○
22.	A ○	B ○	C ○	D ○	E ○
23	A ○	B ○	C ○	D ○	E ○
24	A ○	B ○	C ○	D ○	E ○
25	A ○	B ○	C ○	D ○	E ○
26	A ○	B ○	C ○	D ○	E ○
27	A ○	B ○	C ○	D ○	E ○
28.	A ○	B ○	C ○	D ○	E ○
29.	A ○	B ○	C ○	D ○	E ○
30.	A ○	B ○	C ○	D ○	E ○
31.	A ○	B ○	C ○	D ○	E ○
32.	A ○	B ○	C ○	D ○	E ○

Mock Test 3	Scientific Knowledge and Applications (Section 2)	Questions

1. Identify the vessels shown below.

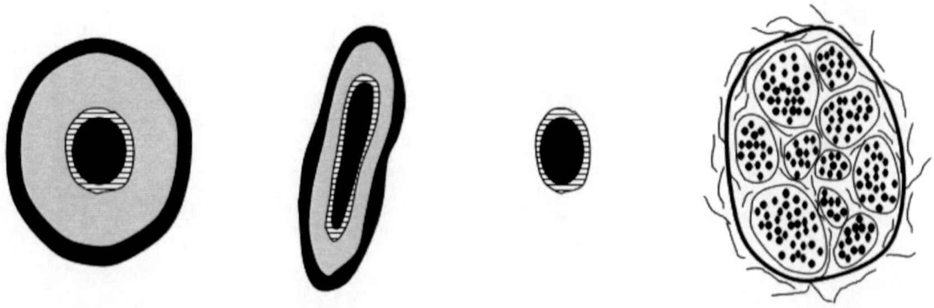

1 2 3 4

	1	2	3	4
A	Artery	Vein	Capillary	Nerve
B	Nerve	Artery	Vein	Capillary
C	Vein	Capillary	Nerve	Artery
D	Capillary	Vein	Artery	Nerve
E	Vein	Artery	Capillary	Nerve

2. What are the half equations at the anode and cathode in the electrolysis of $NaOH_{(aq)}$?

	Anode	Cathode
A	$4OH^- - 4e^- \rightarrow 2H_2O + O_2$	$Na^+ + e^- \rightarrow Na$
B	$2H^+ + 2e^- \rightarrow H_2$	$4OH^- - 4e^- \rightarrow 2H_2O + O_2$
C	$4OH^- - 4e^- \rightarrow 2H_2O + O_2$	$2H^+ + 2e^- \rightarrow H_2$
D	$Na^+ + e \rightarrow Na$	$4OH^- - 4e^- \rightarrow 2H_2O + O_2$
E	$4OH^- \rightarrow 2H_2O + O_2 + 4e^-$	$Na^+ + e^- \rightarrow Na$

3. Which amongst the following statement(s) regarding microwaves is/are correct?

1. Microwave ovens use shorter wavelengths of microwaves than mobile phones.
2. Microwaves show a lot of diffraction.
3. Microwaves can penetrate glass and shiny metal surfaces.
4. Microwaves can cause body tissue to burn.

A. 1 only
B. 2 only
C. 3 only
D. 4 only
E. 1 and 2 only
F. 1 and 3 only
G. 1 and 4 only
H. 1, 2 and 3 only
I. 1, 2 and 4 only
J. 2, 3 and 4 only

Mock Test

4. At the instant the ball is kicked, the velocity of the ball is 'v' and it is inclined at θ degrees from the horizontal.

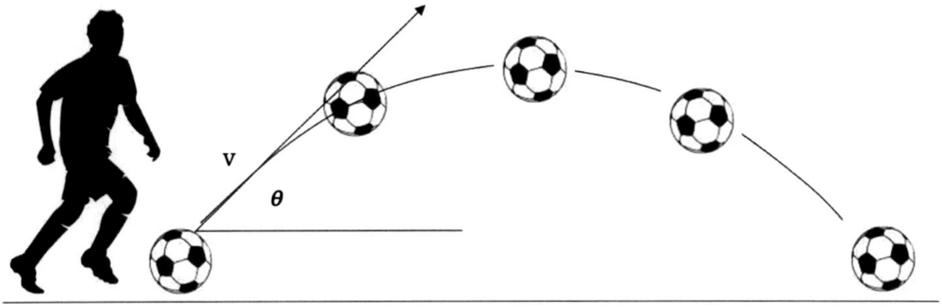

Which of the options below represents the horizontal component of the velocity?

A. v

B. v sinθ

C. v cosθ

D. 0

E. $\frac{v^2}{2}$

5. Vitamin D-resistant rickets is a human X –linked dominant disorder. This is not lethal. Individuals 1 and 2 have a son and a daughter. What is the probability that their children have the disorder?

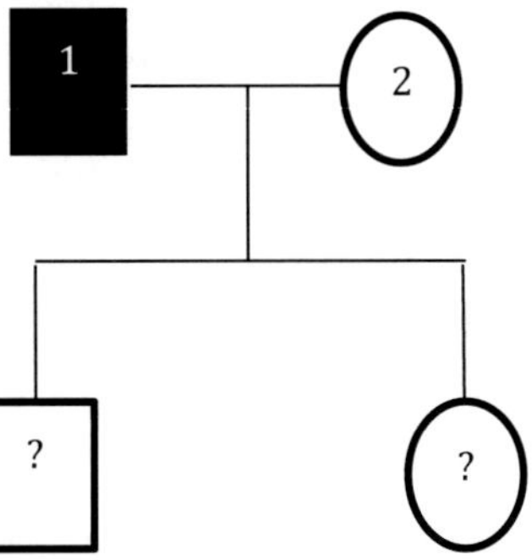

	Daughter	Son
A	0%	100%
B	25%	75%
C	50%	75%
D	100%	0%
E	25%	25%
F	50%	25%
G	50%	50%
H	100%	25%

6. The graph below shows the volume of carbon dioxide produced as limestone reacts with hydrochloric acid.

$$CaCO_3 + 2HCl \rightarrow CaCl_2 + CO_2 + H_2O$$

A Lakshmi, T R Enoch, S Z Y Ooi. Doctors Academy Publications, Cardiff, UK, 2020.

An excess of powdered limestone and 100cm^3 of 0.2moldm^{-3} of hydrochloric acid was used in Reaction 1. The temperature was kept constant at 25°C. An excess of limestone was also used for Reaction 2.

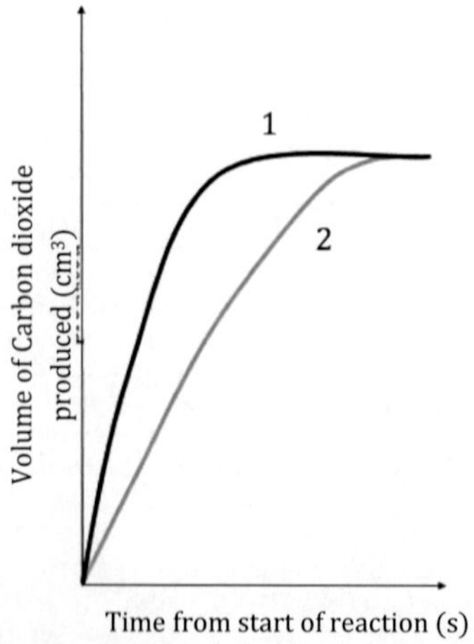

Which line in the table represents the conditions used for Reaction 2?

	Limestone particle size	Temperature (°C)	Volume of hydrochloric acid (cm^3)	Concentration of hydrochloric acid (moldm^{-3})
A	Granules	25	200	0.3
B	Granules	25	200	0.1
C	Granules	30	100	0.4
D	Powdered	25	100	0.2
E	Powdered	30	200	0.2
F	Powdered	25	100	0.4

7. **Harry and Kate walk in a park. Harry walks at a constant speed and Kate walks at a constant velocity.**
   Which of the three diagrams shown below are the potential paths that Harry and Kate could have walked?

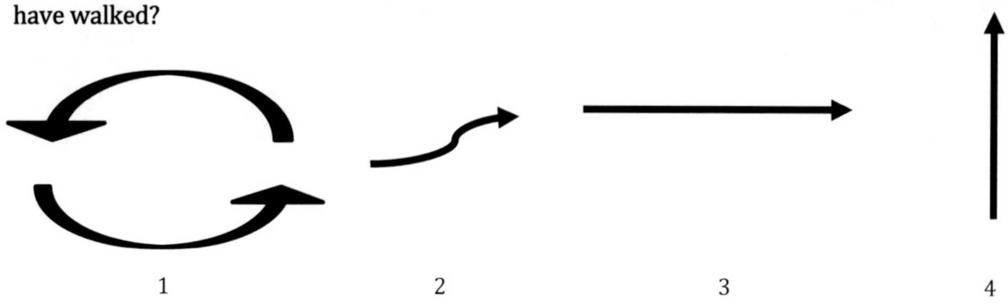

	Harry	Kate
A	1 and 2 only	3 and 4 only
B	3 and 4 only	1 and 2 only
C	2, 3 and 4 only	3 and 4 only
D	1, 2, 3 and 4	2, 3 and 4 only
E	1, 2, 3 and 4	3 and 4 only
F	2 only	1, 2, 3 and 4

Mock Test

8. **A company makes two different sized candles. The candles are similar in shape. The large candle is 7.5 cm tall and the small candle is 5 cm tall.**

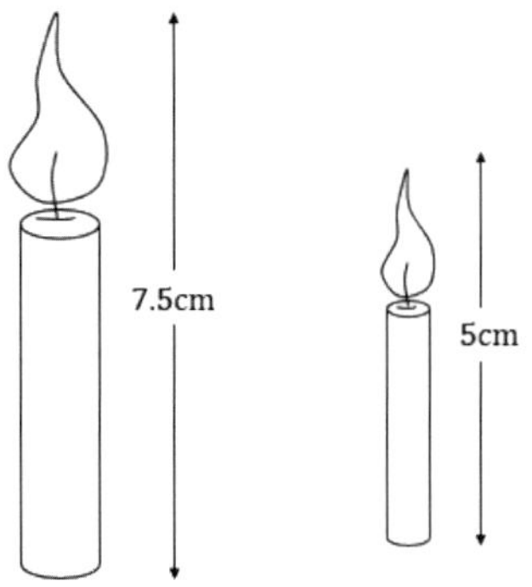

Exactly 200 grams of wax is needed to make the small candle. How much wax is needed to make the larger candle?

A. 59 grams
B. 89 grams
C. 133 grams
D. 300 grams
E. 450 grams
F. 675 grams

9. **Which option correctly identifies the pH of arterial and venous blood?**

	Arterial blood	Venous Blood
A	7.35	7.95
B	6.25	7.40
C	7.95	6.25
D	7.40	7.35
E	7.35	7.40

10. **Ammonia reacts with NaClO to form hydrazine (N2H4), water and a salt. Which of the following statements about this reaction is true?**

1. N is reduced from -2 to -3
2. N is oxidised from -2 to -3
3. N is reduced from -3 to -2
4. N is oxidised from -3 to -2
5. Cl is reduced from +1 to -1
6. Cl is oxidised from +1 to -1
7. Cl is reduced from -1 to +1
8. Cl is oxidised from -1 to +1

A. 1 and 6 only
B. 2 and 5 only
C. 3 and 8 only
D. 4 and 7 only
E. 1 and 8 only
F. 2 and 7 only
G. 3 and 6 only
H. 4 and 5 only

11. A bike accelerates uniformly from rest to a speed of 25 ms^{-1} in a minute. What is the distance travelled in this time?

A. 12.5 m

B. 25 m

C. 240 m

D. 750 m

E. 1500 m

12. Consider the two circles below with centre E and G.

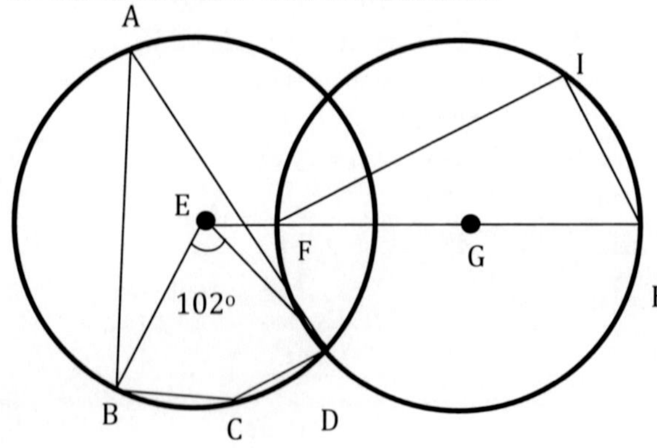

What is the size of the angles BCD and HIF?

	BCD	HIF
A	51°	90°
B	102°	85°
C	258°	90°
D	129°	90°
E	78°	85°

13. Which enzyme is used in the production of milk for those who are intolerant to dairy products?

A. Sucrose

B. Maltose

C. Sucrase

D. Protease

E. Lipase

F. Lactase

G. Ligase

H. Lactose

I. Maltase

14. Silicon has 3 isotopes: ^{28}Si, ^{29}Si, ^{30}Si found in the ratio 18:1:1. Calculate the relative atomic mass of silicon.

A. 28.00

B. 28.15

C. 28.45

D. 28.65

E. 29.00

15. **The table below shows the resistance across four different wires.**

Wire	Resistance in ohms
L	6
M	3
N	6
O	3

Which one amongst the following statements is most likely to explain the different resistances given above?

A. Wire 'L' has the same thickness as 'M'; however, it is shorter.
B. Wire 'L' has the same thickness as 'N'; however, it is shorter.
C. Wire 'L' has the same length as 'M'; however, it is thinner.
D. Wire 'L' has the same length as 'N'; however, it is thicker.
E. Wire 'O' has the same length and thickness as wire 'L'.
F. Wire 'O' has the same length and thickness as wire 'N'.

16. **Find the value of 'm' if $3^{m+2} = 27^{m-6}$:**

A. 6
B. 7
C. 8
D. 9
E. 10
F. 11
G. 12
H. 13

17. **An experiment was conducted to measure the loss of water from the leaves of a plant. A plant is placed in a beaker full of water. The beaker is placed on a balance to measure the change in mass. A layer of oil is put on the surface of the water to prevent it from evaporating from the beaker.**

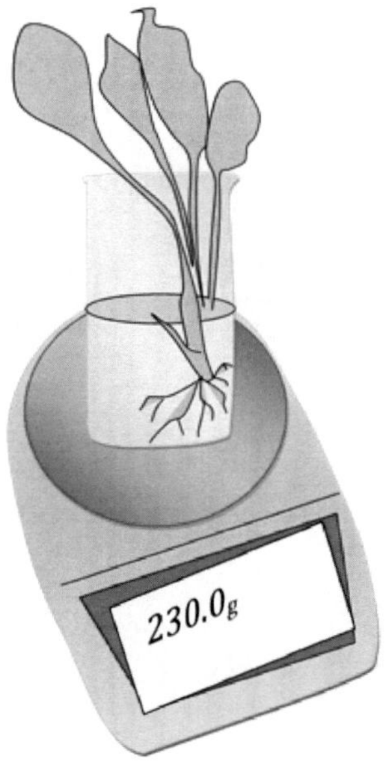

Which of following graphs show the change in mass when the experiment is conducted in a dark room?

A.

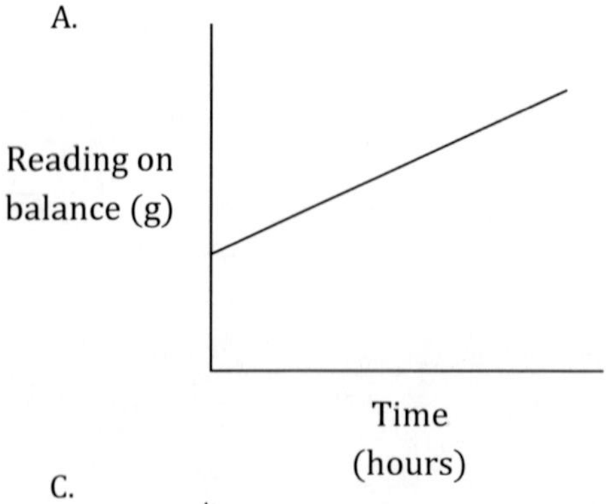

B.

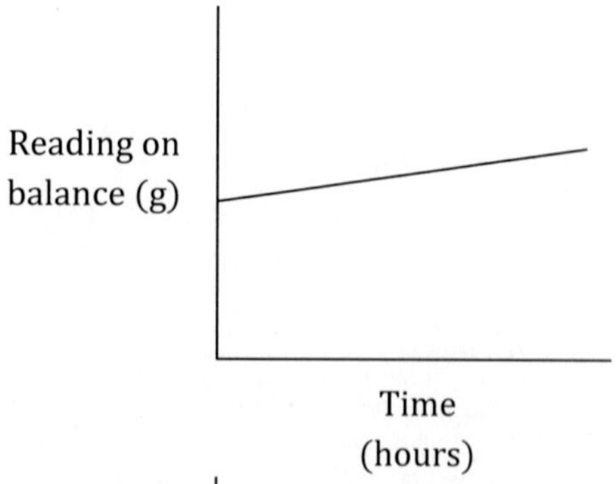

C.

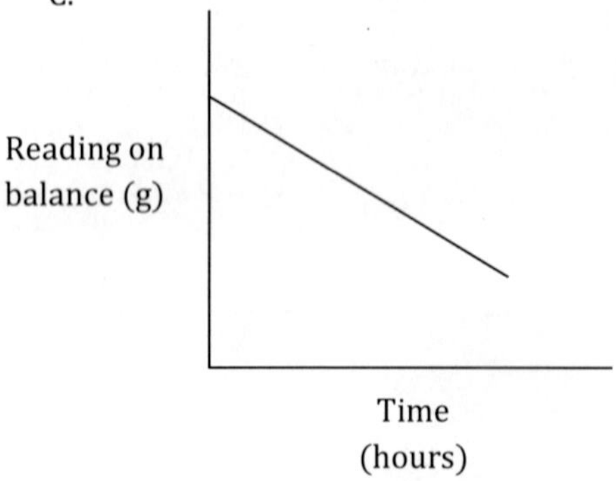

D.

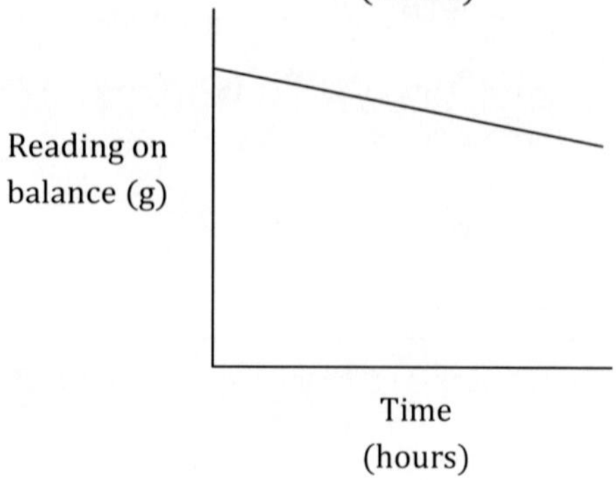

E.

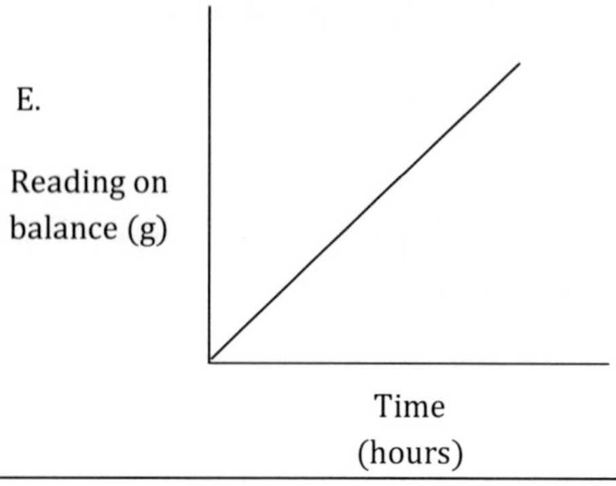

18. Lead nitrate reacts with sodium iodide.

Which of the following is/are the spectator ion(s) in this reaction?

1. Lead ions
2. Nitrate ions
3. Sodium ions
4. Iodide ions

A. 1 only
B. 2 only
C. 3 only

D. 4 only
E. 1 and 2 only
F. 1 and 3 only
G. 1 and 4 only
H. 2 and 3 only
I. 2 and 4 only
J. 3 and 4 only

19. Albert and Celine climb a mountain together. The table below shows the information about their climb. (g = 10 N/kg)

Name	Mass (kg)	Height climbed (m)	Time taken to climb (s)
Albert	70	6.0	150
Celina	60	9.0	180

What is the difference in the power exhibited by Albert and Celina?

A. 0.2 watts
B. 2 watts
C. 5 watts
D. 550 watts
E. 5500 watts

20. Which one of the following is a simplification of $\frac{63p^2q^5}{45p^7q^3}$?

A. $\frac{7}{5}p^{\frac{2}{7}}q^{\frac{5}{3}}$
B. $\frac{7}{5}p^5q^{-2}$
C. $\frac{7}{5}p^{-5}q^2$
D. $\frac{5}{7}p^{-5}q^2$
E. $\frac{5}{7}\ p^5q^{-2}$
F. $\frac{5}{7}\ p^{-1}q^{-2}$

21. Ruby needs a blood transfusion. Her blood group is A negative. The details of some blood available in the hospital are shown below.

Donor	ABO blood group system	Rh blood group system
1	A	+
2	AB	-
3	O	+
4	B	+
5	A	-
6	O	-
7	B	-

Who can she receive blood from?

A. 5 only
B. 1 and 5 only
C. 3 and 5 only
D. 5 and 6 only

Mock Test

E. 3 and 6 only
F. 4 and 7 only
G. 1, 2 and 5 only
H. 1, 3, 5 and 6 only
I. Anyone

22. Which of the following options below shows part of the structure formed by the polymerisation of $H_3C - H_2C - HC = CH - CH_2 - CH_3$?

A.
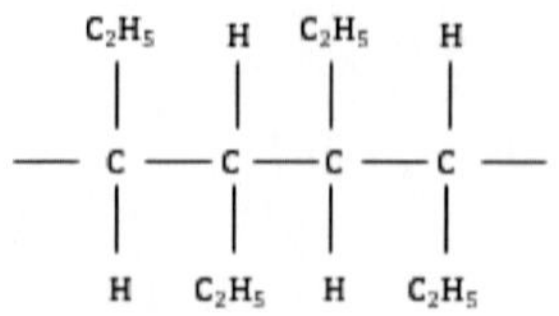

B.
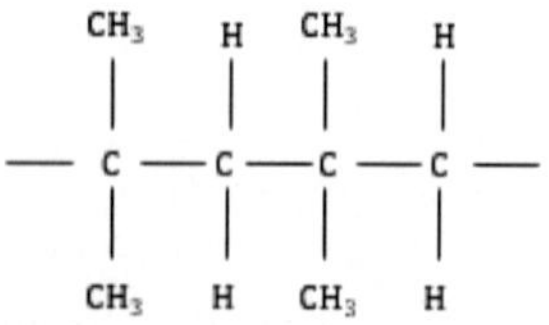

C.
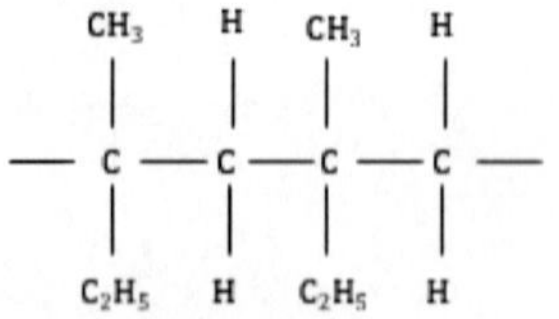

D.
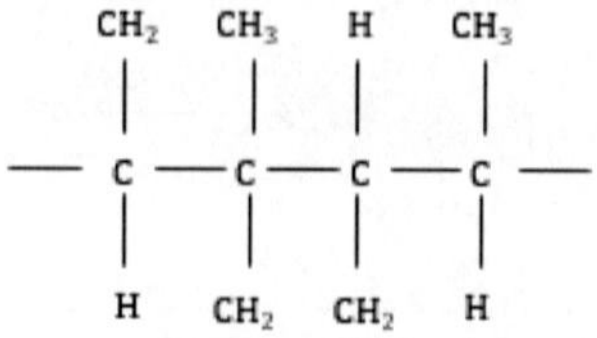

E.
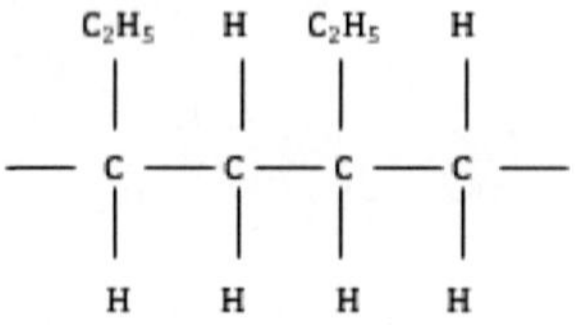

F.
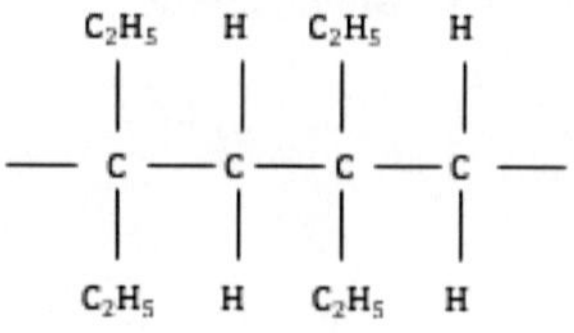

23. Taksh is running a race. When the race begins, he gradually increases his speed. The graph below shows his speed.

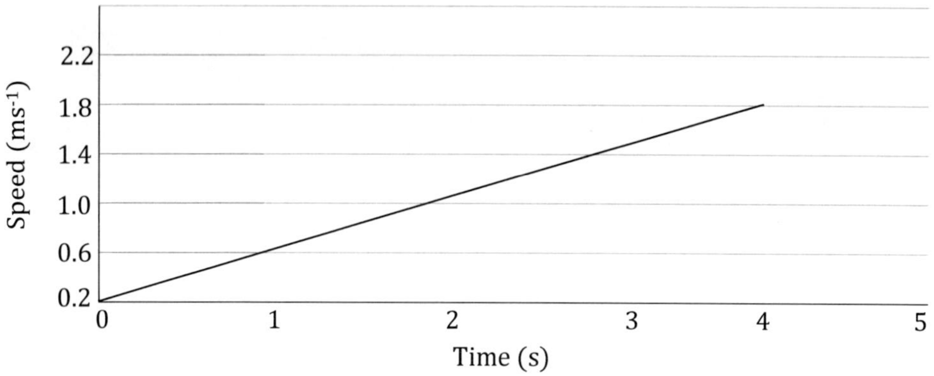

What is the distance travelled in the first 4 seconds given that the acceleration was constant?

A. 2.8 m
B. 3.2 m
C. 3.6 m
D. 5.6 m
E. 6.4 m
F. 7.2 m

Mock Test

24. Of the 30 pupils in a class, 12 play a musical instrument. Of those who do play a musical instrument, 8 are girls. The probability of being a boy, given that he does not play a musical instrument is $\frac{2}{3}$. Find the probability of a girl in this class playing a musical instrument.
   A. $\frac{3}{7}$
   B. $\frac{4}{7}$
   C. $\frac{2}{3}$
   D. $\frac{1}{15}$
   E. $\frac{4}{15}$

25. Which bacteria is used to convert nitrates to nitrogen gas?
   A. Nitrifying bacteria
   B. Nitrogen-fixing bacteria
   C. Denitrifying bacteria
   D. Nitrosomonas
   E. Nitrobacter

26. Compound X is shown below.

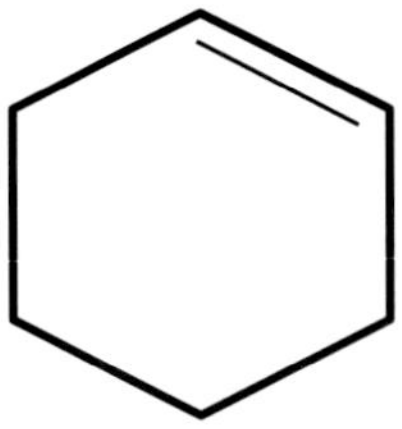

What is the molecule formed when steam is added to this compound using a phosphoric acid catalyst?

A.
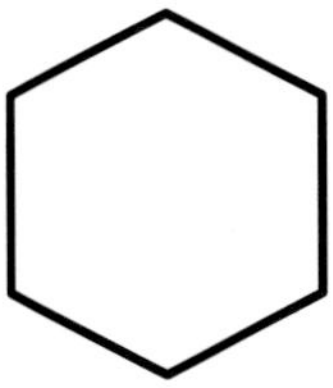

B.
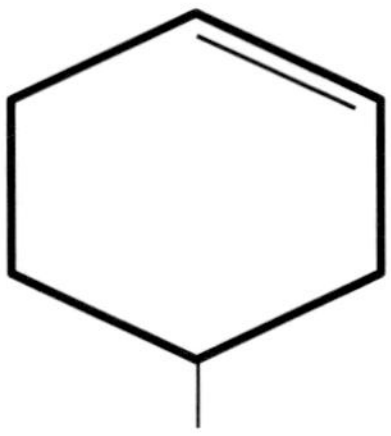

C.
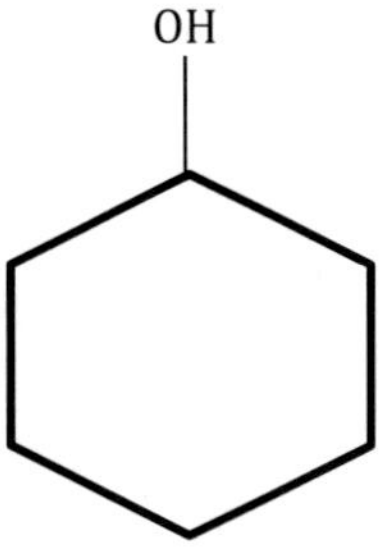

D.
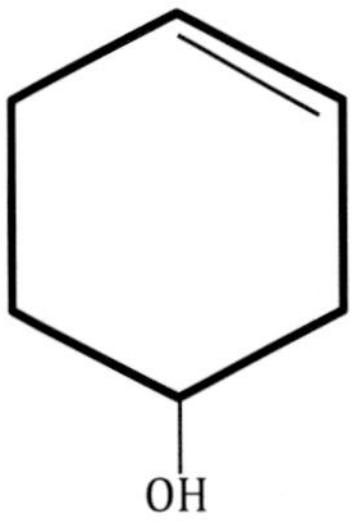

E.
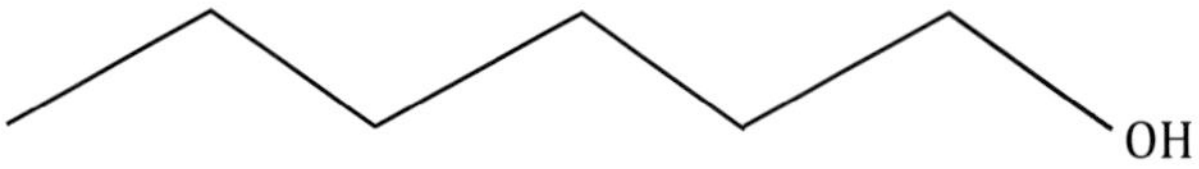

27. **The table below shows the count rate of a radioisotope.**

Time (hours)	0	6	12	18	24
Count rate (counts per minute)	5600	2600	700	250	90

Calculate the half-life of the isotope.

A. 3 hours
B. 4 hours
C. 6 hours
D. 8 hours
E. 12 hours
F. 14 hours

Mock Test 3 | Scientific Knowledge and Applications (Section 2) | Mark Sheet

BioMedical Aptitude Test

SECTION 2 Scientific Knowledge and Applications

BMAT candidate number: B

Centre number

Date of birth (DD MM YYYY)

First name (s)

Surname / Family name

Fill in the appropriate circle for your chosen answer e.g.

A B C D E
○●○○○

Use a soft pencil. If you make a mistake, erase thoroughly and try again.

1. A B C D E
2. A B C D E
3. A B C D E F G H I J
4. A B C D E
5. A B C D E F G H
6. A B C D E F
7. A B C D E F
8. A B C D E F
9. A B C D E
10. A B C D E F G H
11. A B C D E
12. A B C D E
13. A B C D E F G H
14. A B C D E
15. A B C D E F
16. A B C D E F G H
17. A B C D E
18. A B C D E F G H I J
19. A B C D E
20. A B C D E F
21. A B C D E F G H I
22. A B C D E F
23. A B C D E F
24. A B C D E
25. A B C D E
26. A B C D E
27. A B C D E F

Mock Test 3 | Writing Task (Section 3) | Questions

YOU MUST COMPLETE ONLY ONE OF THE FOLLOWING TASKS

Each of the tasks consists of a statement in bold followed by three prompts. It is important that you address all three parts of your chosen task.

Task 1 - Patients should be encouraged to diagnose and possibly treat themselves.

Argue to the contrary of this statement. What are the benefits of reading publications regarding health? How must a doctor communicate with a patient who has been misinformed by an unreliable source?

Task 2 - Medicine is a science and not an art.

What do you think is meant by this statement? Argue to the contrary. To what extent do you agree with the statement?

Task 3 - Science is the great antidote to the poison of enthusiasm and superstition - ***Adam Smith, The Wealth of Nations, 1776***

Explain the reasoning behind this statement. Argue to the contrary that enthusiasm and superstition is required for the advancement of science. To what extent do you agree with the argument?

Mock Test 1	Thinking Skills (Section 1)	Answers

Question	Answer
1.	E
2.	C
3.	E
4.	E
5.	C
6.	D
7.	C
8.	B
9.	A
10.	C
11.	C
12.	C
13.	B
14.	B
15.	C
16.	E
17.	D
18.	A
19.	D
20.	B
21.	A
22.	E
23.	E
24.	D
25.	B
26.	D
27.	C
28.	D
29.	D
30.	A
31.	C
32.	B

1. E

Explanation:
A circular clock always contains 360°.
Since there are 60 minutes on a clock, a minute hand moves 6° a minute:
= **<u>6° a minute</u>**
Since there are 12 hours on a clock, an hour hands moves 30° an hour:
= **<u>30° an hour</u>**
The hour hand is between 10 and 11, because it is not an absolute hour mark.

Between 10 and the hour hand, the angle is: $\frac{25}{60} = \frac{5}{12}$ **of an hour**; $\frac{5}{12}$ x 30 = <u>12.5°</u>

Between 10 and 5, there are <u>5 hours difference</u>; 5 hours: 30° x 5 = <u>150°</u>

Therefore, 150 + 12.5 = <u>162.5°</u>

Since there are 360° in a circle, the largest angle will be: 360 - 162.5 = <u>197.5°</u>

2. C

Explanation:

<u>Conclusion</u> - This new mathematical model provides the most accurate time of death by estimating the temperature change of the body since death, which can be used to calculate the elapsed time.

<u>Evidence</u> - The team of scientists found that the mathematical model, which used skin temperature data from 8 human corpses, was within 38 minutes of the true time elapsed since death, whereas the standard method gives estimates within 3 to 7 hours for the post-mortem interval.

The assumption links the evidence to the conclusion. Since the conclusion and evidence states that the mathematical model relies on skin temperature in order to predict an accurate time of death, <u>Option 'C'</u> is the correct answer. <u>Option 'A'</u> is incorrect because it is stated in the passage - it cannot be an assumption. <u>Option 'D'</u> generalises that skin temperature is the <u>only</u> form of data used. <u>Option 'E'</u> is not supported by the passage - the new mathematical model may be able to predict closer to the true time in further studies.

3. E

Explanation:

Since the average of the eight chocolate bars is £1.50:

The sum of all eight chocolate bars: 8 x £1.50 = <u>£12</u>

In order to calculate the maximum possible value for the most expensive chocolate bar, assume that 7 bars were priced at 50 pence as well.

50 pence x 7 = <u>£3.50</u>

Therefore, the maximum price of the eighth chocolate bar: £12 - £3.50 = <u>£8.50</u>

4. E

Explanation:

<u>Conclusion</u> - Nanomedicine is going to have a tremendous impact on health care and the practice of clinical medicine.

<u>Evidence</u> - Many other subfields have advanced by recent developments in nanomedicine, including tissue engineering, regenerative medicine, medical devices, and vaccines.

Therefore, the conclusion is best stated in <u>Option 'E'</u>. <u>Option 'A'</u> is incorrect because it generalises that <u>all</u> nanoparticles can convert photons into thermal energy for targeted photothermal therapy, when the passage only states that gold nanomaterials can do it. <u>Option 'B'</u> is also factually inaccurate (the passage states that 'magnetic nanoparticles are also attractive for their ability to mediate heat induction') - it does not mention electricity induction. <u>Option 'C'</u> is incorrect because it generalises that <u>only</u> tissue engineering, regenerative medicine, medical devices, and vaccines rely on nanomedicine - this is not supported by the passage. <u>Option 'D'</u> is not supported by the passage - it is not stated that any other therapeutics can also act as drug carriers.

5. C

Explanation:

<u>Conclusion</u> - Preventing obesity by maintaining a healthy weight will reduce the risk of developing certain diseases and its associated complications.

Evidence - If a person is overweight or obese, it can increase his/her risk of developing a number of complications, including metabolic syndrome, arthritis and certain types of cancer.

Therefore, **Option 'C'** is correct because it expresses the main conclusion of the passage. **Option 'A'** is an overgeneralising assertion (all individuals with a BMI between 25 and 29.9 are overweight) – it is incorrect. **Option 'B'** is incorrect because it does not illustrate the main conclusion of the passage. **Option 'D'** is incorrect since it is also a generalisation that all individuals can prevent obesity through a balanced diet. **Option 'E'** is not explicitly mentioned in the passage – it can be eliminated.

6. D

Explanation:

Conclusion - It can be concluded that Johnny suffered from Salmonella in the period of time specified above.

Evidence - The typical symptoms of Salmonella include diarrhoea, fever and stomach cramps.

A flaw is a statement that proves that the conclusion does not lead on from the evidence. The best example of this is **'Option D'**, which indicates that the symptoms common with Salmonella are also common with many other infections - it cannot be proven that Johnny definitely had Salmonella. **'Option A'** is incorrect because it implies that all individuals who have Salmonella must have had all three symptoms - this is not stated in the passage. **Options 'B', 'C' and 'E'** are not relevant to the passage and, therefore, are not flaws in the argument.

7. C

Explanation:

Assume there are 100 cars.

Out of these 100 cars, 60 would function normally and 40 would be faulty.

Consider the 60 normal cars: 10% of 60 = **6 are mistaken for being faulty and rejected**

Therefore, **54 are sold**.

Consider the 40 faulty cars:

85% of 40 = **34 are rejected**. Therefore, **6 are sold in error.**

As a result, there would be: 54 good cars and 6 faulty cars.

The proportion of faulty cars sold is: $\frac{6}{60}$, which is **0.1%.**

8. B

Explanation:

The annual cost at the tennis club is £30 x 6 = **£180**

The number of classes attended at the sports centre where the annual cost is greater than £180 needs to be found.

The membership cost is: £180 – £40 = **£140**

Divide this by £5 to find the number of classes: £140 ÷ £5 = **28**

After 28 classes the annual cost is the same. Therefore, **29 classes need to be attended** before the annual cost at the sports centre is greater than the tennis club.

9. A

Explanation:
Drawing the family tree would help to understand the information. **The gender of each individual must also be considered.**

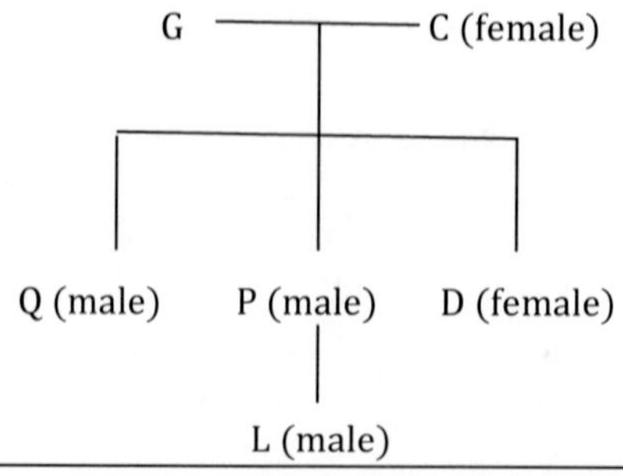

10. C

Explanation:
__ __ 10 __ __
If the numbers are put in order, then 10 will be in the middle. Since the mode is 12, there must be at least two 12s.
__ __ 10 12 12
The range is 8; therefore, the smallest number is: 12 – 8 = 4
4 __ 10 12 12
As the mean is 9, all of the numbers should total to: 9 x 5 = 45
45 = (4 + x + 10 + 12 + 12); $x = 7$ (this is the second largest number).

11. C

Explanation:
The total number of marbles that Abraham owns is **40 – 26 = 14**. Exactly 1 in 7 of these are yellow which is 2 of the marbles.
The total number of yellow marbles are: 40 – (6 + 8 + 10 + 9) = 7
The probability that a yellow marble selected at random belongs to Abraham is 2 in 7. As a result, the probability it **does not belong to him is 5 in 7.**

12. C

Explanation:
Conclusion - A new drug will prevent antibiotic resistance.
Evidence - A study of the bacteria Streptococcus pneumoniae has highlighted a potential drug that stops bacteria from becoming competent in the first place.
The assumption will link the evidence to the conclusion. Since the evidence states that the drug will stop the bacteria from becoming competent, and the drug will also prevent antibiotic resistance, **Option 'C'** is the correct answer. **Option 'A'** is incorrect because it is not related to the evidence or the conclusion. **Options 'B', 'D' and 'E'** are not relevant to the argument that the drug will prevent antibiotic resistance by stopping the bacteria entering the competence stage - these options can be eliminated.

13. B

Explanation:
Conclusion - Frequent and thorough hand-washing with soap (for at least 20 seconds) is the best method for reducing hand germs and curbing disease transmission.

Evidence - According to the Centre for Disease Control and Prevention (CDC), hand-washing with soap kills the most bacteria.

A statement that would weaken the argument will provide evidence that hand-washing is not the best method for reducing hand germs and curbing disease transmission. Therefore, the correct answer is **Option 'B'**. **Option 'A'** is incorrect because it is an assumption that is based but not supported by the passage. **Option 'C'** is implied in the passage - it does not weaken the argument. **Option 'D'** is incorrect because it strengthens the argument by stating that hand-washing with soap kills more bacteria compared to hand sanitiser. **Option 'E'** is not supported or relevant to the passage.

14. B

Explanation:

Conclusion - We shall miss journalists if they disappear.

Evidence - Journalists are being silenced, punched or hit with truncheons for trying to chronicle events.

Therefore, the main conclusion is best stated in **Option 'B'**. **Option 'A'** is incorrect because this statement introduces the topic of the passage - it cannot be the conclusion. **Option 'C'** cannot be the main conclusion because it states some of the evidence that leads to the conclusion. **Option 'D'** is incorrect because it is not supported by any evidence in the passage. **Option 'E'** is not relevant to the conclusion of the passage that journalism may disappear due to the treatment of certain individuals.

15. C

Explanation:

Assume that x is the cost per passenger:

Since the cost per passenger would have been £3 lower if there were 24 friends:

$16x = 24(x - 3)$; $16x = 24x - 72$; $8x = 72$; $x =$ **£9.00**

Since Becca pays with a £20.00 note: 20 - 9 = **£11.00**

16. E

Explanation:

Conclusion - Wearable technology allows humans to perform more complex tasks that require creativity or judgement.

Evidence - Researchers view this robot as being a co-worker when doing chores because it increases productivity by freeing up the user to make decisions based on creativity or judgment.

Since the passage refers to a specific wearable technology (a robotic arm), but the conclusion states that wearable technology allows humans to perform other tasks, the flaw is that the conclusion generalises that all wearable technology can aid humans with certain tasks. Therefore, the correct answer is **Option 'E'**. **Options 'A' and 'C'** are not relevant to the conclusion of the passage - it is incorrect. **Option 'B'** generalises that all humans must use wearable technology - this is not supported by the passage. **Option 'D'** is not relevant because the passage does not state the benefits of other wearable technology.

17. D

Explanation:

Consider Option 'A':

In the first net, the upward arrow points to the tip of the crescent. However, in the corresponding cube, the upward arrow points to the rounded side of the crescent. In the second net, the owl and the giraffe are in opposite faces; therefore, they would not be seen on adjacent faces as displayed by the net.

Option 'A' can be eliminated.

Consider Option 'B':

In the first net, the upward arrow is pointing away from the heart. In the corresponding cube, the upward arrow is pointing towards the right, and not away from the heart. In the second net, the rat and the rooster are in opposite faces; therefore, they would not be seen on adjacent faces as displayed by the net.

Option 'B' can be eliminated.

Consider Option 'C':

In the first net, the upward arrow points to the tip of the crescent. However, in the corresponding cube, the upward arrow points to the concave side of the crescent. In the second net, the owl and the giraffe are in opposite faces; therefore, they would not be seen on adjacent faces as displayed by the net.

Option 'C' can be eliminated.

Option 'D' is correct because the shapes are in their correct relative positions and in the correct orientation.

Consider Option 'E':

In the first net, the downward arrow points to the top of the box. therefore, when folded over, it would point away from the heart. However, in the corresponding cube, the downward arrow does not point to the heart. In the second net, the whale and the monkey are in opposite faces; therefore, they would not be seen on adjacent faces as displayed by the net.

Option 'E' can be eliminated.

18. A

Explanation:

Conclusion - Children and young adults should not be encouraged to use social media because it is detrimental to their health.

Evidence - A survey conducted by the Royal Society for Public Health on 13 to 24-year olds in the UK found that Snapchat, Facebook, Twitter and Instagram all led to increased feelings of depression, anxiety, poor body image and loneliness.

The assumption would link the evidence to the conclusion. Therefore, **Option 'A'** is correct because it states that the drawbacks of social media must outweigh the benefits for the conclusion to follow. **Option 'B'** is incorrect because it is not supported by any evidence in the passage. **Options 'C' and 'E'** generalise that all kids will be happier without social media and only the mentioned social media platforms lead to depression - this is not supported by the passage. **Option 'D'** is not an assumption because it is stated - assumptions are not in the passage.

19. D

Explanation:

The small packet will have an extra 25 grams. The medium packet will have an extra 65 grams. Prior to the offer, if two medium packets are bought, the customer would have a total of 520 grams of biscuits. After the offer, he/she would get the small packet free which contains: 100 + 25 = **125 grams of biscuits**, and 65 x 2 = **130 grams of extra biscuit in the 2 medium packets.**

This would provide an extra of 255 grams: 255 ÷ 520 = **49%**

20. B

Explanation:

The easiest way to approach this question is to draw or circle each different type of tile.

Some of the tiles are rotated within the wall. The different types are:

These are found in the corners; they are rotated in each of the corners:

These are found on the edges:

These three are the found in the centre:

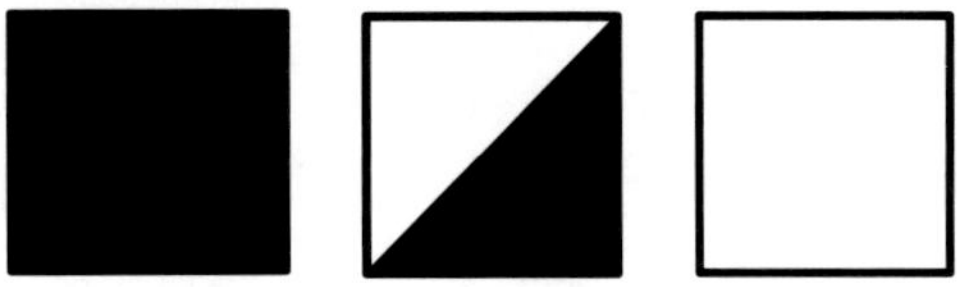

A total of **5 different tiles are used**.

21. A

Explanation:

A table can be drawn quickly to approach this question.

	Plastic	Glass	Total
Red			
Blue		40	
Yellow			
Total	50	100	150

There are $150 \div 3 =$ **50 plastic marbles**

Therefore, the number of glass marbles are $150 - 50 = 100$. If there is a 2 in 5 chance a glass marble is blue, there are $100 \times \frac{2}{5} =$ **40 blue glass marbles**.

Let the number of red marbles be $'x'$. This means the number of yellow and blue marbles are $2x$.

$x + 2x + 2x = 150$; $5x = 150$; $\underline{x = 30}$

	Plastic	Glass	Total
Red			30
Blue		40	60
Yellow			60
Total	50	100	150

The number of blue plastic marbles are $60 - 40 =$ **20**

The chance of a blue marble being plastic is 20 in 60, which simplifies to **1 in 3.**

22. E

Explanation:

All of the 15 friends may want 2 packets of the same flavour. For example, everyone could want 2 packets of ready salted crisps. Therefore, 30 packets of these packets are required. Similarly, everyone may want salt & vinegar or cheese & onion. As a result, Max must buy 30 packets of each of the flavours as it is not possible to know which flavours everyone will choose. The total number of packets he buys is **30 x 3 = 90.**

23. E

Explanation:

Conclusion - A good strategy would be to devote part of the resources for identifying those who are asymptomatic, starting with random testing in the population.

Evidence - People with mild symptoms can be isolated without wasting a test that could be instead used for identifying hidden outbreaks. To reduce the spread of the virus, many researchers think countries need to move to testing those without any signs of disease, instead of focusing on those with symptoms.

Therefore, **Option 'E'** is the conclusion because it states that random testing is a good strategy to identify people who do not have any symptoms. As a result, this will allow any hidden outbreaks to be found. **Option 'A'** is the introductory statement in the passage - it does not provide the full conclusion. **Option 'B'** is incorrect because those who do show symptoms are also tested; the extract is arguing that those without symptoms should be also tested. **Option 'C'** is suggested in the extract; however, it is a supporting statement. **Option 'D'** is mentioning the ideal plan - this is not the main conclusion.

24. D

Explanation:

Considering both charts:

Red Velvet is the smallest section of the pie chart. Therefore, it must show **Thursday** (because on Wednesday, Red Velvet was the most sold)

The largest section must be **Chocolate Sponge** (100).

Since the last two sections are roughly equal in size, it must be depicting:

Fruit Cake (50) and Lemon Drizzle (60).

Therefore, the missing cake is the **Carrot Cake.**

25. B

Explanation:

Conclusion - When schools reopen, children from poorer backgrounds will need more support to catch up compared with children from wealthier families.

Evidence - A survey of families in England suggests better-off children will have studied for around seven days more than their poorer peers by next month. A study of more than 4,000 families, carried out for the Institute for Fiscal Studies (IFS), found the gap in time spent on education activities was slightly bigger for primary age children than older pupils.

The flaw is demonstrated when the conclusion does not follow the evidence. Despite the evidence, not all children from poorer background will require support - therefore, **Option 'B'** is correct. **Option 'A'** contributes to the flaw; however, it is questioning the evidence, rather than the link between the evidence and the conclusion. **Option 'C'** provides a potential explanation to the results from the survey but does not point to a flaw in the argument. <u>**Option 'D'**</u> is not relevant to the argument and <u>**Option 'E'**</u> is explicitly stated in the passage - it cannot be a flaw.

26. D

Explanation:

<u>**Conclusion**</u> - Animals that possess brighter colours have an advantage that will enable them to all survive for a longer period of time.

<u>**Evidence**</u> - Experiments with house finches have also shown that males with the reddest breast feathers are faster at taking flight and escaping from predators. Furthermore, male sex hormones such as testosterone have been shown to work with carotenoids in male zebra finches, increasing the red hue of their beaks and making the birds more aggressive.

Since an assumption links the evidence to the conclusion, it must include the hypothesis that brighter colours may influence an organism's ability to survive. Therefore, <u>**Option 'D'**</u> is correct. <u>**Option 'A'**</u> is not an assumption because it is not related to the colour of the animal. <u>**Options 'B' and 'C'**</u> are also not related to the conclusion of the passage, and therefore cannot be an assumption. <u>**Option 'E'**</u> generalises that <u>only</u> colour determines survival rate - as a result, it is not an assumption.

27. C

Explanation:

Getting on the bus to arriving to school takes: 45 + 10 = <u>**55 minutes**</u>

If Meg gets to school at 8:25am, the bus must have left the bus stop at:

8:25 - 55 minutes = <u>**7:30**</u>

Since there are buses every 25 minutes, the following buses will arrive at:

7:30 + 25 = <u>**7:55**</u>; 7:55 + 25 = <u>**8:20**</u>

Arriving at 8:00 am at the bus station, Meg will take the <u>**8:20 bus**</u>. Since the journey takes 55 minutes, she will arrive at school at <u>**9:15 am.**</u>

28. D

Explanation:

<u>**Conclusion**</u> - Dogs may be able to model a range of human diseases that allows humans to understand the mechanisms of complex diseases.

<u>**Evidence**</u> - A recent study reveals that dogs share certain metabolic conditions - such as obesity - with their human owners. Thus, learning more about dogs' gut microbiota and how they are affected by diet could help humans to understand how best to tackle eating habits.

<u>**Options 'A', 'B' and 'C'**</u> can be concluded from the passage because they are directly stated. <u>**Option 'E'**</u> is implied from information in the passage. <u>**Option 'D'**</u> cannot be reliably concluded because the passage only mentions brain tumours - it cannot be stated that any tumour in a dog has a similar destructive effect to humans.

29. D

Explanation:

Assume 500 friends are invited:

From this, <u>**100**</u> have been counted ($\frac{1}{5}$ x 500); <u>**40**</u> are in favour of a circus theme ($\frac{2}{5}$ x 100); <u>**60**</u> are in favour of a winter wonderland theme ($\frac{3}{5}$ x 100).

<u>For a 3:2 in favour of the circus theme, 300 must be in favour of the circus theme and 200 must be in favour of the winter wonderland theme</u>.

Mock Test

300 - 40 = **260**. Therefore, **260 must be in favour for the circus out of the 400 votes** that remain to be counted. Hence, $\frac{260}{400}$ = **65%**

30. A

Explanation:

Conclusion - In addition to being tied to obesity, heart disease and cancer, poor diets can also permanently damage the nervous system, particularly vision.

Evidence - According to a new report, a teen who ate nothing, but fries, chips and other junk food for years slowly went blind as a result of his poor diet.

The main conclusion is therefore demonstrated in **Option 'A'** because it links the evidence to the statement. **Option 'B'** is not the main conclusion because it does not utilise the evidence given in the passage. **Option 'C'** is incorrect because it is already stated and it does not summarise the overall findings of the passage. **Option 'D'** generalises that most teenagers could become blind due to all diets - this passage only focuses on one such example. **Option 'E'** also generalises that optic nerve damage only occurs due to nutritional deficiencies - there is no evidence of this in the passage.

31. C

Explanation:

Conclusion - Yokota and the team believe that the moon has its own carbon supply.

Evidence - The researchers compared the moon's carbon emissions with estimates of the carbon supplied by two external sources – the solar wind, and collisions with micrometeoroids. They found that they didn't match up. Yokota states that the emission is a bit larger than the supply from outer space.

Option 'C' best illustrates the conclusion of the passage. **Options 'A', 'B', 'D' and 'E'** are mentioned in the extract; however, they are supporting statements of the main conclusion.

32. B

Explanation:

The data only shows the number of individuals from each age group involved in accidents. Despite accidents involving a high percentage of young drivers, it cannot be reliably concluded that they are the most dangerous. Therefore, **Statement 1 is incorrect**. This data could be from a geographical place where people between the ages of 18-25 account for a large proportion of the population. There is no information about the severity of the accidents. Consequently, **Statement 2 is incorrect**. The largest portion of accidents did occur in those between the ages of 18-25 (accounting for 34%). As a result, **Statement 3 is correct**. **Statement 4 is incorrect** as 24% of all the drivers who are involved in the accident are aged 26-45. The exact number of the 26 to 45-year olds in the population whom are involved in accidents is unknown.

Mock Test 1	Scientific Knowledge and Applications (Section 2)	Answers

Question	Answer
1.	B
2.	F
3.	C
4.	H
5.	E
6.	B
7.	A
8.	D
9.	C
10.	C
11.	D
12.	F
13.	B
14.	A
15.	D
16.	B
17.	E
18.	F
19.	D
20.	D
21.	C
22.	B
23.	A
24.	C
25.	E
26.	C
27.	A

1. **B**

Explanation:
The number of elements on the left-hand side must be equal to the right-hand side for the equation to be balanced. Therefore, **Option 'B'** is the correct answer. **Option 'A'** is incorrect because the number of nitrogen atoms on the left (8) does not equal the right-hand side (10). **Option 'C'** is incorrect since the number of oxygen atoms on the left (12) does not equal the right-hand side (13). **Option 'D'** is incorrect because the number of nitrogen atoms on the left (2) does not equal the right-hand side (13). **Option 'E'** is incorrect since the number of copper atoms on the left (8) does not equal the right-hand side (4).

A Lakshmi, T R Enoch, S Z Y Ooi. Doctors Academy Publications, Cardiff, UK, 2020.

2. F

Explanation:
Equation: P = IV
Calculate the total current in the circuit:
$I = \frac{P}{V}; I = \frac{36}{6}; I = \underline{6\,A}$
Assume x is the resistance of Lamp 'B'; therefore, $2x$ is the resistance of Lamp 'A'.
Total resistance of the current circuit:
$x + x + 2x = 4x$
Equation: $R = \frac{V}{I}; 4x = \frac{6}{6}; x = \underline{0.25\,\Omega}$
Lamp 'B' has a resistance of 0.25Ω and Lamp 'A' has a resistance of 0.5 Ω.
Calculate the resistance added to this circuit: $2(0.5) + 0.25 = \underline{1.25\,\Omega}$
Calculate the original resistance: $0.5 + 2(0.25) = \underline{1\,\Omega}$
Therefore, the new resistance: $1 + 1.25 = \underline{2.25\,\Omega}$

3. C

Explanation:
Place all of the fractions as a common denominator of 24:
$\frac{15(2x+2)+1.6\,(10x+5)}{24} = \frac{30}{24}; \frac{30x+30+16x+8}{24} = \frac{30}{24}$
$\frac{46x+38}{24} = \frac{30}{24}; \frac{46x}{24} + \frac{38}{24} = \frac{30}{24}$
$\frac{46x}{24} = -\frac{8}{24}; x = -\frac{4}{23}$

4. H

Explanation:
A hydrolysis reaction requires water in order to break a larger molecule into its smaller constituents. Since Reactions 1 and 4 are both examples of this, they require water as a reactant. When a metal reacts with water, it forms a metal hydroxide and hydrogen gas, as shown in Reaction 2. The fermentation of glucose (Reaction 3) converts glucose into ethanol and carbon dioxide - it does not use water as a reactant. Therefore, Reactions 1, 2 and 4 are the ones which use water as a reactant.

5. E

Explanation:
Since Jack has brown eyes, he could either be Bb or BB.
Since Katie has blue eyes, she must be bb.
Drawing a Punnett diagram for Bb and bb:

	B	b
b	Bb - brown	bb - blue
b	Bb - brown	bb - blue

Therefore, there is a 50% chance of the baby boy having blue eyes in the above scenario.
Drawing a Punnett diagram for BB and bb:

	B	B
b	Bb - brown	Bb - brown
b	Bb - brown	Bb - brown

Therefore, there is a 0% chance of the baby boy having blue eyes in the above scenario.

Since the genotype of Jack is unknown, there is either a 50% chance or a 0% chance of the baby boy having blue eyes.

6. **B**

Explanation:

Equation: $\mathbf{KE = \frac{1}{2} mv^2}$

Use F = ma; $\mathbf{m = \frac{F}{a}}$

Calculate the combined force of the two people: 56 + 24 = 80 kg

W = m x g

Assume g is 10 Nkg^{-1}: W = 80 x 10; W = **800 N**

The acceleration will be the same as the gravitational field strength, g:

Since the combined weight of 800N is leaving the car, it is **negative**.

Mass: $(\frac{-800}{10})$ = **- 80 kg**

Since the car travels 50 metres in 2.5 seconds, it is travelling: $\frac{50}{2.5}$ = **20 ms^{-1}**

Substitute this into the KE equation: KE = $\frac{1}{2}$ x (-80) x 20^2; KE = **-16,000 J**

7. **A**

Explanation:

Temperature change is detected by the hypothalamus - **Options 'B' and 'E'** can be eliminated. When the external temperature increases, the hair muscles relax in order to lie flat - this enables heat to escape. The blood flow in the capillaries increases to allow more heat to be carried by the blood to the skin, where it can be lost to the air. Therefore, **Option 'C'** can be eliminated. The sweat gland secretion increases in order to lose heat to the environment. Arterioles near the skin vasodilate in order to transfer more heat to the skin for it to be lost to the surroundings. As a result, **Option 'D'** can be eliminated. **Option 'A'** is the correct answer.

8. **D**

Explanation:

Due to Le Chatelier's principle, if a system at equilibrium is disturbed, the position of equilibrium will change in order to counteract the change. When the temperature is increased, there will be more endothermic reaction in order to decrease the temperature. As a result, there would be more of the backward reaction (since the forward reaction is exothermic), resulting in **the equilibrium position shifting to the left**. However, since the temperature has increased, the molecules would have more kinetic energy, which **increases the reaction rate**. Catalysts **increase the rate of reaction** by providing an alternate route with a lower activation energy. However, it increases the forward and backward reaction by the same amount, resulting in **no change to the equilibrium position**.

9. **C**

Explanation:

Since 'A' is inversely proportion to the cube root of 'B':

Assume 'k' is the constant: $A = \frac{k}{\sqrt[3]{B}}$

When A = 9, B = 216: $9 = \frac{k}{\sqrt[3]{216}}$; k = 9 x 6; **k = 54**

When A = 6: $6 = \frac{54}{\sqrt[3]{B}}$; $\sqrt[3]{B} = \frac{54}{6}$; $\sqrt[3]{B} = 9$; $B = 9^3$; **B= 729**

Since the square root of 'C' is directly proportional to 'D':

Assume 'k' is the constant: $\sqrt{C} = k \times D$; $\sqrt{324} = 3k$; $18 = 3k$; **k = 6**

When D = 8: $\sqrt{C} = 8 \times 6$; $\sqrt{C} = 48$; $C = \sqrt{48}$; $C = $ **$4\sqrt{3}$**

---

10. C

Find the circumference of the type:

If the diameter is 60 mm, the radius is **30 mm.**

$2\pi r$: 2 x 3.1 x 30 = **186 mm.**

Since the toy tyre travels 24 metres in 1.6 seconds before the slope, it is travelling at: $\frac{24}{1.6}$ = **15 ms^{-1}**

At the bottom of the slope, its speed has reduced by 60%: 15 x 0.4 = **6 ms^{-1}**

At the bottom of the ramp, the tyre was rolling at a speed of 6 ms^{-1}.

Convert 6 m into mm (because the circumference is in mm) = **6000 mm**

Therefore, the number of revolutions per second at the bottom of the ramp:

$\frac{6000}{186}$ is approximately **32 revolutions per second**

---

11. D

Explanation:

Assume 'x' is the price of Laptop 'X', 'y' is the price of Laptop 'Y' and 'z' is the price is the price of Laptop 'Z':

$x + y + z = 950$ **(Equation 1)**

Since Adam had to pay 20% of the price for additional features of Laptop 'X', 45% of the price of Laptop 'Y' and 25% of the price of Laptop 'Z':

$0.2x + 0.45y + 0.25z = 300$ **(Equation 2)**

The price of Laptop 'X' is three times less than Laptop 'Z':

$3x = z$ **(Equation 3)**

Substitute Equation 3 into Equations 1 and 2:

$x + y + 3x = 950$

$4x + y = 950$ **(Equation 4)**

$0.2x + 0.45y + 0.75x = 300$

$0.95x + 0.45y = 300$ **(Equation 5)**

Multiply Equation 4 by 0.45:

$1.8x + 0.45y = 427.5$ **(Equation 6)**

Subtract Equation 6 from Equation 5:

$-0.85x = -127.5$; **$x = 150$**

Substitute x into Equation 3:

$3(150) = z$; **$z = 450$**

Substitute x and z into Equation 1:

$150 + y + 450 = 950$; **$y = 350$**

Therefore, **$x = 150, y = 350, z = 450$**

---

12. F

Explanation:

Since Substance B is not normally found on the rock, it can be assumed that all of Substance B present comes from the decay of Substance A.

Total amount of Substance A at the start: 86% + 6% = **92%**

Mock Test

The half-life of a substance is the time taken for a substance to decay to half of its original amount.

Drawing a table:

Half-life	0	1	2	3	4
Substance A	92%	46%	23%	11.5%	5.75%
Substance B	0%	46%	69%	80.5%	86.25%

Therefore, it takes **approximately 4 half-lives** to obtain the correct amounts of Substances A and B.

Since the half-life is 650 years: 650 x 4 = **2600 years**

13. B

Explanation:

The **collecting duct** is the final section of a nephron (a urine forming tubule within the kidney). The **ureter** takes the urine from the kidney to the **urinary bladder**. The **urethra** is the tube that carries the urine out of the body.

14. A

Explanation:

The empirical formula is the simplest integer ratio of atoms in a compound. Assume that there are 100 grams of the compound:

There would be 57 grams of Carbon (57% of 100), 6 grams of Hydrogen (100%-(57% + 10% + 27%) of 100), 10 grams of Nitrogen (10% of 100) and 27 grams of Oxygen (27% of 100).

As a result, *moles of each element can be found using*

$\text{moles} = \frac{\text{mass}}{M_r}$: Moles of Carbon: $\frac{57}{12}$ =**4.75**; Moles of Hydrogen: $\frac{6}{1} =$ **6**

Moles of Nitrogen: $\frac{10}{14}$ is approximately **0.7..**; Moles of Oxygen: $\frac{27}{16}$= **1.6875**

In order to get the smallest whole number ratio, all three moles must be divided by the smallest number (in this case, 0.7...).

We can approximate numbers in order to make it easier to calculate:

4.75 ÷0.7.. is approximately **7**; 6 ÷0.7... is approximately **9**; 0.7.. ÷0.7.... is **1**. 1.6875 ÷0.7.... is approximately **2.5**

Since 2.5 is not a whole number, times each ratio by 2:

7 x 2=**14**; 9 x 2=**18**; 1 x 2 = **2**; 2.5 x 2 = **5**

Therefore, the empirical formula contains three carbons, 6 hydrogens and 2 oxygens (**$C_{14}H_{18}N_2O_5$**).

15. D

Explanation:

Consider the maximum cost of petrol:

Kelly would travel the **longest distance**, with the **most expensive fuel estimate** and the **least fuel-efficient estimate**.

Calculate the number of litres used: $\frac{6800}{20}$ x 4.5 = **1530 litres**

Therefore, the maximum cost: 1530 x £1.60 = **£2448**

Consider the minimum cost of petrol:

Kelly would travel the **shortest distance**, with the **least expensive fuel estimate** and the **most fuel-efficient estimate**.

Calculate the number of litres used: $\frac{2430}{30} \times 4.5 = \underline{364.5 \text{ litres}}$

Therefore, the minimum cost: 364.5 x £0.80 = **£291.60**

The difference between the maximum and minimum cost: £2448 - £291.60 = **£2156.40**

16. B

Explanation:

Consider Transformer 'A':

Equation: $V_p I_p = V_s I_s$

$V_p = 60$ V; $I_p = 5$ A; $V_s = ?$; $I_s = 1.2$ A; $V_p I_p = V_s I_s$

$V_s = \frac{60 \times 5}{1.2}$; $V_s = \underline{250 \text{ V}}$

Consider Transformer 'B':

Equation: $V_p I_p = V_s I_s$

$V_p = 30$ V; $I_p = 5$ A; $V_s = ?$; $I_s = 20$ A; $V_p I_p = V_s I_s$

$V_s = \frac{40 \times 6}{8}$; $V_s = \underline{30 \text{ V}}$

Therefore, the secondary coil voltage in Transformer 'B' is $\frac{30}{250}$ = **0.12 times larger**

17. E

Explanation:

An oxidising agent is one that oxidises other elements or compounds in the reaction. As a result, it becomes reduced itself. On the left-hand side, Chromium has an oxidation state of +6, but on the right-hand side it has an oxidation state of +3 (due to the ion charge). Therefore, **Chromium is the oxidising agent**. A reducing agent removes oxygen from other elements or compounds - it becomes oxidised itself. On the left-hand side, the N in NO_2^- has an oxidation state of +3, but on the right-hand side it has an oxidation state of +5 (due to three oxygen atoms compared to the two present initially). Since N is present in NO_2^-, the whole molecule is becoming oxidised. **Therefore, NO_2^- is the reducing agent.**

18. F

Explanation:

Consider the red velvet cake:

Calculate the percentage of the cake made from plain flour: $1 - (\frac{1}{5} + \frac{7}{20}) = 0.45$

Let x be the mass of the red velvet cake: $0.45x = 742.5$; $\underline{x = 1650 \text{ grams}}$

Consider the vanilla cake:

Calculate the percentage of the cake made from plain flour: $1 - (\frac{9}{20} + \frac{2}{5}) = 0.15$

Let x be the mass of the vanilla cake: $0.15x = 2(742.5)$; $\underline{x = 9900 \text{ grams}}$

Therefore, the combined mass: 1650 + 9900 = **11550 grams**

19. D

Explanation:

Write an equation that shows the reaction:

$2Fe + 3Cl_2 \rightarrow 2FeCl_3$

Moles of each element can be found using $\textbf{moles} = \frac{\textbf{mass}}{\mathbf{M_r}}$:

Moles of Fe: $\frac{200}{160} = \underline{1.25}$; Moles of Chlorine: $\frac{182}{2(35)} = \underline{2.6}$

Mock Test

To use all of the Fe: $1.25 \times \frac{3 \text{ moles } Cl_2}{2 \text{ moles Fe}}$ = **1.875 moles of Cl_2**

1.875 moles of Cl_2 are required to use up all of the Fe.

To use all of the Cl_2: $2.6 \times \frac{2 \text{ moles Fe}}{3 \text{ moles } Cl_2}$ = **1.73... moles of Fe**

1.73 moles of Fe are required to use up all of the Cl_2.

Therefore, Fe is the limiting reagent since 1.73 moles is required, but there are only 1.25 moles available. The excess reactant is Cl_2.

Excess reactant: 2.6 - 1.875 = 0.725 moles of Cl_2

Since mass = moles x M_r; mass = 0.725 x 70

= **50.75 grams of Cl_2 left over (approximately 51 grams)**

20. D

Explanation:

Consider Statement 1:

The amplitude of the wave is the maximum position from the undisturbed position. The wave has a maximum height of 45 and a minimum height of 10; therefore, its undisturbed position is: $\frac{10+45}{2}$=27.5

The maximum height from the undisturbed position: 45 – 27.5 = **17.5**

Therefore, the amplitude is **17.5 mm**.

Statement 1 is incorrect.

Consider Statement 2:

A complete wave is measured from the same position each time. Therefore, there are only **4 complete waves** (4.5 waves) in the diagram.

Statement 2 is incorrect.

Consider Statement 3:

It takes 25 seconds for two waves to be completed; therefore, the period of each wave is 12.5 seconds.

The frequency is $\frac{1}{\text{period}}$: $\frac{1}{12.5}$ = **0.08 Hz**

Statement 3 is incorrect.

Consider Statement 4:

Each wave has a frequency of 0.08 Hz and a wavelength of 0.15 m (15 cm).

Wave speed: 0.08 x 0.15 = **0.012 ms^{-1}**

Statement 4 is correct. Therefore, **Option 'D'** is the correct answer.

21. C

Explanation:

Consider Organism 'A':

If it has 28% adenine, it must contain 28% thymine (since adenine and thymine always bind together): 100 - (28 + 28) = **44%**

Therefore, **44% is guanine and cytosine.**

Since guanine and cytosine always bind together, there must be equal amounts of each base: 44 ÷ 2 = **22%**

22% of Organism A's DNA is guanine.

Calculate the number of base pairs that are guanine: 0.22 x 4.5 = **0.99 billion base pairs**

Consider Organism 'B':

If it has 36% thymine, it must contain 36% adenine (since adenine and thymine always bind together): 100 - (36 + 36) = 28%
Therefore, **28% is guanine and cytosine.**
Since guanine and cytosine always bind together, there must be equal amounts of each base: 28 ÷ 2 = 14%
14% of Organism B's DNA is guanine.
Calculate the number of base pairs that are guanine: 0.14 x 6 = **0.84 billion base pairs**
Therefore, the difference in the number of guanine base pairs:
0.99 - 0.84 = **0.15 billion guanine base pairs**

22. B

Explanation:
If B = $\frac{1}{3}$ *(since B is divided by 3):* $3\left(\frac{1}{3}\right)^3 = \frac{1}{9}$

Therefore, $\frac{1}{\frac{1}{9}} = 9$; A is multiplied by 9 times.

23. A

Explanation:
Consider Patient X:
The volume of each breath is **800 cm³**. In 2 minutes, the patient takes **36 breaths**.
Therefore, the total volume inhaled in 2 minutes: 36 x 800 = **28800 cm³**
Since 20% of the air is oxygen: 0.2 x 28800 = **5760 cm³ (5.76 dm³)**
Consider Patient Y:
The volume of each breath is: 0.85 x 800 = **680 cm³**
In 2 minutes, the patient takes **40 breaths**.
Therefore, the total volume inhaled in 2 minutes: 40 x 680 = **27200 cm³**
Since 20% of the air is oxygen: 0.2 x 27200 = **5440 cm³ (5.44 dm³)**
Therefore, the difference in oxygen: 5.76 - 5.44 = **0.32 dm³**

24. C

Explanation:
When the lift is at rest, the two people have a combined mass of 25 kg:
W = m x g; W = 25 x 10; W = 250 N
The weight of the two people will be equivalent to the tension in the lift:
Equations when lift is accelerating downwards:
F = ma; F = mg - T (the resultant force is equivalent to the mass x acceleration due to gravity minus the tension working in the opposite direction)
Therefore, m x a = mg - T; (25 x 5) = (25 x 10) - T; T = **125 N**

25. E

Explanation:
The **pain receptor** (U) in the finger is the one which first identifies the sharp sensation of the pin. This impulse then travels along the **sensory neurone** (S), until it reaches a synapse. The impulse is regenerated at the start of the **relay neurone** (Q) until it reaches the synapse of the **motor neurone** (R). The motor neurone is attached to the **effector** (T), which is a muscle. The muscle contracts, causing the finger to retreat from the pin.

26. C

Explanation:
An exothermic reaction is one that transfers energy (usually heat) to the surroundings. Neutralisation reactions (shown in **Reaction 1**) are exothermic since they release energy

to the environment once completed. **Reactions 2, 3 and 5** are all exothermic as well. Since photosynthesis (**Reaction 4**) is the opposite of aerobic respiration, it must be endothermic. **Reaction 6** is an example of thermal decomposition; this requires energy from the surroundings. Therefore, it is an endothermic reaction. Therefore, **Reactions 4 and 6** are the only examples of endothermic reactions.

27. A

Explanation:

Consider Statement 1:

The liver receives oxygenated blood from the heart via the hepatic artery and blood rich in digested nutrients from the intestines through the hepatic portal vein. **Therefore, Statement 1 is correct.**

Consider Statement 2:

Bile is produced in the liver, but it is stored in the gallbladder. From the gallbladder, the stored bile is released into the duodenum. **Therefore, Statement 2 is incorrect.**

Consider Statement 3:

Bile must neutralise stomach acid in order for pancreatic enzymes to work at their optimum pH. In order for the acid to be neutralised, sodium hydrogen carbonate must be an alkali. **Therefore, Statement 3 is incorrect.**

Consider Statement 4:

Carbohydrates are digested in the mouth, stomach and small intestine. The pancreas only secretes digestive enzymes; it does not digest any molecules. **Therefore, Statement 4 is incorrect.**

Statement 1 is the only correct answer.

Mock Test 1	Writing Task (Section 3)	Sample Answers

Task 1 - If the facts do not fit the theory, change the facts.

This statement implies that the proof behind a theory can be altered in order for a theory to be pronounced. A hypothesis is developed first and additional proof is investigated in order to prove the proposed theory. Consequently, if the experiments and data do not match, one may possess the ability to change the facts or alter the results.

However, this statement is flawed because a fact is objective - it cannot be changed. As a result, one must change the theory or the hypothesis, rather than the facts. If a fact is incorrect and published as a seminal article, it could provide misleading information to the society. For example, Mr Andrew Wakefield published an article claiming a strong correlation between MMR vaccines and the risk of developing autism. This resulted in fewer children being vaccinated and, indirectly, increased the prevalence of diseases in the population. Alternatively, with careful observation of a myriad of species, Lamarck's theory of acquired characteristics was refuted by Darwin's Theory of Natural Selection. With regards to the structure of an atom, many theories that were once considered to be established, were disproved due to new or additional knowledge. JJ Thomson's Plum Pudding Model was refuted due to the alpha particle scattering experiment. The discovery of the neutron by James Chadwick finalised the nuclear model of an atom, since it used careful observation and experimental calculations to determine the precise structure.

In conclusion, I believe that facts drive the development of theories because it allows the correct conclusions to be drawn. It is imperative that theories have sufficient proof in order to be pronounced, since this allows the continuous advancement of science.

Task 2 - All essential prescription medicines should be provided to patients free of charge.

The NHS, founded on the 5th July 1948, was designed to be free at the point of delivery and equitable to all citizens. As a result, one may assert that all essential prescriptions of medicine should remain free of charge to ensure that there is no discrimination due to an individual's financial status.

It is one's fundamental civil right to have access to essential medication - one's quality of life should not be governed by income. If a cost is introduced, it may impede the act of distributive justice, since the allocation of medicines would possess an element of bias. Similarly, the additional cost of medication may deter individuals from seeking medical attention; thus, compromising their health and well-being.

However, one may contend that the population should pay for the medicines, since it requires large sums of money to procure them. This could be incorporated in taxes, with a tiered structure implemented to ensure that the amount paid is proportional to the income. Alternatively, one could pay per medication purchased. In order to ensure that the cost does not act as a deterrent, the Government could partially subsidise medicines to make it more affordable for the population.

In conclusion, I concur that all essential prescription medicines should be provided to patients free of charge in order to promote equality and distributive justice. However, a cost may be levied for non-essential medicines, which could contribute towards the research and development of novel pharmacotherapeutics.

Task 3 - The art of healing only requires scientific knowledge in order to improve a patient's health.

Scientific knowledge is the understanding of science that is directly based on objective fact. In medicine, it forms a fundamental basis in diagnosing, investigating and treating patients.

One may contend that only scientific knowledge is required to treat and heal an individual. By understanding the complex interactions of medications on the body and the various metabolic pathways, doctors can prescribe the most efficient medications. A noteworthy example is the use of chemotherapeutic medicines to disrupt the spindle fibre formations during the cell cycle to destroy tumour cells. Likewise, the knowledge that Type I diabetes is caused by a lack of insulin production facilitates scientists to develop replacement insulin therapies.

However, in contrast with the aforementioned paragraph, healing a patient requires more than scientific knowledge. Doctors use a multitude of skills, such as empathy, compassion and communication to comfort the patient, which complements the prescribed medications. With regard to certain psychological illnesses that does not require medical treatment, patients may require therapy sessions, such as Cognitive Behavioural Therapy (CBT), to support them. Amongst others, a doctor's role is to reassure the patient; this has the potential to provide a greater benefit to the patient than complex interventional treatments.

Therefore, I believe that the art of healing requires a balance between scientific knowledge and soft skills in order to achieve an optimum outcome for the patient. Whilst possessing a sound scientific knowledge is essential, a doctor also requires the relevant soft skills to efficiently empathise with a patient.

Mock Test 2	Thinking Skills (Section 1)	Answer

Question	Answer
1.	A
2.	A
3.	C
4.	D
5.	B
6.	D
7.	B
8.	A
9.	D
10.	B
11.	E
12.	C
13.	B
14.	A
15.	C
16.	B
17.	E
18.	D
19.	B
20.	A
21.	A
22.	C
23.	D
24.	E
25.	B
26.	E
27.	D
28.	D
29.	B
30.	D
31.	E
32.	C

1. **A**

Explanation:

If 300 voted for chocolate and caramel, and the ratio is 8:6 :

$\frac{300}{8}$ x 6 =<u>225 customers voted for strawberry and vanilla</u>

Therefore, the total number of regular customers who voted:

225 + 300 = <u>525 customers</u>; The percentage: $\frac{525}{600}$ x 100 = <u>87.5%</u>

2. A

Explanation:

Conclusion - UK universities must employ more staff and encourage students to conduct more research in order to improve their rankings on an international level.

Evidence - Three quarters of British universities have seen a decline in their international league table rankings. According to the data, 66 UK universities saw a drop in their staff to student ratio, while 59 had fewer research citations.

The assumption links the evidence to the conclusion. Since the conclusion and evidence states that the decline in international rankings was due to the staff to student ratio and the amount of research conducted, **Option 'A'** is the correct answer. **Option 'B'** is incorrect because it does not link the evidence to the main conclusion. **Option 'C'** is an assumption that is not supported by the passage - there may be other factors that contribute to the reduction of international students in UK universities. **Option 'D'** is not relevant to the conclusion or the evidence. **Option 'E'** implies that there is a correlation between the number of staff present and the amount of research conducted - this is not indicated in the passage.

3. C

Explanation:

The quickest way to solve this question is to first divide all the given options by 5, as each group in the group stage has 5 participants. This will give 18, 17, 16, 14 and 12 for Options 'A', 'B', 'C', 'D' and 'E' respectively. From this, Option 'B' can be excluded as having 17 groups would mean that the first stage of the knockout round will have 17 participants, hence, making it impossible for pairing to take place fairly. Now, think of the number of knockout matches one can expect to have at this competition. The final round itself is 1 match. The third placing match counts as 1 too. In the semi-final round, 2 matches must have taken place. Before the semi-finals, there must be 4 matches, and the trend goes on where the number of matches in any given round is double of that in the preceeding round. Hence, excluding the third placing match, we have the trend 1, 2, 4, 8, ... Logically, one can stop at 8 because there is no point considering a knockout round with 16 matches as that will involve 32 participants (i.e., not feasible with the options given). From the explanation above, it can be extrapolated that there are: $1 + 1 + 2 + 4 + 8 = 16$ participants who make it to the first knockout round.

Hence, there should be 16 groups. Given that there are 5 participants in each group, a total of 80 participants must have registered for the competition.

4. D

Explanation:

Conclusion - A new algorithm has been designed by a team in Canada that may be able to prevent online bullying and predict the likelihood of suicidal behaviours.

Evidence - These algorithms managed to detect and block almost two-thirds of insults within almost 114,000 posts in English and was more accurate than a simple keyword search. The algorithms were able to predict with an accuracy of 92%, whether a patient would attempt to end his/her life in the week following an instance of self-harm.

Therefore, the main conclusion is stated in **Option 'D'**. **Option 'A'** is not supported by the passage - there is no mention of the difference in detection speed between the keyword search and the new algorithm. **Option 'B'** cannot be determined by the passage - there is no evidence that 92% of all results generated from the algorithm is accurate. **Option 'C'** is also not supported in the passage - there are no statistics regarding human intervention in the passage. **Option 'E'** is incorrect because it generalises that all algorithms are only beneficial to everyday life.

5. **B**

Explanation:

Conclusion - More funding should be allocated to this government campaign in order to raise awareness of the benefits of eating five fruits and vegetables a day.

Evidence - The five-a-day campaign is based on advice from the World Health Organization, which recommends eating a minimum of 400 grams of fruit and vegetables a day to lower the risk of serious health problems, such as heart disease, stroke and some types of cancer.

The flaw is best stated when the conclusion does not link to the evidence. Since the evidence does not discuss the benefits of increasing funding on the five a day campaign, the flaw is illustrated in **'Option B'**. **Option 'A'** is incorrect because it does not include the evidence or conclusion in the passage. **Option 'C', 'D' and 'E'** are incorrect since they do not refer to the conclusion in their statements.

6. **D**

Explanation:

Conclusion - After decades of industry and the Government slow-walking the climate issue, for some, the pandemic is proof that effective action can be achieved.

Evidence - With the global paralysis induced by the coronavirus, levels of pollution and carbon emission are dropping everywhere — leaving bluer skies, visible mountains, splendid wildflowers. Venice's famously murky canals are running clear.

The passage indicates that the global paralysis caused by the coronavirus has improved the environment - which has now become cleaner. This shows that actions can be taken to reduce the pollution in the environment and that it is possible to reverse the damage we have done so far. Therefore, **Option 'D'** is the correct answer. The passage does not indicate which is more important – a cleaner economy or economic growth. It is discussing a method where both the issues are addressed, since they are both important. The passage does not state that improving the economy and keeping the environment clean is not possible.

7. **B**

Explanation:

Conclusion - Scientists found that bad dreams improved the effectiveness of the brain in reacting to frightening experiences when awake.

Evidence - With more than 250 electrodes attached to 18 subjects - and with another 89 people keeping diaries of their sleeping and dreaming patterns - the researchers examined how the emotions experienced during dreams were connected with feelings when awake. It suggested that bad dreams were a way of preparing people for fear in their waking lives.

Therefore, the main conclusion is expressed in **Option 'B'**. **Option 'A'** is incorrect because it states that dreams are used as a therapy, when the passage states that it has only been suggested by scientists. **Option 'C'** also asserts that all emotions experienced during dreams are connected to feelings when awake - this is not supported by the passage. **Option 'D'** is incorrect since there is no mention of the impact of extensive cognitive exercises on the brain. **Option 'E'** generalises that bad dreams are the only way of preparing for fear - this is not stated in the passage.

8. A

Explanation:

Consider the shapes that are supposed to be opposite to each other when the cube is folded. **<u>Option 'B'</u>** is incorrect as this net does not make a cube when it is folded. **<u>Option 'C'</u>** is incorrect as the ring should be opposite the square in the cube but in this net, it is opposite the circle with the cross and adjacent to the square when this net is folded into a cube. **<u>Option 'D'</u>** is wrong because the cross should be opposite the 4 arrows; however, in this net is it adjacent to it. Finally, the net in **<u>Option 'E'</u>** does not form a cube - it is not the right answer. By process of elimination, **<u>Option 'A' is the correct answer</u>**.

9. D

Explanation:

The order of the flowers is:

Tulips——————>

LEFT Roses Lilies Sunflowers *RIGHT*

<——— Poppies——————>

The roses are found to the left of the tulips; however, the position of the tulips in relation to the lilies and sunflower is not known. The poppies are found to the left of the tulips but the position of this in relation to the other flowers is not known. It can be deduced from the passage that the **<u>sunflowers are definitely found to the right of the roses and lilies.</u>**

10. B

Explanation:

The pie chart shows the percentage of girls is much smaller than boys. Therefore, all sports with more girls than boys can be eliminated – namely, **<u>Options 'A', 'C' and 'D'</u>**. The number of boys and girls doing tennis is very similar; as a result, this is not representative of the pie chart. **<u>Option 'B' is the correct answer</u>** as the number of boys doing rowing is almost 3 times the number of girls as shown in the pie chart.

11. E

Explanation:

The set of symbols π^∑œ appears in both the phrases; the word that is common to both the phrases is 'keep'. Therefore, **<u>π^∑œ = 'keep'</u>**. It is not possible to deduce what the other words mean; as a result, it can be extrapolated that the symbols that represent the word 'keys' must either be **<u>¬∂Δ or ç√¥</u>**, since these both appear in the last phrase.

12. C

Explanation:

Time = distance ÷ speed

Ruby: Time = 5 ÷ 1.25 = **<u>4 hours</u>**; *Joe:* Time = 2 ÷ 1.5

Time = 1.33333 hours **<u>(1 hour 20 minutes)</u>**

The difference in time is: 4 hours – 1 hour 20 minutes = **<u>2 hours 40 minutes</u>**

13. B

Explanation:

<u>Conclusion</u> - Current evidence indicates that children are less likely than adults to acquire the coronavirus infection after exposure, less likely to test positive for SARS-CoV-2 at the population-level, and potentially less likely to transmit the infection to others.

Evidence - However, the latter conclusion is based on research performed during a period in which schools have generally been closed, and, therefore, isn't necessarily reflective of the true infectivity of children.

Option 'A' is incorrect as the passage does not mention teenagers. **Option 'B' is the correct answer**. The passage states that children are less likely to transmit the infection; however, this was based on research done after most schools were closed. **Option 'C'** is not mentioned in the passage. **Option 'D'** is not the main conclusion of the passage as it cannot be proven that schools being closed are the main reason for low transmission rates between children. Option 'E' is not explicitly mentioned in the passage as it does not give a reason why children are less likely to acquire the infection.

14. A

Explanation:

Conclusion - The spindle transfer technique, which utilises mitochondrial replacement therapy, is better for age-related infertility.

Evidence - Women aged 40-44 who have undergone this procedure have a 18% chance of a live birth in their first cycle. Without the procedure, women aged 40-44 had an 11% chance of a live birth in their first cycle.

The assumption must link the evidence to the conclusion – **Option 'A'** is the only assertion which mentions the mitochondria and its relation to infertility in older women. **Option 'B'** is not supported in the passage (the passage only mentions IVF and no other infertility treatments). **Options 'C' and 'E'** are incorrect because they generalise that spindle transfer is only successful in older women and that older women can only become fertile due to IVF and spindle transfer. **Option 'D'** is not as assumption because it is directly stated in the passage.

15. C

Explanation:

Conclusion - According to the latest research, reading is the best form of cognitive exercise.

Evidence - A growing body of research indicates that reading could alter the neural pathways in the brain. Using MRI scans, researchers have confirmed that reading involves a complex network of circuits and signals in the brain. As reading ability matures, these networks become stronger and more sophisticated.

Since the conclusion states that reading is the best cognitive exercise, but the passage only mentions the benefits of reading, the flaw is best stated in **Option 'C'**. **Option 'A'** is not supported by the passage - there is no evidence that only reading alters neural pathways. **Option 'B'** is incorrect because it does not refer to the conclusion that reading is the best cognitive exercise. **Options 'D' and 'E'** are not relevant to the conclusion and are not supported by any evidence in the passage.

16. B

Explanation:

Conclusion - Walking is an underrated and important form of exercise.

Evidence - Walking improves fitness, cardiac health, alleviates depression and fatigue, improves mood and creates less stress on joints by reducing pain. When comparing the results of the most recent National Runners' Health Study with the National Walkers' Health Study, researchers found that the energy used for moderate-intensity walking and vigorous-intensity running resulted in similar reductions in risk for high blood pressure, high cholesterol, diabetes and heart disease over the study's six-year period.

Although the passage compares the benefits of walking compared to running, it does not conclude that one is more beneficial than the other. Therefore, the statement that cannot be reliably concluded is **Option 'B'**. **Options 'A', 'C', 'D'** and 'E' are all stated in the passage; therefore, they can all be reliably concluded from the passage.

17. E

Explanation:

From the text, it can be deduced that:

1. Mr Gonville is driving the car and is placed on the right side while his wife who is placed on the left, reads her book during the journey.
2. Roe is sitting in the centre of the middle row.
3. Tia is closest in distance to her mother; hence, she must be placed behind Mrs Gonville.
4. Given that Seth must be placed as far as possible from Tia, Seth must be on the back row on the right.
5. There are now three empty seats, but one is only left with the seat description of two children, Pam and Una. Given that Una sits next to no one else but Pam, this means that they must fill the two seats at the back row. Una must be on the left side of the row while Pam sits in the centre of the back row.

One should be able to get the arrangement as below.

Front of the car

Mrs Gonville		**Mr Gonville (Driver)**
Tia	Roe	
Una	Pam	Seth

Therefore, the child that is seated furthest from the driver is Una.

18. D

Explanation:

Conclusion - Addressing statistics regarding the African population may significantly slow population growth rates globally.

Evidence - The population of Africa is expected to roughly double by 2050. The average woman in Africa today has about 4.7 children. This varies significantly from 2.5 in southern Africa to between 5.5 and 5.8 in central and western Africa. The average in other parts of the world is 2.2 or less, with a global average of 2.5 children per woman.

The assumption will link the evidence to the conclusion. Since the conclusion refers to global overpopulation, but the evidence is exclusively regarding the African population, the assumption is best stated in **Option 'D'**. **Options 'A' and 'C'** generalise that all women in Africa have the most children and the African population will double by 2050 - this is not explicitly stated in the passage. **Option 'B'** is irrelevant to the argument - there is no mention of the Asian population in the passage. **Option 'E'** generalises that overpopulation will become a major issue - this is not relevant to the conclusion of the passage.

19. B

Explanation:

Exactly 60% of the members are adults: 175 x 0.6 = **105 of the members are adults.**

Exactly 40% of the adults are male: 105 x 0.4 = **42 people.**

Since $\frac{1}{7}$ of 42 is 6, 42 – 6 = **36 male adult members left in the club**. The number of male adults who still have a membership as a percentage of the total is:

$\frac{36}{169}$ x 100 = **21.3%.**

Take note that the total number of members also decreases as the six males stop their membership. 21.3% rounds to 21%.

20. A

Explanation:

From the chart, the least number of women prefer musicals; therefore, this should be the smallest sector in the pie chart. This eliminates **Options 'B' and 'E'**. The majority of the women like romance films. Therefore, this would represent the biggest proportion of the pie chart. Knowing this eliminates **Options 'C' and 'D'**. As a result, **Option 'A' is the correct answer**.

21. A

Explanation:

The pie chart is split into one section that represents $\frac{1}{2}$, a section that shows $\frac{1}{4}$ and two sections that represent $\frac{1}{8}$. This means that the two smallest numbers will be the same, the next biggest will be double this and the largest number will be four times bigger than the smallest number. Therefore, **this pie chart represents the time Victoria spent on her homework.**

22. C

Explanation:

The order of the folders is shown below:

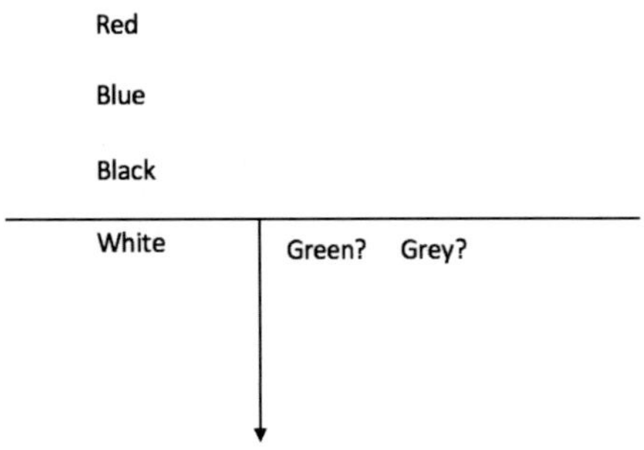

The position of the white and green folders relative to the grey folder is not known. Therefore, **Option 'E'** is not necessarily true. By process of elimination, **Option 'C' is the correct answer.**

Mock Test

23. D

Explanation:

Conclusion - Vaping is not as dangerous as it is perceived to be.

Evidence - In 2019, there were only 66 deaths directly linked to vaping, while there were 146,383 deaths from strokes in the USA.

Statement 1 is a weakness in the argument because these anti-vaping campaigns could be seen as necessary. This necessity may be proven by the low number of deaths related to vaping. If there are more people at risk of developing a stroke, it would follow that more people would die from a stroke. However, this does not mean that vaping is less dangerous to the fewer individuals who may participate in it. Therefore, **Statement 2** is also a weakness in the argument. **Statement 3** is irrelevant since it does not compare vaping with the risk of developing a stroke – it can be eliminated. Therefore, **Option 'D'** is the correct answer.

24. E

Explanation:

Let 'N' be the number of bricks on the bottom row.

Since the row above has 2 bricks less than the bottom row, it will contain 'N-2" bricks; the row above will contain 'N-4' bricks, etc.

There are 120 bricks altogether in the pyramid, and 5 rows:

N + (N-2) + (N-4) + (N-6) + (N-8) = 115; 5N = 135; N = 27

Since the top row is 'N-8': 27 - 8 = 19

25. B

Explanation:

Conclusion - There are many health benefits of living closer to green space compared to urban areas.

Evidence - Researchers found that people living near more green space reported less mental distress, even after adjusting for income, education, and employment (all of which are also correlated with health).

The statement that cannot be reliably concluded from the passage is **Option 'B'**, because it asserts that individuals will not suffer from depression or anxiety if they live close to a green space - this is not supported in the passage. **Options 'A', 'C', 'D' and 'E'** are all stated directly in the passage.

26. E

Explanation:

Conclusion - All children should be encouraged to play video games in order to improve certain skills.

Evidence - In the experiments conducted, the typical finding is that those who play the video game improve on measures of basic perceptual and cognitive abilities while those in the control group do not.

Despite the benefits of playing video games, the conclusion suggests that children should play more video games - the flaw is expressed in **Option 'E'**. **Option 'A'** is not supported by the passage because it does not state that only video games can improve perception, attention, memory and decision-making. **Option 'B'** contributes to the flaw, but it does not mention the advantages of playing video games. **Option 'C'** generalises that video games are the only way of developing vital skills - there is no evidence of this in the passage. **Option 'D'** contributes to a flaw, but it does not refer to the conclusion.

27. D

Explanation:

First, the product of Skye's age and her two pet tortoises is 144.

This can be broken down into its prime factors: **2 x 2 x 2 x 2 x 3 x 3**

Given that the tortoises are of the same age, this means that their ages can be narrowed down to three possibilities: **(1, 1, 144), (2, 2, 36), (4, 4, 9)**

These are the only 3 possible options that satisfy the rule that the tortoises are younger than Skye.

Hence, the possible numbers on Quon's jersey are: **146, 40 and 17**

As a result, **40 is one of the given options.**

---

28. D

Explanation:

Conclusion - The statistical methods that Carlisle used to identify medical fraud in Fujii's work can be used for all medical fraud suspicions.

Evidence - A total of 183 of Yoshitaka Fujii's papers were retracted, which is more retractions than any other individual has had.

The flaw is over-generalising that all fraudulent medical research can be proven using Carlisle's statistical methods, only because Fuji's was. Therefore, **Option 'D'** is correct. **Options 'A' and 'B'** are incorrect – Fujii lost his university job and his papers were retracted because they were fraudulent (not only due to Carlisle's statistical methods). **Option 'C'** is incorrect since it provides more information regarding the statistical method, without addressing the flaw in the argument. **Option 'E'** is incorrect – it is an assumption which is not based on any evidence in the passage.

---

29. B

Explanation:

Consider Statement 1: Those who like football also like cricket. Therefore, those who like cricket do not like hockey. Those who do not like hockey cannot like netball.

Conclusion - Statement 1 is correct.

Consider Statement 2: Those who like netball like hockey. As a result, those who like hockey do not like cricket. Those who do not cricket do not like football.

Conclusion - Statement 2 is incorrect.

Consider Statement 3: Those who like netball also like hockey. Those who like hockey do not like cricket.

Conclusion - Statement 3 is correct.

Consider Statement 4: Those who like hockey do not like cricket. Those who do not like cricket do not like football.

Conclusion - Statement 4 is correct.

Consider Statement 5: Those who like football like cricket. Those who like cricket do not like hockey.

Conclusion - Statement 5 is incorrect.

---

30. D

Explanation:

Conclusion - Travelling is essential in order to reap a number of important health benefits.

Evidence - A study found that women who vacation at least twice a year show a significantly lower risk of suffering a heart attack than those who only travel every six years or so.

The flaw is one that shows that the evidence does not follow on from the conclusion - this is best demonstrated in **Option 'D'**. **Option 'A'** is irrelevant to the argument that travelling is important to an individual's health; therefore, it is incorrect. **Option 'B'** is incorrect because it contradicts the argument. **Option 'C'** generalises that all individuals feel less anxious, more rested and in a better mood after taking a vacation - this is not supported by the passage. **Option 'E'** only mentions heart disease - this is not solely expressed in the conclusion and is consequently not the flaw.

31. E

Explanation:

No information is given regarding the origin of fiction books; **Options 'A' and 'B'** may not be true. There is no information about any other non-fiction books other than the ones with the green sticker from the library. As a result, **Option 'C'** may not be true as she could have some non-fiction books with a different sticker or no sticker. There is no information about stickers on the fiction books (other than the fact that there is no green sticker). Consequently, **Option 'D'** is not the correct answer. **Option 'E' is the correct answer** as the passage states that none of the fiction books have a green sticker on the spine.

32. C

Explanation:

Between 19:00 and 21:00, the time that each of the students spent watching TV are:

Charlie: 30 minutes

Madhav: 37 + 45 = 82 minutes = **1 hour 22 minutes**

Nuan: 1 hour 32 minutes + 1 minute = **1 hour 33 minutes**

Kwame: 12 + 55 = 67 minutes = **1 hour 7 minutes**

Anton: **1 hour 21 minutes**

The exact differences do not need to be found; a rough estimate can help eliminate some of the values – it can easily be identified that Charlie spent a lot less time watching TV in this given time period by looking at the table.

The student who spent the longest amount of time in this two-hour period is **Nuan.**

Mock Test

Mock Test 2 | Scientific Knowledge and Applications (Section 2) | Answer

Question	Answer
1.	B
2.	C
3.	B
4.	E
5.	F
6.	E
7.	C
8.	E
9.	D
10.	C
11.	C
12.	B
13.	E
14.	B
15.	G
16.	B
17.	B
18.	D
19.	C
20.	D
21.	D
22.	A
23.	D
24.	B
25.	G
26.	C
27.	B

1. **B**

Explanation:

The distance travelled is the area under the graph between t=0 and t=45 seconds.

Split the graph into four sections:

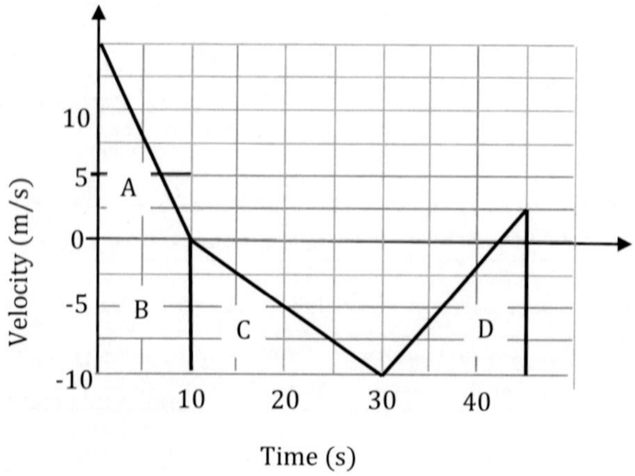

Consider Section 'A':

Area = 0.5 x base x width; Area = 0.5 x 10 x 15; Area = 75 m

Consider Section 'B':

Area = base x width; Area = 10 x 10; Area = 100 m

Consider Section 'C':

Area = 0.5 x base x width; Area = 0.5 x 20 x 10; Area = 100 m

Consider Section 'D':

Area = 0.5 x base x width; Area = 0.5 x 10 x 12.5; Area = 62.5 m

Therefore, the total distance: 75 + 100 + 100 + 62.5 = **337.5 m**

2. **C**

Explanation:

During expiration, the **external intercostal muscles relax**, and the **internal intercostal muscles contract**. The **diaphragm relaxes** and moves upwards, allowing the **lung volume to decrease** and the **air pressure inside the lungs to increase**. As a result of the negative pressure, air is expelled from the lungs and into the surrounding environment.

3. **B**

Explanation:

Substitute $x = 4$ into $y = (x + 7)^3 + 3(x - 2)^2 - 5(x - 3) - 10$:

$y = (4 - 9)^3 + 3(4 - 2)^2 - 5(4 - 3) - 10$; $y = -128$

Therefore, the graph uses the point (4, -128). Point X is **3 mm above the curve.**

4. **E**

Explanation:

These flame tests must be learnt from the BMAT specification **(page 333)**. If an atom or ion is excited by strong heating, electrons can be promoted from their normal unexcited state into higher orbitals. As they fall back down to lower levels (either in one go or in several steps), energy is released as light. Each of these jumps involves a specific amount of energy being released as light energy, and each corresponds to a particular wavelength (or frequency). As a result of all these jumps, a spectrum of lines will be produced, some of which will be in the visible part of the spectrum. The colour seen will be a combination of all these individual colours.

5. **F**

Explanation:

Work done = force x perpendicular distance moved

Calculate force using F= ma: F = 0.9 x 10; F = **9N**; Work Done: 9 x 4 = **36J**

Since the perpendicular distance remains the same when Tommy holds the book at the same height: Work Done: 9 x 0 = **0J**

6. **E**

Explanation:

The percentage of sales from pencils: 100 - (44.8 +26.9 + 6.7 + 3.6) = **18%**

As a circle has 360°, 18% of this will represent pencils: 0.18 x 360 = **64.8°**

7. **C**

Explanation:

Anaerobic respiration in yeast requires enzymes and glucose to produce **carbon dioxide and ethanol**. In humans, anaerobic respiration produces **lactic acid** instead of ethanol.

8. **E**

Explanation:

Consider Electromagnet 'X':

Equation: F = BIL

F (force) = 2.5 N; B (magnetic flux density/magnetic field strength) = 50 T

I = ?; L = 0.1 m

$I = \frac{F}{BL}$; $I = \frac{2.5}{50 \times 0.1}$; I = **0.5 A**

Consider Electromagnet 'Y':

Equation: F = BIL

F (force) = 16.5 N; B (magnetic flux density/magnetic field strength) = 5.5 T; I = ?; L = 0.4 m ; $I = \frac{F}{BL}$; $I = \frac{16.5}{5.5 \times 0.4}$; I = **7.5 A**

Therefore, the total amount of current produced: 7.5 + 0.5 = **8 A**

9. **D**

Explanation:

First, solve the brackets:

Assuming that 'j' is 3 and 'k' is 4: $3 \S 4 = \frac{3^{-1}}{4 \times 3^{-4}}$; $3 \S 4 = \frac{27}{4}$

Assuming that 'j' is 1 and 'k' is $\frac{27}{4}$*:* $1 \S \frac{27}{4} = \frac{1^{-1}}{\frac{27}{4} \times 1^{-\frac{27}{4}}}$; $1 \S \frac{27}{4} = \frac{4}{27}$

10. **C**

Explanation:

Two positive ions, Cu^{2+} and H^+ (from the solution) are attracted to the cathode. When hydrogen is more reactive than the metal (higher up in the reactivity series), **the metal is produced**. This is due to the hydrogen ions being less willing to accept electrons than a less reactive metal, such as copper. At the anode, **Oxygen is produced** (from hydroxide ions), unless halide ions (chloride, bromide or iodide ions) are present. If halides are present, they lose their electrons before oxygen does in order to form the corresponding halogen.

Mock Test

11. C

Explanation:

Metabolic rate (heart rate and respiratory rate) is higher per unit of body mass in small animals (largest surface area to volume ratio) compared to larger ones. This is due to smaller animals having a larger metabolic rate, which is characterised by a higher respiratory and heart rate. Therefore, animals with a higher respiratory rate will have a larger surface area per unit volume of the body. As a result, <u>**Animal 5**</u> has the largest surface area to volume ratio (with the slowest heart rate), and <u>**Animal 2**</u> has the smallest (with the fastest heart rate).

---

12. B

Explanation:

First, find the primary voltage:

V = I x R; V = 16 x 0.8; V = <u>12.8 V</u>

To find the voltage in the secondary transformer, use the equation:

$\frac{V_P}{V_S} = \frac{n_P}{n_S}$; $\frac{12.8}{Vs} = \frac{5}{120}$

Invert fractions: $\frac{V_S}{12.8} = \frac{120}{5}$; $V_s = \frac{120}{5}$ x 12.8; V_s = <u>307.2 V</u>

If the voltage in the secondary coil is larger than the voltage in the primary coil, it is a <u>**step - up transformer**</u>.

---

13. E

Explanation:

Consider $0.\dot{8}$*:*

Let: $x = 0.88888$..... <u>(Equation 1)</u>

Therefore, $10\,x = 8.88888888$.... <u>(Equation 2)</u>

Subtract Equation 1 from Equation 2: $9x = 8$; $x = \frac{8}{9}$

Consider $0.\dot{6}2\dot{5}$*:*

Let: $x = 0.625625625625$..... <u>(Equation 1)</u>

Therefore, $1000\,x = 625.625625625$.... <u>(Equation 2)</u>

Subtract Equation 1 from Equation 2: $999\,x = 625$; $x = \frac{625}{999}$

Therefore, 999 $(\frac{888}{999} - \frac{625}{999})$ = <u>263</u>

---

14. B

Explanation:

Gamma rays have the shortest wavelength since they can carry the most energy. The order of all seven electromagnetic waves from the highest to lowest wavelength is:

<u>Gamma Rays; X-rays; Ultraviolet; Optical; Infrared; Microwaves; Radio waves</u>

---

15. G

Explanation:

Only <u>**photosynthesis**</u> removes carbon from the atmosphere (carbon dioxide + water → glucose + oxygen). <u>**Decomposition, combustion and respiration**</u> add carbon to the atmosphere.

16. B

Explanation:

Methane is an example of a **covalent** substance. As a result, it has **low melting and boiling points** because little energy is required to break the weak intermolecular forces. Methane **does not conduct electricity** since there are no free electrons, and no overall electric charge. At room temperature, methane is a **colourless, odourless gas**.

17. B

Explanation:

Using circle theorems:

Tangents to a circle from the same point are equal; therefore, **WY and WX are equal.**

Triangle WXY must be an isosceles triangle. Angles WYX and WXY are equal.

Let x be angle WYX or angle WXY:

$x + x + 58 = 180$ (angles in a triangle add up to 180°); $2x = 122$; $\underline{x = 61°}$

Using circle theorems:

Alternate segment theorem; angle WXY will be equal to XZY in the opposite segment. **Therefore, XZY = 61°**

18. D

Explanation:

One mole of a gas occupies a set volume at a given temperature and pressure (24 dm^3 at room temperature and pressure).

Firstly, the volume of ethanol gas must be calculated:

M_r of C_2H_6O: $2(12) + 6 + 16 = 46$

Number of moles $= \frac{\text{mass}}{M_r}$; $\frac{345}{46} = \underline{7.5 \text{ moles}}$

Volume (dm^3) = number of moles x 24; 7.5 x 24 = **180 dm^3**

Secondly, the volume of ammonia gas must be calculated:

M_r of ammonia: $14 + 3 = \underline{17}$

Number of moles $= \frac{\text{mass}}{M_r}$; $\frac{272}{17} = \underline{16}$

Volume (dm^3) = number of moles x 24; 16 x 24 = **384 dm^3**

Add the two volumes (in dm^3): 180 + 384 = **564 dm^3**

The question states the volume to be in cm^3.

Convert dm^3 to cm^3: x1000; 564 x 1000 = **564,000 cm^3**

Therefore, **Option 'D' is the correct answer**.

19. C

Explanation:

The small intestine consists of three parts - the **duodenum**, the **jejunum** and the **ileum**. The large intestine is divided into three main regions - the **caecum** (the **appendix** is attached here), the **colon** (ascending, transverse, descending and sigmoid)) and the **rectum**.

20. D

Explanation:

Calculate the car's initial speed:

5400 metres in 120 seconds

$\frac{5400}{120} = 45 \text{ ms}^{-1}$

Mock Test

Consider the 80 kg passenger: Force = $\frac{\text{mass x change in velocity}}{\text{time}}$; Force = $\frac{80 \times 35}{5}$; **Force = 560 N**

Consider the 45kg passenger: Force = $\frac{\text{mass x change in velocity}}{\text{time}}$; Force = $\frac{45 \times 35}{5}$; **Force = 315 N**

Therefore, total force on the two passengers: 315 + 560 = **875 N**

21. D

Explanation:

In order to balance the chemical reaction, the number of each element on both sides must be equal. On the left-hand side, initially there is one molybdenum atom, two sulfur atoms and two oxygen atom. On the right-hand side, there is one molybdenum atom, one sulfur atom and five oxygen atom. By process of elimination, **Option 'D'** results in the equation having equal numbers of molybdenum, oxygen and sulfur atoms on either side.

22. A

Explanation:

Consider the equation:

Thermal energy (J)=

specific heat capacity ($Jkg^{-1}°C^{-1}$) x mass (kg) x temperature change (°C)

Consider 25 grams of vegetable oil: Thermal energy = 1800 x 0.025 x 60

Thermal energy = **2700 J**

Consider 30 grams of water: Thermal energy = 4200 x 0.03 x 25

Thermal energy = **3150 J**

Therefore, difference in thermal energy: 3150 - 2700 = **450 J**

Convert into kJ: $\frac{450}{1000}$ = **0.45 kJ**

23. D

Explanation:

One could choose either one pink and one purple marble, or one purple and one pink marble.

The number of pink marbles in the original bag: 36 - (10 + 12) = 14

There are 36 marbles in the bag:

Probability of getting a pink marble on the first try = $\frac{14}{36}$

This question is regarding dependent probability because the marble is not replaced.

Probability of getting a purple marble on the second try = $\frac{10}{35}$

(There are 35 marbles in the bag as one has been removed in the first try).

Probability of one pink and one purple: $\frac{14}{36} \text{ X } \frac{10}{35} = \frac{1}{9}$

Probability of getting a purple marble on the first try = $\frac{10}{36}$

This question is regarding dependent probability because the marble is not replaced.

Probability of getting a pink marble on the second try = $\frac{14}{35}$

(There are 35 marbles in the bag as one has been removed in the first try).

Probability of one pink and one purple: $\frac{10}{36} \text{ X } \frac{14}{35} = \frac{1}{9}$

Mock Test

Therefore, total probability: $\frac{1}{9}+\frac{1}{9}=\frac{2}{9}$

24. B

Explanation:

The atomic number (35) displays the number of protons present in the nucleus. As a result, **Options 'C' and 'D' can be eliminated**. The mass number (97) illustrates the number of protons and neutrons present in the nucleus. Consequently, by subtracting the atomic number from the mass number the number of neutrons can be found: 97 - 35=**62**

Usually, in atoms, the number of protons is equal to the number of electrons, since there is no overall charge. Since this bromide ion has a negative charge of -1, it has one more electron than protons present (electrons are negatively charged). The correct number of electrons is 35+1=36; hence, the **correct Option is 'B'**.

25. G

Explanation:

Both plant and animal cells possess a **cell membrane** (to control the entry and exit of materials), **chromosomal DNA** (since they are eukaryotes) and **mitochondria** (for aerobic respiration). Only plant cells possess a **vacuole**, **chloroplasts** and a **cellulose cell wall**.

26. C

Explanation:

Pentane (5 carbons) has a longer carbon chain length compared to propene (3 carbons). Along increasing carbon chain length, the **boiling points increase** due to an increased number of intermolecular forces required to overcome. **Viscosity also increases** due to the increasing number of intermolecular forces present with a longer carbon chain length. Longer hydrocarbon chains have a **smaller degree of flammability** because they have a lower proportion of carbon-hydrogen bonds compared to carbon-carbon bonds, for the same number of atoms.

27. B

Explanation:

Adrenaline stimulates the 'fight or flight response' in stressful situations; this leads to an increase in heart rate and respiratory rate, and an increase in glucose production to increase the blood glucose concentration. **Thyroxine** is responsible for metabolism - it aids in heart and digestive function, bone health and muscle control. **Follicle Stimulating Hormone (FSH)** stimulates oestrogen, which causes ovulation to occur (due to an increase in Luteinising Hormone). As a result, **progesterone** inhibits LH in order to prevent further ovulation.

Mock Test 2	Writing Task (Section 3)	Sample Answers

Task 1 - Rich individuals should not be able to buy better medical treatment.

The NHS, founded on the 5th July 1948, was designed to be free at the point of delivery and equitable to all citizens. Consequently, one may postulate that the healthcare sector should not discriminate against an individual's financial status; thus, treatment must not be governed by income.

However, there are two underlying assumptions in this statement. Firstly, it assumes that poor health can be compensated by expensive treatment. An exception, amongst others, is Type II diabetes, which is predominantly influenced by a sedentary lifestyle. Consequently, there is no medical intervention that can prevent the development of the disease - only a healthy diet and regular exercise could help in its prevention. Alternatively, individuals may spend additional money on healthcare for reasons other than better treatment. Private healthcare has shorter waiting times for elective procedures, including dermatology and dental care, and the patient would be able to see the consultant of his or her choice. Although these advantages can contribute to patient outcome, they do not directly influence it.

One may contend that people should be able to spend their own income freely. Individuals may prioritise their finances on healthcare rather than other aspects, such as holidays. Furthermore, all UK citizens pay taxes that fund the NHS, which allows everyone to have access to free healthcare. If one wishes to have additional benefits by paying more money, it is his or her prerogative to do so.

Paying for healthcare may expedite a patient's healthcare journey due to shorter waiting times and an ability to select a specific healthcare provider for his or her treatment. As a result, individuals who have the financial ability should be allowed to access private healthcare and purchase better medical treatment if they wish, since they are also paying taxes that contribute towards the NHS.

Task 2 -Life has a natural end, and doctors and healthcare professionals need to recognise that the point may come in the progression of a patient's condition where death is drawing near. - ***UK General Medical Council, Good Practice***

As per the Hippocratic Oath, doctors and healthcare professionals must ensure that the pillars of medical ethics are upheld. The principle of non-maleficence demonstrates the core tenet of *'primum non nocere'* [first, do no harm] and implies that the benefit of a treatment must outweigh any risk or potential side effects. In addition, the doctor or healthcare professional must act as a patient's advocate in order to maintain beneficence. Consequently, he or she must ensure that the proposed treatment is in the patient's best interest. Furthermore, due to a patient's autonomy, it is his or hers prerogative to refuse treatment; the physician must bear this in mind. Therefore, if all of the treatment options are exhausted, or one of the above criteria is not met, the physician must recognise the imminent outcome of death.

Failure to recognise this outcome could result in a variety of consequences. Firstly, the doctor could induce false hope to the patient, and, therefore, not act in a veracious manner. Secondly, the patient's quality of life may be inadvertently compromised further by offering treatments with no probability of success. For example, regardless of the proposed treatment, an individual with metastasised Stage IV colon cancer that has spread to different organs, such as the liver, possesses a very slim chance of survival. If a doctor or healthcare professional believes that the treatment should be curtailed in the best interest of the patient, and the patient is compos mentis, then he or she must warn the patient in an empathetic manner. As a result, the patient can have important conversations and make necessary arrangements with family and friends.

In conclusion, I concur that doctors and healthcare professionals must be able to recognise the imminent outcome of death in certain individuals. Hence, these individuals are able to maintain a good quality of life until the very end, without undue pain and suffering.

Task 3 -In the next 15 years, biological sciences will be less useful in medicine compared to data sciences and software.

Due to the rapid progression of new technologies, it appears that technology (in the form of data sciences and software) is a greater contributing factor to the development of medicine compared to human knowledge. Analysing data allows trends in the population to be identified, for example, an increased prevalence of melanoma or testicular cancer in the Caucasian population. In addition to this, the human genome was mapped using complex software - this allowed many gene variations, such as the ones present in Polycystic Kidney Disease and Huntington's chorea, to be discovered. Likewise, some individuals were identified as having a genetic predisposition to Type I diabetes. In surgery, the introduction of robots has allowed procedures to be performed in an efficient manner.

However, a sound understanding of biological sciences is essential, since it catalyses the rate at which new software can be developed. For example, interpreting the human genome requires a detailed understanding of genetics. In order to gain data regarding genetic conditions, such as Neurofibromatosis and Tuberous Sclerosis, medical researchers must be able to recognise the disease manifestation so that an individual to be accurately diagnosed. In robotic surgery, although it appears that the machine is performing the procedure, nonetheless, surgeons must be able to rely on their own anatomical knowledge and scientific understanding to control the robot and to be prepared to intervene in case of a machine malfunction.

In conclusion, I believe that the reliance of technology in medicine is increasing; however, it cannot compensate for the essential scientific knowledge required by the physicians. Furthermore, a sound understanding of biological sciences is required to create the software algorithms that can be used in a variety of medical equipment.

Mock Test 3	Thinking Skills (Section 1)	Answers

Question	Answer
1.	D
2.	A
3.	B
4.	C
5.	E
6.	B
7.	B
8.	B
9.	D
10.	C
11.	A
12.	B
13.	C
14.	B
15.	B
16.	B
17.	C
18.	C
19.	C
20.	A
21.	A
22.	C
23.	D
24.	D
25.	E
26.	D
27.	B
28.	E
29.	C
30.	B
31.	C
32.	B

1. D

Explanation:

In Supermarket 'A' she spent £6.

She spent £6 - £2.50 = **£3.50 on bananas and strawberries.**

4+3 = 7; £3.50 ÷ 7 = **£0.50**

Cost of bananas: 4 x £0.50 = **£2.00**; *Cost of strawberries:* 3 x £0.50 = **£1.50**

In Supermarket 'B':

Price of bananas: £2 x 1.25 = **£2.50**; *Price of strawberries:* £1.50 x 1.1 = **£1.65**

Mock Test

Price of orange juice: £2.50 ÷ 2 = **£1.25**
Total cost = £2.50 + £1.65 + £1.25; **Total cost = £5.40**

2. A

Explanation:

It does not matter which flavour is picked out first; therefore, there is a choice of six different chocolate bars from the total of six. Assume the first bar that was picked was caramel, then the next bar will be white chocolate. This has a probability of $\frac{3}{5}$, since one caramel bar has been removed from the bag; however, there are still three white chocolate bars left. The next bar chosen will be caramel. There are two bars left in the bag out of a total of four. The probabilities should all be multiplied together:

$1 \text{ x} \frac{3}{5} \text{x} \frac{2}{4} \text{ x} \frac{2}{3} \text{ x} \frac{1}{2} \text{x } 1 = \mathbf{\frac{1}{10}}$

It does not matter which flavour was chosen first as they both give the same answer - it is the alternating sequence which is the important part of the question.

3. B

Explanation:

Conclusion - Peer interaction is vital for development and is not possible due to the global pandemic.

Evidence - Studies have shown the importance of peer acceptance and peer influence in adolescence. Animal research has shown that social deprivation and isolation have unique effects on brain and behaviour in adolescence compared with other stages of life.

The main conclusion of the passage is best illustrated in **Option 'B'**. However, the use of social media and interacting through technology has reduced the negative impacts brought about by a lack of face-to-face contact. **Options 'A' and 'C'** are statements that are mentioned in the passage; however, they are not the main conclusions. **Option 'D'** does not state the full conclusion which includes the fact that technology makes the lack of face-to-face interaction less detrimental. **Option 'E'** is not mentioned in the passage.

4. C

Explanation:

Conclusion - Masks should be used as part of a comprehensive strategy of measures to suppress transmission and save lives.

Evidence - The use of a mask alone is not sufficient to provide an adequate level of protection against COVID-19. One should also maintain a minimum physical distance of at least one metre from others, frequently wash hands and avoid touching the face or the mask. The use of masks and social distancing will reduce the spread of the virus and provide increased protection. This is achieved by reducing the chances of people getting infected or infected people spreading the virus. Therefore, **Option 'C' is the correct answer**. It does not prevent or stop the spread of COVID – 19; hence, **Options 'A' and 'B'** are incorrect. The passage only states the advantages of the masks; it does not state that everyone should wear one – **Option 'D'** is false. There is no information regarding fabric masks in the extract given in the question; as a result, **Option 'E'** cannot be concluded.

5. E

Explanation:

If 40 family rooms are available and the ratio of the rooms are 4:7, there are **70 single rooms available** (40 ÷ 4 = 10 then 10 x 7 = 70).

The total number of rooms currently available is 40 + 70 = **110**. The percentage is **110 ÷ 150 = 73%**

6. B

Explanation:

Since five builders take three days to build a kitchen, one builder will take 5 x 3 = 15 days to build a kitchen. If two builders don't come to work, there will be three builders left. They will take 15 ÷ 3 = 5 days to complete the work. Therefore, the kitchen in House B will take 2 days longer to be built than the kitchen in House A.

7. B

Explanation:

Conclusion - Maria thinks that she would feel better if she also got prescribed the same antibiotic. She decides to meet and request her GP to prescribe her antibiotics, since she has proof that Jatin is getting better.

Evidence - Jatin and Maria are both feeling unwell. Jatin visits the GP surgery. He was prescribed some antibiotics as his GP said he has a bacterial infection. Jatin starts to feel better after a week.

The passage does not mention that Maria and Jatin have the same illness; therefore, Maria cannot assume that the drug would work to cure her illness as it did with Jatin. As a result, **Option 'B'** best represents the flaw in the argument. Maria could have a viral infection - in which case the GP will not prescribe an antibiotic as this is ineffective against viruses. **Options 'A', 'C' and 'D'** are not relevant flaws in the passage, which is focused on whether Maria would feel better if she was prescribed the same drug as Jatin. **Option 'E'** does not directly address the issue of Maria assuming that the same medication that Jatin was prescribed would help her too.

8. B

Explanation:

The total number of true positives is 12. The actual number of people who have the disease is $6 + 12 = 18$; however, only 12 of these are identified. Therefore, the proportion of true positive patients who are correctly identified are $\frac{12}{18} = \frac{2}{3}$.

9. D

Explanation:

Time from invitation to screening:

(4 months x 2) + 2 weeks = 8 months 2 weeks

Time from screening to next invitation: 2 years

Given that the question asks for his 5th screening, consider 8 months 2 weeks multiplied by 5, which produces: 40 months 10 weeks = 3 years 6 months 2 weeks

The 2-year wait would have occurred 4 times in the period between his 55th birthday and the 5th screening; that gives 8 years.

Hence, the youngest age he would be at his 5th screening is: $55 + 8 + 3 =$ 66 years old (the months and weeks can be ignored in this case as the options are only expressed in years).

10. C

Explanation:

Conclusion - The more training a puppy receives, he or she will be more obedient. This is because the dog will always follow instructions given by the owner.

Evidence - Puppies should be trained from a young age if they are to become obedient and gentle dogs. They will learn more if they are trained early and if the owners often revisit the tricks that they have taught their puppies. The more training a puppy receives, he or she will be more obedient.

Option 'C' best represents the flaw in the argument. **Option 'A'** does not directly relate to the passage of training dogs as puppies. **Option 'B'** could be a point that weakens the argument; however, it is not as directly related to the passage. The passage is talking about training all dogs to become obedient and gentle – **Option 'D'** does not cover all of the relevant points. **Option 'E'** is also not directly related to the argument.

11. A

Explanation:

The total amount of crisps that can be obtained from 10 kg of potatoes is **5 kg.** The packet contains 140 grams of crisps. However, since they decrease this by 15%, there will be **140 x 0.85 = 119 grams of crisps in each packet.** The total amount of crisps is **5 kg = 5000 g.**
5000 ÷ 119 = 42.0168... The maximum number of packets that can be fully filled to 119 grams is 42. This accounts for 42 x 119 = 4998 grams of crisps. The amount is left over is **5000 – 4998 = 2 grams.**

12. B

Explanation:

A total of 30 miles cost £45 and 70 miles cost £80. Therefore, the company charges £35 for 40 miles; this is **£0.875 per mile**. For 30 miles, the cost would be 30 x 0.875 = £26.25. Since the company charges £45, the **base rate is £45 - £26.25 = £18.75.** To travel 120 miles, it would cost: **£18.75 + (120 x 0.875) = £123.75**

13. C

Explanation:

Option 'A' is false as there is nothing in the passage to confirm this. **Option 'B'** is also not the correct answer since it cannot be concluded that some students only play hockey as they could participate in hockey and swimming or hockey and football. **Option 'C'** is the correct answer as it is known that **some students play both hockey and swimming and some play hockey and football, so it could be possible that some play all three sports.** As a result, it is the correct answer because one can definitely state that some students play two sports. **Option 'D'** is false as it does not state anywhere on the text that some students only play football. **Option 'E'** is also incorrect as **it cannot be stated for certain that some students do all three sports** as there is only evidence that some do two for certain – this is the reason why Option 'C' is correct and Option 'E' is not.

14. B

Explanation:

Conclusion - The company would save a lot of money by replacing their workers with the machines. This will increase their profits.

Evidence - The new machines that were bought by the factory are much more efficient and makes fewer mistakes compared to the workers there.

The main argument in the passage is that the machines are more cost-effective than the workers, and, therefore, replacing the workers with the machines would increase profits. As a result, **Option 'B' weakens the argument**. This is because the initial cost of machines would be too high for profits to increase - this is not more cost-effective than having the workers. The other statements do not directly relate to the argument as these do not mention the cost and profits made by this decision.

15. B

Explanation:

Conclusion - Wesley believes involving pupils in more extracurricular activities such as playing a musical instrument or being a part of a sports team will improve their concentration in class. He believes that this will then lead to better examination grades.

Evidence - He states that schools that involve more extracurricular activities into the timetable have shown better examination results and higher pass rates.

Wesley's evidence for his argument is that schools who include more extracurricular activities in their timetable have better examination results. The assumption made to link his evidence to the argument is that examination results are a reliable measure of how well pupils focus in class. Therefore, **Option 'B' is the correct answer.**

16. B

Explanation:

In a 24-hour period, the first app will use: 24 x 2 = 48 (48 lots of 30 minutes in a day), 48 x 1.5 = 72 → 72% of the battery life is consumed by the first app in a day as 1.5% is used up every 30 minutes. The second app uses 20% of battery in 24 hours of this, which is 72 x 0.2 = 14.4%. Therefore, the battery life will decrease by 72 + 14.4 = 86.4%; 100 – 86.4 = 13.6%. The battery percentage on her phone the next day will be 13.6%.

17. C

Explanation:

The current ratio of salted to caramel is 15:17; this could be 15 packets of salted popcorn and 17 packets of caramel flavoured popcorn. Since the number of salted popcorn decreased by 25%, the current number of packets is 75% of original number of packets at the start of the day. Let x be the number of packets of salted popcorn at the start of the day: $\frac{15}{x} = \frac{75}{100}$; $x = \frac{1500}{75}$; $\boldsymbol{x = 20}$. Since half the number of caramel flavoured popcorn was sold, half is now left at the end of the day. This means that the original number of packets of caramel flavoured popcorn was 17 x 2 = 34. The ratio of salted to caramel is therefore 20: 34; this simplifies to 10:17.

18. C

Explanation:

Exactly $\frac{1}{3}$ of the biscuits are custard cream; therefore, $\frac{2}{3}$ of the total number of biscuits are either digestives or shortbreads. Let the number of shortbreads be x; therefore, the number of digestives is $2x$.

$\frac{2}{3} = 2x + x; \frac{2}{3} = 3x; x = \frac{2}{9}$

The proportion of shortbreads in the tin is $\frac{2}{9}$, the proportion of digestives are therefore $\frac{4}{9}$. The minimum number of biscuits in the tin is 9, since $\frac{1}{3} = \frac{3}{9}$; the minimum number of custard creams is 3.

19. C

Explanation:

Conclusion - Teachers without a PhD should not apply for a job at this school.

Evidence - Due to high competition, the physics teachers at a particular school require a PhD qualification in order to be recruited.

The passage states that physics teachers need a PhD, and not that all teachers require a PhD to be recruited. Therefore, **Option 'C' is the correct answer** due to this generalisation being made. **Options 'A', 'B' and 'E'** are incorrect as it does not address the generalisation being made for all teachers. **Option 'D'** is irrelevant since a PhD is a requirement for a new job application for physics teachers. Therefore, the qualifications of the current teachers are not relevant.

20. A

Explanation:

Conclusion - Hobbes argued that people, when left to their own devices, were naturally vicious.

Evidence - Fortunately, they were also gregarious, and it was through their groups, societies and civilisations that people expressed their best selves.

Hobbes argues that humans are naturally vicious, and it is social interactions that allows humans to behave in a more civilised manner. The assumption that can be made is that humans have become more tolerant and adjusting to live in a society that interacts with other humans. Being vicious would prevent humans living in groups. Therefore, **Option 'A' is the correct answer**. **Options 'B' and 'C'** are not directly related to the passage since nothing is mentioned regarding rules or laws. **Option 'D'** is also irrelevant as punishment for such behaviours isn't used in Hobbes' argument. **Option 'E'** is already mentioned in the passage - it is not an assumption.

21. A

Explanation:

Conclusion - Soap bubbles that deliver pollen to flowers could offer an alternative way of fertilising plants as bee populations decline, while being more delicate than other methods.

Evidence - There is a lot of interest in developing new approaches to fertilise flowers, because about 90 percent of flowering plants depend on insect pollinators, such as bees, whose populations are falling due to climate change and pesticide use.

Therefore, **Option 'A' is the main conclusion** of the passage. **Options 'B' and 'E'** mention pesticides - this is not the main subject of the passage. Although **Options 'C' and 'D'** are true, they are just points made in the argument and are not the main conclusions of the entire passage.

22. C

Explanation:

All imported items are expensive; however, it is not known if all items that are expensive in the supermarket are imported. Therefore, **Option 'A'** is incorrect. **Option 'B'** is false as some vegetables are imported, which means they are expensive. **Option 'C' is true** since all fruits are imported; therefore, if it is not imported, it cannot be a fruit. **Option 'D'** is incorrect as all fruits are expensive because they are all imported. It cannot be inferred from the passage if **Option 'E'** is true.

23. D

Explanation:

Let x be the number of marbles in the bag. **There are $\frac{2}{3}$ x marbles remaining in the bag after the first minute** when $\frac{1}{3}$ of the marbles were removed. At the end of the second minute, there are $\frac{2}{3} \times \frac{2}{3} x = \frac{4}{9} x$ marbles left. Therefore, at the end of the fourth minute there are: $\left(\frac{2}{3}\right)^4 x = \frac{16}{81} x$ marbles left. Therefore, $32 = \frac{16}{81} x$; $\mathbf{x = 162}$

Mock Test

24. D

Explanation:

For her first pick, she has a choice of 7 scarves; after this there are only 6 different colours that she can choose from if she is not to wear the same colour scarf on consecutive days. In a week there are 7 days; therefore, she has to pick one on each of the 7 days. Hence, she would choose a scarf 7 different times. The number of different ways that this can be done is 7 x 6 x 6 x 6 x 6 x 6 x 6 = 326,592.

25. E

Explanation:

Conclusion - Layla will become a successful music teacher.

Evidence - To become a successful music teacher, one requires a natural talent, dedication to his/her work and patience. Layla is a very talented singer and has always been hardworking and dedicated to her work. She has also demonstrated a lot of patience during her training.

The passage mentions the qualities to become a successful music teacher; however, this does not mean that these factors are sufficient. The period of time that Layla has been training for is irrelevant to the argument. Option 'A' is incorrect. The passage does not state what the natural talent needs to be. As a result, Option 'B' is not a flaw, since singing could still count as a talent. Option 'C' is not a flaw in the argument laid out. Option 'D' is incorrect as the passage only says that successful music teachers require natural talent, not all music teachers. Consequently, **Option 'E' is the correct answer.**

26. D

Explanation:

The range given by the 3 scales are: **99 g: 95 g - 103 g, 101 g: 97 g - 105 g; 102 g: 98 g - 106 g.** To get the minimum range, take the greatest value of the lower limit and the lowest value of the upper limit. In this case, it would be **98 g to 103 g.**

27. B

Explanation:

The oldest pirate will be able to split the coins to 98-0-1-0-1 among the five pirates from oldest to youngest and still survive.

Let the five pirates be Pirates A, B, C, D and E - arranged from oldest to youngest. With the 98-0-1-0-1 allocation, Pirates A, C and E will agree to the distribution and Pirate A will survive. Pirates C and E will agree to the deal because if Pirate A is killed, Pirate B will allocate the coins by 99-0-1-0. Pirates B and D will agree to this allocation and this would mean that Pirates C and E will not get any coins (which is a loss to them). Pirate D, who is rational, will agree to the 99-0-1-0 allocation for the same reason as to why Pirates C and E accepted Pirate A's deal. If Pirate D disagrees with Pirate B, Pirate C will take over and the deal will be 99-0-1. Pirates C and E will agree to this and thus, Pirate D will not receive any coins at all. It is known that Pirate E will agree to 99-0-1 because if he doesn't, Pirate C will be killed, and Pirate D will take over. When this happens, Pirate D will make the deal 100-0 and his single vote is enough to make it 50%. Pirate E will then have no choice but to accept no coins.

28. E

Explanation:

The front cover of the magazine is always counted as page 1. Hence, it can be extrapolated that the number on the right-hand page will always be odd. This would allow Options 'A', 'B'

and 'D' to be eliminated. The number on the left-hand page at the centre of the newspaper must be half of a multiple of 24 - i.e., a multiple of 12. **Only Option 'E' satisfies this rule**.

29. C

Explanation:

Let the point at which Mr Bebb met Mari be Point 'X'. In the question, it is known that Mr Bebb drives from home to Point 'X' to pick Mari up before driving back home. Let the time for this whole trip be called 'T'. The time taken for Mr Bebb for 'T' allowed Mr Bebb and Mari to arrive home 20 minutes earlier than their usual. This means that the total time usually taken by Mr Bebb to travel the full distance of home-school-home is T + 20 minutes. Hence, the distance that Mr Bebb did not drive on this particular day is 20 minutes long. Given that Mr Bebb drives at a constant speed, the one-way distance between Point 'X' and the school must be a 10-minute drive. Given that Mr Bebb leaves his house at a fixed time to arrive at Mari's school at 4:30 pm each Wednesday, this means that he must have met Mari at Point 'X' at 4:20 pm. Given that Mari has been walking for 30 minutes before she met her father at Point 'X', she must have left the meeting at 3:50 pm. Hence, **she missed 40 minutes of the meeting.**

30. B

Explanation:

First, establish that Judith now has 6 chains altogether. The most intuitive approach would be to break a link on the end of each of the five chains and then reseal the link to the back of the next chain in the loop. This would cost £30 for the six links that are broken and resealed. However, one can do it for £25. Instead of breaking a link in each chain, break all five links in one of the chains and then use those five links to attach the remaining five chains.

31. C

Explanation:

A total of 500 sweets are shared among 6 children. For the child with the third highest number of sweets to have the maximum number of sweets, the other children must have the minimum number of sweets possible. Hence, the three children who have the three least number of sweets must receive 30, 31 and 32 sweets respectively. This is a total of 93 sweets. Hence, there are 407 sweets left. With the remaining sweets, these must be shared such that the children with the two highest numbers of sweets are as close as possible to the third highest child. The integer 407 needs to be divided by three would make the highest get 136, the 2nd highest get 136 and 3rd highest get 135. However, given that no two children can have the same number of sweets, the 3rd highest child must give one sweet to the 1st highest child. Hence, the third child has 134 sweets. This would give: 1st - 137 sweets; 2nd - 136 sweets; 3rd - 134 sweets; 4th - 32 sweets; 5th - 31 sweets; 6th - 30 sweets.

32. B

Explanation:

The quickest way to solve this is to draw out the numbers 0 to 9 in their digital form. Once this is done, some numbers do not share the same light elements as Number 1. Those Numbers are 2, 5 and 6. Hence, any options with 4502, 4505 and 4506 are incorrect. That leaves **Options 'B' and 'D'**. **Option 'D'**, however, has the number 4501. This number should not be excluded as the board, though faulty, will display this number correctly. Therefore, **Option 'B' is the correct answer.**

A Lakshmi, T R Enoch, S Z Y Ooi. Doctors Academy Publications, Cardiff, UK, 2020.

Mock Test 3	Scientific Knowledge and Applications (Section 2)	Answers

Question	Answer
1.	A
2.	C
3.	G
4.	C
5.	D
6.	B
7.	E
8.	F
9.	D
10.	H
11.	D
12.	D
13.	F
14.	B
15.	C
16.	E
17.	D
18.	H
19.	B
20.	C
21.	D
22.	A
23.	B
24.	B
25.	C
26.	C
27.	B

1. A

Explanation:

Image 1 is an artery as it has a thick muscular wall and a smaller lumen compared to a vein. **Image 2** is a vein, which is characterised by the large lumen and less smooth muscle in the wall. **Image 3** is a capillary because it has a thin wall, which is one cell thick. **Image 4** is a nerve since the small circles within it show the axons surrounded by myelin sheath.

2. C

Explanation:

When aqueous sodium hydroxide is electrolysed, **hydrogen forms at the cathode and oxygen forms at the anode**. Hydrogen is made in preference to sodium at the cathode as sodium is higher than hydrogen in the reactivity series. Hence, sodium has less tendency to discharge. Therefore, it remains in the electrolyte solution and will not be discharged.

3. G

Explanation:

Statement 1 is true as less energy is transferred by mobile phones. **Statement 2 is false** as microwaves do not show much diffraction. Microwaves can penetrate glass and plastic; however, they are reflected by shiny metal surfaces – **Statement 3 is incorrect**. **Statement 4 is correct.**

4. C

Explanation:

Let the horizontal component be $'x'$. This must be expressed in terms of 'v'. A right-angle triangle can be formed to analyse the projectile. Therefore, $\mathbf{x = v\cos\theta}$

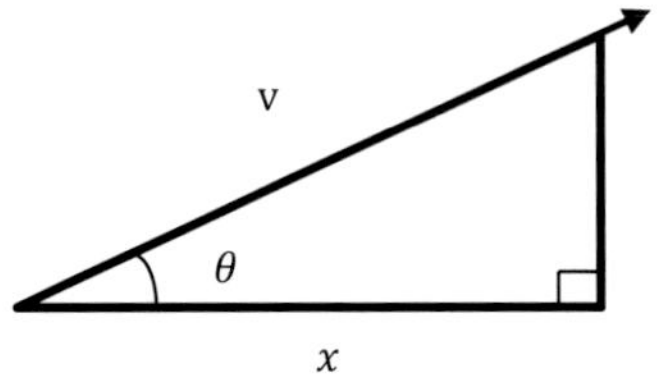

5. D

Explanation:

Since Vitamin D-resistant rickets is an X-linked disorder and Individual 1 (male) is affected, **he will pass his mutation to all his daughters**. This is because all of his daughters will receive an X chromosome from their father. Being a dominant disorder, all of the daughters will be affected. **None of the sons will be affected** as they all inherit the Y chromosome from the father, without the faulty allele.

6. B

Explanation:

Since the final amount of product made is the same, Reaction 2 should have the same number of moles of reactants as Reaction 1. The number of moles of HCl in Reaction 1 is:

n = cv

n = 0.2 x 0.1   ($100cm^3 = 0.1\ dm^3$); **n = 0.02 mol**

Therefore, **Reaction 2 must also have 0.02 moles of HCl**. This leaves **Options 'B' and 'D'**. Since the rate of reaction has decreased, granules of limestone were used instead of powdered limestone. **Granules have a smaller surface area** than the powder; consequently, the rate of reaction decreases. The decrease in concentration of HCl and decrease in surface area of limestone makes Reaction 2 slower than Reaction 1. However, the volume of CO_2 is the same because the same number of moles of the reactants are used. If the **temperature increases, the rate of reaction increases**. However, for this question, the answer can be obtained by looking at the number of moles of HCl and the particle size.

7. E

Explanation:

Velocity is a vector - it has both magnitude and direction. The direction of the path that Kate takes must not change if she is travelling at a constant velocity – her paths can only be **Options 3 or 4**. Since Harry is travelling at a constant speed which is a scalar quantity and has no direction, he can **take any of the 4 paths shown.**

8. F

Explanation:

The larger candle is $\frac{7.5}{5} = \frac{3}{2}$ times taller than the smaller candle.

The length scale factor is $\frac{3}{2}$.

The volume scale factor will be $\left(\frac{3}{2}\right)^3 = \frac{27}{8}$

The wax needed to make the larger candle is: $200 \times \frac{27}{8} =$ **675 grams**

9. D

Explanation:

The body maintains pH at **approximately 7.40** - the pH range of blood is **approximately 7.35 - 7.40**. **Venous blood is slightly more acidic than arterial blood** due to a higher concentration of carbon dioxide. Carbon dioxide is mainly transported in the blood as carbonic acid which decreases the pH (making it more acidic).

10. H

Explanation:

Write the equation for this reaction: $2NH_3 + NaClO \rightarrow NaCl + H_2O + N_2H_4$

The salt formed is NaCl. The oxidation state of N has changed from -3 in NH_3 to -2 in N_2H_4. It has lost an electron; therefore, it has been oxidised. **Statement 4 is correct.** Cl has been reduced from an oxidation state of +1 in NaClO to -1 in NaCl. **Statement 5 is correct.**

11. D

Explanation:

SUVAT equations need to be used in this question.

S = ?; U = 0; V = 25; A ; T = 60 (time must be in seconds since speed is given as ms^{-1})

$S = \frac{U+V}{2} \times T$; $S = \frac{0+25}{2} \times 60$; **S = 750 m**

Mock Test

12. D

Explanation:

This question requires the knowledge of the circle theorems.

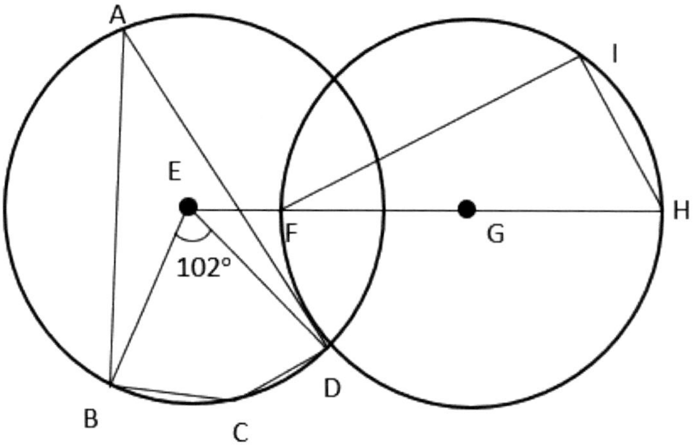

360 – 102 = **258°**

The angle subtended at the centre of the circle is twice that of the circumference (both the angles must be subtended from the same chord or arc).

Angle BCD is: 258 ÷ 2 = **129°**

The angle subtended from either end of the diameter of the circle is a right angle.

HIF = 90°

13. F

Explanation:

Those who are intolerant to dairy products are lactose intolerant; this means that they cannot produce the enzyme lactase. This enzyme is used to make milk for those who are lactose intolerant by converting the lactose in the milk to **glucose and galactose.** This requires the **lactase enzyme.**

14. B

Explanation:

To find the relative atomic mass: $\frac{\text{[Sum of (relative abdundance x Mr) of each isotope]}}{\text{Sum of isotope abundance}}$

$= \frac{[(28 \times 18)+(29 \times 1)+(30 \times 1)]}{18+1+1}$

$\frac{563}{20} = \mathbf{28.15}$

15. C

Explanation:

Longer and thinner wires have more resistance. Therefore, **Option 'C' is the correct answer.**

16. E

Explanation:

$3^{m+2} = 27^{m-6}$; $3^{m+2} = 3^{3(m-6)}$; m+2 = 3m – 18; 20 = 2m; **m = 10**

17. D

Explanation:

Water is lost through the stomata of the plant; therefore, the mass would decrease. The reading of the balance would show a decrease in mass - this leaves **Options 'C' and 'D'.** When the experiment is conducted in a dark room, the stomatal aperture is not open as much as it would be if the experiment was conducted with more light. This is because the guard cells lose water to become flaccid and close some of the stomata. Therefore, **Option 'D' is the correct answer**, since the minimal volume water being lost is shown by a small decrease in the reading on the balance.

18. H

Explanation:

Only lead ions and iodide ions react in this reaction. They form a precipitate out of the solution. The nitrate and sodium ions do not directly take part in the reaction.

Lead nitrate$_{(aq)}$ + Sodium iodide$_{(aq)}$ → Lead iodide$_{(s)}$ + Sodium nitrate$_{(aq)}$

19. B

Explanation:

Work out the power exhibited by Albert and Celina.

Power = force x speed; Power = force x $\frac{\text{distance}}{\text{time}}$

Force is in Newtons; therefore, both the masses have to be converted to weight by multiplying by 10.

Albert: Power = 700 x $\frac{6}{150}$; Power = 28 watts

Celina: Power = 600 x $\frac{9}{180}$; Power = 30 watts

The difference in their power is: 30 – 28 = 2 watts

20. C

Explanation:

$$\frac{63p^2q^5}{45p^7q^3} = \frac{7p^2q^5}{5p^7q^3} = \frac{7}{5}p^{-5}q^2$$

21. D

Explanation:

Blood group 'A' has A antigens in the red blood cells and anti-B antibodies in the plasma. Therefore, blood containing B antigens should not be given to Ruby since the anti-B antibodies in Ruby's plasma would react with the B antigens in the blood – this is called agglutination. She cannot receive from Donors 2, 4 and 7. RhD antigen is another protein that can be present on the red blood cell. If this protein is present then the individual is Rh positive. If it is not present, he or she is Rh negative, such as Ruby. Rh negative individuals cannot receive Rh positive blood. Ruby can **only receive A- or O- blood.**

22. A

Explanation:

Draw out the monomer:

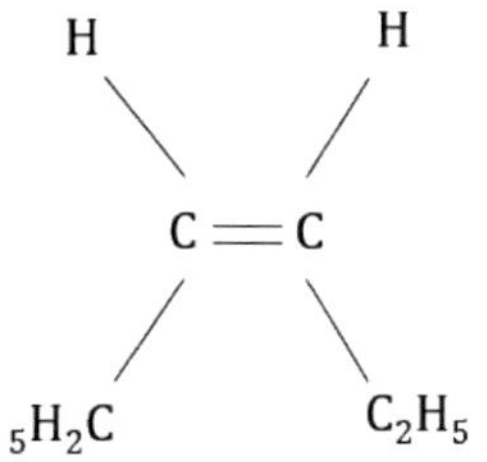

This will help identify the polymer by removing the double bond.

23. B

Explanation:

The area under a speed time graph is distance. If the acceleration n is constant, then the line is a straight line.

<u>The area of the triangle under the line represents the distance travelled</u>.

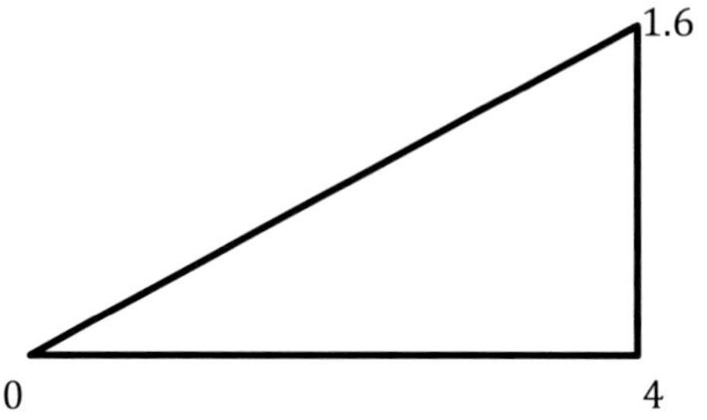

Area of the triangle $= \frac{1}{2}bh;\ \frac{1}{2} \times 4 \times 1.6 = \underline{\mathbf{3.2\ m}}$

Alternatively, SUVAT equations can be used. $s = \frac{u+v}{2}$ x t

$s = \frac{0+1.6}{2}$ x 4; $\underline{\mathbf{s = 3.2\ m}}$

---

24. B

Explanation:

Draw a tree diagram of the information provided.

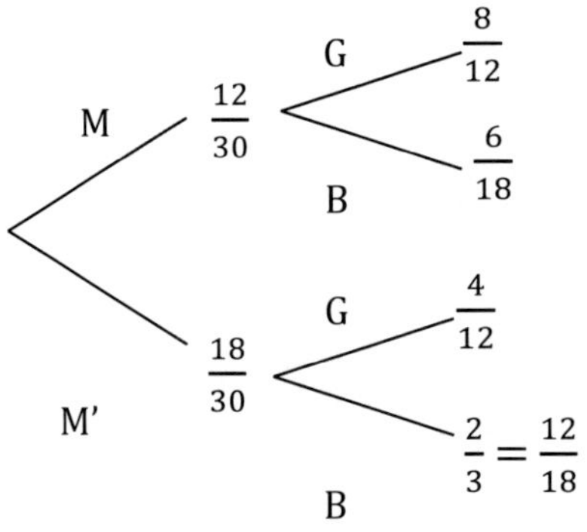

The total number of girls is $\underline{\mathbf{6 + 8 = 14}}$

The number of girls who play a musical instrument is 8.

The probability is $\frac{8}{14} = \frac{\mathbf{4}}{\mathbf{7}}$

Mock Test

25. C

Explanation:

Nitrifying bacteria turns ammonia into nitrates. Nitrifying bacteria include Nitrosomonas to convert ammonia to nitrites, and Nitrobacter to convert nitrites to nitrates. Nitrogen-fixing bacteria convert nitrogen gas to nitrogen compounds.

26. C

Explanation:

This is a hydration reaction of an alkene, in order to convert it to an alcohol.

27. B

Explanation:

After one half-life the count rate will be: $5600 \div 2 =$ <u>2800</u>

After two half-lives it will be: $2800 \div 2 =$ <u>1400</u>

After three half-lives it is: $1400 \div 2 =$ <u>700</u>

Three half-lives have passed in 12 hours. *Therefore, one half-life is:*

$12 \div 3 =$ <u>4 hours</u>

Mock Test 3	Writing Task (Section 3)	Sample Answers

Task 1 - Patients should be encouraged to diagnose and possibly treat themselves.

The abundant availability of health books and medical "advice" on the Internet has led to an increasing number of patients trying to diagnose and even treat themselves. Patients often misdiagnose themselves by comparing their ailments with symptoms that they have found online, and this could result in the patient not visiting his or her GP in a timely manner. The individual might think that he or she can remedy the condition at home by following information retrieved online, or he or she might believe that his or her condition is severe and avoid consulting the GP. The following scenario helps this idea to be better understood. A 51-year-old woman who has a persistent cough attempts to treat it with home remedies found in a magazine. Only after the cough fails to subside and worsens does she visit her GP. It is soon found that she has an advanced lung cancer. Crucial time was lost due to the fact that the patient tried to diagnose and treat herself.

On the other hand, popular health-related publications have increased the public's awareness of a healthy lifestyle by encouraging a balanced diet and regular exercise. This has allowed the general health of the public to improve. Celebrity endorsement of "super foods" and high-intensity exercise routines have also proved effective in motivating the population to be healthy. These simple and manageable ideas have, to a certain extent, contributed to the overall health of our society.

Doctors must always respect the autonomy of the patient whilst simultaneously ensuring that he or she is fully and correctly informed. It is the duty of the physician to advise his or her patient, to offer detailed information in non-technical and understandable terms, and to help the individual to reach the most appropriate decision. The physician has a fundamental role to play in the elimination of misunderstanding and misinformation amongst the general public.

In conclusion, doctors should ensure that patients are fully informed and direct them to authentic sources. However, the doctor must also be certain that he or she does not hinder the doctor-patient relationship or compromise the autonomy of the patient.

Task 2 - Medicine is a science and not an art.

Medicine is considered a branch of science; it is the fusion of biological and chemical notions to understand the mechanisms of the human body. It is argued that medicine is purely a science due to the strong scientific knowledge that doctors must possess in order to treat patients effectively. To prescribe medication, provide medical advice, and perform surgical procedures, the doctor must have a sound understanding of the biological and chemical processes that stimulate the way in which the human body functions. While the more creative side of medicine can be considered as an art, it is arguably underpinned by science; a Plastic Surgeon must ultimately comprehend wound healing in order to leave the patient with a minimal scar. This is the reason for
which the statement asserts that medicine is a science and not an art.

Certain individuals do, however, believe that medicine is an art since the doctor is required to combine scientific principles with practical aspects in a creative and innovative manner. The art of communication is extremely important for a doctor to build a relationship with his or her patients. The doctor must be able to explain the patient's condition in a way in which he or she understands in order to allow him or her to make informed decisions. It can thus be suggested that the art of medicine must
always be demonstrated, especially in a clinical context.

In conclusion, I believe that medicine can be considered as both an art and a science simultaneously. A doctor must be able to tailor the treatment of each patient by applying his or her core scientific knowledge creatively. The skills of the doctor, which are ultimately underpinned by the way in which the human body works, are often used in an artistic manner to achieve aesthetically-pleasing results; this is crucial for Plastic Surgeons.

Overall, it cannot be denied that medicine is largely a science, but doctors must have the ability to apply their knowledge in innovative ways to achieve optimum results.

Task 3 - Science is the great antidote to the poison of enthusiasm and superstition - *Adam Smith, The Wealth Of Nations, 1776*

A core tenet of science is that it is based on facts; it is not an abstract concept. As such, it attempts to challenge excessive emotion, such as enthusiasm, by providing concrete evidence that harnesses the truth. The statement implies that it is necessary for facts (science) to balance sociological factors (in the form of superstition). Science alleviates the unwarranted effects of enthusiasm and superstition and, therefore, allows the progression of novel ideas and approaches.

On the one hand, excessive enthusiasm may have detrimental consequences, since wrong conclusions could be drawn from the conducted research. A superstition is an observation made with limited evidence; it could result in the proclamation of an incorrect assertion. A reasoned error, which has the potential to mislead the general public, could emerge. During the 14th century, individuals believed that illness was caused by the devilish spirit. Yet, the advancement of science has proven that illness cannot be attributed to the Devil.

In contrast to the aforementioned paragraph, science has demystified many processes associated with superstition, such as the shape of the Earth. However, it has not been able to provide evidence for all phenomena, including the vagaries and interactions of the human genome.

In conclusion, superstition leads to questions and ideas, which ultimately results in the progression of science. In addition, enthusiasm is a positive contributing factor since it motivates scientists to uncover the objective truth. At present, science has been unable to provide answers for certain aspects of superstition, but we might hope that it will in the future.

List of Sources Used in the Critical Thinking (CT), Data Analysis (DA) and Mock Tests (MT)

Serial Number	Question Number	Adapted From	Source
1.	CT 1	Science News	https://www.sciencenews.org/article/coronavirus-covid-19-genetic-risk-factors-alzheimers-disease
2.	CT 2	The Conversation	https://theconversation.com/are-autonomous-cars-really-safer-than-human-drivers-90202
3.	CT 4	The NHS	https://www.nhs.uk/live-well/eat-well/red-meat-and-the-risk-of-bowel-cancer/
4.	CT 6	Science News	https://www.sciencenews.org/article/coronavirus-covid19-hydroxychloroquine-prevention-exposure
5.	CT 7	The Guardian	https://www.theguardian.com/news/2017/dec/05/portugals-radical-drugs-policy-is-working-why-hasnt-the-world-copied-it
6.	CT 8	The Conversation	https://theconversation.com/why-rehabilitation-not-harsher-prison-sentences-makes-economic-sense-132213
7.	CT 9	Science Daily	https://www.sciencedaily.com/releases/2019/08/190829101051.htm
8.	CT 10	Psychology Today	https://www.psychologytoday.com/gb/blog/talking-apes/202005/why-does-it-take-longer-go-there-come-back
9.	CT 11	New York Times	https://www.nytimes.com/2020/06/05/science/ocean-biology-larvaceans lasers.html
10.	CT 12	The Conversation	https://theconversation.com/how-ai-could-help-football-managers-spot-weak-links-in-their-teams-90276
11.	CT 13	The Washington Post	https://www.washingtonpost.com/news/animalia/wp/2017/11/03/pets-arent-wonder-drugs-heres-why-we-love-them-anyway/
12.	CT 14	The Washington Post	https://www.washingtonpost.com/business/2019/08/22/school-uniforms-are-rise-even-toddlers-its-changing-back-to-school-shopping/
13.	CT 15	Science Daily	https://www.sciencedaily.com/releases/2020/05/200526134651.htm
14.	CT 16	Science Daily	https://www.sciencedaily.com/releases/2020/04/200422091205.htm
15.	CT 17	New Scientist	https://www.newscientist.com/article/2241614-can-virtual-therapy-help-us-cope-with-the-coronavirus-lockdown/
16.	CT 18	The BMJ	https://www.bmj.com/content/369/bmj.m875
17.	CT 19	New Scientist	https://www.newscientist.com/article/mg24632800-900-is-the-universe-conscious-it-seems-impossible-until-you-do-the-maths/
18.	CT 20	The BMJ	https://www.bmj.com/content/367/bmj.l5373
19.	CT 21	The Guardian	https://www.theguardian.com/politics/2020/may/18/keeping-schools-closed-in-england-will-widen-educational-inequalities-study-ifs
20.	CT 37	Live Science	https://www.livescience.com/32320-how-long-can-a-person-survive-without-water.html).
21.	CT 38	New Scientist	https://www.newscientist.com/article/2245933-ancient-footprints-could-be-from-a-crocodile-that-walked-on-two-legs/
22.	CT 39	The BBC	https://www.bbc.co.uk/news/technology-52033217
23.	CT 40	NCBI	https://www.ncbi.nlm.nih.gov/pmc/articles/PMC2987399/
24.	CT 41	The BMJ	https://www.bmj.com/content/369/bmj.m2303
25.	CT 43	The CNN	https://edition.cnn.com/2020/06/08/health/pool-child-drowning-death-wellness/index.html
26.	CT 44	Science Daily	https://www.sciencedaily.com/releases/2020/05/200526151738.htm
27.	CT 45	NCBI	https://www.ncbi.nlm.nih.gov/pmc/articles/PMC6572041/
28.	CT 46	Medical News Today	https://www.medicalnewstoday.com/articles/323492
29.	CT 48	Independent	https://www.independent.co.uk/news/uk/home-news/homeless-deaths-homelessness-housing-rough-sleeping-a9055671.html
30.	CT 49	The Conversation	https://theconversation.com/reports-of-a-blood-test-for-alzheimers-have-yet-to-show-convincing-evidence-24427
31.	CT 50	Sleep Foundation	https://www.sleepfoundation.org/articles/why-do-we-need-sleep
32.	CT 51	Medical News Today	https://www.medicalnewstoday.com/articles/10566
33.	CT 52	New Scientist	https://www.newscientist.com/article/2242107-tiger-survival-threatened-by-mass-road-building-in-precious-habitats/
34.	DA 153	GOV.UK	https://www.gov.uk/government/publications/rural-population-and-migration/rural-population-201415
35.	DA 154	Alcoholthink again	https://alcoholthinkagain.com.au/Resources/Alcohol-Use-Statistics
36.	DA 155	Research Gate	https://www.researchgate.net/figure/HOUSEHOLD-FINAL-CONSUMPTION-EXPENDITURE-101 tbl2 317383242
37.	MT 1 Section 1, Question 2	News Scientist	https://www.newscientist.com/article/2244859-simulating-dead-bodies-could-help-calculate-an-accurate-time-of-death/

38.	MT 1 Section 1, Question 4	The Scientist	https://www.the-scientist.com/cover-story/nanomedicine-37087
39.	MT 1 Section 1, Question 5	The Scientist	https://www.medicalnewstoday.com/articles/323622
40.	MT 1 Section 1, Question 6	The CNN	https://edition.cnn.com/2013/06/28/health/salmonella-fastfacts/index.html
41.	MT 1 Section 1, Question 12	Live Science	https://www.livescience.com/anti-evolution-drug-could-fight-antibiotic-resistance.html
42.	MT 1 Section 1, Question 13	Live Science	https://www.livescience.com/coronavirus-diy-hand-sanitizer.html
43.	MT 1 Section 1, Question 14	The BBC	https://www.bbc.co.uk/news/entertainment-arts-52923622
44.	MT 1 Section 1, Question 16	The Metro	https://metro.co.uk/2020/06/09/wearable-robotic-arm-powerful-can-smash-walls-12827444/
45.	MT 1 Section 1, Question 18	Child Mind	https://childmind.org/article/how-using-social-media-affects-teenagers/
46.	MT 1 Section 1, Question 23	New Scientist	https://www.newscientist.com/article/mg24632812-700-why-countries-should-start-weekly-covid-19-testing-for-key-workers/#ixzz6LlsZPFPQ
47.	MT 1 Section 1, Question 25	The BBC	https://www.bbc.co.uk/news/education-52701850?intlink_from_url=https://www.bbc.co.uk/news/topics/c6lpr12gep3t/social-inequality&link_location=live-reporting-story
48.	MT 1 Section 1, Question 26	The National Geographic	https://www.nationalgeographic.com/animals/2020/06/pinker-flamingos-more-aggressive/
49.	MT 1 Section 1, Question 28	Medical News Today	https://www.medicalnewstoday.com/articles/322868#What-clinical-research-in-dogs-can-teach-us
50.	MT 1 Section 1, Question 30	Live Science	https://www.livescience.com/teen-fussy-eater-vision-loss.html
51.	MT 1 Section 1, Question 31	New Scientist	https://www.newscientist.com/article/2242725-the-moon-is-emitting-carbon-raising-questions-about-how-it-was-formed/#ixzz6Llon4NmD
52.	MT 2 Section 1, Question 2	Independent	https://www.independent.co.uk/news/education/education-news/uk-university-rankings-world-qs-quacquarelli-symonds-oxford-a9557976.html
53.	MT 2 Section 1, Question 4	The BBC	https://www.bbc.com/future/article/20190207-how-artificial-intelligence-can-help-stop-bullying
54.	MT 2 Section 1, Question 5	The BBC	https://www.bbc.co.uk/news/health-46972101
55.	MT 2 Section 1, Question 6	The BBC	https://www.bbc.co.uk/news/science-environment-51944780
56.	MT 2 Section 1, Question 7	Science Daily	https://www.sciencedaily.com/releases/2019/11/191125100349.htm
57.	MT 2 Section 1, Question 14	NCBI	https://www.ncbi.nlm.nih.gov/pmc/articles/PMC6194288/
58.	MT 2 Section 1, Question 15	Health Line	https://www.healthline.com/health/benefits-of-reading-books#takeaway
59.	MT 2 Section 1, Question 16	NBC News	https://www.nbcnews.com/better/health/why-walking-most-underrated-form-exercise-ncna797271
60.	MT 2 Section 1, Question 18	The Conversation	https://theconversation.com/whats-driving-africas-population-growth-and-what-can-change-it-126362
61.	MT 2 Section 1, Question 25	The BBC	https://www.bbc.co.uk/news/health-22214070
62.	MT 2 Section 1, Question 26	Psychology Today	https://www.psychologytoday.com/gb/blog/freedom-learn/201502/cognitive-benefits-playing-video-games
63.	MT 2 Section 1, Question 28	The Conversation	https://theconversation.com/how-one-nhs-anaesthetist-is-fighting-international-medical-research-fraud-124244
64.	MT 2 Section 1, Question 30	NBC News	https://www.nbcnews.com/better/wellness/5-scientifically-proven-health-benefits-traveling-abroad-n759631
65.	MT 3 Section 1, Question 3	NCBI	https://www.ncbi.nlm.nih.gov/pmc/articles/PMC7292584/
66.	MT 3 Section 1, Question 4	The World Health Organisation	https://www.who.int/emergencies/diseases/novel-coronavirus-2019/question-and-answers-hub/q-a-detail/q-a-on-covid-19-and-masks
67.	MT 3 Section 1, Question 20	New Scientist	https://www.newscientist.com/article/mg24632860-900-humankind-review-a-compelling-case-for-believing-people-are-good/